THE ORWELL READER

George Orwell, whom V. S. Pritchett has called "the conscience of his generation," was born in India in 1903 and was educated at Eton. From 1922 to 1927, he served in the Imperial Police in Burma. He spent the next few years in Paris and in England teaching school, writing, and working at a variety of jobs. He went to Spain when the Civil War broke out, fought on the Republican side, and was severely wounded. Back in England, he joined the Home Guard in World War II, and worked for the B.B.C. He became a literary and political commentator for a variety of British newspapers and magazines, and also contributed to American periodicals. He died in London in 1950. His books include: *Down and Out in Paris and London* (1933), *Burmese Days* (1934), *A Clergyman's Daughter* (1935), *Keep the Aspidistra Flying* (1936), *The Road to Wigan Pier* (1937), *Homage to Catalonia* (1938), *Coming Up for Air* (1939), *Inside the Whale and Other Essays* (1940), *The Lion and the Unicorn* (1941), *Animal Farm* (1945), *Dickens, Dali and Others* (1946), *Nineteen Eighty-four* (1949), *Shooting an Elephant and Other Essays* (1950), and *Such, Such Were the Joys* (1953).

The Orwell Reader

FICTION, ESSAYS, AND REPORTAGE BY

George Orwell

▼

WITH AN INTRODUCTION BY RICHARD H. ROVERE

A HARVEST BOOK

HARCOURT BRACE JOVANOVICH, INC. · NEW YORK

Of the essays in this volume, "Rudyard Kipling" and "In Defense of P. G. Wodehouse" are taken from *Dickens, Dali & Others* (Reynal & Hitchcock, 1946); "Shooting an Elephant," "A Hanging," "How the Poor Die," "Politics vs. Literature: an Examination of 'Gulliver's Travels,' " "Lear, Tolstoy and the Fool," "Reflections on Gandhi," "Second Thoughts on James Burnham," "Politics and the English Language," "The Prevention of Literature," and " 'I Write As I Please' " are taken from *Shooting an Elephant* (Harcourt, Brace, 1950); "England Your England," "Why I Write," and "Such, Such Were the Joys . . ." are taken from *Such, Such Were the Joys* (Harcourt, Brace, 1953).

Some of these essays appeared, before book publication, in the following American magazines: the *Atlantic Monthly,* the *New Republic,* and *Partisan Review.*

CONTENTS

INTRODUCTION
by Richard H. Rovere

The late George Orwell was a novelist, a journalist, an essayist, a literary critic, a political polemicist, an occasional poet, and a man whose mark on his contemporaries was and is large and clear and good. He was central to his time, which is our time from the late 'twenties to the 'fifties and into the plausible terrors of *Nineteen Eighty-Four*.

He was born in India in 1903 and died in England in 1950, of a lung ailment contracted in childhood. George Orwell was a pen name he took in 1934; he had been christened Eric Blair. At the time of his death, he had been a writer for less than twenty years, and for almost half of that period he had been quite obscure. Nevertheless, it is difficult to call to mind any figure of the twentieth century, apart from the seminal thinkers like Freud and Dewey and the literary innovators like Joyce and Eliot, whose influence has been as sharp and visible and cleansing as Orwell's. In the closing years of his life, when *Animal Farm* and *Nineteen Eighty-Four* were being read everywhere, the world had a sense of him as a prophet. *Animal Farm* was published here in 1946 (many publishers rejected it on the ground that it would have a disturbing influence on Soviet-American relations), and I do not think it would be going too far to say that it did as much to clear the air as Winston Churchill's "Iron Curtain" speech of the same year—an oratorical salvo often cited by historians as the starting point of Western resistance to Soviet imperialism. By 1949, when *Nineteen Eighty-Four* appeared, Orwell was by no means a lonely prophet; by then, the wilderness was full of voices. But Orwell's had a stunning clarity and edge. Anyone could see the flower of totalitarianism in Stalin's Russia or Stalin's Poland or Stalin's Czechoslovakia. It took Orwell to uncover the living roots of totalitarianism in contemporary thought and speech, in the puritanism of civic virtue, in our slackening of ties with the usable past, in cravenness before the gods of security, in mass entertainment's deadening of impulses. He put Newspeak and Doublethink into the language, and our habits of speech and thought are the better for this. If we and our offspring never have to endure *Nineteen Eighty-Four,* we and they will have Orwell partly to thank.

Nineteen Eighty-Four was a dazzling illumination, and I suppose that for most people it will always be the first thing to spring to mind whenever Orwell's name is mentioned—just as most of us, in free association, would respond to "Swift" with *"Gulliver's Travels."* But as readers of the selections so discerningly chosen and so admirably arranged here will discover for themselves, it was not Orwell's first illumination but his last. Years earlier, even before *Animal Farm* had won him his first really wide circle of readers, he had exerted a liberating and strengthening influence on a whole generation of writers and intellectuals. That generation, of which I am a member, knew him first as a journalist. In my own case, I did not even know that he had written any fiction until some time after I read his political and literary criticism. (A few of his early novels were published here in the early 'thirties, but they attracted little attention and quickly went out of print. They were not reissued until 1950 or after.) I think my own awareness of him must date from late 1939 or more probably early 1940; in any case, I knew enough about him by 1941 to go to some lengths to get hold of a copy of *The Lion and the Unicorn,* a wartime study of English life and ideals that has never been published here but that is well represented in this volume by "England Your England." Orwell was a socialist when he wrote it, as he was to the day of his death, and the book may justly be regarded as a piece of socialist literature, though it spends less time telling how socialism might improve England than how England might improve socialism.

I followed *The Lion and the Unicorn* with *Homage to Catalonia* and all the fugitive pieces, in English periodicals and in *Partisan Review,* that I could lay hands on. It was not Orwell's view of any particular question that made his work as a journalist so exciting and his example as a writer so bracing to his colleagues. Nor was it merely the verve and acuity of his writing, though this was indeed part of it: quite apart from any special tendencies of his thinking, he was a magnificent performer. But the important and stirring thing was the way he coupled contempt for all the "smelly little orthodoxies" of his time with a continuing interest in ideas and a decent respect for the opinions of mankind. He was free, on the one hand, of pieties of any sort and, on the other, of flippancy. He was at once responsible and absolutely independent, and this in a day when responsibility and independence were customarily disjoined. He fused a moral commitment with a fiercely critical mind and spirit, and if today there are more writers who approach this ideal than there were twenty years ago, it is largely because they have profited by his precepts and have been moved by the magnificent gesture of his career.

Orwell was a writer of great force and distinction. He would be remembered today if he had been only a journalist and critic. But he was far more; he was—among other things, though certainly first among them—an artist, and a many-sided one. The thrust of his moral imagination has been felt by all those who read *Nineteen Eighty-Four*, but that was by no means the end of it, nor was it the beginning. Though *Nineteen Eighty-Four* was no doubt his most important book, that work of apocalyptic fury did not provide the most impressive display of his gifts. The reader of *Burmese Days* and *Coming Up for Air*, which seem to me the two most successful of his early novels, will discover that his imagination was more than moral. He could deal superbly with the individual consciousness and with the intercourse of character. He could be wonderfully evocative of moods and times and scenes and conditions of life. No one who has seen anything of England or encountered any members of the British lower middle class can miss the verisimilitude of *Coming Up for Air*. We have it on excellent authority that *Burmese Days* is as sensitive a rendering of Indian and Anglo-Indian life; in any case, it could scarcely be more memorable. I would rank *Down and Out in Paris and London* with these two novels if I did not think it too directly autobiographical and reportorial a work to be described as a novel at all; whatever its category, it is a matchlessly vivid description of the life of poverty and unemployment and squalor. It is impossible to read the *plongeur* passages without having the sensation of gray soapy water sloshing about the arms up to the elbow. Though Orwell's bent was for such description and for a manner that is ironical, astringent, and detached, he could on occasion be lyrical and quite astonishingly tender, as one may learn from the sections on Tubby Bowling's boyhood in *Coming Up for Air* or from the haunting and pathetic scenes between Julia and Winston in *Nineteen Eighty-Four*.

In all of his novels, including those that might, on balance, be described as failures, one feels oneself always in the presence of a writer who is fully alive and has eyes and an intellect and a vibrant character of his own. The conventions of criticism demand, I suppose, that he be placed as a "minor" novelist. He was not in any

crucial sense an innovator, and he did not penetrate the mysteries
to the depths reached by Dostoevski or Conrad. He did not people
a world as Balzac did—though one has the feeling that something
like this would have been within his powers if he had devoted
himself entirely to fiction or if he had lived and written longer.
He was of the second rank, but he was never second-rate, and to
my mind and taste the distinction is anything but invidious. All
of us, I think, get major satisfactions from certain minor novelists,
and minor satisfactions from certain major novelists. Stendhal, for
example, means less to me than Samuel Butler, and Orwell more
than Joyce. I believe that Orwell is, as Irving Howe has said, "one
of the few contemporary writers who really matter."

John Atkins, the author of a useful critical study of Orwell, has
said that "his uniqueness lay in his having the mind of an intellectual and the feelings of a common man." I cannot quite accept this,
for I recognize no sentient state that can be described as "the feelings of a common man." As for "the mind of an intellectual," that is
what every intellectual has. Still, I think Mr. Atkins is reaching for
a central truth about Orwell and one that is not easy to grasp.
Perhaps one could say that his uniqueness lay to some degree in
his almost studied avoidance of the unique. The experience he
chose to deal with was the kind of experience known to large
numbers of people, to whole social classes, to entire nations. He
did not often concern himself with the single instance. As a novelist,
he was rather old-fashioned in the sense that he did not explore
the extremes of behavior. The merely anomalous, the merely phenomenal, the exotic, the bizarre—none of these attracted his interest
very much. In fact, the most obvious and persistent of his faults
was an intolerance of eccentricity and neurosis. As a critic, he was
rather old-fashioned in the sense that he paid the most attention
to books that have been read by millions and left to other critics
those works of genius that are admired chiefly in genius circles.
It was Dickens and Kipling, staples in a national culture, rather
than, say, Henry James or Gerard Manley Hopkins, who drew
forth his greatest critical efforts. He pioneered in the serious analysis of popular culture, writing brilliantly of "good bad" books,
boys' magazines, patriotic verse and marching songs, penny dread-
fuls, and even the bawdy postcards on sale at seaside resorts. In a
striking essay on Henry Miller, which was, I think, one of his few
appreciations of what some people would call a "coterie" writer,
he found it necessary to convince himself that the lives of the odd
fish of whom Miller wrote "overlap fairly widely with those of

more normal people." Had he been unable to say this, he would have been unable to admire Miller.

He set great store by normality. This is not to say that he despised the extraordinary or placed no value on the uncommon or superior. He was an extraordinary person himself, he detested conformity, and he never celebrated mediocrity. "The average sensual man is out of fashion," he wrote, and he proposed to restore him, giving him "the power of speech, like Balaam's ass" and uncovering his genius. Because we know that he believed there was a great deal in a name, we can assume that in *Nineteen Eighty-Four* he did not settle lightly on one for the central character, Winston Smith, who linked the memory of a most uncommon Englishman with the commonest of English patronymics. What Orwell cared about most deeply was the general quality of human experience in his time. The virtues he honored were the universally accessible ones— candor, courage, love, common sense, integrity, decency, charity. The tyrannies he anatomized were those that could hurt us all.

II

Throughout his career as a writer, Orwell's interests steadily broadened, his insights deepened, and his powers increased. He wrote rather directly from experience, and he recorded, in his journalism and his essays, the development of his convictions. Thus, the arrangement in this volume of his work in terms of its relevance to specific periods has the additional advantages of putting it in roughly the proper chronology of composition and of demonstrating the steady enlargement of his mind and his talent.

Orwell, who was fascinated by the English class structure and enjoyed drawing fine distinctions of status, spoke of his own family as members of the "upper lower middle class." His father was in the Opium Department of the Indian Civil Service and was at Motihari when Orwell was born. Orwell was one of three children; his home life, he said, was drab, and he felt "isolated and undervalued." It is safe to assume that he changed his name because he disliked the memory of the years in which he had borne it. He told friends that he found the name itself unpleasant; he said he did not care for the Scottishness of Blair or the Norseness of Eric and felt more content with a surname taken from an English river he had loved and a resoundingly British Christian name. If his home life was dreary, it was also brief. "I barely saw my father before I was eight," he wrote. And at eight he was sent to a boarding school on the South Coast, the inferior place he calls Crossgates in "Such, Such Were the Joys . . . ," an essay full of that anguishing vividness he scarcely ever failed to achieve. It is possible that the reality of Crossgates was not quite as bad as the memory of it. Cyril Connolly was there at the same time and in *Enemies of Promise* makes the school, which he calls St. Wulfric's, sound a somewhat happier place and Orwell a somewhat happier boy than we find in Orwell's account. But with childhood, it is always the memory that counts. At Crossgates, Orwell did what was expected of him and won a scholarship to Eton. He finished Eton and acknowledged in later life that he had rather liked the place, but he did not go on to a university. He thought it better to see something of "real life." He went back to India and served five years in Burma as a member of the Indian Imperial Police. He was to some extent at least the Flory of *Burmese Days,* a guilt-ridden servant and beneficiary of the Raj.

In the essay "Why I Write," Orwell says that he had known his vocation from the age of five or six but that from the age of seventeen to twenty-four, a period that included all the Burma years, he had sought to escape it, "with the consciousness that I was outraging my true nature." So far as I know, he never explained why he sought to flee what he regarded as his destiny or whether he had in mind some other fulfillment. As a matter of fact, it is difficult to find one's way about in the years between Eric Blair's adolescence and the emergence of George Orwell in 1934, when he was thirty-one. His own writings are vague as to dates and sequences in this period. I think it is quite clear, though, that he was a young man who suffered a good many torments of mind and spirit. His attempt to avoid writing could have resulted from an admixture of insecurity, or fear of failure, and self-denial. There are traces of Calvinist asceticism all through his work. At any rate, not long after his return from Burma, he entered upon the mortification of the flesh that provided him with the materials for *Down and Out in Paris and London.* He sought out poverty, whether to write about it or merely to suffer it we cannot tell. "What I profoundly wanted at that time," he wrote several years later, in *The Road to Wigan Pier,* "was to find some way of getting out of the respectable world altogether." But why did he seek out misery? Why did he embrace poverty instead of Bohemia? John Atkins has said that the moment Orwell thought of anything beyond endurance, he put himself to the test of enduring it. I think there is something to this. It was compulsive behavior, almost masochistic in character, and it makes Orwell's retention of independence and cool judgment all the more interesting and all the more impressive. The

most powerful critic of fanaticism in our time was a man who had
a good many fanatical impulses.

He has said that he spent about two years in all in the lower
depths of Paris and London. It is hard to tell whether or not this
was one continuous experience. At some point between 1928 and
1934, he taught school for a while, and at another time he worked
as a clerk in a bookshop. After 1933, there are few uncertainties. In
that year, his first journalism began to appear—articles and reviews
under the name of Eric Blair in *Adelphi* and other magazines.
Down and Out was published in 1933 and *Burmese Days* in 1934,
when he became Orwell. His surrender to destiny was now complete. He did a book a year for several years, in addition to the
newspaper and magazine work that kept him alive. After *Burmese
Days,* there were three more books dealing with poverty. *A Clergyman's Daughter,* published in 1935, and *Keep the Aspidistra Flying,*
pubiished in 1936, are novels of English life. They have their particular distinctions—the Trafalgar Square scene from *A Clergyman's
Daughter* may well be the finest thing in all of Orwell's fiction—
but they are not his best work. In them, however, one can trace his
growing concern with politics and his drift toward socialism. He
was a socialist by the time he did the fourth of his books on poverty,
The Road to Wigan Pier, which was published in England in 1937
and has not yet been published in this country, doubtless because,
being largely a factual report on the mining communities of South
Wales in the worst part of the depression, it has been thought to
have too antiquarian a flavor. But then the bubonic plague of
which Defoe and Pepys wrote had lost a good deal of its topicality,
and Orwell on life in Swansea and Wigan and Newcastle in 1936
seems to me fully the peer of Defoe and Pepys on London in 1664.

The Road to Wigan Pier is a masterpiece. It is also a basic document in the intellectual history of this century. The book had been
commissioned by Victor Gollancz, the publisher, on behalf of the
Left Book Club, an organization whose tendency is evident in its
title, as a study of human misery in an exploitative social order.
The first half is exactly that. Orwell was never more brilliant as a
journalist. The second part is an examination of socialism as a
remedy. It was perhaps the most rigorous examination that any
doctrine has ever received at the hands of an adherent. It was so
tough, so disrespectful, so rich in heresies that Mr. Gollancz, who,
as proprietor of the Left Book Club was the shepherd of a flock
that scandalized as easily as any Wesleyan congregation, published
the book only after writing an introduction that could not have
been more strained and apologetic if he had actually been a

Wesleyan minister who for some improbable reason found himself the sponsor of a lecture by George Bernard Shaw on the Articles of Religion. Mr. Gollancz's plight was in some respects even more difficult than that hypothetical one, since it was necessary for him to concede that the early chapters "really *are* the kind of thing that makes converts."

In discomfiting his fellow socialists as he did, Orwell performed, for the first time, what was to become his characteristic service to his generation. In 1956, I find it rather awkward—indeed, I find it downright embarrassing—to have the responsibility of explaining exactly what this service was. For it was really nothing more or less than clearing minds of cant, and the service should never have been necessary in the first place. It has to be understood that the typical intellectual of the 'thirties was a man so shocked by social injustice and the ghastly spectacle of Fascism that his brain was easily addled by anyone who proposed a quick and drastic remedy. The humanistic mind in those days was poorly equipped to deal with social and political ideas, and grappled with them almost as awkwardly as in recent years it has grappled with the problems of nuclear physics. We tend now to recall Communism as the only brain-addler of the period, but there were others. Non-Communist liberalism had a way of stiffening into illiberal orthodoxies, as did pacifism. Fascism itself won over a few essentially humanistic intelligences, and so did extreme conservatism. Almost at the onset of social and political consciousness, intellectuals surrendered their critical faculties. Many of them thought they had excellent reasons for doing so. It was perfectly obvious, they would argue, that the conditions that cried out for change would not be changed by individuals. Still less would they be changed by acts of cerebration. They would be changed only by the action of large numbers of people—by parties, by armies, by collectivities of one sort or another. Parties and armies require discipline. Discipline necessarily calls for a ceding of rights and privileges. *Ergo,* for the benefit of mankind, for the prisoners of starvation, for the greatest good of the greatest number, for the Cause, it is necessary to give up the right to be critics, iconoclasts, Bohemians, individualists.

It can be objected, I know, that I am only describing a species of conformity and that conformity continues to be quite a problem. Certainly it does, and that is one of the reasons why Orwell is needed today. But today's conformity is one of assent, and I am talking about a conformity of dissent, which is in many ways a more terrible thing. Twenty years ago, it was the critics of society

who allowed their critical powers to atrophy; it was the inde-
pendent-minded who threw away their independence.

Orwell arrived on the scene in the middle 'thirties and proceeded
to fire the camps of the orthodox wherever he found them. How
he came to this role is, I think, quite a mystery. His acquaintance with social and political ideas and practices was, if anything,
even slighter than that of most of his contemporaries, and there
were, as I have suggested, aspects of his temperament that seemed
to make him rather a promising candidate for fanaticism. Nevertheless, he stood almost alone in his generation as a man of consistent good judgment and as one who never for a moment doubted
that it was possible to be at once humanistic and tough-minded,
to make commitments and avoid the perils of commitment. He
was no less shocked by social injustice and Fascism than the next
man. He had known poverty and had written four books on it, at
least two of which, *Down and Out* and *The Road to Wigan Pier*,
are classics. He saw the point about parties and armies and took
more than his share of responsibilities. For all his heresies as a
socialist, he was no stranger to the grubbiest of political chores,
and in 1936 he went to Spain and bore arms against Fascism—an
experience that led to another classic, *Homage to Catalonia*. He
was not, of course, alone in seeing the perils of commitment, but
most of the others who saw the perils either withdrew their commitments or made silly counter-commitments. Orwell did neither.
He felt that withdrawal was out of the question "unless you are
armored by old age or stupidity or hypocrisy." But of the committed writer he said, "His writings, in so far as they are to have
any value, will always be the product of the saner self that stands
aside, records the things that are done and admits their necessity,
but refuses to be deceived as to their true nature." He was seldom
deceived as to the true nature of anything.

"He was the conscience of his generation," V. S. Pritchett said,
meaning, of course, his generation of writers. Up to 1945, he was
very little known in this country, and his British audience was
pretty well limited to the readers of the weeklies and monthlies
of opinion. He was becoming established as a critic and journalist
when he went to Spain. He was wounded in the neck and hospital-
ized in Lérida; he had joined the P.O.U.M., which opposed the
Communists and was critical of the Popular Front government
from a more or less Trotskyist point of view, and he left Spain
with some difficulty and with a price on his head. He published
Homage to Catalonia in 1938; though it was a passionately Loyalist
book, it gave as great offense to the passionate Loyalists as *The*

Road to Wigan Pier had given to socialists and Communists, and by the time of his death had sold only nine hundred copies. From 1938 to the middle years of World War II, he had a difficult time of it; he was held in great admiration by people whose admiration was worth having, but partly because of his political views and partly because of the general dislocations of the period he had little work and little sense of function. He wanted to join the army, but the army would not have him. In 1939, he published *Coming Up for Air,* and in 1941 *The Lion and the Unicorn,* but these did little to help keep him alive or relieve his sense of frustration. He served in the Home Guard, did occasional scripts for the British Broadcasting Corporation, and wrote brilliantly from London for the *Partisan Review* in New York. It was not until fairly well along in the war that he attracted a sizable British audience for his periodical writing, most of which appeared in the Laborite *Tribune.* His tuberculosis, which he never seems to have done much about, had progressed during the war; it was in an advanced and incurable state by 1945, so that for the short period in which he had a large number of readers, from the publication of *Animal Farm* until his death in a sanatorium a few months after the publication of *Nineteen Eighty-Four,* life held many agonies and few rewards. He once said that *Nineteen Eighty-Four* would have been a less bleak and bitter book if he had not been a dying man when he wrote it.

III

In the past decade, critics in large numbers have been drawn to Orwell's work and have found him for the most part a thorny problem. The truth is that his work does not much lend itself to theirs. His novels were direct and fairly simple narratives in an old tradition. Their meanings are mostly on the surface. Orwell posed no riddles, elaborated no myths, and manipulated no symbols. Even *Nineteen Eighty-Four* offers limited possibilities for exegesis. One need only be alive in the twentieth century to grasp its significance. There is not much to do with Orwell's novels except read them. Nor is there much to be said about his style. It was colloquial in diction and sinewy in construction; it aimed at clarity and unobtrusiveness and achieved both. Cyril Connolly once performed an experiment by scrambling some sentences of Orwell's with some of Ernest Hemingway's and some of Christopher Isherwood's. He defied the reader to tell the writers one from another and argued that, since identification was impossible, all writers who strive for the colloquial throw away a good part of their heritage as writers. He felt that those who worked in a Mandarin Dialect—those, that

is, who strove for elegance of phrase and exquisiteness of texture—
were at least using all the resources of their language, while those
who worked in what he called the New Vernacular needlessly confined themselves to a narrow range of rhythms and tones. I think
Connolly was wrong in saying that his three novelists could not
be told apart and wrong in his dispraise of colloquialism. But beyond saying that Orwell's was simply the style most commonly
used in modern English and American writing and that Orwell
employed it with great vigor, there is really not a great deal for
a critic to say. A writer of Orwell's sort does not give the modern
critic much of a chance to draw upon his imposing collection of
critical utensils and contrivances.

In consequence, there has been a search for the sources of Orwell's
strength in Orwell's character. No doubt that is where the sources
are to be found; *le style est l'homme même,* and so forth. But it
cannot be said that the search has been very productive. What
nearly everyone seems to find in Orwell is rectitude and more rectitude. Lionel Trilling has said that the profoundest statement he
ever heard about Orwell came from a college student who said:
"He was a virtuous man." John Atkins has said, "The common
element in all George Orwell's writing was a sense of decency."
Mr. Atkins also calls him a "social saint." The idea of saintliness
turns up everywhere; there is a touch of hagiography even in the
arguments directed against it. Irving Howe, poking fun at the "old
maids of criticism, hunting for stray bits of morality as if they were
pieces of tatting left in the parlor" and pointing out that Orwell
himself had said that "sainthood is a thing human beings must
avoid," has ventured the opinion that Orwell was a "revolutionary
personality." But what is that except another term, one with secular
and socialist overtones, for a saint? A "revolutionary personality"
is what the Ethical Culturist calls Jesus Christ.

Orwell was an uncommonly decent person, and his moral and
physical courage survived many hard tests. He was not a saint, or
even saintly. I do not think he was any *more* virtuous or decent
than his contemporaries. What is probably behind the use of these
terms is a confusion of the prophet and the saint—that and an appreciation of the fact that Orwell saw through all the pretenses of
his time and never made a fool of himself. None of this really has
much to do with personal "goodness." On the contrary, there is
often a rather direct and visible relationship between folly and
purity of spirit. We all know about the paving stones on the road
to hell. "The surrendering and humbling of the self breed pride
and arrogance," Eric Hoffer has written, and of course pride and

arrogance breed folly. The obverse of this is the old set-a-thief-to-catch-a-thief principle. It takes a certain amount of wickedness to understand the mechanics of wickedness as Orwell did and to perceive that "the essence of being human is that one does not seek perfection, that one *is* sometimes willing to commit sins for the sake of loyalty, that one does not push asceticism to the point where it makes friendly intercourse impossible, and that one is prepared in the end to be defeated and broken up by life, which is the inevitable price of fastening one's love upon other individuals." I think it clear that Orwell's asceticism furnished him with a knowledge of the point to which asceticism should not be pushed and that his impulse toward fanaticism furnished him with a comprehension of it and a determination to resist it. Naturally, there was more than that to it, else he would have succumbed to impulse.

In any event, Orwell had his share of wickedness. He could say cruel things and his fairness of judgment did not always extend to individuals. He called Kipling a "gutter patriot" and W. H. Auden a "gutless Kipling." (He could be remorseful, too; he publicly apologized for this characterization of Auden.) His judgments were not always as charitable as they were sound; there was a bit more to be said for the radical intellectuals of the 'thirties than he could find it in his heart to say. I do not see how, on logical grounds alone, he could be as indulgent as he was toward P. G. Wodehouse and at the same time as bitter about the liberals and radicals, to whom he had a way of referring as "the pansy left." Standing alone, his plea for Wodehouse would have seemed an act of generosity and understanding. But it seems only fair that if one is going to excuse Wodehouse for allowing himself to be exploited by the Nazis, one should be approximately as forgiving to those who allowed themselves to be exploited by the Communists. Orwell was quite frequently unfair in this way, but his unfairness flowed not, I think, from self-righteousness but from ill-temper, from his passion for the truth, and, part of the time, from his use of overstatement as a device of rhetoric. His choler and intemperance had something in common with that of Dr. Johnson and with that of the author of *Gulliver's Travels,* of whom he once wrote: "Politically, Swift was one of those people who are driven into a sort of perverse Toryism by the follies of the progressive party of the moment." It was Orwell's distinction that the follies of his friends never drove him to abandon them, but now and then he did manage to sound like the spokesmen for a perverse Toryism.

Orwell, thank God, was no saint. He was burdened by no excess of purity. I do not think it within the province of the critic to determine what properties of the pneuma account for what we find in a man's work. It should be enough that we find something to which we can respond and that we seek to understand what it is that moves us. In Orwell, we find a mind that did not have to be cleared of cant because it evidently had none to begin with. He had sense and sensibility, a love of language, a nose for fraud, a hunger for truth, a resolute heart, a robust and inquiring intellect, and whatever it is that makes a man an artist.

All of these qualities are to be found in the pages that follow. I am full of envy for the reader who is making his way through them for the first time.

Prologue in Burma

Shooting an Elephant

In Moulmein, in lower Burma, I was hated by large numbers of people—the only time in my life that I have been important enough for this to happen to me. I was sub-divisional police officer of the town, and in an aimless, petty kind of way anti-European feeling was very bitter. No one had the guts to raise a riot, but if a European woman went through the bazaars alone somebody would probably spit betel juice over her dress. As a police officer I was an obvious target and was baited whenever it seemed safe to do so. When a nimble Burman tripped me up on the football field and the referee (another Burman) looked the other way, the crowd yelled with hideous laughter. This happened more than once. In the end the sneering yellow faces of young men that met me everywhere, the insults hooted after me when I was at a safe distance, got badly on my nerves. The young Buddhist priests were the worst of all. There were several thousands of them in the town and none of them seemed to have anything to do except stand on street corners and jeer at Europeans.

All this was perplexing and upsetting. For at that time I had already made up my mind that imperialism was an evil thing and the sooner I chucked up my job and got out of it the better. Theoretically—and secretly, of course—I was all for the Burmese and all against their oppressors, the British. As for the job I was doing, I hated it more bitterly than I can perhaps make clear. In a job like that you see the dirty work of Empire at close quarters. The wretched prisoners huddling in the stinking cages of the lock-ups, the gray, cowed faces of the long-term convicts, the scarred buttocks of the men who had been flogged with bamboos—all these oppressed me with an intolerable sense of guilt. But I could get nothing into perspective. I was young and ill educated and I had had to think out my problems in the utter silence that is imposed on every Englishman in the East. I did not even know that the British Empire is dying, still less did I know that it is a great deal better than the younger empires that are going to supplant it. All I knew was that I was stuck between my hatred of the empire I served and my rage against the evil-spirited little beasts who tried to make my job impossible. With one part of my mind I thought of the British Raj as an unbreakable tyranny, as something clamped down, in *saecula saeculorum,* upon the will of prostrate peoples; with another part I thought that the greatest joy in the world would be to drive a bayonet into a Buddhist priest's guts. Feelings like these are the normal by-products of imperialism; ask any Anglo-Indian official, if you can catch him off duty.

One day something happened which in a roundabout way was enlightening. It was a tiny incident in itself, but it gave me a better glimpse than I had had before of the real nature of imperialism—the real motives for which despotic governments act. Early one morning the sub-inspector at a police station the other end of the town rang me up on the 'phone and said that an elephant was ravaging the bazaar. Would I please come and do something about it? I did not know what I could do, but I wanted to see what was happening and I got on to a pony and started out. I took my rifle, an old .44 Winchester and much too small to kill an elephant, but I thought the noise might be useful *in terrorem.* Various Burmans stopped me on the way and told me about the elephant's doings. It was not, of course, a wild elephant, but a tame one which had gone "must." It had been chained up, as tame elephants always are when their attack of "must" is due, but on the previous night it had broken its chain and escaped. Its mahout, the only person who could manage it when it was in that state, had set out in pursuit, but had taken the wrong direction and was now twelve hours' journey away, and in the morning the elephant had suddenly re appeared in the town. The Burmese population had no weapons and were quite helpless against it. It had already destroyed somebody's bamboo hut, killed a cow and raided some fruit-stalls and devoured the stock; also it had met the municipal rubbish van and, when the driver jumped out and took to his heels, had turned the van over and inflicted violences upon it.

The Burmese sub-inspector and some Indian constables were waiting for me in the quarter where the elephant had been seen. It was a very poor quarter, a labyrinth of squalid bamboo huts, thatched with palm-leaf, winding all over a steep hillside. I remember that it was a cloudy, stuffy morning at the beginning of the rains. We began questioning the people as to where the elephant had gone and, as usual, failed to get any definite information. That is invariably the case in the East; a story always sounds clear enough at a distance, but the nearer you get to the scene of events the vaguer it becomes. Some of the people said that the elephant had gone in one direction, some said that he had gone in another, some professed not even to have heard of any elephant. I had almost made up my mind that the whole story was a pack of lies, when we heard yells a little distance away. There was a loud, scandalized cry of "Go away, child! Go away this instant!" and an old woman with a switch in her hand came round the corner of a hut, violently shooing away a crowd of naked children. Some more women followed, clicking their tongues and exclaiming; evidently there was something that the children ought not to have seen. I rounded the hut and saw a man's dead body sprawling in the mud. He was an Indian, a black Dravidian coolie, almost naked, and he could not have been dead many minutes. The people said that the elephant had come suddenly upon him round the corner of the hut, caught him with its trunk, put its foot on his back and ground him into the earth. This was the rainy season and the ground was soft, and his face had scored a trench a foot deep and a couple of yards long. He was lying on his belly with arms crucified and head sharply twisted to one side. His face was coated with mud, the eyes wide open, the teeth bared and grinning with an expression of unendurable agony. (Never tell me, by the way, that the dead look peaceful. Most of the corpses I have seen looked devilish.) The friction of the great beast's foot had stripped the skin from his back as neatly as one skins a rabbit. As soon as I saw the dead man I sent an orderly to a friend's house nearby to borrow an elephant rifle. I had already sent back the pony, not wanting it to go mad with fright and throw me if it smelt the elephant.

The orderly came back in a few minutes with a rifle and five cartridges, and meanwhile some Burmans had arrived and told us that the elephant was in the paddy fields below, only a few hundred yards away. As I started forward practically the whole population of the quarter flocked out of the houses and followed me. They had seen the rifle and were all shouting excitedly that I was going to shoot the elephant. They had not shown much interest in the elephant when he was merely ravaging their homes, but it was different now that he was going to be shot. It was a bit of fun to them, as it would be to an English crowd; besides they wanted the meat. It made me vaguely uneasy. I had no intention of shooting the elephant—I had merely sent for the rifle to defend myself if necessary—and it is always unnerving to have a crowd following you. I marched down the hill, looking and feeling a fool, with the rifle over my shoulder and an ever-growing army of people jostling at my heels. At the bottom, when you got away from the huts, there was a metalled road and beyond that a miry waste of paddy fields a thousand yards across, not yet ploughed but soggy from the first rains and dotted with coarse grass. The elephant was standing eight yards from the road, his left side toward us. He took not the slightest notice of the crowd's approach. He was tearing up bunches of grass, beating them against his knees to clean them, and stuffing them into his mouth.

I had halted on the road. As soon as I saw the elephant I knew with perfect certainty that I ought not to shoot him. It is a serious matter to shoot a working elephant—it is comparable to destroying a huge and costly piece of machinery—and obviously one ought not to do it if it can possibly be avoided. And at that distance, peacefully eating, the elephant looked no more dangerous than a cow. I thought then and I think now that his attack of "must" was already passing off; in which case he would merely wander harmlessly about until the mahout came back and caught him. Moreover, I did not in the least want to shoot him. I decided that I would watch him for a little while to make sure that he did not turn savage again, and then go home.

But at that moment I glanced round at the crowd that had followed me. It was an immense crowd, two thousand at the least and growing every minute. It blocked the road for a long distance on either side. I looked at the sea of yellow faces above the garish clothes—faces all happy and excited over this bit of fun, all certain that the elephant was going to be shot. They were watching me as they would watch a conjurer about to perform a trick. They did not like me, but with the magical rifle in my hands I was momentarily worth watching. And suddenly I realized that I should have to shoot the elephant after all. The people expected it of me and I had got to do it; I could feel their two thousand wills pressing me forward, irresistibly. And it was at this moment, as I stood there with the rifle in my hands, that I first grasped the hollowness, the futility of the white man's dominion in the East. Here was I, the white man with his gun, standing in front of the unarmed native crowd—seemingly the leading actor of the piece; but in reality I was only an absurd puppet pushed to and fro by the will of those yellow faces behind. I perceived in this moment that when the white man turns tyrant it is his own freedom that he destroys. He becomes a sort of hollow, posing dummy, the conventionalized figure of a sahib. For it is the condition of his rule that he shall spend his life in trying to impress the "natives," and so in every crisis he has got to do what the "natives" expect of him. He

wears a mask, and his face grows to fit it. I had got to shoot the
elephant. I had committed myself to doing it when I sent for the
rifle. A sahib has got to act like a sahib; he has got to appear resolute, to know his own mind and do definite things. To come all
that way, rifle in hand, with two thousand people marching at my
heels, and then to trail feebly away, having done nothing—no, that
was impossible. The crowd would laugh at me. And my whole life,
every white man's life in the East, was one long struggle not to be
laughed at.

But I did not want to shoot the elephant. I watched him beating his bunch of grass against his knees with that preoccupied
grandmotherly air that elephants have. It seemed to me that it
would be murder to shoot him. At that age I was not squeamish
about killing animals, but I had never shot an elephant and never
wanted to. (Somehow it always seems worse to kill a *large* animal.)
Besides, there was the beast's owner to be considered. Alive, the
elephant was worth at least a hundred pounds; dead, he would
only be worth the value of his tusks, five pounds, possibly. But I
had got to act quickly. I turned to some experienced-looking Burmans who had been there when we arrived, and asked them how
the elephant had been behaving. They all said the same thing: he
took no notice of you if you left him alone, but he might charge
if you went too close to him.

It was perfectly clear to me what I ought to do. I ought to walk
up to within, say, twenty-five yards of the elephant and test his
behavior. If he charged, I could shoot; if he took no notice of me,
it would be safe to leave him until the mahout came back. But
also I knew that I was going to do no such thing. I was a poor shot
with a rifle and the ground was soft mud into which one would
sink at every step. If the elephant charged and I missed him, I
should have about as much chance as a toad under a steam-roller.
But even then I was not thinking particularly of my own skin, only
of the watchful yellow faces behind. For at that moment, with the
crowd watching me, I was not afraid in the ordinary sense, as I
would have been if I had been alone. A white man mustn't be
frightened in front of "natives"; and so, in general, he isn't frightened. The sole thought in my mind was that if anything went
wrong those two thousand Burmans would see me pursued, caught,
trampled on, and reduced to a grinning corpse like that Indian up
the hill. And if that happened it was quite probable that some of
them would laugh. That would never do. There was only one al
ternative. I shoved the cartridges into the magazine and lay down
on the road to get a better aim.

The crowd grew very still, and a deep, low, happy sigh, as of people who see the theater curtain go up at last, breathed from innumerable throats. They were going to have their bit of fun after all. The rifle was a beautiful German thing with cross-hair sights. I did not then know that in shooting an elephant one would shoot to cut an imaginary bar running from ear-hole to ear-hole. I ought, therefore, as the elephant was sideways on, to have aimed straight at his ear-hole; actually I aimed several inches in front of this, thinking the brain would be further forward.

When I pulled the trigger I did not hear the bang or feel the kick—one never does when a shot goes home—but I heard the dev- ilish roar of glee that went up from the crowd. In that instant, in too short a time, one would have thought, even for the bullet to get there, a mysterious, terrible change had come over the elephant. He neither stirred nor fell, but every line of his body had altered. He looked suddenly stricken, shrunken, immensely old, as though the frightful impact of the bullet had paralyzed him without knock- ing him down. At last, after what seemed a long time—it might have been five seconds, I dare say—he sagged flabbily to his knees. His mouth slobbered. An enormous senility seemed to have settled upon him. One could have imagined him thousands of years old. I fired again into the same spot. At the second shot he did not col- lapse but climbed with desperate slowness to his feet and stood weakly upright, with legs sagging and head drooping. I fired a third time. That was the shot that did for him. You could see the agony of it jolt his whole body and knock the last remnant of strength from his legs. But in falling he seemed for a moment to rise, for as his hind legs collapsed beneath him he seemed to tower upward like a huge rock toppling, his trunk reaching skyward like a tree. He trumpeted, for the first and only time. And then down he came, his belly toward me, with a crash that seemed to shake the ground even where I lay.

I got up. The Burmans were already racing past me across the mud. It was obvious that the elephant would never rise again, but he was not dead. He was breathing very rhythmically with long rattling gasps, his great mound of a side painfully rising and fall- ing. His mouth was wide open—I could see far down into caverns of pale pink throat. I waited a long time for him to die, but his breathing did not weaken. Finally I fired my two remaining shots into the spot where I thought his heart must be. The thick blood welled out of him like red velvet, but still he did not die. His body did not even jerk when the shots hit him, the tortured breathing continued without a pause. He was dying, very slowly and in great agony, but in some world remote from me where not even a bullet could damage him further. I felt that I had got to put an end to that dreadful noise. It seemed dreadful to see the great beast lying there, powerless to move and yet powerless to die, and not even to be able to finish him. I sent back for my small rifle and poured shot after shot into his heart and down his throat. They seemed to make no impression. The tortured gasps continued as steadily as the ticking of a clock.

In the end I could not stand it any longer and went away. I heard later that it took him half an hour to die. Burmans were bringing dahs and baskets even before I left, and I was told they had stripped his body almost to the bones by the afternoon.

Afterward, of course, there were endless discussions about the shooting of the elephant. The owner was furious, but he was only an Indian and could do nothing. Besides, legally I had done the right thing, for a mad elephant has to be killed, like a mad dog, if its owner fails to control it. Among the Europeans opinion was divided. The older men said I was right, the younger men said it was a damn shame to shoot an elephant for killing a coolie, because an elephant was worth more than any damn Coringhee coolie. And afterward I was very glad that the coolie had been killed; it put me legally in the right and it gave me a sufficient pretext for shooting the elephant. I often wondered whether any of the others grasped that I had done it solely to avoid looking a fool.

1936

△

A Hanging

▽

It was in Burma, a sodden morning of the rains. A sickly light, like yellow tinfoil, was slanting over the high walls into the jail yard. We were waiting outside the condemned cells, a row of sheds fronted with double bars, like small animal cages. Each cell measured about ten feet by ten and was quite bare within except for a plank bed and a pot for drinking water. In some of them brown silent men were squatting at the inner bars, with their blankets draped round them. These were the condemned men, due to be hanged within the next week or two.

One prisoner had been brought out of his cell. He was a Hindu, a puny wisp of a man, with a shaven head and vague liquid eyes. He had a thick, sprouting moustache, absurdly too big for his body, rather like the moustache of a comic man on the films. Six tall Indian warders were guarding him and getting him ready for the gallows. Two of them stood by with rifles and fixed bayonets, while the others handcuffed him, passed a chain through his handcuffs and fixed it to their belts, and lashed his arms tight to his sides. They crowded very close about him, with their hands always on him in a careful, caressing grip, as though all the while feeling him to make sure he was there. It was like men handling a fish which is still alive and may jump back into the water. But he stood quite unresisting, yielding his arms limply to the ropes, as though he hardly noticed what was happening.

Eight o'clock struck and a bugle call, desolately thin in the wet air, floated from the distant barracks. The superintendent of the jail, who was standing apart from the rest of us, moodily prodding the gravel with his stick, raised his head at the sound. He was an army doctor, with a gray toothbrush moustache and a gruff voice. "For God's sake hurry up, Francis," he said irritably. "The man ought to have been dead by this time. Aren't you ready yet?"

Francis, the head jailer, a fat Dravidian in a white drill suit and gold spectacles, waved his black hand. "Yes sir, yes sir," he bubbled. "All iss satisfactorily prepared. The hangman iss waiting. We shall proceed."

"Well, quick march, then. The prisoners can't get their breakfast till this job's over."

We set out for the gallows. Two warders marched on either side of the prisoner, with their rifles at the slope; two others marched close against him, gripping him by arm and shoulder, as though at once pushing and supporting him. The rest of us, magistrates and the like, followed behind. Suddenly, when we had gone ten yards, the procession stopped short without any order or warning. A dreadful thing had happened—a dog, come goodness knows whence, had appeared in the yard. It came bounding among us with a loud volley of barks, and leapt round us wagging its whole body, wild with glee at finding so many human beings together. It was a large woolly dog, half Airedale, half pariah. For a moment it pranced round us, and then, before anyone could stop it, it had made a dash for the prisoner and, jumping up, tried to lick his face. Everyone stood aghast, too taken aback even to grab at the dog.

"Who let that bloody brute in here?" said the superintendent angrily. "Catch it, someone!"

A warder, detached from the escort, charged clumsily after the dog, but it danced and gamboled just out of his reach, taking everything as part of the game. A young Eurasian jailer picked up a handful of gravel and tried to stone the dog away, but it dodged the stones and came after us again. Its yaps echoed from the jail walls. The prisoner, in the grasp of the two warders, looked on incuriously, as though this was another formality of the hanging. It was several minutes before someone managed to catch the dog. Then we put my handkerchief through its collar and moved off once more, with the dog still straining and whimpering.

It was about forty yards to the gallows. I watched the bare brown back of the prisoner marching in front of me. He walked clumsily with his bound arms, but quite steadily, with that bobbing gait of the Indian who never straightens his knees. At each step his muscles slid neatly into place, the lock of hair on his scalp danced up and down, his feet printed themselves on the wet gravel. And once, in spite of the men who gripped him by each shoulder, he stepped slightly aside to avoid a puddle on the path.

It is curious, but till that moment I had never realized what it means to destroy a healthy, conscious man. When I saw the prisoner step aside to avoid the puddle I saw the mystery, the unspeakable wrongness, of cutting a life short when it is in full tide. This man was not dying, he was alive just as we are alive. All the organs of his body were working—bowels digesting food, skin renewing itself, nails growing, tissues forming—all toiling away in solemn foolery. His nails would still be growing when he stood on the drop, when he was falling through the air with a tenth of a second to live. His eyes saw the yellow gravel and the gray walls, and his brain still remembered, foresaw, reasoned—reasoned even about puddles. He and we were a party of men walking together, seeing, hearing, feeling, understanding the same world; and in two minutes, with a sudden snap, one of us would be gone—one mind less, one world less.

The gallows stood in a small yard, separate from the main grounds of the prison, and overgrown with tall prickly weeds. It was a brick erection like three sides of a shed, with planking on top, and above that two beams and a crossbar with the rope dangling. The hangman, a gray-haired convict in the white uniform of the prison, was waiting beside his machine. He greeted us with a servile crouch as we entered. At a word from Francis the two warders, gripping the prisoner more closely than ever, half led half pushed him to the gallows and helped him clumsily up the ladder. Then the hangman climbed up and fixed the rope round the prisoner's neck.

We stood waiting, five yards away. The warders had formed in a rough circle round the gallows. And then, when the noose was fixed, the prisoner began crying out to his god. It was a high, re-iterated cry of "Ram! Ram! Ram! Ram!" not urgent and fearful like a prayer or cry for help, but steady, rhythmical, almost like the tolling of a bell. The dog answered the sound with a whine. The hangman, still standing on the gallows, produced a small cotton bag like a flour bag and drew it down over the prisoner's face. But the sound, muffled by the cloth, still persisted, over and over again: "Ram! Ram! Ram! Ram! Ram!"

The hangman climbed down and stood ready, holding the lever. Minutes seemed to pass. The steady, muffled crying from the prisoner went on and on, "Ram! Ram! Ram!" never faltering for an instant. The superintendent, his head on his chest, was slowly poking the ground with his stick; perhaps he was counting the cries, allowing the prisoner a fixed number—fifty, perhaps, or a hundred. Everyone had changed color. The Indians had gone gray like bad coffee, and one or two of the bayonets were wavering. We looked at the lashed, hooded man on the drop, and listened to his cries—each cry another second of life; the same thought was in all our minds: oh, kill him quickly, get it over, stop that abominable noise!

Suddenly the superintendent made up his mind. Throwing up his head he made a swift motion with his stick. "Chalo!" he shouted almost fiercely.

There was a clanking noise, and then dead silence. The prisoner had vanished, and the rope was twisting on itself. I let go of the dog, and it galloped immediately to the back of the gallows; but when it got there it stopped short, barked, and then retreated into a corner of the yard, where it stood among the weeds, looking timorously out at us. We went round the gallows to inspect the prisoner's body. He was dangling with his toes pointed straight downward, very slowly revolving, as dead as a stone.

The superintendent reached out with his stick and poked the bare brown body; it oscillated slightly. *"He's* all right," said the superintendent. He backed out from under the gallows, and blew out a deep breath. The moody look had gone out of his face quite suddenly. He glanced at his wrist watch. "Eight minutes past eight. Well, that's all for this morning, thank God."

The warders unfixed bayonets and marched away. The dog, sobered and conscious of having misbehaved itself, slipped after

hem. We walked out of the gallows yard, past the condemned cells
with their waiting prisoners, into the big central yard of the prison.
The convicts, under the command of warders armed with lathis,
were already receiving their breakfast. They squatted in long rows,
each man holding a tin pannikin, while two warders with buckets
marched round ladling out rice; it seemed quite a homely, jolly
scene, after the hanging. An enormous relief had come upon us now
that the job was done. One felt an impluse to sing, to break into a
run, to snigger. All at once everyone began chattering gaily.

The Eurasian boy walking beside me nodded toward the way we
had come, with a knowing smile: "Do you know, sir, our friend [he
meant the dead man] when he heard his appeal had been dismissed,
he pissed on the floor of his cell. From fright. Kindly take one of my
cigarettes, sir. Do you not admire my new silver case, sir? From the
boxwalah, two rupees eight annas. Classy European style."

Several people laughed—at what, nobody seemed certain.

Francis was walking by the superintendent, talking garrulously:
Well, sir, all hass passed off with the utmost satisfactoriness. It was
all finished—flick! like that. It iss not always so—oah, no! I have
known cases where the doctor wass obliged to go beneath the gallows
and pull the prissoner's legs to ensure decease. Most disagreeable!"

"Wriggling about, eh? That's bad," said the superintendent.

"Ach, sir, it iss worse when they become refractory! One man, I
recall, clung to the bars of hiss cage when we went to take him out.
You will scarcely credit, sir, that it took six warders to dislodge him,
three pulling at each leg. We reasoned with him. 'My dear fellow,'
we said, 'think of all the pain and trouble you are causing to us!'
But no, he would not listen! Ach, he wass very troublesome!"

I found that I was laughing quite loudly. Everyone was laughing.
Even the superintendent grinned in a tolerant way. "You'd better
all come out and have a drink," he said quite genially. "I've got a
bottle of whisky in the car. We could do with it."

We went through the big double gates of the prison into the
road. "Pulling at his legs!" exclaimed a Burmese magistrate suddenly,
and burst into a loud chuckling. We all began laughing again. At
that moment Francis' anecdote seemed extraordinarily funny. We
all had a drink together, native and European alike, quite ami-
ably. The dead man was a hundred yards away.

                                                                1931

△

From "Burmese Days"

▽

IV

. . . Flory stood in the middle of the room, yawning. Should he go down to the Club for tennis after all? No, it meant shaving, and he could not face the effort of shaving until he had a few drinks inside him. He felt his scrubby chin and lounged across to the mirror to examine it, but then turned away. He did not want to see the yellow, sunken face that would look back at him. For several minutes he stood, slack-limbed, watching the *tuktoo* stalk a moth above the book shelves. The cigarette that Ma Hla May had dropped burned down with an acrid smell, browning the paper. Flory took a book from the shelves, opened it, and then threw it away in distaste. He had not even the energy to read. Oh God, God, what to do with the rest of this bloody evening?

Flo waddled into the room, wagging her tail and asking to be taken for a walk. Flory went sulkily into the little stone-floored bathroom that gave on to the bedroom, splashed himself with lukewarm water, and put on his shirt and shorts. He must take some kind of exercise before the sun went down. In India it is in some way evil to spend a day without being once in a muck-sweat. It gives one a deeper sense of sin than a thousand lecheries. In the dark evening, after a quite idle day, one's ennui reaches a pitch that is frantic, suicidal. Work, prayer, books, drinking, talking—they are all power-less against it; it can only be sweated out through the pores of the skin.

Flory went out and followed the road uphill into the jungle. It was scrub jungle at first, with dense stunted bushes, and the only trees were half-wild mangoes, bearing little turpentiny fruits the size of plums. Then the road struck among taller trees. The jungle was dried up and lifeless at this time of year. The trees lined the road in close, dusty ranks, with leaves a dull olive-green. No birds were visible except some ragged brown creatures like disreputable thrushes, which hopped clumsily under the bushes; in the distance some other bird uttered a cry of "*Ah* ha ha! *Ah* ha ha!"—a lonely, hollow sound like the echo of a laugh. There was a poisonous, ivy-like smell of crushed leaves. It was still hot, though the sun was losing its glare and the slanting light was yellow.

After two miles the road ended at the ford of a shallow stream. The jungle grew greener here, because of the water, and the trees were taller. At the edge of the stream there was a huge dead pyinkado tree festooned with spidery orchids, and there were some wild lime bushes with white, waxen flowers. They had a sharp scent like bergamot. Flory had walked fast and the sweat had drenched his shirt and dribbled, stinging, into his eyes. He had sweated himself into a better mood. Also, the sight of this stream always heartened him; its water was quite clear, rarest of sights in a miry country. He crossed the stream by the stepping stones, Flo splashing after him, and turned into a narrow track he knew, which led through the bushes. It was a track that cattle had made, coming to the stream to drink, and few human beings ever followed it. It led to a pool fifty yards upstream. Here a peepul tree grew, a great buttressed thing six feet thick, woven of innumerable strands of wood, like a wooden cable twisted by a giant. The roots of the tree made a natural cavern, under which the clear greenish water bubbled. Above and all round dense foliage shut out the light, turning the place into a green grotto walled with leaves.

Flory threw off his clothes and stepped into the water. It was a shade cooler than the air, and it came up to his neck when he sat down. Shoals of silvery *mahseer,* no bigger than sardines, came nosing and nibbling at his body. Flo had also flopped into the water, and she swam round silently, otter-like, with her webbed feet. She knew the pool well, for they often came here when Flory was at Kyauktada.

There was a stirring high up in the peepul tree, and a bubbling noise like pots boiling. A flock of green pigeons were up there, eating the berries. Flory gazed up into the great green dome of the tree, trying to distinguish the birds; they were invisible, they matched the leaves so perfectly, and yet the whole tree was alive with them, shimmering, as though the ghosts of birds were shaking it. Flo rested herself against the roots and growled up at the invisible creatures. Then a single green pigeon fluttered down and perched on a lower branch. It did not know that it was being watched. It was a tender thing, smaller than a tame dove, with jade-green back as smooth as velvet, and neck and breast of iridescent colors. Its legs were like the pink wax that dentists use.

The pigeon rocked itself backward and forward on the bough, swelling out its breast feathers and laying its coraline beak upon them. A pang went through Flory. Alone, alone, the bitterness of being alone! So often like this, in lonely places in the forest, he would come upon something—bird, flower, tree—beautiful beyond all words, if there had been a soul with whom to share it. Beauty is meaningless until it is shared. If he had one person, just one, to halve his loneliness! Suddenly the pigeon saw the man and dog below, sprang into the air, and dashed away swift as a bullet, with a rattle of wings. One does not often see green pigeons so closely when they are alive. They are high-flying birds, living in the tree-tops, and they do not come to the ground, or only to drink. When one shoots them, if they are not killed outright, they cling to the branch until they die, and drop long after one has given up waiting and gone away.

Flory got out of the water, put on his clothes and recrossed the stream. He did not go home by the road, but followed a foot-track southward into the jungle, intending to make a detour and pass through a village that lay in the fringe of the jungle not far from his house. Flo frisked in and out of the undergrowth, yelping sometimes when her long ears caught in the thorns. She had once turned up a hare near here. Flory walked slowly. The smoke of his pipe floated straight upward in still plumes. He was happy and at peace after the walk and the clear water. It was cooler now, except for patches of heat lingering under the thicker trees, and the light was gentle. Bullock-cart wheels were screaming peacefully in the distance.

Soon they had lost their way in the jungle, and were wandering in a maze of dead trees and tangled bushes. They came to an impasse where the path was blocked by large ugly plants like magnified aspidistras, whose leaves terminated in long lashes armed with thorns. A firefly glowed greenish at the bottom of a bush; it was getting twilight in the thicker places. Presently the bullock-cart wheels screamed nearer, taking a parallel course.

"Hey, *saya gyi, saya gyi!*" Flory shouted, taking Flo by the collar to prevent her running away.

"*Ba le-de?*" the Burman shouted back. There was the sound of plunging hooves and of yells to the bullocks.

"Come here, if you please, O venerable and learned sir! We have lost our way. Stop a moment, O great builder of pagodas!"

The Burman left his cart and pushed through the jungle, slicing the creepers with his *dah*. He was a squat middle-aged man with one eye. He led the way back to the track, and Flory climbed on to the flat, uncomfortable bullock cart. The Burman took up the string reins, yelled to the bullocks, prodded the roots of their tails with his short stick, and the cart jolted on with a shriek of wheels. The

Burmese bullock-cart drivers seldom grease their axles, probably because they believe that the screaming keeps away evil spirits, though when questioned they will say that it is because they are too poor to buy grease.

They passed a whitewashed wooden pagoda, no taller than a man and half hidden by the tendrils of creeping plants. Then the track wound into the village, which consisted of twenty ruinous wooden huts roofed with thatch, and a well beneath some barren date palms. The egrets that roosted in the palms were streaming homeward over the treetops like white flights of arrows. A fat yellow woman with her *longyi* hitched under her armpits was chasing a dog round a hut, smacking at it with a bamboo and laughing, and the dog was also laughing in its fashion. The village was called Nyaungle-bin—"the four peepul trees"; there were no peepul trees there now, probably they had been cut down and forgotten a century ago. The villagers cultivated a narrow strip of fields that lay between the town and the jungle, and they also made bullock carts which they sold in Kyauktada. Bullock-cart wheels were littered everywhere under the houses; massive things five feet across, with spokes roughly but strongly carved.

Flory got off the cart and gave the driver a present of four annas. Some brindled curs hurried from beneath the houses to sniff at Flo, and a flock of pot-bellied, naked children, with their hair tied in top-knots, also appeared, curious about the white man but keeping their distance. The village headman, a weazened, leaf-brown old man, came out of his house, and there were shikoings. Flory sat down on the steps of the headman's house and relighted his pipe. He was thirsty.

"Is the water in your well good to drink, *thugyi-min?*" The headman reflected, scratching the calf of his left leg with his right big toenail. "Those who drink it, drink it, *thakin*. And those who do not drink it, do not drink it."

"Ah. That is wisdom."

The fat woman who had chased the pariah brought a blackened earthenware teapot and a handleless bowl, and gave Flory some pale green tea, tasting of wood-smoke.

"I must be going, *thugyi-min*. Thank you for the tea."

"God go with you, *thakin*."

Flory went home by a path that led out on to the maidan. It was dark now. Ko S'la had put on a clean *ingyi* and was waiting in the bedroom. He had heated two kerosene tins of bath-water, lighted the petrol lamps, and laid out a clean suit and shirt for Flory. The clean clothes were intended as a hint that Flory should shave, dress

himself, and go down to the Club after dinner. Occasionally he spent
the evening in Shan trousers, loafing in a chair with a book, and Ko
S'la disapproved of this habit. He hated to see his master behaving
differently from other white men. The fact that Flory often came
back from the Club drunk, whereas he remained sober when he
stayed at home, did not alter Ko S'la's opinion, because getting
drunk was normal and pardonable in a white man. . . .

V

In spite of the whisky he had drunk at the Club, Flory had little
sleep that night. The pariah curs were baying the moon—it was
only a quarter full and nearly down by midnight, but the dogs slept
all day in the heat, and they had begun their moon-choruses already.
One dog had taken a dislike to Flory's house, and had settled down
to bay at it systematically. Sitting on its bottom fifty yards from the
gate, it let out sharp, angry yelps, one to half a minute, as regularly
as a clock. It would keep this up for two or three hours, until the
cocks began crowing.

Flory lay turning from side to side, his head aching. Some fool
has said that one cannot hate an animal; he should try a few nights
in India, when the dogs are baying the moon. In the end Flory
could stand it no longer. He got up, rummaged in the tin uniform
case under his bed for a rifle and a couple of cartridges, and went
out on to the veranda.

It was fairly light in the quarter moon. He could see the dog, and
he could see his foresight. He rested himself against the wooden
pillar of the veranda and took aim carefully; then, as he felt the
hard vulcanite butt against his bare shoulder, he flinched. The rifle
had a heavy kick, and it left a bruise when one fired it. The soft
flesh of his shoulder quailed. He lowered the rifle. He had not the
nerve to fire it in cold blood.

It was no use trying to sleep. Flory got his jacket and some cigarettes, and began to stroll up and down the garden path, between
the ghostly flowers. It was hot, and the mosquitoes found him out
and came droning after him. Phantoms of dogs were chasing one
another on the maidan. Over to the left the gravestones of the
English cemetery glittered whitish, rather sinister, and one could see
the mounds nearby, that were the remains of old Chinese tombs.
The hillside was said to be haunted, and the Club *chokras* cried
when they were sent up the road at night.

"Cur, spineless cur," Flory was thinking to himself; without heat,
however, for he was too accustomed to the thought. "Sneaking
idling, boozing, fornicating, soul-examining, self-pitying cur. All

those fools at the Club, those dull louts to whom you are so pleased to think yourself superior—they are all better than you, every man of them. At least they are men in their oafish way. Not cowards, not liars. Not half-dead and rotting. But you——"

He had reason to call himself names. There had been a nasty, dirty affair at the Club that evening. Something quite ordinary, quite according to precedent; but still dingy, cowardly, dishonoring.

When Flory had arrived at the Club only Ellis and Maxwell were there. The Lackersteens had gone to the station with the loan of Mr. Macgregor's car, to meet their niece, who was to arrive by the night train. The three men were playing three-handed bridge fairly amicably when Westfield came in, his sandy face quite pink with rage, bringing a copy of a Burmese paper called the *Burmese Patriot*. There was a libelous article in it, attacking Mr. Macgregor. The rage of Ellis and Westfield was devilish. They were so angry that Flory had the greatest difficulty in pretending to be angry enough to satisfy them. Ellis spent five minutes in cursing and then, by some extraordinary process, made up his mind that Dr. Veraswami was responsible for the article. And he had thought of a counterstroke already. They would put a notice on the board—a notice answering and contradicting the one Mr. Macgregor had posted the day before. Ellis wrote it out immediately, in his tiny, clear handwriting:

"In view of the cowardly insult recently offered to our Deputy Commissioner, we the undersigned wish to give it as our opinion that this is the worst possible moment to consider the election of niggers to this Club," etc., etc.

Westfield demurred to "niggers." It was crossed out by a single thin line and "natives" substituted. The notice was signed "R. West-field, P. W. Ellis, C. W. Maxwell, J. Flory."

Ellis was so pleased with his idea that quite half of his anger evaporated. The notice would accomplish nothing in itself, but the news of it would travel swiftly round the town, and would reach Dr. Veraswami tomorrow. In effect, the doctor would have been publicly called a nigger by the European community. This delighted Ellis. For the rest of the evening he could hardly keep his eyes from the notice board, and every few minutes he exclaimed in glee, "That'll give little fat-belly something to think about, eh? Teach the little sod what we think of him. That's the way to put 'em in their place, eh?" etc.

Meanwhile, Flory had signed a public insult to his friend. He had done it for the same reason as he had done a thousand such things in his life; because he lacked the small spark of courage that was needed to refuse. For, of course, he could have refused if he had

chosen; and, equally of course, refusal would have meant a row with
Ellis and Westfield. And oh, how he loathed a row! The nagging,
the jeers! At the very thought of it he flinched; he could feel his
birthmark palpable on his cheek, and something happening in his
throat that made his voice go flat and guilty. Not that! It was easier
to insult his friend, knowing that his friend must hear of it.

Flory had been fifteen years in Burma, and in Burma one learns
not to set oneself up against public opinion. . . .

He was not quite twenty when he came to Burma. His parents,
good people and devoted to him, had found him a place in a timber
firm. They had had great difficulty in getting him the job, had paid
a premium they could not afford; later, he had rewarded them by
answering their letters with careless scrawls at intervals of months.
His first six months in Burma he had spent in Rangoon, where he
was supposed to be learning the office side of his business. He had
lived in a "chummery" with four other youths who devoted their
entire energies to debauchery. And what debauchery! They swilled
whisky which they privately hated, they stood round the piano
bawling songs of insane filthiness and silliness, they squandered
rupees by the hundred on aged Jewish whores with the faces of
crocodiles. That too had been a formative period.

From Rangoon he had gone to a camp in the jungle, north of
Mandalay, extracting teak. The jungle life was not a bad one, in
spite of the discomfort, the loneliness, and what is almost the worst
thing in Burma, the filthy, monotonous food. He was very young
then, young enough for hero worship, and he had friends among
the men in his firm. There were also shooting, fishing, and perhaps
once in a year a hurried trip to Rangoon—pretext, a visit to the
dentist. Oh, the joy of those Rangoon trips! The rush to Smart and
Mookerdum's bookshop for the new novels out from England, the
dinner at Anderson's with beefsteaks and butter that had traveled
eight thousand miles on ice, the glorious drinking bout! He was too
young to realize what this life was preparing for him. He did not
see the years stretching out ahead, lonely, eventless, corrupting.

He acclimatized himself to Burma. His body grew attuned to the
strange rhythms of the tropical seasons. Every year from February
to May the sun glared in the sky like an angry god, then suddenly
the monsoon blew westward, first in sharp squalls, then in a heavy
ceaseless downpour that drenched everything until neither one's
clothes, one's bed, nor even one's food ever seemed to be dry. It was
still hot, with a stuffy, vaporous heat. The lower jungle paths turned
into morasses, and the paddy fields were great wastes of stagnant
water with a stale, mousy smell. Books and boots were mildewed.

Naked Burmans in yard-wide hats of palm-leaf ploughed the paddy fields, driving their buffaloes through knee-deep water. Later, the women and children planted the green seedlings of paddy, dabbing each plant into the mud with little three-pronged forks. Through July and August there was hardly a pause in the rain. Then one night, high overhead, one heard a squawking of invisible birds. The snipe were flying southward from Central Asia. The rains tailed off, ending in October. The fields dried up, the paddy ripened, the Burmese children played hopscotch with gonyin seeds and flew kites in the cool winds. It was the beginning of the short winter, when Upper Burma seemed haunted by the ghost of England. Wild flowers sprang into bloom everywhere, not quite the same as the English ones, but very like them—honeysuckle in thick bushes, field roses smelling of peardrops, even violets in dark places of the forest. The sun circled low in the sky, and the nights and early mornings were bitterly cold, with white mists that poured through the valleys like the steam of enormous kettles. One went shooting after duck and snipe. There were snipe in countless myriads, and wild geese in flocks that rose from the jeel with a roar like a goods train crossing an iron bridge. The ripening paddy, breast high and yellow, looked like wheat. The Burmans went to their work with muffled heads and their arms clasped across their breasts, their faces yellow and pinched with the cold. In the morning one marched through misty, incongruous wildernesses, clearings of drenched, almost English grass and naked trees where monkeys squatted in the upper branches, waiting for the sun. At night, coming back to camp through the cold lanes, one met herds of buffaloes which the boys were driving home, with their huge horns looming through the mist like crescents. One had three blankets on one's bed, and game pies instead of the eternal chicken. After dinner one sat on a log by the vast camp fire, drinking beer and talking about shooting. The flames danced like red holly, casting a circle of light at the edge of which servants and coolies squatted, too shy to intrude on the white men and yet edging up to the fire like dogs. As one lay in bed one could hear the dew dripping from the trees like large but gentle rain. It was a good life while one was young and need not think about the future or the past.

Flory was twenty-four, and due for home leave, when the war broke out. He had dodged military service, which was easy to do and seemed natural at the time. The civilians in Burma had a comforting theory that "sticking by one's job" (wonderful language, English! "Sticking *by*"—how different from "sticking *to*") was the truest patriotism; there was even a covert hostility toward the men who threw up their jobs in order to join the Army. In reality, Flory had dodged the war because the East had already corrupted him, and he did not want to exchange his whisky, his servants, and his Burmese girls for the boredom of the parade ground and the strain of cruel marches. The war rolled on, like a storm beyond the horizon. The hot, blowzy country, remote from danger, had a lonely, forgotten feeling. Flory took to reading voraciously, and learned to live in books when life was tiresome. He was growing adult, tiring of boyish pleasures, learning to think for himself, almost willy nilly.

He celebrated his twenty-seventh birthday in hospital, covered from head to foot with hideous sores which were called mud-sores, but were probably caused by whisky and bad food. They left little pits in his skin which did not disappear for two years. Quite suddenly he had begun to look and feel very much older. His youth was finished. Eight years of Eastern life, fever, loneliness, and intermittent drinking, had set their mark on him.

Since then, each year had been lonelier and more bitter than the last. What was at the center of all his thoughts now, and what poisoned everything, was the ever bitterer hatred of the atmosphere of imperialism in which he lived. For as his brain developed—you cannot stop your brain developing, and it is one of the tragedies of the half-educated that they develop late, when they are already committed to some wrong way of life—he had grasped the truth about the English and their Empire. The Indian Empire is a despotism —benevolent, no doubt, but still a despotism with theft as its final object. And as to the English of the East, the *sahiblog*, Flory had come so to hate them from living in their society, that he was quite incapable of being fair to them. For after all, the poor devils are no worse than anybody else. They lead unenviable lives; it is a poor bargain to spend thirty years, ill paid, in an alien country, and then come home with a wrecked liver and a pineapple backside from sitting in cane chairs, to settle down as the bore of some second-rate club. On the other hand, the *sahiblog* are not to be idealized. There is a prevalent idea that the men at the "outposts of Empire" are at least able and hardworking. It is a delusion. Outside the scientific services—the Forest Department, the Public Works Department, and the like—there is no particular need for a British official in India to do his job competently. Few of them work as hard or as intelligently as the postmaster of a provincial town in England. The real work of administration is done mainly by native subordinates; and the real backbone of the despotism is not the officials but the Army. Given the Army, the officials and the business men can rub along safely enough even if they are fools. And most of them *are* fools. A dull, decent people, cherishing and fortifying their dullness behind a quarter of a million bayonets.

It is a stifling, stultifying world in which to live. It is a world in which every word and every thought is censored. In England it is hard even to imagine such an atmosphere. Everyone is free in England; we sell our souls in public and buy them back in private, among our friends. But even friendship can hardly exist when every white man is a cog in the wheels of despotism. Free speech is unthinkable. All other kinds of freedom are permitted. You are free to be a drunkard, an idler, a coward, a backbiter, a fornicator; but you are not free to think for yourself. Your opinion on every subject of any conceivable importance is dictated for you by the pukka sahibs' code.

In the end the secrecy of your revolt poisons you like a secret disease. Your whole life is a life of lies. Year after year you sit in Kipling-haunted little clubs, whisky to right of you, *Pink'un* to left of you, listening and eagerly agreeing while Colonel Bodger develops his theory that these bloody Nationalists should be boiled in oil. You hear your Oriental friends called "greasy little babus," and you admit, dutifully, that they *are* greasy little babus. You see louts fresh from school kicking gray-haired servants. The time comes when you burn with hatred of your own countrymen, when you long for a native rising to drown their Empire in blood. And in this there is nothing honorable, hardly even any sincerity. For, *au fond,* what do you care if the Indian Empire is a despotism, if Indians are bullied and exploited? You only care because the right of free speech is denied you. You are a creature of the despotism, a pukka sahib, tied tighter than a monk or a savage by an unbreakable system of tabus.

Time passed, and each year Flory found himself less at home in the world of the sahibs, more liable to get into trouble when he talked seriously on any subject whatever. So he had learned to live inwardly, secretly, in books and secret thoughts that could not be uttered. Even his talks with the doctor were a kind of talking to himself; for the doctor, good man, understood little of what was said to him. But it is a corrupting thing to live one's real life in secret. One should live with the stream of life, not against it. It would be better to be the thickest-skulled pukka sahib who ever hiccuped over "Forty years on," than to live silent, alone, consoling oneself in secret, sterile worlds.

Flory had never been home to England. Why, he could not have explained, though he knew well enough. In the beginning accidents had prevented him. First there was the war, and after the war his

firm were so short of trained assistants that they would not let him
go for two years more. Then at last he had set out. He was pining for England, though he dreaded facing it, as one dreads facing
a pretty girl when one is collarless and unshaven. When he left
home he had been a boy, a promising boy and handsome in spite
of his birthmark; now, only ten years later, he was yellow, thin,
drunken, almost middle aged in habits and appearance. Still, he
was pining for England. The ship rolled westward over wastes of
sea like rough-beaten silver, with the winter trade wind behind her.
Flory's thin blood quickened with the good food and the smell of
the sea. And it occurred to him—a thing he had actually forgotten
in the stagnant air of Burma—that he was still young enough to
begin over again. He would live a year in civilized society, he would
find some girl who did not mind his birthmark—a civilized girl,
not a pukka memsahib—and he would marry her and endure ten,
fifteen more years of Burma. Then they would retire—he would be
worth twelve or fifteen thousand pounds on retirement, perhaps.
They would buy a cottage in the country, surround themselves with
friends, books, their children, animals. They would be free for ever
of the small of pukka sahibdom. He would forget Burma, the horrible country that had come near ruining him.

When he reached Colombo he found a cable waiting for him.
Three men in his firm had died suddenly of blackwater fever. The
firm were sorry, but would he please return to Rangoon at once?
He should have his leave at the earliest possible opportunity.

Flory boarded the next boat for Rangoon, cursing his luck, and
took the train back to his headquarters. He was not at Kyauktada
then, but at another Upper Burma town. All the servants were
waiting for him on the platform. He had handed them over *en
bloc* to his successor, who had died. It was so queer to see their
familiar faces again! Only ten days ago he had been speeding for
England, almost thinking himself in England already; and now
back in the old stale scene, with the naked black coolies squab-
bling over the luggage and a Burman shouting at his bullocks down
the road.

The servants came crowding round him, a ring of kindly brown
faces, offering presents. Ko S'la had brought a sambhur skin, the
Indians some sweetmeats and a garland of marigolds, Ba Pe, a
young boy then, a squirrel in a wicker cage. There were bullock
carts waiting for the luggage. Flory walked up to the house, looking ridiculous with the big garland dangling from his neck. The
light of the cold weather evening was yellow and kind. At the gate
an old Indian, the color of earth, was cropping grass with a tiny

sickle. The wives of the cook and the *mali* were kneeling in front of the servants' quarters, grinding curry paste on the stone slab.

Something turned over in Flory's heart. It was one of those moments when one becomes conscious of a vast change and deterioration in one's life. For he had realized, suddenly, that in his heart he was glad to be coming back. This country which he hated was now his native country, his home. He had lived here ten years, and every particle of his body was compounded of Burmese soil. Scenes like these—the sallow evening light, the old Indian cropping grass, the creak of the cartwheels, the streaming egrets—were more native to him than England. He had sent deep roots, perhaps his deepest, into a foreign country.

Since then he had not even applied for home leave. His father had died, then his mother, and his sisters, disagreeable horsefaced women whom he had never liked, had married and he had almost lost touch with them. He had no tie with Europe now, except the tie of books. For he had realized that merely to go back to England was no remedy for loneliness; he had grasped the special nature of the hell that is reserved for Anglo-Indians. Ah, those poor prosing old wrecks in Bath and Cheltenham! Those tomblike boarding-houses with Anglo-Indians littered about in all stages of decomposition, all talking and talking about what happened in Boggleywalah in '88! Poor devils, they know what it means to have left one's heart in an alien and hated country. There was, he saw clearly, only one way out. To find someone who would share his life in Burma—but really share it, share his inner, secret life, carry away from Burma the same memories as he carried. Someone who would love Burma as he loved it and hate it as he hated it. Who would help him to live with nothing hidden, nothing unexpressed. Someone who understood him: a friend, that was what it came down to.

A friend. Or a wife? That quite impossible she. Someone like Mrs. Lackersteen, for instance? Some damned memsahib, yellow and thin, scandalmongering over cocktails, making kit-kit with the servants, living twenty years in the country without learning a word of the language. Not one of those, please God.

Flory leaned over the gate. The moon was vanishing behind the dark wall of the jungle, but the dogs were still howling. Some lines from Gilbert came into his mind, a vulgar silly jingle but appropriate—something about "discoursing on your complicated state of mind." Gilbert was a gifted little skunk. Did all his trouble, then, simply boil down to that? Just complicated, unmanly whinings; poor-little-rich-girl stuff? Was he no more than a loafer using his idleness to invent imaginary woes? A spiritual Mrs. Wititterly? A

Hamlet without poetry? Perhaps. And if so, did that make it any more bearable? It is not the less bitter because it is perhaps one's own fault, to see oneself drifting, rotting, in dishonor and horrible futility, and all the while knowing that somewhere within one there is the possibility of a decent human being.

Oh well, God save us from self-pity! Flory went back to the veranda, took up the rifle, and, wincing slightly, let drive at the pariah dog. There was an echoing roar, and the bullet buried itself in the maidan, wide of the mark. A mulberry-colored bruise sprang out on Flory's shoulder. The dog gave a yell of fright, took to its heels, and then, sitting down fifty yards farther away, once more began rhythmically baying.

VIII

That evening Flory told Ko S'la to send for the barber—he was the only barber in the town, an Indian, and he made a living by shaving the Indian coolies at the rate of eight annas a month for a dry shave every other day. The Europeans patronized him for lack of any other. The barber was waiting on the veranda when Flory came back from tennis, and Flory sterilized the scissors with boiling water and Condy's fluid and had his hair cut.

"Lay out my best Palm Beach suit," he told Ko S'la, "and a silk shirt and my sambhur-skin shoes. Also that new tie that came from Rangoon last week."

"I have done so, *thakin*," said Ko S'la, meaning that he would do so. When Flory came into the bedroom he found Ko S'la waiting beside the clothes he had laid out, with a faintly sulky air. It was immediately apparent that Ko S'la knew why Flory was dressing himself up (that is, in hopes of meeting Elizabeth) and that he disapproved of it.

"What are you waiting for?" Flory said.

"To help you dress, *thakin*."

"I shall dress myself this evening. You can go."

He was going to shave—the second time that day—and he did not want Ko S'la to see him take his shaving things into the bathroom. It was several years since he had shaved twice in one day. What providential luck that he had sent for that new tie only last week, he thought. He dressed himself very carefully, and spent nearly a quarter of an hour in brushing his hair, which was stiff and would never lie down after it had been cut.

Almost the next moment, as it seemed, he was walking with Elizabeth down the bazaar road. He had found her alone in the Club "library," and with a sudden burst of courage asked her to come out with him; and she had come with a readiness that surprised him, not even stopping to say anything to her uncle and aunt. He had lived so long in Burma, he had forgotten English ways. It was very dark under the peepul trees of the bazaar road, the foliage hiding the quarter moon, but the stars here and there in a gap blazed white and low, like lamps hanging on invisible threads. Successive waves of scent came rolling, first the cloying sweetness of frangipani, then a cold putrid stench of dung or decay from the huts opposite Dr. Veraswami's bungalow. Drums were throbbing a little distance away.

As he heard the drums Flory remembered that a *pwe* was being acted a little farther down the road, opposite U Po Kyin's house; in fact, it was U Po Kyin who had made arrangements for the *pwe*, though someone else had paid for it. A daring thought occurred to Flory. He would take Elizabeth to the *pwe!* She would love it—she must; no one with eyes in his head could resist a *pwe* dance. Probably there would be a scandal when they came back to the Club together after a long absence; but damn it! what did it matter? She was different from that herd of fools at the Club. And it would be such fun to go to the *pwe* together! At this moment the music burst out with a fearful pandemonium—a strident squeal of pipes, a rattle like castanets, and the hoarse thump of drums, above which a man's voice was brassily squalling.

"Whatever is that noise?" said Elizabeth, stopping. "It sounds just like a jazz band!"

"Native music. They're having a *pwe*—that's a kind of Burmese play; a cross between a historical drama and a revue, if you can imagine that. It'll interest you, I think. Just round the bend of the road here."

"Oh," she said rather doubtfully.

They came round the bend into a glare of light. The whole road for thirty yards was blocked by the audience watching the *pwe*. At the back there was a raised stage, under humming petrol lamps, with the orchestra squalling and banging in front of it; on the stage two men dressed in clothes that reminded Elizabeth of Chinese pagodas were posturing with curved swords in their hands. All down the roadway it was a sea of white muslin backs of women, pink scarves flung round their shoulders, and black hair-cylinders. A few sprawled on their mats, fast asleep. An old Chinese with a tray of peanuts was threading his way through the crowd, intoning mournfully, *"Myaype! Myaype!"*

"We'll stop and watch a few minutes if you like," Flory said.

The blaze of lights and the appalling din of the orchestra had almost dazed Elizabeth, but what startled her most of all was the sight of this crowd of people sitting in the road as though it had been the pit of a theater.

"Do they always have their plays in the middle of the road?" she said.

"As a rule. They put up a rough stage and take it down in the morning. The show lasts all night."

"But are they *allowed* to—blocking up the whole roadway?"

"Oh yes. There are no traffic regulations here. No traffic to regulate, you see."

It struck her as very queer. By this time almost the entire audience had turned round on their mats to stare at the "Ingaleikma." There were half a dozen chairs in the middle of the crowd, where some clerks and officials were sitting. U Po Kyin was among them, and he was making efforts to twist his elephantine body round and greet the Europeans. As the music stopped the pock-marked Ba Taik came hastening through the crowd and shikoed low to Flory, with his timorous air.

"Most holy one, my master U Po Kyin asks whether you and the young white lady will not come and watch our *pwe* for a few minutes. He has chairs ready for you."

"They're asking us to come and sit down," Flory said to Elizabeth. "Would you like to? It's rather fun. Those two fellows will clear off in a moment and there'll be some dancing. If it wouldn't bore you for a few minutes?"

Elizabeth felt very doubtful. Somehow it did not seem right or even safe to go in among that smelly native crowd. However, she trusted Flory, who presumably knew what was proper, and allowed him to lead her to the chairs. The Burmans made way on their mats, gazing after her and chattering; her shins brushed against warm, muslin-clad bodies, there was a feral reek of sweat. U Po Kyin leaned over toward her, bowing as well as he could and saying nasally:

"Kindly to sit down, madam! I am most honored to make your acquaintance. Good evening, Mr. Flory, sir! A most unexpected pleasure. Had we known that you were to honor us with your company, we would have provided whiskies and other European refreshments. Ha ha!"

He laughed, and his betel-reddened teeth gleamed in the lamplight like red tinfoil. He was so vast and so hideous that Elizabeth could not help shrinking from him. A slender youth in a purple *longyi* was bowing to her and holding out a tray with two glasses of yellow sherbet, iced. U Po Kyin clapped his hands sharply, *"Hey haung galay!"* he called to a boy beside him. He gave some instructions in Burmese, and the boy pushed his way to the edge of the stage.

"He's telling them to bring on their best dancer in our honor," Flory said. "Look, here she comes."

A girl who had been squatting at the back of the stage, smoking, stepped forward into the lamplight. She was very young, slim-shouldered, breastless, dressed in a pale-blue satin *longyi* that hid her feet. The skirts of her *ingyi* curved outward above her hips in little panniers, according to the ancient Burmese fashion. They were like the petals of a downward-pointing flower. She threw her cigar languidly to one of the men in the orchestra, and then, holding out one slender arm, writhed it as though to shake the muscles loose.

The orchestra burst into a sudden loud squalling. There were pipes like bagpipes, a strange instrument consisting of plaques of bamboo which a man struck with a little hammer, and in the middle there was a man surrounded by twelve tall drums of different sizes. He reached rapidly from one to another, thumping them with the heel of his hand. In a moment the girl began to dance. But at first it was not a dance, it was a rhythmic nodding, posturing, and twisting of the elbows, like the movements of one of those jointed wooden figures on an old-fashioned roundabout. The way her neck and elbows rotated was precisely like a jointed doll, and yet incredibly sinuous. Her hands, twisting like snakeheads with the fingers close together, could lie back until they were almost along her forearms. By degrees her movements quickened. She began to leap from side to side, flinging herself down in a kind of curtsy and springing up again with extraordinary agility, in spite of the long *longyi* that imprisoned her feet. Then she danced in a grotesque posture as though sitting down, knees bent, body leaned forward, with her arms extended and writhing, her head also moving to the beat of the drums. The music quickened to a climax. The girl rose upright and whirled round as swiftly as a top, the panniers of her *ingyi* flying out about her like the petals of a snowdrop. Then the music stopped as abruptly as it had begun, and the girl sank again into a curtsy, amid raucous shouting from the audience.

Elizabeth watched the dance with a mixture of amazement, boredom, and something approaching horror. She had sipped her drink and found that it tasted like hair oil. On a mat by her feet three Burmese girls lay fast asleep with their heads on the same pillow, their small oval faces side by side like the faces of kittens. Under cover of the music Flory was speaking in a low voice into Elizabeth's ear, commenting on the dance.

"I knew this would interest you; that's why I brought you here. You've read books and been in civilized places, you're not like the rest of us miserable savages here. Don't you think this is worth watching, in its queer way? Just look at that girl's movements—look at that strange, bent-forward pose like a marionette, and the way her arms twist from the elbow like a cobra rising to strike. It's grotesque, it's even ugly, with a sort of wilful ugliness. And there's something sinister in it too. There's a touch of the diabolical in all Mongols. And yet when you look closely, what art, what centuries of culture you can see behind it! Every movement that girl makes has been studied and handed down through innumerable generations. Whenever you look closely at the art of these Eastern peoples you can see that—a civilization stretching back and back, practically the same, into times when we were dressed in woad. In some way that I can't define to you, the whole life and spirit of Burma is summed up in the way that girl twists her arms. When you see her you can see the rice fields, the villages under the teak trees, the pagodas, the priests in their yellow robes, the buffaloes swimming the rivers in the early morning, Thibaw's palace——"

His voice stopped abruptly as the music stopped. There were certain things, and a *pwe* dance was one of them, that pricked him to talk discursively and incautiously; but now he realized that he had only been talking like a character in a novel, and not a very good novel. He looked away. Elizabeth had listened to him with a chill of discomfort. What *was* the man talking about? was her first thought. Moreover, she had caught the hated word *Art* more than once. For the first time she remembered that Flory was a total stranger and that it had been unwise to come out with him alone. She looked round her, at the sea of dark faces and the lurid glare of the lamps; the strangeness of the scene almost frightened her. What was she doing in this place? Surely it was not right to be sitting among the black people like this, almost touching them, in the scent of their garlic and their sweat? Why was she not back at the Club with the other white people? Why had he brought her here, among this horde of natives, to watch this hideous and savage spectacle?

The music struck up, and the *pwe* girl began dancing again. Her face was powdered so thickly that it gleamed in the lamplight like a chalk mask with live eyes behind it. With that dead-white oval face and those wooden gestures she was monstrous, like a demon. The music changed its tempo, and the girl began to sing in a brassy voice. It was a song with a swift trochaic rhythm, gay yet fierce. The crowd took it up, a hundred voices chanting the harsh syllables in unison. Still in that strange bent posture the girl turned round and danced with her buttocks protruded toward the audience. Her silk *longyi* gleamed like metal. With hands and elbows still rotating she wagged her posterior from side to side. Then—astonishing feat, quite visible through the *longyi*—she began to wriggle her two buttocks independently in time with the music.

There was a shout of applause from the audience. The three girls asleep on the mat woke up at the same moment and began clapping their hands wildly. A clerk shouted nasally "Bravo! Bravo!" in English for the Europeans' benefit. But U Po Kyin frowned and waved his hand. He knew all about European women. Elizabeth, however, had already stood up.

"I'm going. It's time we were back," she said abruptly. She was looking away, but Flory could see that her face was pink.

He stood up beside her, dismayed. "But, I say! Couldn't you stay a few minutes longer? I know it's late, but—they brought this girl on two hours before she was due, in our honor. Just a few minutes?"

"I can't help it, I ought to have been back ages ago. I don't know *what* my uncle and aunt will be thinking."

She began at once to pick her way through the crowd, and he followed her, with not even time to thank the *pwe* people for their trouble. The Burmans made way with a sulky air. How like these English people, to upset everything by sending for the best dancer and then go away almost before she had started! There was a fearful row as soon as Flory and Elizabeth had gone, the *pwe* girl refusing to go on with her dance and the audience demanding that she should continue. However, peace was restored when two clowns hurried on to the stage and began letting off crackers and making obscene jokes.

Flory followed the girl abjectly up the road. She was walking quickly, her head turned away, and for some moments she would not speak. What a thing to happen, when they had been getting on so well together! He kept trying to apologize.

"I'm so sorry! I'd no idea you'd mind——"

"It's nothing. What is there to be sorry about? I only said it was time to go back, that's all."

"I ought to have thought. One gets not to notice that kind of thing in this country. These people's sense of decency isn't the same as ours—it's stricter in some ways—but——"

"It's not that! It's not that!" she exclaimed quite angrily.

He saw that he was only making it worse. They walked on in silence, he behind. He was miserable. What a bloody fool he had

been! And yet all the while he had no inkling of the real reason
why she was angry with him. It was not the *pwe* girl's behavior,
in itself, that had offended her; it had only brought things to a
head. But the whole expedition—the very notion of *wanting* to rub
shoulders with all those smelly natives—had impressed her badly.
She was perfectly certain that that was not how white men ought
to behave. And that extraordinary rambling speech that he had
begun, with all those long words—almost, she thought bitterly, as
though he were quoting poetry! It was how those beastly artists
that you met sometimes in Paris used to talk. She had thought him
a manly man till this evening. Then her mind went back to the
morning's adventure, and how he had faced the buffalo barehanded,
and some of her anger evaporated. By the time they reached the
Club gate she felt inclined to forgive him. Flory had by now plucked
up courage to speak again. He stopped, and she stopped too, in a
patch where the boughs let through some starlight and he could
see her face dimly.

"I say. I say, I do hope you're not really angry about this?"

"No, of course I'm not. I told you I wasn't."

"I oughtn't to have taken you there. Please forgive me.—Do you
know, I don't think I'd tell the others where you've been. Perhaps
it would be better to say you've just been out for a stroll, out in
the garden—something like that. They might think it queer, a white
girl going to a *pwe*. I don't think I'd tell them."

"Oh, of course I won't!" she agreed with a warmness that surprised him. After that he knew that he was forgiven. But what it
was that he was forgiven, he had not yet grasped. . . .

XIV

Like long curved needles threading through embroidery, the two
canoes that carried Flory and Elizabeth threaded their way up the
creek that led inland from the eastern bank of the Irrawaddy. It
was the day of the shooting trip—a short afternoon trip, for they
could not stay a night in the jungle together. They were to shoot
for a couple of hours in the comparative cool of the evening, and
be back at Kyauktada in time for dinner.

The canoes, each hollowed out of a single tree-trunk, glided
swiftly, hardly rippling the dark brown water. Water hyacinth with
profuse spongy foliage and blue flowers had choked the stream so
that the channel was only a winding ribbon four feet wide. The
light filtered, greenish, through interlacing boughs. Sometimes one
could hear parrots scream overhead, but no wild creatures showed

themselves, except once a snake that swam hurriedly away and disappeared among the water hyacinth.

"How long before we get to the village?" Elizabeth called back to Flory. He was in a larger canoe behind, together with Flo and Ko S'la, paddled by a wrinkly old woman dressed in rags.

"How far, grandmama?" Flory asked the canoe-woman.

The old woman took her cigar out of her mouth and rested her paddle on her knees to think. "The distance a man can shout," she said after reflection.

"About half a mile," Flory translated.

They had come two miles. Elizabeth's back was aching. The canoes were liable to upset at a careless movement, and you had to sit bolt upright on the narrow backless seat, keeping your feet as well as possible out of the bilge, with dead prawns in it, that sagged to and fro at the bottom. The Burman who paddled Elizabeth was sixty years old, half naked, leaf-brown, with a body as perfect as that of a young man. His face was battered, gentle, and humorous. His black cloud of hair, finer than that of most Burmans, was knotted loosely over one ear, with a wisp or two tumbling across his cheek. Elizabeth was nursing her uncle's gun across her knees. Flory had offered to take it, but she had refused; in reality, the feel of it delighted her so much that she could not bring herself to give it up. She had never had a gun in her hand until today. She was wearing a rough skirt with brogue shoes and a silk shirt like a man's, and she knew that with her Terai hat they looked well on her. She was very happy, in spite of her aching back and the hot sweat that tickled her face, and the large, speckled mosquitoes that hummed round her ankles.

The stream narrowed and the beds of water hyacinth gave place to steep banks of glistening mud, like chocolate. Rickety thatched huts leaned far out over the stream, their piles driven into its bed. A naked boy was standing between two of the huts, flying a green beetle on a piece of thread like a kite. He yelled at the sight of the Europeans, whereat more children appeared from nowhere. The old Burman guided the canoe to a jetty made of a single palm-trunk laid in the mud—it was covered with barnacles and so gave foothold—and sprang out and helped Elizabeth ashore. The others followed with the bags and cartridges, and Flo, as she always did on these occasions, fell into the mud and sank as deep as the shoulder. A skinny old gentleman wearing a magenta *paso*, with a mole on his cheek from which four yard-long gray hairs sprouted, came forward shikoing and cuffing the heads of the children who had gathered round the jetty.

"The village headman," Flory said.

The old man led the way to his house, walking ahead with an extraordinary crouching gait, like a letter L upside down—the result of rheumatism combined with the constant shikoing needed in a minor government official. A mob of children marched rapidly after the Europeans, and more and more dogs, all yapping and causing Flo to shrink against Flory's heels. In the doorway of every hut clusters of moon-like, rustic faces gaped at the "Ingaleikma." The village was darkish, under the shade of broad leaves. In the rains the creek would flood, turning the lower parts of the village into a squalid wooden Venice where the villagers stepped from their front doors into their canoes.

The headman's house was a little bigger than the others, and it had a corrugated iron roof, which, in spite of the intolerable din it made during the rains, was the pride of the headman's life. He had foregone the building of a pagoda, and appreciably lessened his chances of Nirvana, to pay for it. He hastened up the steps and gently kicked in the ribs a youth who was lying asleep on the veranda. Then he turned and shikoed again to the Europeans, asking them to come inside.

"Shall we go in?" Flory said. "I expect we shall have to wait half an hour."

"Couldn't you tell him to bring some chairs out on the veranda?" Elizabeth said. After her experience in Li Yeik's house she had privately decided that she would never go inside a native house again, if she could help it.

There was a fuss inside the house, and the headman, the youth, and some women dragged forth two chairs decorated in an extraordinary manner with red hibiscus flowers, and also some begonias growing in kerosene tins. It was evident that a sort of double throne had been prepared within for the Europeans. When Elizabeth had sat down the headman reappeared with a teapot, a bunch of very long, bright green bananas, and six coal-black cheroots. But when he had poured her out a cup of tea Elizabeth shook her head, for the tea looked, if possible, worse even than Li Yeik's.

The headman looked abashed and rubbed his nose. He turned to Flory and asked him whether the young *thakin-ma* would like some milk in her tea. He had heard that Europeans drank milk in their tea. The villagers should, if it were desired, catch a cow and milk it. However, Elizabeth still refused the tea; but she was thirsty, and she asked Flory to send for one of the bottles of soda water that Ko S'la had brought in his bag. Seeing this, the headman retired, feeling guiltily that his preparations had been insufficient, and left the veranda to the Europeans.

Elizabeth was still nursing her gun on her knees, while Flory leaned against the veranda rail pretending to smoke one of the head-man's cheroots. Elizabeth was pining for the shooting to begin. She plied Flory with innumerable questions.

"How soon can we start out? Do you think we've got enough cartridges? How many beaters shall we take? Oh, I do so hope we have some luck! You do think we'll get something, don't you?"

"Nothing wonderful, probably. We're bound to get a few pigeons, and perhaps jungle fowl. They're out of season, but it doesn't matter shooting the cocks. They say there's a leopard round here, that killed a bullock almost in the village last week."

"Oh, a leopard! How lovely if we could shoot it!"

"It's very unlikely, I'm afraid. The only rule with this shooting in Burma is to hope for nothing. It's invariably disappointing. The jungles teem with game, but as often as not you don't even get a chance to fire your gun."

"Why is that?"

"The jungle is so thick. An animal may be five yards away and quite invisible, and half the time they manage to dodge back past the beaters. Even when you see them it's only for a flash of a second. And again, there's water everywhere, so that no animal is tied down to one particular spot. A tiger, for instance, will roam hundreds of miles if it suits him. And with all the game there is, they need never come back to a kill if there's anything suspicious about it. Night after night, when I was a boy, I've sat up over horrible stinking dead cows, waiting for tigers that never came."

Elizabeth wriggled her shoulder blades against the chair. It was a movement that she made sometimes when she was deeply pleased. She loved Flory, really loved him, when he talked like this. The most trivial scrap of information about shooting thrilled her. If only he would always talk about shooting, instead of about books and Art and that mucky poetry! In a sudden burst of admiration she decided that Flory was really quite a handsome man, in his way. He looked so splendidly manly, with his pagri-cloth shirt open at the throat, and his shorts and puttees and shooting boots! And his face, lined, sunburned, like a soldier's face. He was standing with his birthmarked cheek away from her. She pressed him to go on talking.

"*Do* tell me some more about tiger-shooting. It's so awfully interesting!"

He described the shooting, years ago, of a mangy old man-eater who had killed one of his coolies. The wait in the mosquito-ridden *machan;* the tiger's eyes approaching through the dark jungle, like great green lanterns; the panting, slobbering noise as he devoured the coolie's body, tied to a stake below. Flory told it all perfunctorily enough—did not the proverbial Anglo-Indian bore always talk about tiger-shooting?—but Elizabeth wriggled her shoulders delightedly once more. He did not realize how such talk as this reassured her and made up for all the times when he had bored her and disquieted her. Six shock-headed youths came down the path, carrying *dahs* over their shoulders, and headed by a stringy but active old man with gray hair. They halted in front of the headman's house, and one of them uttered a hoarse whoop, whereat the headman appeared and explained that these were the beaters. They were ready to start now, if the young *thakin-ma* did not find it too hot.

They set out. The side of the village away from the creek was protected by a hedge of cactus six feet high and twelve thick. One went up a narrow lane of cactus, then along a rutted, dusty bullock-cart track, with bamboos as tall as flagstaffs growing densely on either side. The beaters marched rapidly ahead in single file, each with his broad *dah* laid along his forearm. The old hunter was marching just in front of Elizabeth. His *longyi* was hitched up like a loincloth, and his meager thighs were tattooed with dark blue patterns, so intricate that he might have been wearing drawers of blue lace. A bamboo the thickness of a man's wrist had fallen and hung across the path. The leading beater severed it with an upward flick of his *dah;* the prisoned water gushed out of it with a diamond-flash. After half a mile they reached the open fields, and everyone was sweating, for they had walked fast and the sun was savage.

"That's where we're going to shoot, over there," Flory said.

He pointed across the stubble, a wide dust-colored plain, cut up into patches of an acre or two by mud boundaries. It was horribly flat, and lifeless save for the snowy egrets. At the far edge a jungle of great trees rose abruptly, like a dark green cliff. The beaters had gone across to a small tree like a hawthorn twenty yards away. One of them was on his knees, shikoing to the tree and gabbling, while the old hunter poured a bottle of some cloudy liquid on to the ground. The others stood looking on with serious, bored faces, like men in church.

"What *are* those men doing?" Elizabeth said.

"Only sacrificing to the local gods. Nats, they call them—a kind of dryad. They're praying to him to bring us good luck."

The hunter came back and in a cracked voice explained that they were to beat a small patch of scrub over to the right before proceeding to the main jungle. Apparently the Nat had counseled this. The hunter directed Flory and Elizabeth where to stand, pointing with his *dah*. The six beaters plunged into the scrub; they would make a detour and beat back toward the paddy fields. There were some bushes of the wild rose thirty yards from the jungle's edge, and Flory and Elizabeth took cover behind one of these, while Ko S'la squatted down behind another bush a little distance away, holding Flo's collar and stroking her to keep her quiet. Flory always sent Ko S'la to a distance when he was shooting, for he had an irritating trick of clicking his tongue if a shot was missed. Presently there was a far-off echoing sound—a sound of tapping and strange hollow cries; the beat had started. Elizabeth at once began trembling so uncontrollably that she could not keep her gun-barrel still. A wonderful bird, a little bigger than a thrush, with gray wings and body of blazing scarlet, broke from the trees and came toward them with a dipping flight. The tapping and the cries came nearer. One of the bushes at the jungle's edge waved violently—some large animal was emerging. Elizabeth raised her gun and tried to steady it. But it was only a naked yellow beater, *dah* in hand. He saw that he had emerged and shouted to the others to join him.

Elizabeth lowered her gun. "What's happened?"

"Nothing. The beat's over."

"So there was nothing there!" she cried in bitter disappointment.

"Never mind, one never gets anything the first beat. We'll have better luck next time."

They crossed the lumpy stubble, climbing over the mud boundaries that divided the fields, and took up their position opposite the high green wall of the jungle. Elizabeth had already learned how to load her gun. This time the beat had hardly started when Ko S'la whistled sharply.

"Look out!" Flory cried. "Quick, here they come!"

A flight of green pigeons were dashing toward them at incredible speed, forty yards up. They were like a handful of catapulted stones whirling through the sky. Elizabeth was helpless with excitement. For a moment she could not move, then she flung her barrel into the air, somewhere in the direction of the birds, and tugged violently at the trigger. Nothing happened—she was pulling at the trigger-guard. Just as the birds passed overhead she found the triggers and pulled both of them simultaneously. There was a deafening roar and she was thrown backward a pace with her collar-bone almost broken. She had fired thirty yards behind the birds. At the same moment she saw Flory turn and level his gun. Two of the pigeons, suddenly checked in their flight, swirled over and dropped to the ground like arrows. Ko S'la yelled, and he and Flo raced after them.

"Look out!" said Flory, "here's an imperial pigeon. Let's have him!"

A large heavy bird, with flight much slower than the others, was flapping overhead. Elizabeth did not care to fire after her previous failure. She watched Flory thrust a cartridge into the breech and raise his gun, and the white plume of smoke leapt up from the muzzle. The bird planed heavily down, his wing broken. Flo and Ko S'la came running excitedly up, Flo with the big imperial pigeon in her mouth, and Ko S'la grinning and producing two green pigeons from his Kachin bag.

Flory took one of the little green corpses to show to Elizabeth. "Look at it. Aren't they lovely things? The most beautiful bird in Asia."

Elizabeth touched its smooth feathers with her finger-tip. It filled her with bitter envy, because she had not shot it. And yet it was curious, but she felt almost an adoration for Flory now that she had seen how he could shoot.

"Just look at its breast-feathers; like a jewel. It's murder to shoot them. The Burmese say that when you kill one of these birds they vomit, meaning to say, 'Look, here is all I possess, and I've taken nothing of yours. Why do you kill me?' I've never seen one do it, I must admit."

"Are they good to eat?"

"Very. Even so, I always feel it's a shame to kill them."

"I wish I could do it like you do!" she said enviously.

"It's only a knack, you'll soon pick it up. You know how to hold your gun, and that's more than most people do when they start."

However, at the next two beats, Elizabeth could hit nothing. She had learned not to fire both barrels at once, but she was too paralyzed with excitement ever to take aim. Flory shot several more pigeons, and a small bronze-wing dove with back as green as verdigris. The jungle fowl were too cunning to show themselves, though one could hear them cluck-clucking all round, and once or twice the sharp trumpet call of a cock. They were getting deeper into the jungle now. The light was grayish, with dazzling patches of sunlight. Whichever way one looked one's view was shut in by the multitudinous ranks of trees, and the tangled bushes and creepers that struggled round their bases like the sea round the piles of a pier. It was so dense, like a bramble bush extending mile after mile, that one's eyes were oppressed by it. Some of the creepers were huge, like serpents. Flory and Elizabeth struggled along narrow game-tracks, up slippery banks, thorns tearing at their clothes. Both their shirts were drenched with sweat. It was stifling hot, with a scent of crushed leaves. Sometimes for minutes together invisible cicadas would keep up a shrill, metallic pinging like the twanging of a steel guitar, and then, by stopping, make a silence that startled one.

As they were walking to the fifth beat they came to a great peepul tree in which, high up, one could hear imperial pigeons cooing. It was a sound like the far-off lowing of cows. One bird fluttered out and perched alone on the topmost bough, a small grayish shape.

"Try a sitting shot," Flory said to Elizabeth. "Get your sight on him and pull off without waiting. Don't shut your left eye."

Elizabeth raised her gun, which had begun trembling as usual. The beaters halted in a group to watch, and some of them could not refrain from clicking their tongues; they thought it queer and rather shocking to see a woman handle a gun. With a violent effort of will Elizabeth kept her gun still for a second, and pulled the trigger. She did not hear the shot; one never does when it has gone home. The bird seemed to jump upward from the bough, then down it came, tumbling over and over, and stuck in a fork ten yards up. One of the beaters laid down his *dah* and glanced appraisingly at the tree; then he walked to a great creeper, thick as a man's thigh and twisted like a stick of barley sugar, that hung far out from a bough. He ran up the creeper as easily as though it had been a ladder, walked upright along the broad bough, and brought the pigeon to the ground. He put it limp and warm into Elizabeth's hand.

She could hardly give it up, the feel of it so ravished her. She could have kissed it, hugged it to her breast. All the men, Flory and Ko S'la and the beaters, smiled at one another to see her fondling the dead bird. Reluctantly, she gave it to Ko S'la to put in the bag. She was conscious of an extraordinary desire to fling her arms round Flory's neck and kiss him; and in some way it was the killing of the pigeon that made her feel this.

After the fifth beat the hunter explained to Flory that they must cross a clearing that was used for growing pineapples, and would beat another patch of jungle beyond. They came out into sunlight, dazzling after the jungle gloom. The clearing was an oblong of an acre or two hacked out of the jungle like a patch mown in long grass, with the pineapples, prickly cactus-like plants, growing in rows, almost smothered by weeds. A low hedge of thorns divided the field in the middle. They had nearly crossed the field when there was a sharp cock-a-doodle-doo from beyond the hedge.

"Oh, listen!" said Elizabeth, stopping. "Was that a jungle cock?"

"Yes. They come out to feed about this time."

"Couldn't we go and shoot him?"

"We'll have a try if you like. They're cunning beggars. Look, we'll stalk up the hedge until we get opposite where he is. We'll have to go without making a sound."

He sent Ko S'la and the beaters on, and the two of them skirted the field and crept along the hedge. They had to bend double to keep themselves out of sight. Elizabeth was in front. The hot sweat trickled down her face, tickling her upper lip, and her heart was knocking violently. She felt Flory touch her heel from behind. Both of them stood upright and looked over the hedge together.

Ten yards away a little cock the size of a bantam, was pecking vigorously at the ground. He was beautiful, with his long silky neck feathers, bunched comb, and arching, laurel-green tail. There were six hens with him, smaller brown birds, with diamond-shaped feathers like snake scales on their backs. All this Elizabeth and Flory saw in the space of a second, then with a squawk and a whirr the birds were up and flying like bullets for the jungle. Instantly, automatically as it seemed, Elizabeth raised her gun and fired. It was one of those shots where there is no aiming, no consciousness of the gun in one's hand, when one's mind seems to fly behind the charge and drive it to the mark. She knew the bird was doomed even before she pulled the trigger. He tumbled, showering feathers thirty yards away. "Good shot, good shot!" cried Flory. In their excitement both of them dropped their guns, broke through the thorn hedge, and raced side by side to where the bird lay.

"Good shot!" Flory repeated, as excited as she. "By Jove, I've never seen anyone kill a flying bird their first day, never! You got your gun off like lightning. It's marvelous!"

They were kneeling face to face with the dead bird between them. With a shock they discovered that their hands, his right and her left, were clasped tightly together. They had run to the place hand in hand without noticing it.

A sudden stillness came on them both, a sense of something momentous that must happen. Flory reached across and took her other hand. It came yieldingly, willingly. For a moment they knelt with their hands clasped together. The sun blazed upon them and the warmth breathed out of their bodies; they seemed to be floating upon clouds of heat and joy. He took her by the upper arms to draw her toward him.

Then suddenly he turned his head away and stood up, pulling Elizabeth to her feet. He let go of her arms. He had remembered his birthmark. He dared not do it. Not here, not in daylight! The snub it invited was too terrible. To cover the awkwardness of the moment he bent down and picked up the jungle cock.

"It was splendid," he said. "You don't need any teaching. You can shoot already. We'd better get on to the next beat."

They had just crossed the hedge and picked up their guns when there was a series of shouts from the edge of the jungle. Two of the beaters were running towards them with enormous leaps, waving their arms wildly in the air.

"What is it?" Elizabeth said.

"I don't know. They've seen some animal or other. Something good, by the look of them."

"Oh, hurry! Come on!"

They broke into a run and hurried across the field, breaking through the pineapples and the stiff prickly weeds. Ko S'la and five of the beaters were standing in a knot all talking at once, and the other two were beckoning excitedly to Flory and Elizabeth. As they came up they saw in the middle of the group an old woman who was holding up her ragged *longyi* with one hand and gesticulating with a big cigar in the other. Elizabeth could hear some word that sounded like "Char" repeated over and over again.

"What is it they're saying?" she said.

The beaters came crowding round Flory, all talking eagerly and pointing into the jungle. After a few questions he waved his hand to silence them and turned to Elizabeth:

"I say, here's a bit of luck! This old girl was coming through the jungle, and she says that at the sound of the shot you fired just now, she saw a leopard run across the path. These fellows know where he's likely to hide. If we're quick they may be able to surround him before he sneaks away, and drive him out. Shall we try it?"

"Oh, do let's! Oh, what awful fun! How lovely, how lovely if we could get that leopard!"

"You understand it's dangerous? We'll keep close together and it'll probably be all right, but it's never absolutely safe on foot. Are you ready for that?"

"Oh, of course, of course! I'm not frightened. Oh, do let's be quick and start!"

"One of you come with us, and show us the way," he said to the beaters. "Ko S'la, put Flo on the leash and go with the others. She'll never keep quiet with us. We'll have to hurry," he added to Elizabeth.

Ko S'la and the beaters hurried off along the edge of the jungle. They would strike in and begin beating farther up. The other beater, the same youth who had climbed the tree after the pigeon, dived into the jungle, Flory and Elizabeth following. With short rapid steps, almost running, he led them through a labyrinth of game-tracks. The bushes trailed so low that sometimes one had almost to crawl, and creepers hung across the path like tripwires. The ground was dusty and silent underfoot. At some landmark in the jungle the beater halted, pointed to the ground as a sign that this spot would do, and put his finger on his lips to enjoin silence. Flory took four SG cartridges from his pockets and took Elizabeth's gun to load it silently.

There was a faint rustling behind them, and they all started. A nearly naked youth with a pellet-bow, come goodness knows whence, had parted the bushes. He looked at the beater, shook his head and pointed up the path. There was a dialogue of signs between the two youths, then the beater seemed to agree. Without speaking all four stole forty yards along the path, round a bend, and halted again. At the same moment a frightful pandemonium of yells, punctuated by barks from Flo, broke out a few hundred yards away.

Elizabeth felt the beater's hand on her shoulder, pushing her downward. They all four squatted down under cover of a prickly bush, the Europeans in front, the Burmans behind. In the distance there was such a tumult of yells and the rattle of *dahs* against tree-trunks that one could hardly believe six men could make so much noise. The beaters were taking good care that the leopard should not turn back upon them. Elizabeth watched some large, pale-yellow ants marching like soldiers over the thorns of the bush. One fell on to her hand and crawled up her forearm. She dared not move to brush it away. She was praying silently, "Please God, let the leopard come! Oh please, God, let the leopard come!"

There was a sudden loud pattering on the leaves. Elizabeth raised her gun, but Flory shook his head sharply and pushed the barrel down again. A jungle fowl scuttled across the path with long noisy strides.

The yells of the beaters seemed hardly to come any closer, and this end of the jungle the silence was like a pall. The ant on Elizabeth's arm bit her painfully and dropped to the ground. A dreadful despair had begun to form in her heart; the leopard was not coming, he had slipped away somewhere, they had lost him. She almost wished they had never heard of the leopard, the disappointment was so agonizing. Then she felt the beater pinch her elbow. He was craning his face forward, his smooth, dull-yellow cheek only a few inches from her own; she could smell the coconut oil in his hair. His coarse lips were puckered as in a whistle; he had heard something. Then Flory and Elizabeth heard it too, the faintest whisper, as though some creature of air were gliding through the jungle, just brushing the ground with its foot. At the same moment the leopard's

head and shoulders emerged from the undergrowth, fifteen yards
down the path.

He stopped with his forepaws on the path. They could see his
low, flat-eared head, his bare eyetooth and his thick, terrible forearm. In the shadow he did not look yellow but gray. He was listening
intently. Elizabeth saw Flory spring to his feet, raise his gun, and
pull the trigger instantly. The shot roared, and almost simultaneously there was a heavy crash as the brute dropped flat in the weeds.
"Look out!" Flory cried. "He's not done for!" He fired again, and
there was a fresh thump as the shot went home. The leopard gasped.
Flory threw open his gun and felt in his pocket for a cartridge, then
flung all his cartridges on to the path and fell on his knees, searching
rapidly among them.

"Damn and blast it!" he cried. "There isn't a single SG among
them. Where in hell did I put them?"

The leopard had disappeared as he fell. He was thrashing about
in the undergrowth like a great, wounded snake, and crying out
with a snarling, sobbing noise, savage and pitiful. The noise seemed
to be coming nearer. Every cartridge Flory turned up had 6 or 8
marked on the end. The rest of the large-shot cartridges had, in fact,
been left with Ko S'la. The crashing and snarling were now hardly
five yards away, but they could see nothing, the jungle was so thick.

The two Burmans were crying out "Shoot! Shoot! Shoot!" The
sound of "Shoot! Shoot!" got farther away—they were skipping for
the nearest climbable trees. There was a crash in the undergrowth
so close that it shook the bush by which Elizabeth was standing.

"By God, he's almost on us!" Flory said. "We must turn him
somehow. Let fly at the sound."

Elizabeth raised her gun. Her knees were knocking like castanets,
but her hand was as steady as stone. She fired rapidly, once, twice.
The crashing noise receded. The leopard was crawling away, crippled
but swift, and still invisible.

"Well done! You've scared him," Flory said.

"But he's getting away! He's getting away!" Elizabeth cried, dancing about in agitation. She made to follow him. Flory jumped to his
feet and pulled her back.

"No fear! You stay here. Wait!"

He slipped two of the small-shot cartridges into his gun and ran
after the sound of the leopard. For a moment Elizabeth could not
see either beast or man, then they reappeared in a bare patch thirty
yards away. The leopard was writhing along on his belly, sobbing
as he went. Flory leveled his gun and fired at four yards' distance.
The leopard jumped like a cushion when one hits it, then rolled

over, curled up, and lay still. Flory poked the body with his gun-barrel. It did not stir.

"It's all right, he's done for," he called. "Come and have a look at him."

The two Burmans jumped down from their tree, and they and Elizabeth went across to where Flory was standing. The leopard—it was a male—was lying curled up with his head between his forepaws. He looked much smaller than he had looked alive; he looked rather pathetic, like a dead kitten. Elizabeth's knees were still quivering. She and Flory stood looking down at the leopard, close together, but not clasping hands this time.

It was only a moment before Ko S'la and the others came up, shouting with glee. Flo gave one sniff at the dead leopard, then down went her tail and she bolted fifty yards, whimpering. She could not be induced to come near him again. Everyone squatted down round the leopard and gazed at him. They stroked his beautiful white belly, soft as a hare's, and squeezed his broad pugs to bring out the claws, and pulled back his black lips to examine the fangs. Presently two of the beaters cut down a tall bamboo and slung the leopard upon it by his paws, with his long tail trailing down, and then they marched back to the village in triumph. There was no talk of further shooting, though the light still held. They were all, including the Europeans, too anxious to get home and boast of what they had done.

Flory and Elizabeth walked side by side across the stubble field. The others were thirty yards ahead with the guns and the leopard, and Flo was slinking after them a long way in the rear. The sun was going down beyond the Irrawaddy. The light shone level across the field, gilding the stubble stalks, and striking into their faces with a yellow, gentle beam. Elizabeth's shoulder was almost touching Flory's as they walked. The sweat that had drenched their shirts had dried again. They did not talk much. They were happy with that inordinate happiness that comes of exhaustion and achievement, and with which nothing else in life—no joy of either the body or the mind—is even able to be compared.

"The leopard skin is yours," Flory said as they approached the village.

"Oh, but you shot him!"

"Never mind, you stick to the skin. By Jove, I wonder how many of the women in this country would have kept their heads like you did! I can just see them screaming and fainting. I'll get the skin cured for you in Kyauktada jail. There's a convict there who can

ure skins as soft as velvet. He's doing a seven-year sentence, so he's
ad time to learn the job."

"Oh well, thanks awfully."

No more was said for the present. Later, when they had washed
ff the sweat and dirt, and were fed and rested, they would meet
gain at the Club. They made no rendezvous, but it was understood
etween them that they would meet. Also, it was understood that
lory would ask Elizabeth to marry him, though nothing was said
bout this either.

At the village Flory paid the beaters eight annas each, superin-
nded the skinning of the leopard, and gave the headman a bottle
f beer and two of the imperial pigeons. The skin and skull were
acked into one of the canoes. All the whiskers had been stolen, in
ite of Ko S'la's efforts to guard them. Some young men of the village
rried off the carcass in order to eat the heart and various other
rgans, the eating of which they believed would make them strong
nd swift like the leopard.

1934

The Thirties

Δ

From "Down and Out in Paris and London"

∇

I

The Rue du Coq d'Or, Paris, seven in the morning. A succession of furious, choking yells from the street. Madame Monce, who kept the little hotel opposite mine, had come out on to the pavement to address a lodger on the third floor. Her bare feet were stuck into sabots and her gray hair was streaming down.

Madame Monce: "Salope! Salope! How many times have I told you not to squash bugs on the wallpaper? Do you think you've bought the hotel, eh? Why can't you throw them out of the window like everyone else? *Putain! Salope!"*

The woman on the third floor: "Vache!"

Thereupon a whole variegated chorus of yells, as windows were flung open on every side and half the street joined in the quarrel. They shut up abruptly ten minutes later, when a squadron of cavalry rode past and people stopped shouting to look at them.

I sketch this scene, just to convey something of the spirit of the Rue du Coq d'Or. Not that quarrels were the only thing that happened there—but still, we seldom got through the morning without at least one outburst of this description. Quarrels, and the desolate cries of street hawkers, and the shouts of children chasing orange-peel over the cobbles, and at night loud singing and the sour reek of the refuse-carts, made up the atmosphere of the street.

It was a very narrow street—a ravine of tall, leprous houses, lurching toward one another in queer attitudes, as though they had all been frozen in the act of collapse. All the houses were hotels and packed to the tiles with lodgers, mostly Poles, Arabs, and Italians. At the foot of the hotels were tiny *bistros,* where you could be drunk for the equivalent of a shilling. On Saturday nights about a third of the male population of the quarter was drunk. There was fighting over women, and the Arab navvies who lived in the cheapest hotels

49

used to conduct mysterious feuds, and fight them out with chairs and occasionally revolvers. At night the policemen would only come through the street two together. It was a fairly rackety place. And yet amid the noise and dirt lived the usual respectable French shop-keepers, bakers and laundresses and the like, keeping themselves to themselves and quietly piling up small fortunes. It was quite a representative Paris slum.

My hotel was called the Hôtel des Trois Moineaux. It was a dark, rickety warren of five storeys, cut up by wooden partitions into forty rooms. The rooms were small and inveterately dirty, for there was no maid, and Madame F., the *patronne*, had no time to do any sweeping. The walls were as thin as matchwood, and to hide the cracks they had been covered with layer after layer of pink paper, which had come loose and housed innumerable bugs. Near the ceiling long lines of bugs marched all day like columns of soldiers, and at night came down ravenously hungry, so that one had to get up every few hours and kill them in hecatombs. Sometimes when the bugs got too bad one used to burn sulphur and drive them into the next room; whereupon the lodger next door would retort by having *his* room sulphured, and drive the bugs back. It was a dirty place, but home-like, for Madame F. and her husband were good sorts. The rent of the rooms varied between thirty and fifty francs a week.

The lodgers were a floating population, largely foreigners, who used to turn up without luggage, stay a week, and then disappear again. They were of every trade—cobblers, bricklayers, stonemasons, navvies, students, prostitutes, rag-pickers. Some of them were fantastically poor. In one of the attics there was a Bulgarian student who made fancy shoes for the American market. From six to twelve he sat on his bed, making a dozen pairs of shoes and earning thirty-five francs; the rest of the day he attended lectures at the Sorbonne. He was studying for the Church, and books of theology lay face down on his leather-strewn floor. In another room lived a Russian woman and her son, who called himself an artist. The mother worked sixteen hours a day, darning socks at twenty-five centimes a sock, while the son, decently dressed, loafed in the Montparnasse cafés. One room was let to two different lodgers, one a day worker and the other a night worker. In another room a widower shared the same bed with his two grown-up daughters, both consumptive.

There were eccentric characters in the hotel. The Paris slums are a gathering place for eccentric people—people who have fallen into solitary, half-mad grooves of life and given up trying to be normal or decent. Poverty frees them from ordinary standards of behavior, just as money frees people from work. Some of the lodgers in our hotel lived lives that were curious beyond words.

There were the Rougiers, for instance, an old, ragged, dwarfish couple who plied an extraordinary trade. They used to sell postcards on the Boulevard St. Michel. The curious thing was that the postcards were sold in sealed packets as pornographic ones, but were actually photographs of châteaux on the Loire; the buyers did not discover this till too late, and of course never complained. The Rougiers earned about a hundred francs a week, and by strict economy managed to be always half starved and half drunk. The filth of their room was such that one could smell it on the floor below. According to Madame F., neither of the Rougiers had taken off their clothes for four years.

Or there was Henri, who worked in the sewers. He was a tall, melancholy man with curly hair, rather romantic-looking in his long, sewer-man's boots. Henri's peculiarity was that he did not speak, except for the purposes of work, literally for days together. Only a year before he had been a chauffeur in good employ and saving money. One day he fell in love, and when the girl refused him he lost his temper and kicked her. On being kicked the girl fell desperately in love with Henri, and for a fortnight they lived together and spent a thousand francs of Henri's money. Then the girl was unfaithful; Henri planted a knife in her upper arm and was sent to prison for six months. As soon as she had been stabbed the girl fell more in love with Henri than ever, and the two made up their quarrel and agreed that when Henri came out of jail he should buy a taxi and they would marry and settle down. But a fortnight later the girl was unfaithful again, and when Henri came out she was with child. Henri did not stab her again. He drew out all his savings and went on a drinking bout that ended in another month's imprisonment; after that he went to work in the sewers. Nothing would induce Henri to talk. If you asked him why he worked in the sewers he never answered, but simply crossed his wrists to signify handcuffs, and jerked his head southward, toward the prison. Bad luck seemed to have turned him half-witted in a single day.

Or there was R., an Englishman, who lived six months of the year in Putney with his parents and six months in France. During his time in France he drank four liters of wine a day, and six liters on Saturdays; he had once traveled as far as the Azores, because the wine there is cheaper than anywhere in Europe. He was a gentle, domesticated creature, never rowdy or quarrelsome, and never sober. He would lie in bed till midday, and from then till midnight he was in his corner of the *bistro,* quietly and methodically soaking. While he soaked he talked, in a refined, womanish voice, about antique furniture. Except myself, R. was the only Englishman in the quarter.

There were plenty of other people who lived lives just as eccentric as these: Monsieur Jules, the Roumanian, who had a glass eye and would not admit it, Furex the Limousin stonemason, Roucolle the miser—he died before my time, though—old Laurent the rag-merchant, who used to copy his signature from a slip of paper he carried in his pocket. It would be fun to write some of their biographies, if one had time. I am trying to describe the people in our quarter, not for the mere curiosity, but because they are all part of the story. Poverty is what I am writing about, and I had my first contact with poverty in this slum. . . .

III

I lived in the Coq d'Or quarter for about a year and a half. One day, in summer, I found that I had just four hundred and fifty francs left, and beyond this nothing but thirty-six francs a week, which I earned by giving English lessons. Hitherto I had not thought about the future, but I now realized that I must do something at once. I decided to start looking for a job, and—very luckily, as it turned out—I took the precaution of paying two hundred francs for a month's rent in advance. With the other two hundred and fifty francs, besides the English lessons, I could live a month, and in a month I should probably find work. I aimed at becoming a guide to one of the tourist companies, or perhaps an interpreter. However, a piece of bad luck prevented this.

One day there turned up at the hotel a young Italian who called himself a compositor. He was rather an ambiguous person, for he wore side whiskers, which are the mark either of an apache or an intellectual, and nobody was quite certain in which class to put him. Madame F. did not like the look of him, and made him pay a week's rent in advance. The Italian paid the rent and stayed six nights at the hotel. During this time he managed to prepare some duplicate keys, and on the last night he robbed a dozen rooms, including mine. Luckily, he did not find the money that was in my pockets, so I was not left penniless. I was left with just forty-seven francs. . . .

This put an end to my plans of looking for work. I had now got to live at the rate of about six francs a day, and from the start it was too difficult to leave much thought for anything else. It was now that my experiences of poverty began—for six francs a day, if not actual poverty, is on the fringe of it. Six francs is a shilling, and you can live on a shilling a day in Paris if you know how. But it is a complicated business.

It is altogether curious, your first contact with poverty. You have thought so much about poverty—it is the thing you have feared all your life, the thing you knew would happen to you sooner or later; and it is all so utterly and prosaically different. You thought it would be quite simple; it is extraordinarily complicated. You thought it would be terrible; it is merely squalid and boring. It is the peculiar *lowness* of poverty that you discover first; the shifts that it puts you to, the complicated meanness, the crust-wiping.

You discover, for instance, the secrecy attaching to poverty. At a sudden stroke you have been reduced to an income of six francs a day. But of course you dare not admit it—you have got to pretend that you are living quite as usual. From the start it tangles you in a net of lies, and even with the lies you can hardly manage it. You stop sending clothes to the laundry, and the laundress catches you in the street and asks you why; you mumble something, and she, thinking you are sending the clothes elsewhere, is your enemy for life. The tobacconist keeps asking why you have cut down your smoking. There are letters you want to answer, and cannot, because stamps are too expensive. And then there are your meals—meals are the worst difficulty of all. Every day at meal times you go out, ostensibly to a restaurant, and loaf an hour in the Luxembourg Gardens, watching the pigeons. Afterward you smuggle your food home in your pockets. Your food is bread and margarine, or bread and wine, and even the nature of the food is governed by lies. You have to buy rye bread instead of household bread, because the rye loaves, though dearer, are round and can be smuggled in your pockets. This wastes you a franc a day. Sometimes, to keep up appearances, you have to spend sixty centimes on a drink, and go correspondingly short of food. Your linen gets filthy, and you run out of soap and razor blades. Your hair wants cutting, and you try to cut it yourself, with such fearful results that you have to go to the barber after all, and spend the equivalent of a day's food. All day you are telling lies, and expensive lies.

You discover the extreme precariousness of your six francs a day. Mean disasters happen and rob you of food. You have spent your last eighty centimes on half a liter of milk, and are boiling it over the spirit lamp. While it boils a bug runs down your forearm; you give the bug a flick with your nail, and it falls, plop! straight into the milk. There is nothing for it but to throw the milk away and go foodless.

You go to the baker's to buy a pound of bread, and you wait while the girl cuts a pound for another customer. She is clumsy, and cuts more than a pound. *"Pardon, monsieur,"* she says, "I suppose you don't mind paying two sous extra?" Bread is a franc a pound, and you have exactly a franc. When you think that you too might be asked to pay two sous extra, and would have to confess that you could not, you bolt in panic. It is hours before you dare venture into a baker's shop again.

You go to the greengrocer's to spend a franc on a kilogram of potatoes. But one of the pieces that make up the franc is a Belgium piece, and the shopman refuses it. You slink out of the shop, and can never go there again.

You have strayed into a respectable quarter, and you see a prosperous friend coming. To avoid him you dodge into the nearest café. Once in the café you must buy something, so you spend your last fifty centimes on a glass of black coffee with a dead fly in it. One could multiply these disasters by the hundred. They are part of the process of being hard up.

You discover what it is like to be hungry. With bread and margarine in your belly, you go out and look into the shop windows. Everywhere there is food insulting you in huge, wasteful piles; whole dead pigs, baskets of hot loaves, great yellow blocks of butter, strings of sausages, mountains of potatoes, vast Gruyère cheeses like grindstones. A sniveling self-pity comes over you at the sight of so much food. You plan to grab a loaf and run, swallowing it before they catch you; and you refrain, from pure funk.

You discover the boredom which is inseparable from poverty; the times when you have nothing to do and, being underfed, can interest yourself in nothing. For half a day at a time you lie on your bed, feeling like the *jeune squelette* in Baudelaire's poem. Only food could rouse you. You discover that a man who has gone even a week on bread and margarine is not a man any longer, only a belly with a few accessory organs.

This—one could describe it further, but it is all in the same style— is life on six francs a day. Thousands of people in Paris live it— struggling artists and students, prostitutes when their luck is out, out-of-work people of all kinds. It is the suburbs, as it were, of poverty.

I continued in this style for about three weeks. The forty-seven francs were soon gone, and I had to do what I could on thirty-six francs a week from the English lessons. Being inexperienced, I handled the money badly, and sometimes I was a day without food. When this happened I used to sell a few of my clothes, smuggling them out of the hotel in small packets and taking them to a second-hand shop in the Rue de la Montagne St. Geneviève. The shopman was a red-haired Jew, an extraordinary disagreeable man, who used to fall into furious rages at the sight of a client. From his manner one would have supposed that we had done him some injury by coming to him. *"Merde!"* he used to shout, *"you* here again? What do you think this is? A soup kitchen?" And he paid incredibly low prices. For a hat which I had bought for twenty-five shillings and scarcely worn he gave five francs; for a good pair of shoes, five francs; for shirts, a franc each. He always preferred to exchange rather than buy, and he had a trick of thrusting some useless article into one's hand and then pretending that one had accepted it. Once I saw him take a good overcoat from an old woman, put two white billiard balls into her hand, and then push her rapidly out of the shop before she could protest. It would have been a pleasure to flatten the Jew's nose, if only one could have afforded it.

These three weeks were squalid and uncomfortable, and evidently there was worse coming, for my rent would be due before long. Nevertheless, things were not a quarter as bad as I had expected. For, when you are approaching poverty, you make one discovery which outweighs some of the others. You discover boredom and mean complications and the beginnings of hunger, but you also discover the great redeeming feature of poverty: the fact that it annihilates the future. Within certain limits, it is actually true that the less money you have, the less you worry. When you have a hundred francs in the world you are liable to the most craven panics. When you have only three francs you are quite indifferent; for three francs will feed you till tomorrow, and you cannot think further than that. You are bored, but you are not afraid. You think vaguely, "I shall be starving in a day or two—shocking, isn't it?" And then the mind wanders to other topics. A bread-and-margarine diet does, to some extent, provide its own anodyne.

And there is another feeling that is a great consolation in poverty. I believe everyone who has been hard up has experienced it. It is a feeling of relief, almost of pleasure, at knowing yourself at last genuinely down and out. You have talked so often of going to the dogs—and well, here are the dogs, and you have reached them, and you can stand it. It takes off a lot of anxiety.

IV

One day my English lessons ceased abruptly. The weather was getting hot and one of my pupils, feeling too lazy to go on with his lessons, dismissed me. The other disappeared from his lodgings without notice, owing me twelve francs. . . .

It was now absolutely necessary to find work, and I remembered a friend of mine, a Russian waiter named Boris, who might be able to help me. I had first met him in the public ward of a hospital, where he was being treated for arthritis in the left leg. He had told me to come to him if I were ever in difficulties.

I must say something about Boris, for he was a curious character and my close friend for a long time. He was a big, soldierly man of about thirty-five, and had been good-looking, but since his illness he had grown immensely fat from lying in bed. Like most Russian refugees, he had had an adventurous life. His parents, killed in the Revolution, had been rich people, and he had served through the war in the Second Siberian Rifles, which, according to him, was the best regiment in the Russian Army. After the war he had first worked in a brush factory, then as a porter at Les Halles, then had become a dishwasher, and had finally worked his way up to be a waiter. When he fell ill he was at the Hôtel Scribe, and taking a hundred francs a day in tips. His ambition was to become a *maître d'hôtel,* save fifty thousand francs, and set up a small, select restaurant on the Right Bank.

Boris always talked of the war as the happiest time of his life. War and soldiering were his passion; he had read innumerable books of strategy and military history, and could tell you all about the theories of Napoleon, Kutuzof, Clausewitz, Moltke, and Foch. Anything to do with soldiers pleased him. His favorite café was the Closerie des Lilas in Montparnasse, simply because the statue of Marshal Ney stands outside it. Later on, Boris and I sometimes went to the Rue du Commerce together. If we went by Metro, Boris always got out at Cambronne station instead of Commerce, though Commerce was nearer; he liked the association with General Cambronne, who was called on to surrender at Waterloo, and answered simply, *"Merde!"*

The only things left to Boris by the Revolution were his medals and some photographs of his old regiment; he had kept these when everything else went to the pawnshop. Almost every day he would spread the photographs out on the bed and talk about them:

"Voilà, mon ami! There you see me at the head of my company. Fine big men, eh? Not like these little rats of Frenchmen. A captain at twenty—not bad, eh? Yes, a captain in the Second Siberian Rifles; and my father was a colonel.

"Ah, mais, mon ami, the ups and downs of life! A captain in the Russian Army, and then, piff! the Revolution—every penny gone. In 1916 I stayed a week at the Hôtel Edouard Sept; in 1920 I was trying for a job as night watchman there. I have been night watchman, cellarman, floor-scrubber, dishwasher, porter, lavatory attendant. I have tipped waiters, and I have been tipped by waiters.

"Ah, but I have known what it is to live like a gentleman, *mon ami*. I do not say it to boast, but the other day I was trying to compute how many mistresses I have had in my life, and I made it out to be over two hundred. Yes, at least two hundred . . . Ah, well, *ça reviendra*. Victory is to him who fights the longest. Courage!" etc. etc.

Boris had a queer, changeable nature. He always wished himself back in the army, but he had also been a waiter long enough to acquire the waiter's outlook. Though he had never saved more than a few thousand francs, he took it for granted that in the end he would be able to set up his own restaurant and grow rich. All waiters, I afterward found, talk and think of this; it is what reconciles them to being waiters. . . .

I liked Boris, and we had interesting times together, playing chess and talking about war and hotels. Boris used often to suggest that I should become a waiter. "The life would suit you," he used to say; "when you are in work, with a hundred francs a day and a nice mistress, it's not bad. You say you go in for writing. Writing is bosh. There is only one way to make money at writing, and that is to marry a publisher's daughter. But you would make a good waiter if you shaved that moustache off. You are tall and you speak English—those are the chief things a waiter needs. Wait till I can bend this accursed leg, *mon ami*. And then, if you are ever out of a job, come to me."

Now that I was short of my rent, and getting hungry, I remembered Boris's promise, and decided to look him up at once. I did not hope to become a waiter so easily as he had promised, but of course I knew how to scrub dishes, and no doubt he could get me a job in the kitchen. He had said that dishwashing jobs were to be had for the asking during the summer. It was a great relief to remember that I had after all one influential friend to fall back on.

V

A short time before, Boris had given me an address in the Rue du Marché des Blancs Manteaux. All he had said in his letter was that "things were not marching too badly," and I assumed that he was back at the Hôtel Scribe, touching his hundred francs a day. I was full of hope, and wondered why I had been fool enough not to go to Boris before. I saw myself in a cosy restaurant, with jolly cooks singing love songs as they broke eggs into the pan, and five solid meals a day. I even squandered two francs-fifty on a packet of Gaulois Bleu, in anticipation of my wages.

In the morning I walked down to the Rue du Marché des Blancs

Manteaux; with a shock, I found it a slummy back street as bad
as my own. Boris's hotel was the dirtiest hotel in the street. From
its dark doorway there came out a vile, sour odor, a mixture of
slops and synthetic soup—it was Bouillon Zip, twenty-five centimes
a packet. A misgiving came over me. People who drink Bouillon
Zip are starving, or near it. Could Boris possibly be earning a hundred francs a day? A surly *patron,* sitting in the office, said to me,
Yes, the Russian was at home—in the attic. I went up six flights
of narrow, winding stairs, the Bouillon Zip growing stronger as
one got higher. Boris did not answer when I knocked at his door,
so I opened it and went in.

The room was an attic, ten feet square, lighted only by a skylight, its sole furniture a narrow iron bedstead, a chair, and a
washhand-stand with one game leg. A long S-shaped chain of bugs
marched slowly across the wall above the bed. Boris was lying
asleep, naked, his large belly making a mound under the grimy
sheet. His chest was spotted with insect bites. As I came in he woke
up, rubbed his eyes, and groaned deeply.

"Name of Jesus Christ!" he exclaimed, "oh, name of Jesus Christ,
my back! Curse it, I believe my back is broken!"

"What's the matter?" I exclaimed.

"My back is broken, that is all. I have spent the night on the
floor. Oh, name of Jesus Christ! If you knew what my back feels
like!"

"My dear Boris, are you ill?"

"Not ill, only starving—yes, starving to death if this goes on much
longer. Besides sleeping on the floor, I have lived on two francs a
day for weeks past. It is fearful. You have come at a bad moment,
mon ami."

It did not seem much use to ask whether Boris still had his job
at the Hôtel Scribe. I hurried downstairs and bought a loaf of
bread. Boris threw himself on the bread and ate half of it, after
which he felt better, sat up in bed, and told me what was the matter with him. He had failed to get a job after leaving the hospital,
because he was still very lame, and he had spent all his money and
pawned everything, and finally starved for several days. He had
slept a week on the quay under the Pont d'Austerlitz, among some
empty wine barrels. For the past fortnight he had been living in
this room, together with a Jew, a mechanic. It appeared (there was
some complicated explanation) that the Jew owed Boris three hundred francs, and was repaying this by letting him sleep on the floor
and allowing him two francs a day for food. Two francs would buy
a bowl of coffee and three rolls. The Jew went to work at seven in

the mornings, and after that Boris would leave his sleeping place (it was beneath the skylight, which let in the rain) and get into the bed. He could not sleep much even there owing to the bugs, but it rested his back after the floor.

It was a great disappointment, when I had come to Boris for help, to find him even worse off than myself. I explained that I had only about sixty francs left and must get a job immediately. By this time, however, Boris had eaten the rest of the bread and was feeling cheerful and talkative. He said carelessly:

"Good heavens, what are you worrying about? Sixty francs—why, it's a fortune! Please hand me that shoe, *mon ami*. I'm going to smash some of those bugs if they come within reach."

"But do you think there's any chance of getting a job?"

"Chance? It's a certainty. In fact, I have got something already. There is a new Russian restaurant which is to open in a few days in the Rue du Commerce. It is *une chose entendue* that I am to be *maître d'hôtel*. I can easily get you a job in the kitchen. Five hundred francs a month and your food—tips, too, if you are lucky."

"But in the meantime? I've got to pay my rent before long."

"Oh, we shall find something. I have got a few cards up my sleeve. There are people who owe me money, for instance—Paris is full of them. One of them is bound to pay up before long. Then think of all the women who have been my mistress! A woman never forgets, you know—I have only to ask and they will help me. Besides, the Jew tells me he is going to steal some magnetos from the garage where he works, and he will pay us five francs a day to clean them before he sells them. That alone would keep us. Never worry, *mon ami*. Nothing is easier to get than money."

"Well, let's go out now and look for a job."

"Presently, *mon ami*. We shan't starve, don't you fear. This is only the fortune of war—I've been in a worse hole scores of times. It's only a question of persisting. Remember Foch's maxim: '*Attaquez! Attaquez! Attaquez!*'"

It was midday before Boris decided to get up. All the clothes he now had left were one suit, with one shirt, collar, and tie, a pair of shoes almost worn out, and a pair of socks all holes. He had also an overcoat which was to be pawned in the last extremity. He had a suitcase, a wretched twenty-franc cardboard thing, but very important, because the *patron* of the hotel believed that it was full of clothes—without that, he would probably have turned Boris out of doors. What it actually contained were the medals and photographs, various odds and ends, and huge bundles of love-letters. In spite of all this Boris managed to keep a fairly smart appearance. He shaved without soap and with a razor blade two months old, tied his tie so that the holes did not show, and carefully stuffed the soles of his shoes with newspaper. Finally, when he was dressed, he produced an ink bottle and inked the skin of his ankles where it showed through his socks. You would never have thought, when it was finished, that he had recently been sleeping under the Seine bridges. . . .

We went to the Hôtel Scribe and waited an hour on the pavement, hoping that the manager would come out, but he never did. Then we dragged ourselves down to the Rue du Commerce, only to find that the new restaurant, which was being redecorated, was shut up and the *patron* away. It was now night. We had walked fourteen kilometers over pavement, and we were so tired that we had to waste one franc-fifty on going home by Metro. Walking was agony to Boris with his game leg, and his optimism wore thinner and thinner as the day went on. When he got out of the Metro at the Place d'Italie he was in despair. He began to say that it was no use looking for work—there was nothing for it but to try crime.

"Sooner rob than starve, *mon ami.* I have often planned it. A fat, rich American—some dark corner down Montparnasse way—a cobblestone in a stocking—bang! And then go through his pockets and bolt. It is feasible, do you not think? I would not flinch—I have been a soldier, remember."

He decided against the plan in the end, because we were both foreigners and easily recognized.

When we had got back to my room we spent another one franc-fifty on bread and chocolate. Boris devoured his share, and at once cheered up like magic; food seemed to act on his system as rapidly as a cocktail. He took out a pencil and began making a list of the people who would probably give us jobs. There were dozens of them, he said.

"Tomorrow we shall find something, *mon ami,* I know it in my bones. The luck always changes. Besides, we both have brains—a man with brains can't starve.

"What things a man can do with brains! Brains will make money out of anything. I had a friend once, a Pole, a real man of genius; and what do you think he used to do? He would buy a gold ring and pawn it for fifteen francs. Then—you know how carelessly the clerks fill up the tickets—where the clerk had written '*en or*' he would add '*et diamants*' and he would change 'fifteen francs' to 'fifteen thousand.' Neat, eh? Then, you see, he could borrow a thousand francs on the security of the ticket. That is what I mean by brains. . . ."

For the rest of the evening Boris was in a hopeful mood, talking of the times we should have together when we were waiters together at Nice or Biarritz, with smart rooms and enough money to set up mistresses. He was too tired to walk the three kilometers back to his hotel, and slept the night on the floor of my room, with his coat rolled round his shoes for a pillow.

VI

We again failed to find work the next day, and it was three weeks before the luck changed. My two hundred francs saved me from trouble about the rent, but everything else went as badly as possible. Day after day Boris and I went up and down Paris, drifting at two miles an hour through the crowds, bored and hungry, and finding nothing. One day, I remember, we crossed the Seine eleven times. We loitered for hours outside service doorways, and when the manager came out we would go up to him ingratiatingly, cap in hand. We always got the same answer: they did not want a lame man, nor a man without experience. . . .

We enrolled our names at agencies and answered advertisements, but walking everywhere made us slow, and we seemed to miss every job by half an hour. Once we very nearly got a job swabbing out railway trucks, but at the last moment they rejected us in favor of Frenchmen. Once we answered an advertisement calling for hands at a circus. You had to shift benches and clean up litter, and, during the performance, stand on two tubs and let a lion jump through your legs. When we got to the place, an hour before the time named, we found a queue of fifty men already waiting. There is some attraction in lions, evidently. . . .

Once Boris suggested that I should go to Les Halles and try for a job as a porter. I arrived at half-past four in the morning, when the work was getting into its swing. Seeing a short, fat man in a bowler hat directing some porters, I went up to him and asked for work. Before answering he seized my right hand and felt the palm.

"You are strong, eh?" he said.

"Very strong," I said untruly.

"*Bien.* Let me see you lift that crate."

It was a huge wicker basket full of potatoes. I took hold of it, and found that, so far from lifting it, I could not even move it. The man in the bowler hat watched me, then shrugged his shoulders and turned away. I made off. When I had gone some distance I looked back and saw *four* men lifting the basket on to a cart. It weighed three hundredweight, possibly. The man had seen that I was no use, and taken this way of getting rid of me.

Sometimes in his hopeful moments Boris spent fifty centimes on a stamp and wrote to one of his ex-mistresses, asking for money. Only one of them ever replied. It was a woman who, besides having been his mistress, owed him two hundred francs. When Boris saw the letter waiting and recognized the handwriting, he was wild with hope. We seized the letter and rushed up to Boris's room to read it, like a child with stolen sweets. Boris read the letter, then handed it silently to me. It ran:

My Little Cherished Wolf,

With what delight did I open thy charming letter, reminding me of the days of our perfect love, and of the so dear kisses which I have received from thy lips. Such memories linger for ever in the heart, like the perfume of a flower that is dead.

As to thy request for two hundred francs, alas! it is impossible. Thou dost not know, my dear one, how I am desolated to hear of thy embarrassments. But what wouldst thou? In this life which is so sad, trouble comes to everyone. I too have had my share. My little sister has been ill (ah, the poor little one, how she suffered!) and we are obliged to pay I know not what to the doctor. All our money is gone and we are passing, I assure thee, very difficult days.

Courage, my little wolf, always the courage! Remember that the bad days are not for ever, and the trouble which seems so terrible will disappear at last.

Rest assured, my dear one, that I will remember thee always. And receive the most sincere embraces of her who has never ceased to love thee, thy

YVONNE.

This letter disappointed Boris so much that he went straight to bed and would not look for work again that day.

My sixty francs lasted about a fortnight. I had given up the pretense of going out to restaurants, and we used to eat in my room, one of us sitting on the bed and the other on the chair. Boris would contribute his two francs and I three or four francs, and we would buy bread, potatoes, milk, and cheese, and make soup over my spirit lamp. We had a saucepan and a coffee-bowl and one spoon; every day there was a polite squabble as to who should eat out of the saucepan and who out of the coffee-bowl (the saucepan held more), and every day, to my secret anger, Boris gave in first and had the saucepan. Sometimes we had more bread in the evening, sometimes not. Our linen was getting filthy, and it was three weeks since I had had a bath; Boris, so he said, had not had a bath for months. It was tobacco that made everything tolerable. We had plenty of tobacco, for some time before Boris had met a soldier (the soldiers are given their tobacco free) and bought twenty or thirty packets at fifty centimes each.

All this was far worse for Boris than for me. The walking and sleeping on the floor kept his leg and back in constant pain, and with his vast Russian appetite he suffered torments of hunger, though he never seemed to grow thinner. On the whole he was surprisingly gay, and he had vast capacities for hope. He used to say seriously that he had a patron saint who watched over him, and when things were very bad he would search the gutter for money, saying that the saint often dropped a two-franc piece there. One day we were waiting in the Rue Royale; there was a Russian restaurant near by, and we were going to ask for a job there. Suddenly, Boris made up his mind to go into the Madeleine and burn a fifty-centime candle to his patron saint. Then, coming out, he said that he would be on the safe side, and solemnly put a match to a fifty-centime stamp, as a sacrifice to the immortal gods. Perhaps the gods and the saints did not get on together; at any rate, we missed the job. . . .

IX

. . . the *patron* of the new restaurant in the Rue du Commerce had at last come back. We went down in the afternoon and saw him. On the way Boris talked of the vast fortunes we should make if we got this job, and on the importance of making a good impression on the *patron*.

"Appearance—appearance is everything, *mon ami*. Give me a new suit and I will borrow a thousand francs by dinner time. What a pity I did not buy a collar when we had money. I turned my collar inside out this morning; but what is the use, one side is as dirty as the other. Do you think I look hungry, *mon ami?*"

"You look pale."

"Curse it, what can one do on bread and potatoes? It is fatal to look hungry. It makes people want to kick you. Wait."

He stopped at a jeweler's window and smacked his cheeks sharply to bring the blood into them. Then, before the flush had faded, we hurried into the restaurant and introduced ourselves to the *patron*.

The *patron* was a short, fattish, very dignified man with wavy gray hair, dressed in a smart, double-breasted flannel suit and smelling of scent. Boris told me that he too was an ex-colonel of the Russian Army. His wife was there too, a horrid, fat French-woman with a dead-white face and scarlet lips, reminding me of cold veal and tomatoes. The *patron* greeted Boris genially, and they talked together in Russian for a few minutes. I stood in the background, preparing to tell some big lies about my experience as a dishwasher.

Then the *patron* came over toward me. I shuffled uneasily, trying to look servile. Boris had rubbed it into me that a *plongeur* is a slave's slave, and I expected the patron to treat me like dirt. To my astonishment, he seized me warmly by the hand.

"So you are an Englishman!" he exclaimed. "But how charming! I need not ask, then, whether you are a golfer?"

"*Mais certainement,*" I said, seeing that this was expected of me.

"All my life I have wanted to play golf. Will you, my dear *monsieur,* be so kind as to show me a few of the principal strokes?"

Apparently this was the Russian way of doing business. The *patron* listened attentively while I explained the difference between a driver and an iron, and then suddenly informed me that it was all *entendu;* Boris was to be *maître d'hôtel* when the restaurant opened, and I *plongeur,* with a chance of rising to lavatory attendant if trade was good. When would the restaurant open? I asked. "Exactly a fortnight from today," the *patron* answered grandly (he had a manner of waving his hand and flicking off his cigarette ash at the same time, which looked very grand), "exactly a fortnight from today, in time for lunch." Then, with obvious pride, he showed us over the restaurant.

It was a smallish place, consisting of a bar, a dining room, and a kitchen no bigger than the average bathroom. The *patron* was decorating it in a trumpery "picturesque" style (he called it "*le Normand*"; it was a matter of sham beams stuck on the plaster, and the like) and proposed to call it the Auberge de Jehan Cottard, to give a medieval effect. He had a leaflet printed, full of lies about the historical associations of the quarter, and this leaflet actually claimed, among other things, that there had once been an inn on the site of the restaurant which was frequented by Charlemagne. The *patron* was very pleased with this touch. He was also having the bar decorated with indecent pictures by an artist from the Salon. Finally he gave us each an expensive cigarette, and after some more talk he went home.

I felt strongly that we should never get any good from this restaurant. The *patron* had looked to me like a cheat, and, what was worse, an incompetent cheat, and I had seen two unmistakable duns hanging about the back door. But Boris, seeing himself a *maître d'hôtel* once more, would not be discouraged.

"We've brought it off—only a fortnight to hold out. What is a fortnight? Food? *Je m'en f——.* To think that in only three weeks

I shall have my mistress! Will she be dark or fair, I wonder? I don't mind, so long as she is not too thin."

Two bad days followed. We had only sixty centimes left, and we spent it on half a pound of bread, with a piece of garlic to rub it with. The point of rubbing garlic on bread is that the taste lingers and gives one the illusion of having fed recently. We sat most of that day in the Jardin des Plantes. Boris had shots with stones at the tame pigeons, but always missed them, and after that we wrote dinner menus on the backs of envelopes. We were too hungry even to try and think of anything except food. I remember the dinner Boris finally selected for himself. It was: a dozen oysters, borsch soup (the red, sweet, beetroot soup with cream on top), crayfishes, a young chicken *en casserole,* beef with stewed plums, new potatoes, a salad, suet pudding, and Roquefort cheese, with a liter of Burgundy and some old brandy. Boris had international tastes in food. Later on, when we were prosperous, I occasionally saw him eat meals almost as large without difficulty.

When our money came to an end I stopped looking for work, and was another day without food. I did not believe that the Auberge de Jehan Cottard was really going to open, and I could see no other prospect, but I was too lazy to do anything but lie in bed. Then the luck changed abruptly. At night, at about ten o'clock, I heard an eager shout from the street. I got up and went to the window. Boris was there, waving his stick and beaming. Before speaking he dragged a bent loaf from his pocket and threw it up to me.

"*Mon ami, mon cher ami,* we're saved! What do you think?"

"Surely you haven't got a job!"

"At the Hôtel X., near the Place de la Concorde—five hundred francs a month, and food. I have been working there today. Name of Jesus Christ, how I have eaten!"

After ten or twelve hours' work, and with his game leg, his first thought had been to walk three kilometers to my hotel and tell me the good news! What was more, he told me to meet him in the Tuileries the next day during his afternoon interval, in case he should be able to steal some food for me. At the appointed time I met Boris on a public bench. He undid his waistcoat and produced a large, crushed, newspaper packet; in it were some minced veal, a wedge of Camembert cheese, bread, and an éclair, all jumbled together.

"*Voilà!*" said Boris, "that's all I could smuggle out for you. The doorkeeper is a cunning swine."

It is disagreeable to eat out of a newspaper on a public seat, especially in the Tuileries, which are generally full of pretty girls, but I was too hungry to care. While I ate, Boris explained that he was working in the cafeterie of the hotel—that is, in English, the stillroom. It appeared that the cafeterie was the very lowest post in the hotel, and a dreadful come-down for a waiter, but it would do until the Auberge de Jehan Cottard opened. Meanwhile I was to meet Boris every day in the Tuileries, and he would smuggle out as much food as he dared. For three days we continued with this arrangement, and I lived entirely on the stolen food. Then all our troubles came to an end, for one of the *plongeurs* left the Hôtel X., and on Boris's recommendation I was given a job there myself.

X

The Hôtel X. was a vast, grandiose place with a classical façade, and at one side a little, dark doorway like a rat-hole, which was the service entrance. I arrived at a quarter to seven in the morning. A stream of men with greasy trousers were hurrying in and being checked by a doorkeeper who sat in a tiny office. I waited, and presently the *chef du personnel,* a sort of assistant manager, arrived and began to question me. He was an Italian, with a round, pale face, haggard from overwork. He asked whether I was an experienced dishwasher, and I said that I was; he glanced at my hands and saw that I was lying, but on hearing that I was an Englishman he changed his tone and engaged me.

"We have been looking for someone to practice our English on," he said. "Our clients are all Americans, and the only English we know is——" He repeated something that little boys write on the walls in London. "You may be useful. Come downstairs."

He led me down a winding staircase into a narrow passage, deep underground, and so low that I had to stoop in places. It was stiflingly hot and very dark, with only dim, yellow bulbs several yards apart. There seemed to be miles of dark labyrinthine passages—actually, I suppose, a few hundred yards in all—that reminded one queerly of the lower decks of a liner; there were the same heat and cramped space and warm reek of food, and a humming, whirring noise (it came from the kitchen furnaces) just like the whir of engines. We passed doorways which let out sometimes a shouting of oaths, sometimes the red glare of a fire, once a shuddering draught from an ice chamber. As we went along, something struck me violently in the back. It was a hundred-pound block of ice, carried by a blue-aproned porter. After him came a boy with a great slab of veal on his shoulder, his cheek pressed into the damp, spongy flesh. They shoved me aside with a cry of *"Sauve-*

toi, idiot!" and rushed on. On the wall, under one of the lights, someone had written in a very neat hand: "Sooner will you find a cloudless sky in winter, than a woman at the Hôtel X. who has her maidenhead." It seemed a queer sort of place.

One of the passages branched off into a laundry, where an old, skull-faced woman gave me a blue apron and a pile of dishcloths. Then the *chef du personnel* took me to a tiny underground den— a cellar below a cellar, as it were—where there were a sink and some gas-ovens. It was too low for me to stand quite upright, and the temperature was perhaps 110 degrees Fahrenheit. The *chef du personnel* explained that my job was to fetch meals for the higher hotel employees, who fed in a small dining room above, clean their room and wash their crockery. When he had gone, a waiter, another Italian, thrust a fierce, fuzzy head into the doorway and looked down at me.

"English, eh?" he said. "Well, I'm in charge here. If you work well"—he made the motion of up-ending a bottle and sucked noisily. "If you don't"—he gave the doorpost several vigorous kicks. "To me, twisting your neck would be no more than spitting on the floor. And if there's any trouble, they'll believe me, not you. So be careful."

After this I set to work rather hurriedly. Except for about an hour, I was at work from seven in the morning till a quarter-past nine at night; first at washing crockery, then at scrubbing the tables and floors of the employees' dining room, then at polishing glasses and knives, then at fetching meals, then at washing crockery again, then at fetching more meals and washing more crockery. It was easy work, and I got on well with it except when I went to the kitchen to fetch meals. The kitchen was like nothing I had ever seen or imagined—a stifling, low-ceilinged inferno of a cellar, red-lit from the fires, and deafening with oaths and the clanging of pots and pans. It was so hot that all the metal work except the stoves had to be covered with cloth. In the middle were furnaces, where twelve cooks skipped to and fro, their faces dripping sweat in spite of their white caps. Round that were counters where a mob of waiters and *plongeurs* clamored with trays. Scullions, naked to the waist, were stoking the fires and scouring huge copper saucepans with sand. Everyone seemed to be in a hurry and a rage. The head cook, a fine, scarlet man with big moustachios, stood in the middle booming continuously, "*Ça marche deux œufs brouillés! Ça marche un Chateau-briand aux pommes sautées!*" except when he broke off to curse at a *plongeur*. There were three counters, and the first time I went to the kitchen I took my tray unknowingly to the wrong one. The head cook walked up to me, twisted his moustaches, and looked me up and down. Then he beckoned to the breakfast cook and pointed at me.

"Do you see *that*? That is the type of *plongeur* they send us nowadays. Where do you come from, idiot? From Charenton, I suppose?" (There is a large lunatic asylum at Charenton.)

"From England," I said.

"I might have known it. Well, *mon cher monsieur l'Anglais*, may I inform you that you are the son of a whore? And now —— the camp to the other counter, where you belong."

I got this kind of reception every time I went to the kitchen, for I always made some mistake; I was expected to know the work, and was cursed accordingly. From curiosity I counted the number of times I was called *maquereau* during the day, and it was thirty-nine.

At half-past four the Italian told me that I could stop working, but that it was not worth going out, as we began again at five. I went to the lavatory for a smoke; smoking was strictly forbidden, and Boris had warned me that the lavatory was the only safe place. After that I worked again till a quarter-past nine, when the waiter put his head into the doorway and told me to leave the rest of the crockery. To my astonishment, after calling me pig, mackerel, etc., all day, he had suddenly grown quite friendly. I realized that the curses I had met with were only a kind of probation.

"That'll do, *mon p'tit*," said the waiter. *"Tu n'es pas débrouillard*, but you work all right. Come up and have your dinner. The hotel allows us two liters of wine each, and I've stolen another bottle. We'll have a fine booze."

We had an excellent dinner from the leavings of the higher employees. The waiter, grown mellow, told me stories about his love affairs, and about two men whom he had stabbed in Italy, and about how he had dodged his military service. He was a good fellow when one got to know him; he reminded me of Benvenuto Cellini, somehow. I was tired and drenched with sweat, but I felt a new man after a day's solid food. The work did not seem difficult, and I felt that this job would suit me. It was not certain, however, that it would continue, for I had been engaged as an "extra" for the day only, at twenty-five francs. The sour-faced doorkeeper counted out the money, less fifty centimes which he said was for insurance (a lie, I discovered afterward). Then he stepped out into the passage, made me take off my coat, and carefully prodded me all over, searching for stolen food. After this the *chef du personnel* appeared and spoke to me. Like the waiter, he had grown more genial on seeing that I was willing to work.

"We will give you a permanent job if you like," he said. "The head waiter says he would enjoy calling an Englishman names. . . ."

XI

. . . I worked . . . four days a week in the cafeterie, one day helping the waiter on the fourth floor, and one day replacing the woman who washed up for the dining room. My day off, luckily, was Sunday, but sometimes another man was ill and I had to work that day as well. The hours were from seven in the morning till two in the afternoon, and from five in the evening till nine—eleven hours; but it was a fourteen-hour day when I washed up for the dining room. By the ordinary standards of a Paris *plongeur,* these are exceptionally short hours. The only hardship of life was the fearful heat and stuffiness of these labyrinthine cellars. Apart from this the hotel, which was large and well organized, was considered a comfortable one.

Our cafeterie was a murky cellar measuring twenty feet by seven by eight high, and so crowded with coffee-urns, bread-cutters and the like that one could hardly move without banging against something. It was lighted by one dim electric bulb, and four or five gas fires that sent out a fierce red breath. There was a thermometer there, and the temperature never fell below 110 degrees Fahrenheit —it neared 130 at some times of the day. At one end were five service lifts, and at the other an ice cupboard where we stored milk and butter. When you went into the ice cupboard you dropped a hundred degrees of temperature at a single step; it used to remind me of the hymn about Greenland's icy mountains and India's coral strand. Two men worked in the cafeterie besides Boris and myself. One was Mario, a huge, excitable Italian—he was like a city policeman with operatic gestures—and the other, a hairy, uncouth animal whom we called the Magyar; I think he was a Transylvanian, or something even more remote. Except the Magyar we were all big men, and at the rush hours we collided incessantly.

The work in the cafeterie was spasmodic. We were never idle, but the real work only came in bursts of two hours at a time—we called each burst *"un coup de feu."* The first *coup de feu* came at eight, when the guests upstairs began to wake up and demand breakfast. At eight a sudden banging and yelling would break out all through the basement; bells rang on all sides, blue-aproned men rushed through the passages, our service lifts came down with a simultaneous crash, and the waiters on all five floors began shouting Italian oaths down the shafts. I don't remember all our duties, but they included making tea, coffee, and chocolate, fetching meals from the kitchen, wines from the cellar, and fruit and so forth from the dining room, slicing bread, making toast, rolling pats of butter, measuring jam, opening milk cans, counting lumps of sugar, boiling eggs, cooking porridge, pounding ice, grinding coffee—all this for from a hundred to two hundred customers. The kitchen was thirty yards away, and the dining room sixty or seventy yards. Everything we sent up in the service lifts had to be covered by a voucher, and the vouchers had to be carefully filed, and there was trouble if even a lump of sugar was lost. Besides this, we had to supply the staff with bread and coffee, and fetch the meals for the waiters upstairs. All in all, it was a complicated job.

I calculated that one had to walk and run about fifteen miles during the day, and yet the strain of the work was more mental than physical. Nothing could be easier, on the face of it, than this stupid scullion work, but it is astonishingly hard when one is in a hurry. One has to leap to and fro between a multitude of jobs —it is like sorting a pack of cards against the clock. You are, for example, making toast, when bang! down comes a service lift with an order for tea, rolls, and three different kinds of jam, and simultaneously bang! down comes another demanding scrambled eggs, coffee, and grapefruit; you run to the kitchen for the eggs and to the dining room for the fruit, going like lightning so as to be back before your toast burns, and having to remember about the tea and coffee, besides half a dozen other orders that are still pending; and at the same time some waiter is following you and making trouble about a lost bottle of soda water, and you are arguing with him. It needs more brains than one might think. Mario said, no doubt truly, that it took a year to make a reliable cafetier.

The time between eight and half-past ten was a sort of delirium. Sometimes we were going as though we had only five minutes to live; sometimes there were sudden lulls when the orders stopped and everything seemed quiet for a moment. Then we swept up the litter from the floor, threw down fresh sawdust, and swallowed gallipots of wine or coffee or water—anything, so long as it was wet. Very often we used to break off chunks of ice and suck them while we worked. The heat among the gas fires was nauseating; we swallowed quarts of drink during the day, and after a few hours even our aprons were drenched with sweat. At times we were hopelessly behind with the work, and some of the customers would have gone without their breakfast, but Mario always pulled us through. He had worked fourteen years in the cafeterie, and he had the skill that never wastes a

second between jobs. The Magyar was very stupid and I was inexperienced, and Boris was inclined to shirk, partly because of his
lame leg, partly because he was ashamed of working in the cafeterie
after being a waiter; but Mario was wonderful. The way he would
stretch his great arms right across the cafeterie to fill a coffee-pot
with one hand and boil an egg with the other, at the same time
watching toast and shouting directions to the Magyar, and between
whiles singing snatches from *Rigoletto,* was beyond all praise. The
patron knew his value, and he was paid a thousand francs a month,
instead of five hundred like the rest of us.

The breakfast pandemonium stopped at half-past ten. Then we
scrubbed the cafeterie tables, swept the floor and polished the brass-
work, and, on good mornings, went one at a time to the lavatory
for a smoke. This was our slack time—only relatively slack, however,
for we had only ten minutes for lunch, and we never got through
it uninterrupted. The customers' luncheon hour, between twelve
and two, was another period of turmoil like the breakfast hour.
Most of our work was fetching meals from the kitchen, which meant
constant *engueulades* from the cooks. By this time the cooks had
sweated in front of their furnaces for four or five hours, and their
tempers were all warmed up.

At two we were suddenly free men. We threw off our aprons and
put on our coats, hurried out of doors, and, when we had money,
dived into the nearest *bistro.* It was strange, coming up into the
street from those firelit cellars. The air seemed blindingly clear and
cold, like arctic summer; and how sweet the petrol did smell, after
the stenches of sweat and food! Sometimes we met some of our cooks
and waiters in the *bistros,* and they were friendly and stood us
drinks. Indoors we were their slaves, but it is an etiquette in hotel
life that between hours everyone is equal, and the *engueulades* do
not count.

At a quarter to five we went back to the hotel. Till half-past six
there were no orders, and we used this time to polish silver, clean
out the coffee-urns, and do other odd jobs. Then the grand turmoil
of the day started—the dinner hour. I wish I could be Zola for a
little while, just to describe that dinner hour. The essence of the
situation was that a hundred or two hundred people were demanding individually different meals of five or six courses, and that fifty
or sixty people had to cook and serve them and clean up the mess
afterward; anyone with experience of catering will know what that
means. And at this time when the work was doubled, the whole staff
was tired out, and a number of them were drunk. I could write
pages about the scene without giving a true idea of it. The chargings

to and fro in the narrow passages, the collisions, the yells, the struggling with crates and trays and blocks of ice, the heat, the darkness,
the furious festering quarrels which there was no time to fight out—
they pass description. Anyone coming into the basement for the
first time would have thought himself in a den of maniacs. It was
only later, when I understood the working of a hotel, that I saw
order in all this chaos.

At half-past eight the work stopped very suddenly. We were not
free till nine, but we used to throw ourselves full length on the floor,
and lie there resting our legs, too lazy even to go to the ice cupboard
for a drink. Sometimes the *chef du personnel* would come in with
bottles of beer, for the hotel stood us an extra beer when we had
had a hard day. The food we were given was no more than eatable,
but the *patron* was not mean about drink; he allowed us two liters
of wine a day each, knowing that if a *plongeur* is not given two
liters he will steal three. We had the heeltaps of bottles as well, so
that we often drank too much—a good thing, for one seemed to work
faster when partially drunk.

Four days of the week passed like this; of the other two working
days, one was better and one worse. After a week of this life I felt
in need of a holiday. It was Saturday night, so the people in our
bistro were busy getting drunk, and with a free day ahead of me I
was ready to join them. We all went to bed, drunk, at two in the
morning, meaning to sleep till noon. At half-past five I was suddenly
awakened. A night watchman, sent from the hotel, was standing at
my bedside. He stripped the clothes back and shook me roughly.

"Get up!" he said. "*Tu t'es bien saoulé la gueule, eh?* Well, never
mind that, the hotel's a man short. You've got to work today."

"Why should I work?" I protested. "This is my day off."

"Day off, nothing! The work's got to be done. Get up!"

I got up and went out, feeling as though my back were broken
and my skull filled with hot cinders. I did not think that I could
possibly do a day's work. And yet, after only an hour in the basement, I found that I was perfectly well. It seemed that in the heat
of those cellars, as in a Turkish bath, one could sweat out almost
any quantity of drink. *Plongeurs* know this, and count on it. The
power of swallowing quarts of wine, and then sweating it out before
it can do much damage, is one of the compensations of their life.

XII

By far my best time at the hotel was when I went to help the waiter
on the fourth floor. We worked in a small pantry which communi-
cated with the cafeterie by service lifts. It was delightfully cool after

the cellars, and the work was chiefly polishing silver and glasses, which is a humane job. Valenti, the waiter, was a decent sort, and treated me almost as an equal when we were alone, though he had to speak roughly when there was anyone else present, for it does not do for a waiter to be friendly with *plongeurs.* He used sometimes to tip me five francs when he had had a good day. He was a comely youth, aged twenty-four but looking eighteen, and, like most waiters, he carried himself well and knew how to wear his clothes. With his black tail coat and white tie, fresh face and sleek brown hair, he looked just like an Eton boy; yet he had earned his living since he was twelve, and worked his way up literally from the gutter. Crossing the Italian frontier without a passport, and selling chestnuts from a barrow on the northern boulevards, and being given fifty days' imprisonment in London for working without a permit, and being made love to by a rich old woman in a hotel, who gave him a diamond ring and afterward accused him of stealing it, were among his experiences. I used to enjoy talking to him, at slack times when we sat smoking down the lift shaft.

My bad day was when I washed up for the dining room. I had not to wash the plates, which were done in the kitchen, but only the other crockery, silver, knives and glasses; yet, even so, it meant thirteen hours' work, and I used between thirty and forty dishcloths during the day. The antiquated methods used in France double the work of washing up. Plate racks are unheard of, and there are no soap flakes, only the treacly soft soap, which refuses to lather in the hard, Paris water. I worked in a dirty, crowded little den, a pantry and scullery combined, which gave straight on the dining room. Besides washing up, I had to fetch the waiters' food and serve them at table; most of them were intolerably insolent, and I had to use my fists more than once to get common civility. The person who normally washed up was a woman, and they made her life a misery.

It was amusing to look round the filthy little scullery and think that only a double door was between us and the dining room. There sat the customers in all their splendor—spotless table-cloths, bowls of flowers, mirrors and gilt cornices and painted cherubim; and here, just a few feet away, we in our disgusting filth. For it really was disgusting filth. There was no time to sweep the floor till evening, and we slithered about in a compound of soapy water, lettuce-leaves, torn paper, and trampled food. A dozen waiters with their coats off, showing their sweaty armpits, sat at the table mixing salads and sticking their thumbs into the cream pots. The room had a dirty, mixed smell of food and sweat. Everywhere in the cupboards, behind the piles of crockery, were squalid stores of food that the waiters had stolen. There were only two sinks, and no washing basin, and it was nothing unusual for a waiter to wash his face in the water in which clean crockery was rinsing. But the customers saw nothing of this. There were a coconut mat and a mirror outside the dining-room door, and the waiters used to preen themselves up and go in looking the picture of cleanliness.

It is an instructive sight to see a waiter going into a hotel dining room. As he passes the door a sudden change comes over him. The set of his shoulders alters; all the dirt and hurry and irritation have dropped off in an instant. He glides over the carpet, with a solemn priest-like air. I remember our assistant *maître d'hôtel,* a fiery Italian, pausing at the dining-room door to address an apprentice who had broken a bottle of wine. Shaking his fist above his head he yelled (luckily the door was more or less soundproof):

"Tu me fais —— Do you call yourself a waiter, you young bastard? You a waiter! You're not fit to scrub floors in the brothel your mother came from. *Maquereau!"*

Words failing him, he turned to the door; and as he opened it he delivered a final insult in the same manner as Squire Western in *Tom Jones.*

Then he entered the dining room and sailed across it dish in hand, graceful as a swan. Ten seconds later he was bowing reverently to a customer. And you could not help thinking, as you saw him bow and smile, with that benign smile of the trained waiter, that the customer was put to shame by having such an aristocrat to serve him.

This washing up was a thoroughly odious job—not hard, but boring and silly beyond words. It is dreadful to think that some people spend their whole decades at such occupations. The woman whom I replaced was quite sixty years old, and she stood at the sink thirteen hours a day, six days a week, the year round; she was, in addition, horribly bullied by the waiters. She gave out that she had once been an actress—actually, I imagine, a prostitute; most prostitutes end as charwomen. It was strange to see that in spite of her age and her life she still wore a bright blonde wig, and darkened her eyes and painted her face like a girl of twenty. So apparently even a seventy-eight-hour week can leave one with some vitality.

XVII

With thirty francs a week to spend on drinks I could take part in the social life of the quarter. We had some jolly evenings, on Saturdays, in the little *bistro* at the foot of the Hôtel des Trois Moineaux.

The brick-floored room, fifteen feet square, was packed with twenty people, and the air dim with smoke. The noise was deafening, for everyone was either talking at the top of his voice or singing. Sometimes it was just a confused din of voices; sometimes everyone would burst out together in the same song—the "Marseillaise," or the "Internationale," or "Madelon," or "Les Fraises et les Framboises." Azaya, a great clumping peasant girl who worked fourteen hours a day in a glass factory, sang a song about *"Il a perdu ses pantalons, tout en dansant le Charleston."* Her friend Marinette, a thin, dark Corsican girl of obstinate virtue, tied her knees together and danced the *danse du ventre*. The old Rougiers wandered in and out, cadging drinks and trying to tell a long, involved story about someone who had once cheated them over a bedstead. R., cadaverous and silent, sat in his corner quietly boozing. Charlie, drunk, half danced, half staggered to and fro with a glass of sham absinthe balanced in one fat hand, pinching the women's breasts and declaiming poetry. People played darts and diced for drinks. Manuel, a Spaniard, dragged the girls to the bar and shook the dice-box against their bellies, for luck. Madame F. stood at the bar rapidly pouring *chopines* of wine through the pewter funnel, with a wet dishcloth always handy, because every man in the room tried to make love to her. Two children, bastards of big Louis the bricklayer, sat in a corner sharing a glass of *sirop*. Everyone was very happy, overwhelmingly certain that the world was a good place and we a notable set of people.

For an hour the noise scarcely slackened. Then about midnight there was a piercing shout of *"Citoyens!"* and the sound of a chair falling over. A blond, red-faced workman had risen to his feet and was banging a bottle on the table. Everyone stopped singing; the word went round, "Sh! Furex is starting!" Furex was a strange creature, a Limousin stonemason who worked steadily all the week and drank himself into a kind of paroxysm on Saturdays. He had lost his memory and could not remember anything before the war, and he would have gone to pieces through drink if Madame F. had not taken care of him. On Saturday evenings at about five o'clock she would say to someone, "Catch Furex before he spends his wages," and when he had been caught she would take away his money, leaving him enough for one good drink. One week he escaped, and, rolling blind drunk in the Place Monge, was run over by a car and badly hurt.

The queer thing about Furex was that, though he was a Communist when sober, he turned violently patriotic when drunk. He started the evening with good Communist principles, but after four or five liters he was a rampant chauvinist, denouncing spies, challenging all foreigners to fight, and, if he was not prevented, throwing bottles. It was at this stage that he made his speech—for he made a patriotic speech every Saturday night. The speech was always the same, word for word. It ran:

"Citizens of the Republic, are there any Frenchmen here? If there are any Frenchmen here, I rise to remind them—to remind them in effect, of the glorious days of the war. When one looks back upon that time of comradeship and heroism—one looks back, in effect, upon that time of comradeship and heroism. When one remembers the heroes who are dead—one remembers, in effect, the heroes who are dead. Citizens of the Republic, I was wounded at Verdun——"

Here he partially undressed and showed the wound he had received at Verdun. There were shouts of applause. We thought nothing in the world could be funnier than this speech of Furex's. He was a well-known spectacle in the quarter; people used to come in from other *bistros* to watch him when his fit started.

The word was passed round to bait Furex. With a wink to the others someone called for silence, and asked him to sing the "Marseillaise." He sang it well, in a fine bass voice, with patriotic gurgling noises deep down in his chest when he came to *"Aux arrmes, citoyens! Forrmez vos bataillons!"* Veritable tears rolled down his cheeks; he was too drunk to see that everyone was laughing at him. Then, before he had finished, two strong workmen seized him by either arm and held him down, while Azaya shouted, *"Vive l'Allemagne!"* just out of his reach. Furex's face went purple at such infamy. Everyone in the *bistro* began shouting together, *"Vive l'Allemagne! A bas la France!"* while Furex struggled to get at them. But suddenly he spoiled the fun. His face turned pale and doleful, his limbs went limp, and before anyone could stop him he was sick on the table. Then Madame F. hoisted him like a sack and carried him up to bed. In the morning he reappeared quiet and civil, and bought a copy of *L'Humanité*.

The table was wiped with a cloth, Madame F. brought more liter bottles and loaves of bread, and we settled down to serious drinking. There were more songs. An itinerant singer came in with his banjo and performed for five-sou pieces. An Arab and a girl from the *bistro* down the street did a dance, the man wielding a painted wooden phallus the size of a rolling-pin. There were gaps in the noise now. People had begun to talk about their love affairs, and the war, and the barbel-fishing in the Seine, and the best way to *faire la révolution,* and to tell stories. Charlie, grown sober again, captured the conversation and talked about his soul for five minutes.

The doors and windows were opened to cool the room. The street was emptying, and in the distance one could hear the lonely milk train thundering down the Boulevard St. Michel. The air blew cold on our foreheads, and the coarse African wine still tasted good: we were still happy, but meditatively, with the shouting and hilarious mood finished.

By one o'clock we were not happy any longer. We felt the joy of the evening wearing thin, and called hastily for more bottles, but Madame F. was watering the wine now, and it did not taste the same. Men grew quarrelsome. The girls were violently kissed and hands thrust into their bosoms and they made off lest worse should happen. Big Louis, the bricklayer, was drunk, and crawled about the floor barking and pretending to be a dog. The others grew tired of him and kicked at him as he went past. People seized each other by the arm and began long rambling confessions, and were angry when these were not listened to. The crowd thinned. Manuel and another man, both gamblers, went across to the Arab *bistro,* where card-playing went on till daylight. Charlie suddenly borrowed thirty francs from Madame F. and disappeared, probably to a brothel. Men began to empty their glasses, call briefly, " *'Sieurs, dames!*" and go off to bed.

By half-past one the last drop of pleasure had evaporated, leaving nothing but headaches. We perceived that we were not splendid inhabitants of a splendid world, but a crew of underpaid workmen grown squalidly and dismally drunk. We went on swallowing the wine, but it was only from habit, and the stuff seemed suddenly nauseating. One's head had swollen up like a balloon, the floor rocked, one's tongue and lips were stained purple. At last it was no use keeping it up any longer. Several men went out into the yard behind the *bistro* and were sick. We crawled up to bed, tumbled down half dressed, and stayed there ten hours.

Most of my Saturday nights went in this way. On the whole, the two hours when one was perfectly and wildly happy seemed worth the subsequent headache. For many men in the quarter, unmarried and with no future to think of, the weekly drinking bout was the one thing that made life worth living.

XIX

One day, when we had been at the Hôtel X. five or six weeks, Boris disappeared without notice. In the evening I found him waiting for me in the Rue de Rivoli. He slapped me gaily on the shoulder.

"Free at last, *mon ami!* You can give notice in the morning. The Auberge opens tomorrow."

"Tomorrow?"

"Well, possibly we shall need a day or two to arrange things. But at any rate, no more cafeterie! *Nous sommes lancés, mon ami!* My tail coat is out of pawn already."

His manner was so hearty that I felt sure there was something wrong, and I did not at all want to leave my safe and comfortable job at the hotel. However, I had promised Boris, so I gave notice, and the next morning at seven went down to the Auberge de Jehan Cottard. It was locked, and I went in search of Boris, who had once more bolted from his lodgings and taken a room in the Rue de la Croix Nivert. I found him asleep, together with a girl whom he had picked up the night before, and who he told me was "of a very sympathetic temperament." As to the restaurant, he said that it was all arranged; there were only a few little things to be seen to before we opened.

At ten I managed to get Boris out of bed, and we unlocked the restaurant. At a glance I saw what the "few little things" amounted to. It was briefly this: that the alterations had not been touched since our last visit. The stoves for the kitchen had not arrived, the water and electricity had not been laid on, and there was all manner of painting, polishing, and carpentering to be done. Nothing short of a miracle could open the restaurant within ten days, and by the look of things it might collapse without even opening. It was obvious what had happened. The *patron* was short of money, and he had engaged the staff (there were four of us) in order to use us instead of workmen. He would be getting our services almost free, for waiters are paid no wages, and though he would have to pay me, he would not be feeding me till the restaurant opened. In effect, he had swindled us of several hundred francs by sending for us before the restaurant was open. We had thrown up a good job for nothing.

Boris, however, was full of hope. He had only one idea in his head, namely, that here at last was a chance of being a waiter and wearing a tail coat once more. For this he was quite willing to do ten days' work unpaid, with the chance of being left jobless in the end. "Patience!" he kept saying. "That will arrange itself. Wait till the restaurant opens, and we'll get it all back. Patience, *mon ami!*"

We needed patience, for days passed and the restaurant did not even progress towards opening. We cleaned out the cellars, fixed the shelves, distempered the walls, polished the woodwork, whitewashed the ceiling, stained the floor; but the main work, the plumbing and gas-fitting and electricity, was still not done, because the *patron* could not pay the bills. Evidently he was almost penniless, for he refused the smallest charges, and he had a trick of swiftly disappearing when asked for money. His blend of shiftiness and aristocratic manners made him very hard to deal with. Melancholy duns came looking for him at all hours, and by instruction we always told them that he was at Fontainebleau, or Saint Cloud, or some other place that was safely distant. Meanwhile, I was getting hungrier and hungrier. I had left the hotel with thirty francs, and I had to go back immediately to a diet of dry bread. Boris had managed in the beginning to extract an advance of sixty francs from the *patron,* but he had spent half of it, in redeeming his waiter's clothes, and half on the girl of sympathetic temperament. He borrowed three francs a day from Jules, the second waiter, and spent it on bread. Some days we had not even money for tobacco.

Sometimes the cook came to see how things were getting on, and when she saw that the kitchen was still bare of pots and pans she usually wept. Jules, the second waiter, refused steadily to help with the work. He was a Magyar, a little dark, sharp-featured fellow in spectacles, and very talkative; he had been a medical student, but had abandoned his training for lack of money. He had a taste for talking while other people were working, and he told me all about himself and his ideas. It appeared that he was a Communist, and had various strange theories (he could prove to you by figures that it was wrong to work), and he was also, like most Magyars, passionately proud. Proud and lazy men do not make good waiters. It was Jules's dearest boast that once when a customer in a restaurant had insulted him, he had poured a plate of hot soup down the customer's neck, and then walked straight out without even waiting to be sacked.

As each day went by Jules grew more and more enraged at the trick the *patron* had played on us. He had a spluttering, oratorical way of talking. He used to walk up and down shaking his fist, and trying to incite me not to work:

"Put that brush down, you fool! You and I belong to proud races; we don't work for nothing, like these damned Russian serfs. I tell you, to be cheated like this is torture to me. There have been times in my life, when someone has cheated me even of five sous, when I have vomited—yes, vomited with rage.

"Besides, *mon vieux,* don't forget that I'm a Communist. *A bas la bourgeoisie!* Did any man alive ever see me working when I could avoid it? No. And not only I don't wear myself out working, like you other fools, but I steal, just to show my independence. Once I was in a restaurant where the *patron* thought he could treat me like a dog. Well, in revenge I found out a way to steal milk from the milk cans and seal them up again so that no one should know. I tell you

I just swilled that milk down night and morning. Every day I drank four liters of milk, besides half a liter of cream. The *patron* was at his wits' end to know where the milk was going. It wasn't that I wanted milk, you understand, because I hate the stuff; it was principle, just principle.

"Well, after three days I began to get dreadful pains in my belly, and I went to the doctor. 'What have you been eating?' he said. I said: 'I drink four liters of milk a day, and half a liter of cream.' 'Four liters!' he said. 'Then stop it at once. You'll burst if you go on.' 'What do I care?' I said. 'With me principle is everything. I shall go on drinking that milk, even if I do burst.'

"Well, the next day the *patron* caught me stealing milk. 'You're sacked,' he said; 'you leave at the end of the week.' '*Pardon, monsieur,*' I said, 'I shall leave this morning.' 'No, you won't,' he said, 'I can't spare you till Saturday.' 'Very well, *mon patron,*' I thought to myself, 'we'll see who gets tired of it first.' And then I set to work to smash the crockery. I broke nine plates the first day and thirteen the second; after that the *patron* was glad to see the last of me.

"Ah, I'm not one of your Russian *moujiks* . . ."

Ten days passed. It was a bad time. I was absolutely at the end of my money, and my rent was several days overdue. We loafed about the dismal empty restaurant, too hungry even to get on with the work that remained. Only Boris now believed that the restaurant would open. He had set his heart on being *maître d'hôtel,* and he invented a theory that the *patron's* money was tied up in shares and he was waiting a favorable moment for selling. On the tenth day I had nothing to eat or smoke, and I told the *patron* that I could not continue working without an advance on my wages. As blandly as usual, the *patron* promised the advance, and then, according to his custom, vanished. I walked part of the way home, but I did not feel equal to a scene with Madame F. over the rent, so I passed the night on a bench on the boulevard. It was very uncomfortable—the arm of the seat cuts into your back—and much colder than I had expected. There was plenty of time, in the long boring hours between dawn and work, to think what a fool I had been to deliver myself into the hands of these Russians.

Then, in the morning, the luck changed. Evidently the *patron* had come to an understanding with his creditors, for he arrived with money in his pockets, set the alterations going, and gave me my advance. Boris and I bought macaroni and a piece of horse's liver, and had our first hot meal in ten days.

The workmen were brought in and the alterations made, hastily and with incredible shoddiness. The tables, for instance, were to be covered with baize, but when the *patron* found that baize was expensive he bought instead disused army blankets, smelling incorrigibly of sweat. The table-cloths (they were check, to go with the "Norman" decorations) would cover them, of course. On the last night we were at work till two in the morning, getting things ready. The crockery did not arrive till eight, and, being new, had all to be washed. The cutlery did not arrive till the next morning, nor the linen either, so that we had to dry the crockery with a shirt of the *patron's* and an old pillowslip belonging to the concierge. Boris and I did all the work. Jules was skulking, and the *patron* and his wife sat in the bar with a dun and some Russian friends, drinking success to the restaurant. The cook was in the kitchen with her head on the table, crying, because she was expected to cook for fifty people, and there were not pots and pans enough for ten. About midnight there was a fearful interview with some duns, who came intending to seize eight copper saucepans which the *patron* had obtained on credit. They were bought off with half a bottle of brandy.

Jules and I missed the last Metro home and had to sleep on the floor of the restaurant. The first thing we saw in the morning were two large rats sitting on the kitchen table, eating from a ham that stood there. It seemed a bad omen, and I was surer than ever that the Auberge de Jehan Cottard would turn out a failure.

XX

The *patron* had engaged me as kitchen *plongeur;* that is, my job was to wash up, keep the kitchen clean, prepare vegetables, make tea, coffee, and sandwiches, do the simpler cooking, and run errands. The terms were, as usual, five hundred francs a month and food, but I had no free day and no fixed working hours. At the Hôtel X. I had seen catering at its best, with unlimited money and good organization. Now, at the Auberge, I learned how things are done in a thoroughly bad restaurant. It is worth describing, for there are hundreds of similar restaurants in Paris, and every visitor feeds in one of them occasionally.

I should add, by the way, that the Auberge was not the ordinary cheap eating house frequented by students and workmen. We did not provide an adequate meal at less than twenty-five francs, and we were picturesque and artistic, which sent up our social standing. There were the indecent pictures in the bar, and the Norman decorations—sham beams on the walls, electric lights done up as candlesticks, "peasant" pottery, even a mounting-block at the door—and the *patron* and the head waiter were Russian officers, and many of the customers titled Russian refugees. In short, we were decidedly chic.

Nevertheless, the conditions behind the kitchen door were suitable for a pigsty. For this is what our service arrangements were like.

The kitchen measured fifteen feet long by eight broad, and half this space was taken up by the stoves and tables. All the pots had to be kept on shelves out of reach, and there was only room for one dustbin. This dustbin used to be crammed full by midday, and the floor was normally an inch deep in a compost of trampled food.

For firing we had nothing but three gas stoves, without ovens, and all joints had to be sent out to the bakery.

There was no larder. Our substitute for one was a half-roofed shed in the yard, with a tree growing in the middle of it. The meat, vegetables, and so forth lay there on the bare earth, raided by rats and cats.

There was no hot water laid on. Water for washing up had to be heated in pans, and, as there was no room for these on the stoves when meals were cooking, most of the plates had to be washed in cold water. This, with soft soap and the hard Paris water, meant scraping the grease off with bits of newspaper.

We were so short of saucepans that I had to wash each one as soon as it was done with, instead of leaving them till the evening. This alone wasted probably an hour a day.

Owing to some scamping of expense in the installation, the electric light usually fused at eight in the evening. The *patron* would only allow us three candles in the kitchen, and the cook said three were unlucky, so we had only two.

Our coffee-grinder was borrowed from a *bistro* near by, and our dustbin and brooms from the concierge. After the first week a quantity of linen did not come back from the wash, as the bill was not paid. We were in trouble with the inspector of labor, who had discovered that the staff included no Frenchmen; he had several private interviews with the *patron*, who, I believe, was obliged to bribe him. The electric company was still dunning us, and when the duns found that we would buy them off with *apéritifs*, they came every morning. We were in debt at the grocery, and credit would have been stopped, only the grocer's wife (a moustachio'd woman of sixty) had taken a fancy to Jules, who was sent every morning to cajole her. Similarly I had to waste an hour every day haggling over vegetables in the Rue du Commerce, to save a few centimes.

These are the results of starting a restaurant on insufficient capital. And in these conditions the cook and I were expected to serve thirty or forty meals a day, and would later on be serving a hundred. From the first day it was too much for us. The cook's working hours were from eight in the morning till midnight, and mine from seven in the morning till half-past twelve the next morning—seventeen and a half hours, almost without a break. We never had time to sit down till five in the afternoon, and even then there was no seat except the top of the dustbin. Boris, who lived near by and had not to catch the last Metro home, worked from eight in the morning till two the next morning—eighteen hours a day, seven days a week. Such hours, though not usual, are nothing extraordinary in Paris.

Life settled at once into a routine that made the Hôtel X. seem like a holiday. Every morning at six I drove myself out of bed, did not shave, sometimes washed, hurried up to the Place d'Italie and fought for a place on the Metro. By seven I was in the desolation of the cold, filthy kitchen, with the potato skins and bones and fish-tails littered on the floor, and a pile of plates, stuck together in their grease, waiting from overnight. I could not start on the plates yet, because the water was cold, and I had to fetch milk and make coffee, for the others arrived at eight and expected to find coffee ready. Also, there were always several copper saucepans to clean. Those copper saucepans are the bane of a *plongeur's* life. They have to be scoured with sand and bunches of chain, ten minutes to each one, and then polished on the outside with Brasso. Fortunately, the art of making them has been lost and they are gradually vanishing from French kitchens, though one can still buy them second-hand.

When I had begun on the plates the cook would take me away from the plates to begin skinning onions, and when I had begun on the onions the *patron* would arrive and send me out to buy cabbages. When I came back with the cabbages the *patron's* wife would tell me to go to some shop half a mile away and buy a pot of rouge; by the time I came back there would be more vegetables waiting, and the plates were still not done. In this way our incompetence piled one job on another throughout the day, everything in arrears.

Till ten, things went comparatively easily, though we were working fast, and no one lost his temper. The cook would find time to talk about her artistic nature, and say did I not think Tolstoi was *épatant,* and sing in a fine soprano voice as she minced beef on the board. But at ten the waiters began clamoring for their lunch, which they had early, and at eleven the first customers would be arriving. Suddenly everything became hurry and bad temper. There was not the same furious rushing and yelling as at the Hôtel X., but an atmosphere of muddle, petty spite, and exasperation. Discomfort was at the bottom of it. It was unbearably cramped in the kitchen, and dishes had to be put on the floor, and one had to be thinking constantly about not stepping on them. The cook's vast buttocks banged against me as she moved to and fro. A ceaseless, nagging chorus of orders streamed from her:

"Unspeakable idiot! How many times have I told you not to bleed the beetroots? Quick, let me get to the sink! Put those knives away; get on with the potatoes. What have you done with my strainer? Oh, leave those potatoes alone. Didn't I tell you to skim the *bouillon?* Take that can of water off the stove. Never mind the washing up, chop this celery. No, not like that, you fool, like this. There! Look at you letting those peas boil over! Now get to work and scale these herrings. Look, do you call this plate clean? Wipe it on your apron. Put that salad on the floor. That's right, put it where I'm bound to step in it! Look out, that pot's boiling over! Get me down that sauce-pan. No, the other one. Put this on the grill. Throw those potatoes away. Don't waste time, throw them on the floor. Tread them in. Now throw down some sawdust; this floor's like a skating-rink. Look, you fool, that steak's burning! *Mon Dieu,* why did they send me an idiot for a *plongeur?* Who are you talking to? Do you realize that my aunt was a Russian countess?" etc. etc. etc.

This went on till three o'clock without much variation, except that about eleven the cook usually had a *crise de nerfs* and a flood of tears. From three to five was a fairly slack time for the waiters, but the cook was still busy, and I was working my fastest, for there was a pile of dirty plates waiting, and it was a race to get them done, or partly done, before dinner began. The washing up was doubled by the primitive conditions—a cramped draining board, tepid water, sodden cloths, and a sink that got blocked once in an hour. By five the cook and I were feeling unsteady on our feet, not having eaten or sat down since seven. We used to collapse, she on the dustbin and I on the floor, drink a bottle of beer, and apologize for some of the things we had said in the morning. Tea was what kept us going. We took care to have a pot always stewing, and drank pints during the day.

At half-past five the hurry and quarreling began again, and now worse than before, because everyone was tired out. The cook had a *crise de nerfs* at six and another at nine; they came on so regularly that one could have told the time by them. She would flop down on the dustbin, begin weeping hysterically, and cry out that never, no, never had she thought to come to such a life as this; her nerves would not stand it; she had studied music at Vienna; she had a bed-ridden husband to support, etc. etc. At another time one would have been sorry for her, but, tired as we all were, her whimpering voice merely infuriated us. Jules used to stand in the doorway and mimic her weeping. The *patron's* wife nagged, and Boris and Jules quarreled all day, because Jules shirked his work, and Boris, as head waiter, claimed the larger share of the tips. Only the second day after the restaurant opened, they came to blows in the kitchen over a two-franc tip, and the cook and I had to separate them. The only person who never forgot his manners was the *patron*. He kept the same hours as the rest of us, but he had no work to do, for it was his wife who really managed things. His sole job, besides ordering the supplies, was to stand in the bar smoking cigarettes and looking gentlemanly, and he did that to perfection.

The cook and I generally found time to eat our dinner between ten and eleven o'clock. At midnight the cook would steal a packet of food for her husband, stow it under her clothes, and make off, whimpering that these hours would kill her and she would give notice in the morning. Jules also left at midnight, usually after a dispute with Boris, who had to look after the bar till two. Between twelve and half-past I did what I could to finish the washing up. There was no time to attempt doing the work properly, and I used simply to rub the grease off the plates with table-napkins. As for the dirt on the floor, I let it lie, or swept the worst of it out of sight under the stoves.

At half-past twelve I would put on my coat and hurry out. The *patron*, bland as ever, would stop me as I went down the alley-way past the bar. "*Mais, mon cher monsieur,* how tired you look! Please do me the favor of accepting this glass of brandy."

He would hand me the glass of brandy as courteously as though I had been a Russian duke instead of a *plongeur*. He treated all of us like this. It was our compensation for working seventeen hours a day.

As a rule the last Metro was almost empty—a great advantage, for one could sit down and sleep for a quarter of an hour. Generally I was in bed by half-past one. Sometimes I missed the train and had to sleep on the floor of the restaurant, but it hardly mattered, for I could have slept on cobblestones at that time.

1933

△

How the Poor Die

▽

In the year 1929 I spent several weeks in the Hôpital X, in the fifteenth arrondissement of Paris. The clerks put me through the usual third degree at the reception desk, and indeed I was kept answering questions for some twenty minutes before they would let me in. If you have ever had to fill up forms in a Latin country you will know the kind of questions I mean. For some days past I had been unequal to translating Reaumur into Fahrenheit, but I know that my temperature was round about 103, and by the end of the interview I had some difficulty in standing on my feet. At my back a resigned little knot of patients, carrying bundles done up in colored handkerchiefs, waited their turn to be questioned.

After the questioning came the bath—a compulsory routine for all newcomers, apparently, just as in prison or the workhouse. My clothes were taken away from me, and after I had sat shivering for some minutes in five inches of warm water I was given a linen nightshirt and a short blue flannel dressing gown—no slippers, they had none big enough for me, they said—and led out into the open air. This was a night in February and I was suffering from pneumonia. The ward we were going to was two hundred yards away and it seemed that to get to it you had to cross the hospital grounds. Someone stumbled in front of me with a lantern. The gravel path was frosty underfoot, and the wind whipped the nightshirt round my bare calves. When we got into the ward I was aware of a strange feeling of familiarity whose origin I did not succeed in pinning down till later in the night. It was a long, rather low, ill-lit room, full of murmuring voices and with three rows of beds surprisingly close together. There was a foul smell, fecal and yet sweetish. As I lay down I saw on a bed nearly opposite me a small, round-shouldered, sandy-haired man sitting half naked while a doctor and a student performed some strange operation on him. First the doctor produced from his black bag a dozen small glasses like wine glasses, then the student burned a match inside each glass to exhaust the air, then the glass was popped on to the man's back or chest and the vacuum drew up a huge yellow blister. Only after some moments did I realize what they were doing to him. It was something called cupping, a treatment which you can read about in old medical textbooks but which till then I had vaguely thought of as one of those things they do to horses.

The cold air outside had probably lowered my temperature, and I watched this barbarous remedy with detachment and even a certain amount of amusement. The next moment, however, the doctor and the student came across to my bed, hoisted me upright, and without a word began applying the same set of glasses, which had not been sterilized in any way. A few feeble protests that I uttered got no more response than if I had been an animal. I was very much impressed by the impersonal way in which the two men started on me. I had never been in the public ward of a hospital before, and it was my first experience of doctors who handle you without speaking to you or, in a human sense, taking any notice of you. They only put on six glasses in my case, but after doing so they scarified the blisters and applied the glasses again. Each glass now drew out about a dessert-spoonful of dark-colored blood. As I lay down again, humiliated, disgusted, and frightened by the thing that had been done to me, I reflected that now at least they would leave me alone. But no, not a bit of it. There was another treatment coming, the mustard poultice, seemingly a matter of routine like the hot bath. Two slatternly nurses had already got the poultice ready, and they lashed it round my chest as tight as a straitjacket while some men who were wandering about the ward in shirt and trousers began to collect round my bed with half-sympathetic grins. I learned later that watching a patient have a mustard poultice was a favorite pastime in the ward. These things are normally applied for a quarter of an hour and certainly they are funny enough if you don't happen to be the person inside. For the first five minutes the pain is severe, but you believe you can bear it. During the second five minutes this belief evaporates, but the poultice is buckled at the back and you can't get it off. This is the period the onlookers enjoy most. During the last five minutes, I noted, a sort of numbness supervenes. After the poultice had been removed a waterproof pillow packed with ice was thrust beneath my head and I was left alone. I did not sleep, and to the best of my knowledge this was the only night of my life— I mean the only night spent in bed—in which I have not slept at all, not even a minute.

During my first hour in the Hôpital X I had had a whole series of different and contradictory treatments, but this was misleading,

for in general you got very little treatment at all, either good or
bad, unless you were ill in some interesting and instructive way.
At five in the morning the nurses came round, woke the patients,
and took their temperatures, but did not wash them. If you were
well enough you washed yourself, otherwise you depended on the
kindness of some walking patient. It was generally patients, too,
who carried the bedbottles and the grim bedpan, nicknamed *la
casserole*. At eight breakfast arrived, called army-fashion *la soupe*.
It was soup, too, a thin vegetable soup with slimy hunks of bread
floating about in it. Later in the day the tall, solemn, black-bearded
doctor made his rounds, with an interne and a troop of students
following at his heels, but there were about sixty of us in the ward
and it was evident that he had other wards to attend to as well.
There were many beds past which he walked day after day, sometimes followed by imploring cries. On the other hand if you had
some disease with which the students wanted to familiarize themselves you got plenty of attention of a kind. I myself, with an exceptionally fine specimen of a bronchial rattle, sometimes had as
many as a dozen students queuing up to listen to my chest. It was
a very queer feeling—queer, I mean, because of their intense interest in learning their job, together with a seeming lack of any
perception that the patients were human beings. It is strange to
relate, but sometimes as some young student stepped forward to
take his turn at manipulating you, he would be actually tremulous
with excitement, like a boy who has at last got his hands on some
expensive piece of machinery. And then ear after ear—ears of young
men, of girls, of Negroes—pressed against your back, relays of fingers solemnly but clumsily tapping, and not from any one of them
did you get a word of conversation or a look direct in your face.
As a non-paying patient, in the uniform nightshirt, you were primarily *a specimen*, a thing I did not resent but could never quite
get used to.

After some days I grew well enough to sit up and study the surrounding patients. The stuffy room, with its narrow beds so close
together that you could easily touch your neighbor's hand, had
every sort of disease in it except, I suppose, acutely infectious cases.
My right-hand neighbor was a little red-haired cobbler with one
leg shorter than the other, who used to announce the death of any
other patient (this happened a number of times, and my neighbor
was always the first to hear of it) by whistling to me, exclaiming
"Numero 43!" (or whatever it was) and flinging his arms above his
head. This man had not much wrong with him, but in most of the
other beds within my angle of vision some squalid tragedy or some

plain horror was being enacted. In the bed that was foot to foot with mine there lay, until he died (I didn't see him die—they moved him to another bed), a little weazened man who was suffering from I do not know what disease, but something that made his whole body so intensely sensitive that any movement from side to side, sometimes even the weight of the bedclothes, would make him shout out with pain. His worst suffering was when he urinated, which he did with the greatest difficulty. A nurse would bring him the bedbottle and then for a long time stand beside his bed, whistling, as grooms are said to do with horses, until at last with an agonized shriek of *"Je pisse!"* he would get started. In the bed next to him the sandy-haired man whom I had seen being cupped used to cough up blood-streaked mucus at all hours. My left-hand neighbor was a tall, flaccid-looking young man who used periodically to have a tube inserted into his back and astonishing quantities of frothy liquid drawn off from some part of his body. In the bed beyond that a veteran of the war of 1870 was dying, a handsome old man with a white imperial, round whose bed, at all hours when visiting was allowed, four elderly female relatives dressed all in black sat exactly like crows, obviously scheming for some pitiful legacy. In the bed opposite me in the further row was an old bald-headed man with drooping moustaches and greatly swollen face and body, who was suffering from some disease that made him urinate almost incessantly. A huge glass receptacle stood always beside his bed. One day his wife and daughter came to visit him. At sight of them the old man's bloated face lit up with a smile of surprising sweetness, and as his daughter, a pretty girl of about twenty, approached the bed I saw that his hand was slowly working its way from under the bedclothes. I seemed to see in advance the gesture that was coming—the girl kneeling beside the bed, the old man's hand laid on her head in his dying blessing. But no, he merely handed her the bedbottle, which she promptly took from him and emptied into the receptacle.

About a dozen beds away from me was Numero 57—I think that was his number—a cirrhosis of the liver case. Everyone in the ward knew him by sight because he was sometimes the subject of a medical lecture. On two afternoons a week the tall, grave doctor would lecture in the ward to a party of students, and on more than one occasion old Numero 57 was wheeled in on a sort of trolley into the middle of the ward, where the doctor would roll back his nightshirt, dilate with his fingers a huge flabby protuberance on the man's belly—the diseased liver, I suppose—and explain solemnly that this was a disease attributable to alcoholism, commoner in the wine-drinking countries. As usual he neither spoke to his patient nor gave him a smile, a nod or any kind of recognition. While he talked, very grave and upright, he would hold the wasted body beneath his two hands, sometimes giving it a gentle roll to and fro, in just the attitude of a woman handling a rolling-pin. Not that Numero 57 minded this kind of thing. Obviously he was an old hospital inmate, a regular exhibit at lectures, his liver long since marked down for a bottle in some pathological museum. Utterly uninterested in what was said about him, he would lie with his colorless eyes gazing at nothing, while the doctor showed him off like a piece of antique china. He was a man of about sixty, astonishingly shrunken. His face, pale as vellum, had shrunken away till it seemed no bigger than a doll's.

One morning my cobbler neighbor woke me up plucking at my pillow before the nurses arrived. "Numero 57!"—he flung his arms above his head. There was a light in the ward, enough to see by. I could see old Numero 57 lying crumpled up on his side, his face sticking out over the side of the bed, and toward me. He had died some time during the night, nobody knew when. When the nurses came they received the news of his death indifferently and went about their work. After a long time, an hour or more, two other nurses marched in abreast like soldiers, with a great clumping of sabots, and knotted the corpse up in the sheets, but it was not removed till some time later. Meanwhile, in the better light, I had had time for a good look at Numero 57. Indeed I lay on my side to look at him. Curiously enough he was the first dead European I had seen. I had seen dead men before, but always Asiatics and usually people who had died violent deaths. Numero 57's eyes were still open, his mouth also open, his small face contorted into an expression of agony. What most impressed me, however, was the whiteness of his face. It had been pale before, but now it was little darker than the sheets. As I gazed at the tiny, screwed-up face it struck me that this disgusting piece of refuse, waiting to be carted away and dumped on a slab in the dissecting room, was an example of "natural" death, one of the things you pray for in the Litany. There you are, then, I thought, that's what is waiting for you, twenty, thirty, forty years hence: that is how the lucky ones die, the one who lives to be old. One wants to live, of course, indeed one only stays alive by virtue of the fear of death, but I think now, as I thought then, that it's better to die violently and not too old. People talk about the horrors of war, but what weapon has man invented that even approaches in cruelty some of the commoner diseases? "Natural" death, almost by definition, means something slow, smelly, and painful. Even at that, it makes a difference if you can achieve it in your own home and not in a public institution. This poor old wretch who had just flickered out like a candle end was not even important enough to have anyone watching by his deathbed. He was merely a number, then a "subject" for the students' scalpels. And the sordid publicity of dying in such a place! In the Hôpital X the beds were very close together and there were no screens. Fancy, for instance, dying like the little man whose bed was for a while foot to foot with mine, the one who cried out when the bedclothes touched him! I dare say *"Je pisse!"* were his last recorded words. Perhaps the dying don't bother about such things—that at least would be the standard answer: nevertheless dying people are often more or less normal in their minds till within a day or so of the end.

In the public wards of a hospital you see horrors that you don't seem to meet with among people who manage to die in their own homes, as though certain diseases only attacked people at the lower income levels. But it is a fact that you would not in any English hospitals see some of the things I saw in the Hôpital X. This business of people just dying like animals, for instance, with nobody standing by, nobody interested, the death not even noticed till the morning—this happened more than once. You certainly would not see that in England, and still less would you see a corpse left exposed to the view of the other patients. I remember that once in a cottage hospital in England a man died while we were at tea, and though there were only six of us in the ward the nurses managed things so adroitly that the man was dead and his body removed without our even hearing about it till tea was over. A thing we perhaps underrate in England is the advantage we enjoy in having large numbers of well-trained and rigidly disciplined nurses. No doubt English nurses are dumb enough, they may tell fortunes with tea leaves, wear Union Jack badges, and keep photographs of the Queen on their mantelpieces, but at least they don't let you lie unwashed and constipated on an unmade bed, out of sheer laziness. The nurses at the Hôpital X still had a tinge of Mrs. Gamp about them, and later, in the military hospitals of Republican Spain, I was to see nurses almost too ignorant to take a temperature. You wouldn't, either, see in England such dirt as existed in the Hôpital X. Later on, when I was well enough to wash myself in the bathroom, I found that there was kept there a huge packing case into which the scraps of food and dirty dressings from the ward were flung, and the wainscotings were infested by crickets.

When I had got back my clothes and grown strong on my legs

I fled from the Hôpital X, before my time was up and without
waiting for a medical discharge. It was not the only hospital I
have fled from, but its gloom and bareness, its sickly smell and,
above all, something in its mental atmosphere stand out in my
memory as exceptional. I had been taken there because it was the
hospital belonging to my arrondissement, and I did not learn till
after I was in it that it bore a bad reputation. A year or two later
the celebrated swindler, Madame Hanaud, who was ill while on
remand, was taken to the Hôpital X, and after a few days of it
she managed to elude her guards, took a taxi, and drove back to
the prison, explaining that she was more comfortable there. I have
no doubt that the Hôpital X was quite untypical of French hospitals even at that date. But the patients, nearly all of them working men, were surprisingly resigned. Some of them seemed to find
the conditions almost comfortable, for at least two were destitute
malingerers who found this a good way of getting through the
winter. The nurses connived because the malingerers made themselves useful by doing odd jobs. But the attitude of the majority
was: of course this is a lousy place, but what else do you expect?
It did not seem strange to them that you should be woken at five
and then wait three hours before starting the day on watery soup,
or that people should die with no one at their bedside, or even
that your chance of getting medical attention should depend on
catching the doctor's eye as he went past. According to their tra-
ditions that was what hospitals were like. If you are seriously ill,
and if you are too poor to be treated in your own home, then you
must go into hospital, and once there you must put up with harshness and discomfort, just as you would in the army. But on top of
this I was interested to find a lingering belief in the old stories
that have now almost faded from memory in England—stories, for
instance, about doctors cutting you open out of sheer curiosity or
thinking it funny to start operating before you were properly "under." There were dark tales about a little operating room said to
be situated just beyond the bathroom. Dreadful screams were said
to issue from this room. I saw nothing to confirm these stories and
no doubt they were all nonsense, though I did see two students
kill a sixteen-year-old boy, or nearly kill him (he appeared to be
dying when I left the hospital, but he may have recovered later)
by a mischievous experiment which they probably could not have
tried on a paying patient. Well within living memory it used to
be believed in London that in some of the big hospitals patients
were killed off to get dissection subjects. I didn't hear this tale repeated at the Hôpital X, but I should think some of the men there

would have found it credible. For it was a hospital in which not
the methods, perhaps, but something of the atmosphere of the nineteenth century had managed to survive, and therein lay its peculiar
interest.

During the past fifty years or so there has been a great change
in the relationship between doctor and patient. If you look at almost any literature before the later part of the nineteenth century,
you find that a hospital is popularly regarded as much the same
thing as a prison, and an old-fashioned, dungeon-like prison at that.
A hospital is a place of filth, torture, and death, a sort of ante-
chamber to the tomb. No one who was not more or less destitute
would have thought of going into such a place for treatment. And
especially in the early part of the last century, when medical science had grown bolder than before without being any more successful, the whole business of doctoring was looked on with horror
and dread by ordinary people. Surgery, in particular, was believed
to be no more than a peculiarly gruesome form of sadism, and
dissection, possible only with the aid of body-snatchers, was even
confused with necromancy. From the nineteenth century you could
collect a large horror-literature connected with doctors and hospitals. Think of poor old George III, in his dotage, shrieking for
mercy as he sees his surgeons approaching to "bleed him till he
faints"! Think of the conversations of Bob Sawyer and Benjamin
Allen, which no doubt are hardly parodies, or the field hospitals
in *La Débâcle* and *War and Peace,* or that shocking description of
an amputation in Melville's *Whitejacket!* Even the names given
to doctors in nineteenth-century English fiction, Slasher, Carver,
Sawyer, Fillgrave, and so on, and the generic nickname "sawbones,"
are about as grim as they are comic. The anti-surgery tradition is
perhaps best expressed in Tennyson's poem, *The Children's Hospital,* which is essentially a pre-chloroform document though it
seems to have been written as late as 1880. Moreover, the outlook
which Tennyson records in this poem had a lot to be said for it.
When you consider what an operation without anaesthetics must
have been like, what it notoriously *was* like, it is difficult not to
suspect the motives of people who would undertake such things.
For these bloody horrors which the students so eagerly looked forward to ("A magnificent sight if Slasher does it!") were admittedly
more or less useless: the patient who did not die of shock usually
died of gangrene, a result which was taken for granted. Even now
doctors can be found whose motives are questionable. Anyone who
has had much illness, or who has listened to medical students talking, will know what I mean. But anaesthetics were a turning point,

and disinfectants were another. Nowhere in the world, probably, would you now see the kind of scene described by Axel Munthe in *The Story of San Michele,* when the sinister surgeon in top-hat and frock-coat, his starched shirtfront spattered with blood and pus, carves up patient after patient with the same knife and flings the severed limbs into a pile beside the table. Moreover, national health insurance has partly done away with the idea that a working-class patient is a pauper who deserves little consideration. Well into this century it was usual for "free" patients at the big hospitals to have their teeth extracted with no anaesthetic. They didn't pay, so why should they have an anaesthetic—that was the attitude. That too has changed.

And yet every institution will always bear upon it some lingering memory of its past. A barrack-room is still haunted by the ghost of Kipling, and it is difficult to enter a workhouse without being reminded of *Oliver Twist.* Hospitals began as a kind of casual ward for lepers and the like to die in, and they continued as places where medical students learned their art on the bodies of the poor. You can still catch a faint suggestion of their history in their characteristically gloomy architecture. I would be far from complaining about the treatment I have received in any English hospital, but I do know that it is a sound instinct that warns people to keep out of hospitals if possible, and especially out of the public wards. Whatever the legal position may be, it is unquestionable that you have far less control over your own treatment, far less certainty that frivolous experiments will not be tried on you, when it is a case of "accept the discipline or get out." And it is a great thing to die in your own bed, though it is better still to die in your boots. However great the kindness and the efficiency, in every hospital death there will be some cruel, squalid detail, something perhaps too small to be told but leaving terribly painful memories behind, arising out of the haste, the crowding, the impersonality of a place where every day people are dying among strangers.

The dread of hospitals probably still survives among the very poor, and in all of us it has only recently disappeared. It is a dark patch not far beneath the surface of our minds. I have said earlier that when I entered the ward at the Hôpital X I was conscious of a strange feeling of familiarity. What the scene reminded me of, of course, was the reeking, pain-filled hospitals of the nineteenth century, which I had never seen but of which I had a traditional knowledge. And something, perhaps the black-clad doctor with his frowsy black bag, or perhaps only the sickly smell, played the queer trick of unearthing from my memory that poem of Tennyson's, *The*

Children's Hospital, which I had not thought of for twenty years. It happened that as a child I had had it read aloud to me by a sick-nurse whose own working life might have stretched back to the time when Tennyson wrote the poem. The horrors and sufferings of the old-style hospitals were a vivid memory to her. We had shuddered over the poem together, and then seemingly I had forgotten it. Even its name would probably have recalled nothing to me. But the first glimpse of the ill-lit murmurous room, with the beds so close together, suddenly roused the train of thought to which it belonged, and in the night that followed I found myself remembering the whole story and atmosphere of the poem, with many of its lines complete.

△

From "A Clergyman's Daughter"

▽

Chapter Three

I

(*Scene:* Trafalgar Square. Dimly visible through the mist, a dozen people, Dorothy among them, are grouped about one of the benches near the north parapet.)

Charlie (singing): " 'Ail Mary, 'ail Mary, 'a-il Ma-ary——"

(Big Ben strikes ten.)

Snouter (mimicking the noise): "Ding dong, ding dong! Shut your —— noise, can't you? Seven more hours of it on this —— square before we got the chance of a set-down and a bit of sleep! Cripes!"

Mr. Tallboys (to himself): *"Non sum qualis eram boni sub regno Edwardii!* In the days of my innocence, before the Devil carried me up into a high place and dropped me into the Sunday newspapers—that is to say when I was Rector of Little Fawley-cum-Dewsbury . . ."

Deafie (singing): "With my willy willy, *with* my willy willy——"

Mrs. Wayne: "Ah, dearie, as soon as I set eyes on you I knew as you was a lady born and bred. You and me've known what it is to come down in the world, haven't we, dearie? It ain't the same for us as what it is for some of these others here."

Charlie (singing): " 'Ail Mary, 'ail Mary, 'a-il Ma-ary, full of grace!"

Mrs. Bendigo: "Calls himself a bloody husband, does he? Four pound a week in Covent Garden and 'is wife doing a starry in the bloody Square! Husband!"

Mr. Tallboys (to himself): "Happy days, happy days! My ivied church under the sheltering hillside—my red-tiled Rectory slumbering among Elizabethan yews! My library, my vinery, my cook, house-parlormaid and groom-gardener! My cash in the bank, my name in Crockford! My black suit of irreproachable cut, my collar back to front, my watered silk cassock in the church precincts . . ."

Mrs. Wayne: "Of course the one thing I *do* thank God for, dearie, is that my poor dear mother never lived to see this day. Because if she ever *had* of lived to see the day when her eldest daughter—as was brought up, mind you, with no expense spared and milk straight from the cow . . ."

Mrs. Bendigo: "Husband!"

Ginger: "Come on, less 'ave a drum of tea while we got the chance. Last we'll get tonight—coffee shop shuts at 'ar-parse ten."

The Kike: "Oh Jesus! This bloody cold's gonna kill me! I ain't got nothing on under my trousers. Oh Je-e-e-*eeze!*"

Charlie (singing): " 'Ail Mary, 'ail Mary——"

Snouter: "Fourpence! Fourpence for six —— hours on the bum! And that there nosing sod with the wooden leg queering our pitch at every boozer between Aldgate and the Mile End Road. With 'is —— wooden leg and 'is war medals as 'e bought in Lambeth Cut! Bastard!"

Deafie (singing): "With my willy willy, *with* my willy willy——"

Mrs. Bendigo: "Well, I told the bastard what I thought of 'im, anyway. 'Call yourself a man?' I says. 'I've seen things like you kep' in a bottle at the 'orspital,' I says. . . ."

Mr. Tallboys (to himself): "Happy days, happy days! Roast beef and bobbing villagers, and the peace of God that passeth all understanding! Sunday mornings in my oaken stall, cool flower scent and frou-frou of surplices mingling in the sweet corpse-laden air! Summer evenings when the late sun slanted through my study window—I pensive, boozed with tea, in fragrant wreaths of Cavendish, thumbing drowsily some half-calf volume—*Poetical Works of William Shenstone, Esq.,* Percy's *Rel-*

iques of Ancient English Poetry, J. Lempriere, D.D., professor of immoral theology . . ."

Ginger: "Come on, 'oo's for that drum of riddleme-ree? We got the milk and we got the tea. Question is, 'oo's got any bleeding sugar?"

Dorothy: "This cold, this cold! It seems to go right through you! Surely it won't be like this all night?"

Mrs. Bendigo: "Oh, cheese it! I 'ate these sniveling tarts."

Charlie: "Ain't it going to be a proper perisher, too? Look at the perishing river mist creeping up that there column. Freeze the fishhooks off of ole Nelson before morning."

Mrs. Wayne: "Of course, at the time that I'm speaking of we still had our little tobacco and sweetstuff business on the corner, you'll understand. . . ."

The Kike: "Oh Je-e-e-eeze! Lend's that overcoat of yours, Ginger. I'm bloody freezing!"

Snouter: "——double-crossing bastard! P'raps I won't bash 'is navel in when I get a 'old of 'im!"

Charlie: "Fortunes o' war, boy, fortunes o' war. Perishing Square tonight—rump steak and kip on feathers tomorrow. What else d'you expect on perishing Thursday?"

Mrs. Bendigo: "Shove up, Daddy, shove up! Think I want your lousy old 'ed on my shoulder—me a married woman?"

Mr. Tallboys (to himself): "For preaching, chanting, and intoning I was unrivaled. My 'Lift up your Hearts' was renowned throughout the diocese. All styles I could do you, High Church, Low Church, Broad Church, and No Church. Throaty Anglo-Cat Warblings, straight from the shoulder muscular Anglican, or the adenoidal Low Church whine in which still lurk the Houyhnhnm-notes of neighing chapel elders. . . ."

Deafie (singing): *"With my willy willy——"*

Ginger: "Take your 'ands off that bleeding overcoat, Kikie. You don't get no clo'es of mine while you got the chats on you."

Charlie (singing):

> "As pants the 'art for cooling streams,
>   When 'eated in the chase——"

Mrs. McElligot (in her sleep): "Was 'at you, Michael dear?"

Mrs. Bendigo: "It's my belief as the sneaking bastard 'ad another wife living when 'e married me."

Mr. Tallboys (from the roof of his mouth, stage curate-wise, reminiscently): "If any of you know cause or just impediment why

these two persons should not be joined together in holy mat-
rimony . . ."

The Kike: "A pal! A bloody pal! And won't lend his bloody overcoat!"

Mrs. Wayne: "Well, now as you've mentioned it, I must admit as
I never *was* one to refuse a nice cup of tea. I know that when
our poor dear mother was alive, pot after pot we used to . . ."

Nosy Watson (to himself, angrily): "Sod! . . . Gee'd into it and
then a stretch all round. . . . Never even done the bloody
job. . . . Sod!"

Deafie (singing): "*With* my willy willy——"

Mrs. McElligot (half asleep): "*Dear* Michael. . . . He was real loving, Michael was. Tender an' true. . . . Never looked at another man since dat evenin' when I met'm outside Kronk's
slaughter-house an' he gimme de two pound o' sausage as he'd
bummed off de International Stores for his own supper. . . ."

Mrs. Bendigo: "Well, I suppose we'll get that bloody tea this time
tomorrow."

Mr. Tallboys (chanting, reminiscently): "By the waters of Babylon we sat down and wept, when we remembered thee, O
Zion! . . ."

Dorothy: "Oh, this cold, this cold!"

Snouter: "Well, I don't do no more —— starries this side of Christmas. I'll 'ave my kip tomorrow if I 'ave to cut it out of their
bowels."

Nosy Watson: "Detective, is he? Smith of the Flying Squad! Flying Judas more likely! All they can bloody do—copping the
old offenders what no beak won't give a fair chance to."

Ginger: "Well, I'm off for the fiddlede-dee. 'Oo's got a couple of
clods for the water?"

Mrs. McElligot (waking): "Oh dear, oh dear! If my back ain't fair
broke! Oh holy Jesus, if dis bench don't catch you across de
kidneys! An' dere was me dreamin' I was warm in kip wid a
nice cup o' tea an' two o' buttered toast waitin' by me bedside. Well, dere goes me last wink o' sleep till I gets into Lambeth public lib'ry tomorrow."

Daddy (his head emerging from within his overcoat like a tortoise's
from within its shell): "Wassat you said, boy? Paying money
for water! How long've you bin on the road, you ignorant
young scut? Money for bloody water? Bum it, boy, bum it!
Don't buy what you can bum and don't bum what you can
steal. That's my word—fifty year on the road, man and boy."
(Retires within his coat.)

Mr. Tallboys (chanting): "O all ye works of the Lord——"
Deafie (singing): *"With* my willy willy——"
Charlie: " 'Oo was it copped you, Nosy?"
The Kike: "Oh Je-e-e-*eeze!*"
Mrs. Bendigo: "Shove up, shove up! Seems to me some folks think
    they've took a mortgage on this bloody seat."
Mr. Tallboys (chanting): "O all ye works of the Lord, curse ye the
    Lord, curse Him and vilify Him for ever!"
Mrs. McElligot: "What I always says is, it's always us poor bloody
    Catholics dat's down in de bloody dumps."
Nosy Watson: "Smithy. Flying Squad—flying sod! Give us the plans
    of the house and everything, and then had a van full of cop-
    pers waiting and nipped the lot of us. I wrote it up in the
    Black Maria:

> 'Detective Smith knows how to gee;
>   Tell him he's a —— from me.' "

Snouter: " 'Ere, what about our —— tea? Go on, Kikie, you're a
    young 'un; shut that —— noise and take the drums. Don't you
    pay nothing. Worm it out of the old tart. Snivel. Do the dole-
    ful."
Mr. Tallboys (chanting): "O all ye children of men, curse ye the
    Lord, curse Him and vilify Him for ever!"
Charlie: "What, is Smithy crooked too?"
Mrs. Bendigo: "I tell you what, girls, I tell you what gets *me* down,
    and that's to think of my bloody husband snoring under four
    blankets and me freezing in this bloody Square. That's what
    I can't stomach. The unnatural sod!"
Ginger (singing): " '*There* they go—*in* their joy——' Don't take that
    there drum with the cold sausage in it, Kikie."
Nosy Watson: "Crooked? *Crooked?* Why, a corkscrew 'ud look like
    a bloody bradawl beside of him! There isn't one of them
    double —— sons of whores in the Flying Squad but 'ud sell
    his grandmother to the knackers for two pound ten and then
    sit on her gravestone eating potato crisps. The geeing, nark-
    ing toe-rag!"
Charlie: "Perishing tough. 'Ow many convictions you got?"
Ginger (singing):

> "*There* they go—*in* their joy—
>   '*Ap*py girl—*luc*ky boy——"

Nosy Watson: "Fourteen. You don't stand no chance with that lot
    against you."

Mrs. Wayne: "What, don't he keep you, then?"

Mrs. Bendigo: "No, I'm married to this one, sod 'im!"

Charlie: "I got perishing nine myself."

Mr. Tallboys (chanting): "O Ananias, Azarias, and Misael, curse ye the Lord, curse Him and vilify Him for ever!"

Ginger (singing):

> "*There* they go—*in* their joy—
> '*Ap*py girl—*luc*ky boy—
> But 'ere am *I-I-I*—
> Broken—'*a-a-aar*ted!

God, I ain't 'ad a dig in the grave for three days. 'Ow long since you washed your face, Snouter?"

Mrs. McElligot: "Oh dear, oh dear! If dat boy don't come soon wid de tea me insides'll dry up like a bloody kippered herring."

Charlie: "*You* can't sing, none of you. Ought to 'ear Snouter and me 'long towards Christmas time when we pipe up 'Good King Wenceslas' outside the boozers. 'Ymns, too. Blokes in the bar weep their perishing eyes out to 'ear us. 'Member when we tapped twice at the same 'ouse by mistake, Snouter? Old tart fair tore the innards out of us."

Mr. Tallboys (marching up and down behind an imaginary drum and singing):

> "All things vile and damnable,
>   All creatures great and small——"

(Big Ben strikes half-past ten.)

Snouter (mimicking the clock): "Ding dong, ding dong! Six and a —— half hours of it! Cripes!"

Ginger: "Kikie and me knocked off four of them safety-razor blades in Woolworths 's afternoon. I'll 'ave a dig in the bleeding fountains tomorrow if I can bum a bit of soap."

Deafie: "When I was a stooard in the P. and O., we used to meet them black Indians two days out at sea, in them there great canoes as they call catamarans, catching sea-turtles the size of dinner tables."

Mrs. Wayne: "Did you used to be a clergyman, then, sir?"

Mr. Tallboys (halting): "After the order of Melchizedec. There is no question of 'used to be,' Madam. Once a priest always a priest. *Hoc est corpus* hocus pocus. Even though unfrocked—

un-Crocked, we call it—and dog-collar publicly torn off by the
bishop of the diocese."

Ginger (singing): " '*There* they go—*in* their joy——' Thank Christ!
'Ere comes Kikie. Now for the consultation-free!"

Mrs. Bendigo: "Not before it's bloody needed."

Charlie: " 'Ow come they give you the sack, mate? Usual story?
Choirgirls in the family way?"

Mrs. McElligot: "You've took your time, ain't you, young man?
But come on, let's have a sup of it before me tongue falls
out o' me bloody mouth."

Mrs. Bendigo: "Shove up, Daddy! You're sitting on my packet of
bloody sugar."

Mr. Tallboys: "Girls is a euphemism. Only the usual flannel-bloom-
ered hunters of the unmarried clergy. Church hens—altar-dress-
ers and brass-polishers—spinsters growing bony and desperate.
There is a demon that enters into them at thirty-five."

The Kike: "The old bitch wouldn't give me the hot water. Had
to tap a toff in the street and pay a penny for it."

Snouter: "—— likely story! Bin swigging it on the way more likely."

Daddy (emerging from his overcoat): "Drum o' tea, eh? I could
sup a drum o' tea." (Belches slightly.)

Charlie: "When their bubs get like perishing razor strops? *I* know."

Nosy Watson: "Tea—bloody catlap. Better'n that cocoa in the stir,
though. Lend's your cup, matie."

Ginger: "Jest wait'll I knock a 'ole in this tin of milk. Shy us a
money or your life, someone."

Mrs. Bendigo: "Easy with that bloody sugar! 'Oo paid for it, I
sh'd like to know?"

Mr. Tallboys: "When their bubs get like razor strops. I thank thee
for that humor. *Pippin's Weekly* made quite a feature of the
case. 'Missing Canon's Sub Rosa Romance. Intimate Revela-
tions.' And also an Open Letter in *John Bull:* 'To a Skunk
in Shepherd's Clothing.' A pity—I was marked out for preferment. (To Dorothy) Gaiters in the family, if you understand
me. You would not think, would you, that the time has been
when this unworthy backside dented the plush cushions of a
cathedral stall?"

Charlie: " 'Ere comes Florry. Thought she'd be along soon as we
got the tea going. Got a nose like a perishing vulture for tea,
that girl 'as."

Snouter: "Ay, always on the tap. (Singing)

   'Tap, tap, tapetty tap,
   I'm a perfec' devil at that——' "

Mrs. McElligot: "De poor kid, she ain't got no sense. Why don't she go up to Piccadilly Circus where she'd get her five bob reg'lar? She won't do herself no good bummin' round de Square wid a set of miserable ole Tobies."

Dorothy: "Is that milk all right?"

Ginger: "All right?" (Applies his mouth to one of the holes in the tin and blows. A sticky grayish stream dribbles from the other.)

Charlie: "What luck, Florry? 'Ow 'bout that perishing toff as I see you get off with just now?"

Dorothy: "It's got 'Not fit for babies' on it."

Mrs. Bendigo: "Well, you ain't a bloody baby, are you? You can drop your Buckingham Palace manners 'ere, dearie."

Florry: "Stood me a coffee and a fag—mingy bastard! That tea you got there, Ginger? You always *was* my favorite, Ginger dear."

Mrs. Wayne: "There's jest thirteen of us."

Mr. Tallboys: "As we are not going to have any dinner you need not disturb yourself."

Ginger: "What-o, ladies and gents! Tea is served. Cups forward, please!"

The Kike: "Oh Jeez! You ain't filled my bloody cup half full!"

Mrs. McElligot: "Well, here's luck to us all, an' a better bloody kip tomorrow. I'd ha' took shelter in one o' dem dere churches meself, only de b——s won't let you in if so be as dey t'ink you got de chats on you." (Drinks.)

Mrs. Wayne: "Well, I can't say as this is exactly the way as I've been *accustomed* to drinking a cup of tea—but still——" (Drinks.)

Charlie: "Perishing good cup of tea." (Drinks.)

Deafie: "And there was flocks of them there green parakeets in the coconut palms, too." (Drinks.)

Mr. Tallboys:

> "What potions have I drunk of siren tears,
>   Distilled from limbecs foul as Hell within!"

(Drinks.)

Snouter: "Last we'll get till five in the —— morning." (Drinks.)

(Florry produces a broken shop-made cigarette from her stocking, and cadges a match. The men, except Daddy, Deafie and Mr. Tallboys, roll cigarettes from picked-up fag-ends. The red ends glow through the misty twilight, like a crooked constellation, as the smokers sprawl on the bench, the ground or the slope of the parapet.)

Mrs. Wayne: "Well, there now! A nice cup of tea do seem to warm you up, don't it, now? Not but what I don't feel it a bit different, as you might say, not having no nice clean table-cloth like I've been accustomed to, and the beautiful china tea service as our mother used to have; and always, of course, the very best tea as money could buy—real Pekoe Points at two and nine a pound. . . ."

Ginger (singing):

> *"There* they go—*in* their joy—
> '*Appy* girl—*lucky* boy——"

Mr. Tallboys (singing, to the tune of "Deutschland, Deutschland über alles"): "Keep the aspidistra flying——"

Charlie: "'Ow long you two kids been in Smoke?"

Snouter: "I'm going to give them boozers such a doing tomorrow as they won't know if they're on their 'eads or their —— 'eels. I'll 'ave my 'alf dollar if I 'ave to 'old them upside down and —— shake 'em."

Ginger: "Three days. We come down from York—skippering 'alf the way. God, wasn't it jest about bleeding nine-carat gold, too!"

Florry: "Got any more tea there, Ginger dear? Well, so long, folks, See you all at Wilkins's tomorrow morning."

Mrs. Bendigo: "Thieving little tart! Swallers 'er tea and then jacks off without so much as a thank you. Can't waste a bloody moment."

Mrs. McElligot: "Cold? Ay, I b'lieve you. Skipperin' in de long grass wid no blanket an' de bloody dew fit to drown you, an' den can't get your bloody fire goin' in de mornin', an' got to tap de milkman 'fore you can make yourself a drum o' tea. I've had some'v it when me and Michael was on de toby."

Mrs. Bendigo: "Even go with blackies and Chinamen she will, the dirty little cow."

Dorothy: "How much does she get each time?"

Snouter: "Tanner."

Dorothy: "Sixpence?"

Charlie: "Bet your life. Do it for a perishing fag along toward morning."

Mrs. McElligot: "I never took less'n a shilling, never."

Ginger: "Kikie and me skippered in a boneyard one night. Woke up in the morning and found I was lying on a bleeding gravestone."

The Kike: "She ain't half got the crabs on her, too."

Mrs. McElligot: "Michael an' me skippered in a pigsty once. We was just a-creepin' in, when, 'Holy Mary!' says Michael, 'dere's a pig in here!' 'Pig be ——!' I says, 'he'll keep us warm anyway.' So in we goes, an' dere was an old sow lay on her side snorin' like a traction engine. I creeps up agen her an' puts me arms round her, an' begod she kept me warm all night. I've skippered worse."

Deafie (singing): *"With* my willy willy——"

Charlie: "Don't ole Deafie keep it up? Sets up a kind of a 'umming inside of 'im, 'e says."

Daddy: "When I was a boy we didn't live on this 'ere bread and marg. and tea and suchlike trash. Good solid tommy we 'ad in them days. Beef stoo. Black pudden. Bacon dumpling. Pig's 'ead. Fed like a fighting-cock on a tanner a day. And now fifty year I've 'ad of it on the toby. Spud-grabbing, pea-picking, lambing, turnip-topping—everythink. And sleeping in wet straw and not once in a year you don't fill your guts right full. Well——!" (Retires within his coat.)

Mrs. McElligot: "But he was real bold, Michael was. He'd go in any-where. Many's de time we've broke into an empty house an' kipped in de best bed. 'Other people got homes,' he'd say. 'Why shouldn't we have'm too?' "

Ginger (singing): "But I'm dan-cing with tears—in my eyes——"

Mr. Tallboys (to himself): *"Absumet haeres Caecuba dignior!* To think that there were twenty-one bottles of Clos St. Jacques 1911 in my cellar still, that night when the baby was born and I left for London on the milk train! . . ."

Mrs. Wayne: "And as for the *wreaths* we 'ad sent us when our mother died—well, you wouldn't believe! 'Uge, they was. . . ."

Mrs. Bendigo: "If I 'ad my time over again I'd marry for bloody money."

Ginger (singing):

> "But I'm dan-cing with tears—in my eyes—
> Cos the girl—in my arms—isn't you-o-ou!"

Nosy Watson: "Some of you lot think you got a bloody lot to howl about, don't you? What about a poor sod like me? You wasn't narked into the stir when you was eighteen year old, was you?"

The Kike: "Oh Je-e-e-*eeze!*"

Charlie: "Ginger, you can't sing no more'n a perishing tomcat with the guts-ache. Just you listen to me. I'll give y'a treat. (Singing) Jesu, lover *of* my soul——"

Mr. Tallboys (to himself): *"Et ego* in Crockford. . . . With Bishops and Archbishops and with all the Company of Heaven. . . ."

Nosy Watson: "D'you know how I got in the stir the first time? Narked by my own sister—yes, my own bloody sister! My sister's a cow if ever there was one. She got married to a religious maniac—he's so bloody religious that she's got fifteen kids now —well, it was him put her up to narking me. But I got back on 'em, *I* can tell you. First thing I done when I come out of the stir, I buys a hammer and goes round to my sister's house, and smashed her piano to bloody matchwood. 'There!' I says, 'that's what you get for narking *me!* You nosing mare!' I says."

Dorothy: "This cold, this cold! I don't know whether my feet are there or not."

Mrs. McElligot: "Bloody tea don't warm you for long, do it? I'm fair froze meself."

Mr. Tallboys (to himself): "My curate days, my curate days! My fancywork bazaars and morris dances in aid of on the village green, my lectures to the Mothers' Union—missionary work in Western China with fourteen magic lantern slides! My Boys' Cricket Club, teetotalers only, my confirmation classes—purity lecture once monthly in the Parish Hall—my Boy Scout orgies! The Wolf Cubs will deliver the Grand Howl. Household Hints for the Parish Magazine, 'Discarded fountain-pen fillers can be used as enemas for canaries. . . .'"

Charlie (singing): "Jesu, lover *of* my soul——"

Ginger: " 'Ere comes the bleeding flattie! Get up off the ground, all of you." (Daddy emerges from his overcoat.)

The policeman (shaking the sleepers on the next bench): "Now then, wake up, wake up! Rouse up, you! Got to go home if you want to sleep. This isn't a common lodging house. Get up, there!" etc., etc.

Mrs. Bendigo: "It's that nosy young sod as wants promotion. Wouldn't let you bloody breathe if 'e 'ad 'is way."

Charlie (singing):

> "Jesu, lover *of* my soul,
>   Let me *to* Thy bosom fly——"

The policeman: "Now then, *you!* What you think *this* is? Baptist prayer meeting? (To the Kike) Up you get, and look sharp about it!"

Charlie: "I can't 'elp it, sergeant. It's my toonful nature. It comes out of me natural-like."

The policeman (shaking Mrs. Bendigo): "Wake up, mother, wake up!"

Mrs. Bendigo: "Mother! *Mother,* is it? Well, if I am a mother, thank God I ain't got a bloody son like you! And I'll tell you another little secret, constable. Next time I want a man's fat 'ands feeling round the back of my neck, I won't ask *you* to do it. I'll 'ave someone with a bit more sex appeal."

The policeman: "Now then, now then! No call to get abusive, you know. We got our orders to carry out." (Exit majestically.)

Snouter (sotto voce): "—— off, you —— son of a ——!"

Charlie (singing):

> "While the gathering waters roll,
>   While the tempest still is 'igh!

Sung bass in the choir my last two years in Dartmoor, I did."

Mrs. Bendigo: "I'll bloody mother 'im! (Shouting after the policeman) 'I! Why don't you get after them bloody cat burglars 'stead of coming nosing round a respectable married woman?"

Ginger: "Kip down, blokes. 'E's jacked." (Daddy retires within his coat.)

Nosy Watson: "Wassit like in Dartmoor now? D'they give you jam now?"

Mrs. Wayne: "Of course, you can see as they couldn't reely allow people to sleep in the streets—I mean, it wouldn't be quite nice —and then you've got to remember as it'd be encouraging of all the people as haven't got homes of their own—the kind of riff-raff, if you take my meaning. . . ."

Mr. Tallboys (to himself): "Happy days, happy days! Outings with the Girl Guides in Epping Forest—hired brake and sleek roan horses, and I on the box in my gray flannel suit, speckled straw hat, and discreet layman's necktie. Buns and ginger pop under the green elms. Twenty Girl Guides pious yet susceptible frisking in the breast-high bracken, and I a happy curate sporting among them, in loco parentis pinching the girls' backsides. . . ."

Mrs. McElligot: "Well, you may talk about kippin' down, but begod dare won't be much sleep for my poor ole bloody bones tonight. I can't skipper it now de way me and Michael used to."

Charlie: "Not jam. Gets cheese, though, twice a week."

The Kike: "Oh Jeez! I can't stand it no longer. I going down to the M.A.B."

(Dorothy stands up, and then, her knees having stiffened with the cold, almost falls.)

Ginger: "Only send you to the bleeding Labor Home. What you say we all go up to Covent Garden tomorrow morning? Bum a few pears if we get there early enough."

Charlie: "I've 'ad my perishing bellyful of Dartmoor, b'lieve me. Forty on us went through 'ell for getting off with the ole women down on the allotments. Ole trots seventy years old they was—spud-grabbers. Didn't we cop it just! Bread and water, chained to the wall—perishing near murdered us."

Mrs. Bendigo: "No fear! Not while my bloody husband's there. One black eye in a week's enough for me, thank you."

Mr. Tallboys (chanting, reminiscently): "As for our harps, we hangèd them up, upon the willow trees of Babylon! . . ."

Mrs. McElligot: "Hold up, kiddie! Stamp your feet an' get de blood back into 'm. I'll take y'a walk up to Paul's in a coupla minutes."

Deafie (singing): *"With my willy willy——"*

(Big Ben strikes eleven.)

Snouter: "Six more —— hours! Cripes!"

(An hour passes. Big Ben stops striking. The mist thins and the cold increases. A grubby-faced moon is seen sneaking among the clouds of the southern sky.

A dozen hardened old men remain on the benches, and still contrive to sleep, doubled up and hidden in their greatcoats. Occasionally they groan in their sleep. The others set out in all directions, intending to walk all night and so keep their blood flowing, but nearly all of them have drifted back to the Square by midnight. A new policeman comes on duty. He strolls through the Square at intervals of half an hour, scrutinizing the faces of the sleepers but letting them alone when he has made sure that they are only asleep and not dead. Round each bench revolves a knot of people who take it in turns to sit down and are driven to their feet by the cold after a few minutes. Ginger and Charlie fill two drums at the fountains and set out in the desperate hope of boiling some tea over the navvies' clinker fire in Chandos Street; but a policeman is warming himself at the fire, and orders them away. The Kike suddenly vanishes, probably to beg a bed at the M.A.B. Toward one o'clock a rumor goes round that a lady is distributing hot coffee, ham sandwiches, and packets of cigarettes under Charing Cross Bridge; there is a rush to the spot, but the rumor turns out to be unfounded. As the Square fills again the ceaseless changing of places upon the benches quickens until it is like a game of musical chairs. Sitting down, with one's hands under one's arm-pits, it is possible to get into a kind of sleep, or doze, for two or three minutes on end. In this state, enormous ages seem to pass. One sinks into complex, troubling dreams which leave one conscious of one's surroundings and of the bitter cold. The night is growing clearer and colder every minute. There is a chorus of varying sounds—groans, curses, bursts of laughter and singing, and through them all the uncontrollable chattering of teeth.)

Mr. Tallboys (chanting): "I am poured out like water, and all my bones are out of joint! . . ."

Mrs. McElligot: "Ellen an' me bin wanderin' round de City dis two hours. Begod it's like a bloody tomb wid dem great lamps glarin' down on you an' not a soul stirrin' excep' de flatties strollin' two an' two."

Snouter: "Five past —— one and I ain't 'ad a bite since dinner! Course it 'ad to 'appen to us on a —— night like this!"

Mr. Tallboys: "A drinking night I should have called it. But every man to his taste. (Chanting) 'My strength is dried like a pot-sherd, and my tongue cleaveth to my gums!' . . ."

Charlie: "Say, what you think? Nosy and me done a smash jest now. Nosy sees a tobacconist's showcase full of them fancy boxes of Gold Flake, and 'e says, 'By cripes I'm going to 'ave some of them fags if they give me a perishing stretch for it!' 'e says. So 'e wraps 'is scarf round 'is 'and, and we waits till there's a perishing great van passing as'll drown the noise, and then Nosy lets fly —biff! We nipped a dozen packets of fags, and then I bet you didn't see our a——s for dust. And when we gets round the cor-ner and opens them, there wasn't no perishing fags inside! Perishing dummy boxes. I 'ad to laugh."

Dorothy: "My knees are giving way. I can't stand up much longer."

Mrs. Bendigo: "Oh, the sod, the sod! To turn a woman out of doors on a night like bloody this! You wait'll I get 'im drunk o' Satur-day night an' 'e can't 'it back. I'll mash 'im to bloody shin of beef, I will. 'E'll look like two pennorth of pieces after I've swiped 'im with the bloody flatiron."

Mrs. McElligot: "Here, make room'n let de kid sit down. Press up agen ole Daddy, dear. Put his arm round you. He's chatty, but he'll keep you warm."

Ginger (double marking time): "Stamp your feet on the ground—

only bleeding thing to do. Strike up a song, someone, and less all stamp our bleeding feet in time to it."

Daddy (waking and emerging): "Wassat?" (Still half asleep, he lets his head fall back, with mouth open and Adam's apple protruding from his withered throat like the blade of a tomahawk.)

Mrs. Bendigo: "There's women what if they'd stood what *I've* stood, they'd 'ave put spirits of salts in 'is cup of bloody tea."

Mr. Tallboys (beating an imaginary drum and singing): "Onward, heathen so-oldiers——"

Mrs. Wayne: "Well, reely now! If any of us'd ever of thought, in the dear old days when we used to sit round our own Silkstone coal fire, with the kettle on the hob and a nice dish of toasted crumpets from the baker's over the way . . ." (The chattering of her teeth silences her.)

Charlie: "No perishing church trap now, matie. I'll give y'a bit of smut—something as we can perishing dance to. You listen t'me."

Mrs. McElligot: "Don't you get talkin' about crumpets, Missis. Me bloody belly's rubbin' agen me backbone already."

(Charlie draws himself up, clears his throat, and in an enormous voice roars out a song entitled "Rollicking Bill the Sailor." A laugh that is partly a shudder bursts from the people on the bench. They sing the song through again, with increasing volume of noise, stamping and clapping in time. Those sitting down, packed elbow to elbow, sway grotesquely from side to side, working their feet as though stamping on the pedals of a harmonium. Even Mrs. Wayne joins in after a moment, laughing in spite of herself. They are all laughing, though with chattering teeth. Mr. Tallboys marches up and down behind his vast swag belly, pretending to carry a banner or crozier in front of him. The night is now quite clear, and an icy wind comes shuddering at intervals through the Square. The stamping and clapping rise to a kind of frenzy as the people feel the deadly cold penetrate to their bones. Then the policeman is seen wandering into the Square from the eastern end, and the singing ceases abruptly.)

Charlie: "There! You can't say as a bit of music don't warm you up."

Mrs. Bendigo: "This bloody wind! And I ain't even got any drawers on, the bastard kicked me out in such a 'urry."

Mrs. McElligot: "Well, glory be to Jesus, 'twon't be long before dat dere church in de Gray's Inn Road opens up for de winter. Dey gives you a roof over your head of a night, 't any rate."

The policeman: "Now then, now *then!* D'you think this is the time of night to begin singing like a blooming bear garden? I shall have to send you back to your homes if you can't keep quiet."

Snouter (sotto voce): "You —— son of a ——!"

Ginger: "Yes—they lets you kip on the bleeding stone floor with three newspaper posters 'stead of blankets. Might as well be in the Square and 'ave done with it. God, I wish I was in the bleeding spike."

Mrs. McElligot: "Still, you gets a cup o' Horlicks an' two slices. I bin glad to kip dere often enough."

Mr. Tallboys (chanting): "I was glad when they said unto me, We will go into the house of the Lord! . . ."

Dorothy (starting up): "Oh, this cold, this cold! I don't know whether it's worse when you're sitting down or when you're standing up. Oh, how can you all stand it? Surely you don't have to do this every night of your lives?"

Mrs. Wayne: "You mustn't think, dearie, as there isn't *some* of us as wasn't brought up respectable."

Charlie (singing): "Cheer up, cully, you'll soon be dead! Brrh! Perishing Jesus! Ain't my fishhooks blue!" (Double marks time and beats his arms against his sides.)

Dorothy: "Oh, but how can you stand it? How can you go on like this, night after night, year after year? It's not possible that people can live so! It's so absurd that one wouldn't believe it if one didn't know it was true. It's impossible!"

Snouter: "—— possible if you ask me."

Mr. Tallboys (stage curate-wise): "With God, all things are possible."

(Dorothy sinks back on to the bench, her knees still being unsteady.)

Charlie: "Well, it's jest on 'ar-parse one. Either we got to get moving, or else make a pyramid on that perishing bench. Unless we want to perishing turn up our toes. 'Oo's for a little constitootional up to the Tower of London?"

Mrs. McElligot: " 'Twon't be me dat'll walk another step tonight. Me bloody legs've given out on me."

Ginger: "What-o for the pyramid! This is a bit too bleeding nine-day-old for me. Less scrum into that bench—beg pardon, Ma!"

Daddy (sleepily): "Wassa game? Can't a man get a bit of kip but what you must come worriting 'im and shaking of 'im?"

Charlie: "That's the stuff! Shove in! Shift yourself, Daddy, and make room for my little sit-me-down. Get one atop of each other.

That's right. Never mind the chats. Jam all together like pilchards in a perishing tin."

Mrs. Wayne: "Here! I didn't ask you to sit on my lap, young man!"

Ginger: "Sit on mine, then, mother—'sall the same. What-o! First bit of stuff I've 'ad my arm round since Easter."

(They pile themselves in a monstrous shapeless clot, men and women clinging indiscriminately together, like a bunch of toads at spawning time. There is a writhing movement as the heap settles down, and a sour stench of clothes diffuses itself. Only Mr. Tallboys remains marching up and down.)

Mr. Tallboys (declaiming): "O ye nights and days, ye light and darkness, ye lightnings and clouds, curse ye the Lord!"

(Deafie, someone having sat on his diaphragm, utters a strange, unreproducible sound.)

Mrs. Bendigo: "Get off my bad leg, can't you? What you think I am? Bloody drawing-room sofa?"

Charlie: "Don't ole Daddy stink when you get up agen 'im?"

Ginger: "Bleeding Bank 'oliday for the chats this'll be."

Dorothy: "Oh, God, God!"

Mr. Tallboys (halting): "Why call on God, you puling deathbed penitent? Stick to your guns and call on the Devil as I do. Hail to thee, Lucifer, Prince of the Air! (Singing to the tune of 'Holy, holy, holy') Incubi and Succubi, falling down before Thee! . . ."

Mrs. Bendigo: "Oh, shut up, you blarsphemous old sod! 'E's too bloody fat to feel the cold, that's what's wrong with 'im."

Charlie: "Nice soft be'ind you got, Ma. Keep an eye out for the perishing flattie, Ginger."

Mr. Tallboys: "*Maledicite, omnia opera!* The Black Mass! Why not? Once a priest always a priest. Hand me a chunk of toke and I will work the miracle. Sulphur candles, Lord's Prayer backwards, crucifix upside down. (To Dorothy) If we had a black he-goat you would come in useful."

(The animal heat of the piled bodies has already made itself felt. A drowsiness is descending upon everyone.)

Mrs. Wayne: "You mustn't think as I'm *accustomed* to sitting on a gentleman's knee, you know . . ."

Mrs. McElligot (drowsily): "I took my sacraments reg'lar till de bloody priest wouldn't give me absolution along o' my Michael De ole get, de ole getsie! . . ."

Mr. Tallboys (striking an attitude): *"Per aquam sacratam quam nunc spargo, signumque crucis quod nunc facio . . ."*

Ginger: " 'Oo's got a fill of 'ard-up? I've smoked my last bleeding fag-end."

Mr. Tallboys (as at the altar): "Dearly beloved brethren, we are gathered together in the sight of God for the solemnization of unholy blasphemy. He has afflicted us with dirt and cold, with hunger and solitude, with the pox and the itch, with the head-louse and the crablouse. Our food is damp crusts and slimy meat scraps handed out in packets from hotel doorways. Our pleasure is stewed tea and sawdust cakes bolted in reeking cellars, bar-rinsings and spittle of common ale, the embraces of toothless hags. Our destiny is the pauper's grave, twenty-five deep in deal coffins, the kip-house of underground. It is very meet, right, and our bounden duty at all times and in all places to curse Him and revile Him. Therefore with Demons and Archdemons," etc., etc., etc.

Mrs. McElligot (drowsily): "By holy Jesus, I'm half asleep right now, only some b——'s lyin' across me legs an' crushin' 'em."

Mr. Tallboys: "Amen. Evil from us deliver, but temptation into not us lead," etc., etc., etc.

(As he reaches the first word of the prayer he tears the consecrated bread across. The blood runs out of it. There is a rolling sound, as of thunder, and the landscape changes. Dorothy's feet are very cold. Monstrous winged shapes of Demons and Archdemons are dimly visible, moving to and fro. Something, beak or claw, closes upon Dorothy's shoulder, reminding her that her feet and hands are aching with cold.)

The policeman (shaking Dorothy by the shoulder): "Wake up, now, wake up, wake up! Haven't you got an overcoat? You're as white as death. Don't you know better than to let yourself sprawl about in the cold like that?"

(Dorothy finds that she is stiff with cold. The sky is now quite clear, with gritty little stars twinkling like electric lamps enormously remote. The pyramid has unrolled itself.)

Mrs. McElligot: "De poor kid, she ain't used to roughin' it de way us others are."

Ginger (beating his arms): "Brrr! Woo! 'Taters in the bleeding mould!"

Mrs. Wayne: "She's a lady born and bred."

The policeman: "Is that so?—See here, Miss, you best come down to the M.A.B. with me. They'll give you a bed all right. Anyone can see with half an eye as you're a cut above these others here."

Mrs. Bendigo: "Thank you, constable, *thank* you! 'Ear that, girls? 'A cut above us,' 'e says. Nice, ain't it? (To the policeman) Proper bloody Ascot swell yourself, ain't you?"

Dorothy: "No, no! Leave me. I'd rather stay here."

The policeman: "Well, please yourself. You looked real bad just now. I'll be along later and take a look at you." (Moves off doubtfully.)

Charlie: "Wait'll the perisher's round the corner and then pile up agen. Only perishing way we'll keep warm."

Mrs. McElligot: "Come on, kid. Get underneath an' let'm warm you."

Snouter: "Ten minutes to —— two. Can't last for ever, I s'pose."

Mr. Tallboys (chanting): "I am poured out like water, and all my bones are out of joint: My heart also in the midst of my body is like unto melting wax! . . ."

(Once more the people pile themselves on the bench. But the temperature is now not many degrees above freezing point, and the wind is blowing more cuttingly. The people wriggle their wind-nipped faces into the heap like sucking pigs struggling for their mother's teats. One's interludes of sleep shrink to a few seconds, and one's dreams grow more monstrous, troubling, and undreamlike. There are times when the nine people are talking almost normally, times when they can even laugh at their situation, and times when they press themselves together in a kind of frenzy, with deep groans of pain. Mr. Tallboys suddenly becomes exhausted and his monologue degenerates into a stream of nonsense. He drops his vast bulk on top of the others, almost suffocating them. The heap rolls apart. Some remain on the bench, some slide to the ground and collapse against the parapet or against the others' knees. The policeman enters the Square and orders those on the ground to their feet. They get up, and collapse again the moment he is gone. There is no sound from the ten people save of snores that are partly groans. Their heads nod like those of jointed porcelain Chinamen as they fall asleep and re-awake as rhythmically as the ticking of a clock. Three strikes somewhere. A voice yells like a trumpet from the eastern end of the Square: "Boys! Up you get! The noospapers is come!")

Charlie (starting from his sleep): "The perishing papers! C'm on, Ginger! Run like Hell!"

(They run, or shamble, as fast as they can to the corner of the Square, where three youths are distributing surplus posters given away in charity by the morning newspapers. Charlie and Ginger come back with a thick wad of posters. The five largest men now jam themselves together on the bench, Deafie and the four women sitting across their knees; then, with infinite difficulty (as it has to be done from the inside), they wrap themselves in a monstrous cocoon of paper, several sheets thick, tucking the loose ends into their necks or breasts or between their shoulders and the back of the bench. Finally nothing is uncovered save their heads and the lower part of their legs. For their heads they fashion hoods of paper. The paper constantly comes loose and lets in cold shafts of wind, but it is now possible to sleep for as much as five minutes consecutively. At this time —between three and five in the morning—it is customary with the police not to disturb the Square sleepers. A measure of warmth steals through everyone and extends even to their feet. There is some furtive fondling of the women under cover of the paper. Dorothy is too far gone to care.

By a quarter-past four the paper is all crumpled and torn to nothing, and it is far too cold to remain sitting down. The people get up, swear, find their legs somewhat rested, and begin to slouch to and fro in couples, frequently halting from mere lassitude. Every belly is now contorted with hunger. Ginger's tin of condensed milk is torn open and the contents devoured, everyone dipping their fingers into it and licking them. Those who have no money at all leave the Square for the Green Park, where they will be undisturbed till seven. Those who can command even a halfpenny make for Wilkins's café not far from the Charing Cross Road. It is known that the café will not open till five o'clock; nevertheless, a crowd is waiting outside the door by twenty to five.)

Mrs. McElligot: "Got your halfpenny, dearie? Dey won't let more'n four of us in on one cup o' tea, de stingy ole gets!"

Mr. Tallboys (singing): "The roseate hu-ues of early da-awn—"

Ginger: "God, that bit of sleep we 'ad under the newspapers done me some good. (Singing) But I'm dan-cing with tears—in my eyes——"

Charlie: "Oh, boys, boys! Look through that perishing window, will you? Look at the 'eat steaming down the window pane! Look at the tea-urns jest on the boil, and them great piles of 'ot toast and 'am sandwiches, and them there sausages sizzling in the pan! Don't it make your belly turn perishing summersaults to see 'em?"

Dorothy: "I've got a penny. I can't get a cup of tea for that, can I?"

Snouter: "—— lot of sausages we'll get this morning with fourpence between us. 'Alf a cup of tea and a —— doughnut more likely. There's a breakfus' for you!"

Mrs. McElligot: "You don't need buy a cup o' tea all to yourself. I got a halfpenny an' so's Daddy, an' we'll put'm to your penny an' have a cup between de t're of us. He's got sores on his lip, but Hell! who cares? Drink near de handle an' dere's no harm done."

(A quarter to five strikes.)

Mrs. Bendigo: "I'd bet a dollar my ole man's got a bit of 'addock to 'is breakfast. I 'ope it bloody chokes 'im."

Ginger (singing): "But I'm dan-cing with tears—in my eyes——"

Mr. Tallboys (singing): "Early in the morning my song shall rise to Thee!"

Mrs. McElligot: "You gets a bit o' kip in dis place, dat's one comfort. Dey lets you sleep wid your head on de table till seven o'clock. It's a bloody godsend to us Square Tobies."

Charlie (slavering like a dog): "Sausages! Perishing sausages! Welsh rabbit! 'Ot dripping toast! And a rump steak two inches thick with chips and a pint of Ole Burton! Oh, perishing Jesus!" (He bounds forward, pushes his way through the crowd and rattles the handle of the glass door. The whole crowd of people, about forty strong, surge forward and attempt to storm the door, which is stoutly held within by Mr. Wilkins, the proprietor of the café. He menaces them through the glass. Some press their breasts and faces against the window as though warming themselves. With a whoop and a rush Florry and four other girls,

comparatively fresh from having spent part of the night in bed,
debouch from a neighboring alley, accompanied by a gang of
youths in blue suits. They hurl themselves upon the rear of the
crowd with such momentum that the door is almost broken.
Mr. Wilkins pulls it furiously open and shoves the leaders back.
A fume of sausages, kippers, coffee, and hot bread streams into
the outer cold.)

Youths' voices from the rear: "Why can't he —— open before five?
We're starving for our —— tea! Ram the —— door in!" etc., etc.

Mr. Wilkins: "Get out! Get out, the lot of you! Or by God not one
of you comes in this morning!"

Girls' voices from the rear: "Mis-ter Wil-kins! Mis-ter Wil-kins! *Be*
a sport and let us in! I'll give y'a kiss all free for nothing. *Be*
a sport now!" etc., etc.

Mr. Wilkins: "Get on out of it! We don't open before five, and you
know it." (Slams the door.)

Mrs. McElligot: "Oh, holy Jesus, if dis ain't de longest ten minutes
o' de whole bloody night! Well, I'll give me poor ole legs a rest,
anyway." (Squats on her heels coal-miner fashion. Many others
do the same.)

Ginger: " 'Oo's got a 'alfpenny? I'm ripe to go fifty-fifty on a doughnut."

Youths' voices (imitating military music, then singing):

> " '——!' was all the band could play;
> " '——! ——!' And the same to you!"

Dorothy (to Mrs. McElligot): "Look at us all! Just look at us! What
clothes! What faces!"

Mrs. Bendigo: "You're no Greta Garbo yourself, if you don't mind
my mentioning it."

Mrs. Wayne: "Well, now, the time *do* seem to pass slowly when
you're waiting for a nice cup of tea, don't it now?"

Mr. Tallboys (chanting): "For our soul is brought low, even unto
the dust: our belly cleaveth unto the ground!"

Charlie: "Kippers! Perishing piles of 'em! I can smell 'em through
the perishing glass."

Ginger (singing):

> "But I'm dan-cing with tears—in my eyes—
> Cos the girl—in my arms—isn't you-o-ou!"

(Much time passes. Five strikes. Intolerable ages seem to pass.
Then the door is suddenly wrenched open and the people stam-

pede in to fight for the corner seats. Almost swooning in the
hot air, they fling themselves down and sprawl across the tables,
drinking in the heat and the smell of food through all their
pores.)

Mr. Wilkins: "Now then, all! You know the rules, I s'pose. No
hokey-pokey this morning! Sleep till seven if you like, but if
I see any man asleep after that, out he goes on his neck. Get busy
with that tea, girls!"

A deafening chorus of yells: "Two teas 'ere! Large tea and a doughnut between us four! Kippers! Mis-ter Wil-kins! 'Ow much them
sausages? Two slices! Mis-ter Wil-kins! Got any fag papers?
Kipp-*ers!*" etc., etc.

Mr. Wilkins: "Shut up, shut up! Stop that hollering or I don't serve
any of you."

Mrs. McElligot: "D'you feel de blood runnin' back into your toes,
dearie?"

Mrs. Wayne: "He do speak rough to you, don't he? Not what I'd
call a reely gentlemanly kind of man."

Snouter: "This is —— Starvation Corner, this is. Cripes! Couldn't I
do a couple of them sausages!"

The tarts (in chorus): "Kippers 'ere! 'Urry up with them kippers!
Mis-ter Wil-kins! Kippers all round! *And* a doughnut!"

Charlie: "Not 'alf! Got to fill up on the smell of 'em this morning.
Sooner be 'ere than on the perishing Square, *all* the same."

Ginger: " 'Ere, Deafie! You've 'ad your 'alf! Gimme that bleeding
cup."

Mr. Tallboys (chanting): "Then was our mouth filled with laughter,
and our tongue with joy! . . ."

Mrs. McElligot: "Begod I'm half asleep already. It's de heat o' de
room as does it."

Mr. Wilkins: "Stop that singing there! You know the rules."

The tarts (in chorus): "Kipp-*ers!*"

Snouter: "—— doughnuts! Cold prog! It turns my belly sick."

Daddy: "Even the tea they give you ain't no more than water with
a bit of dust in it." (Belches.)

Charlie: "Bes' thing—'ave a bit of shut-eye and forget about it. Dream
about perishing cut off the joint and two veg. Less get our 'eads
on the table and pack up comfortable."

Mrs. McElligot: "Lean up agen me shoulder, dearie. I've got more
flesh on me bones'n what you have."

Ginger: "I'd give a tanner for a bleeding fag, if I 'ad a bleeding
tanner."

Charlie: "Pack up. Get your 'ead agenst mine, Snouter. That's right. Jesus, won't I perishing sleep!"

(A dish of smoking kippers is borne past to the tarts' table.)

Snouter (drowsily): "More —— kippers. Wonder 'ow many times she's bin on 'er back to pay for that lot."

Mrs. McElligot (half asleep): " 'Twas a pity, 'twas a real pity, when Michael went off on his jack an' left me wid de bloody baby an' all. . . ."

Mrs. Bendigo (furiously, following the dish of kippers with accusing finger): "Look at that, girls! Look at that! *Kippers!* Don't it make you bloody wild? *We* don't get kippers for breakfast, do we, girls? Bloody tarts swallering down kippers as fast as they can turn 'em out of the pan, and us 'ere with a cup of tea between four of us and lucky to get that! Kippers!"

Mr. Tallboys (stage curate-wise): "The wages of sin is kippers."

Ginger: "Don't breathe in my face, Deafie. I can't bleeding stand it."

Charlie (in his sleep): "Charles-Wisdom-drunk-and-incapable-drunk?- yes-six-shillings-move-on-*next!*"

Dorothy (on Mrs. McElligot's bosom): "Oh, joy, joy!"

(They are asleep.)

1935

△

From "Keep the Aspidistra Flying"

▽

Chapter One

The clock struck half-past two. In the little office at the back of Mr. McKechnie's bookshop, Gordon—Gordon Comstock, last member of the Comstock family, aged twenty-nine and rather moth-eaten already—lounged across the table, pushing a fourpenny packet of Player's Weights open and shut with his thumb.

The dingdong of another, remoter clock—from the Prince of Wales, the other side of the street—rippled the stagnant air. Gordon made an effort, sat upright, and stowed his packet of cigarettes away in his inside pocket. He was perishing for a smoke. However, there were only four cigarettes left. Today was Wednesday and he had no money coming to him till Friday. It would be too bloody to be without tobacco tonight as well as all tomorrow.

Bored in advance by tomorrow's tobaccoless hours, he got up and moved toward the door—a small frail figure, with delicate bones and fretful movements. His coat was out at elbow in the right sleeve and its middle button was missing; his ready-made flannel trousers were stained and shapeless. Even from above you could see that his shoes needed resoling.

The money clinked in his trouser pocket as he got up. He knew the precise sum that was there. Fivepence halfpenny—twopence halfpenny and a Joey. He paused, took out the miserable little threepenny-bit and looked at it. Beastly, useless thing! And bloody fool to have taken it! It had happened yesterday, when he was buying cigarettes. "Don't mind a threepenny-bit, do you, sir?" the little bitch of a shopgirl had chirped. And of course he had let her give it him. "Oh no, not at all!" he had said—fool, bloody fool!

His heart sickened to think that he had only fivepence halfpenny in the world, threepence of which couldn't even be spent. Because how can you buy anything with a threepenny-bit? It isn't a coin, it's the answer to a riddle. You look such a fool when you take it out of your pocket, unless it's in among a whole handful of other coins. "How much?" you say. "Threepence," the shopgirl says. And then you feel all round your pocket and fish out that absurd little thing, all by itself, sticking on the end of your finger like a tiddlywink. The shopgirl sniffs. She spots immediately that it's your last threepence in the world. You see her glance quickly at it—she's wondering whether there's a piece of Christmas pudding still sticking to it. And you stalk out with your nose in the air, and can't ever go to that shop again. No! We won't spend our Joey. Twopence halfpenny left—twopence halfpenny to last till Friday.

This was the lonely after-dinner hour, when few or no customers were to be expected. He was alone with seven thousand books. The small dark room, smelling of dust and decayed paper, that gave on the office, was filled to the brim with books, mostly aged and unsaleable. On the top shelves near the ceiling the quarto volumes of extinct encyclopedias slumbered on their sides in piles like the tiered coffins in common graves. Gordon pushed aside the blue, dust-sodden curtains that served as a doorway to the next room. This, better lighted than the other, contained the lending library. It was one of those "twopenny no-deposit" libraries beloved of book-pinchers. No books in it except novels, of course. And *what* novels! But that too was a matter of course.

Eight hundred strong, the novels lined the room on three sides ceiling high, row upon row of gaudy oblong backs, as though the walls had been built of many-colored bricks laid upright. They were arranged alphabetically. Arlen, Burroughs, Deeping, Dell, Frankau, Galsworthy, Gibbs, Priestley, Sapper, Walpole. Gordon eyed them with inert hatred. At this moment he hated all books, and novels most of all. Horrible to think of all that soggy, half-baked trash massed together in one place. Pudding, suet pudding. Eight hundred slabs of pudding, walling him in—a vault of puddingstone. The thought was oppressive. He moved on through the open doorway into the front part of the shop. In doing so, he smoothed his hair. It was an habitual movement. After all, there might be girls outside the glass door. Gordon was not impressive to look at. He was just five feet seven inches high, and because his hair was usually too long he gave the impression that his head was a little too big for his body. He was never quite unconscious of his small stature. When he knew that anyone was looking at him he carried himself very upright, throwing a chest, with a you-be-damned air which occasionally deceived simple people.

However, there was nobody outside. The front room, unlike the rest of the shop, was smart and expensive-looking, and it contained about two thousand books, exclusive of those in the window. On the right there was a glass showcase in which children's books were kept. Gordon averted his eyes from a beastly Rackhamesque dust-jacket; elvish children tripping Wendily through a bluebell glade. He gazed out through the glass door. A foul day, and the wind rising. The sky was leaden, the cobbles of the street were slimy. It was St. Andrew's day, the thirtieth of November. McKechnie's stood on a corner, on a sort of shapeless square where four streets converged. To the left, just within sight from the door, stood a great elm tree, leafless now, its multitudinous twigs making sepia-colored lace against the sky. Opposite, next to the Prince of Wales, were tall hoardings covered with ads for patent foods and patent medicines. A gallery of monstrous doll-faces—pink vacuous faces, full of goofy optimism. Q.T. Sauce, Truweet Breakfast Crisps ("Kiddies clamour for their Breakfast Crisps"), Kangaroo Burgundy, Vitamalt Chocolate, Bovex. Of them all, the Bovex one oppressed Gordon the most. A spectacled rat-faced clerk, with patent-leather hair, sitting at a café table grinning over a white mug of Bovex. "Corner Table enjoys his meal with Bovex," the legend ran.

Gordon shortened the focus of his eyes. From the dust-dulled pane the reflection of his own face looked back at him. Not a good face. Not thirty yet, but moth-eaten already. Very pale, with bitter, ineradicable lines. What people call a "good" forehead— high, that is—but a small pointed chin, so that the face as a whole was pear-shaped rather than oval. Hair mouse-colored and unkempt, mouth unamiable, eyes hazel inclining to green. He lengthened the focus of his eyes again. He hated mirrors nowadays. Outside, all was bleak and wintry. A tram, like a raucous swan of steel, glided groaning over the cobbles, and in its wake the wind swept a debris of trampled leaves. The twigs of the elm tree were swirling, strain- ing eastward. The poster that advertised Q.T. Sauce was torn at the edge; a ribbon of paper fluttered fitfully like a tiny pennant. In the side street too, to the right, the naked poplars that lined the pavement bowed sharply as the wind caught them. A nasty raw wind. There was a threatening note in it as it swept over; the first growl of winter's anger. Two lines of a poem struggled for birth in Gordon's mind:

Sharply the something wind—for instance, threatening wind? No, better, menacing wind. The menacing wind blows over—no, sweeps over, say.

The something poplars—yielding poplars? No, better, bending poplars. Assonance between bending and menacing? No matter. The bending poplars, newly bare. Good.

> Sharply the menacing wind sweeps over
> The bending poplars, newly bare.

Good. "Bare" is a sod to rhyme; however, there's always "air," which every poet since Chaucer has been struggling to find rhymes for. But the impulse died away in Gordon's mind. He turned the money over in his pocket. Twopence halfpenny and a Joey—two- pence halfpenny. His mind was sticky with boredom. He couldn't cope with rhymes and adjectives. You can't, with only twopence halfpenny in your pocket.

His eyes refocused themselves upon the posters opposite. He had his private reasons for hating them. Mechanically he reread their slogans. "Kangaroo Burgundy—the wine for Britons." "Asthma was choking her!" "Q.T. Sauce Keeps Hubby Smiling." "Hike all day on a Slab of Vitamalt!" "Curve Cut—the Smoke for Outdoor Men." "Kiddies clamour for their Breakfast Crisps." "Corner Table enjoys his meal with Bovex."

Ha! A customer—potential, at any rate. Gordon stiffened himself. Standing by the door, you could get an oblique view out of the front window without being seen yourself. He looked the potential customer over.

A decentish middle-aged man, black suit, bowler hat, umbrella and dispatch-case—provincial solicitor or town clerk—peeking at the window with large pale-colored eyes. He wore a guilty look. Gordon followed the direction of his eyes. Ah! So that was it! He had nosed out those D. H. Lawrence first editions in the far corner. Pining for a bit of smut, of course. He had heard of Lady Chatterley afar off. A bad face he had, Gordon thought. Pale, heavy, downy, with bad contours. Welsh, by the look of him—Nonconformist, anyway. He had the regular Dissenting pouches round the corners of his mouth. At home, president of the local Purity League or Seaside Vigilance Committee (rubber-soled slippers and electric torch, spotting kissing couples along the beach parade), and now up in town on the razzle. Gordon wished he would come in. Sell him a copy of *Women in Love*. How it would disappoint him!

But no! The Welsh solicitor had funked it. He tucked his umbrella under his arm and moved off with righteously turned backside. But doubtless tonight, when darkness hid his blushes, he'd slink into one of the rubber shops and buy *High Jinks in a Parisian Convent*, by Sadie Blackeyes.

Gordon turned away from the door and back to the book-shelves. In the shelves to your left as you came out of the library the new and nearly new books were kept—a patch of bright color that was meant to catch the eye of anyone glancing through the glass door. Their sleek unspotted backs seemed to yearn at you from the shelves. "Buy me, buy me!" they seemed to be saying. Novels fresh from the press—still unravished brides, pining for the paperknife to deflower them—and review copies, like youthful widows, blooming still though virgin no longer, and here and there, in sets of half a dozen, those pathetic spinster-things, "remainders," still guarding hopefully their long preserv'd virginity. Gordon turned his eyes away from the "remainders." They called up evil memories. The single wretched little book that he himself had published, two years ago, had sold exactly a hundred and fifty-three copies and then been "remaindered"; and even as a "remainder" it hadn't sold. He passed the new books by and paused in front of the shelves which ran at right angles to them and which contained more second-hand books.

Over to the right were shelves of poetry. Those in front of him were prose, a miscellaneous lot. Upward and downward they were graded, from clean and expensive at eye level to cheap and dingy at top and bottom. In all bookshops there goes on a savage Dar-

winian struggle in which the works of living men gravitate to eye
level and the works of dead men go up or down—down to Gehenna
or up to the throne, but always away from any position where
they will be noticed. Down in the bottom shelves the "classics,"
the extinct monsters of the Victorian age, were quietly rotting.
Scott, Carlyle, Meredith, Ruskin, Pater, Stevenson—you could hardly
read the names upon their broad dowdy backs. In the top shelves,
almost out of sight, slept the pudgy biographies of dukes. Below
those, saleable still and therefore placed within reach, was "religious" literature—all sects and all creeds, lumped indiscriminately
together. *The World Beyond*, by the author of *Spirit Hands Have
Touched Me*. Dean Farrar's *Life of Christ*. *Jesus the First Rotar-
ian*. Father Hilaire Chestnut's book of R.C. propaganda. Religion
always sells provided it is soppy enough. Below, exactly at eye
level, was the contemporary stuff. Priestley's latest. Dinky little
books of reprinted "middles." Cheer-up "humor" from Herbert
and Knox and Milne. Some highbrow stuff as well. A novel or
two by Hemingway and Virginia Woolf. Smart pseudo-Strachey
predigested biographies. Snooty, refined books on safe painters and
safe poets by those moneyed young beasts who glide so gracefully
from Eton to Cambridge and from Cambridge to the literary reviews.

Dull-eyed, he gazed at the wall of books. He hated the whole
lot of them, old and new, highbrow and lowbrow, snooty and
chirpy. The mere sight of them brought home to him his own
sterility. For here was he, supposedly a "writer," and he couldn't
even "write"! It wasn't merely a question of not getting published;
it was that he produced nothing, or next to nothing. And all that
tripe cluttering the shelves—well, at any rate it existed; it was an
achievement of sorts. Even the Dells and Deepings do at least turn
out their yearly acre of print. But it was the snooty "cultured"
kind of books that he hated the worst. Books of criticism and
belles lettres. The kind of thing that those moneyed young beasts
from Cambridge write almost in their sleep—and that Gordon himself might have written if he had had a little more money. Money
and culture! In a country like England you can no more be cultured without money than you can join the Cavalry Club. With
the same instinct that makes a child waggle a loose tooth, he took
out a snooty-looking volume—*Some Aspects of the Italian Baroque*
—opened it, read a paragraph and shoved it back with mingled
loathing and envy. That devastating omniscience! That noxious,
horn-spectacled refinement! And the money that such refinement
means! For after all, what is there behind it, except money? Money

for the right kind of education, money for influential friends, money for leisure and peace of mind, money for trips to Italy. Money writes books, money sells them. Give me not righteousness, O Lord, give me money, only money.

He jingled the coins in his pocket. He was nearly thirty and had accomplished nothing; only his miserable book of poems that had fallen flatter than any pancake. And ever since, for two whole years, he had been struggling in the labyrinth of a dreadful book that never got any further, and which, as he knew in his moments of clarity, never would get any further. It was the lack of money, simply the lack of money, that robbed him of the power to "write." He clung to that as to an article of faith. Money, money, all is money! Could you write even a penny novelette without money to put heart in you? Invention, energy, wit, style, charm—they've all got to be paid for in hard cash.

Nevertheless, as he looked along the shelves he felt himself a little comforted. So many of the books were faded and unreadable. After all, we're all in the same boat. Memento mori. For you and for me and for the snooty young men from Cambridge, the same oblivion waits—though doubtless it'll wait rather longer for those snooty young men from Cambridge. He looked at the time-dulled "classics" near his feet. Dead, all dead. Carlyle and Ruskin and Meredith and Stevenson—all are dead, God rot them. He glanced over their faded titles. *Collected Letters of Robert Louis Stevenson.* Ha, ha! That's good. *Collected Letters of Robert Louis Stevenson!* Its top edge was black with dust. Dust thou art, to dust returnest. Gordon kicked Stevenson's buckram backside. Art there, old false-penny? You're cold meat, if ever Scotchman was.

Ping! The shop bell. Gordon turned round. Two customers, for the library.

A dejected, round-shouldered, lower-class woman, looking like a draggled duck nosing among garbage, seeped in, fumbling with a rush basket. In her wake hopped a plump little sparrow of a woman, red-cheeked, middle-middle class, carrying under her arm a copy of *The Forsyte Saga*—title outward, so that passers-by could spot her for a highbrow.

Gordon had taken off his sour expression. He greeted them with the homey, family-doctor geniality reserved for library-subscribers.

"Good afternoon, Mrs. Weaver. Good afternoon, Mrs. Penn. What terrible weather!"

"Shocking!" said Mrs. Penn.

He stood aside to let them pass. Mrs. Weaver upset her rush basket and spilled on to the floor a much-thumbed copy of Ethel

M. Dell's *Silver Wedding.* Mrs. Penn's bright bird-eye lighted upon it. Behind Mrs. Weaver's back she smiled up at Gordon, archly, as highbrow to highbrow. Dell! The lowness of it! The books these lower classes read! Understandingly, he smiled back. They passed into the library, highbrow to highbrow smiling.

Mrs. Penn laid *The Forsyte Saga* on the table and turned her sparrow-bosom upon Gordon. She was always very affable to Gordon. She addressed him as Mister Comstock, shopwalker though he was, and held literary conversations with him. There was the freemasonry of highbrows between them.

"I hope you enjoyed *The Forsyte Saga,* Mrs. Penn?"

"What a perfectly *marvelous* achievement that book is, Mr. Comstock! Do you know that that makes the fourth time I've read it? An epic, a real epic!"

Mrs. Weaver nosed among the books, too dim-witted to grasp that they were in alphabetical order.

"I don't know what to 'ave this week, that I don't," she mumbled through untidy lips. "My daughter she keeps on at me to 'ave a try at Deeping. She's great on Deeping, my daughter is. But my son-in-law, now, 'e's more for Burroughs. I don't know, I'm sure."

A spasm passed over Mrs. Penn's face at the mention of Burroughs. She turned her back markedly on Mrs. Weaver.

"What I feel, Mr. Comstock, is that there's something so *big* about Galsworthy. He's so broad, so universal, and yet at the same time so thoroughly English in spirit, so *human.* His books are real *human* documents."

"And Priestley, too," said Gordon. "I think Priestley's such an awfully fine writer, don't you?"

"Oh, he is! So big, so broad, so human! And so essentially English!"

Mrs. Weaver pursed her lips. Behind them were three isolated yellow teeth.

"I think p'raps I can't do better'n 'ave another Dell," she said. "You 'ave got some more Dells, 'aven't you? I *do* enjoy a good read of Dell, I must say. I says to my daughter, I says, 'You can keep your Deepings and your Burroughses. Give me Dell,' I says."

Ding Dong Dell! Dukes and dogwhips! Mrs. Penn's eye signaled highbrow irony. Gordon returned her signal. Keep in with Mrs. Penn! A good, steady customer.

"Oh, certainly, Mrs. Weaver. We've got a whole shelf by Ethel M. Dell. Would you like *The Desire of His Life?* Or perhaps you've read that. Then what about *The Altar of Honour?*"

"l wonder whether you have Hugh Walpole's latest book?" said Mrs. Penn. "I feel in the mood this week for something epic, something *big*. Now Walpole, you know, I consider a really *great* writer, I put him second only to Galsworthy. There's something so *big* about him. And yet he's so human with it."

"And so essentially English," said Gordon.

"Oh, of course! So essentially English!"

"I b'lieve I'll jest 'ave *The Way of an Eagle* over again," said Mrs. Weaver finally. "You don't never seem to get tired of *The Way of an Eagle*, do you, now?"

"It's certainly astonishingly popular," said Gordon, diplomatically, his eye on Mrs. Penn.

"Oh, as*ton*ishingly!" echoed Mrs. Penn, ironically, her eye on Gordon.

He took their twopences and sent them happy away, Mrs. Penn with Walpole's *Rogue Herries* and Mrs. Weaver with *The Way of an Eagle*.

Soon he had wandered back to the other room and toward the shelves of poetry. A melancholy fascination, those shelves had for him. His own wretched book was there—skied, of course, high up among the unsaleable. *Mice*, by Gordon Comstock; a sneaky little foolscap octavo, price three and sixpence but now reduced to a bob. Of the thirteen B.F.s who had reviewed it (and *The Times Lit. Supp.* had declared that it showed "exceptional promise") not one had seen the none too subtle joke of that title. And in the two years he had been at McKechnie's bookshop, not a single customer, not a single one, had ever taken *Mice* out of its shelf.

There were fifteen or twenty shelves of poetry. Gordon regarded them sourly. Dud stuff, for the most part. A little above eye level, already on their way to heaven and oblivion, were the poets of yesteryear, the stars of his earlier youth. Yeats, Davies, Housman, Thomas, De la Mare, Hardy. Dead stars. Below them, exactly at eye level, were the squibs of the passing minute. Eliot, Pound, Auden, Campbell, Day Lewis, Spender. Very damp squibs, that lot. Dead stars above, damp squibs below. Shall we ever again get a writer worth reading? But Lawrence was all right, and Joyce even better before he went off his coconut. And if we did get a writer worth reading, should we know him when we saw him, so choked as we are with trash?

Ping! Shop bell. Gordon turned. Another customer.

A youth of twenty, cherry-lipped, with gilded hair, tripped Nancifully in. Moneyed, obviously. He had the golden aura of money. He hadn't been in the shop before. Gordon assumed the gentlemanly servile mien reserved for new customers. He repeated the usual formula:

"Good afternoon. Can I do anything for you? Are you looking for any particular book?"

"Oh, no, not weally." An R-less Nancy voice. "May I just *bwowse?* I simply couldn't wesist your fwont window. I have such a tew-wible weakness for bookshops! So I just floated in—tee-hee!"

Float out again, then, Nancy. Gordon smiled a cultured smile, as booklover to booklover.

"Oh, please do. We like people to look round. Are you interested in poetry, by any chance?"

"Oh, of course! I *adore* poetwy!"

Of course! Mangy little snob. There was a subartistic look about his clothes. Gordon slid a "slim" red volume from the poetry shelves.

"These are just out. They might interest you, perhaps. They're translations—something rather out of the common. Translations from the Bulgarian."

Very subtle, that. Now leave him to himself. That's the proper way with customers. Don't hustle them; let them browse for twenty minutes or so; then they get ashamed and buy something. Gordon moved to the door, discreetly, keeping out of Nancy's way; yet casually, one hand in his pocket, with the insouciant air proper to a gentleman.

Outside, the slimy street looked gray and drear. From somewhere round the corner came the clatter of hooves, a cold hollow sound. Caught by the wind, the dark columns of smoke from the chimneys veered over and rolled flatly down the sloping roofs. Ah!

> Sharply the menacing wind sweeps over
> The bending poplars, newly bare,
> And the dark ribbons of the chimneys
> Veer downward *tumty tumty (something like "murky")* air.

Good. But the impulse faded. His eye fell again upon the ad-posters across the street.

He almost wanted to laugh at them, they were so feeble, so dead-alive, so unappetizing. As though anybody could be tempted by *those!* Like succubi with pimply backsides. But they depressed him all the same. The money-stink, everywhere the money-stink. He stole a glance at the Nancy, who had drifted away from the poetry shelves and taken out a large expensive book on the Russian ballet. He was holding it delicately between his pink non-prehensile paws, as a squirrel holds a nut, studying the photographs. Gordon knew his type. The moneyed "artistic" young man. Not an artist himself, exactly, but a hanger-on of the arts; frequenter of studios, retailer of scandal. A nice-looking boy, though, for all his Nancitude. The skin at the back of his neck was as silky smooth as the inside of a shell. You can't have a skin like that under five hundred a year. A sort of charm he had, a glamour, like all moneyed people. Money and charm; who shall separate them?

Gordon thought of Ravelston, his charming, rich friend, editor of *Antichrist,* of whom he was extravagantly fond, and whom he did not see so often as once in a fortnight; and of Rosemary, his girl, who loved him—adored him, so she said—and who, all the same, had never slept with him. Money, once again; all is money. All human relationships must be purchased with money. If you have no money, men won't care for you, women won't love you; won't, that is, care for you or love you the last little bit that matters. And how right they are, after all! For, moneyless, you are unlovable. Though I speak with the tongues of men and of angels. But then, if I haven't money, I *don't* speak with the tongues of men and of angels.

He looked again at the ad-posters. He really hated them this time. That Vitamalt one, for instance! "Hike all day on a Slab of Vitamalt!" A youthful couple, boy and girl, in clean-minded hiking kit, their hair picturesquely tousled by the wind, climbing a stile against a Sussex landscape. That girl's face! The awful bright tomboy cheeriness of it! The kind of girl who goes in for Plenty of Clean Fun. Windswept. Tight khaki shorts but that doesn't mean you can pinch her backside. And next to them—Corner Table. "Corner Table enjoys his meal with Bovex." Gordon examined the thing with the intimacy of hatred. The idiotic grinning face, like the face of a self-satisfied rat, the slick black hair, the silly spectacles. Corner Table, heir of the ages; victor of Waterloo, Corner Table, Modern man as his masters want him to be. A docile little porker, sitting in the money-sty, drinking Bovex.

Faces passed, wind-yellowed. A tram boomed across the square, and the clock over the Prince of Wales struck three. A couple of old creatures, a tramp or beggar and his wife, in long greasy overcoats that reached almost to the ground, were shuffling toward the shop. Book-pinchers, by the look of them. Better keep an eye on the boxes outside. The old man halted on the curb a few yards away while his wife came to the door. She pushed it open and looked up at Gordon, between gray strings of hair, with a sort of hopeful malevolence.

"Ju buy books?" she demanded hoarsely.

"Sometimes. It depends what books they are."

"I gossome *lovely* books 'ere."

She came in, shutting the door with a clang. The Nancy glanced over his shoulder distastefully and moved a step or two away, into the corner. The old woman had produced a greasy little sack from under her overcoat. She moved confidentially nearer to Gordon. She smelt of very, very old breadcrusts.

"Will you 'ave 'em?" she said, clasping the neck of the sack. "Only 'alf a crown the lot."

"What are they? Let me see them, please."

"*Lovely* books, they are," she breathed, bending over to open the sack and emitting a sudden very powerful whiff of breadcrusts.

"'Ere!" she said, and thrust an armful of filthy-looking books almost into Gordon's face.

They were an 1884 edition of Charlotte M. Yonge's novels, and had the appearance of having been slept on for many years. Gordon stepped back, suddenly revolted.

"We can't possibly buy those," he said shortly.

"Can't buy 'em? *Why* can't yer buy 'em?"

"Because they're no use to us. We can't sell that kind of thing."

"Wotcher make me take 'em out o' me bag for, then?" demanded the old woman ferociously.

Gordon made a detour round her, to avoid the smell, and held the door open, silently. No use arguing. You had people of this type coming into the shop all day long. The old woman made off, mumbling, with malevolence in the hump of her shoulders, and joined her husband. He paused on the curb to cough, so fruitily that you could hear him through the door. A clot of phlegm, like a little white tongue, came slowly out between his lips and was ejected into the gutter. Then the two old creatures shuffled away beetle-like in the long greasy overcoats that hid everything except their feet.

Gordon watched them go. They were just by-products. The throw-outs of the money-god. All over London, by tens of thousands, draggled old beasts of that description; creeping like unclean beetles to the grave.

He gazed out at the graceless street. At this moment it seemed to him that in a street like this, in a town like this, every life that is lived must be meaningless and intolerable. The sense of disintegration, of decay, that is endemic in our time, was strong upon him. Somehow it was mixed up with the ad-posters opposite. He looked now with more seeing eyes at those grinning yard-wide faces. After all, there was more there than mere silliness, greed and vulgarity. Corner Table grins at you, seemingly optimistic, with a flash of false teeth. But what is behind the grin? Desolation, emptiness, prophecies of doom. For can you not see, if you know how to look, that behind that slick self-satisfaction, that tittering fat-bellied triviality, there is nothing but a frightful emptiness, a secret despair? The great death wish of the modern world. Suicide pacts. Heads stuck in gas ovens in lonely maisonettes. French letters and Amen Pills. And the reverberations of future wars. Enemy aeroplanes flying over London; the deep threatening hum of the propellers, the shattering thunder of the bombs. It is all written in Corner Table's face.

More customers coming. Gordon stood back, gentlemanly servile.

The doorbell clanged. Two upper-middle-class ladies sailed noisily in. One pink and fruity, thirty-fivish, with voluptuous bosom burgeoning from her coat of squirrel-skin, emitting a super-feminine scent of Parma violets; the other middle-aged, tough, and curried—India, presumably. Close behind them a dark, grubby, shy young man slipped through the doorway as apologetically as a cat. He was one of the shop's best customers—a flitting, solitary creature who was almost too shy to speak and who by some strange manipulation kept himself always a day away from a shave.

Gordon repeated his formula:

"Good afternoon. Can I do anything for you? Are you looking for any particular book?"

Fruity-face overwhelmed him with a smile, but curry-face decided to treat the question as an impertinence. Ignoring Gordon, she drew fruity-face across to the shelves next the new books where the dog-books and cat-books were kept. The two of them immediately began taking books out of the shelves and talking loudly. Curry-face had the voice of a drill sergeant. She was no doubt a colonel's wife, or widow. The Nancy, still deep in the big book on the Russian ballet, edged delicately away. His face said that he would leave the shop if his privacy were disturbed again. The shy young man had already found his way to the poetry shelves. The two ladies were fairly frequent visitors to the shop. They always wanted to see books about cats and dogs, but never actually bought anything. There were two whole shelves of dog books and cat books. "Ladies' Corner," old McKechnie called it.

Another customer arrived, for the library. An ugly girl of twenty, hatless, in a white overall, with a sallow, blithering, honest face and powerful spectacles that distorted her eyes. She was assistant at a chemist's shop. Gordon put on his homey library manner.

She smiled at him, and with a gait as clumsy as a bear's followed him into the library.

"What kind of book would you like this time, Miss Weeks?"

"Well—" She clutched the front of her overall. Her distorted black-treacle eyes beamed trustfully into his. "Well, what I'd *really* like's a good hot-stuff love story. You know—something *modern.*"

"Something modern? Something by Barbara Bedworthy, for instance? Have you read *Almost a Virgin?*"

"Oh no, not her. She's too Deep. I can't bear Deep books. But I want something—well, *you* know—*modern.* Sex problems and divorce and all that. *You* know."

"Modern, but not Deep," said Gordon, as lowbrow to lowbrow.

He ranged among the hot-stuff modern love stories. There were not less than three hundred of them in the library. From the front room came the voices of the two upper-middle-class ladies, the one fruity, the other curried, disputing about dogs. They had taken out one of the dog books and were examining the photographs. Fruity-voice enthused over the photograph of a Peke, the ickle angel pet, wiv his gweat big Soulful eyes and his ickle black nosie —oh, so ducky-duck! But curry-voice—yes, undoubtedly a colonel's widow—said Pekes were soppy. Give her dogs with guts—dogs that would fight, she said; she hated these soppy lapdogs, she said. "You have no Soul, Bedelia, no Soul," said fruity-voice plaintively. The doorbell pinged again. Gordon handed the chemist's girl *Seven Scarlet Nights* and booked it on her ticket. She took a shabby leather purse out of her overall pocket and paid him twopence.

He went back to the front room. The Nancy had put his book back in the wrong shelf and vanished. A lean, straight-nosed, brisk woman, with sensible clothes and gold-rimmed pince-nez—school-marm possibly, feminist certainly—came in and demanded Mrs. Wharton-Beverley's history of the suffrage movement. With secret joy Gordon told her that they hadn't got it. She stabbed his male incompetence with gimlet eyes and went out again. The thin young man stood apologetically in the corner, his face buried in D. H. Lawrence's *Collected Poems*, like some long-legged bird with its head buried under its wing.

Gordon waited by the door. Outside, a shabby-genteel old man with a strawberry nose and a khaki muffler round his throat was picking over the books in the sixpenny box. The two upper-middle-class ladies suddenly departed, leaving a litter of open books on the table. Fruity-face cast reluctant backward glances at the dog-books, but curry-face drew her away, resolute not to buy anything.

Gordon held the door open. The two ladies sailed noisily out, ignoring him.

He watched their fur-coated upper-middle-class backs go down the street. The old strawberry-nosed man was talking to himself as he pawed over the books. A bit wrong in the head, presumably. He would pinch something if he wasn't watched. The wind blew colder, drying the slime of the street. Time to light up presently. Caught by a swirl of air, the torn strip of paper on the Q.T. Sauce advertisement fluttered sharply, like a piece of washing on the line. Ah!

> Sharply the menacing wind sweeps over
> The bending poplars, newly bare,
> And the dark ribbons of the chimneys
> Veer downward; flicked by whips of air,
> Torn posters flutter.

Not bad, not bad at all. But he had no wish to go on—could not go on, indeed. He fingered the money in his pocket, not chinking it, lest the shy young man should hear. Twopence halfpenny. No tobacco all tomorrow. His bones ached.

A light sprang up in the Prince of Wales. They would be swabbing out the bar. The old strawberry-nosed man was reading an Edgar Wallace out of the twopenny box. A tram boomed in the distance. In the room upstairs Mr. McKechnie, who seldom came down to the shop, drowsed by the gas fire, white-haired and white-bearded, with snuffbox handy, over his calf-bound folio of Middleton's *Travels in the Levant*.

The thin young man suddenly realized that he was alone and looked up guiltily. He was an habitué of bookshops, yet never stayed longer than ten minutes in any one shop. A passionate hunger for books, and the fear of being a nuisance, were constantly at war in him. After ten minutes in any shop he would grow uneasy, feel himself de trop, and take to flight, having bought something out of sheer nervousness. Without speaking he held out the copy of Lawrence's poems and awkwardly extracted three florins from his pocket. In handing them to Gordon he dropped one. Both dived for it simultaneously; their heads bumped against one another. The young man stood back, blushing sallowly.

"I'll wrap it up for you," said Gordon.

But the shy young man shook his head—he stammered so badly that he never spoke when it was avoidable. He clutched his book to him and slipped out with the air of having committed some disgraceful action.

Gordon was alone. He wandered back to the door. The straw-berry-nosed man glanced over his shoulder, caught Gordon's eye and moved off, foiled. He had been on the point of slipping Edgar Wallace into his pocket. The clock over the Prince of Wales struck a quarter past three.

Ding Dong! A quarter-past three. Light up at half-past. Four and three-quarter hours till closing time. Five and a quarter hours till supper. Twopence halfpenny in pocket. No tobacco tomorrow.

Suddenly a ravishing, irresistible desire to smoke came over Gordon. He had made up his mind not to smoke this afternoon. He had only four cigarettes left. They must be saved for tonight, when he intended to "write"; for he could no more "write" without tobacco than without air. Nevertheless, he had got to have a smoke. He took out his packet of Player's Weights and extracted one of the dwarfish cigarettes. It was sheer stupid indulgence; it meant half an hour off tonight's "writing" time. But there was no re-sisting it. With a sort of shameful joy he sucked the soothing smoke into his lungs.

The reflection of his own face looked back at him from the grayish pane. Gordon Comstock, author of *Mice; en l'an tren-tièsme de son eage,* and moth-eaten already. Only twenty-six teeth left. However, Villon at the same age was poxed, on his own showing. Let's be thankful for small mercies.

He watched the ribbon of torn paper whirling, fluttering on the Q.T. Sauce advertisement. Our civilization is dying. It *must* be dying. But it isn't going to die in its bed. Presently the aeroplanes are coming. Zoom—whizz—crash! The whole western world going up in a roar of high explosives.

He looked at the darkening street, at the grayish reflection of his face in the pane, at the shabby figures shuffling past. Almost involuntarily he repeated:

> *C'est l'Ennui—l'œil chargé d'un pleur involontaire,*
> *Il rêve d'échafauds en fumant son houka!*

Money, money! Corner Table! The humming of the aeroplanes and the crash of the bombs.

Gordon squinted up at the leaden sky. Those aeroplanes are coming. In imagination he saw them coming now; squadron after squadron, innumerable, darkening the sky like clouds of gnats. With his tongue not quite against his teeth he made a buzzing, blue-bottle-on-the-window-pane sound to represent the humming of the aeroplanes. It was a sound which, at that moment, he ardently desired to hear.

Chapter Eleven

Spring, spring! Bytuene Mershe ant Averil, when spray biginneth to spring! When shaws be sheene and swards full fayre, and leaves both large and longe! When the hounds of spring are on winter's traces, in the spring time, the only pretty ring time, when the birds do sing, hey-ding-a-ding ding, cuckoo, jug-jug, pu-wee, ta-witta-woo! And so on and so on and so on. See almost any poet between the Bronze Age and 1850.

But how absurd that even now, in the era of central heating and tinned peaches, a thousand so-called poets are still writing in the same strain! For what difference does spring or winter or any other time of year make to the average civilized person nowadays? In a town like London the most striking seasonal change, apart from the mere change of temperature, is in the things you see lying about on the pavement. In late winter it is mainly cabbage leaves. In July you tread on cherry stones, in November on burnt-out fireworks. Toward Christmas the orange peel grows thicker. It was a different matter in the Middle Ages. There was some sense in writing poems about spring when spring meant fresh meat and green vegetables after months of frowsting in some windowless hut on a diet of salt fish and mouldy bread.

If it was spring Gordon failed to notice it. March in Lambeth did not remind you of Persephone. The days grew longer, there were vile dusty winds and sometimes in the sky patches of harsh blue appeared. Probably there were a few sooty buds on the trees if you cared to look for them. The aspidistra, it turned out, had not died after all; the withered leaves had dropped off it, but it was putting forth a couple of dull green shoots near its base.

Gordon had been three months at the library now. The stupid slovenly routine did not irk him. The library had swelled to a thousand "assorted titles" and was bringing Mr. Cheeseman a pound a week clear profit, so Mr. Cheeseman was happy after his fashion. He was, nevertheless, nurturing a secret grudge against Gordon. Gordon had been sold to him, so to speak, as a drunkard. He had expected Gordon to get drunk and miss a day's work at least once, thus giving a sufficient pretext for docking his wages; but Gordon had failed to get drunk. Queerly enough, he had no impulse to drink nowadays. He would have gone without beer even if he could have afforded it. Tea seemed a better poison. All his desires and discontents had dwindled. He was better off on thirty bob a week than he had been previously on two pounds. The thirty bob covered, without too much stretching, his rent, cigarettes, a washing bill of about a shilling a week, a little fuel, and his meals, which consisted almost entirely of bacon, bread-and-marg and tea, and cost about two bob a day, gas included. Sometimes he even had sixpence over for a seat at a cheap but lousy picture-house near the Westminster Bridge Road. He still carried the grimy manuscript of *London Pleasures* to and fro in his pocket, but it was from mere force of habit; he had dropped even the pretense of working. All his evenings were spent in the same way. There in the remote frowzy attic, by the fire if there was any coal left, in bed if there wasn't, with teapot and cigarettes handy, read-ing, always reading. He read nothing nowadays except twopenny weekly papers. *Tit Bits, Answers, Peg's Paper, The Gem, The Mag-net, Home Notes, The Girl's Own Paper*—they were all the same. He used to get them a dozen at a time from the shop. Mr. Cheese-man had great dusty stacks of them, left over from his uncle's day and used for wrapping paper. Some of them were as much as twenty years old.

He had not seen Rosemary for weeks past. She had written a number of times and then, for some reason, abruptly stopped writ-ing. Ravelston had written once, asking him to contribute an ar-ticle on twopenny libraries to *Antichrist*. Julia had sent a desolate little letter, giving family news. Aunt Angela had had bad colds all the winter, and Uncle Walter was complaining of bladder trou-ble. Gordon did not answer any of their letters. He would have forgotten their existence if he could. They and their affection were only an encumbrance. He would not be free, free to sink down into the ultimate mud, till he had cut his links with all of them, even with Rosemary.

One afternoon he was choosing a book for a tow-headed factory girl, when someone he only saw out of the corner of his eye came into the library and hesitated just inside the door.

"What kind of book did you want?" he asked the factory girl.

"Oo—jest a kind of a romance, please."

Gordon selected a romance. As he turned, his heart bounded violently. The person who had just come in was Rosemary. She did not make any sign, but stood waiting, pale and worried-look-ing, with something ominous in her appearance.

He sat down to enter the book on the girl's ticket, but his hands had begun trembling so that he could hardly do it. He pressed the rubber stamp in the wrong place. The girl trailed out, peep-ing into the book as she went. Rosemary was watching Gordon's face. It was a long time since she had seen him by daylight, and she was struck by the change in him. He was shabby to the point of raggedness, his face had grown much thinner and had the dingy, grayish pallor of people who live on bread and margarine. He looked much older—thirty-five at the least. But Rosemary herself did not look quite as usual. She had lost her gay trim bearing, and her clothes had the appearance of having been thrown on in a hurry. It was obvious that there was something wrong.

He shut the door after the factory girl. "I wasn't expecting you," he began.

"I had to come. I got away from the studio at lunch time. I told them I was ill."

"You don't look well. Here, you'd better sit down."

There was only one chair in the library. He brought it out from behind the desk and was moving toward her, rather vaguely, to offer some kind of caress. Rosemary did not sit down, but laid her small hand, from which she had removed the glove, on the top rung of the chair-back. By the pressure of her fingers he could see how agitated she was.

"Gordon, I've a most awful thing to tell you. It's happened after all."

"What's happened?"

"I'm going to have a baby."

"A baby? Oh, Christ!"

He stopped short. For a moment he felt as though someone had struck him a violent blow under the ribs. He asked the usual fatuous question:

"Are you sure?"

"Absolutely. It's been weeks now. If you knew the time I've had! I kept hoping and hoping—I took some pills—oh, it was too beastly!"

"A baby! Oh, God, what fools we were! As though we couldn't have foreseen it!"

"I know. I suppose it was my fault. I——"

"Damn! Here comes somebody."

The doorbell ping'd. A fat, freckled woman with an ugly underlip came in at a rolling gait and demanded "Something with a murder in it." Rosemary had sat down and was twisting her glove round and round her fingers. The fat woman was exacting. Each book that Gordon offered her she refused on the ground that she had "had it already" or that it "looked dry." The deadly news that Rosemary had brought had unnerved Gordon. His heart pounding, his entrails constricted, he had to pull out book after book and assure the fat woman that this was the very book she was looking for. At last, after nearly ten minutes, he managed to fob her off with something which she said grudgingly she "didn't think she'd had before."

He turned back to Rosemary. "Well, what the devil are we going to do about it?" he said as soon as the door had shut.

"I don't see what I can do. If I have this baby I'll lose my job, of course. But it isn't only that I'm worrying about. It's my people finding out. My mother—oh, dear! It simply doesn't bear thinking of."

"Ah, your people! I hadn't thought of them. One's people! What a cursed incubus they are!"

"*My* people are all right. They've always been good to me. But it's different with a thing like this."

He took a pace or two up and down. Though the news had scared him he had not really grasped it as yet. The thought of a baby, his baby, growing in her womb had awoken in him no emotion except dismay. He did not think of the baby as a living creature; it was a disaster pure and simple. And already he saw where it was going to lead.

"We shall have to get married, I suppose," he said flatly.

"Well, shall we? That's what I came here to ask you."

"But I suppose you want me to marry you, don't you?"

"Not unless *you* want to. I'm not going to tie you down. I know it's against your ideas to marry. You must decide for yourself."

"But we've no alternative—if you're really going to have this baby."

"Not necessarily. That's what you've got to decide. Because after all there *is* another way."

"What way?"

"Oh, *you* know. A girl at the studio gave me an address. A friend of hers had it done for only five pounds."

That pulled him up. For the first time he grasped, with the only kind of knowledge that matters, what they were really talking about. The words "a baby" took on a new significance. They did not mean any longer a mere abstract disaster, they meant a bud of flesh, a bit of himself, down there in her belly, alive and growing. His eyes met hers. They had a strange moment of sympathy such as they had never had before. For a moment he did feel that in some mysterious way they were one flesh. Though they were feet apart he felt as though they were joined together—as though some invisible living cord stretched from her entrails to his. He knew then that it was a dreadful thing they were contemplating—a blasphemy, if that word had any meaning. Yet if it had been put otherwise he might not have recoiled from it. It was the squalid detail of the five pounds that brought it home.

"No fear!" he said. "Whatever happens we're not going to do *that*. It's disgusting."

"I know it is. But I can't have the baby without being married."

"No! If that's the alternative I'll marry you. I'd sooner cut my right hand off than do a thing like that."

Ping! went the doorbell. Two ugly louts in cheap bright blue suits, and a girl with a fit of the giggles, came in. One of the youths asked with a sort of sheepish boldness for "something with a kick in it—something smutty." Silently, Gordon indicated the shelves where the "sex" books were kept. There were hundreds of them in the library. They had titles like *Secrets of Paris* and *The Man She Trusted;* on their tattered yellow jackets were pictures of half-naked girls lying on divans with men in dinner jackets standing over them. The stories inside, however, were painfully harmless. The two youths and the girl ranged among them, sniggering over the pictures on their covers, the girl letting out little squeals and pretending to be shocked. They disgusted Gordon so much that he turned his back on them till they had chosen their books.

When they had gone he came back to Rosemary's chair. He stood behind her, took hold of her small firm shoulders, then slid a hand inside her coat and felt the warmth of her breast. He liked the strong springy feeling of her body; he liked to think that down there, a guarded seed, his baby was growing. She put a hand up and caressed the hand that was on her breast, but did not speak. She was waiting for him to decide.

"If I marry you I shall have to turn respectable," he said musingly.

"Could you?" she said with a touch of her old manner.

"I mean I shall have to get a proper job—go back to the New Albion. I suppose they'd take me back."

He felt her grow very still and knew that she had been waiting for this. Yet she was determined to play fair. She was not going to bully him or cajole him.

"I never said I wanted you to do that. I want you to marry me —yes, because of the baby. But it doesn't follow you've got to keep me."

"There's no sense in marrying if I can't keep you. Suppose I married you when I was like I am at present—no money and no proper job? What would you do then?"

"I don't know. I'd go on working as long as I could. And afterwards, when the baby got too obvious—well, I suppose I'd have to go home to father and mother."

"That would be jolly for you, wouldn't it? But you were so anxious for me to go back to the New Albion before. You haven't changed your mind?"

"I've thought things over. I know you'd hate to be tied to a regular job. I don't blame you. You've got your own life to live."

He thought it over a little while longer. "It comes down to this. Either I marry you and go back to the New Albion, or you go to one of those filthy doctors and get yourself messed about for five pounds."

At that she twisted herself out of his grasp and stood up facing him. His blunt words had upset her. They had made the issue clearer and uglier than before.

"Oh, why did you say that?"

"Well, those *are* the alternatives."

"I'd never thought of it like that. I came here meaning to be fair. And now it sounds as if I was trying to bully you into it—trying to play on your feelings by threatening to get rid of the baby. A sort of beastly blackmail."

"I didn't mean that. I was only stating facts."

Her face was full of lines, the black brows drawn together. But she had sworn to herself that she would not make a scene. He could guess what this meant to her. He had never met her people, but he could imagine them. He had some notion of what it might mean to go back to a country town with an illegitimate baby; or, what was almost as bad, with a husband who couldn't keep you. But she was going to play fair. No blackmail! She drew a sharp inward breath, taking a decision.

"All right, then, I'm not going to hold *that* over your head. It's too mean. Marry me or don't marry me, just as you like. But I'll have the baby, anyway."

"You'd do that? Really?"

"Yes, I think so."

He took her in his arms. Her coat had come open, her body was warm against him. He thought he would be a thousand kinds of fool if he let her go. Yet the alternative was impossible, and he did not see it any less clearly because he held her in his arms.

"Of course, you'd like me to go back to the New Albion," he said.

"No, I wouldn't. Not if you don't want to."

"Yes, you would. After all, it's natural. You want to see me earning a decent income again. In a *good* job, with four pounds a week and an aspidistra in the window. Wouldn't you, now? Own up."

"All right, then—yes, I would. But it's only something I'd *like* to see happening; I'm not going to *make* you do it. I'd just hate you to do it if you didn't really want to. I want you to feel free."

"Really and truly free?"

"Yes."

"You know what that means? Supposing I decided to leave you and the baby in the lurch?"

"Well—if you really wanted to. You're free—quite free."

After a little while she went away. Later in the evening or tomorrow he would let her know what he decided. Of course it was not absolutely certain that the New Albion would give him a job even if he asked them; but presumably they would, considering what Mr. Erskine had said. Gordon tried to think and could not. There seemed to be more customers than usual this afternoon. It maddened him to have to bounce out of his chair every time he had sat down and deal with some fresh influx of fools demanding crime stories and sex stories and romances. Suddenly, about six o'clock, he turned out the lights, locked up the library and went out. He had got to be alone. The library was not due to shut for two hours yet. God knew what Mr. Cheeseman would say when he found out. He might even give Gordon the sack. Gordon did not care.

He turned westward, up Lambeth Cut. It was a dull sort of evening, not cold. There was muck underfoot, white lights, and hawkers screaming. He had got to think this thing out, and he could think better walking. But it was so hard, so hard! Back to the New Albion, or leave Rosemary in the lurch; there was no other alternative. It was no use thinking, for instance, that he might find some "good" job which would offend his sense of decency a bit less. There aren't so many "good" jobs waiting for moth-eaten people of thirty. The New Albion was the only chance he had or ever would have.

At the corner, on the Westminster Bridge Road, he paused a moment. There were some posters opposite, livid in the lamplight. A monstrous one, ten feet high at least, advertised Bovex. The Bovex people had dropped Corner Table and got on to a new tack. They were running a series of four-line poems—Bovex Ballads, they were called. There was a picture of a horribly eupeptic family, with grinning ham-pink faces, sitting at breakfast; underneath, in blatant lettering:

Why should you be thin and white?
And have that washed-out feeling?

Just take hot Bovex every night—
Invigorating—healing!

ordon gazed at the thing. He drank in its puling silliness. God,
hat trash! "Invigorating—healing!" The weak incompetence of
It hadn't even the vigorous badness of the slogans that really
ick. Just soppy, lifeless drivel. It would have been almost pathetic
its feebleness if one hadn't reflected that all over London and all
er every town in England that poster was plastered, rotting the
inds of men. He looked up and down the graceless street. Yes, war
coming soon. You can't doubt it when you see the Bovex ads.
he electric drills in our streets presage the rattle of the machine
ins. Only a little while before the aeroplanes come. Zoom—bang!
few tons of T.N.T. to send our civilization back to hell where it
:longs.

He crossed the road and walked on, southward. A curious thought
id struck him. He did not any longer want that war to happen.
was the first time in months—years, perhaps—that he had thought
it and not wanted it.

If he went back to the New Albion, in a month's time he might
: writing Bovex Ballads himself. To go back to *that!* Any "good"
b was bad enough; but to be mixed up in *that!* Christ! Of course
: oughtn't to go back. It was just a question of having the guts to
and firm. But what about Rosemary? He thought of the kind of
fe she would live at home, in her parents' house, with a baby and
) money; and of the news running through that monstrous family
iat Rosemary had married some awful rotter who couldn't even
:ep her. She would have the whole lot of them nagging at her to-
:ther. Besides, there was the baby to think about. The money-god
so cunning. If he only baited his traps with yachts and race-horses,
rts and champagne, how easy it would be to dodge him. It is when
: gets at you through your sense of decency that he finds you help-
ss.

The Bovex Ballad jingled in Gordon's head. He ought to stand
rm. He had made war on money—he ought to stick it out. After
1, hitherto he *had* stuck it out, after a fashion. He looked back over
is life. No use deceiving himself. It had been a dreadful life—lonely,
jualid, futile. He had lived thirty years and achieved nothing ex-
:pt misery. But that was what he had chosen. It was what he *wanted,*
ren now. He wanted to sink down, down into the muck where
oney does not rule. But this baby business had upset everything.
was a pretty banal predicament, after all. Private vices, public
rtues—the dilemma is as old as the world.

He looked up and saw that he was passing a public library. /
thought struck him. That baby. What did it mean, anyway, having
baby? What was it that was actually happening to Rosemary at thi
moment? He had only vague and general ideas of what pregnanc
meant. No doubt they would have books in there that would tel
him about it. He went in. The lending library was on the left. I
was there that you had to ask for works of reference.

The woman at the desk was a university graduate, young, colo
less, spectacled and intensely disagreeable. She had a fixed suspicio
that no one—at least, no male person—ever consulted works of refer
ence except in search of pornography. As soon as you approache
she pierced you through and through with a flash of her pince-ne
and let you know that your dirty secret was no secret from *he*
After all, all works of reference are pornographical, except perhap
Whitaker's *Almanac*. You can put even the Oxford Dictionary t
evil purposes by looking up words like —— and ——.

Gordon knew her type at a glance, but he was too preoccupie
to care.

"Have you any books on gynecology?" he said.

"Any *what?*" demanded the young woman with a pince-nez flas
of unmistakable triumph. As usual! Another male in search of dirt

"Well, any books on midwifery? About babies being born, an
so forth."

"We don't issue books of that description to the general public,
said the young woman frostily.

"I'm sorry—there's a point I particularly want to look up."

"Are you a medical student?"

"No."

"Then I don't *quite* see what you want with books on midwifery.

Curse the woman! Gordon thought. At another time he woul
have been afraid of her; at present, however, she merely bored him

"If you want to know, my wife's going to have a baby. We neithe
of us know much about it. I want to see whether I can find out an
thing useful."

The young woman did not believe him. He looked too shabb
and worn, she decided, to be a newly married man. However, it wa
her job to lend out books, and she seldom actually refused them
except to children. You always got your book in the end, after yo
had been made to feel yourself a dirty swine. With an aseptic ai
she led Gordon to a small table in the middle of the library an
presented him with two fat books in brown covers. Thereafter sh
left him alone, but kept an eye on him from whatever part of th
library she happened to be in. He could feel her pince-nez probin

the back of his neck at long range, trying to decide from his demeanor whether he was really searching for information or merely picking out the dirty bits.

He opened one of the books and searched inexpertly through it. There were acres of close-printed text full of Latin words. That was no use. He wanted something simple—pictures, for choice. How long had this thing been going on? Six weeks—nine weeks, perhaps. Ah! This must be it.

He came on a print of a nine weeks' fetus. It gave him a shock to see it, for he had not expected it to look in the least like that. It was a deformed, gnomelike thing, a sort of clumsy caricature of a human being, with a huge domed head as big as the rest of its body. In the middle of the great blank expanse of head there was a tiny button of an ear. The thing was in profile; its boneless arm was bent, and one hand, crude as a seal's flipper, covered its face—fortunately, perhaps. Below were little skinny legs, twisted like a monkey's, with the toes turned in. It was a monstrous thing, and yet strangely human. It surprised him that they should begin looking human so soon. He had pictured something much more rudimentary; a mere blob with a nucleus, like a bubble of frog-spawn. But it must be very tiny, of course. He looked at the dimensions marked below. Length 30 millimeters. About the size of a large gooseberry.

But perhaps it had not been going on quite so long as that. He turned back a page or two and found a print of a six weeks' fetus. A really dreadful thing this time—a thing he could hardly even bear to look at. Strange that our beginnings and endings are so ugly —the unborn as ugly as the dead. This thing looked as if it were dead already. Its huge head, as though too heavy to hold upright, was bent over at right angles at the place where its neck ought to have been. There was nothing you could call a face, only a wrinkle representing the eye—or was it the mouth? It had no human semblance this time; it was more like a dead puppy dog. Its short thick arms were very doglike, the hands being mere stumpy paws. 15.5 millimeters long—no bigger than a hazelnut.

He pored for a long time over the two pictures. Their ugliness made them more credible and therefore more moving. His baby had seemed real to him from the moment when Rosemary spoke of abortion; but it had been a reality without visual shape—something that happened in the dark and was only important after it had happened. But here was the actual process taking place. Here was the poor ugly thing, no bigger than a gooseberry, that he had created by his heedless act. Its future, its continued existence perhaps, depended on him. Besides, it was a bit of himself—it *was* himself. Dare one dodge such a responsibility as that?

But what about the alternative? He got up, handed over his books to the disagreeable young woman, and went out; then, on an impulse, turned back and went into the other part of the library, where the periodicals were kept. The usual crowd of mangy-looking people were dozing over the papers. There was one table set apart for women's papers. He picked up one of them at random and bore it off to another table.

It was an American paper of the more domestic kind, mainly adverts with a few stories lurking apologetically among them. And *what* adverts! Quickly he flicked over the shiny pages. Lingerie, jewelry, cosmetics, fur coats, silk stockings flicked up and down like the figures in a child's peepshow. Page after page, advert after advert. Lipsticks, undies, tinned food, patent medicines, slimming cures, face creams. A sort of cross section of the money-world. A panorama of ignorance, greed, vulgarity, snobbishness, whoredom and disease.

And *that* was the world they wanted him to re-enter! *That* was the business in which he had a chance of Making Good. He flicked over the pages more slowly. Flick, flick. Adorable—until she smiles. The food that is shot out of a gun. Do you let foot-fag affect your personality? Get back that peach-bloom on a Beautyrest Mattress. Only a *penetrating* face cream will reach that under-surface dirt. Pink toothbrush is *her* trouble. How to alkalize your stomach almost instantly. Roughage for husky kids. Are you one of the four out of five? The world-famed Culturequick Scrapbook. Only a drummer and yet he quoted Dante.

Christ, what muck!

But of course it was an American paper. The Americans always go one better on any kind of beastliness, whether it is ice-cream soda, racketeering, or theosophy. He went over to the women's table and picked up another paper. An English one this time. Perhaps the ads in an English paper wouldn't be quite so bad—a little less brutally offensive?

He opened the paper. Flick, flick. Britons never shall be slaves!

Flick, flick. Get that waistline back to normal! She *said,* "Thanks awfully for the lift," but she *thought,* "Poor boy, why doesn't somebody tell him?" How a woman of thirty-two stole her young man from a girl of twenty. Prompt relief for feeble kidneys. Silkyseam— the smooth-sliding bathroom tissue. Asthma was choking her! Are *you* ashamed of your undies? Kiddies clamour for their Breakfast Crisps. Now I'm school-girl complexion all over. Hike all day on a slab of Vitamalt!

To be mixed up in *that!* To be in it and of it—part and parcel of it! God, God, God!

Presently he went out. The dreadful thing was that he knew already what he was going to do. His mind was made up—had been made up for a long time past. When this problem appeared it had brought its solution with it; all his hesitation had been a kind of make-believe. He felt as though some force outside himself were pushing him. There was a telephone booth near by. Rosemary's hostel was on the phone—she ought to be at home by now. He went into the booth, feeling in his pocket. Yes, exactly two pennies. He dropped them into the slot, swung the dial.

A refined, adenoidal feminine voice answered him: "Who's thyah, please?"

He pressed Button A. So the die was cast.

"Is Miss Waterlow in?"

"Who's *thyah,* please?"

"Say it's Mr. Comstock. She'll know. Is she at home?"

"Ay'll see. Hold the lane, please."

A pause.

"Hullo! Is that you, Gordon?"

"Hullo! Hullo! Is that you, Rosemary? I just wanted to tell you. I've thought it over—I've made up my mind."

"Oh!" There was another pause. With difficulty mastering her voice, she added: "Well, what did you decide?"

"It's all right. I'll take the job—if they'll give it me, that is."

"Oh, Gordon, I'm so glad! You're not angry with me? You don't feel I've sort of bullied you into it?"

"No, it's all right. It's the only thing I can do. I've thought everything out. I'll go up to the office and see them tomorrow."

"I *am* so glad!"

"Of course, I'm assuming they'll give me the job. But I suppose they will, after what old Erskine said."

"I'm sure they will. But, Gordon, there's just one thing. You will go there nicely dressed, won't you? It might make a lot of difference."

"I know. I'll have to get my best suit out of pawn. Ravelston will lend me the money."

"Never mind about Ravelston. I'll lend you the money. I've got four pounds put away. I'll run out and wire it you before the post office shuts. I expect you'll want some new shoes and a new tie as well. And, oh, Gordon!"

"What?"

"Wear a hat when you go up to the office, won't you? It looks better, wearing a hat."

"A hat! God! I haven't worn a hat for two years. Must I?"

"Well—it does look more business-like, doesn't it?"

"Oh, all right. A bowler hat, even, if you think I ought."

"I think a soft hat would do. But get your hair cut, won't you, there's a dear?"

"Yes, don't you worry. I'll be a smart young business man. Well groomed, and all that."

"Thanks ever so, Gordon dear. I must run out and wire that money. Good night and good luck."

"Good night."

He came out of the booth. So that was that. He had torn it now, right enough.

He walked rapidly away. What had he done? Chucked up the sponge! Broken all his oaths! His long and lonely war had ended in ignominious defeat. Circumcise ye your foreskins, saith the Lord. He was coming back to the fold, repentant. He seemed to be walking faster than usual. There was a peculiar sensation, an actual physical sensation, in his heart, in his limbs, all over him. What was it? Shame, misery, despair? Rage at being back in the clutch of money? Boredom when he thought of the deadly future? He dragged the sensation forth, faced it, examined it. It was relief.

Yes, that was the truth of it. Now that the thing was done he felt nothing but relief; relief that now at last he had finished with dirt, cold, hunger, and loneliness and could get back to decent, fully human life. His resolutions, now that he had broken them, seemed nothing but a frightful weight that he had cast off. Moreover, he was aware that he was only fulfilling his destiny. In some corner of his mind he had always known that this would happen. He thought of the day when he had given them notice at the New Albion; and Mr. Erskine's kind, red, beefish face, gently counseling him not to chuck up a "good" job for nothing. How bitterly he had sworn, then, that he was done with "good" jobs forever! Yet it was foredoomed that he should come back, and he had known it even then. And it was not merely because of Rosemary and the baby that he had done it. That was the obvious cause, the precipitating cause, but even without it the end would have been the same; if there had been no baby to think about, something else would have forced his hand. For it was what, in his secret heart, he had desired.

After all he did not lack vitality, and that moneyless existence to which he had condemned himself had thrust him ruthlessly out of the stream of life. He looked back over the last two frightful years. He had blasphemed against money, rebelled against money, tried to live like an anchorite outside the money-world; and it had brought him not only misery, but also a frightful emptiness, an inescapable sense of futility. To abjure money is to abjure life. Be not righteous over much; why shouldst thou die before thy time? Now he was back in the money-world, or soon would be. Tomorrow he would go up to the New Albion, in his best suit and overcoat (he must remember to get his overcoat out of pawn at the same time as his suit), in Homburg hat of the correct gutter-crawling pattern, neatly shaved and with his hair cut short. He would be as though born anew. The sluttish poet of today would be hardly recognizable in the natty young business man of tomorrow. They would take him back, right enough; he had the talent they needed. He would buckle to work, sell his soul and hold down his job.

And what about the future? Perhaps it would turn out that these last two years had not left much mark upon him. They were merely a gap, a small setback in his career. Quite quickly, now that he had taken the first step, he would develop the cynical, blinkered business mentality. He would forget his fine disgusts, cease to rage against the tyranny of money—cease to be aware of it, even—cease to squirm at the ads for Bovex and Breakfast Crisps. He would sell his soul so utterly that he would forget it had ever been his. He would get married, settle down, prosper moderately, push a pram, have a villa and a radio and an aspidistra. He would be a law-abiding little cit like any other law-abiding little cit—a soldier in the strap-hanging army. Probably it was better so.

He slowed his pace a little. He was thirty and there was gray in his hair, yet he had a queer feeling that he had only just grown up. It occurred to him that he was merely repeating the destiny of every human being. Everyone rebels against the money-code, and everyone sooner or later surrenders. He had kept up his rebellion a little longer than most, that was all. And he had made such a wretched failure of it! He wondered whether every anchorite in his dismal cell pines secretly to be back in the world of men. Perhaps there were a few who did not. Somebody or other had said that the modern world is only habitable by saints and scoundrels. He, Gordon, wasn't a saint. Better, then, to be an unpretending scoundrel along with the others. It was what he had secretly pined for; now that he had acknowledged his desire and surrendered to it, he was at peace.

He was making roughly in the direction of home. He looked up at the houses he was passing. It was a street he did not know. Oldish houses, mean-looking and rather dark, let off in flatlets and single rooms for the most part. Railed areas, smoke-grimed bricks, whited steps, dingy lace curtains. "Apartments" cards in half the windows, aspidistras in nearly all. A typical lower-middle-class street. But not, on the whole, the kind of street that he wanted to see blown to hell by bombs.

He wondered about the people in houses like those. They would be, for example, small clerks, shop assistants, commercial travelers, insurance touts, tram-conductors. Did *they* know that they were only puppets dancing when money pulled the strings? You bet they didn't. And if they did, what would they care? They were too busy being born, being married, begetting, working, dying. It mightn't be a bad thing, if you could manage it, to feel yourself one of them, one of the ruck of men. Our civilization is founded on greed and fear, but in the lives of common men the greed and fear are mysteriously transmuted into something nobler. The lower-middle-class people in there, behind their lace curtains, with their children and their scraps of furniture and their aspidistras—they lived by the money code, sure enough, and yet they contrived to keep their decency. The money code as they interpreted it was not merely cynical and hoggish. They had their standards, their inviolable points of honor. They "kept themselves respectable"—kept the aspidistra flying. Besides, they were *alive*. They were bound up in the bundle of life. They begot children, which is what the saints and the soul-savers never by any chance do.

The aspidistra is the tree of life, he thought suddenly. . . .

1936

Δ

From "The Road to Wigan Pier"

∇

PART I

Chapter Two

Our civilization, *pace* Chesterton, *is* founded on coal, more completely than one realizes until one stops to think about it. The machines that keep us alive, and the machines that make the machines, are all directly or indirectly dependent upon coal. In the metabolism of the Western world the coal miner is second in importance only to the man who ploughs the soil. He is a sort of grimy caryatid upon whose shoulders nearly everything that is *not* grimy is supported.

For this reason the actual process by which coal is extracted is well worth watching, if you get the chance and are willing to take the trouble.

When you go down a coal mine it is important to try and get to the coal face when the "fillers" are at work. This is not easy, because when the mine is working visitors are a nuisance and are not encouraged, but if you go at any other time, it is possible to come away with a totally wrong impression. On a Sunday, for instance, a mine seems almost peaceful. The time to go there is when the machines are roaring and the air is black with coal dust, and when you can actually see what the miners have to do. At those times the place is like hell, or at any rate like my own mental picture of hell. Most of the things one imagines in hell are there—heat, noise, confusion, darkness, foul air, and, above all, unbearably cramped space. Everything except the fire, for there is no fire down there except the feeble beams of Davy lamps and electric torches which scarcely penetrate the clouds of coal dust.

When you have finally got there—and getting there is a job in itself: I will explain that in a moment—you crawl through the last line of pit props and see opposite you a shiny black wall three or four feet high. This is the coal face. Overhead is the smooth ceiling made by the rock from which the coal has been cut; underneath is the rock again, so that the gallery you are in is only as high as the ledge of coal itself, probably not much more than a yard. The first impression of all, overmastering everything else for a while, is the frightful, deafening din from the conveyor belt which carries the coal away. You cannot see very far, because the fog of coal dust throws back the beam of your lamp, but you can see on either side of you the line of half-naked kneeling men, one to every four or five yards, driving their shovels under the fallen coal and flinging it swiftly over their left shoulders. They are feeding it on to the conveyor belt, a moving rubber belt a couple of feet wide which runs a yard or two behind them. Down this belt a glittering river of coal races constantly. In a big mine it is carrying away several tons of coal every minute. It bears it off to some place in the main roads where it is shot into tubs holding half a ton, and thence dragged to the cages and hoisted to the outer air.

It is impossible to watch the "fillers" at work without feeling a pang of envy for their toughness. It is a dreadful job that they do, an almost superhuman job by the standards of an ordinary person. For they are not only shifting monstrous quantities of coal, they are also doing it in a position that doubles or trebles the work. They have got to remain kneeling all the while—they could hardly rise from their knees without hitting the ceiling—and you can easily see by trying it what a tremendous effort this means. Shoveling is comparatively easy when you are standing up, because you can use your knee and thigh to drive the shovel along; kneeling down, the whole of the strain is thrown upon your arm and belly muscles. And the other conditions do not exactly make things easier. There is the heat —it varies, but in some mines it is suffocating—and the coal dust that stuffs up your throat and nostrils and collects along your eyelids, and the unending rattle of the conveyor belt, which in that confined space is rather like the rattle of a machine gun. But the fillers look and work as though they were made of iron. They really do look like iron—hammered iron statues—under the smooth coat of coal dust which clings to them from head to foot. It is only when you see miners down the mine and naked that you realize what splendid men they are. Most of them are small (big men are at a disadvantage in that job) but nearly all of them have the most noble bodies: wide shoulders tapering to slender supple waists, and small pronounced buttocks and sinewy thighs, with not an ounce of waste flesh anywhere. In the hotter mines they wear only a pair of thin drawers, clogs and knee-pads; in the hottest mines of all, only the clogs and knee-pads. You can hardly tell by the look of them whether they are young or old. They may be any age up to sixty or even sixty-five, but when they are black and naked they all look alike. No one could do their work who had not a young man's body, and a figure fit for a guardsman at that; just a few pounds of extra flesh on the waistline, and the constant bending would be impossible. You can never forget that spectacle once you have seen it—the line of bowed, kneeling figures, sooty black all over, driving their huge shovels under the coal with stupendous force and speed. They are on the job for seven and a half hours, theoretically without a break, for there is no time "off." Actually they snatch a quarter of an hour or so at some time during the shift to eat the food they have brought with them, usually a hunk of bread and dripping and a bottle of cold tea. The first time I was watching the "fillers" at work I put my hand upon some dreadful slimy thing among the coal dust. It was a chewed quid of tobacco. Nearly all the miners chew tobacco, which is said to be good against thirst.

Probably you have to go down several coal mines before you can get much grasp of the processes that are going on round you. This is chiefly because the mere effort of getting from place to place makes it difficult to notice anything else. In some ways it is even disappointing, or at least is unlike what you have expected. You get into the cage, which is a steel box about as wide as a telephone box and two or three times as long. It holds ten men, but they pack it like pilchards in a tin, and a tall man cannot stand upright in it. The steel door shuts upon you, and somebody working the winding gear above drops you into the void. You have the usual momentary qualm in your belly and a bursting sensation in the ears, but not much sensation of movement till you get near the bottom, when the cage slows down so abruptly that you could swear it is going upward again. In the middle of the run the cage probably touches sixty miles an hour; in some of the deeper mines it touches even more. When you crawl out at the bottom you are perhaps four hundred yards under ground. That is to say you have a tolerable-sized mountain on top of you; hundreds of yards of solid rock, bones of extinct beasts, subsoil, flints, roots of growing things, green grass and cows grazing on it—all this suspended over your head and held back only by wooden props as thick as the calf of your leg. But because of the speed at which the cage has brought you down, and the complete blackness through which you have traveled, you hardly feel yourself deeper down than you would at the bottom of the Piccadilly tube.

What *is* surprising, on the other hand, is the immense horizontal distances that have to be traveled underground. Before I had been down a mine I had vaguely imagined the miner stepping out of the cage and getting to work on a ledge of coal a few yards away. I had not realized that before he even gets to his work he may have to creep through passages as long as from London Bridge to Oxford Circus. In the beginning, of course, a mine shaft is sunk somewhere near a seam of coal. But as that seam is worked out and fresh seams are followed up, the workings get farther and farther from the pit bottom. If it is a mile from the pit bottom to the coal face, that is probably an average distance; three miles is a fairly normal one; there are even said to be a few mines where it is as much as five miles. But these distances bear no relation to distances above ground. For in all that mile or three miles as it may be, there is hardly anywhere outside the main road, and not many places even there, where a man can stand upright.

You do not notice the effect of this till you have gone a few hundred yards. You start off, stooping slightly, down the dim-lit gallery, eight or ten feet wide and about five high, with the walls built up with slabs of shale, like the stone walls in Derbyshire. Every yard or two there are wooden props holding up the beams and girders; some of the girders have buckled into fantastic curves under which you have to duck. Usually it is bad going underfoot—thick dust or jagged chunks of shale, and in some mines where there is water it is as mucky as a farmyard. Also there is the track for the coal tubs, like a miniature railway track with sleepers a foot or two apart, which is tiresome to walk on. Everything is gray with shale dust; there is a dusty fiery smell which seems to be the same in all mines. You see mysterious machines of which you never learn the purpose, and bundles of tools slung together on wires, and sometimes mice darting away from the beam of the lamps. They are surprisingly common, especially in mines where there are or have been horses. It would be interesting to know how they got there in the first place; possibly by falling down the shaft—for they say a mouse can fall any distance uninjured, owing to its surface area being so large relative to its weight. You press yourself against the wall to make way for lines of tubs jolting slowly toward the shaft, drawn by an endless steel cable operated from the surface. You creep through sacking curtains and thick wooden doors which, when they are opened, let out fierce blasts of air. These doors are an important part of the ventilation system. The exhausted air is sucked out of one shaft by means of fans, and the fresh air enters the other of its own accord. But if left to itself the air will take the shortest way round, leaving the deeper workings unventilated; so all short-cuts have to be partitioned off.

At the start to walk stooping is rather a joke, but it is a joke that soon wears off. I am handicapped by being exceptionally tall, but when the roof falls to four feet or less it is a tough job for anybody except a dwarf or a child. You have not only got to bend double, you have also got to keep your head up all the while so as to see the beams and girders and dodge them when they come. You have, therefore, a constant crick in the neck, but this is nothing to the pain in your knees and thighs. After half a mile it becomes (I am not exaggerating) an unbearable agony. You begin to wonder whether you will ever get to the end—still more, how on earth you are going to get back. Your pace grows slower and slower. You come to a stretch of a couple of hundred yards where it is all exceptionally low and you have to work yourself along in a squatting position. Then suddenly the roof opens out to a mysterious height—scene of an old fall of rock, probably—and for twenty whole yards you can stand upright. The relief is overwhelming. But after this there is another low stretch of a hundred yards and then a succession of beams which you have to crawl under. You go down on all fours; even this is a relief after the squatting business. But when you come to the end of the beams and try to get up again, you find that your knees have temporarily struck work and refuse to lift you. You call a halt, ignominiously, and say that you would like to rest for a minute or two. Your guide (a miner) is sympathetic. He knows that your muscles are not the same as his. "Only another four hundred yards," he says encouragingly; you feel that he might as well say another four hundred miles. But finally you do somehow creep as far as the coal face. You have gone a mile and taken the best part of an hour; a miner would do it in not much more than twenty minutes. Having got there, you have to sprawl in the coal dust and get your strength back for several minutes before you can even watch the work in progress with any kind of intelligence.

Coming back is worse than going, not only because you are already tired out but because the journey back to the shaft is probably slightly uphill. You get through the low places at the speed of a tortoise, and you have no shame now about calling a halt when your knees give way. Even the lamp you are carrying becomes a nuisance and probably when you stumble you drop it; whereupon, if it is a Davy lamp, it goes out. Ducking the beams becomes more and more of an effort, and sometimes you forget to duck. You try walking head down as the miners do, and then you bang your backbone. Even the miners bang their backbones fairly often. This is the reason why in very hot mines, where it is necessary to go about half naked, most of the miners have what they call "buttons down the back"—that is, a permanent scab on each vertebra. When the track is downhill the miners sometimes fit their clogs, which are hollow underneath, on to the trolley rails and slide down. In mines where the "traveling" is very bad all the miners carry sticks about two and a half feet long, hollowed out below the handle. In normal places you keep your hand on top of the stick and in the low places you slide your hand down into the hollow. These sticks are a great help, and the wooden crash-helmets—a comparatively recent invention—are a godsend. They look like a French or Italian steel helmet, but they are made of some kind of pith and very light, and so strong that you can take a violent blow on the head without feeling it. When finally you get back to the surface you have been perhaps three hours underground and traveled two miles, and you are more exhausted than you would be by a twenty-five-mile walk above ground. For a week afterward your thighs are so stiff that coming downstairs is quite a difficult feat; you have to work your way down in a peculiar sidelong manner, without bending the knees. Your miner friends notice the stiffness of your walk and chaff you about it. ("How'd ta like to work down pit, eh?" etc.) Yet even a miner who has been long away from work—from illness, for instance—when he comes back to the pit, suffers badly for the first few days.

It may seem that I am exaggerating, though no one who has been down an old-fashioned pit (most of the pits in England are old-fashioned) and actually gone as far as the coal face, is likely to say so. But what I want to emphasize is this. Here is this frightful business of crawling to and fro, which to any normal person is a hard day's work in itself; and it is not part of the miner's work at all, it is merely an extra, like the City man's daily ride in the tube. The miner does that journey to and fro, and sandwiched in between there are seven and a half hours of savage work. I have never traveled much more than a mile to the coal face; but often it is three miles, in which case I and most people other than coal miners would never get there at all. This is the kind of point that one is always liable to miss. When you think of a coal mine you think of depth, heat, darkness, blackened figures hacking at walls of coal; you don't think, necessarily, of those miles of creeping to and fro. There is the question of time, also. A miner's working shift of seven and a half hours does not sound very long, but one has got to add on to it at least an hour a day for "traveling," more often two hours and sometimes three. Of course, the "traveling" is not technically work and the miner is not paid for it; but it is as like work as makes no difference. It is easy to say that miners don't mind all this. Certainly, it is not the same for them as it would be for you or me. They have done it since childhood, they have the right muscles hardened, and they can move to and fro underground with a startling and rather horrible agility. A miner puts his head down and *runs*, with a long swinging stride, through places where I can only stagger. At the workings you see them on all fours, skipping round the pit props almost like dogs. But it is quite a mistake to think that they enjoy it. I have talked about this to scores of miners and they all admit that the "traveling" is hard work; in any case when you hear them discussing a pit among themselves the "traveling" is always one of the things they discuss. It is said that a shift always returns from work faster than it goes; nevertheless the miners all say that it is the coming away, after a hard day's work, that is especially irksome. It is part of their work and they are equal to it, but certainly it is an effort. It is comparable, perhaps, to climbing a smallish mountain before and after your day's work.

When you have been down two or three pits you begin to get some grasp of the processes that are going on underground. (I ought to say, by the way, that I know nothing whatever about the technical side of mining: I am merely describing what I have seen.) Coal lies in thin seams between enormous layers of rock, so that essentially the process of getting it out is like scooping the central layer from a Neapolitan ice. In the old days the miners used to cut straight into the coal with pick and crowbar—a very slow job because coal, when lying in its virgin state, is almost as hard as rock. Nowadays the preliminary work is done by an electrically driven coal-cutter, which in principle is an immensely tough and powerful band-saw, running horizontally instead of vertically, with teeth a couple of inches long and half an inch or an inch thick. It can move backward or forward on its own power, and the men operating it can rotate it this way and that. Incidentally it makes one of the most awful noises I have ever heard, and sends forth clouds of coal dust which make it impossible to see more than two or three feet and almost impossible to breathe. The machine travels along the coal face cutting into the base of the coal and undermining it to the depth of five feet or five feet and a half; after this it is comparatively easy to extract the coal to the depth to which it has been undermined. Where it is "difficult getting," however, it has also to be loosened with explosives. A man with an electric drill, like a rather smaller version of the drills used in street-mending, bores holes at intervals in the coal, inserts blasting powder, plugs it with clay, goes round the corner if there is one handy (he is supposed to retire to twenty-five yards distance) and touches off the charge with an electric current. This is not intended to bring the coal out, only to loosen it. Occasionally, of course, the charge is too powerful, and then it not only brings the coal out but brings the roof down as well.

After the blasting has been done the "fillers" can tumble the coal out, break it up, and shovel it on to the conveyor belt. It comes out at first in monstrous boulders which may weigh anything up to twenty tons. The conveyor belt shoots it on to tubs, and the tubs are shoved into the main road and hitched on to an endlessly revolving steel cable which drags them to the cage. Then they are hoisted, and at the surface the coal is sorted by being run over screens, and if necessary is washed as well. As far as possible the "dirt"—the shale, that is—is used for making the roads below. All that cannot be used is sent to the surface and dumped; hence the monstrous "dirt-heaps," like hideous gray mountains, which are the characteristic scenery of the coal areas. When the coal has been extracted to the depth to which the machine has cut, the coal face has advanced by five feet. Fresh props are put in to hold up the newly exposed roof, and during the next shift the conveyor belt is taken to pieces, moved five feet forward and re-assembled. As far as possible the three operations of cutting, blasting, and extraction are done in three separate shifts, the cutting in the afternoon, the blasting at night (there is a law, not always kept, that forbids its being done when there are other men working near by), and the "filling" in the morning shift, which lasts from six in the morning until half-past one.

Even when you watch the process of coal-extraction you probably only watch it for a short time, and it is not until you begin making a few calculations that you realize what a stupendous task the "fillers" are performing. Normally each man has to clear a space four or five yards wide. The cutter has undermined the coal to the depth of five feet, so that if the seam of coal is three or four feet high, each man has to cut out, break up and load on to the belt something between seven and twelve cubic yards of coal. This is to say, taking a cubic yard as weighing twenty-seven hundredweight, that each man is shifting coal at a speed approaching two tons an hour. I have just enough experience of pick-and-shovel work to be able to grasp what this means. When I am digging trenches in my garden, if I shift two tons of earth during the afternoon, I feel that I have earned my tea. But earth is tractable stuff compared with coal, and I don't have to work kneeling down, a thousand feet underground, in suffocating heat and swallowing coal dust with every breath I take; nor do I have to walk a mile bent double before I begin. The miner's job would be as much beyond my power as it would be to perform on the flying trapeze or to win the Grand National. I am not a manual laborer and please God I never shall be one, but there are some kinds of manual work that I could do if I had to. At a pitch I could be a tolerable road-sweeper or an inefficient gardener or even a tenth-rate farm hand. But by no conceivable amount of effort or training could I become a coal miner; the work would kill me in a few weeks.

Watching coal miners at work, you realize momentarily what different universes different people inhabit. Down there where coal is dug it is a sort of world apart which one can quite easily go through life without ever hearing about. Probably a majority of people would even prefer not to hear about it. Yet it is the absolutely necessary counterpart of our world above. Practically everything we do, from eating an ice to crossing the Atlantic, and from baking a loaf to writing a novel, involves the use of coal, directly or indirectly. For all the arts of peace coal is needed; if war breaks out it is needed all the more. In time of revolution the miner must go on working or the revolution must stop, for revolution as much as reaction needs coal. Whatever may be happening on the surface, the hacking and shoveling have got to continue without a pause, or at any rate without pausing for more than a few weeks at the most. In order that Hitler may march the goosestep, that the Pope may denounce Bolshevism, that the cricket crowds may assemble at

Lord's, that the Nancy poets may scratch one another's backs, coal has got to be forthcoming. But on the whole we are not aware of it; we all know that we "must have coal," but we seldom or never remember what coal-getting involves. Here am I, sitting writing in front of my comfortable coal fire. It is April but I still need a fire. Once a fortnight the coal cart drives up to the door and men in leather jerkins carry the coal indoors in stout sacks smelling of tar and shoot it clanking into the coal-hole under the stairs. It is only very rarely, when I make a definite mental effort, that I connect this coal with that far-off labor in the mines. It is just "coal"— something that I have got to have; black stuff that arrives mysteriously from nowhere in particular, like manna except that you have to pay for it. You could quite easily drive a car right across the north of England and never once remember that hundreds of feet below the road you are on the miners are hacking at the coal. Yet in a sense it is the miners who are driving your car forward. Their lamp-lit world down there is as necessary to the daylight world above as the root is to the flower.

It is not long since conditions in the mines were worse than they are now. There are still living a few very old women who in their youth have worked underground, with a harness round their waists and a chain that passed between their legs, crawling on all fours and dragging tubs of coal. They used to go on doing this even when they were pregnant. And even now, if coal could not be produced without pregnant women dragging it to and fro, I fancy we should let them do it rather than deprive ourselves of coal. But most of the time, of course, we should prefer to forget that they were doing it. It is so with all types of manual work; it keeps us alive, and we are oblivious of its existence. More than anyone else, perhaps, the miner can stand as the type of the manual worker, not only because his work is so exaggeratedly awful, but also because it is so vitally necessary and yet so remote from our experience, so invisible, as it were, that we are capable of forgetting it as we forget the blood in our veins. In a way it is even humiliating to watch coal miners working. It raises in you a momentary doubt about your own status as an "intellectual" and a superior person generally. For it is brought home to you, at least while you are watching, that it is only because miners sweat their guts out that superior persons can remain superior. You and I and the editor of the *Times Lit. Supp.*, and the Nancy poets and the Archbishop of Canterbury and Comrade X, author of *Marxism for Infants*—all of us *really* owe the comparative decency of our lives to poor drudges underground, blackened to the

eyes, with their throats full of coal dust, driving their shovels forward with arms and belly muscles of steel.

Chapter Three

When the miner comes up from the pit his face is so pale that it is
noticeable even through the mask of coal dust. This is due to the
foul air that he has been breathing, and will wear off presently. To
a Southerner, new to the mining districts, the spectacle of a shift of
several hundred miners streaming out of the pit is strange and
slightly sinister. Their exhausted faces, with the grime clinging in
all the hollows, have a fierce, wild look. At other times, when their
faces are clean, there is not much to distinguish them from the rest
of the population. They have a very upright square-shouldered walk,
a reaction from the constant bending underground, but most of
them are shortish men and their thick ill-fitting clothes hide the
splendor of their bodies. The most definitely distinctive thing about
them is the blue scars on their noses. Every miner has blue scars on
his nose and forehead, and will carry them to his death. The coal
dust of which the air underground is full enters every cut, and then
the skin grows over it and forms a blue stain like tattooing, which in
fact it is. Some of the older men have their foreheads veined like
Roquefort cheeses from this cause.

As soon as the miner comes above ground he gargles a little water
to get the worst of the coal dust out of his throat and nostrils, and
then goes home and either washes or does not wash according to his
temperament. From what I have seen I should say that a majority
of miners prefer to eat their meal first and wash afterward, as I
should do in their circumstances. It is the normal thing to see a
miner sitting down to his tea with a Christy-minstrel face, completely black except for very red lips which become clean by eating.
After his meal he takes a largish basin of water and washes very
methodically, first his hands, then his chest, neck, and armpits, then
his forearms, then his face and scalp (it is on the scalp that the grime
clings thickest), and then his wife takes the flannel and washes his
back. He has only washed the top half of his body and probably his
navel is still a nest of coal dust, but even so it takes some skill to get
passably clean in a single basin of water. For my own part I found
I needed two complete baths after going down a coal mine. Getting
the dirt out of one's eyelids is a ten minutes' job in itself.

At some of the larger and better appointed collieries there are
pithead baths. This is an enormous advantage, for not only can
the miner wash himself all over every day, in comfort and even
luxury, but at the baths he has two lockers where he can keep his

pit clothes separate from his day clothes, so that within twenty
minutes of emerging as black as a Negro he can be riding off to
a football match dressed up to the nines. But it is only comparatively few mines that have baths, partly because a seam of coal
does not last for ever, so that it is not necessarily worth building
a bath every time a shaft is sunk. I cannot get hold of exact figures, but it seems likely that rather less than one miner in three
has access to a pithead bath. Probably a large majority of miners
are completely black from the waist down for at least six days a
week. It is almost impossible for them to wash all over in their
own homes. Every drop of water has got to be heated up, and in
a tiny living room which contains, apart from the kitchen range
and a quantity of furniture, a wife, some children and probably
a dog, there is simply not room to have a proper bath. Even with
a basin one is bound to splash the furniture. Middle-class people
are fond of saying that the miners would not wash themselves properly even if they could, but this is nonsense, as is shown by the
fact that where pithead baths exist practically all the men use them.
Only among the very old men does the belief still linger that washing one's legs "causes lumbago." Moreover the pithead baths, where
they exist, are paid for wholly or partly by the miners themselves,
out of the Miners' Welfare Fund. Sometimes the colliery company
subscribes, sometimes the Fund bears the whole cost. But doubtless even at this late date the old ladies in Brighton boarding-
houses are saying that "if you give those miners baths they only
use them to keep coal in."

As a matter of fact it is surprising that miners wash as regularly as they do, seeing how little time they have between work
and sleep. It is a great mistake to think of a miner's working day
as being only seven and a half hours. Seven and a half hours is
the time spent actually on the job, but, as I have already explained,
one has got to add on to this time taken up in "traveling," which
is seldom less than an hour and may often be three hours. In addition most miners have to spend a considerable time in getting to
and from the pit. Throughout the industrial districts there is acute
shortage of houses, and it is only in the small mining villages,
where the village is grouped round the pit, that the men can be
certain of living near their work. In the larger mining towns where
I have stayed, nearly everyone went to work by bus; half a crown
a week seemed to be the normal amount to spend on fares. One
miner I stayed with was working on the morning shift, which was
from six in the morning till half-past one. He had to be out of
bed at a quarter to four and got back somewhere after three in

the afternoon. In another house where I stayed a boy of fifteen was working on the night shift. He left for work at nine at night and got back at eight in the morning, had his breakfast and then promptly went to bed and slept till six in the evening; so that his leisure time amounted to about four hours a day—actually a good deal less, if you take off the time for washing, eating, and dressing.

The adjustments a miner's family have to make when he is changed from one shift to another must be tiresome in the extreme. If he is on the night shift he gets home in time for breakfast, on the morning shift he gets home in the middle of the afternoon, and on the afternoon shift he gets home in the middle of the night; and in each case, of course, he wants his principal meal of the day as soon as he returns. I notice that the Reverend W. R. Inge, in his book *England,* accuses the miners of gluttony. From my own observation I should say that they eat astonishingly little. Most of the miners I stayed with ate slightly less than I did. Many of them declare that they cannot do their day's work if they have had a heavy meal beforehand, and the food they take with them is only a snack, usually bread-and-dripping and cold tea. They carry it in a flat tin called a snap-can which they strap to their belts. When a miner gets back late at night his wife waits up for him, but when he is on the morning shift it seems to be the custom for him to get his breakfast for himself. Apparently the old superstition that it is bad luck to see a woman before going to work on the morning shift is not quite extinct. In the old days, it is said, a miner who happened to meet a woman in the early morning would often turn back and do no work that day. . . .

The rate of accidents among miners is so high, compared with that in other trades, that casualties are taken for granted almost as they would be in a minor war. Every year one miner in about nine hundred is killed and one in about six is injured; most of these injuries, of course, are petty ones, but a fair number amount to total disablement. This means that if a miner's working life is forty years the chances are nearly seven to one against his escaping injury and not much more than twenty to one against his being killed outright. No other trade approaches this in dangerousness; the next most dangerous is the shipping trade, one sailor in a little under 1,300 being killed every year. The figures I have given apply, of course, to mine workers as a whole; for those actually working underground the proportion of injuries would be very much higher. Every miner of long standing that I have talked to had either been in a fairly serious accident himself or had seen some of his mates killed, and in every mining family they tell you tales of fathers, brothers or uncles killed at work. ("And he fell seven hundred feet, and they wouldn't never have collected t'pieces only he were wearing a new suit of oilskins," etc., etc., etc.) Some of these tales are appalling in the extreme. One miner, for instance, described to me how a mate of his, a "dataller," was buried by a fall of rock. They rushed to him and managed to uncover his head and shoulders so that he could breathe, and he was alive and spoke to them. Then they saw that the roof was coming down again and had to run to save themselves; the "dataller" was buried a second time. Once again they rushed to him and got his head and shoulders free, and again he was alive and spoke to them. Then the roof came down a third time, and this time they could not uncover him for several hours, after which, of course, he was dead. But the miner who told me the story (he had been buried himself on one occasion, but he was lucky enough to have his head jammed between his legs so that there was a small space in which he could breathe) did not think it was a particularly appalling one. Its significance, for him, was that the "dataller" had known perfectly well that the place where he was working was unsafe, and had gone there in daily expectation of an accident. "And it worked on his mind to that extent that he got to kissing his wife before he went to work. And she told me afterward that it were over twenty year since he'd kissed her."

The most obviously understandable cause of accidents is explosions of gas, which is always more or less present in the atmosphere of the pit. There is a special lamp which is used to test the air for gas, and when it is present in at all large quantities it can be detected by the flame of an ordinary Davy lamp burning blue. If the wick can be turned up to its full extent and the flame is still blue, the proportion of gas is dangerously high; it is, nevertheless, difficult to detect, because it does not distribute itself evenly throughout the atmosphere but hangs about in cracks and crevices. Before starting work a miner often tests for gas by poking his lamp into all the corners. The gas may be touched off by a spark during blasting operations, or by a pick striking a spark from a stone, or by a defective lamp, or by "gob fires"—spontaneously generated fires which smoulder in the coal dust and are very hard to put out. The great mining disasters which happen from time to time, in which several hundred men are killed, are usually caused by explosions; hence one tends to think of explosions as the chief danger of mining. Actually, the great majority of accidents are due to the normal everyday dangers of the pit; in particular, to falls of roof. There are, for instance, "pot-holes"—circular holes from which a lump of stone big enough to kill a man shoots out with the promptitude of a bullet. With, so far as I can remember, only one exception, all the miners I have talked to declared that the new machinery, and "speeding up" generally, has made the work more dangerous. This may be partly due to conservatism, but they can give plenty of reasons. To begin with, the speed at which the coal is now extracted means that for hours at a time a dangerously large stretch of roof remains unpropped. Then there is the vibration, which tends to shake everything loose, and the noise, which makes it harder to detect signs of danger. One must remember that a miner's safety underground depends largely on his own care and skill. An experienced miner claims to know by a sort of instinct when the roof is unsafe; the way he puts it is that he "can feel the weight on him." He can, for instance, hear the faint creaking of the props. The reason why wooden props are still generally preferred to iron girders is that a wooden prop which is about to collapse gives warning by creaking, whereas a girder flies out unexpectedly. The devastating noise of the machines makes it impossible to hear anything else, and thus the danger is increased.

When a miner is hurt it is of course impossible to attend to him immediately. He lies crushed under several hundredweight of stone in some dreadful cranny underground, and even after he has been extricated it is necessary to drag his body a mile or more, perhaps, through galleries where nobody can stand upright. Usually when you talk to a man who has been injured you find that it was a couple of hours or so before they got him to the surface. Sometimes, of course, there are accidents to the cage. The cage is shooting several hundred yards up or down at the speed of an express train, and it is operated by somebody on the surface who cannot see what is happening. He has very delicate indicators to tell him how far the cage has got, but it is possible for him to make a mistake, and there have been cases of the cage crashing into the pit-bottom at its very maximum speed. This seems to me a dreadful way to die. For as that tiny steel box whizzes through the blackness there must come a moment when the ten men who are locked inside it *know* that something has gone wrong; and the remaining seconds before they are smashed to pieces hardly bear thinking about. A miner told me he was once in a cage in which something went wrong. It did not slow up when it should have done, and they thought the cable must have snapped. As it happened they got to the bottom safely, but when he stepped out he found that he had broken a tooth; he had been clenching his teeth so hard in expectation of that frightful crash.

Apart from accidents miners seem to be healthy, as obviously they have got to be, considering the muscular efforts demanded of them. They are liable to rheumatism and a man with defective lungs does not last long in that dust-impregnated air, but the most characteristic industrial disease is nystagmus. This is a disease of the eyes which makes the eyeballs oscillate in a strange manner when they come near a light. It is due presumably to working in half-darkness, and sometimes results in total blindness. Miners who are disabled in this way or any other way are compensated by the colliery company, sometimes with a lump sum, sometimes with a weekly pension. This pension never amounts to more than twenty-nine shillings a week; if it falls below fifteen shillings the disabled man can also get something from the dole or the P.A.C. If I were a disabled miner I should very much prefer the lump sum, for then at any rate I should know that I had got my money. Disability pensions are not guaranteed by any centralized fund, so that if the colliery company goes bankrupt that is the end of the disabled miner's pension, though he does figure among the other creditors.

In Wigan I stayed for a while with a miner who was suffering from nystagmus. He could see across the room but not much farther. He had been drawing compensation of twenty-nine shillings a week for the past nine months, but the colliery company were now talking of putting him on "partial compensation" of fourteen shillings a week. It all depended on whether the doctor passed him as fit for light work "on top." Even if the doctor did pass him there would, needless to say, be no light work available, but he could draw the dole and the company would have saved itself fifteen shillings a week. Watching this man go to the colliery to draw his compensation, I was struck by the profound differences that are still made by *status*. Here was a man who had been half blinded in one of the most useful of all jobs and was drawing a pension to which he had a perfect right, if anybody has a right to anything. Yet he could not, so to speak, *demand* this pension—he could not, for instance, draw it when and how he wanted it. He had to go to the colliery once a week at a time named by the company, and when he got there he was kept waiting about for hours in the cold wind. For all I know he was also expected to touch his cap and show gratitude to whoever paid him; at any rate he had to waste an afternoon and spend sixpence in bus fares. It is very different for a member of the bourgeoisie, even such a down-at-heel member as I am. Even when I am on the verge of starvation I have certain rights attaching to my bourgeois status. 1 do not earn much more than a miner earns, but I do at least get it paid into my bank in a gentlemanly manner and can draw it out when I choose. And even when my account is exhausted the bank people are still passably polite.

This business of petty inconvenience and indignity, of being kept waiting about, of having to do everything at other people's convenience, is inherent in working-class life. A thousand influences constantly press a working man down into a *passive* role. He does not act, he is acted upon. He feels himself the slave of mysterious authority and has a firm conviction that "they" will never allow him to do this, that and the other. Once when I was hop-picking I asked the sweated pickers (they earn something under sixpence an hour) why they did not form a union. I was told immediately that "they" would never allow it. Who were "they"? I asked. Nobody seemed to know; but evidently "they" were omnipotent.

A person of bourgeois origin goes through life with some expectation of getting what he wants, within reasonable limits. Hence the fact that in times of stress "educated" people tend to come to the front; they are no more gifted than the others and their "education" is generally quite useless in itself, but they are accustomed to a certain amount of deference and consequently have the cheek necessary to a commander. That they *will* come to the front seems to be taken for granted, always and everywhere. In Lissagaray's *History of the Commune* there is an interesting passage describing the shootings that took place after the Commune had been suppressed. The authorities were shooting the ringleaders, and as they did not know who the ringleaders were, they were picking them out on the principle that those of better class would be the ringleaders. An officer walked down a line of prisoners, picking out likely-looking types. One man was shot because he was wearing a watch, another because he "had an intelligent face." I should not like to be shot for having an intelligent face, but I do agree that in almost any revolt the leaders would tend to be people who could pronounce their aitches.

1937

△

From "Homage to Catalonia"

▽

Chapter One

In the Lenin Barracks in Barcelona, the day before I joined the militia, I saw an Italian militiaman standing in front of the officers' table.

He was a tough-looking youth of twenty-five or -six, with reddish-yellow hair and powerful shoulders. His peaked leather cap was pulled fiercely over one eye. He was standing in profile to me, his chin on his breast, gazing with a puzzled frown at a map which one of the officers had open on the table. Something in his face deeply moved me. It was the face of a man who would commit murder and throw away his life for a friend—the kind of face you would expect in an Anarchist, though as likely as not he was a Communist. There were both candor and ferocity in it; also the pathetic reverence that illiterate people have for their supposed superiors. Obviously he could not make head or tail of the map; obviously he regarded map-reading as a stupendous intellectual feat. I hardly know why, but I have seldom seen anyone—any man, I mean—to whom I have taken such an immediate liking. While they were talking round the table some remark brought it out that I was a foreigner. The Italian raised his head and said quickly: "*Italiano?*"

I answered in my bad Spanish: "*No, Ingles. Y tu?*"

"*Italiano.*"

As he went out he stepped across the room and gripped my hand very hard. Queer, the affection you can feel for a stranger! It was as though his spirit and mine had momentarily succeeded in bridging the gulf of language and tradition and meeting in utter intimacy. I hoped he liked me as well as I liked him. But I also knew that to retain my first impression of him I must not see him again; and needless to say I never did see him again. One was always making contacts of that kind in Spain.

I mention this Italian militiaman because he has stuck vividly in my memory. With his shabby uniform and fierce pathetic face he typifies for me the special atmosphere of that time. He is bound up with all my memories of that period of the war—the red flags in Barcelona, the gaunt trains full of shabby soldiers creeping to the front, the gray war-stricken towns farther up the line, the muddy, ice-cold trenches in the mountains.

This was in late December, 1936, less than seven months ago as I write, and yet it is a period that has already receded into enormous distance. Later events have obliterated it much more completely than they have obliterated 1935, or 1905, for that matter. I had come to Spain with some notion of writing newspaper articles, but I had joined the militia almost immediately, because at that time and in that atmosphere it seemed the only conceivable thing to do. The Anarchists were still in virtual control of Catalonia and the revolution was still in full swing. To anyone who had been there since the beginning it probably seemed even in December or January that the revolutionary period was ending; but when one came straight from England the aspect of Barcelona was something startling and overwhelming. It was the first time that I had ever been in a town where the working class was in the saddle. Practically every building of any size had been seized by the workers and was draped with red flags or with the red-and-black flag of the Anarchists; every wall was scrawled with the hammer and sickle and with the initials of the revolutionary parties; almost every church had been gutted and its images burnt. Churches here and there were being systematically demolished by gangs of workmen. Every shop and café had an inscription saying that it had been collectivized; even the bootblacks had been collectivized and their boxes painted red and black. Waiters and shop-walkers looked you in the face and treated you as an equal. Servile and even ceremonial forms of speech had temporarily disappeared. Nobody said *"Señor"* or *"Don"* or even *"Usted"*; everyone called everyone else "Comrade" and "Thou," and said *"Salud!"* instead of *"Buenos dias."* Tipping had been forbidden by law since the time of Primo de Rivera; almost my first experience was receiving a lecture from an hotel manager for trying to tip a lift-boy. There were no private motor cars, they had all been commandeered, and all the trams and taxis and much of the other transport were painted red and black. The revolutionary posters were everywhere, flaming from the walls in clean reds and blues that made the few remaining advertisements look like daubs of mud. Down the Ramblas, the wide central artery of the town where crowds of people streamed constantly to and fro, the loudspeakers were bellowing revolutionary songs all day and far into the night. And it was the aspect of the crowds that was the queerest thing of all. In outward appearance it was a town in which the wealthy classes had practically ceased to exist. Except for a small number of women and foreigners there were no "well-dressed" people at all. Practically everyone wore rough working-class clothes or blue overalls or some variant of the militia uniform. All this was queer and moving. There was much in it that I did not understand, in some ways I did not even like it, but I recognized it immediately as a state of affairs worth fighting for. Also I believed that things were as they appeared, that this was really a workers' state and that the entire bourgeoisie had either fled, been killed, or voluntarily come over to the workers' side; I did not realize that great numbers of well-to-do bourgeois were simply lying low and disguising themselves as proletarians for the time being.

Together with all this there was something of the evil atmosphere of war. The town had a gaunt untidy look, roads and buildings were in poor repair, the streets at night were dimly lit for fear of air raids, the shops were mostly shabby and half empty. Meat was scarce and milk practically unobtainable, there was a shortage of coal, sugar, and petrol, and a really serious shortage of bread. Even at this period the bread queues were often hundreds of yards long. Yet so far as one could judge the people were contented and hopeful. There was no unemployment, and the price of living was still extremely low; you saw very few conspicuously destitute people, and no beggars except the gypsies. Above all, there was a belief in the revolution and the future, a feeling of having suddenly emerged into an era of equality and freedom. Human beings were trying to behave as human beings and not as cogs in the capitalist machine. In the barbers' shops were Anarchist notices (the barbers were mostly Anarchists) solemnly explaining that barbers were no longer slaves. In the streets were colored posters appealing to prostitutes to stop being prostitutes. To anyone from the hard-boiled, sneering civilization of the English-speaking races there was something rather pathetic in the literalness with which these idealistic Spaniards took the hackneyed phrases of revolution. At that time revolutionary ballads of the naïvest kind, all about proletarian brotherhood and the wickedness of Mussolini, were being sold on the streets for a few centimes each. I have often seen an illiterate militiaman buy one of these ballads, laboriously spell out the words, and then, when he had got the hang of it, begin singing it to an appropriate tune.

All this time I was at the Lenin Barracks, ostensibly in training for the front. When I joined the militia I had been told that

I should be sent to the front the next day, but in fact I had to wait while a fresh *centuria* was got ready. The workers' militias, hurriedly raised by the trade unions at the beginning of the war, had not yet been organized on an ordinary army basis. The units of command were the "section," of about thirty men, the *centuria*, of about a hundred men, and the "column," which in practice meant any large number of men. The Lenin Barracks was a block of splendid stone buildings with a riding school and enormous cobbled courtyards; it had been a cavalry barracks and had been captured during the July fighting. My *centuria* slept in one of the stables, under the stone mangers where the names of the cavalry chargers were still inscribed. All the horses had been seized and sent to the front, but the whole place still smelt of horse-piss and rotten oats. I was at the barracks about a week. Chiefly I remember the horsy smells, the quavering bugle calls (all our buglers were amateurs—I first learned the Spanish bugle calls by listening to them outside the Fascist lines), the tramp-tramp of hobnailed boots in the barrack yard, the long morning parades in the wintry sunshine, the wild games of football, fifty a side, in the graveled riding school. There were perhaps a thousand men at the barracks, and a score or so of women, apart from the militiamen's wives who did the cooking. There were still women serving in the militias, though not very many. In the early battles they had fought side by side with the men as a matter of course. It is a thing that seems natural in time of revolution. Ideas were changing already, however. The militiamen had to be kept out of the riding school while the women were drilling there, because they laughed at the women and put them off. A few months earlier no one would have seen anything comic in a woman handling a gun.

The whole barracks was in the state of filth and chaos to which the militia reduced every building they occupied and which seems to be one of the by-products of revolution. In every corner you came upon piles of smashed furniture, broken saddles, brass cavalry helmets, empty saber-scabbards, and decaying food. There was frightful wastage of food, especially bread. From my barrack-room alone a basketful of bread was thrown away at every meal—a disgraceful thing when the civilian population was short of it. We ate at long trestle tables out of permanently greasy tin pannikins, and drank out of a dreadful thing called a *poron*. A *poron* is a sort of glass bottle with a pointed spout from which a thin jet of wine spurts out whenever you tip it up; you can thus drink from a distance, without touching it with your lips, and it can be passed from hand to hand. I went on strike and demanded a drinking cup as soon as I saw a *poron* in use. To my eye the things were altogether too like bedbottles, especially when they were filled with white wine.

By degrees they were issuing the recruits with uniforms, and because this was Spain everything was issued piecemeal, so that it was never quite certain who had received what, and various of the things we most needed, such as belts and cartridge boxes, were not issued till the last moment, when the train was actually waiting to take us to the front. I have spoken of the militia "uniform," which probably gives a wrong impression. It was not exactly a uniform. Perhaps a "multiform" would be the proper name for it. Everyone's clothes followed the same general plan, but they were never quite the same in any two cases. Practically everyone in the army wore corduroy kneebreeches, but there the uniformity ended. Some wore puttees, others corduroy gaiters, others leather leggings or high boots. Everyone wore a zipper jacket, but some of the jackets were of leather, others of wool and of every conceivable color. The kinds of cap were about as numerous as their wearers. It was usual to adorn the front of your cap with a party badge, and in addition nearly every man wore a red or red-and-black handkerchief round his throat. A militia column at that time was an extraordinary-looking rabble. But the clothes had to be issued as this or that factory rushed them out, and they were not bad clothes considering the circumstances. The shirts and socks were wretched cotton things, however, quite useless against cold. I hate to think of what the militiamen must have gone through in the earlier months before anything was organized. I remember coming upon a newspaper of only about two months earlier in which one of the P.O.U.M.* leaders, after a visit to the front, said that he would try to see to it that "every militiaman had a blanket." A phrase to make you shudder if you have ever slept in a trench.

On my second day at the barracks there began what was comically called "instruction." At the beginning there were frightful scenes of chaos. The recruits were mostly boys of sixteen or seventeen from the back streets of Barcelona, full of revolutionary ardor but completely ignorant of the meaning of war. It was impossible even to get them to stand in line. Discipline did not exist; if a man disliked an order he would step out of the ranks and argue fiercely with the officer. The lieutenant who instructed us was a stout, fresh-faced, pleasant young man who had previously been a Regular Army officer, and still looked like one, with his smart

* Party of Marxist Unification (*Partido Obrero de Unificacion Marxista*).

carriage and spick-and-span uniform. Curiously enough he was a sincere and ardent Socialist. Even more than the men themselves he insisted upon complete social equality between all ranks. I remember his pained surprise when an ignorant recruit addressed him as "*Señor.*" "What! *Señor!* Who is that calling me *Señor?* Are we not all comrades?" I doubt whether it made his job any easier. Meanwhile the raw recruits were getting no military training that could be of the slightest use to them. I had been told that foreigners were not obliged to attend "instruction" (the Spaniards, I noticed, had a pathetic belief that all foreigners knew more of military matters than themselves), but naturally I turned out with the others. I was very anxious to learn how to use a machine gun; it was a weapon I had never had a chance to handle. To my dismay I found that we were taught nothing about the use of weapons. The so-called instruction was simply parade-ground drill of the most antiquated, stupid kind; right turn, left turn, about turn, marching at attention in column of threes and all the rest of that useless nonsense which I had learned when I was fifteen years old. It was an extraordinary form for the training of a guerilla army to take. Obviously if you have only a few days in which to train a soldier, you must teach him the things he will most need; how to take cover, how to advance across open ground, how to mount guards and build a parapet—above all, how to use his weapons. Yet this mob of eager children, who were going to be thrown into the front line in a few days' time, were not even taught how to fire a rifle or pull the pin out of a bomb. At the time I did not grasp that this was because there were no weapons to be had. In the P.O.U.M. militia the shortage of rifles was so desperate that fresh troops reaching the front always had to take their rifles from the troops they relieved in the line. In the whole of the Lenin Barracks there were, I believe, no rifles except those used by the sentries.

After a few days, though still a complete rabble by any ordinary standard, we were considered fit to be seen in public, and in the mornings we were marched out to the public gardens on the hill beyond the Plaza de España. This was the common drill ground of all the party militias, besides the Carabineros and the first contingents of the newly formed Popular Army. Up in the public gardens it was a strange and heartening sight. Down every path and alley-way, amid the formal flower-beds, squads and companies of men marched stiffly to and fro, throwing out their chests and trying desperately to look like soldiers. All of them were unarmed and none completely in uniform, though on most of them the militia uniform was breaking out in patches here and there. The procedure was always very much the same. For three hours we strutted to and fro (the Spanish marching step is very short and rapid), then we halted, broke the ranks and flocked thirstily to a little grocer's shop which was halfway down the hill and was doing a roaring trade in cheap wine. Everyone was very friendly to me. As an Englishman I was something of a curiosity, and the Carabinero officers made much of me and stood me drinks. Meanwhile, whenever I could get our lieutenant into a corner, I was clamoring to be instructed in the use of a machine gun. I used to drag my Hugo's dictionary out of my pocket and start on him in my villainous Spanish:

"*Yo se manejar fusil. No se manejar ametralladora. Quiero apprender ametralladora. Quando vamos apprender ametralladora?*"

The answer was always a harassed smile and a promise that there should be machine-gun instruction *mañana*. Needless to say *mañana* never came. Several days passed and the recruits learned to march in step and spring to attention almost smartly, but if they knew which end of a rifle the bullet came out of, that was all they knew. One day an armed Carabinero strolled up to us when we were halting and allowed us to examine his rifle. It turned out that in the whole of my section no one except myself even knew how to load the rifle, much less how to take aim.

All this time I was having the usual struggles with the Spanish language. Apart from myself there was only one Englishman at the barracks, and nobody even among the officers spoke a word of French. Things were not made easier for me by the fact that when my companions spoke to one another they generally spoke in Catalan. The only way I could get along was to carry everywhere a small dictionary which I whipped out of my pocket in moments of crisis. But I would sooner be a foreigner in Spain than in most countries. How easy it is to make friends in Spain! Within a day or two there was a score of militiamen who called me by my Christian name, showed me the ropes, and overwhelmed me with hospitality. I am not writing a book of propaganda and I do not want to idealize the P.O.U.M. militia. The whole militia system had serious faults, and the men themselves were a mixed lot, for by this time voluntary recruitment was falling off and many of the best men were already at the front or dead. There was always among us a certain percentage who were completely useless. Boys of fifteen were being brought up for enlistment by their parents, quite openly for the sake of the ten pesetas a day which was the militiaman's wage; also for the sake of the bread which the militia received in plenty and could smuggle home to their parents. But I defy anyone to be thrown as I was among the Spanish working class—I ought perhaps to say the Catalan working class, for apart from a few Aragonese and Andalusians I mixed only with Catalans—and not be struck by their essential decency; above all, their straightforwardness and generosity. A Spaniard's generosity, in the ordinary sense of the word, is at times almost embarrassing. If you ask him for a cigarette he will force the whole packet upon you. And beyond this there is generosity in a deeper sense, a real largeness of spirit, which I have met with again and again in the most unpromising circumstances. Some of the journalists and other foreigners who traveled in Spain during the war have declared that in secret the Spaniards were bitterly jealous of foreign aid. All I can say is that I never observed anything of the kind. I remember that a few days before I left the barracks a group of men returned on leave from the front. They were talking excitedly about their experiences and were full of enthusiasm for some French troops who had been next to them at Huesca. The French were very brave, they said; adding enthusiastically: *"Mas valientes que nosotros"*—"Braver than we are!" Of course I demurred, whereupon they explained that the French knew more of the art of war—were more expert with bombs, machine guns, and so forth. Yet the remark was significant. An Englishman would cut his hand off sooner than say a thing like that.

Every foreigner who served in the militia spent his first few weeks in learning to love the Spaniards and in being exasperated by certain of their characteristics. In the front line my own exasperation sometimes reached the pitch of fury. The Spaniards are good at many things, but not at making war. All foreigners alike are appalled by their inefficiency, above all their maddening unpunctuality. The one Spanish word that no foreigner can avoid learning is *mañana*—"tomorrow" (literally, "the morning"). Whenever it is conceivably possible, the business of today is put off until *mañana*. This is so notorious that even the Spaniards themselves make jokes about it. In Spain nothing, from a meal to a battle, ever happens at the appointed time. As a general rule things happen too late, but just occasionally—just so that you shan't even be able to depend on their happening late—they happen too early. A train which is due to leave at eight will normally leave at any time between nine and ten, but perhaps once a week, thanks to some private whim of the engine-driver, it leaves at half-past seven. Such things can be a little trying. In theory I rather admire the paniards for not sharing our Northern time-neurosis; but unfortunately I share it myself.

After endless rumors, *mañanas,* and delays we were suddenly ordered to the front at two hours' notice, when much of our equipment was still unissued. There were terrible tumults in the quartermaster's store; in the end numbers of men had to leave without their full equipment. The barracks had promptly filled with women who seemed to have sprung up from the ground and were helping their menfolk to roll their blankets and pack their kitbags. It was rather humiliating that I had to be shown how to put on my new leather cartridge boxes by a Spanish girl, the wife of Williams, the other English militiaman. She was a gentle, dark-eyed, intensely feminine creature who looked as though her life work was to rock a cradle, but who as a matter of fact had fought bravely in the street battles of July. At this time she was carrying a baby which was born just ten months after the outbreak of war and had perhaps been begotten behind a barricade.

The train was due to leave at eight, and it was about ten past eight when the harassed, sweating officers managed to marshal us in the barrack square. I remember very vividly the torchlit scene—the uproar and excitement, the red flags flapping in the torchlight, the massed ranks of militiamen with their knapsacks on their backs and their rolled blankets worn bandolier-wise across the shoulder; and the shouting and the clatter of boots and tin pannikins, and then a tremendous and finally successful hissing for silence; and then some political commissar standing beneath a huge rolling red banner and making us a speech in Catalan. Finally they marched us to the station, taking the longest route, three or four miles, so as to show us to the whole town. In the Ramblas they halted us while a borrowed band played some revolutionary tune or other. Once again the conquering-hero stuff—shouting and enthusiasm, red flags and red-and-black flags everywhere, friendly crowds thronging the pavement to have a look at us, women waving from the windows. How natural it all seemed then; how remote and improbable now! The train was packed so tight with men that there was barely room even on the floor, let alone on the seats. At the last moment Williams's wife came rushing down the platform and gave us a bottle of wine and a foot of that bright red sausage which tastes of soap and gives you diarrhoea. The train crawled out of Catalonia and on to the plateau of Aragon at the normal wartime speed of something under twenty kilometers an hour.

Chapter Three

In trench warfare five things are important: firewood, food, tobacco, candles, and the enemy. In winter on the Zaragoza front they were important in that order, with the enemy a bad last. Except at night, when a surprise attack was always conceivable, nobody bothered about the enemy. They were simply remote black insects whom one occasionally saw hopping to and fro. The real preoccupation of both armies was trying to keep warm.

I ought to say in passing that all the time I was in Spain I saw very little fighting. I was on the Aragon front from January to May, and between January and late March little or nothing happened on that front, except at Teruel. In March there was heavy fighting round Huesca, but I personally played only a minor part in it. Later, in June, there was the disastrous attack on Huesca in which several thousand men were killed in a single day, but I had been wounded and disabled before that happened. The things that one normally thinks of as the horrors of war seldom happened to me. No aeroplane ever dropped a bomb anywhere near me, I do not think a shell ever exploded within fifty yards of me, and I was only in hand-to-hand fighting once (once is once too often, I may say). Of course I was often under heavy machine-gun fire, but usually at longish ranges. Even at Huesca you were generally safe enough if you took reasonable precautions.

Up here, in the hills round Zaragoza, it was simply the mingled boredom and discomfort of stationary warfare. A life as uneventful as a city clerk's, and almost as regular. Sentry-go, patrols, digging; digging, patrols, sentry-go. On every hilltop, Fascist or Loyalist, a knot of ragged, dirty men shivering round their flag and trying to keep warm. And all day and night the meaningless bullets wandering across the empty valleys and only by some rare improbable chance getting home on a human body.

Often I used to gaze round the wintry landscape and marvel at the futility of it all. The inconclusiveness of such a kind of war! Earlier, about October, there had been savage fighting for all these hills; then, because the lack of men and arms, especially artillery, made any large-scale operation impossible, each army had dug itself in and settled down on the hilltops it had won. Over to our right there was a small outpost, also P.O.U.M., and on the spur to our left, at seven o'clock of us, a P.S.U.C.* position faced a taller

---

* Socialist Party of Catalonia (*Partido Socialista de Catalunya*). Elsewhere in *Homage to Catalonia* Orwell writes of the P.S.U.C. that it was "a fusion of various Marxist parties, including the Catalan Communist Party, but it was now entirely under Communist control and was affiliated to the Third International."

spur with several small Fascist posts dotted on its peaks. The so-called line zigzagged to and fro in a pattern that would have been quite unintelligible if every position had not flown a flag. The P.O.U.M. and P.S.U.C. flags were red, those of the Anarchists red and black; the Fascists generally flew the monarchist flag (red-yellow-red), but occasionally they flew the flag of the Republic (red-yellow-purple).* The scenery was stupendous, if you could forget that every mountain-top was occupied by troops and was therefore littered with tin cans and crusted with dung. To the right of us the sierra bent southeastward and made way for the wide, veined valley that stretched across to Huesca. In the middle of the plain a few tiny cubes sprawled like a throw of dice; this was the town of Robres, which was in Loyalist possession. Often in the mornings the valley was hidden under seas of cloud, out of which the hills rose flat and blue, giving the landscape a strange resemblance to a photographic negative. Beyond Huesca there were more hills of the same formation as our own, streaked with a pattern of snow which altered day by day. In the far distance the monstrous peaks of the Pyrenees, where the snow never melts, seemed to float upon nothing. Even down in the plain everything looked dead and bare. The hills opposite us were gray and wrinkled like the skins of elephants. Almost always the sky was empty of birds. I do not think I have ever seen a country where there were so few birds. The only birds one saw at any time were a kind of magpie, and the coveys of partridges that startled one at night with their sudden whirring, and, very rarely, the flights of eagles that drifted slowly over, generally followed by rifle shots which they did not deign to notice.

At night and in misty weather patrols were sent out in the valley between ourselves and the Fascists. The job was not popular, it was too cold and too easy to get lost, and I soon found that I could get leave to go out on patrol as often as I wished. In the huge jagged ravines there were no paths or tracks of any kind; you could only find your way about by making successive journeys and noting fresh landmarks each time. As the bullet flies the nearest Fascist post was seven hundred meters from our own, but it was a mile and a half by the only practicable route. It was rather fun wandering about the dark valleys with the stray bullets flying high overhead like redshanks whistling. Better than nighttime were the heavy mists, which often lasted all day and which had a habit of

---

* An errata note found in Orwell's papers after his death: "Am not now completely certain that I ever saw Fascists flying the Republican flag, though I *think* they sometimes flew it with a small imposed swastika."

clinging round the hilltops and leaving the valleys clear. When you were anywhere near the Fascist lines you had to creep at a snail's pace; it was very difficult to move quietly on those hillsides, among the crackling shrubs and tinkling limestones. It was only at the third or fourth attempt that I managed to find my way to the Fascist lines. The mist was very thick, and I crept up to the barbed wire to listen. I could hear the Fascists talking and singing inside. Then to my alarm I heard several of them coming down the hill toward me. I cowered behind a bush that suddenly seemed very small, and tried to cock my rifle without noise. However, they branched off and did not come within sight of me. Behind the bush where I was hiding I came upon various relics of the earlier fighting—a pile of empty cartridge cases, a leather cap with a bullet hole in it, and a red flag, obviously one of our own. I took it back to the position, where it was unsentimentally torn up for cleaning-rags.

I had been made a corporal, or *cabo,* as it was called, as soon as we reached the front, and was in command of a guard of twelve men. It was no sinecure, especially at first. The *centuria* was an untrained mob composed mostly of boys in their teens. Here and there in the militia you came across children as young as eleven or twelve, usually refugees from Fascist territory who had been enlisted as militiamen as the easiest way of providing for them. As a rule they were employed on light work in the rear, but sometimes they managed to worm their way to the front line, where they were a public menace. I remember one little brute throwing a hand grenade into the dugout fire "for a joke." At Monte Pocero I do not think there was anyone younger than fifteen, but the average age must have been well under twenty. Boys of this age ought never to be used in the front line, because they cannot stand the lack of sleep which is inseparable from trench warfare. At the beginning it was almost impossible to keep our position properly guarded at night. The wretched children of my section could only be roused by dragging them out of their dugouts feet foremost, and as soon as your back was turned they left their posts and slipped into shelter; or they would even, in spite of the frightful cold, lean up against the wall of the trench and fall fast asleep. Luckily the enemy were very unenterprising. There were nights when it seemed to me that our position could be stormed by twenty Boy Scouts armed with air guns, or twenty Girl Guides armed with battledores, for that matter.

At this time and until much later the Catalan militias were still on the same basis as they had been at the beginning of the war. In the early days of Franco's revolt the militias had been hurriedly raised by the various trade unions and political parties; each was essentially a political organization, owing allegiance to its party as much as to the central government. When the Popular Army, which was a "non-political" army organized on more or less ordinary lines, was raised at the beginning of 1937, the party militias were theoretically incorporated in it. But for a long time the only changes that occurred were on paper; the new Popular Army troops did not reach the Aragon front in any numbers till June, and until that time the militia system remained unchanged. The essential point of the system was social equality between officers and men. Everyone from general to private drew the same pay, ate the same food, wore the same clothes, and mingled on terms of complete equality. If you wanted to slap the general commanding the division on the back and ask him for a cigarette, you could do so, and no one thought it curious. In theory at any rate each militia was a democracy and not a hierarchy. It was understood that orders had to be obeyed, but it was also understood that when you gave an order you gave it as comrade to comrade and not as superior to inferior. There were officers and N.C.O.s, but there was no military rank in the ordinary sense; no titles, no badges, no heel-clicking and saluting. They had attempted to produce within the militias a sort of temporary working model of the classless society. Of course there was not perfect equality, but there was a nearer approach to it than I had ever seen or than I would have thought conceivable in time of war.

But I admit that at first sight the state of affairs at the front horrified me. How on earth could the war be won by an army of this type? It was what everyone was saying at the time, and though it was true it was also unreasonable. For in the circumstances the militias could not have been much better than they were. A modern mechanized army does not spring up out of the ground, and if the government had waited until it had trained troops at its disposal, Franco would never have been resisted. Later it became the fashion to decry the militias, and therefore to pretend that the faults which were due to lack of training and weapons were the result of the equalitarian system. Actually, a newly raised draft of militia was an undisciplined mob not because the officers called the privates "Comrade" but because raw troops are *always* an undisciplined mob. In practice the democratic "revolutionary" type of discipline is more reliable than might be expected. In a workers' army discipline is theoretically voluntary. It is based on class loyalty, whereas the discipline of a bourgeois conscript army is based ultimately on fear. (The Popular Army that replaced the militias was midway between the two types.) In the militias the bullying and abuse that go on in an ordinary army would never have been tolerated for a moment. The normal military punishments existed, but they were only invoked for very serious offenses. When a man refused to obey an order you did not immediately get him punished; you first appealed to him in the name of comradeship. Cynical people with no experience of handling men will say instantly that this would never "work," but as a matter of fact it does "work" in the long run. The discipline of even the worst drafts of militia visibly improved as time went on. In January the job of keeping a dozen raw recruits up to the mark almost turned my hair gray. In May for a short while I was acting lieutenant in command of about thirty men, English and Spanish. We had all been under fire for months, and I never had the slightest difficulty in getting an order obeyed or in getting men to volunteer for a dangerous job. "Revolutionary" discipline depends on political consciousness—on an understanding of *why* orders must be obeyed; it takes time to diffuse this, but it also takes time to drill a man into an automaton on the barrack square. The journalists who sneered at the militia system seldom remembered that the militias had to hold the line while the Popular Army was training in the rear. And it is a tribute to the strength of "revolutionary" discipline that the militias stayed in the field at all. For until about June, 1937, there was nothing to keep them there, except class loyalty. Individual deserters could be shot—were shot, occasionally—but if a thousand men had decided to walk out of the line together there was no force to stop them. A conscript army in the same circumstances—with its battle-police removed—would have melted away. Yet the militias held the line, though God knows they won very few victories, and even individual desertions were not common. In four or five months in the P.O.U.M. militia I only heard of four men deserting, and two of those were fairly certainly spies who had enlisted to obtain information. At the beginning the apparent chaos, the general lack of training, the fact that you often had to argue for five minutes before you could get an order obeyed, appalled and infuriated me. I had British Army ideas, and certainly the Spanish militias were very unlike the British Army. But considering the circumstances they were better troops than one had any right to expect.

Meanwhile, firewood—always firewood. Throughout that period there is probably no entry in my diary that does not mention firewood, or rather the lack of it. We were between two and three thousand feet above sea level, it was midwinter and the cold was unspeakable. The temperature was not exceptionally low, on many nights it did not even freeze, and the wintry sun often shone for an hour in the middle of the day; but even if it was not really cold, I assure you that it seemed so. Sometimes there were shrieking winds that tore your cap off and twisted your hair in all directions, sometimes there were mists that poured into the trench like a liquid and seemed to penetrate your bones; frequently it rained, and even a quarter of an hour's rain was enough to make conditions intolerable. The thin skin of earth over the limestone turned promptly into a slippery grease, and as you were always walking on a slope it was impossible to keep your footing. On dark nights I have often fallen half a dozen times in twenty yards; and this was dangerous, because it meant that the lock of one's rifle became jammed with mud. For days together clothes, boots, blankets, and rifles were more or less coated with mud. I had brought as many thick clothes as I could carry, but many of the men were terribly underclad. For the whole garrison, about a hundred men, there were only twelve great-coats, which had to be handed from sentry to sentry, and most of the men had only one blanket. One icy night I made a list in my diary of the clothes I was wearing. It is of some interest as showing the amount of clothes the human body can carry. I was wearing a thick vest and pants, a flannel shirt, two pullovers, a woolen jacket, a pigskin jacket, corduroy breeches, puttees, thick socks, boots, a stout trench-coat, a muffler, lined leather gloves, and a woolen cap. Nevertheless I was shivering like a jelly. But I admit I am unusually sensitive to cold.

Firewood was the one thing that really mattered. The point about the firewood was that there was practically no firewood to be had. Our miserable mountain had not even at its best much vegetation, and for months it had been ranged over by freezing militiamen, with the result that everything thicker than one's finger had long since been burnt. When we were not eating, sleeping, on guard or on fatigue duty we were in the valley behind the position, scrounging for fuel. All my memories of that time are memories of scrambling up and down the almost perpendicular slopes, over the jagged limestone that knocked one's boots to pieces, pouncing eagerly on tiny twigs of wood. Three people searching for a couple of hours could collect enough fuel to keep the dugout fire alight for about an hour. The eagerness of our search for firewood turned us all into botanists. We classified according to their burning qualities every plant that grew on the mountainside; the various heaths and grasses that were good to start a fire with but burnt out in a few minutes, the wild rosemary and the tiny whin bushes that would burn when the fire was well alight, the stunted oak tree, smaller than a gooseberry bush, that was practically unburnable. There was a kind of dried-up reed that was very good for starting fires with, but these grew only on the hilltop to the left of the position, and you had to go under fire to get them. If the Fascist machine-gunners saw you they gave you a drum of ammunition all to yourself. Generally their aim was high and the bullets sang overhead like birds, but sometimes they crackled and chipped the limestone uncomfortably close, whereupon you flung yourself on your face. You went on gathering reeds, however; nothing mattered in comparison with firewood.

Beside the cold the other discomforts seemed petty. Of course all of us were permanently dirty. Our water, like our food, came on muleback from Alcubierre, and each man's share worked out at about a quart a day. It was beastly water, hardly more transparent than milk. Theoretically it was for drinking only, but I always stole a pannikinful for washing in the mornings. I used to wash one day and shave the next; there was never enough water for both. The position stank abominably, and outside the little enclosure of the barricade there was excrement everywhere. Some of the militiamen habitually defecated in the trench, a disgusting thing when one had to walk round it in the darkness. But the dirt never worried me. Dirt is a thing people make too much fuss about. It is astonishing how quickly you get used to doing without a handkerchief and to eating out of the tin pannikin in which you also wash. Nor was sleeping in one's clothes any hardship after a day or two. It was of course impossible to take one's clothes and especially one's boots off at night; one had to be ready to turn out instantly in case of an attack. In eighty nights I only took my clothes off three times, though I did occasionally manage to get them off in the daytime. It was too cold for lice as yet, but rats and mice abounded. It is often said that you don't find rats and mice in the same place, but you do when there is enough food for them.

In other ways we were not badly off. The food was good enough and there was plenty of wine. Cigarettes were still being issued at the rate of a packet a day, matches were issued every other day, and there was even an issue of candles. They were very thin candles, like those on a Christmas cake, and were popularly supposed to have been looted from churches. Every dugout was issued daily with three inches of candle, which would burn for about twenty minutes. At that time it was still possible to buy candles, and I had brought several pounds of them with me. Later on the famine of matches and candles made life a misery. You do not realize the importance of these things until you lack them. In a night alarm, for instance, when everyone in the dugout is scrambling for his rifle and treading on everybody else's face, being able to strike a light may make the difference between life and death. Every militiaman possessed a tinder-lighter and several yards of yellow wick. Next to his rifle it was his most important possession. The tinder-lighters had the great advantage that they could be struck in a wind, but they would only smolder, so that they were no use for lighting a fire. When the match famine was at its worst our only way of producing a flame was to pull the bullet out of a cartridge and touch the cordite off with a tinder-lighter.

It was an extraordinary life that we were living—an extraordinary way to be at war, if you could call it war. The whole militia chafed against the inaction and clamored constantly to know why we were not allowed to attack. But it was perfectly obvious that there would be no battle for a long while yet, unless the enemy started it. Georges Kopp,* on his periodical tours of inspection, was quite frank with us. "This is not a war," he used to say, "it is a comic opera with an occasional death." As a matter of fact the stagnation on the Aragon front had political causes of which I knew nothing at that time; but the purely military difficulties—quite apart from the lack of reserves of men—were obvious to anybody.

To begin with, there was the nature of the country. The front line, ours and the Fascists', lay in positions of immense natural strength, which as a rule could only be approached from one side. Provided a few trenches have been dug, such places cannot be taken by infantry, except in overwhelming numbers. In our own position or most of those round us a dozen men with two machine guns could have held off a battalion. Perched on the hilltops as we were, we should have made lovely marks for artillery; but there was no artillery. Sometimes I used to gaze round the landscape and long— oh, how passionately!—for a couple of batteries of guns. One could have destroyed the enemy positions one after another as easily as smashing nuts with a hammer. But on our side the guns simply did not exist. The Fascists did occasionally manage to bring a gun or two from Zaragoza and fire a very few shells, so few that they never even found the range and the shells plunged harmlessly into the empty ravines. Against machine guns and without artillery there are only three things you can do: dig yourself in at a safe distance —four hundred yards, say—advance across the open and be mas-

* A Belgian who was Orwell's commandant.

sacred, or make small-scale night attacks that will not alter the general situation. Practically the alternatives are stagnation or suicide.

And beyond this there was the complete lack of war materials of every description. It needs an effort to realize how badly the militias were armed at this time. Any public school O.T.C. in England is far more like a modern army than we were. The badness of our weapons was so astonishing that it is worth recording in detail.

For this sector of the front the entire artillery consisted of four trench mortars with *fifteen rounds* for each gun. Of course they were far too precious to be fired and the mortars were kept in Alcubierre. There were machine guns at the rate of approximately one to fifty men; they were oldish guns, but fairly accurate up to three or four hundred yards. Beyond this we had only rifles, and the majority of the rifles were scrap iron. There were three types of rifle in use. The first was the long Mauser. These were seldom less than twenty years old, their sights were about as much use as a broken speedometer, and in most of them the rifling was hopelessly corroded; about one rifle in ten was not bad, however. Then there was the short Mauser, or *mousqueton,* really a cavalry weapon. These were more popular than the others because they were lighter to carry and less nuisance in a trench, also because they were comparatively new and looked efficient. Actually they were almost useless. They were made out of reassembled parts, no bolt belonged to its rifle, and three-quarters of them could be counted on to jam after five shots. There were also a few Winchester rifles. These were nice to shoot with, but they were wildly inaccurate, and as their cartridges had no clips they could only be fired one shot at a time. Ammunition was so scarce that each man entering the line was only issued with fifty rounds, and most of it was exceedingly bad. The Spanish-made cartridges were all refills and would jam even the best rifles. The Mexican cartridges were better and were therefore reserved for the machine guns. Best of all was the German-made ammunition, but as this came only from prisoners and deserters there was not much of it. I always kept a clip of German or Mexican ammunition in my pocket for use in an emergency. But in practice when the emergency came I seldom fired my rifle; I was too frightened of the beastly thing jamming and too anxious to reserve at any rate one round that would go off.

We had no tin hats, no bayonets, hardly any revolvers or pistols, and not more than one bomb between five or ten men. The bomb in use at this time was a frightful object known as the "F.A.I. bomb," it having been produced by the Anarchists in the early days of the war. It was on the principle of a Mills bomb, but the lever was held down not by a pin but a piece of tape. You broke the tape and then got rid of the bomb with the utmost possible speed. It was said of these bombs that they were "impartial"; they killed the man they were thrown at and the man who threw them. There were several other types, even more primitive but probably a little less dangerous —to the thrower, I mean. It was not till late March that I saw a bomb worth throwing.

And apart from weapons there was a shortage of all the minor necessities of war. We had no maps or charts, for instance. Spain has never been fully surveyed, and the only detailed maps of this area were the old military ones, which were almost all in the possession of the Fascists. We had no range-finders, no telescopes, no periscopes, no field glasses except a few privately owned pairs, no flares or Very lights, no wire-cutters, no armorers' tools, hardly even any cleaning materials. The Spaniards seemed never to have heard of a pull-through and looked on in surprise when I constructed one. When you wanted your rifle cleaned you took it to the sergeant, who possessed a long brass ramrod which was invariably bent and therefore scratched the rifling. There was not even any gun oil. You greased your rifle with olive oil, when you could get hold of it; at different times I have greased mine with vaseline, with cold cream, and even with bacon fat. Moreover, there were no lanterns or electric torches—at this time there was not, I believe, such a thing as an electric torch throughout the whole of our sector of the front, and you could not buy one nearer than Barcelona, and only with difficulty even there.

As time went on, and the desultory rifle fire rattled among the hills, I began to wonder with increasing skepticism whether anything would ever happen to bring a bit of life, or rather a bit of death, into this cockeyed war. It was pneumonia that we were fighting against, not against men. When the trenches are more than five hundred yards apart no one gets hit except by accident. Of course there were casualties, but the majority of them were self-inflicted. If I remember rightly, the first five men I saw wounded in Spain were all wounded by our own weapons—I don't mean intentionally, but owing to accident or carelessness. Our worn-out rifles were a danger in themselves. Some of them had a nasty trick of going off if the butt was tapped on the ground; I saw a man shoot himself through the hand owing to this. And in the darkness the raw recruits were always firing at one another. One evening when it was barely even dusk a sentry let fly at me from a distance of twenty yards; but he missed me by a yard—goodness knows how many times the Spanish standard of marksmanship has saved my life. Another time I had gone out on patrol in the mist and had carefully warned the guard commander beforehand. But in coming back I stumbled against a bush, the startled sentry called out that the Fascists were coming, and I had the pleasure of hearing the guard commander order everyone to open rapid fire in my direction. Of course I lay down and the bullets went harmlessly over me. Nothing will convince a Spaniard, at least a young Spaniard, that firearms are dangerous. Once, rather later than this, I was photographing some machine-gunners with their gun, which was pointed directly towards me.

"Don't fire," I said half-jokingly as I focused the camera.

"Oh, no, we won't fire."

The next moment there was a frightful roar and a stream of bullets tore past my face so close that my cheek was stung by grains of cordite. It was unintentional, but the machine-gunners considered it a great joke. Yet only a few days earlier they had seen a mule-driver accidentally shot by a political delegate who was playing the fool with an automatic pistol and had put five bullets in the mule-driver's lungs.

The difficult passwords which the army was using at this time were a minor source of danger. They were those tiresome double passwords in which one word has to be answered by another. Usually they were of an elevating and revolutionary nature, such as *Cultura—progreso,* or *Seremos—invencibles,* and it was often impossible to get illiterate sentries to remember these highfalutin words. One night, I remember, the password was *Cataluña—eroica,* and a moon-faced peasant lad named Jaime Domenech approached me, greatly puzzled, and asked me to explain.

"*Eroica*—what does *eroica* mean?"

I told him that it meant the same as *valiente.* A little while later he was stumbling up the trench in the darkness, and the sentry challenged him:

"*Alto! Cataluña!*"

"*Valiente!*" yelled Jaime, certain that he was saying the right thing.

Bang!

However, the sentry missed him. In this war everyone always did miss everyone else, when it was humanly possible.

Chapter Eight

The days grew hotter and even the nights grew tolerably warm. On a bullet-chipped tree in front of our parapet thick clusters of cherries were forming. Bathing in the river ceased to be an agony

and became almost a pleasure. Wild roses with pink blooms the size
of saucers straggled over the shell holes round Torre Fabian. Behind the line you met peasants wearing wild roses over their ears.
In the evenings they used to go out with green nets, hunting quails.
You spread the net over the tops of the grasses and then lay down
and made a noise like a female quail. Any male quail that was
within hearing then came running toward you, and when he was
underneath the net you threw a stone to scare him, whereupon he
sprang into the air and was entangled in the net. Apparently only
male quails were caught, which struck me as unfair.

There was a section of Andalusians next to us in the line now.
I do not know quite how they got to this front. The current explanation was that they had run away from Malaga so fast that they
had forgotten to stop at Valencia; but this, of course, came from
the Catalans, who professed to look down on the Andalusians as a
race of semi-savages. Certainly the Andalusians were very ignorant.
Few if any of them could read, and they seemed not even to know
the one thing that everybody knows in Spain—which political party
they belonged to. They thought they were Anarchists, but were not
quite certain; perhaps they were Communists. They were gnarled,
rustic-looking men, shepherds or laborers from the olive groves,
perhaps, with faces deeply stained by the ferocious suns of farther
south. They were very useful to us, for they had an extraordinary
dexterity at rolling the dried-up Spanish tobacco into cigarettes. The
issue of cigarettes had ceased, but in Monflorite it was occasionally
possible to buy packets of the cheapest kind of tobacco, which in
appearance and texture was very like chopped chaff. Its flavor was
not bad, but it was so dry that even when you had succeeded in
making a cigarette the tobacco promptly fell out and left an empty
cylinder. The Andalusians, however, could roll admirable cigarettes
and had a special technique for tucking the ends in.

Two Englishmen were laid low by sunstroke. My salient memories of that time are the heat of the midday sun, and working half-
naked with sandbags punishing one's shoulders which were already
flayed by the sun; and the lousiness of our clothes and boots, which
were literally dropping to pieces; and the struggles with the mule
which brought our rations and which did not mind rifle fire but
took to flight when shrapnel burst in the air; and the mosquitoes
(just beginning to be active) and the rats, which were a public
nuisance and would even devour leather belts and cartridge pouches.
Nothing was happening except an occasional casualty from a sniper's
bullet and the sporadic artillery fire and air raids on Huesca. Now
that the trees were in full leaf we had constructed snipers' platforms,

like machans, in the poplar trees that fringed the line. On the other side of Huesca the attacks were petering out. The Anarchists had had heavy losses and had not succeeded in completely cutting the Jaca road. They had managed to establish themselves close enough on either side to bring the road itself under machine-gun fire and make it impassable for traffic; but the gap was a kilometer wide and the Fascists had constructed a sunken road, a sort of enormous trench, along which a certain number of lorries could come and go. Deserters reported that in Huesca there were plenty of munitions and very little food. But the town was evidently not going to fall. Probably it would have been impossible to take it with the fifteen thousand ill-armed men who were available. Later, in June, the government brought troops from the Madrid front and concentrated thirty thousand men on Huesca, with an enormous quantity of aeroplanes, but still the town did not fall.

When we went on leave I had been a hundred and fifteen days in the line, and at the time this period seemed to me to have been one of the most futile of my whole life. I had joined the militia in order to fight against Fascism, and as yet I had scarcely fought at all, had merely existed as a sort of passive object, doing nothing in return for my rations except to suffer from cold and lack of sleep. Perhaps that is the fate of most soldiers in most wars. But now that I can see this period in perspective I do not altogether regret it. I wish, indeed, that I could have served the Spanish Government a little more effectively; but from a personal point of view—from the point of view of my own development—those first three or four months that I spent in the line were less futile than I then thought. They formed a kind of interregnum in my life, quite different from anything that had gone before and perhaps from anything that is to come, and they taught me things that I could not have learned in any other way.

The essential point is that all this time I had been isolated—for at the front one was almost completely isolated from the outside world: even of what was happening in Barcelona one had only a dim conception—among people who could roughly but not too inaccurately be described as revolutionaries. This was the result of the militia system, which on the Aragon front was not radically altered till about June, 1937. The workers' militias, based on the trade unions and each composed of people of approximately the same political opinions, had the effect of canalizing into one place all the most revolutionary sentiment in the country. I had dropped more or less by chance into the only community of any size in Western Europe where political consciousness and disbelief in capitalism were more normal than their opposites. Up here in Aragon one was among tens of thousands of people, mainly though not entirely of working-class origin, all living at the same level and mingling on terms of equality. In theory it was perfect equality, and even in practice it was not far from it. There is a sense in which it would be true to say that one was experiencing a fore-taste of socialism, by which I mean that the prevailing mental at-mosphere was that of socialism. Many of the normal motives of civilized life—snobbishness, money-grubbing, fear of the boss, etc.— had simply ceased to exist. The ordinary class division of society had disappeared to an extent that is almost unthinkable in the money-tainted air of England; there was no one there except the peasants and ourselves, and no one owned anyone else as his mas-ter. Of course such a state of affairs could not last. It was simply a temporary and local phase in an enormous game that is being played over the whole surface of the earth. But it lasted long enough to have its effect upon anyone who experienced it. How-ever much one cursed at the time, one realized afterward that one had been in contact with something strange and valuable. One had been in a community where hope was more normal than apathy or cynicism, where the word "comrade" stood for comradeship and not, as in most countries, for humbug. One had breathed the air of equality. I am well aware that it is now the fashion to deny that socialism has anything to do with equality. In every country in the world a huge tribe of party hacks and sleek little profes-sors are busy "proving" that socialism means no more than a planned state capitalism with the grab-motive left intact. But for-tunately there also exists a vision of socialism quite different from this. The thing that attracts ordinary men to socialism and makes them willing to risk their skins for it, the "mystique" of socialism, is the idea of equality; to the vast majority of people socialism means a classless society, or it means nothing at all. And it was here that those few months in the militia were valuable to me. For the Spanish militias, while they lasted, were a sort of mi-crocosm of a classless society. In that community where no one was on the make, where there was a shortage of everything but no privilege and no bootlicking, one got, perhaps, a crude forecast of what the opening stages of socialism might be like. And, after all, instead of disillusioning me it deeply attracted me. The effect was to make my desire to see socialism established much more actual than it had been before. Partly, perhaps, this was due to the good luck of being among Spaniards, who, with their innate decency and their ever-present Anarchist tinge, would make even the opening stages of socialism tolerable if they had the chance.

Of course at the time I was hardly conscious of the changes that were occurring in my own mind. Like everyone about me I was chiefly conscious of boredom, heat, cold, dirt, lice, privation, and occasional danger. It is quite different now. This period which then seemed so futile and eventless is now of great importance to me. It is so different from the rest of my life that already it has taken on the magic quality which, as a rule, belongs only to memories that are years old. It was beastly while it was happening, but it is a good patch for my mind to browse upon. I wish I could convey to you the atmosphere of that time. I hope I have done so, a little, in the earlier chapters of this book. It is all bound up in my mind with the winter cold, the ragged uniforms of militiamen, the oval Spanish faces, the Morse-like tapping of machine guns, the smells of urine and rotting bread, the tinny taste of bean stews wolfed hurriedly out of unclean pannikins.

The whole period stays by me with curious vividness. In my memory I live over incidents that might seem too petty to be worth recalling. I am in the dugout at Monte Pocero again, on the ledge of limestone that serves as a bed, and young Ramon is snoring with his nose flattened between my shoulder blades. I am stumbling up the mucky trench, through the mist that swirls round me like cold steam. I am halfway up a crack in the mountainside, struggling to keep my balance and to tug a root of wild rosemary out of the ground. High overhead some meaningless bullets are singing.

I am lying hidden among small fir trees on the low ground west of Monte Oscuro, with Kopp and Bob Edwards and three Spaniards. Up the naked gray hill to the right of us a string of Fascists are climbing like ants. Close in front a bugle call rings out from the Fascist lines. Kopp catches my eye and, with a schoolboy gesture, thumbs his nose at the sound.

I am in the mucky yard at La Granja, among the mob of men who are struggling with their tin pannikins round the cauldron of stew. The fat and harassed cook is warding them off with the ladle. At a table nearby a bearded man with a huge automatic pistol strapped to his belt is hewing loaves of bread into five pieces. Behind me a Cockney voice (Bill Chambers, with whom I quarreled bitterly and who was afterward killed outside Huesca) is singing:

> There are rats, rats,
> Rats as big as cats,
> In the . .

A shell comes screaming over. Children of fifteen fling themselves on their faces. The cook dodges behind the cauldron. Everyone rises with a sheepish expression as the shell plunges and booms a hundred yards away.

I am walking up and down the line of sentries, under the dark boughs of the poplars. In the flooded ditch outside the rats are paddling about, making as much noise as otters. As the yellow dawn comes up behind us, the Andalusian sentry, muffled in his cloak, begins singing. Across no man's land, a hundred or two hundred yards away, you can hear the Fascist sentry also singing.

On April 25, after the usual *mañanas,* another section relieved us and we handed over our rifles, packed our kits and marched back to Monflorite. I was not sorry to leave the line. The lice were multiplying in my trousers far faster than I could massacre them, and for a month past I had had no socks and my boots had very little sole left, so that I was walking more or less barefoot. I wanted a hot bath, clean clothes, and a night between sheets more passionately than it is possible to want anything when one has been living a normal civilized life. We slept a few hours in a barn in Monflorite, jumped a lorry in the small hours, caught the five o'clock train at Barbastro and—having the luck to connect with a fast train at Lerida—were in Barcelona by three o'clock in the afternoon of the twenty-sixth. And after that the trouble began.

Chapter Nine

From Mandalay, in Upper Burma, you can travel by train to Maymyo, the principal hill-station of the province, on the edge of the Shan plateau. It is rather a queer experience. You start off in the typical atmosphere of an eastern city—the scorching sunlight, the dusty palms, the smells of fish and spices and garlic, the squashy tropical fruits, the swarming dark-faced human beings—and because you are so used to it you carry this atmosphere intact, so to speak, in your railway carriage. Mentally you are still in Mandalay when the train stops at Maymyo, four thousand feet above sea level. But in stepping out of the carriage you step into a different hemisphere. Suddenly you are breathing cool sweet air that might be that of England, and all round you are green grass, bracken, fir trees, and hill women with pink cheeks selling baskets of strawberries.

Getting back to Barcelona, after three and a half months at the front, reminded me of this. There was the same abrupt and startling change of atmosphere. In the train, all the way to Barcelona, the atmosphere of the front persisted; the dirt, the noise, the discomfort, the ragged clothes, the feeling of privation, comradeship and equality. The train, already full of militiamen when it left Barbastro, was invaded by more and more peasants at every station on the line; peasants with bundles of vegetables, with terrified fowls which they carried head-downward, with sacks which looped and writhed all over the floor and were discovered to be full of live rabbits—finally with a quite considerable flock of sheep which were driven into the compartments and wedged into every empty space. The militiamen shouted revolutionary songs which drowned the rattle of the train and kissed their hands or waved red and black handkerchiefs to every pretty girl along the line. Bottles of wine and of anis, the filthy Aragonese liqueur, traveled from hand to hand. With the Spanish goatskin water-bottles you can squirt a jet of wine right across a railway carriage into your friend's mouth, which saves a lot of trouble. Next to me a black-eyed boy of fifteen was recounting sensational and, I do not doubt, completely untrue stories of his own exploits at the front to two old leather-faced peasants who listened open-mouthed. Presently the peasants undid their bundles and gave us some sticky dark-red wine. Everyone was profoundly happy, more happy than I can convey. But when the train had rolled through Sabadell and into Barcelona, we stepped into an atmosphere that was scarcely less alien and hostile to us and our kind than if this had been Paris or London.

Everyone who has made two visits, at intervals of months, to Barcelona during the war has remarked upon the extraordinary changes that took place in it. And curiously enough, whether they went there first in August and again in January, or, like myself, first in December and again in April, the thing they said was always the same: that the revolutionary atmosphere had vanished. No doubt to anyone who had been there in August, when the blood was scarcely dry in the streets and militia were quartered in the smart hotels, Barcelona in December would have seemed bourgeois; to me, fresh from England, it was liker to a workers' city than anything I had conceived possible. Now the tide had rolled back. Once again it was an ordinary city, a little pinched and chipped by war, but with no outward sign of working-class predominance.

The change in the aspect of the crowds was startling. The militia uniform and the blue overalls had almost disappeared; everyone seemed to be wearing the smart summer suits in which Spanish tailors specialize. Fat prosperous men, elegant women, and sleek cars were everywhere. (It appeared that there were still no private cars; nevertheless, anyone who "was anyone" seemed able to command a car.) The officers of the new Popular Army, a type that had scarcely existed when I left Barcelona, swarmed in surprising numbers. The Popular Army was officered at the rate of one officer to ten men. A certain number of these officers had served in the militia and been brought back from the front for technical instruction, but the majority were young men who had gone to the School of War in preference to joining the militia. Their relation to their men was not quite the same as in a bourgeois army, but there was a definite social difference, expressed by the difference of pay and uniform. The men wore a kind of coarse brown overalls, the officers wore an elegant khaki uniform with a tight waist, like a British Army officer's uniform, only a little more so. I do not suppose that more than one in twenty of them had yet been to the front, but all of them had automatic pistols strapped to their belts; we, at the front, could not get pistols for love or money. As we made our way up the street I noticed that people were staring at our dirty exteriors. Of course, like all men who have been several months in the line, we were a dreadful sight. I was conscious of looking like a scarecrow. My leather jacket was in tatters, my woolen cap had lost its shape and slid perpetually over one eye, my boots consisted of very little beyond splayed-out uppers. All of us were in more or less the same state, and in addition we were dirty and unshaven, so it was no wonder that the people stared. But it dismayed me a little, and brought it home to me that some queer things had been happening in the last three months.

During the next few days I discovered by innumerable signs that my first impression had not been wrong. A deep change had come over the town. There were two facts that were the keynote of all else. One was that the people—the civil population—had lost much of their interest in the war; the other was that the normal division of society into rich and poor, upper class and lower class, was reasserting itself.

The general indifference to the war was surprising and rather disgusting. It horrified people who came to Barcelona from Madrid or even from Valencia. Partly it was due to the remoteness of Barcelona from the actual fighting; I noticed the same thing a month later in Tarragona, where the ordinary life of a smart seaside town was continuing almost undisturbed. But it was significant that all over Spain voluntary enlistment had dwindled from about January onward. In Catalonia, in February, there had been a wave of enthusiasm over the first big drive for the Popular Army, but it had not led to any great increase in recruiting. The war was only six months old or thereabouts when the Spanish Government had to resort to conscription, which would be natural in a foreign war, but seems anomalous in a civil war. Undoubtedly it was bound up with the disappointment of the revolutionary hopes with which the war had started. The trade-union members who formed themselves into militias and chased the Fascists back to Zaragoza in the first few weeks of war had done so largely because they believed themselves to be fighting for working-class control; but it was becoming more and more obvious that working-class control was a lost cause, and the common people, especially the town proletariat, who have to fill the ranks in any war, civil or foreign, could not be blamed for a certain apathy. Nobody wanted to lose the war, but the majority were chiefly anxious for it to be over. You noticed this wherever you went. Everywhere you met with the same perfunctory remark: "This war—terrible, isn't it? When is it going to end?" Politically conscious people were far more aware of the internecine struggle between Anarchist and Communist than of the fight against Franco. To the mass of the people the food shortage was the most important thing. "The front" had come to be thought of as a mythical far-off place to which young men disappeared and either did not return or returned after three or four months with vast sums of money in their pockets. (A militiaman usually received his back pay when he went on leave.) Wounded men, even when they were hopping about on crutches, did not receive any special consideration. To be in the militia was no longer fashionable. The shops, always the barometers of public taste, showed this clearly. When I first reached Barcelona the shops, poor and shabby though they were, had specialized in militiamen's equipment. Forage caps, zipper jackets, Sam Browne belts, hunting knives, water-bottles, revolver-holsters were displayed in every window. Now the shops were markedly smarter, but the war had been thrust into the background. As I discovered later, when buying my kit before going back to the front, certain things that one badly needed at the front were very difficult to procure.

Meanwhile there was going on a systematic propaganda against the party militias and in favor of the Popular Army. The position here was rather curious. Since February the entire armed forces had theoretically been incorporated in the Popular Army, and the militias were, on paper, reconstructed along Popular Army lines, with differential pay rates, gazetted rank, etc., etc. The divisions were made up of "mixed brigades," which were supposed to consist partly of Popular Army troops and partly of militia. But the only changes that had actually taken place were changes of name. The P.O.U.M. troops, for instance, previously called the Lenin Division, were now known as the 29th Division. Until June very few Popular Army troops reached the Aragon front, and in consequence the militias were able to retain their separate structure and their special character. But on every wall the government agents had stenciled: "We need a Popular Army," and over the radio and in the Communist Press there was a ceaseless and sometimes very malignant jibing against the militias, who were described as ill trained, undisciplined, etc., etc.; the Popular Army was always described as "heroic." From much of this propaganda you would have derived the impression that there was something disgraceful in having gone to the front voluntarily and something praiseworthy in waiting to be conscripted. For the time being, however, the militias were holding the line while the Popular Army was training in the rear, and this fact had to be advertised as little as possible. Drafts of militia returning to the front were no longer marched throught the streets with drums beating and flags flying. They were smuggled away by train or lorry at five o'clock in the morning. A few drafts of the Popular Army were now beginning to leave for the front, and these, as before, were marched ceremoniously through the streets; but even they, owing to the general waning of interest in the war, met with comparatively little enthusiasm. The fact that the militia troops were also, on paper, Popular Army troops, was skillfully used in the press propaganda. Any credit that happened to be going was automatically handed to the Popular Army, while all blame was reserved for the militias. It sometimes happened that the same troops were praised in one capacity and blamed in the other.

But besides all this there was the startling change in the social atmosphere—a thing difficult to conceive unless you have actually experienced it. When I first reached Barcelona I had thought it a town where class distinctions and great differences of wealth hardly existed. Certainly that was what it looked like. "Smart" clothes were an abnormality, nobody cringed or took tips, waiters and flower-women and bootblacks looked you in the eye and called you "Comrade." I had not grasped that this was mainly a mixture of hope and camouflage. The working class believed in a revolution that had been begun but never consolidated, and the bourgeoisie were scared and temporarily disguising themselves as workers. In the first months of revolution there must have been many thousands of people who deliberately put on overalls and shouted revolutionary slogans as a way of saving their skins. Now things were returning to normal. The smart restaurants and hotels were full of rich people wolfing expensive meals, while for the working-class population food prices had jumped enormously without any corresponding rise in wages. Apart from the expensiveness of everything, there were recurrent shortages of this and that, which, of course, always hit the poor rather than the rich. The restaurants and hotels seemed to have little difficulty in getting whatever they wanted, but in the working-class quarters the queues for bread, olive oil, and other necessaries were hundreds of yards long. Previously in Barcelona I had been struck by the absence of beggars; now there were quantities of them. Outside the delicatessen shops at the top of the Ramblas gangs of barefooted children were always waiting to swarm round anyone who came out and clamor for scraps of food. The "revolutionary" forms of speech were dropping out of use. Strangers seldom addressed you as *tu* and *cama-rada* nowadays; it was usually *señor* and *usted. Buenos dias* was beginning to replace *salud*. The waiters were back in their boiled shirts and the shop-walkers were cringing in the familiar manner. My wife and I went into a hosiery shop on the Ramblas to buy some stockings. The shopman bowed and rubbed his hands as they do not do even in England nowadays, though they used to do it twenty or thirty years ago. In a furtive indirect way the practice of tipping was coming back. The workers' patrols had been ordered to dissolve and the pre-war police forces were back on the streets. One result of this was that the cabaret shows and high-class brothels, many of which had been closed by the workers' patrols, had promptly re-opened.* A small but significant instance of the way in which everything was now orientated in favor of the wealthier classes could be seen in the tobacco shortage. For the mass of the people the shortage of tobacco was so desperate that cigarettes filled with sliced liquorice-root were being sold in the streets. I tried some of these once. (A lot of people tried them once.) Franco held the Canaries, where all the Spanish tobacco is grown; consequently the only stocks of tobacco left on the government side were those that had been in existence before the war. These were running so low that the tobacconists' shops only opened once a week; after waiting for a couple of hours in a queue you might, if you were lucky, get a three-quarter-ounce packet of tobacco. Theoretically the government would not allow tobacco to

---

* Orwell's footnote to the original edition read: "The workers' patrols are said to have closed 75 per cent of the brothels." An errata note found after his death says: "Remark should be modified. I have no good evidence that prostitution decreased 75 per cent in the early days of the war, and I believe the Anarchists went on the principle of 'collectivizing' the brothels, not suppressing them. But there was a drive against prostitution (posters, etc.) and it is a fact that the smart brothel and naked cabaret shows were shut in the early months of the war and open again when the war was about a year old."

be purchased from abroad, because this meant reducing the gold reserves, which had got to be kept for arms and other necessities. Actually there was a steady supply of smuggled foreign cigarettes of the more expensive kinds, Lucky Strikes and so forth, which gave a grand opportunity for profiteering. You could buy the smuggled cigarettes openly in the smart hotels and hardly less openly in the streets, provided that you could pay ten pesetas (a militiaman's daily wage) for a packet. The smuggling was for the benefit of wealthy people, and was therefore connived at. If you had enough money there was nothing that you could not get in any quantity, with the possible exception of bread, which was rationed fairly strictly. This open contrast of wealth and poverty would have been impossible a few months earlier, when the working class still were or seemed to be in control. But it would not be fair to attribute it solely to the shift of political power. Partly it was a result of the safety of life in Barcelona, where there was little to remind one of the war except an occasional air raid. Everyone who had been in Madrid said that it was completely different there. In Madrid the common danger forced people of almost all kinds into some sense of comradeship. A fat man eating quails while children are begging for bread is a disgusting sight, but you are less likely to see it when you are within sound of the guns.

A day or two after the street fighting * I remember passing through one of the fashionable streets and coming upon a confectioner's shop with a window full of pastries and bon-bons of the most elegant kinds, at staggering prices. It was the kind of shop you see in Bond Street or the Rue de la Paix. And I remember feeling a vague horror and amazement that money could still be wasted upon such things in a hungry war-stricken country. But God forbid that I should pretend to any personal superiority. After several months of discomfort I had a ravenous desire for decent food and wine, cocktails, American cigarettes, and so forth, and I admit to having wallowed in every luxury that I had money to buy. During that first week, before the street fighting began, I had several preoccupations which interacted upon one another in a curious way. In the first place, as I have said, I was busy making myself as comfortable as I could. Secondly, thanks to overeating and overdrinking, I was slightly out of health all that week. I would feel a little unwell, go to bed for half a day, get up and eat an-

---

* Street fighting, which Orwell describes in Chapter Ten of *Homage to Catalonia,* broke out in Barcelona on May 3 when the Spanish Government sent Assault Guards to take over the Telephone Exchange, hitherto held by the Anarchists

other excessive meal, and then feel ill again. At the same time I was making secret negotiations to buy a revolver. I badly wanted a revolver—in trench-fighting much more useful than a rifle—and they were very difficult to get hold of. The government issued them to policemen and Popular Army officers, but refused to issue them to the militia; you had to buy them, illegally, from the secret stores of the Anarchists. After a lot of fuss and nuisance an Anarchist friend managed to procure me a tiny 26-inch automatic pistol, a wretched weapon, useless at more than five yards, but better than nothing. And besides all this I was making preliminary arrangements to leave the P.O.U.M. militia and enter some other unit that would ensure my being sent to the Madrid front.

I had told everyone for a long time past that I was going to leave the P.O.U.M. As far as my purely personal preferences went I would have liked to join the Anarchists. If one became a member of the C.N.T. it was possible to enter the F.A.I. militia, but I was told that the F.A.I. were likelier to send me to Teruel than to Madrid. If I wanted to go to Madrid I must join the International Column, which meant getting a recommendation from a member of the Communist Party. I sought out a Communist friend, attached to the Spanish Medical Aid, and explained my case to him. He seemed very anxious to recruit me and asked me, if possible, to persuade some of the other I.L.P. Englishmen to come with me. If I had been in better health I should probably have agreed there and then. It is hard to say now what difference this would have made. Quite possibly I should have been sent to Albacete before the Barcelona fighting started; in which case, not having seen the fighting at close quarters, I might have accepted the official version of it as truthful. On the other hand, if I had been in Barcelona during the fighting, under Communist orders but still with a sense of personal loyalty to my comrades in the P.O.U.M., my position would have been impossible. But I had another week's leave due to me and I was very anxious to get my health back before returning to the line. Also—the kind of detail that is always deciding one's destiny—I had to wait while the bootmakers made me a new pair of marching boots. (The entire Spanish army had failed to produce a pair of boots big enough to fit me.) I told my Communist friend that I would make definite arrangements later. Meanwhile I wanted a rest. I even had a notion that we—my wife and I—might go to the seaside for two or three days. What an idea! The political atmosphere ought to have warned me that that was not the kind of thing one could do nowadays.

For under the surface aspect of the town, under the luxury and growing poverty, under the seeming gaiety of the streets, with their flower-stalls, their many-colored flags, their propaganda posters, and thronging crowds, there was an unmistakable and horrible feeling of political rivalry and hatred. People of all shades of opinion were saying forebodingly: "There's going to be trouble before long." The danger was quite simple and intelligible. It was the antagonism between those who wished the revolution to go forward and those who wished to check or prevent it—ultimately, between Anarchists and Communists. Politically there was now no power in Catalonia except the P.S.U.C. and their Liberal allies. But over against this there was the uncertain strength of the C.N.T., less well armed and less sure of what they wanted than their adversaries, but powerful because of their numbers and their predominance in various key industries. Given this alignment of forces there was bound to be trouble. From the point of view of the P.S.U.C.-controlled Generalite, the first necessity, to make their position secure, was to get the weapons out of the C.N.T. workers' hands. As I have pointed out earlier, the move to break up the party militias was at bottom a maneuver toward this end. At the same time the pre-war armed police forces, Civil Guards, and so forth, had been brought back into use and were being heavily reinforced and armed. This could mean only one thing. The Civil Guards, in particular, were a gendarmerie of the ordinary continental type, who for nearly a century past had acted as the bodyguards of the possessing class. Meanwhile a decree had been issued that all arms held by private persons were to be surrendered. Naturally this order had not been obeyed; it was clear that the Anarchists' weapons could only be taken from them by force. Throughout this time there were rumors, always vague and contradictory owing to newspaper censorship, of minor clashes that were occurring all over Catalonia. In various places the armed police forces had made attacks on Anarchist strongholds. At Puigcerda, on the French frontier, a band of Carabineros were sent to seize the Customs Office, previously controlled by Anarchists, and Antonio Martin, a well-known Anarchist, was killed.* Similar incidents had occurred at Figueras and, I think, at Tarragona. In Barcelona there had been a series of more or less unofficial brawls in the working-class suburbs. C.N.T. and U.G.T. members had been murdering one another for some time past; on several occasions the murders were followed by huge, provocative funerals which were

* Errata note found after Orwell's death: "I am told my reference to this incident is incorrect and misleading."

quite deliberately intended to stir up political hatred. A short time earlier a C.N.T. member had been murdered, and the C.N.T. had turned out in hundreds of thousands to follow the cortège. At the end of April, just after I got to Barcelona, Roldan Cortada, a prominent member of the U.G.T., was murdered, presumably by someone in the C.N.T. The government ordered all shops to close and staged an enormous funeral procession, largely of Popular Army troops, which took two hours to pass a given point. From the hotel window I watched it without enthusiasm. It was obvious that the so-called funeral was merely a display of strength; a little more of this kind of thing and there might be bloodshed. The same night my wife and I were woken by a fusillade of shots from the Plaza de Catalunya, a hundred or two hundred yards away. We learned next day that it was a C.N.T. man being bumped off, presumably by someone in the U.G.T. It was of course distinctly possible that all these murders were committed by agents provocateurs. One can gauge the attitude of the foreign capitalist press toward the Communist-Anarchist feud by the fact that Roldan's murder was given wide publicity, while the answering murder was carefully unmentioned.

The 1st of May was approaching, and there was talk of a monster demonstration in which both the C.N.T. and the U.G.T. were to take part. The C.N.T. leaders, more moderate than many of their followers, had long been working for a reconciliation with the U.G.T.; indeed the keynote of their policy was to try and form the two blocks of unions into one huge coalition. The idea was that the C.N.T. and U.G.T. should march together and display their solidarity. But at the last moment the demonstration was called off. It was perfectly clear that it would only lead to rioting. So nothing happened on May 1. It was a queer state of affairs. Barcelona, the so-called revolutionary city, was probably the only city in non-Fascist Europe that had no celebrations that day. But I admit I was rather relieved. The I.L.P. contingent was expected to march in the P.O.U.M. section of the procession, and everyone expected trouble. The last thing I wished for was to be mixed up in some meaningless street fight. To be marching up the street behind red flags inscribed with elevating slogans, and then to be bumped off from an upper window by some total stranger with a sub-machine gun—that is not my idea of a useful way to die.

Chapter Fourteen

The worst of being wanted by the police in a town like Barcelona is that everything opens so late. When you sleep out of doors you always wake about dawn, and none of the Barcelona cafés opens much before nine. It was hours before I could get a cup of coffee or a shave. It seemed queer, in the barber's shop, to see the Anarchist notice still on the wall, explaining that tips were prohibited. "The Revolution has struck off our chains," the notice said. I felt like telling the barbers that their chains would soon be back again if they didn't look out.

I wandered back to the center of the town. Over the P.O.U.M. buildings the red flags had been torn down, Republican flags were floating in their place, and knots of armed Civil Guards were lounging in the doorways. At the Red Aid center on the corner of the Plaza de Catalunya the police had amused themselves by smashing most of the windows. The P.O.U.M. bookstalls had been emptied of books and the notice board farther down the Ramblas had been plastered with an anti-P.O.U.M. cartoon—the one representing the mask and the Fascist face beneath. Down at the bottom of the Ramblas, near the quay, I came upon a queer sight: a row of militiamen, still ragged and muddy from the front, sprawling exhaustedly on the chairs placed there for the bootblacks. I knew who they were—indeed, I recognized one of them. They were P.O.U.M. militiamen who had come down the line on the previous day to find that the P.O.U.M. had been suppressed, and had had to spend the night in the streets because their homes had been raided. Any P.O.U.M. militiaman who returned to Barcelona at this time had the choice of going straight into hiding or into jail —not a pleasant reception after three or four months in the line.

It was a queer situation that we were in. At night one was a hunted fugitive, but in the daytime one could live an almost normal life. Every house known to harbor P.O.U.M. supporters was— or at any rate was likely to be—under observation, and it was impossible to go to a hotel or boarding-house, because it had been decreed that on the arrival of a stranger the hotel-keeper must inform the police immediately. Practically this meant spending the night out of doors. In the daytime, on the other hand, in a town the size of Barcelona, you were fairly safe. The streets were thronged by Civil Guards, Assault Guards, Carabineros, and ordinary police, besides God knows how many spies in plain clothes; still, they could not stop everyone who passed, and if you looked normal you might escape notice. The thing to do was to avoid hanging round P.O.U.M. buildings and going to cafés and restaurants where the waiters knew you by sight. I spent a long time that day, and the next, in having a bath at one of the public baths. This struck me as a good way of putting in the time and keeping out of sight.

Unfortunately the same idea occurred to a lot of people, and a few days later—after I left Barcelona—the police raided one of the public baths and arrested a number of "Trotskyists" in a state of nature.

Halfway up the Ramblas I ran into one of the wounded men from the Sanatorium Maurin. We exchanged the sort of invisible wink that people were exchanging at that time, and managed in an unobtrusive way to meet in a café farther up the street. He had escaped arrest when the Maurin was raided, but, like the others, had been driven into the street. He was in shirtsleeves—had had to flee without his jacket—and had no money. He described to me how one of the Civil Guards had torn the large colored portrait of Maurin from the wall and kicked it to pieces. Maurin (one of the founders of the P.O.U.M.) was a prisoner in the hands of the Fascists and at that time was believed to have been shot by them.

I met my wife at the British Consulate at ten o'clock. McNair and Cottman turned up shortly afterward. The first thing they told me was that Bob Smillie was dead. He had died in prison at Valencia—of what, nobody knew for certain. He had been buried immediately, and the I.L.P. representative on the spot, David Murray, had been refused permission to see his body.

Of course I assumed at once that Smillie had been shot. It was what everyone believed at the time, but I have since thought that I may have been wrong. Later the cause of his death was given out as appendicitis, and we heard afterward from another prisoner who had been released that Smillie had certainly been ill in prison. So perhaps the appendicitis story was true. The refusal to let Murray see his body may have been due to pure spite. I must say this, however. Bob Smillie was only twenty-two years old and physically he was one of the toughest people I have met. He was, I think, the only person I knew, English or Spanish, who went three months in the trenches without a day's illness. People so tough as that do not usually die of appendicitis if they are properly looked after. But when you saw what the Spanish jails were like—the makeshift jails used for political prisoners—you realized how much chance there was of a sick man getting proper attention. The jails were places that could only be described as dungeons. In England you would have to go back to the eighteenth century to find anything comparable. People were penned together in small rooms where there was barely space for them to lie down, and often they were kept in cellars and other dark places. This was not as a temporary measure—there were cases of people being kept four and five months almost without sight of daylight. And they were fed on a filthy and insufficient diet of two plates of soup and two pieces of bread a day. (Some months later, however, the food seems to have improved a little.) I am not exaggerating; ask any political suspect who was imprisoned in Spain. I have had accounts of the Spanish jails from a number of separate sources, and they agree with one another too well to be disbelieved; besides, I had a few glimpses into one Spanish jail myself. Another English friend who was imprisoned later writes that his experiences in jail "make Smillie's case easier to understand." Smillie's death is not a thing I can easily forgive. Here was this brave and gifted boy, who had thrown up his career at Glasgow University in order to come and fight against Fascism, and who, as I saw for myself, had done his job at the front with faultless courage and willingness; and all they could find to do with him was to fling him into jail and let him die like a neglected animal. I know that in the middle of a huge and bloody war it is no use making too much fuss over an individual death. One aeroplane bomb in a crowded street causes more suffering than quite a lot of political persecution. But what angers one about a death like this is its utter pointlessness. To be killed in battle—yes, that is what one expects; but to be flung into jail, not even for any imaginary offense, but simply owing to dull blind spite, and then left to die in solitude—that is a different matter. I fail to see how this kind of thing—and it is not as though Smillie's case were exceptional—brought victory any nearer.

My wife and I visited Kopp that afternoon. You were allowed to visit prisoners who were not *incomunicado,* though it was not safe to do so more than once or twice. The police watched the people who came and went, and if you visited the jails too often you stamped yourself as a friend of "Trotskyists" and probably ended in jail yourself. This had already happened to a number of people.

Kopp was not *incomunicado* and we got a permit to see him without difficulty. As they led us through the steel doors into the jail, a Spanish militiaman whom I had known at the front was being led out between two Civil Guards. His eye met mine; again the ghostly wink. And the first person we saw inside was an American militiaman who had left for home a few days earlier; his papers were in good order, but they had arrested him at the frontier all the same, probably because he was still wearing corduroy breeches and was therefore identifiable as a militiaman. We walked past one another as though we had been total strangers. That was dreadful. I had known him for months, had shared a dugout with him, he had helped to carry me down the line when I was wounded; but it was the only thing one could do. The blue-clad guards were snooping everywhere. It would be fatal to recognize too many people.

The so-called jail was really the ground floor of a shop. Into two rooms each measuring about twenty feet square, close on a hundred people were penned. The place had the real eighteenth-century Newgate Calendar appearance, with its frowsy dirt, its huddle of human bodies, its lack of furniture—just the bare stone floor, one bench, and a few ragged blankets—and its murky light, for the corrugated steel shutters had been drawn over the windows. On the grimy walls revolutionary slogans—*"Visca P.O.U.M.!"* *"Viva la Revolucion!"* and so forth—had been scrawled. The place had been used as a dump for political prisoners for months past. There was a deafening racket of voices. This was the visiting hour, and the place was so packed with people that it was difficult to move. Nearly all of them were of the poorest of the working-class population. You saw women undoing pitiful packets of food which they had brought for their imprisoned menfolk. There were several of the wounded men from the Sanatorium Maurin among the prisoners. Two of them had amputated legs; one of them had been brought to prison without his crutch and was hopping about on one foot. There was also a boy of not more than twelve; they were even arresting children, apparently. The place had the beastly stench that you always get when crowds of people are penned together without proper sanitary arrangements.

Kopp elbowed his way through the crowd to meet us. His plump fresh-colored face looked much as usual, and in that filthy place he had kept his uniform neat and had even contrived to shave. There was another officer in the uniform of the Popular Army among the prisoners. He and Kopp saluted as they struggled past one another; the gesture was pathetic, somehow. Kopp seemed in excellent spirits. "Well, I suppose we shall all be shot," he said cheerfully. The word "shot" gave me a sort of inward shudder. A bullet had entered my own body recently and the feeling of it was fresh in my memory; it is not nice to think of that happening to anyone you know well. At that time I took it for granted that all the principal people in the P.O.U.M., and Kopp among them, *would* be shot. The first rumor of Nin's death had just filtered through, and we knew that the P.O.U.M. were being accused of treachery and espionage. Everything pointed to a huge frame-up trial followed by a massacre of leading "Trotskyists." It is a terrible thing to see your friend in jail and to know yourself impotent to help him. For there was nothing that one could do; use-less even to appeal to the Belgian authorities, for Kopp had broken the law of his own country by coming here. I had to leave most of the talking to my wife; with my squeaking voice * I could not make myself heard in the din. Kopp was telling us about the friends he had made among the other prisoners, about the guards, some of whom were good fellows, but some of whom abused and beat the more timid prisoners, and about the food, which was "pig-wash." Fortunately we had thought to bring a packet of food, also ciga-rettes. Then Kopp began telling us about the papers that had been taken from him when he was arrested. Among them was his letter from the Ministry of War, addressed to the colonel commanding engineering operations in the Army of the East. The police had seized it and refused to give it back; it was said to be lying in the Chief of Police's office. It might make a very great difference if it were recovered.

I saw instantly how important this might be. An official letter of that kind, bearing the recommendation of the Ministry of War and of General Pozas, would establish Kopp's bona fides. But the trouble was to prove that the letter existed; if it were opened in the Chief of Police's office one could be sure that some nark or other would destroy it. There was only one person who might pos-sibly be able to get it back, and that was the officer to whom it was addressed. Kopp had already thought of this, and he had writ-ten a letter which he wanted me to smuggle out of the jail and post. But it was obviously quicker and surer to go in person. I left my wife with Kopp, rushed out, and, after a long search, found a taxi. I knew that time was everything. It was now about half-past five, the colonel would probably leave his office at six, and by tomorrow the letter might be God knew where—destroyed, per-haps, or lost somewhere in the chaos of documents that was pre-sumably piling up as suspect after suspect was arrested. The colo-nel's office was at the War Department down by the quay. As I hurried up the steps the Assault Guard on duty at the door barred the way with his long bayonet and demanded "papers." I waved my discharge ticket at him; evidently he could not read, and he let me pass, impressed by the vague mystery of "papers." Inside, the place was a huge complicated warren running round a central courtyard, with hundreds of offices on each floor; and, as this was Spain, nobody had the vaguest idea where the office I was looking

---

* Orwell had been wounded in the neck and had not yet regained full use of his voice.

for was. I kept repeating: *"El coronel ——, jefe de ingenieros, Ejer-cito de Este!"* People smiled and shrugged their shoulders grace-fully. Everyone who had an opinion sent me in a different direc-tion; up these stairs, down those, along interminable passages which turned out to be blind alleys. And time was slipping away. I had the strangest sensation of being in a nightmare: the rushing up and down flights of stairs, the mysterious people coming and go-ing, the glimpses through open doors of chaotic offices with papers strewn everywhere and typewriters clicking; and time slipping away and a life perhaps in the balance.

However, I got there in time, and slightly to my surprise I was granted a hearing. I did not see Colonel ——, but his aide-de-camp or secretary, a little slip of an officer in smart uniform, with large and squinting eyes, came out to interview me in the ante-room. I began to pour forth my story. I had come on behalf of my su-perior officer, Major Jorge Kopp, who was on an urgent mission to the front and had been arrested by mistake. The letter to Colo-nel —— was of a confidential nature and should be recovered with-out delay. I had served with Kopp for months, he was an officer of the highest character, obviously his arrest was a mistake, the police had confused him with someone else, etc., etc., etc. I kept piling it on about the urgency of Kopp's mission to the front, knowing that this was the strongest point. But it must have sounded a strange tale, in my villainous Spanish which lapsed into French at every crisis. The worst was that my voice gave out almost at once and it was only by violent straining that I could produce a sort of croak. I was in dread that it would disappear altogether and the little officer would grow tired of trying to listen to me. I have often wondered what he thought was wrong with my voice —whether he thought I was drunk or merely suffering from a guilty conscience.

However, he heard me patiently, nodded his head a great num-ber of times and gave a guarded assent to what I said. Yes, it sounded as though there might have been a mistake. Clearly the matter should be looked into. *Mañana—.* I protested. Not *mañana!* The matter was urgent; Kopp was due at the front already. Again the officer seemed to agree. Then came the question I was dreading:

"This Major Kopp—what force was he serving in?"

The terrible word had to come out: "In the P.O.U.M. militia."

"P.O.U.M.!"

I wish I could convey to you the shocked alarm in his voice. You have got to remember how the P.O.U.M. was regarded at that moment. The spy scare was at its height; probably all good Republicans did believe for a day or two that the P.O.U.M. was a huge spying organization in German pay. To have to say such a thing to an officer in the Popular Army was like going into the Cavalry Club immediately after the Red Letter scare and announcing yourself a Communist. His dark eyes moved obliquely across my face. Another long pause, then he said slowly:

"And you say you were with him at the front. Then you were serving in the P.O.U.M. militia yourself?"

"Yes."

He turned and dived into the colonel's room. I could hear an agitated conversation. "It's all up," I thought. We should never get Kopp's letter back. Moreover I had had to confess that I was in the P.O.U.M. myself, and no doubt they would ring up the police and get me arrested, just to add another Trotskyist to the bag. Presently, however, the officer reappeared, fitting on his cap, and sternly signed to me to follow. We were going to the Chief of Police's office. It was a long way, twenty minutes' walk. The little officer marched stiffly in front with a military step. We did not exchange a single word the whole way. When we got to the Chief of Police's office a crowd of the most dreadful-looking scoundrels, obviously police narks, informers, and spies of every kind, were hanging about outside the door. The little officer went in; there was a long, heated conversation. You could hear voices furiously raised; you pictured violent gestures, shruggings of the shoulders, bangings on the table. Evidently the police were refusing to give the letter up. At last, however, the officer emerged, flushed, but carrying a large official envelope. It was Kopp's letter. We had won a tiny victory—which, as it turned out, made not the slightest difference. The letter was duly delivered, but Kopp's military superiors were quite unable to get him out of jail.

The officer promised me that the letter should be delivered. But what about Kopp? I said. Could we not get him released? He shrugged his shoulders. That was another matter. They did not know what Kopp had been arrested for. He would only tell me that the proper inquiries would be made. There was no more to be said; it was time to part. Both of us bowed slightly. And then there happened a strange and moving thing. The little officer hesitated a moment, then stepped across and shook hands with me.

I do not know if I can bring home to you how deeply that action touched me. It sounds a small thing, but it was not. You have got to realize what was the feeling of the time—the horrible atmosphere of suspicion and hatred, the lies and rumors circulating everywhere, the posters screaming from the hoardings that I and

everyone like me was a Fascist spy. And you have got to remember
that we were standing outside the Chief of Police's office, in front
of that filthy gang of tale-bearers and agents provocateurs, any one
of whom might know that I was "wanted" by the police. It was
like publicly shaking hands with a German during the Great War.
I suppose he had decided in some way that I was not really a
Fascist spy; still, it was good of him to shake hands.

I record this, trivial though it may sound, because it is somehow typical of Spain—of the flashes of magnanimity that you get
from Spaniards in the worst of circumstances. I have the most evil
memories of Spain, but I have very few bad memories of Spaniards.
I only twice remember even being seriously angry with a Spaniard,
and on each occasion, when I look back, I believe I was in the
wrong myself. They have, there is no doubt, a generosity, a species
of nobility, that do not really belong to the twentieth century. It
is this that makes one hope that in Spain even Fascism may take
a comparatively loose and bearable form. Few Spaniards possess the
damnable efficiency and consistency that a modern totalitarian state
needs. There had been a queer little illustration of this fact a few
nights earlier, when the police had searched my wife's room. As a
matter of fact that search was a very interesting business, and I
wish I had seen it, though perhaps it is as well that I did not, for
I might not have kept my temper.

The police conducted the search in the recognized Ogpu or Gestapo style. In the small hours of the morning there was a pounding on the door, and six men marched in, switched on the light,
and immediately took up various positions about the room, obviously agreed upon beforehand. They then searched both rooms
(there was a bathroom attached) with inconceivable thoroughness.
They sounded the walls, took up the mats, examined the floor,
felt the curtains, probed under the bath and the radiator, emptied
every drawer and suitcase, and felt every garment and held it up
to the light. They impounded all papers, including the contents
of the waste-paper basket, and all our books into the bargain. They
were thrown into ecstasies of suspicion by finding that we possessed
a French translation of Hitler's *Mein Kampf*. If that had been the
only book they found our doom would have been sealed. It is obvious that a person who reads *Mein Kampf* must be a Fascist. The
next moment, however, they came upon a copy of Stalin's pamphlet, *Ways of Liquidating Trotskyists and other Double Dealers*,
which reassured them somewhat. In one drawer there was a number of packets of cigarette papers. They picked each packet to
pieces and examined each paper separately, in case there should

be messages written on them. Altogether they were on the job for nearly two hours. Yet all this time they *never searched the bed.* My wife was lying in bed all the while; obviously there might have been half a dozen sub-machine guns under the mattress, not to mention a library of Trotskyist documents under the pillow. Yet the detectives made no move to touch the bed, never even looked underneath it. I cannot believe that this is a regular feature of the Ogpu routine. One must remember that the police were almost entirely under Communist control, and these men were probably Communist Party members themselves. But they were also Spaniards, and to turn a woman out of bed was a little too much for them. This part of the job was silently dropped, making the whole search meaningless.

That night McNair, Cottman, and I slept in some long grass at the edge of a derelict building lot. It was a cold night for the time of year and no one slept much. I remember the long dismal hours of loitering about before one could get a cup of coffee. For the first time since I had been in Barcelona I went to have a look at the cathedral—a modern cathedral, and one of the most hideous buildings in the world. It has four crenellated spires exactly the shape of hock bottles. Unlike most of the churches in Barcelona it was not damaged during the revolution—it was spared because of its "artistic value," people said. I think the Anarchists showed bad taste in not blowing it up when they had the chance, though they did hang a red-and-black banner between its spires. That afternoon my wife and I went to see Kopp for the last time. There was nothing that we could do for him, absolutely nothing, except to say good-bye and leave money with Spanish friends who would take him food and cigarettes. A little while later, however, after we had left Barcelona, he was placed *incomunicado* and not even food could be sent to him. That night, walking down the Ramblas, we passed the Café Moka, which the Civil Guards were still holding in force. On an impulse I went in and spoke to two of them who were leaning against the counter with their rifles slung over their shoulders. I asked them if they knew which of their comrades had been on duty here at the time of the May fighting. They did not know, and, with the usual Spanish vagueness, did not know how one could find out. I said that my friend Jorge Kopp was in prison and would perhaps be put on trial for something in connection with the May fighting; that the men who were on duty here would know that he had stopped the fighting and saved some of their lives; they ought to come forward and give evidence to that effect. One of the men I was talking to was a dull, heavy-looking man who kept shaking his head because he could not hear my voice in the din of the traffic. But the other was different. He said he had heard of Kopp's action from some of his comrades; Kopp was *buen chico* (a good fellow). But even at the time I knew that it was all useless. If Kopp were ever tried, it would be, as in all such trials, with faked evidence. If he has been shot (and I am afraid it is quite likely), that will be his epitaph: the *buen chico* of the poor Civil Guard who was part of a dirty system but had remained enough of a human being to know a decent action when he saw one.

It was an extraordinary, insane existence that we were leading. By night we were criminals, but by day we were prosperous English visitors—that was our pose, anyway. Even after a night in the open, a shave, a bath, and a shoeshine do wonders with your appearance. The safest thing at present was to look as bourgeois as possible. We frequented the fashionable residential quarter of the town, where our faces were not known, went to expensive restaurants, and were very English with the waiters. For the first time in my life I took to writing things on walls. The passage-ways of several smart restaurants had *"Visca P.O.U.M.!"* scrawled on them as large as I could write it. All the while, though I was technically in hiding, I could not feel myself in danger. The whole thing seemed too absurd. I had the ineradicable English belief that "they" cannot arrest you unless you have broken the law. It is a most dangerous belief to have during a political pogrom. There was a warrant out for McNair's arrest, and the chances were that the rest of us were on the list as well. The arrests, raids, searchings were continuing without pause; practically everyone we knew, except those who were still at the front, was in jail by this time. The police were even boarding the French ships that periodically took off refugees and seizing suspected "Trotskyists."

Thanks to the kindness of the British consul, who must have had a very trying time during that week, we had managed to get our passports into order. The sooner we left the better. There was a train that was due to leave for Port Bou at half-past seven in the evening and might normally be expected to leave at about half-past eight. We arranged that my wife should order a taxi beforehand and then pack her bags, pay her bill, and leave the hotel at the last possible moment. If she gave the hotel people too much notice they would be sure to send for the police. I got down to the station at about seven to find that the train had already gone —it had left at ten to seven. The engine-driver had changed his mind, as usual. Fortunately we managed to warn my wife in time.

There was another train early the following morning. McNair, Cott-man, and I had dinner at a little restaurant near the station and by cautious questioning discovered that the restaurant-keeper was a C.N.T. member and friendly. He let us a three-bedded room and forgot to warn the police. It was the first time in five nights that I had been able to sleep with my clothes off.

Next morning my wife slipped out of the hotel successfully. The train was about an hour late in starting. I filled in the time by writing a long letter to the Ministry of War, telling them about Kopp's case—that without a doubt he had been arrested by mistake, that he was urgently needed at the front, that countless people would testify that he was innocent of any offense, etc., etc., etc. I wonder if anyone read that letter, written on pages torn out of a notebook in wobbly handwriting (my fingers were still partly paralyzed) and still more wobbly Spanish. At any rate, neither this letter nor anything else took effect. As I write, six months after the event, Kopp (if he has not been shot) is still in jail, untried and uncharged. At the beginning we had two or three letters from him, smuggled out by released prisoners and posted in France. They all told the same story—imprisonment in filthy dark dens, bad and insufficient food, serious illness due to the conditions of imprisonment, and refusal of medical attention. I have had all this confirmed from several other sources, English and French. More recently he disappeared into one of the "secret prisons" with which it seems impossible to make any kind of communication. His case is the case of scores or hundreds of foreigners and no one knows how many thousands of Spaniards.

In the end we crossed the frontier without incident. The train had a first class and a dining car, the first I had seen in Spain. Until recently there had been only one class on the trains in Catalonia. Two detectives came round the train taking the names of foreigners, but when they saw us in the dining car they seemed satisfied that we were respectable. It was queer how everything had changed. Only six months ago, when the Anarchists still reigned, it was looking like a proletarian that made you respectable. On the way down from Perpignan to Cerbères a French commercial traveler in my carriage had said to me in all solemnity: "You mustn't go into Spain looking like that. Take off that collar and tie. They'll tear them off you in Barcelona." He was exaggerating, but it showed how Catalonia was regarded. And at the frontier the Anarchist guards had turned back a smartly dressed Frenchman and his wife, solely—I think—because they looked too bourgeois. Now it was the other way about; to look bourgeois was the one salvation. At the passport office they looked us up in the card-index of suspects, but thanks to the inefficiency of the police our names were not listed, not even McNair's. We were searched from head to foot, but we possessed nothing incriminating, except my discharge papers, and the carabineros who searched me did not know that the 29th Division was the P.O.U.M. So we slipped through the barrier, and after just six months I was on French soil again. My only souvenirs of Spain were a goatskin water-bottle and one of those tiny iron lamps in which the Aragon peasants burn olive oil —lamps almost exactly the shape of the terra-cotta lamps that the Romans used two thousand years ago—which I had picked up in some ruined hut, and which had somehow got stuck in my luggage.

After all, it turned out that we had come away none too soon. The very first newspaper we saw announced McNair's arrest for espionage. The Spanish authorities had been a little premature in announcing this. Fortunately, "Trotskyism" is not extraditable.

I wonder what is the appropriate first action when you come from a country at war and set foot on peaceful soil. Mine was to rush to the tobacco kiosk and buy as many cigars and cigarettes as I could stuff into my pockets. Then we all went to the buffet and had a cup of tea, the first tea with fresh milk in it that we had had for many months. It was several days before I could get used to the idea that you could buy cigarettes whenever you wanted them. I always half expected to see the tobacconists' doors barred and the forbidding notice *"No hay tobaco"* in the window.

McNair and Cottman were going on to Paris. My wife and I got off the train at Banyuls, the first station up the line, feeling that we would like a rest. We were not too well received in Banyuls when they discovered that we had come from Barcelona. Quite a number of times I was involved in the same conversation: "You come from Spain? Which side were you fighting on? The government? Oh!"—and then a marked coolness. The little town seemed solidly pro-Franco, no doubt because of the various Spanish Fascist refugees who had arrived there from time to time. The waiter at the café I frequented was a pro-Franco Spaniard and used to give me lowering glances as he served me with an apéritif. It was otherwise in Perpignan, which was stiff with government partisans and where all the different factions were cabaling against one another almost as in Barcelona. There was one café where the word "P.O.U.M." immediately procured you French friends and smiles from the waiter.

I think we stayed three days in Banyuls. It was a strangely restless time. In this quiet fishing town, remote from bombs, machine guns, food queues, propaganda, and intrigue, we ought to have felt profoundly relieved and thankful. We felt nothing of the kind. The things we had seen in Spain did not recede and fall into proportion now that we were away from them; instead they rushed back upon us and were far more vivid than before. We thought, talked, dreamed incessantly of Spain. For months past we had been telling ourselves that "when we get out of Spain" we would go somewhere beside the Mediterranean and be quiet for a little while and perhaps do a little fishing; but now that we were here it was merely a bore and a disappointment. It was chilly weather, a persistent wind blew off the sea, the water was dull and choppy, round the harbor's edge a scum of ashes, corks, and fish guts bobbed against the stones. It sounds like lunacy, but the thing that both of us wanted was to be back in Spain. Though it could have done no good to anybody, might indeed have done serious harm, both of us wished that we had stayed to be imprisoned along with the others. I suppose I have failed to convey more than a little of what those months in Spain mean to me. I have recorded some of the outward events, but I cannot record the feeling they have left me with. It is all mixed up with sights, smells, and sounds that cannot be conveyed in writing: the smell of the trenches, the mountain dawns stretching away into inconceivable distances, the frosty crackle of bullets, the roar and glare of bombs; the clear cold light of the Barcelona mornings, and the stamp of boots in the barrack yard, back in December when people still believed in the revolution; and the food queues and the red-and-black flags and the faces of Spanish militiamen; above all the faces of militiamen—men whom I knew in the line and who are now scattered Lord knows where, some killed in battle, some maimed, some in prison —most of them, I hope, still safe and sound. Good luck to them all; I hope they win their war and drive all the foreigners out of Spain, Germans, Russians, and Italians alike. This war, in which I played so ineffectual a part, has left me with memories that are mostly evil, and yet I do not wish that I had missed it. When you have had a glimpse of such a disaster as this—and however it ends the Spanish war will turn out to have been an appalling disaster, quite apart from the slaughter and physical suffering—the result is not necessarily disillusionment and cynicism. Curiously enough the whole experience has left me with not less but more belief in the decency of human beings. And I hope the account I have given is not too misleading. I believe that on such an issue as this no one is or can be completely truthful. It is difficult to be certain about anything except what you have seen with your own eyes, and consciously or unconsciously everyone writes as a partisan. In case I have not said this somewhere earlier in the book I will say it now: beware of my partisanship, my mistakes of fact, and the distortion inevitably caused by my having seen only one corner of events. And beware of exactly the same things when you read any other book on this period of the Spanish war.

Because of the feeling that we ought to be doing something, though actually there was nothing we could do, we left Banyuls earlier than we had intended. With every mile that you went northward France grew greener and softer. Away from the mountain and the vine, back to the meadow and the elm. When I had passed through Paris on my way to Spain it had seemed to me decayed and gloomy, very different from the Paris I had known eight years earlier, when living was cheap and Hitler was not heard of. Half the cafés I used to know were shut for lack of custom, and everyone was obsessed with the high cost of living and the fear of war. Now, after poor Spain, even Paris seemed gay and prosperous. And the Exhibition was in full swing, though we managed to avoid visiting it.

And then England—southern England, probably the sleekest landscape in the world. It is difficult when you pass that way, especially when you are peacefully recovering from seasickness with the plush cushions of a boat-train carriage under your bum, to believe that anything is really happening anywhere. Earthquakes in Japan, famines in China, revolutions in Mexico? Don't worry, the milk will be on the doorstep tomorrow morning, the *New Statesman* will come out on Friday. The industrial towns were far away, a smudge of smoke and misery hidden by the curve of the earth's surface. Down here it was still the England I had known in my childhood: the railway cuttings smothered in wild flowers, the deep meadows where the great shining horses browse and meditate, the slow-moving streams bordered by willows, the green bosoms of the elms, the larkspurs in the cottage gardens; and then the huge peaceful wilderness of outer London, the barges on the miry river, the familiar streets, the posters telling of cricket matches and Royal weddings, the men in bowler hats, the pigeons in Trafalgar Square, the red buses, the blue policemen—all sleeping the deep, deep sleep of England, from which I sometimes fear that we shall never wake till we are jerked out of it by the roar of bombs.

1938

△

From "Coming Up for Air"

▽

PART II

Chapter One

. . . I suppose by this time you've got a kind of picture of me in your mind—a fat middle-aged bloke with false teeth and a red face —and subconsciously you've been imagining that I was just the same even when I was in my cradle. But forty-five years is a long time, and though some people don't change and develop, others do. I've changed a great deal, and I've had my ups and downs, mostly ups. It may seem queer, but my father would probably be rather proud of me if he could see me now. He'd think it a wonderful thing that a son of his should own a motor car and live in a house with a bathroom. Even now I'm a little above my origin, and at other times I've touched levels that we should never have dreamed of in those old days before the war.

Before the war! How long shall we go on saying that, I wonder? How long before the answer will be "Which war?" In my case the never-never land that people are thinking of when they say "before the war" might almost be before the Boer War. I was born in '93, and I can actually remember the outbreak of the Boer War, because of the first-class row that Father and Uncle Ezekiel had about it. I've several other memories that would date from about a year earlier than that.

The very first thing I remember is the smell of sainfoin chaff. You went up the stone passage that led from the kitchen to the shop, and the smell of sainfoin got stronger all the way. Mother had fixed a wooden gate in the doorway to prevent Joe and myself (Joe was my elder brother) from getting into the shop. I can still remember standing there clutching the bars, and the smell of sainfoin mixed up with the damp plastery smell that belonged to the passage. It wasn't till years later that I somehow managed to crash the gate and get into the shop when nobody was there. A mouse that had been having a go at one of the meal bins suddenly plopped out and ran between my feet. It was quite white with meal. This must have happened when I was about six.

When you're very young you seem to suddenly become conscious of things that have been under your nose for a long time past. The things round about you swim into your mind one at a time, rather as they do when you're waking from sleep. For instance, it was only when I was nearly four that I suddenly realized that we owned a dog. Nailer, his name was, an old white English terrier of the breed that's gone out nowadays. I met him under the kitchen table and in some way seemed to grasp, having only learnt it that moment, that he belonged to us and that his name was Nailer. In the same way, a bit earlier, I'd discovered that beyond the gate at the end of the passage there was a place where the smell of sainfoin came from. And the shop itself, with the huge scales and the wooden measures and the tin shovel, and the white lettering on the window, and the bullfinch in its cage—which you couldn't see very well even from the pavement, because the window was always dusty—all these things dropped into place in my mind one by one, like bits of a jigsaw puzzle.

Time goes on, you get stronger on your legs, and by degrees you begin to get a grasp of geography. I suppose Lower Binfield was just like any other market town of about two thousand inhabitants. It was in Oxfordshire—I keep saying *was*, you notice, though after all the place still exists—about five miles from the Thames. It lay in a bit of a valley, with a low ripple of hills between itself and the Thames, and higher hills behind. On top of the hills there were woods in sort of dim blue masses among which you could see a great white house with a colonnade. This was Binfield House ("The Hall," everybody called it), and the top of the hill was known as Upper Binfield, though there was no village there and hadn't been for a hundred years or more. I must have been nearly seven before I noticed the existence of Binfield House. When you're very small you don't look into the distance. But by that time I knew every inch of the town, which was shaped roughly like a cross with the market place in the middle. Our shop was in the High Street a little before you got to the market place, and on the corner there was Mrs. Wheeler's sweetshop where you spent a halfpenny when you had one. Mother Wheeler was a dirty old witch and people suspected her of sucking the bull's-eyes and putting them back in the bottle, though this was never proved. Farther down there was the barber's shop with the advert for Abdulla cigarettes—the one with the Egyptian soldiers on it, and curiously enough they're using the same ad to this day—and the rich boozy smell of bay rum and Latakia. Behind the houses you could see the chimneys of the brewery. In the middle of the market place there was the stone horse-trough, and on top of the water there was always a fine film of dust and chaff.

Before the war, and especially before the Boer War, it was summer all the year round. I'm quite aware that that's a delusion. I'm merely trying to tell you how things come back to me. If I shut my eyes and think of Lower Binfield any time before I was, say, eight, it's always in summer weather that I remember it. Either it's the market place at dinner time, with a sort of sleepy dusty hush over everything and the carrier's horse with his nose dug well into his nosebag, munching away, or it's a hot afternoon in the great green juicy meadows round the town, or it's about dusk in the lane behind the allotments, and there's a smell of pipe tobacco and night stocks floating through the hedge. But in a sense I do remember different seasons, because all my memories are bound up with things to eat, which varied at different times of the year. Especially the things you used to find in the hedges. In July there were dewberries—but they're very rare—and the blackberries were getting red enough to eat. In September there were sloes and hazelnuts. The best hazelnuts were always out of reach. Later on there were beechnuts and crab apples. Then there were the kind of minor foods that you used to eat when there was nothing better going. Haws—but they're not much good—and hips, which have a nice sharp taste if you clean the hairs out of them. Angelica is good in early summer, especially when you're thirsty, and so are the stems of various grasses. Then there's sorrel, which is good with bread and butter, and pignuts, and a kind of wood shamrock which has a sour taste. Even plantain seeds are better than nothing when you're a long way from home and very hungry.

Joe was two years older than myself. When we were very small Mother used to pay Katie Simmons eighteen pence a week to take us out for walks in the afternoons. Katie's father worked in the brewery and had fourteen children, so that the family were always on the lookout for odd jobs. She was only twelve when Joe was seven and I was five, and her mental level wasn't very different from ours. She used to drag me by the arm and call me "Baby," and she had just enough authority over us to prevent us from being run over by dogcarts or chased by bulls, but so far as conversation went we were almost on equal terms. We used to go for long, trailing kind of walks—always, of course, picking and eating things all the way—down the lane past the allotments, across Roper's Meadows and down to the Mill Farm, where there was

a pool with newts and tiny carp in it (Joe and I used to go fishing there when we were a bit older), and back by the Upper Binfield Road so as to pass the sweetshop that stood on the edge of
the town. . . .

It always seems to be summer when I look back. I can feel the
grass round me as tall as myself, and the heat coming out of the
earth. And the dust in the lane, and the warm greeny light coming through the hazel boughs. I can see the three of us trailing
along, eating stuff out of the hedge, with Katie dragging at my
arm and saying, "Come on, Baby!" and sometimes yelling ahead
to Joe, "Joe! You come back 'ere this minute! You'll catch it!"
Joe was a hefty boy with a big, lumpy sort of head and tremendous calves, the kind of boy who's always doing something dangerous. At seven he'd already got into short trousers, with the thick
black stockings drawn up over the knee and the great clumping
boots that boys had to wear in those days. I was still in frocks—
a kind of holland overall that Mother used to make for me. Katie
used to wear a dreadful ragged parody of a grown-up dress that
descended from sister to sister in her family. She had a ridiculous
great hat with her pigtails hanging down behind it, and a long,
draggled skirt which trailed on the ground, and button boots with
the heels trodden down. She was a tiny thing, not much taller
than Joe, but not bad at "minding" children. In a family like that
a child is "minding" other children about as soon as it's weaned.
At times she'd try to be grown-up and ladylike, and she had a
way of cutting you short with a proverb, which to her mind was
something unanswerable. If you said "Don't care," she'd answer
immediately:

> Don't care was made to care,
> Don't care was hung,
> Don't care was put in a pot
> And boiled till he was done.

Or if you called her names it would be "Hard words break no
bones," or, when you'd been boasting, "Pride comes before a fall."
This came very true one day when I was strutting along pretending to be a soldier and fell into a cowpat. Her family lived in
a filthy little rat-hole of a place in the slummy street behind the
brewery. The place swarmed with children like a kind of vermin.
The whole family had managed to dodge going to school, which
was fairly easy to do in those days, and started running errands
and doing other odd jobs as soon as they could walk. One of her
elder brothers got a month for stealing turnips. She stopped tak-

ing us out for walks a year later when Joe was eight and getting too tough for a girl to handle. He'd discovered that in Katie's home they slept five in a bed, and used to tease the life out of her about it. . . .

Chapter Three

. . . Joe was only eight when he got in with a tough gang of boys who called themselves the Black Hand. The leader was Sid Love-grove, the saddler's younger son, who was about thirteen, and there were two other shopkeepers' sons, an errand boy from the brewery and two farm lads who sometimes managed to cut work and go off with the gang for a couple of hours. The farm lads were great lumps bursting out of corduroy breeches, with very broad accents and rather looked down on by the rest of the gang, but they were tolerated because they knew twice as much about animals as any of the others. One of them, nicknamed Ginger, would even catch a rabbit in his hands occasionally. If he saw one lying in the grass he used to fling himself on it like a spread-eagle. There was a big social distinction between the shopkeepers' sons and the sons of laborers and farmhands, but the local boys didn't usually pay much attention to it till they were about sixteen. The gang had a secret password and an "ordeal" which included cutting your finger and eating an earthworm, and they gave themselves out to be fright-ful desperadoes. Certainly they managed to make a nuisance of themselves, broke windows, chased cows, tore the knockers off doors, and stole fruit by the hundredweight. Sometimes in winter they managed to borrow a couple of ferrets and go ratting, when the farmers would let them. They all had catapults and squailers, and they were always saving up to buy a saloon pistol, which in those days cost five shillings, but the savings never amounted to more than about threepence. In summer they used to go fishing and birdnesting. When Joe was at Mrs. Howlett's he used to cut school at least once a week, and even at the Grammar School he man-aged it about once a fortnight. There was a boy at the Grammar School, an auctioneer's son, who could copy any handwriting and for a penny he'd forge a letter from your mother saying you'd been ill yesterday. Of course I was wild to join the Black Hand, but Joe always choked me off and said they didn't want any blasted kids hanging round.

It was the thought of going fishing that really appealed to me. At eight years old I hadn't yet been fishing, except with a penny net, with which you can sometimes catch a stickleback. Mother was always terrified of letting us go anywhere near water. She "forbade" fishing, in the way in which parents in those days "forbade" almost everything, and I hadn't yet grasped that grown-ups can't see round corners. But the thought of fishing sent me wild with excitement. Many a time I'd been past the pool at the Mill Farm and watched the small carp basking on the surface, and sometimes under the willow tree at the corner a great diamond-shaped carp that to my eyes looked enormous—six inches long, I suppose —would suddenly rise to the surface, gulp down a grub and sink again. I'd spent hours gluing my nose against the window of Wallace's in the High Street, where fishing tackle and guns and bicycles were sold. I used to lie awake on summer mornings thinking of the tales Joe had told me about fishing, how you mixed bread paste, how your float gives a bob and plunges under and you feel the rod bending and the fish tugging at the line. Is it any use talking about it, I wonder—the sort of fairy light that fish and fishing tackle have in a kid's eyes? Some kids feel the same about guns and shooting, some feel it about motor bikes or aeroplanes or horses. It's not a thing that you can explain or rationalize, it's merely magic. One morning—it was in June and I must have been eight—I knew that Joe was going to cut school and go out fishing, and I made up my mind to follow. In some way Joe guessed what I was thinking about, and he started on me while we were dressing.

"Now then, young George! Don't you get thinking you're coming with the gang today. You stay back home."

"No, I didn't. I didn't think nothing about it."

"Yes, you did! You thought you were coming with the gang."

"No, I didn't!"

"Yes, you did!"

"No, I didn't!"

"Yes, you did! You stay back home. We don't want any bloody kids along."

Joe had just learned the word "bloody" and was always using it. Father overheard him once and swore that he'd thrash the life out of Joe, but as usual he didn't do so. After breakfast Joe started off on his bike, with his satchel and his Grammar School cap, five minutes early as he always did when he meant to cut school, and when it was time for me to leave for Mother Howlett's I sneaked off and hid in the lane behind the allotments. I knew the gang were going to the pond at the Mill Farm, and I was going to follow them if they murdered me for it. Probably they'd give me a hiding, and probably I wouldn't get home to dinner, and then Mother would know that I'd cut school and I'd get another hid-

ing, but I didn't care. I was just desperate to go fishing with the
gang. I was cunning, too. I allowed Joe plenty of time to make
a circuit round and get to the Mill Farm by road, and then I
followed down the lane and skirted round the meadows on the
far side of the hedge, so as to get almost to the pond before the
gang saw me. It was a wonderful June morning. The buttercups
were up to my knees. There was a breath of wind just stirring
the tops of the elms, and the great green clouds of leaves were
sort of soft and rich like silk. And it was nine in the morning
and I was eight years old, and all round me it was early summer,
with great tangled hedges where the wild roses were still in bloom,
and bits of soft white cloud drifting overhead, and in the distance
the low hills and the dim blue masses of the woods round Upper
Binfield. And I didn't give a damn for any of it. All I was thinking of was the green pool and the carp and the gang with their
hooks and lines and bread paste. It was as though they were in
paradise and I'd got to join them. Presently I managed to sneak
up on them—four of them, Joe and Sid Lovegrove and the errand
boy and another shopkeeper's son, Harry Barnes I think his name
was.

Joe turned and saw me. "Christ!" he said. "It's the kid." He
walked up to me like a tom-cat that's going to start a fight. "Now
then, you! What'd I tell you? You get back 'ome double quick."

Both Joe and I were inclined to drop our aitches if we were at
all excited. I backed away from him.

"I'm not going back 'ome."

"Yes you are."

"Clip his ear, Joe," said Sid. "We don't want no kids along."

"*Are* you going back 'ome?" said Joe.

"No."

"Righto, my boy! Right-*ho!*"

Then he started on me. The next minute he was chasing me
round, catching me one clip after another. But I didn't run away
from the pool, I ran in circles. Presently he'd caught me and got
me down, and then he knelt on my upper arms and began screw-
ing my ears, which was his favorite torture and one I couldn't
stand. I was blubbing by this time, but still I wouldn't give in
and promise to go home. I wanted to stay and go fishing with
the gang. And suddenly the others swung round in my favor and
told Joe to get up off my chest and let me stay if I wanted to.
So I stayed after all.

The others had some hooks and lines and floats and a lump
of bread paste in a rag, and we all cut ourselves willow switches

from the tree at the corner of the pool. The farmhouse was only about two hundred yards away, and you had to keep out of sight because old Brewer was very down on fishing. Not that it made any difference to him, he only used the pool for watering his cattle, but he hated boys. The others were still jealous of me and kept telling me to get out of the light and reminding me that I was only a kid and knew nothing about fishing. They said that I was making such a noise I'd scare all the fish away, though actually I was making about half as much noise as anyone else there. Finally they wouldn't let me sit beside them and sent me to another part of the pool where the water was shallower and there wasn't so much shade. They said a kid like me was sure to keep splashing the water and frighten the fish away. It was a rotten part of the pool, a part where no fish would ordinarily come. I knew that. I seemed to know by a kind of instinct the places where a fish would lie. Still, I was fishing at last. I was sitting on the grass bank with the rod in my hands, with the flies buzzing round and the smell of wild peppermint fit to knock you down, watching the red float on the green water, and I was happy as a tinker although the tearmarks mixed up with dirt were still all over my face.

Lord knows how long we sat there. The morning stretched out and out, and the sun got higher and higher, and nobody had a bite. It was a hot still day, too clear for fishing. The floats lay on the water with never a quiver. You could see deep down into the water as though you were looking into a kind of dark green glass. Out in the middle of the pool you could see the fish lying just under the surface, sunning themselves, and sometimes in the weeds near the side a newt would come gliding upwards and rest there with his fingers on the weeds and his nose just out of the water. But the fish weren't biting. The others kept shouting that they'd got a nibble, but it was always a lie. And the time stretched out and out and it got hotter and hotter, and the flies ate you alive and the wild peppermint under the bank smelt like Mother Wheeler's sweetshop. I was getting hungrier and hungrier, all the more because I didn't know for certain where my dinner was coming from. But I sat as still as a mouse and never took my eyes off my float. The others had given me a lump of bait about the size of a marble, telling me that would have to do for me, but for a long time I didn't even dare to rebait my hook, because every time I pulled my line up they swore I was making enough noise to frighten every fish within five miles.

I suppose we must have been there about two hours when suddenly my float gave a quiver. I knew it was a fish. It must have been a fish that was just passing accidentally and saw my bait. There's no mistaking the movement your float gives when it's a real bite. It's quite different from the way it moves when you twitch your line accidentally. The next moment it gave a sharp bob and almost went under. I couldn't hold myself in any longer. I yelled to the others:

"I've got a bite!"

"Rats!" yelled Sid Lovegrove instantly.

But the next moment there wasn't any doubt about it. The float dived straight down, I could still see it under the water, kind of dim red, and I felt the rod tighten in my hand. Christ, that feeling! The line jerking and straining and a fish on the other end of it! The others saw my rod bending, and the next moment they'd all flung their rods down and rushed round to me. I gave a terrific haul and the fish—a great huge silvery fish—came flying up through the air. The same moment all of us gave a yell of agony. The fish had slipped off the hook and fallen into the wild peppermint under the bank. But he'd fallen into shallow water where he couldn't turn over, and for perhaps a second he lay there on his side helpless. Joe flung himself into the water, splashing us all over, and grabbed him in both hands. "I got 'im!" he yelled. The next moment he'd flung the fish on to the grass and we were all kneeling round it. How we gloated! The poor dying brute flapped up and down and his scales glistened all the colors of the rainbow. It was a huge carp, seven inches long at least, and must have weighed a quarter of a pound. How we shouted to see him! But the next moment it was as though a shadow had fallen across us. We looked up, and there was old Brewer standing over us, with his tall billycock hat—one of those hats they used to wear that were a cross between a top-hat and a bowler—and his cowhide gaiters and a thick hazel stick in his hand.

We suddenly cowered like partridges when there's a hawk overhead. He looked from one to other of us. He had a wicked old mouth with no teeth in it, and since he'd shaved his beard off his chin looked like a nutcracker.

"What are you boys doing here?" he said.

There wasn't much doubt about what we were doing. Nobody answered.

"I'll learn 'ee come fishing in my pool!" he suddenly roared, and the next moment he was on us, whacking out in all directions.

The Black Hand broke and fled. We left all the rods behind and also the fish. Old Brewer chased us half across the meadow. His legs were stiff and he couldn't move fast, but he got in some good swipes before we were out of his reach. We left him in the middle of the field, yelling after us that he knew all our names and was going to tell our fathers. I'd been at the back and most of the wallops had landed on me. I had some nasty red weals on the calves of my legs when we got to the other side of the hedge.

I spent the rest of the day with the gang. They hadn't made up their mind whether I was really a member yet, but for the time being they tolerated me. The errand boy, who'd had the morning off on some lying pretext or other, had to go back to the brewery. The rest of us went for a long, meandering, scrounging kind of walk, the sort of walk that boys go for when they're away from home all day, and especially when they're away without permission. It was the first real boy's walk I'd had, quite different from the walks we used to go with Katie Simmons. We had our dinner in a dry ditch on the edge of the town, full of rusty cans and wild fennel. The others gave me bits of their dinner, and Sid Lovegrove had a penny, so someone fetched a Penny Monster which we had between us. It was very hot, and the fennel smelt very strong, and the gas of the Penny Monster made us belch. Afterward we wandered up the dusty white road to Upper Binfield, the first time I'd been that way, I believe, and into the beechwoods with the carpets of dead leaves and the great smooth trunks that soar up into the sky so that the birds in the upper branches look like dots. You could go wherever you liked in the woods in those days. Binfield House was shut up, they didn't preserve the pheasants any longer, and at the worst you'd only meet a carter with a load of wood. There was a tree that had been sawn down, and the rings on the trunk looked like a target, and we had shots at it with stones. Then the others had shots at birds with their catapults, and Sid Lovegrove swore he'd hit a chaffinch and it had stuck in a fork of the tree. Joe said he was lying, and they argued and almost fought. Then we went down into a chalk hollow full of beds of dead leaves and shouted to hear the echo. Someone shouted a dirty word, and then we said over all the dirty words we knew, and the others jeered at me because I only knew three. Sid Lovegrove said he knew how babies were born and it was just the same as rabbits except that the baby came out of the woman's navel. Harry Barnes started to carve the word —— on a beech tree, but got fed up with it after the first two letters. Then we went round by the lodge of Binfield House. There was a rumor that somewhere in the grounds there was a pond with enormous fish in it, but no one ever dared go inside because old Hodges, the lodge-keeper who acted as a kind of caretaker, was "down" on boys. He was digging in his vegetable garden by the lodge when we passed. We cheeked him over the fence until he chased us off, and then we went down to the Walton Road and cheeked the carters, keeping on the other side of the hedge so that they couldn't reach us with their whips. Beside the Walton Road there was a place that had been a quarry and then a rubbish dump, and finally had got overgrown with blackberry bushes. There were great mounds of rusty old tin cans and bicycle frames and saucepans with holes in them and broken bottles with weeds growing all over them, and we spent nearly an hour and got ourselves filthy from head to foot routing out iron fence posts, because Harry Barnes swore that the blacksmith in Lower Binfield would pay sixpence a hundredweight for old iron. Then Joe found a late thrush's nest with half-fledged chicks in it in a blackberry bush. After a lot of argument about what to do with them we took the chicks out, had shots at them with stones, and finally stamped on them. There were four of them, and we each had one to stamp on. It was getting on towards teatime now. We knew that old Brewer would be as good as his word and there was a hiding ahead of us, but we were getting too hungry to stay out much longer. Finally we trailed home, with one more row on the way, because when we were passing the allotments we saw a rat and chased it with sticks, and old Bennet the station-master, who worked at his allotment every night and was very proud of it, came after us in a tearing rage because we'd trampled on his onion-bed.

I'd walked ten miles and I wasn't tired. All day I'd trailed after the gang and tried to do everything they did, and they'd called me "the kid" and snubbed me as much as they could, but I'd more or less kept my end up. I had a wonderful feeling inside me, a feeling you can't know about unless you've had it—but if you're a man you'll have had it some time. I knew that I wasn't a kid any longer, I was a boy at last. And it's a wonderful thing to be a boy, to go roaming where grown-ups can't catch you, and to chase rats and kill birds and shy stones and cheek carters and shout dirty words. It's a kind of strong, rank feeling, a feeling of knowing everything and fearing nothing, and it's all bound up with breaking rules and killing things. The white dusty roads, the hot sweaty feeling of one's clothes, the smell of fennel and wild peppermint, the dirty words, the sour stink of the rubbish dump, the taste of fizzy lemonade and the gas that made one belch, the stamping on the young birds, the feel of the fish straining on the line—it was all part of it. Thank God I'm a man, because no woman ever has that feeling.

Sure enough, old Brewer had sent round and told everybody. Father looked very glum, fetched a strap out of the shop and said he was going to "thrash the life out of" Joe. But Joe struggled and yelled and kicked, and in the end Father didn't get in more than a couple of whacks at him. However, he got a caning from the headmaster of the Grammar School next day. I tried to struggle too, but I was small enough for Mother to get me across her knee, and she gave me what-for with the strap. So I'd had three hidings that day, one from Joe, one from old Brewer, and one from Mother. Next day the gang decided that I wasn't really a member yet and that I'd got to go through the "ordeal" (a word they'd got out of the Red Indian stories) after all. They were very strict in insisting that you had to bite the worm before you swallowed it. Moreover, because I was the youngest and they were jealous of me for being the only one to catch anything, they all made out afterward that the fish I'd caught wasn't really a big one. In a general way the tendency of fish, when people talk about them, is to get bigger and bigger, but this one got smaller and smaller, until to hear the others talk you'd have thought it was no bigger than a minnow.

But it didn't matter. I'd been fishing. I'd seen the float dive under the water and felt the fish tugging at the line, and however many lies they told they couldn't take that away from me.

Chapter Four

For the next seven years, from when I was eight to when I was fifteen, what I chiefly remember is fishing.

Don't think that I did nothing else. It's only that when you look back over a long period of time, certain things seem to swell up till they overshadow everything else. I left Mother Howlett's and went to the Grammar School, with a leather satchel and a black cap with yellow stripes, and got my first bicycle and a long time afterward my first long trousers. My first bike was a fixed-wheel—free-wheel bikes were very expensive then. When you went downhill you put your feet up on the front rests and let the pedals go whizzing round. That was one of the characteristic sights of the early nineteen hundreds—a boy sailing downhill with his head back and his feet up in the air. I went to the Grammar School in fear and trembling, because of the frightful tales Joe had told me about old Whiskers (his name was Wicksey) the headmaster, who was certainly a dreadful-looking little man, with a face just like a wolf, and at the end of the big schoolroom he had a glass case with canes in it, which he'd sometimes take out and swish through the air in a terrifying manner. But to my surprise I did rather well at school. It had never occurred to me that I might be cleverer than Joe, who was two years older than me and had bullied me ever since he could walk. Actually Joe was an utter dunce, got the cane about once a week, and stayed somewhere near the bottom of the school till he was sixteen. My second term I took a prize in arithmetic and another in some queer stuff that was mostly concerned with pressed flowers and went by the name of Science, and by the time I was fourteen Whiskers was talking about scholarships and Reading University. Father, who had ambitions for Joe and me in those days, was very anxious that I should go to "college." There was an idea floating round that I was to be a schoolteacher and Joe was to be an auctioneer.

But I haven't many memories connected with school. When I've mixed with chaps from the upper classes, as I did during the war, I've been struck by the fact that they never really get over that frightful drilling they go through at public schools. Either it flattens them out into half-wits or they spend the rest of their lives kicking against it. It wasn't so with boys of our class, the sons of shopkeepers and farmers. You went to the Grammar School and you stayed there till you were sixteen, just to show that you weren't a prole, but school was chiefly a place that you wanted to get away from. You'd no sentiment of loyalty, no goofy feeling about the old gray stones (and they *were* old, right enough, the school had been founded by Cardinal Wolsey), and there was no Old Boy's tie and not even a school song. You had your half-holidays to yourself, because games weren't compulsory and as often as not you cut them. We played football in braces, and though it was considered proper to play cricket in a belt, you wore your ordinary shirt and trousers. The only game I really cared about was the stump cricket we used to play in the gravel yard during the break, with a bat made out of a bit of packing case and a compo ball.

But I remember the smell of the big schoolroom, a smell of ink and dust and boots, and the stone in the yard that had been a mounting block and was used for sharpening knives on, and the little baker's shop opposite where they sold a kind of Chelsea bun, twice the size of the Chelsea buns you get nowadays, which were called Lardy Busters and cost a halfpenny. I did all the things you do at school. I carved my name on a desk and got the cane for it— you were always caned for it if you were caught, but it was the etiquette that you had to carve your name. And I got inky fingers and bit my nails and made darts out of penholders and played conkers and passed round dirty stories and learned to masturbate and cheeked old Blowers, the English master, and bullied the life out of little Willy Simeon, the undertaker's son, who was half-witted and believed everything you told him. Our favorite trick was to send him to shops to buy things that didn't exist. All the old gags —the ha'porth of penny stamps, the rubber hammer, the left-handed screwdriver, the pot of striped paint—poor Willy fell for all of them. We had grand sport one afternoon, putting him in a tub and telling him to lift himself up by the handles. He ended up in an asylum, poor Willy. But it was in the holidays that one really lived.

There were good things to do in those days. In winter we used to borrow a couple of ferrets—Mother would never let Joe and me keep them at home, "nasty smelly things" she called them—and go round the farms and ask leave to do a bit of ratting. Sometimes they let us, sometimes they told us to hook it and said we were more trouble than the rats. Later in winter we'd follow the threshing machine and help kill the rats when they threshed the stacks. One winter, 1908 it must have been, the Thames flooded and then froze and there was skating for weeks on end, and Harry Barnes broke his collar-bone on the ice. In early spring we went after squirrels with squailers, and later on we went birdnesting. We had a theory that birds can't count and it's all right if you leave one egg, but we were cruel little beasts and sometimes we'd just knock the nest down and trample on the eggs or chicks. There was another game we had when the toads were spawning. We used to catch toads, ram the nozzle of a bicycle pump up their backsides and blow them up till they burst. That's what boys are like, I don't know why. In summer we used to bike over to Burford Weir and bathe. Wally Lovegrove, Sid's young cousin, was drowned in 1906. He got tangled in the weeds at the bottom, and when the drag-hooks brought his body to the surface his face was jet black.

But fishing was the real thing. We went many a time to old Brewer's pool, and took tiny carp and tench out of it, and once a whopping eel, and there were other cow-ponds that had fish in them and were within walking distance on Saturday afternoons. But after we got bicycles we started fishing in the Thames below Burford Weir. It seemed more grown-up than fishing in cow-ponds. There were no farmers chasing you away, and there are some thumping fish in the Thames—though, so far as I know, nobody's ever been known to catch one.

It's queer, the feeling I had for fishing—and still have, really. I can't call myself a fisherman. I've never in my life caught a fish two feet long, and it's thirty years now since I've had a rod in my hands. And yet when I look back the whole of my boyhood from eight to fifteen seems to have revolved round the days when we went fishing. Every detail has stuck clear in my memory. I can remember individual days and individual fish, there isn't a cow-pond or a backwater that I can't see a picture of if I shut my eyes and think. I could write a book on the technique of fishing. When we were kids we didn't have much in the way of tackle, it cost too much and most of our threepence a week (which was the usual pocket-money in those days) went on sweets and Lardy Busters. Very small kids generally fish with a bent pin, which is too blunt to be much use, but you can make a pretty good hook (though of course it's got no barb) by bending a needle in a candle flame with a pair of pliers. The farm lads knew how to plait horsehair so that it was almost as good as gut, and you can take a small fish on a single horsehair. Later we got to having two-shilling fishing rods and even reels of sorts. God, what hours I've spent gazing into Wallace's window! Even the .410 guns and saloon pistols didn't thrill me so much as the fishing tackle. And the copy of Gamage's catalogue that I picked up somewhere, on a rubbish dump I think, and studied as though it had been the Bible! Even now I could give you all the details about gut-substitute and gimp and Limerick hooks and priests and disgorgers and Nottingham reels and God knows how many other technicalities.

Then there were the kinds of bait we used to use. In our shop there were always plenty of mealworms, which were good but not very good. Gentles were better. You had to beg them off old Gravitt, the butcher, and the gang used to draw lots or do ena-mena-mina-mo to decide who should go and ask, because Gravitt wasn't usually too pleasant about it. He was a big, rough-faced old devil with a voice like a mastiff, and when he barked, as he generally did when speaking to boys, all the knives and steels on his blue apron would give a jangle. You'd go in with an empty treacle tin in your hand, hang round till any customers had disappeared and then say very humbly:

"Please, Mr. Gravitt, y'got any gentles today?"

Generally he'd roar out: "What! Gentles! Gentles in my shop! Ain't seen such a thing in years. Think I got blow-flies in my shop?"

He had, of course. They were everywhere. He used to deal with them with a strip of leather on the end of a stick, with which he could reach out to enormous distances and smack a fly into paste. Sometimes you had to go away without any gentles, but as a rule he'd shout after you just as you were going:

" 'Ere! Go round the back yard an' 'ave a look. P'raps you might find one or two if you looked careful."

You used to find them in little clusters everywhere. Gravitt's back yard smelt like a battlefield. Butchers didn't have refrigerators in those days. Gentles live longer if you keep them in sawdust.

Wasp grubs are good, though it's hard to make them stick on the hook, unless you bake them first. When someone found a wasps' nest we'd go out at night and pour turpentine down it and plug up the hole with mud. Next day the wasps would all be dead and you could dig out the nest and take the grubs. Once something went wrong, the turps missed the hole or something, and when we took the plug out the wasps, which had been shut up all night, came out all together with a zoom. We weren't very badly stung, but it was a pity there was no one standing by with a stop-watch. Grasshoppers are about the best bait there is, especially for chub. You stick them on the hook without any shot and just flick them to and fro on the surface—"dapping," they call it. But you can never get more than two or three grasshoppers at a time. Greenbottle flies, which are also damned difficult to catch, are the best bait for dace, especially on clear days. You want to put them on the hook alive, so that they wriggle. A chub will even take a wasp, but it's a ticklish job to put a live wasp on the hook.

God knows how many other baits there were. Bread paste you make by squeezing water through white bread in a rag. Then there are cheese paste and honey paste and paste with aniseed in it. Boiled wheat isn't bad for roach. Redworms are good for gudgeon. You find them in very old manure heaps. And you also find another kind of worm called a brandling, which is striped and smells like an earwig, and which is very good bait for perch. Ordinary earthworms are good for perch. You have to put them in moss to keep them fresh and lively. If you try to keep them in earth they die. Those brown flies you find on cow-dung are pretty good for roach. You can take a chub on a cherry, so they say, and I've seen a roach taken with a currant out of a bun.

In those days, from the sixteenth of June (when the coarse-fishing season starts) till midwinter I wasn't often without a tin of worms or gentles in my pocket. I had some fights with Mother about it, but in the end she gave in, fishing came off the list of forbidden things and Father even gave me a two-shilling fishing rod for Christmas in 1903. Joe was barely fifteen when he started going after girls, and from then on he seldom came out fishing, which he said was a kid's game. But there were about half a dozen others who were as mad on fishing as I was. Christ, those fishing days! The hot sticky afternoons in the big schoolroom when I've sprawled across my desk, with old Blowers's voice grating away about predicates and subjunctives and relative clauses, and all that's in my mind is the backwater near Burford Weir and the green pool under the willows with the dace gliding to and fro. And then the terrific rush on bicycles after tea, up Chamford Hill and down to the river to get in an hour's fishing before dark. The still summer evening, the faint splash of the weir, the rings on the water where the fish are rising, the midges eating you alive, the shoals of dace swarming round your hook and never biting. And the kind of passion with which you'd watch the black backs of the fish swarming round, hoping and praying (yes, literally praying) that one of them would change his mind and grab your bait before it got too dark. And then it was always "Let's have five minutes more," and then "Just five minutes more," until in the end you had to walk your bike into the town because Towler, the copper, was prowling round and you could be "had up" for riding without a light. And the times in the summer holidays when we went out to make a day of it with boiled eggs and bread and butter and a bottle of lemonade, and fished and bathed and then fished again and did occasionally catch something. At night you'd come home with filthy hands and so hungry that you'd eaten what was left of your bread paste, with three or four smelly dace wrapped up in your handkerchief. Mother always refused to cook the fish I brought home. She would never allow that river fish were edible, except trout and salmon. "Nasty muddy things," she called them. The fish I remembered best of all are the ones I didn't catch. Especially the monstrous fish you always used to see when you went for a walk along the towpath on Sunday afternoons and hadn't a rod with you. There was no fishing on Sundays, even the Thames Conservancy Board didn't allow it. On Sundays you had to go for what was called a "nice walk" in your thick black suit and the Eton collar that sawed your head off. It was on a Sunday that I saw a pike a yard long asleep in shallow water by the bank and nearly got him with a stone. And sometimes in the green pools on the edge of the reeds you'd see a huge Thames trout go sailing past. The trout grow to vast sizes in the Thames, but they're practically never caught. They say that one of the real Thames fishermen, the old bottle-nosed blokes that you see muffled up in overcoats on camp stools with twenty-foot roach-poles at all seasons of the year, will willingly give up a year of his life to catching a Thames trout. I don't blame them, I see their point entirely, and still better I saw it then.

Of course other things were happening. I grew three inches in a year, got my long trousers, won some prizes at school, went to confirmation classes, told dirty stories, took to reading and had crazes for white mice, fretwork, and postage stamps. But it's always fishing that I remember. Summer days, and the flat water-meadows and the blue hills in the distance, and the willows up the backwater and the pools underneath like a kind of deep green glass. Summer evenings, the fish breaking the water, the nightjars hawking round your head, the smell of night stocks and Latakia. Don't mistake what I'm talking about. It's not that I'm trying to put across any of that poetry of childhood stuff. I know that's all baloney. Old Porteous (a friend of mine, a retired schoolmaster, I'll tell you about him later) is great on the poetry of childhood. Sometimes he reads me stuff about it out of books. Wordsworth. Lucy Gray. *There was a time when meadow, grove*—and all that. Needless to say he's got no kids of his own. The truth is that kids aren't in any way poetic, they're merely savage little animals, except that no animal is a quarter as selfish. A boy isn't interested in meadows, groves, and so forth. He never looks at a landscape, doesn't give a damn for flowers, and unless they affect him in some way, such as being good to eat, he doesn't know one plant from another. Killing things—that's about as near to poetry as a boy gets. And yet all the while there's that peculiar intensity, the power of longing for things as you can't long when you're grown up, and the feeling that time stretches out and out in front of you and that whatever you're doing you could go on for ever.

I was rather an ugly little boy, with butter-colored hair which was always cropped short except for a quiff in front. I don't idealize my childhood, and unlike many people I've no wish to be young again. Most of the things I used to care for would leave me something more than cold. I don't care if I never see a cricket ball again, and I wouldn't give you threepence for a hundredweight of sweets. But I've still got, I've always had, that peculiar feeling for fishing. You'll think it damned silly, no doubt, but I've actually half a wish to go fishing even now, when I'm fat and forty-five and got two kids and a house in the suburbs. Why? Because in a manner of speaking I *am* sentimental about my childhood—not my own particular childhood, but the civilization which I grew up in and which is now, I suppose, just about at its last kick. And fishing is somehow typical of that civilization. As soon as you think of fishing you think of things that don't belong to the modern world. The very idea of sitting all day under a willow tree beside a quiet pool—and being able to find a quiet pool to sit beside—belongs to the time before the war, before the radio, before aeroplanes, before Hitler. There's a kind of peacefulness even in the names of English coarse fish. Roach, rudd, dace, bleak, barbel, bream, gudgeon, pike, chub, carp, tench. They're solid kind of names. The people who made them up hadn't heard of machine guns, they didn't live in terror of the sack or spend their time eating aspirins, going to the pictures, and wondering how to keep out of the concentration camp.

Does anyone go fishing nowadays, I wonder? Anywhere within a hundred miles of London there are no fish left to catch. A few dismal fishing clubs plant themselves in rows along the banks of canals, and millionaires go trout-fishing in private waters round Scotch hotels, a sort of snobbish game of catching hand-reared fish with artificial flies. But who fishes in mill streams or moats or cowponds any longer? Where are the English coarse fish now? When I was a kid every pond and stream had fish in it. Now all the ponds are drained, and when the streams aren't poisoned with chemicals from factories they're full of rusty tins and motor-bike tires.

My best fishing memory is about some fish that I never caught. That's usual enough, I suppose.

When I was about fourteen Father did a good turn of some kind to old Hodges, the caretaker at Binfield House. I forget what it was —gave him some medicine that cured his fowls of the worms, or something. Hodges was a crabby old devil, but he didn't forget a good turn. One day a little while afterward when he'd been down to the shop to buy chicken corn he met me outside the door and stopped me in his surly way. He had a face like something carved out of a bit of root, and only two teeth, which were dark brown and very long.

"Hey, young 'un! Fisherman, ain't you?"

"Yes."

"Thought you was. You listen, then. If so be you wanted to, you could bring your line and have a try in that they pool up ahind the Hall. There's plenty bream and jack in there. But don't you tell no one as I told you. And don't you go for to bring any of them other young whelps, or I'll beat the skin off their backs."

Having said this he hobbled off with his sack of corn over his shoulder, as though feeling that he'd said too much already. The next Saturday afternoon I biked up to Binfield House with my pockets full of worms and gentles, and looked for old Hodges at the lodge. At that time Binfield House had already been empty for ten or twenty years. Mr. Farrel, the owner, couldn't afford to live in it and either couldn't or wouldn't let it. He lived in London on the rent of his farms and let the house and grounds go to the devil. All the fences were green and rotting, the park was a mass of nettles, the plantations were like a jungle and even the gardens had gone back to meadow, with only a few old gnarled rose bushes to show you where the beds had been. But it was a very beautiful house,

especially from a distance. It was a great white place with colon-
nades and long-shaped windows, which had been built, I suppose,
about Queen Anne's time by someone who'd traveled in Italy. If
I went there now I'd probably get a certain kick out of wandering
round the general desolation and thinking about the life that used
to go on there, and the people who built such places because they
imagined that the good days would last for ever. As a boy I didn't
give either the house or the grounds a second look. I dug out old
Hodges, who'd just finished his dinner and was a bit surly, and got
him to show me the way down to the pool. It was several hundred
yards behind the house and completely hidden in the beech woods,
but it was a good-sized pool, almost a lake, about a hundred and
fifty yards across. It was astonishing, and even at that age it astonished me, that there, a dozen miles from Reading and not fifty from
London, you could have such solitude. You felt as much alone as
if you'd been on the banks of the Amazon. The pool was ringed
completely round by the enormous beech trees, which in one place
came down to the edge and were reflected in the water. On the other
side there was a patch of grass where there was a hollow with beds
of wild peppermint, and up at one end of the pool an old wooden
boathouse was rotting among the bulrushes.

The pool was swarming with bream, small ones, about four to
six inches long. Every now and again you'd see one of them turn
half over and gleam reddy-brown under the water. There were pike
there too, and they must have been big ones. You never saw them,
but sometimes one that was basking among the weeds would turn
over and plunge with a splash that was like a brick being bunged
into the water. It was no use trying to catch them, though of course
I always tried every time I went there. I tried them with dace and
minnows I'd caught in the Thames and kept alive in a jam jar, and
even with a spinner made out of a bit of tin. But they were gorged
with fish and wouldn't bite, and in any case they'd have broken any
tackle I possessed. I never came back from the pool without at least
a dozen small bream. Sometimes in the summer holidays I went
there for a whole day, with my fishing rod and a copy of *Chums* or
the *Union Jack* or something, and a hunk of bread and cheese which
Mother had wrapped up for me. And I've fished for hours and then
lain in the grass hollow and read the *Union Jack*, and then the smell
of my bread paste and the plop of a fish jumping somewhere would
send me wild again, and I'd go back to the water and have another
go, and so on all through a summer's day. And the best of all was
to be alone, utterly alone, though the road wasn't a quarter of a
mile away. I was just old enough to know that it's good to be alone

occasionally. With the trees all round you it was as though the pool belonged to you, and nothing ever stirred except the fish ringing the water and the pigeons passing overhead. And yet, in the two years or so that I went fishing there, how many times did I really go, I wonder? Not more than a dozen. It was a three-mile bike ride from home and took up a whole afternoon at least. And sometimes other things turned up, and sometimes when I'd meant to go it rained. You know the way things happen.

One afternoon the fish weren't biting and I began to explore at the end of the pool farthest from Binfield House. There was a bit of an overflow of water and the ground was boggy, and you had to fight your way through a sort of jungle of blackberry bushes and rotten boughs that had fallen off the trees. I struggled through it for about fifty yards, and then suddenly there was a clearing and I came to another pool which I had never known existed. It was a small pool not more than twenty yards wide, and rather dark because of the boughs that overhung it. But it was very clear water and immensely deep. I could see ten or fifteen feet down into it. I hung about for a bit, enjoying the dampness and the rotten boggy smell, the way a boy does. And then I saw something that almost made me jump out of my skin.

It was an enormous fish. I don't exaggerate when I say it was enormous. It was almost the length of my arm. It glided across the pool, deep under water, and then became a shadow and disappeared into the darker water on the other side. I felt as if a sword had gone through me. It was far the biggest fish I'd ever seen, dead or alive. I stood there without breathing, and in a moment another huge thick shape glided through the water, and then another and then two more close together. The pool was full of them. They were carp, I suppose. Just possibly they were bream or tench, but more probably carp. Bream or tench wouldn't grow so huge. I knew what had happened. At some time this pool had been connected with the other, and then the stream had dried up and the woods had closed round the small pool and it had just been forgotten. It's a thing that happens occasionally. A pool gets forgotten somehow, nobody fishes in it for years and decades and the fish grow to monstrous sizes. The brutes that I was watching might be a hundred years old. And not a soul in the world knew about them except me. Very likely it was twenty years since anyone had so much as looked at the pool, and probably even old Hodges and Mr. Farrel's bailiff had forgotten its existence.

Well, you can imagine what I felt. After a bit I couldn't even bear the tantalization of watching. I hurried back to the other pool and got my fishing things together. It was no use trying for those colossal brutes with the tackle I had. They'd snap it as if it had been a hair. And I couldn't go on fishing any longer for the tiny bream. The sight of the big carp had given me a feeling in my stomach almost as if I was going to be sick. I got on to my bike and whizzed down the hill and home. It was a wonderful secret for a boy to have. There was the dark pool hidden away in the woods and the monstrous fish sailing round it—fish that had never been fished for and would grab the first bait you offered them. It was only a question of getting hold of a line strong enough to hold them. Already I'd made all the arrangements. I'd buy the tackle that would hold them if I had to steal the money out of the till. Somehow, God knew how, I'd get hold of half a crown and buy a length of silk salmon line and some thick gut or gimp and Number 5 hooks, and come back with cheese and gentles and paste and mealworms and brandlings and grasshoppers and every mortal bait a carp might look at. The very next Saturday afternoon I'd come back and try for them.

But as it happened I never went back. One never does go back. I never stole the money out of the till or bought the bit of salmon line or had a try for those carp. Almost immediately afterward something turned up to prevent me, but if it hadn't been that it would have been something else. It's the way things happen.

I know, of course, that you think I'm exaggerating about the size of those fish. You think, probably, that they were just medium-sized fish (a foot long, say) and that they've swollen gradually in my memory. But it isn't so. People tell lies about the fish they've caught and still more about the fish that are hooked and get away, but I never caught any of these or even tried to catch them, and I've no motive for lying. I tell you they were enormous.

Chapter Seven

That's all, really.

I've tried to tell you something about the world before the war, the world I got a sniff of when I saw King Zog's name on the poster, and the chances are that I've told you nothing. Either you remember before the war and don't need to be told about it, or you don't remember, and it's no use telling you. So far I've only spoken about the things that happened to me before I was sixteen. Up to that time things had gone pretty well with the family. It was a bit before my sixteenth birthday that I began to get glimpses of what people call "real life," meaning unpleasantness.

About three days after I'd seen the big carp at Binfield House, Father came in to tea looking very worried and even more gray and mealy than usual. He ate his way solemnly through his tea and didn't talk much. In those days he had a rather preoccupied way of eating, and his moustache used to work up and down with a sidelong movement, because he hadn't many back teeth left. I was just getting up from the table when he called me back.

"Wait a minute, George, my boy. I got suthing to say to you. Sit down jest a minute. Mother, you heard what I got to say last night."

Mother, behind the huge brown teapot, folded her hands in her lap and looked solemn. Father went on, speaking very seriously but rather spoiling the effect by trying to deal with a crumb that lodged somewhere in what was left of his back teeth:

"George, my boy, I got suthing to say to you. I been thinking it over, and it's about time you left school. 'Fraid you'll have to get to work now and start earning a bit to bring home to your mother. I wrote to Mr. Wicksey last night and told him as I should have to take you away."

Of course this was quite according to precedent—his writing to Mr. Wicksey before telling me, I mean. Parents in those days, as a matter of course, always arranged everything over their children's heads.

Father went on to make some rather mumbling and worried explanations. He'd "had bad times lately," things had "been a bit difficult," and the upshot was that Joe and I would have to start earning our living. At that time I didn't either know or greatly care whether the business was really in a bad way or not. I hadn't even enough commercial instinct to see the reason why things were "difficult." The fact was that Father had been hit by competition. Sarazins', the big retail seedsmen who had branches all over the home counties, had stuck a tentacle into Lower Binfield. Six months earlier they'd taken the lease of a shop in the market place and dolled it up until what with bright green paint, gilt lettering, gardening tools painted red and green and huge advertisements for sweet peas, it hit you in the eye at a hundred yards' distance. Sarazins', besides selling flower seeds, described themselves as "universal poultry and live-stock providers," and apart from wheat and oats and so forth they went in for patent poultry mixtures, birdseed done up in fancy packets, dog biscuits of all shapes and colors, medicines, embrocations, and conditioning powders, and branched off into such things as rat traps, dog chains, incubators, sanitary eggs, bird-netting, bulbs, weed-killer, insecticide, and even, in some branches, into what they called a "livestock department," meaning rabbits and day-old chicks. Father, with his dusty old shop and his refusal to stock new lines, couldn't compete with that kind of thing and didn't want to. The tradesmen with their van-horses, and such of the farmers as dealt with the retail seedsmen, fought shy of Sarazins', but in six months they'd gathered in the petty gentry of the neighborhood, who in those days had carriages or dogcarts and therefore horses. This meant a big loss of trade for Father and the other corn merchant, Winkle. I didn't grasp any of this at the time. I had a boy's attitude toward it all. I'd never taken any interest in the business. I'd never or hardly ever served in the shop, and when, as occasionally happened, Father wanted me to run an errand or give a hand with something, such as hoisting sacks of grain up to the loft or down again, I'd always dodged it whenever possible. Boys in our class aren't such complete babies as public schoolboys, they know that work is work and sixpence is sixpence, but it seems natural for a boy to regard his father's business as a bore. Up till that time fishing rods, bicycles, fizzy lemonade, and so forth had seemed to me a good deal more real than anything that happened in the grown-up world.

Father had already spoken to old Grimmett, the grocer, who wanted a smart lad and was willing to take me into the shop immediately. Meanwhile Father was going to get rid of the errand boy, and Joe was to come home and help with the shop till he got a regular job. Joe had left school some time back and had been more or less loafing ever since. Father had sometimes talked of "getting him into" the accounts department at the brewery, and earlier had even had thoughts of making him into an auctioneer. Both were completely hopeless because Joe, at seventeen, wrote a hand like a ploughboy and couldn't repeat the multiplication table. At present he was supposed to be "learning the trade" at a big bicycle shop on the outskirts of Walton. Tinkering with bicycles suited Joe, who, like most half-wits, had a slight mechanical turn, but he was quite incapable of working steadily and spent all his time loafing about in greasy overalls, smoking Woodbines, getting into fights, drinking (he'd started that already), getting "talked of" with one girl after another and sticking Father for money. Father was worried, puzzled, and vaguely resentful. I can see him yet, with the meal on his bald head, and the bit of gray hair over his ears, and his spectacles and his gray moustache. He couldn't understand what was happening to him. For years his profits had gone up, slowly and steadily, ten pounds this year, twenty pounds that year, and now suddenly they'd gone down with a bump. He couldn't understand it. He'd inherited the business from his father, he'd done an honest trade, worked hard, sold sound goods, swindled nobody—and his profits were going down. He said a number of times, between sucking at his teeth to get the crumb out, that times were very bad, trade seemed very slack, he couldn't think what had come over people, it wasn't as if the horses didn't have to eat. Perhaps it was these here motors, he decided finally. "Nasty smelly things!" Mother put in. She was a little worried, and knew that she ought to be more so. Once or twice while Father was talking there was a far-away look in her eyes and I could see her lips moving. She was trying to decide whether it should be a round of beef and carrots tomorrow or another leg of mutton. Except when there was something in her own line that needed foresight, such as buying linen or saucepans, she wasn't really capable of thinking beyond tomorrow's meals. The shop was giving trouble and Father was worried— that was about as far as she saw into it. None of us had any grasp of what was happening. Father had had a bad year and lost money, but was he really frightened by the future? I don't think so. This was 1909, remember. He didn't know what was happening to him, he wasn't capable of foreseeing that these Sarazin people would systematically undersell him, ruin him, and eat him up. How could he? Things hadn't happened like that when he was a young man. All he knew was that times were bad, trade was very "slack," very "slow" (he kept repeating these phrases), but probably things would "look up presently."

It would be nice if I could tell you that I was a great help to my father in his time of trouble, suddenly proved myself a man and developed qualities which no one had suspected in me—and so on and so forth, like the stuff you used to read in the uplift novels of thirty years ago. Or alternatively I'd like to be able to record that I bitterly resented having to leave school, my eager young mind, yearning for knowledge and refinement, recoiled from the soulless mechanical job into which they were thrusting me—and so on and so forth, like the stuff you read in the uplift novels today. Both would be complete bunkum. The truth is that I was pleased and excited at the idea of going to work, especially when I grasped that old Grimmett was going to pay me real wages, twelve shillings a week, of which I could keep four for myself. The big carp at Bin-field House, which had filled my mind for three days past, faded right out of it. I'd no objection to leaving school a few terms early. It generally happened the same way with boys at our school. A boy was always "going to" go to Reading University, or study to be an engineer, or "go into business" in London, or run away to sea—and then suddenly, at two days' notice, he'd disappear from school, and a fortnight later you'd meet him on a bicycle, delivering vegetables. Within five minutes of Father telling me that I should have to leave

school I was wondering about the new suit I should wear to go to
work in. I instantly started demanding a "grown-up suit," with a
kind of coat that was fashionable at that time, a "cutaway," I think
it was called. Of course both Mother and Father were scandalized
and said they'd "never heard of such a thing." For some reason that
I've never fully fathomed, parents in those days always tried to
prevent their children wearing grown-up clothes as long as possible.
In every family there was a stand-up fight before a boy had his first
tall collars or a girl put her hair up.

So the conversation veered away from Father's business troubles
and degenerated into a long, nagging kind of argument, with Father
gradually getting angry and repeating over and over—dropping an
aitch now and again, as he was apt to do when he got angry—"Well,
you can't 'ave it. Make up your mind to that—you can't 'ave it." So
I didn't have my "cutaway," but went to work for the first time in
a ready-made black suit and a broad collar in which I looked an
overgrown lout. Any distress I felt over the whole business really
arose from that. Joe was even more selfish about it. He was furious
at having to leave the bicycle shop, and for the short time that he
remained at home he merely loafed about, made a nuisance of himself and was no help to Father whatever.

I worked in old Grimmett's shop for nearly six years. Grimmett
was a fine, upstanding, white-whiskered old chap, like a rather
stouter version of Uncle Ezekiel, and like Uncle Ezekiel a good
Liberal. But he was less of a firebrand and more respected in the
town. He'd trimmed his sails during the Boer War, he was a bitter
enemy of trade unions and once sacked an assistant for possessing
a photograph of Keir Hardie, and he was "chapel"—in fact he was
a big noise, literally, in the Baptist Chapel, known locally as the
Tin Tab—whereas my family were "church" and Uncle Ezekiel was
an infidel at that. Old Grimmett was a town councillor and an
official of the local Liberal Party. With his white whiskers, his cant-
ing talk about liberty of conscience and the Grand Old Man, his
thumping bank balance and the extempore prayers you could sometimes hear him letting loose when you passed the Tin Tab, he was
a little like a legendary nonconformist grocer in the story—you've
heard it, I expect:

"James!"

"Yessir!"

"Have you sanded the sugar?"

"Yessir!"

"Have you watered the treacle?"

"Yessir!"

"Then come up to prayers."

God knows how often I heard that story whispered in the shop. We did actually start the day with a prayer before we put up the shutters. Not that old Grimmett sanded the sugar. He knew that that doesn't pay. But he was a sharp man in business, he did all the high-class grocery trade of Lower Binfield and the country round, and he had three assistants in the shop besides the errand boy, the van-man and his own daughter (he was a widower) who acted as cashier. I was the errand boy for my first six months. Then one of the assistants left to "set up" in Reading and I moved into the shop and wore my first white apron. I learned to tie a parcel, pack a bag of currants, grind coffee, work the bacon-slicer, carve ham, put an edge on a knife, sweep the floor, dust eggs without breaking them, pass off an inferior article as a good one, clean a window, judge a pound of cheese by eye, open a packing case, whack a slab of butter into shape and—what was a good deal the hardest—remember where the stock was kept. I haven't such detailed memories of grocering as I have of fishing, but I remember a good deal. To this day I know the trick of snapping a bit of string in my fingers. If you put me in front of a bacon-slicer I could work it better than I can a typewriter. I could spin you some pretty fair technicalities about grades of China tea and what margarine is made of and the average weight of eggs and the price of paper bags per thousand.

Well, for more than five years that was me—an alert young chap with a round, pink, snubby kind of face and butter-colored hair (no longer cut short but carefully greased and slicked back in what people used to call a "smarm"), hustling about behind the counter in a white apron with a pencil behind my ear, tying up bags of coffee like lightning and jockeying the customer along with "Yes, ma'am! Certainly, ma'am! *And* the next order, ma'am!" in a voice with just a trace of a Cockney accent. Old Grimmett worked us pretty hard, it was an eleven-hour day except on Thursdays and Sundays, and Christmas week was a nightmare. Yet it's a good time to look back on. Don't think that I had no ambitions. I knew I wasn't going to remain a grocer's assistant for ever, I was merely "learning the trade." Some time, somehow or other, there'd be enough money for me to "set up" on my own. That was how people felt in those days. This was before the war, remember, and before the slumps and before the dole. The world was big enough for everyone. Anyone could "set up in trade," there was always room for another shop. And time was slipping on. 1909, 1910, 1911. King Edward died and the papers came out with a black border round the edge. Two cinemas opened in Walton. The cars got commoner on the roads and cross-country motor buses began to run. An aero-plane—a flimsy, rickety-looking thing with a chap sitting in the middle on a kind of chair—flew over Lower Binfield and the whole town rushed out of their houses to yell at it. People began to say rather vaguely that this here German Emperor was getting too big for his boots and "it" (meaning war with Germany) was "coming some time." My wages went gradually up, until finally, just before the war, they were twenty-eight shillings a week. I paid Mother ten shillings a week for my board, and later, when times got worse, fifteen shillings, and even that left me feeling richer than I've felt since. I grew another inch, my moustache began to sprout, I wore button boots and collars three inches high. In church on Sundays, in my natty dark gray suit, with my bowler hat and black dogskin gloves on the pew beside me, I looked the perfect gent, so that Mother could hardly contain her pride in me. In between work and "walking out" on Thursdays, and thinking about clothes and girls, I had fits of ambition and saw myself developing into a Big Business Man like Lever or William Whiteley. Between sixteen and eighteen I made serious efforts to "improve my mind" and train myself for a business career. I cured myself of dropping aitches and got rid of most of my Cockney accent. (In the Thames Valley the country accents were going out. Except for the farm lads, nearly everyone who was born later than 1890 talked Cockney.) I did a correspondence course with Littleburns' Commercial Academy, learnt bookkeeping and business English, read solemnly through a book of frightful blah called *The Art of Salesmanship,* and improved my arithmetic and even my handwriting. When I was as old as seventeen I've sat up late at night with my tongue hanging out of my mouth, practising copperplate by the little oil-lamp on the bedroom table. At times I read enormously, generally crime and adventure stories, and sometimes paper-covered books which were furtively passed round by the chaps at the shop and described as "hot." (They were translations of Maupassant and Paul de Kock.) But when I was eighteen I suddenly turned highbrow, got a ticket for the County Library and began to stodge through books by Marie Corelli and Hall Caine and Anthony Hope. It was at about that time that I joined the Lower Binfield Reading Circle, which was run by the vicar and met one evening a week all through the winter for what was called "literary discussion." Under pressure from the vicar I read bits of *Sesame and Lilies* and even had a go at Browning.

And time was slipping away. 1910, 1911, 1912. And Father's business was going down—not slumping suddenly into the gutter, but it was going down. Neither Father nor Mother was ever quite the same after Joe ran away from home. This happened not long after I went to work at Grimmett's.

Joe, at eighteen, had grown into an ugly ruffian. He was a hefty chap, much bigger than the rest of the family, with tremendous shoulders, a big head and a sulky, lowering kind of face on which he already had a respectable moustache. When he wasn't in the tap-room of the George he was loafing in the shop doorway, with his hands dug deep into his pockets, scowling at the people who passed, except when they happened to be girls, as though he'd like to knock them down. If anyone came into the shop he'd move aside just enough to let them pass and, without taking his hands out of his pockets, yell over his shoulders, "Da-ad! Shop!" This was as near as he ever got to helping. Father and Mother said despairingly that they "didn't know what to do with him," and he was costing the devil of a lot with his drinking and endless smoking. Late one night he walked out of the house and was never heard of again. He'd prised open the till and taken all the money that was in it, luckily not much, about eight pounds. That was enough to get him a steer-age passage to America. He'd always wanted to go to America, and I think he probably did so, though we never knew for certain. It made a bit of a scandal in the town. The official theory was that Joe had bolted because he'd put a girl in the family way. There was a girl named Sally Chivers who lived in the same street as the Sim-monses and was going to have a baby, and Joe had certainly been with her, but so had about a dozen others, and nobody knew whose baby it was. Mother and Father accepted the baby theory and even, in private, used it to excuse their "poor boy" for stealing the eight pounds and running away. They weren't capable of grasping that Joe had cleared out because he couldn't stand a decent respectable life in a little country town and wanted a life of loafing, fights, and women. We never heard of him again. Perhaps he went utterly to the bad, perhaps he was killed in the war, perhaps he merely didn't bother to write. Luckily the baby was born dead, so there were no complications. As for the fact that Joe had stolen the eight pounds, Mother and Father managed to keep it a secret till they died. In their eyes it was a much worse disgrace than Sally Chivers's baby.

The trouble over Joe aged Father a great deal. To lose Joe was merely to cut a loss, but it hurt him and made him ashamed. From that time forward his moustache was much grayer and he seemed to have grown a lot smaller. Perhaps my memory of him as a little gray man, with a round, lined, anxious face and dusty spectacles, really dates from that time. By slow degrees he was getting more and more involved in money worries and less and less interested in other things.

He talked less about politics and the Sunday papers, and more about
the badness of trade. Mother seemed to have shrunk a little, too.
In my childhood I'd known her as something vast and overflowing,
with her yellow hair and her beaming face and her enormous
bosom, a sort of great opulent creature like the figurehead of a
battleship. Now she'd got smaller and more anxious and older than
her years. She was less lordly in the kitchen, went in more for neck
of mutton, worried over the price of coal and began to use margarine, a thing which in the old days she'd never have allowed into
the house. After Joe had gone Father had to hire an errand boy
again, but from then on he employed very young boys whom he
only kept for a year or two and who couldn't lift heavy weights. I
sometimes lent him a hand when I was at home. I was too selfish
to do it regularly. I can still see him working his way slowly across
the yard, bent double and almost hidden under an enormous sack,
like a snail under its shell. The huge, monstrous sack, weighing a
hundred and fifty pounds, I suppose, pressing his neck and shoulders
almost to the ground, and the anxious, spectacled face looking up
from underneath it. In 1911 he ruptured himself and had to spend
weeks in hospital and hire a temporary manager for the shop, which
ate another hole in his capital. A small shopkeeper going down the
hill is a dreadful thing to watch, but it isn't sudden and obvious like
the fate of a working man who gets the sack and promptly finds
himself on the dole. It's just a gradual chipping away of trade, with
little ups and downs, a few shillings to the bad here, a few sixpences
to the good there. Somebody who's dealt with you for years suddenly
deserts and goes to Sarazins'. Somebody else buys a dozen hens and
gives you a weekly order for corn. You can still keep going. You're
still "your own master," always a little more worried and a little
shabbier, with your capital shrinking all the time. You can go on
like that for years, for a lifetime if you're lucky. Uncle Ezekiel died
in 1911, leaving £120 which must have made a lot of difference to
Father. It wasn't till 1913 that he had to mortgage his life-insurance
policy. That I didn't hear about at the time, or I'd have understood
what it meant. As it was I don't think I ever got further than realizing that Father "wasn't doing well," trade was "slack," there'd be a
bit longer to wait before I had the money to "set up." Like Father
himself, I looked on the shop as something permanent, and I was
a bit inclined to be angry with him for not managing things better.
I wasn't capable of seeing, and neither was he nor anyone else, that
he was being slowly ruined, that his business would never pick up
again and if he lived to be seventy he'd certainly end in the workhouse. Many a time I've passed Sarazins' shop in the market place
and merely thought how much I preferred their slick window-front

to Father's dusty old shop, with the "S. Bowling" which you could hardly read, the chipped white lettering and the faded packets of birdseed. It didn't occur to me that Sarazins' were tapeworms who were eating him alive. Sometimes I used to repeat to him some of the stuff I'd been reading in my correspondence-course textbooks, about salesmanship and modern methods. He never paid much attention. He'd inherited an old, established business, he'd always worked hard, done a fair trade and supplied sound goods, and things would look up presently. It's a fact that very few shopkeepers in those days actually ended in the workhouse. With any luck you died with a few pounds still your own. It was a race between death and bankruptcy, and, thank God, death got Father first, and Mother too. . . .

Christ! What's the use of saying that one oughtn't to be sentimental about "before the war"? I *am* sentimental about it. So are you if you remember it. It's quite true that if you look back on any special period of time you tend to remember the pleasant bits. That's true even of the war. But it's also true that people then had something that we haven't got now.

What? It was simply that they didn't think of the future as something to be terrified of. It isn't that life was softer then than now. Actually it was harsher. People on the whole worked harder, lived less comfortably and died more painfully. The farm hands worked frightful hours for fourteen shillings a week and ended up as worn-out cripples with a five-shilling old-age pension and an occasional half-crown from the parish. And what was called "respectable" poverty was even worse. When little Watson, a small draper at the other end of the High Street, "failed" after years of struggling, his personal assets were £2 9s. 6d., and he died almost immediately of what was called "gastric trouble," but the doctor let it out that it was starvation. Yet he'd clung to his frock coat to the last. Old Crimp, the watchmaker's assistant, a skilled workman who'd been at the job, man and boy, for fifty years, got cataract and had to go into the workhouse. His grandchildren were howling in the street when they took him away. His wife went out charring, and by desperate efforts managed to send him a shilling a week for pocket money. You saw ghastly things happening sometimes. Small business sliding down the hill, solid tradesmen turning gradually into broken-down bankrupts, people dying by inches of cancer and liver disease, drunken husbands signing the pledge every Monday and breaking it every Saturday, girls ruined for life by an illegitimate baby. The houses had no bathrooms, you broke the ice in your basin on winter mornings, the back streets stank like the devil in hot weather, and the churchyard was bang in the middle of the town, so that you never went a day without remembering how you'd got to end. And yet what was it that people had in those days? A feeling of security, even when they weren't secure. More exactly, it was a feeling of continuity. All of them knew they'd got to die, and I suppose a few of them knew they were going to go bankrupt, but what they didn't know was that the order of things could change. Whatever might happen to themselves, things would go on as they'd known them. I don't believe it made very much difference that what's called religious belief was still prevalent in those days. It's true that nearly everyone went to church, at any rate in the country . . . and if you asked people whether they believed in a life after death they generally answered that they did. But I've never met anyone who gave me the impression of really believing in a future life. I think that, at most, people believe in that kind of thing in the same way as kids believe in Father Christmas. But it's precisely in a settled period, a period when civilization seems to stand on its four legs like an elephant, that such things as a future life don't matter. It's easy enough to die if the things you care about are going to survive. You've had your life, you're getting tired, it's time to go underground—that's how people used to see it. Individually they were finished, but their way of life would continue. Their good and evil would remain good and evil. They didn't feel the ground they stood on shifting under their feet.

Father was failing, and he didn't know it. It was merely that times were very bad, trade seemed to dwindle and dwindle, his bills were harder and harder to meet. Thank God, he never even knew that he was ruined, never actually went bankrupt, because he died very suddenly (it was influenza that turned into pneumonia) at the beginning of 1915. To the end he believed that with thrift, hard work, and fair dealing a man can't go wrong. There must have been plenty of small shopkeepers who carried that belief not merely on to bankrupt deathbeds but even into the workhouse. Even Lovegrove the saddler, with cars and motor vans staring him in the face, didn't realize that he was as out of date as the rhinoceros. And Mother too—Mother never lived to know that the life she'd been brought up to, the life of a decent God-fearing shopkeeper's daughter and a decent God-fearing shopkeeper's wife in the reign of good Queen Vic, was finished for ever. Times were difficult and trade was bad, Father was worried and this and that was "aggravating," but you carried on much the same as usual. The old English order of life couldn't change. For ever and ever decent God-fearing women would cook Yorkshire pudding and apple dumplings on enormous coal ranges, wear woolen underclothes and sleep on feathers, make plum jam in

July and pickles in October, and read *Hilda's Home Companion* in the afternoons, with the flies buzzing round, in a sort of cosy little underworld of stewed tea, bad legs and happy endings. I don't say that either Father or Mother was quite the same to the end. They were a bit shaken, and sometimes a little dispirited. But at least they never lived to know that everything they'd believed in was just so much junk. They lived at the end of an epoch, when everything was dissolving into a sort of ghastly flux, and they didn't know it. They thought it was eternity. You couldn't blame them. That was what it felt like.

Then came the end of July, and even Lower Binfield grasped that things were happening. For days there was tremendous vague excitement and endless leading articles in the papers, which Father actually brought in from the shop to read aloud to Mother. And then suddenly the posters everywhere:

GERMAN ULTIMATUM; FRANCE MOBILIZING

For several days (four days, wasn't it? I forget the exact dates) there was a strange stifled feeling, a kind of waiting hush, like the moment before a thunderstorm breaks, as though the whole of England was silent and listening. It was very hot, I remember. In the shop it was as though we couldn't work, though already everyone in the neighborhood who had five bob to spare was rushing in to buy quantities of tinned stuff and flour and oatmeal. It was as if we were too feverish to work, we only sweated and waited. In the evenings people went down to the railway station and fought like devils over the evening papers which arrived on the London train. And then one afternoon a boy came rushing down the High Street with an armful of papers, and people were coming into their doorways to shout across the street. Everyone was shouting, "We've come in! We've come in!" The boy grabbed a poster from his bundle and stuck it on the shop front opposite:

ENGLAND DECLARES WAR ON GERMANY

We rushed out on to the pavement, all three assistants, and cheered. Everybody was cheering. Yes, cheering. But old Grimmett, though he'd already done pretty well out of the war scare, still held on to a little of his Liberal principles, "didn't hold" with the war and said it would be a bad business.

Two months later I was in the Army. Seven months later I was in France.

1939

World War II
and After

From "The Lion and the Unicorn"

SOCIALISM AND THE ENGLISH GENIUS

I. ENGLAND YOUR ENGLAND

I

As I write, highly civilized human beings are flying overhead, trying to kill me.

They do not feel any enmity against me as an individual, nor I against them. They are "only doing their duty," as the saying goes. Most of them, I have no doubt, are kindhearted law-abiding men who would never dream of committing murder in private life. On the other hand, if one of them succeeds in blowing me to pieces with a well-placed bomb, he will never sleep any the worse for it. He is serving his country, which has the power to absolve him from evil.

One cannot see the modern world as it is unless one recognizes the overwhelming strength of patriotism, national loyalty. In certain circumstances it can break down, at certain levels of civilization it does not exist, but as a *positive* force there is nothing to set beside it. Christianity and international socialism are as weak as straw in comparison with it. Hitler and Mussolini rose to power in their own countries very largely because they could grasp this fact and their opponents could not.

Also, one must admit that the divisions between nation and nation are founded on real differences of outlook. Till recently it was thought proper to pretend that all human beings are very much alike, but in fact anyone able to use his eyes knows that the average of human behavior differs enormously from country to country. Things that could happen in one country could not happen in another. Hitler's June Purge, for instance, could not have happened in England. And, as Western peoples go, the English are very highly differentiated. There is a sort of backhanded admission of this in the dislike which nearly all foreigners feel for our national way of life. Few Europeans can endure living in England, and even Americans often feel more at home in Europe.

When you come back to England from any foreign country, you have immediately the sensation of breathing a different air. Even in the first few minutes dozens of small things conspire to give you this feeling. The beer is bitterer, the coins are heavier, the grass is greener, the advertisements are more blatant. The crowds in the big towns, with their mild knobby faces, their bad teeth, and gentle manners, are different from a European crowd. Then the vastness of England swallows you up, and you lose for a while your feeling that the whole nation has a single identifiable character. Are there really such things as nations? Are we not 46 million individuals, all different? And the diversity of it, the chaos! The clatter of clogs in the Lancashire mill towns, the to-and-fro of the lorries on the Great North Road, the queues outside the Labor Exchanges, the rattle of pin-tables in the Soho pubs, the old maids biking to Holy Communion through the mists of the autumn mornings—all these are not only fragments, but *characteristic* fragments, of the English scene. How can one make a pattern out of this muddle?

But talk to foreigners, read foreign books or newspapers, and you are brought back to the same thought. Yes, there *is* something distinctive and recognizable in English civilization. It is a culture as individual as that of Spain. It is somehow bound up with solid breakfasts and gloomy Sundays, smoky towns and winding roads, green fields and red pillar-boxes. It has a flavor of its own. Moreover it is continuous, it stretches into the future and the past, there is something in it that persists, as in a living creature. What can the England of 1940 have in common with the England of 1840? But then, what have you in common with the child of five whose photograph your mother keeps on the mantelpiece? Nothing, except that you happen to be the same person.

And above all, it is *your* civilization, it is *you*. However much you hate it or laugh at it, you will never be happy away from it for any length of time. The suet puddings and the red pillar-boxes have entered into your soul. Good or evil, it is yours, you belong to it, and this side the grave you will never get away from the marks that it has given you.

Meanwhile England, together with the rest of the world, is changing. And like everything else it can change only in certain directions, which up to a point can be foreseen. That is not to say that the future is fixed, merely that certain alternatives are possible and others not. A seed may grow or not grow, but at any rate a turnip seed never grows into a parsnip. It is therefore of the deepest importance to try and determine what England *is,* before guessing what part England *can play* in the huge events that are happening.

II

National characteristics are not easy to pin down, and when pinned down they often turn out to be trivialities or seem to have no connection with one another. Spaniards are cruel to animals, Italians can do nothing without making a deafening noise, the Chinese are addicted to gambling. Obviously such things don't matter in themselves. Nevertheless, nothing is causeless, and even the fact that Englishmen have bad teeth can tell one something about the realities of English life.

Here are a couple of generalizations about England that would be accepted by almost all observers. One is that the English are not gifted artistically. They are not as musical as the Germans or Italians, painting and sculpture have never flourished in England as they have in France. Another is that, as Europeans go, the English are not intellectual. They have a horror of abstract thought, they feel no need for any philosophy or systematic "world view." Nor is this because they are "practical," as they are so fond of claiming for themselves. One has only to look at their methods of town-planning and water-supply, their obstinate clinging to everything that is out of date and a nuisance, a spelling system that defies analysis and a system of weights and measures that is intelligible only to the compilers of arithmetic books, to see how little they care about mere efficiency. But they have a certain power of acting without taking thought. Their world-famed hypocrisy—their double-faced attitude toward the Empire, for instance—is bound up with this. Also, in moments of supreme crisis the whole nation can suddenly draw together and act upon a species of instinct, really a code of conduct which is understood by almost everyone, though never formulated. The phrase that Hitler coined for the Germans, "a sleep-walking people," would have been better applied to the English. Not that there is anything to be proud of in being a sleep-walker.

But here it is worth noticing a minor English trait which is extremely well marked though not often commented on, and that is a love of flowers. This is one of the first things that one notices when one reaches England from abroad, especially if one is coming from southern Europe. Does it not contradict the English indifference to the arts? Not really, because it is found in people who have no aesthetic feelings whatever. What it does link up with, however, is another English characteristic which is so much a part of us that we barely notice it, and that is the addiction to hobbies and spare-time occupations, the *privateness* of English life. We are a nation of flower-lovers, but also a nation of stamp-collectors, pigeon-fanciers, amateur carpenters, coupon-snippers, darts-players, crossword-puzzle fans. All the culture that is most truly native centers round things which even when they are communal are not official—the pub, the football match, the back garden, the fireside, and the "nice cup of tea." The liberty of the individual is still believed in, almost as in the nineteenth century. But this has nothing to do with economic liberty, the right to exploit others for profit. It is the liberty to have a home of your own, to do what you like in your spare time, to choose your own amusements instead of having them chosen for you from above. The most hateful of all names in an English ear is Nosey Parker. It is obvious, of course, that even this purely private liberty is a lost cause. Like all other modern peoples, the English are in process of being numbered, labeled, conscripted, "coordinated." But the pull of their impulses is in the other direction, and the kind of regimentation that can be imposed on them will be modified in consequence. No party rallies, no Youth Movements, no colored shirts, no Jew-baiting or "spontaneous" demonstrations. No Gestapo either, in all probability.

But in all societies the common people must live to some extent *against* the existing order. The genuinely popular culture of England is something that goes on beneath the surface, unofficially and more or less frowned on by the authorities. One thing one notices if one looks directly at the common people, especially in the big towns, is that they are not puritanical. They are inveterate gamblers, drink as much beer as their wages will permit, are devoted to bawdy jokes, and use probably the foulest language in the world. They have to satisfy these tastes in the face of astonishing, hypocritical laws (licensing laws, lottery acts, etc., etc.) which are designed to interfere with everybody but in practice allow everything to happen. Also, the common people are without definite religious belief, and have been so for centuries. The Anglican Church never had a real hold on them, it was simply a preserve of the landed gentry, and the Nonconformist sects only influenced minorities. And yet they have retained a deep tinge of Christian feeling, while almost forgetting the name of Christ. The power-worship which is the new religion of Europe, and which has infected the English intelligentsia, has never touched the common people. They have never caught up with power politics. The "realism" which is preached in Japanese and Italian newspapers would horrify them.

One can learn a good deal about the spirit of England from the comic colored postcards that you see in the windows of cheap stationers' shops. These things are a sort of diary upon which the English people have unconsciously recorded themselves. Their old-fashioned outlook, their graded snobberies, their mixture of bawdiness and hypocrisy, their extreme gentleness, their deeply moral attitude to life, are all mirrored there.

The gentleness of the English civilization is perhaps its most marked characteristic. You notice it the instant you set foot on English soil. It is a land where the bus conductors are good-tempered and the policemen carry no revolvers. In no country inhabited by white men is it easier to shove people off the pavement. And with this goes something that is always written off by European observers as "decadence" or hypocrisy, the English hatred of war and militarism. It is rooted deep in history, and it is strong in the lower-middle class as well as the working class. Successive wars have shaken it but not destroyed it. Well within living memory it was common for "the redcoats" to be booed at in the street and for the landlords of respectable public-houses to refuse to allow soldiers on the premises. In peacetime, even when there are two million unemployed, it is difficult to fill the ranks of the tiny standing army, which is officered by the county gentry and a specialized stratum of the middle class, and manned by farm laborers and slum proletarians. The mass of the people are without military knowledge or tradition, and their attitude toward war is invariably defensive. No politician could rise to power by promising them conquests or military "glory," no Hymn of Hate has ever made any appeal to them. In the 1914-18 war the songs which the soldiers made up and sang of their own accord were not vengeful but humorous and mock-defeatist.* The only enemy they ever named was the sergeant-major.

In England all the boasting and flag-wagging, the "Rule Britannia" stuff, is done by small minorities. The patriotism of the common people is not vocal or even conscious. They do not retain among their historical memories the name of a single military vic-

* For example:

> I don't want to join the bloody Army,
> I don't want to go into the war;
> I want no more to roam,
> I'd rather stay at home
> Living on the earnings of a whore.

But it was not in that spirit that they fought.

tory. English literature, like other literatures, is full of battle poems, but it is worth noticing that the ones that have won for themselves a kind of popularity are always a tale of disasters and retreats. There is no popular poem about Trafalgar or Waterloo, for instance. Sir John Moore's army at Corunna, fighting a desperate rear-guard action before escaping overseas (just like Dunkirk!) has more appeal than a brilliant victory. The most stirring battle poem in English is about a brigade of cavalry which charged in the wrong direction. And of the last war, the four names which have really engraved themselves on the popular memory are Mons, Ypres, Gallipoli, and Passchendaele, every time a disaster. The names of the great battles that finally broke the German armies are simply unknown to the general public.

The reason why the English anti-militarism disgusts foreign observers is that it ignores the existence of the British Empire. It looks like sheer hypocrisy. After all, the English absorbed a quarter of the earth and held on to it by means of a huge navy. How dare they then turn round and say that war is wicked?

It is quite true that the English are hypocritical about their Empire. In the working class this hypocrisy takes the form of not knowing that the Empire exists. But their dislike of standing armies is a perfectly sound instinct. A navy employs comparatively few people, and it is an external weapon which cannot affect home politics directly. Military dictatorships exist everywhere, but there is no such thing as a naval dictatorship. What English people of nearly all classes loathe from the bottom of their hearts is the swaggering officer type, the jingle of spurs, and the crash of boots. Decades before Hitler was ever heard of, the word "Prussian" had much the same significance in England as "Nazi" has today. So deep does this feeling go that for a hundred years past the officers of the British Army, in peacetime, have always worn civilian clothes when off duty.

One rapid but fairly sure guide to the social atmosphere of a country is the parade-step of its army. A military parade is really a kind of ritual dance, something like a ballet, expressing a certain philosophy of life. The goose-step, for instance, is one of the most horrible sights in the world, far more terrifying than a dive bomber. It is simply an affirmation of naked power; contained in it, quite consciously and intentionally, is the vision of a boot crashing down on a face. Its ugliness is part of its essence, for what it is saying is "Yes, I *am* ugly, and you daren't laugh at me," like the bully who makes faces at his victim. Why is the goose-step not used in England? There are, heaven knows, plenty of army officers who would be only too glad to introduce some such thing. It is not used because the people in the street would laugh. Beyond a certain point, military display is only possible in countries where the common people dare not laugh at the army. The Italians adopted the goose-step at about the time when Italy passed definitely under German control, and, as one would expect, they do it less well than the Germans. The Vichy Government, had it survived, was bound to introduce a stiffer parade-ground discipline into what was left of the French Army. In the British Army the drill is rigid and complicated, full of memories of the eighteenth century, but without definite swagger; the march is merely a formalized walk. It belongs to a society which is ruled by the sword, no doubt, but a sword which must never be taken out of the scabbard.

And yet the gentleness of English civilization is mixed up with barbarities and anachronisms. Our criminal law is as out of date as the muskets in the Tower. Over against the Nazi storm trooper you have got to set that typically English figure, the hanging judge, some gouty old bully with his mind rooted in the nineteenth century, handing out savage sentences. In England until recently people were still hanged by the neck and flogged with the cat o' nine tails. Both of these punishments are obscene as well as cruel, but there has never been any genuinely popular outcry against them. People accept them (and Dartmoor, and Borstal) almost as they accept the weather. They are part of "the law," which is assumed to be unalterable.

Here one comes upon an all-important English trait: the respect for constitutionalism and legality, the belief in "the law" as something above the State and above the individual, something which is cruel and stupid, of course, but at any rate *incorruptible*.

It is not that anyone imagines the law to be just. Everyone knows that there is one law for the rich and another for the poor. But no one accepts the implications of this, everyone takes it for granted that the law, such as it is, will be respected, and feels a sense of outrage when it is not. Remarks like "They can't run me in; I haven't done anything wrong," or "They can't do that; it's against the law," are part of the atmosphere of England. The professed enemies of society have this feeling as strongly as anyone else. One sees it in prison-books like Wilfred Macartney's *Walls Have Mouths* or Jim Phelan's *Jail Journey*, in the solemn idiocies that take place at the trials of conscientious objectors, in letters to the papers from eminent Marxist professors, pointing out that this or that is a "miscarriage of British justice." Everyone believes in his heart that the law can be, ought to be, and, on the whole, will be impartially administered. The totalitarian idea that there is no such thing as law, there is only power, has never taken root. Even the intelligentsia have only accepted it in theory.

An illusion can become a half-truth, a mask can alter the expression of a face. The familiar arguments to the effect that democracy is "just the same as" or "just as bad as" totalitarianism never take account of this fact. All such arguments boil down to saying that half a loaf is the same as no bread. In England such concepts as justice, liberty, and objective truth are still believed in. They may be illusions, but they are very powerful illusions. The belief in them influences conduct, national life is different because of them. In proof of which, look about you. Where are the rubber truncheons, where is the castor oil? The sword is still in the scabbard, and while it stays there corruption cannot go beyond a certain point. The English electoral system, for instance, is an all but open fraud. In a dozen obvious ways it is gerrymandered in the interest of the monied class. But until some deep change has occurred in the public mind, it cannot become *completely* corrupt. You do not arrive at the polling booth to find men with revolvers telling you which way to vote, nor are the votes miscounted, nor is there any direct bribery. Even hypocrisy is a powerful safeguard. The hanging judge, that evil old man in scarlet robe and horsehair wig, whom nothing short of dynamite will ever teach what century he is living in, but who will at any rate interpret the law according to the books and will in no circumstances take a money bribe, is one of the symbolic figures of England. He is a symbol of the strange mixture of reality and illusion, democracy and privilege, humbug and decency, the subtle network of compromises, by which the nation keeps itself in its familiar shape.

III

I have spoken all the while of "the nation," "England," "Britain," as though 46 million souls could somehow be treated as a unit. But is not England notoriously two nations, the rich and the poor? Dare one pretend that there is anything in common between people with £100,000 a year and people with £1 a week? And even Welsh and Scottish readers are likely to have been offended because I have used the word "England" oftener than "Britain," as though the whole population dwelt in London and the Home Counties and neither north nor west possessed a culture of its own.

One gets a better view of this question if one considers the minor point first. It is quite true that the so-called races of Britain feel themselves to be very different from one another. A Scotsman, for instance, does not thank you if you call him an Englishman. You can see the hesitation we feel on this point by the fact that we call our islands by no less than six different names, England, Britain, Great Britain, the British Isles, the United Kingdom, and, in very exalted moments, Albion. Even the differences between north and south England loom large in our own eyes. But somehow these differences fade away the moment that any two Britons are confronted by a European. It is very rare to meet a foreigner, other than an American, who can distinguish between English and Scots or even English and Irish. To a Frenchman, the Breton and the Auvergnat seem very different beings, and the accent of Marseilles is a stock joke in Paris. Yet we speak of "France" and "the French," recognizing France as an entity, a single civilization, which in fact it is. So also with ourselves. Looked at from the outside, even the cockney and the Yorkshireman have a strong family resemblance.

And even the distinction between rich and poor dwindles somewhat when one regards the nation from the outside. There is no question about the inequality of wealth in England. It is grosser than in any European country, and you have only to look down the nearest street to see it. Economically, England is certainly two nations, if not three or four. But at the same time the vast majority of the people *feel* themselves to be a single nation and are conscious of resembling one another more than they resemble foreigners. Patriotism is usually stronger than class hatred, and always stronger than any kind of internationalism. Except for a brief moment in 1920 (the "Hands off Russia" movement) the British working class have never thought or acted internationally. For two and a half years they watched their comrades in Spain slowly strangled, and never aided them by even a single strike.* But when their own country (the country of Lord Nuffield and Mr. Montagu Norman) was in danger, their attitude was very different. At the moment when it seemed likely that England might be invaded, Anthony Eden appealed over the radio for Local Defence Volunteers. He got a quarter of a million men in the first twenty-four hours, and another million in the subsequent month. One has only to compare these figures with, for instance, the num-

---

* It is true that they aided them to a certain extent with money. Still, the sums raised for the various aid-Spain funds would not equal 5 per cent of the turnover of the Football Pools during the same period.

ber of conscientious objectors to see how vast is the strength of
traditional loyalties compared with new ones.

In England patriotism takes different forms in different classes,
but it runs like a connecting thread through nearly all of them.
Only the Europeanized intelligentsia are really immune to it. As
a positive emotion it is stronger in the middle class than in the
upper class—the cheap public schools, for instance, are more given
to patriotic demonstrations than the expensive ones—but the number of definitely treacherous rich men, the Laval-Quisling type, is
probably very small. In the working class patriotism is profound,
but it is unconscious. The working man's heart does not leap when
he sees a Union Jack. But the famous "insularity" and "xeno-
phobia" of the English is far stronger in the working class than
in the bourgeoisie. In all countries the poor are more national
than the rich, but the English working class are outstanding in
their abhorrence of foreign habits. Even when they are obliged to
live abroad for years they refuse either to accustom themselves to
foreign food or to learn foreign languages. Nearly every Englishman of working-class origin considers it effeminate to pronounce
a foreign word correctly. During the war of 1914-18 the English
working class were in contact with foreigners to an extent that is
rarely possible. The sole result was that they brought back a hatred
of all Europeans, except the Germans, whose courage they admired.
In four years on French soil they did not even acquire a liking
for wine. The insularity of the English, their refusal to take foreigners seriously, is a folly that has to be paid for very heavily
from time to time. But it plays its part in the English *mystique,*
and the intellectuals who have tried to break it down have generally done more harm than good. At bottom it is the same quality
in the English character that repels the tourist and keeps out the
invader.

Here one comes back to two English characteristics that I pointed
out, seemingly rather at random, at the beginning of the last chapter. One is the lack of artistic ability. This is perhaps another way
of saying that the English are outside the European culture. For
there is one art in which they have shown plenty of talent, namely
literature. But this is also the only art that cannot cross frontiers.
Literature, especially poetry, and lyric poetry most of all, is a kind
of family joke, with little or no value outside its own language
group. Except for Shakespeare, the best English poets are barely
known in Europe, even as names. The only poets who are widely
read are Byron, who is admired for the wrong reasons, and Oscar
Wilde, who is pitied as a victim of English hypocrisy. And linked

up with this, though not very obviously, is the lack of philosophical faculty, the absence in nearly all Englishmen of any need for
an ordered system of thought or even for the use of logic.

Up to a point, the sense of national unity is a substitute for a
"world view." Just because patriotism is all but universal and not
even the rich are uninfluenced by it, there can come moments
when the whole nation suddenly swings together and does the
same thing, like a herd of cattle facing a wolf. There was such a
moment, unmistakably, at the time of the disaster in France. After
eight months of vaguely wondering what the war was about, the
people suddenly knew what they had got to do: first, to get the
army away from Dunkirk, and secondly to prevent invasion. It
was like the awakening of a giant. Quick! Danger! The Philistines
be upon thee, Samson! And then the swift unanimous action—and
then, alas, the prompt relapse into sleep. In a divided nation that
would have been exactly the moment for a big peace movement
to arise. But does this mean that the instinct of the English will
always tell them to do the right thing? Not at all, merely that it
will tell them to do the same thing. In the 1931 General Election,
for instance, we all did the wrong thing in perfect unison. We
were as single-minded as the Gadarene swine. But I honestly doubt
whether we can say that we were shoved down the slope against
our will.

It follows that British democracy is less of a fraud than it sometimes appears. A foreign observer sees only the huge inequality of
wealth, the unfair electoral system, the governing-class control over
the press, the radio, and education, and concludes that democracy
is simply a polite name for dictatorship. But this ignores the considerable agreement that does unfortunately exist between the leaders and the led. However much one may hate to admit it, it is almost certain that between 1931 and 1940 the National Government represented the will of the mass of the people. It tolerated
slums, unemployment, and a cowardly foreign policy. Yes, but so
did public opinion. It was a stagnant period, and its natural leaders were mediocrities.

In spite of the campaigns of a few thousand left-wingers, it is
fairly certain that the bulk of the English people were behind
Chamberlain's foreign policy. More, it is fairly certain that the
same struggle was going on in Chamberlain's mind as in the minds
of ordinary people. His opponents professed to see in him a dark
and wily schemer, plotting to sell England to Hitler, but it is far
likelier that he was merely a stupid old man doing his best according to his very dim lights. It is difficult otherwise to explain

the contradictions of his policy, his failure to grasp any of the courses that were open to him. Like the mass of the people, he did not want to pay the price either of peace or of war. And public opinion was behind him all the while, in policies that were completely incompatible with one another. It was behind him when he went to Munich, when he tried to come to an understanding with Russia, when he gave the guarantee to Poland, when he honored it, and when he prosecuted the war half-heartedly. Only when the results of his policy became apparent did it turn against him; which is to say that it turned against its own lethargy of the past seven years. Thereupon the people picked a leader nearer to their mood, Churchill, who was at any rate able to grasp that wars are not won without fighting. Later, perhaps, they will pick another leader who can grasp that only socialist nations can fight effectively.

Do I mean by all this that England is a genuine democracy? No, not even a reader of the *Daily Telegraph* could quite swallow that.

England is the most class-ridden country under the sun. It is a land of snobbery and privilege, ruled largely by the old and silly. But in any calculation about it one has got to take into account its emotional unity, the tendency of nearly all its inhabitants to feel alike and act together in moments of supreme crisis. It is the only great country in Europe that is not obliged to drive hundreds of thousands of its nationals into exile or the concentration camp. At this moment, after a year of war, newspapers and pamphlets abusing the government, praising the enemy and clamouring for surrender are being sold on the streets, almost without interference. And this is less from a respect for freedom of speech than from a simple perception that these things don't matter. It is safe to let a paper like *Peace News* be sold, because it is certain that 95 per cent of the population will never want to read it. The nation is bound together by an invisible chain. At any normal time the ruling class will rob, mismanage, sabotage, lead us into the muck; but let popular opinion really make itself heard, let them get a tug from below that they cannot avoid feeling, and it is difficult for them not to respond. The left-wing writers who denounce the whole of the ruling class as "pro-Fascist" are grossly oversimplifying. Even among the inner clique of politicians who brought us to our present pass, it is doubtful whether there were any *conscious* traitors. The corruption that happens in England is seldom of that kind. Nearly always it is more in the nature of self-deception, of the right hand not knowing what the left hand doeth.

And being unconscious, it is limited. One sees this at its most obvious in the English press. Is the English press honest or dishonest? At normal times it is deeply dishonest. All the papers that matter live off their advertisements, and the advertisers exercise an indirect censorship over news. Yet I do not suppose there is one paper in England that can be straightforwardly bribed with hard cash. In the France of the Third Republic all but a very few of the newspapers could notoriously be bought over the counter like so many pounds of cheese. Public life in England has never been *openly* scandalous. It has not reached the pitch of disintegration at which humbug can be dropped.

England is not the jeweled isle of Shakespeare's much-quoted passage, nor is it the inferno depicted by Dr. Goebbels. More than either it resembles a family, a rather stuffy Victorian family, with not many black sheep in it but with all its cupboards bursting with skeletons. It has rich relations who have to be kowtowed to and poor relations who are horribly sat upon, and there is a deep conspiracy of silence about the source of the family income. It is a family in which the young are generally thwarted and most of the power is in the hands of irresponsible uncles and bedridden aunts. Still, it is a family. It has its private language and its common memories, and at the approach of an enemy it closes its ranks. A family with the wrong members in control—that, perhaps, is as near as one can come to describing England in a phrase.

IV

Probably the battle of Waterloo *was* won on the playing-fields of Eton, but the opening battles of all subsequent wars have been lost there. One of the dominant facts in English life during the past three-quarters of a century has been the decay of ability in the ruling class.

In the years between 1920 and 1940 it was happening with the speed of a chemical reaction. Yet at the moment of writing it is still possible to speak of a ruling class. Like the knife which has had two new blades and three new handles, the upper fringe of English society is still almost what it was in the mid-nineteenth century. After 1832 the old landowning aristocracy steadily lost power, but instead of disappearing or becoming a fossil they simply intermarried with the merchants, manufacturers, and financiers who had replaced them, and soon turned them into accurate copies of themselves. The wealthy shipowner or cotton-miller set up for himself an alibi as a country gentleman, while his sons learned the right mannerisms at public schools which had been designed for just that purpose. England was ruled by an aristocracy constantly recruited from parvenus. And considering what energy the self-made men possessed, and considering that they were buying their way into a class which at any rate had a tradition of public service, one might have expected that able rulers could be produced in some such way.

And yet somehow the ruling class decayed, lost its ability, its daring, finally even its ruthlessness, until a time came when stuffed shirts like Eden or Halifax could stand out as men of exceptional talent. As for Baldwin, one could not even dignify him with the name of stuffed shirt. He was simply a hole in the air. The mishandling of England's domestic problems during the nineteen-twenties had been bad enough, but British foreign policy between 1931 and 1939 is one of the wonders of the world. Why? What had happened? What was it that at every decisive moment made every British statesman do the wrong thing with so unerring an instinct?

The underlying fact was that the whole position of the monied class had long ceased to be justifiable. There they sat, at the center of a vast empire and a worldwide financial network, drawing interest and profits and spending them—on what? It was fair to say that life within the British Empire was in many ways better than life outside it. Still, the Empire was undeveloped, India slept in the Middle Ages, the Dominions lay empty, with foreigners jealously barred out, and even England was full of slums and unemployment. Only half a million people, the people in the country houses, definitely benefited from the existing system. Moreover, the tendency of small businesses to merge together into large ones robbed more and more of the monied class of their function and turned them into mere *owners,* their work being done for them by salaried managers and technicians. For long past there had been in England an entirely functionless class, living on money that was invested they hardly knew where, the "idle rich," the people whose photographs you can look at in the *Tatler* and the *Bystander,* always supposing that you want to. The existence of these people was by any standard unjustifiable. They were simply parasites, less useful to society than his fleas are to a dog.

By 1920 there were many people who were aware of all this. By 1930 millions were aware of it. But the British ruling class obviously could not admit to themselves that their usefulness was at an end. Had they done that they would have had to abdicate. For it was not possible for them to turn themselves into mere bandits, like the American millionaires, consciously clinging to unust privileges and beating down opposition by bribery and tear-gas bombs. After all, they belonged to a class with a certain tradition, they had been to public schools where the duty of dying for your country, if necessary, is laid down as the first and greatest of the Commandments. They had to *feel* themselves true patriots, even while they plundered their countrymen. Clearly there was only one escape for them—into stupidity. They could keep society in its existing shape only by being *unable* to grasp that any improvement was possible. Difficult though this was, they achieved it, largely by fixing their eyes on the past and refusing to notice the changes that were going on round them.

There is much in England that this explains. It explains the decay of country life, due to the keeping-up of a sham feudalism which drives the more spirited workers off the land. It explains the immobility of the public schools, which have barely altered since the eighties of the last century. It explains the military incompetence which has again and again startled the world. Since the fifties every war in which England has engaged has started off with a series of disasters, after which the situation has been saved by people comparatively low in the social scale. The higher commanders, drawn from the aristocracy, could never prepare for modern war, because in order to do so they would have had to admit to themselves that the world was changing. They have always clung to obsolete methods and weapons, because they inevitably saw each war as a repetition of the last. Before the Boer War they prepared for the Zulu War, before 1914 for the Boer War, and before the present war for 1914. Even at this moment hundreds of thousands of men in England are being trained with the bayonet, a weapon entirely useless except for opening tins. It is worth noticing that the Navy and, latterly, the Air Force, have always been more efficient than the regular army. But the navy is only partially, and the Air Force hardly at all, within the ruling-class orbit.

It must be admitted that so long as things were peaceful the methods of the British ruling class served them well enough. Their own people manifestly tolerated them. However unjustly England might be organized, it was at any rate not torn by class warfare or haunted by secret police. The Empire was peaceful as no area of comparable size has ever been. Throughout its vast extent, nearly a quarter of the earth, there were fewer armed men than would be found necessary by a minor Balkan state. As people to live under, and looking at them merely from a liberal, *negative* standpoint, the British ruling class had their points. They were preferable to the truly modern men, the Nazis and Fascists. But

it had long been obvious that they would be helpless against an
serious attack from the outside.

They could not struggle against Nazism or Fascism, because the
could not understand them. Neither could they have struggle
against Communism, if Communism had been a serious force i
Western Europe. To understand Fascism they would have had t
study the theory of socialism, which would have forced them t
realize that the economic system by which they lived was unjus
inefficient, and out of date. But it was exactly this fact that the
had trained themselves never to face. They dealt with Fascism a
the cavalry generals of 1914 dealt with the machine-gun—by igno
ing it. After years of aggression and massacres, they had graspe
only one fact, that Hitler and Mussolini were hostile to Commu
nism. Therefore, it was argued, they *must* be friendly to the Bri
ish dividend-drawer. Hence the truly frightening spectacle of Con
servative M.P.s wildly cheering the news that British ships, brin
ing food to the Spanish Republican Government, had been bombe
by Italian aeroplanes. Even when they had begun to grasp tha
Fascism was dangerous, its essentially revolutionary nature, th
huge military effort it was capable of making, the sort of tactic
it would use, were quite beyond their comprehension. At the tim
of the Spanish civil war, anyone with as much political knowledg
as can be acquired from a sixpenny pamphlet on socialism kne
that if Franco won, the result would be strategically disastrous fo
England; and yet generals and admirals who had given their live
to the study of war were unable to grasp this fact. This vein o
political ignorance runs right through English official life, throug
cabinet ministers, ambassadors, consuls, judges, magistrates, police
men. The policeman who arrests the "Red" does not understan
the theories the "Red" is preaching; if he did, his own positio
as bodyguard of the monied class might seem less pleasant to him
There is reason to think that even military espionage is hopelessl
hampered by ignorance of the new economic doctrines and th
ramifications of the underground parties.

The British ruling class were not altogether wrong in thinkin
that Fascism was on their side. It is a fact that any rich man, un
less he is a Jew, has less to fear from Fascism than from eithe
Communism or democratic socialism. One ought never to forge
this, for nearly the whole of German and Italian propaganda i
designed to cover it up. The natural instinct of men like Simon
Hoare, Chamberlain, etc., was to come to an agreement with Hitle
But—and here the peculiar feature of English life that I hav
spoken of, the deep sense of national solidarity, comes in—the

could only do so by breaking up the Empire and selling their own people into semi-slavery. A truly corrupt class would have done this without hesitation, as in France. But things had not gone that distance in England. Politicians who would make cringing speeches about "the duty of loyalty to our conquerors" are hardly to be found in English public life. Tossed to and fro between their incomes and their principles, it was impossible that men like Chamberlain should do anything but make the worst of both worlds.

One thing that has always shown that the English ruling class are *morally* fairly sound, is that in time of war they are ready enough to get themselves killed. Several dukes, earls, and what-not were killed in the recent campaign in Flanders. That could not happen if these people were the cynical scoundrels that they are sometimes declared to be. It is important not to misunderstand their motives, or one cannot predict their actions. What is to be expected of them is not treachery or physical cowardice, but stupidity, unconscious sabotage, an infallible instinct for doing the wrong thing. They are not wicked, or not altogether wicked; they are merely unteachable. Only when their money and power are gone will the younger among them begin to grasp what century they are living in.

v

The stagnation of the Empire in the between-war years affected everyone in England, but it had an especially direct effect upon two important sub-sections of the middle class. One was the military and imperialist middle class, generally nicknamed the Blimps, and the other the left-wing intelligentsia. These two seemingly hostile types, symbolic opposites—the half-pay colonel with his bull neck and diminutive brain, like a dinosaur, the highbrow with his domed forehead and stalk-like neck—are mentally linked together and constantly interact upon one another; in any case they are born to a considerable extent into the same families.

Thirty years ago the Blimp class was already losing its vitality. The middle-class families celebrated by Kipling, the prolific low-brow families whose sons officered the Army and Navy and swarmed over all the waste places of the earth from the Yukon to the Irrawaddy, were dwindling before 1914. The thing that had killed them was the telegraph. In a narrowing world, more and more governed from Whitehall, there was every year less room for individual initiative. Men like Clive, Nelson, Nicholson, Gordon would find no place for themselves in the modern British Empire. By 1920 nearly every inch of the colonial empire was in the grip of Whitehall. Well-meaning, overcivilized men, in dark suits and black felt hats, with neatly rolled umbrellas crooked over the left forearm, were imposing their constipated view of life on Malaya and Nigeria, Mombasa, and Mandalay. The one-time empire-builders were reduced to the status of clerks, buried deeper and deeper under mounds of paper and red tape. In the early twenties one could see, all over the Empire, the older officials, who had known more spacious days, writhing impotently under the changes that were happening. From that time onward it has been next door to impossible to induce young men of spirit to take any part in imperial administration. And what was true of the official world was true also of the commercial. The great monopoly companies swallowed up hosts of petty traders. Instead of going out to trade adventurously in the Indies one went to an office stool in Bombay or Singapore. And life in Bombay or Singapore was actually duller and safer than life in London. Imperialist sentiment remained strong in the middle class, chiefly owing to family tradition, but the job of administering the Empire had ceased to appeal. Few able men went east of Suez if there was any way of avoiding it.

But the general weakening of imperialism, and to some extent of the whole British morale, that took place during the nineteen-thirties, was partly the work of the left-wing intelligentsia, itself a kind of growth that had sprouted from the stagnation of the Empire.

It should be noted that there is now no intelligentsia that is not in some sense "Left." Perhaps the last right-wing intellectual was T. E. Lawrence. Since about 1930 everyone describable as an "intellectual" has lived in a state of chronic discontent with the existing order. Necessarily so, because society as it was constituted had no room for him. In an Empire that was simply stagnant, neither being developed nor falling to pieces, and in an England ruled by people whose chief asset was their stupidity, to be "clever" was to be suspect. If you had the kind of brain that could understand the poems of T. S. Eliot or the theories of Karl Marx, the higher-ups would see to it that you were kept out of any important job. The intellectuals could find a function for themselves only in the literary reviews and the left-wing political parties.

The mentality of the English left-wing intelligentsia can be studied in half a dozen weekly and monthly papers. The immediately striking thing about all these papers is their generally negative, querulous attitude, their complete lack at all times of any constructive suggestion. There is little in them except the irresponsible carping of people who have never been and never expect to be in a position of power. Another marked characteristic is the emotional shallowness of people who live in a world of ideas and have little contact with physical reality. Many intellectuals of the Left were flabbily pacifist up to 1935, shrieked for war against Germany in the years 1935-39, and then promptly cooled off when the war started. It is broadly though not precisely true that the people who were most "anti-Fascist" during the Spanish civil war are most defeatist now. And underlying this is the really important fact about so many of the English intelligentsia—their severance from the common culture of the country.

In intention, at any rate, the English intelligentsia are Europeanized. They take their cookery from Paris and their opinions from Moscow. In the general patriotism of the country they form a sort of island of dissident thought. England is perhaps the only great country whose intellectuals are ashamed of their own nationality. In left-wing circles it is always felt that there is something slightly disgraceful in being an Englishman and that it is a duty to snigger at every English institution, from horseracing to suet puddings. It is a strange fact, but it is unquestionably true, that almost any English intellectual would feel more ashamed of standing to attention during "God save the King" than of stealing from a poor box. All through the critical years many left-wingers were chipping away at English morale, trying to spread an outlook that was sometimes squashily pacifist, sometimes violently pro-Russian, but always anti-British. It is questionable how much effect this had, but it certainly had some. If the English people suffered for several years a real weakening of morale, so that the Fascist nations judged that they were "decadent" and that it was safe to plunge into war, the intellectual sabotage from the Left was partly responsible. Both the *New Statesman* and the *News-Chronicle* cried out against the Munich settlement, but even they had done something to make it possible. Ten years of systematic Blimp-baiting affected even the Blimps themselves and made it harder than it had been before to get intelligent young men to enter the armed forces. Given the stagnation of the Empire the military middle class must have decayed in any case, but the spread of a shallow Leftism hastened the process.

It is clear that the special position of the English intellectuals during the past ten years, as purely *negative* creatures, mere anti-Blimps, was a by-product of ruling-class stupidity. Society could not use them, and they had not got it in them to see that devotion to one's country implies "for better, for worse." Both Blimps and highbrows took for granted, as though it were a law of nature, the divorce between patriotism and intelligence. If you were a patriot you read *Blackwood's Magazine* and publicly thanked God that you were "not brainy." If you were an intellectual you sniggered at the Union Jack and regarded physical courage as barbarous. It is obvious that this preposterous convention cannot continue. The Bloomsbury highbrow, with his mechanical snigger, is as out of date as the cavalry colonel. A modern nation cannot afford either of them. Patriotism and intelligence will have to come together again. It is the fact that we are fighting a war, and a very peculiar kind of war, that may make this possible.

VI

One of the most important developments in England during the past twenty years has been the upward and downward extension of the middle class. It has happened on such a scale as to make the old classification of society into capitalists, proletarians, and petit bourgeois (small property-owners) almost obsolete.

England is a country in which property and financial power are concentrated in very few hands. Few people in modern England *own* anything at all, except clothes, furniture, and possibly a house. The peasantry have long since disappeared, the independent shopkeeper is being destroyed, the small businessman is diminishing in numbers. But at the same time modern industry is so complicated that it cannot get along without great numbers of managers, salesmen, engineers, chemists, and technicians of all kinds, drawing fairly large salaries. And these in turn call into being a professional class of doctors, lawyers, teachers, artists, etc., etc. The tendency of advanced capitalism has therefore been to enlarge the middle class and not to wipe it out as it once seemed likely to do.

But much more important than this is the spread of middle-class ideas and habits among the working class. The British working class are now better off in almost all ways than they were thirty years ago. This is partly due to the efforts of the trade unions, but partly to the mere advance of physical science. It is not always realized that within rather narrow limits the standard of life of a country can rise without a corresponding rise in real wages. Up to a point, civilization can lift itself up by its boot-tags. However unjustly society is organized, certain technical advances are bound to benefit the whole community, because certain kinds of goods are necessarily held in common. A millionaire cannot, for example, light the streets for himself while darkening them for other people. Nearly all citizens of civilized countries now enjoy the use of good roads, germ-free water, police protection, free libraries, and probably free education of a kind. Public education in England has been meanly starved of money, but it has nevertheless improved, largely owing to the devoted efforts of the teachers, and the habit of reading has become enormously more widespread. To an increasing extent the rich and the poor read the same books, and they also see the same films and listen to the same radio programs. And the differences in their way of life have been diminished by the mass production of cheap clothes and improvements in housing. So far as outward appearance goes, the clothes of rich and poor, especially in the case of women, differ far less than they did thirty or even fifteen years ago. As to housing, England still has slums which are a blot on civilization, but much building has been done during the past ten years, largely by the local authorities. The modern Council house, with its bathroom and electric light, is smaller than the stockbroker's villa, but it is recognizably the same kind of house, which the farm laborer's cottage is not. A person who has grown up in a Council housing estate is likely to be—indeed, visibly *is*—more middle class in outlook than a person who has grown up in a slum.

The effect of all this is a general softening of manners. It is enhanced by the fact that modern industrial methods tend always to demand less muscular effort and therefore to leave people with more energy when their day's work is done. Many workers in the light industries are less truly manual laborers than is a doctor or a grocer. In tastes, habits, manners, and outlook the working class and the middle class are drawing together. The unjust distinctions remain, but the real differences diminish. The old-style "proletarian" —collarless, unshaven, and with muscles warped by heavy labor— still exists, but he is constantly decreasing in numbers; he only predominates in the heavy-industry areas of the north of England.

After 1918 there began to appear something that had never existed in England before: people of indeterminate social class. In 1910 every human being in these islands could be "placed" in an instant by his clothes, manners, and accent. That is no longer the case. Above all, it is not the case in the new townships that have developed as a result of cheap motor cars and the southward shift of industry. The place to look for the germs of the future England is in the light-industry areas and along the arterial roads. In Slough, Dagenham, Barnet, Letchworth, Hayes—everywhere, indeed, on the outskirts of great towns—the old pattern is gradually changing into something new. In those vast new wildernesses of glass and brick the sharp distinctions of the older kind of town, with its slums and mansions, or of the country, with its manor houses and squalid cottages, no longer exist. There are wide gradations of income, but it is the same kind of life that is being lived at different levels, in labor-saving flats or Council houses, along the concrete roads and in the naked democracy of the swimming pools. It is a rather restless, cultureless life, centering round tinned food, *Picture Post,* the radio, and the internal combustion engine. It is a civilization in which children grow up with an intimate knowledge of magnetos and in complete ignorance of the Bible. To that civilization belong the people who are most at home in and most definitely *of* the modern world, the technicians and the higher-paid skilled workers, the airmen and their mechanics, the radio experts, film producers, popular journalists, and industrial chemists. They are the indeterminate stratum at which the older class distinctions are beginning to break down.

This war, unless we are defeated, will wipe out most of the existing class privileges. There are every day fewer people who wish them to continue. Nor need we fear that as the pattern changes life in England will lose its peculiar flavor. The new red cities of Greater London are crude enough, but these things are only the rash that accompanies a change. In whatever shape England emerges from the war, it will be deeply tinged with the characteristics that I have spoken of earlier. The intellectuals who hope to see it Russianized or Germanized will be disappointed. The gentleness, the hypocrisy, the thoughtlessness, the reverence for law, and the hatred of uniforms will remain, along with the suet puddings and the misty skies. It needs some very great disaster, such as prolonged subjugation by a foreign enemy, to destroy a national culture. The Stock Exchange will be pulled down, the horse plough will give way to the tractor, the country houses will be turned into children's holiday camps, the Eton and Harrow match will be forgotten, but England will still be England, an everlasting animal stretching into the future and the past, and, like all living things, having the power to change out of recognition and yet remain the same.

1941

△

Rudyard Kipling

▽

It was a pity that Mr. Eliot should be so much on the defensive in the long essay with which he prefaces this selection of Kipling's poetry,* but it was not to be avoided, because before one can even speak about Kipling one has to clear away a legend that has been created by two sets of people who have not read his works. Kipling is in the peculiar position of having been a byword for fifty years. During five literary generations every enlightened person has despised him, and at the end of that time nine-tenths of those enlightened persons are forgotten and Kipling is in some sense still there. Mr. Eliot never satisfactorily explains this fact, because in answering the shallow and familiar charge that Kipling is a "Fascist," he falls into the opposite error of defending him where he is not defensible. It is no use pretending that Kipling's view of life, as a whole, can be accepted or even forgiven by any civilized person. It is no use claiming, for instance, that when Kipling describes a British soldier beating a "nigger" with a cleaning rod in order to get money out of him, he is acting merely as a reporter and does not necessarily approve what he describes. There is not the slightest sign anywhere in Kipling's work that he disapproves of that kind of conduct—on the contrary, there is a definite strain of sadism in him, over and above the brutality which a writer of that type has to have. Kipling *is* a jingo imperialist, he *is* morally insensitive and aesthetically disgusting. It is better to start by admitting that, and then to try to find out why it is that he survives while the refined people who have sniggered at him seem to wear so badly.

And yet the "Fascist" charge has to be answered, because the first clue to any understanding of Kipling, morally or politically, is the fact that he was *not* a Fascist. He was further from being one than the most humane or the most "progressive" person is able to be nowadays. An interesting instance of the way in which quotations

* *A Choice of Kipling's Verse*, made by T. S. Eliot (Faber & Faber, London).

are parroted to and fro without any attempt to look up their context or discover their meaning is the line from "Recessional," "Lesser breeds without the Law." This line is always good for a snigger in pansy-left circles. It is assumed as a matter of course that the "lesser breeds" are "natives," and a mental picture is called up of some pukka sahib in a pith helmet kicking a coolie. In its context the sense of the line is almost the exact opposite of this. The phrase "lesser breeds" refers almost certainly to the Germans, and especially the pan-German writers, who are "without the Law" in the sense of being lawless, not in the sense of being powerless. The whole poem, conventionally thought of as an orgy of boasting, is a denunciation of power politics, British as well as German. Two stanzas are worth quoting (I am quoting this as politics, not as poetry):

> If, drunk with sight of power, we loose
> Wild tongues that have not Thee in awe,
> Such boastings as the Gentiles use,
> Or lesser breeds without the Law—
> Lord God of hosts, be with us yet,
> Lest we forget—lest we forget!
>
> For heathen heart that puts her trust
> In reeking tube and iron shard,
> All valiant dust that builds on dust,
> And guarding, calls not Thee to guard,
> For frantic boast and foolish word—
> Thy mercy on Thy People, Lord!

Much of Kipling's phraseology is taken from the Bible, and no doubt in the second stanza he had in mind the text from Psalm cxxvii: "Except the Lord build the house, they labour in vain that build it; except the Lord keep the city, the watchman waketh but in vain." It is not a text that makes much impression on the post-Hitler mind. No one, in our time, believes in any sanction greater than military power; no one believes that it is possible to overcome force except by greater force. There is no "law," there is only power. I am not saying that that is a true belief, merely that it is the belief which all modern men do actually hold. Those who pretend otherwise are either intellectual cowards, or power-worshipers under a thin disguise, or have simply not caught up with the age they are living in. Kipling's outlook is pre-Fascist. He still believes that pride comes before a fall and that the gods punish *hubris*. He does not foresee the tank, the bombing plane, the radio, and the secret police or their psychological results.

But in saying this, does not one unsay what I said above about Kipling's jingoism and brutality? No, one is merely saying that the nineteenth-century imperialist outlook and the modern gangster outlook are two different things. Kipling belongs very definitely to the period 1885-1902. The Great War and its aftermath embittered him, but he shows little sign of having learned anything from any event later than the Boer War. He was the prophet of British Imperialism in its expansionist phase (even more than his poems, his solitary novel, *The Light that Failed,* gives you the atmosphere of that time) and also the unofficial historian of the British Army, the old mercenary army which began to change its shape in 1914. All his confidence, his bouncing vulgar vitality, sprang out of limitations which no Fascist or near-Fascist shares.

Kipling spent the later part of his life in sulking, and no doubt it was political disappointment rather than literary vanity that accounted for this. Somehow history had not gone according to plan. After the greatest victory she had ever known, Britain was a lesser world power than before, and Kipling was quite acute enough to see this. The virtue had gone out of the classes he idealized, the young were hedonistic or disaffected, the desire to paint the map red had evaporated. He could not understand what was happening, because he had never had any grasp of the economic forces underlying imperial expansion. It is notable that Kipling does not seem to realize, any more than the average soldier or colonial administrator, that an empire is primarily a money-making concern. Imperialism as he sees it is a sort of forcible evangelizing. You turn a Gatling gun on a mob of unarmed "natives," and then you establish "the Law," which includes roads, railways, and a courthouse. He could not foresee, therefore, that the same motives which brought the Empire into existence would end by destroying it. It was the same motive, for example, that caused the Malayan jungles to be cleared for rubber estates, and which now causes those estates to be handed over intact to the Japanese. The modern totalitarians know what they are doing, and the nineteenth-century English did not know what they were doing. Both attitudes have their advantages, but Kipling was never able to move forward from one into the other. His outlook, allowing for the fact that after all he was an artist, was that of the salaried bureaucrat who despises the "box-wallah" and often lives a lifetime without realizing that the "box-wallah" calls the tune.

But because he identifies himself with the official class, he does possess one thing which "enlightened" people seldom or never possess, and that is a sense of responsibility. The middle-class Left hate him for this quite as much as for his cruelty and vulgarity. All left-wing parties in the highly industrialized countries are at bottom a sham, because they make it their business to fight against something which they do not really wish to destroy. They have internationalist aims, and at the same time they struggle to keep up a standard of life with which those aims are incompatible. We all live by robbing Asiatic coolies, and those of us who are "enlightened" all maintain that those coolies ought to be set free; but our standard of living, and hence our "enlightenment," demands that the robbery shall continue. A humanitarian is always a hypocrite, and Kipling's understanding of this is perhaps the central secret of his power to create telling phrases. It would be difficult to hit off the one-eyed pacifism of the English in fewer words than in the phrase, "making mock of uniforms that guard you while you sleep." It is true that Kipling does not understand the economic aspect of the relationship between the highbrow and the Blimp. He does not see that the map is painted red chiefly in order that the coolie may be exploited. Instead of the coolie he sees the Indian civil servant; but even on that plane his grasp of function, of who protects whom, is very sound. He sees clearly that men can only be highly civilized while other men, inevitably less civilized, are there to guard and feed them.

How far does Kipling really identify himself with the administrators, soldiers, and engineers whose praises he sings? Not so completely as is sometimes assumed. He had traveled very widely while he was still a young man, he had grown up with a brilliant mind in mainly philistine surroundings, and some streak in him that may have been partly neurotic led him to prefer the active man to the sensitive man. The nineteenth-century Anglo-Indians, to name the least sympathetic of his idols, were at any rate people who did things. It may be that all that they did was evil, but they changed the face of the earth (it is instructive to look at a map of Asia and compare the railways system of India with that of the surrounding countries), whereas they could have achieved nothing, could not have maintained themselves in power for a single week, if the normal Anglo-Indian outlook had been that of, say, E. M. Forster. Tawdry and shallow though it is, Kipling's is the only literary picture that we possess of nineteenth-century Anglo-India, and he could only make it because he was just coarse enough to be able to exist and keep his mouth shut in clubs and regimental messes. But he did not greatly resemble the people he admired. I know from several private sources that many of the Anglo-Indians who were Kipling's contemporaries did not like or approve of him. They said, no doubt truly, that he knew nothing about India, and on the other hand, he was from their point of view too much of a highbrow. While in India he tended to mix with "the wrong" people, and because of his dark complexion he was wrongly suspected of having a streak of Asiatic blood. Much in his development is traceable to his having been born in India and having left school early. With a slightly different background he might have been a good novelist or a superlative writer of music-hall songs. But how true is it that he was a vulgar flag-waver, a sort of publicity agent for Cecil Rhodes? It is true, but it is not true that he was a yes-man or a time-server. After his early days, if then, he never courted public opinion. Mr. Eliot says that what is held against him is that he expressed unpopular views in a popular style. This narrows the issue by assuming that "unpopular" means unpopular with the intelligentsia, but it is a fact that Kipling's "message" was one that the big public did not want, and, indeed, has never accepted. The mass of the people, in the 'nineties as now, were anti-militarist, bored by the Empire, and only unconsciously patriotic. Kipling's official admirers are and were the "service" middle class, the people who read *Blackwood's.* In the stupid early years of this century, the Blimps, having at last discovered someone who could be called a poet and who was on their side, set Kipling on a pedestal, and some of his more sententious poems, such as "If," were given almost Biblical status. But it is doubtful whether the Blimps have ever read him with attention, any more than they have read the Bible. Much of what he says they could not possibly approve. Few people who have criticized England from the inside have said bitterer things about her than this gutter patriot. As a rule it is the British working class that he is attacking, but not always. That phrase about "the flanneled fools at the wicket and the muddied oafs at the goal" sticks like an arrow to this day, and it is aimed at the Eton and Harrow match as well as the Cup-Tie Final. Some of the verses he wrote about the Boer War have a curiously modern ring, so far as their subject matter goes. "Stellenbosch," which must have been written about 1902, sums up what every intelligent infantry officer was saying in 1918, or is saying now, for that matter.

Kipling's romantic ideas about England and the Empire might not have mattered if he could have held them without having the class prejudices which at that time went with them. If one examines his best and most representative work, his soldier poems, especially *Barrack-Room Ballads*, one notices that what more than anything else spoils them is an underlying air of patronage. Kipling idealizes the army officer, especially the junior officer, and that to an idiotic extent, but the private soldier, though lovable and romantic, has to be a comic. He is always made to speak in a sort of stylized

cockney, not very broad but with all the aitches and final "g's" carefully omitted. Very often the result is as embarrassing as the humorous recitation at a church social. And this accounts for the curious
fact that one can often improve Kipling's poems, make them less
facetious and less blatant, by simply going through them and trans-
planting them from cockney into standard speech. This is especially
true of his refrains, which often have a truly lyrical quality. Two
examples will do (one is about a funeral and the other about a wedding):

>   So it's knock out your pipes and follow me!
>   And it's finish up your swipes and follow me!
>   Oh, hark to the big drum calling,
>   Follow me—follow me home!

and again:

>   Cheer for the Sergeant's wedding—
>   Give them one cheer more!
>   Grey gun-horses in the lando,
>   And a rogue is married to a whore!

Here I have restored the aitches, etc. Kipling ought to have known
better. He ought to have seen that the two closing lines of the first
of these stanzas are very beautiful lines, and that ought to have over-
ridden his impulse to make fun of a working-man's accent. In the
ancient ballads the lord and the peasant speak the same language.
This is impossible to Kipling, who is looking down a distorting
class perspective, and by a piece of poetic justice one of his best lines
is spoiled—for "follow me 'ome" is much uglier than "follow me
home." But even where it makes no difference musically the facetiousness of his stage cockney dialect is irritating. However, he is
more often quoted aloud than read on the printed page, and most
people instinctively make the necessary alterations when they quote
him.

Can one imagine any private soldier, in the 'nineties or now, reading *Barrack-Room Ballads* and feeling that here was a writer who
spoke for him? It is very hard to do so. Any soldier capable of reading a book of verse would notice at once that Kipling is almost
unconscious of the class war that goes on in an army as much as
elsewhere. It is not only that he thinks the soldier comic, but that
he thinks him patriotic, feudal, a ready admirer of his officers, and
proud to be a soldier of the Queen. Of course that is partly true, or
battles could not be fought, but "What have I done for thee, England, my England?" is essentially a middle-class query. Almost any
working man would follow it up immediately with "What has Eng-

land done for me?" In so far as Kipling grasps this, he simply sets it down to "the intense selfishness of the lower classes" (his own phrase). When he is writing not of British but of "loyal" Indians he carries the "Salaam, sahib" motif to sometimes disgusting lengths. Yet it remains true that he has far more interest in the common soldier, far more anxiety that he shall get a fair deal, than most of the "liberals" of his day or our own. He sees that the soldier is neglected, meanly underpaid, and hypocritically despised by the people whose incomes he safeguards. "I came to realize," he says in his posthumous memoirs, "the bare horrors of the private's life, and the unnecessary torments he endured." He is accused of glorifying war, and perhaps he does so, but not in the usual manner, by pretending that war is a sort of football match. Like most people capable of writing battle poetry, Kipling had never been in battle, but his vision of war is realistic. He knows that bullets hurt, that under fire everyone is terrified, that the ordinary soldier never knows what the war is about or what is happening except in his own corner of the battlefield, and that British troops, like other troops, frequently run away:

> I 'eard the knives be'ind me, but I dursn't face my man,
> Nor I don't know where I went to, 'cause I didn't stop to see,
> Till I 'eard a beggar squealin' out for quarter as 'e ran,
> An' I thought I knew the voice an'—it was me!

Modernize the style of this, and it might have come out of one of the debunking war books of the nineteen-twenties. Or again:

> An' now the hugly bullets come peckin' through the dust,
> An' no one wants to face 'em, but every beggar must;
> So, like a man in irons, which isn't glad to go,
> They moves 'em off by companies uncommon stiff an' slow.

Compare this with:

> Forward the Light Brigade!
> Was there a man dismayed?
> No! though the soldier knew
> Someone had blundered.

If anything, Kipling overdoes the horrors, for the wars of his youth were hardly wars at all by our standards. Perhaps that is due to the neurotic strain in him, the hunger for cruelty. But at least he knows that men ordered to attack impossible objectives *are* dismayed, and also that fourpence a day is not a generous pension.

How complete or truthful a picture has Kipling left us of the long-service, mercenary Army of the late nineteenth century? One must say of this, as of what Kipling wrote about nineteenth-century Anglo-India, that it is not only the best but almost the only literary picture we have. He has put on record an immense amount of stuff that one could otherwise only gather from verbal tradition or from unreadable regimental histories. Perhaps his picture of army life seems fuller and more accurate than it is because any middle-class English person is likely to know enough to fill up the gaps. At any rate, reading the essay on Kipling that Mr. Edmund Wilson has just published,* I was struck by the number of things that are boringly familiar to us and seem to be barely intelligible to an American. But from the body of Kipling's early work there does seem to emerge a vivid and not seriously misleading picture of the old pre-machine-gun army—the sweltering barracks in Gibraltar or Lucknow, the red coats, the pipeclayed belts and the pillbox hats, the beer, the fights, the floggings, hangings, and crucifixions, the bugle-calls, the smell of oats and horse-piss, the bellowing sergeants with foot-long moustaches, the bloody skirmishes, invariably mismanaged, the crowded troopships, the cholera-stricken camps, the "native" concubines, the ultimate death in the workhouse. It is a crude, vulgar picture, in which a patriotic music-hall term seems to have got mixed up with one of Zola's gorier passages, but from it future generations will be able to gather some idea of what a long-term volunteer army was like. On about the same level they will be able to learn something of British India in the days when motor cars and refrigerators were unheard of. It is an error to imagine that we might have had better books on these subjects if, for example, George Moore, or Gissing, or Thomas Hardy had had Kipling's opportunities. That is the kind of accident that cannot happen. It was not possible that nineteenth-century England should produce a book like *War and Peace,* or like Tolstoy's minor stories of army life, such as *Sebastopol* or *The Cossacks,* not because the talent was necessarily lacking but because no one with sufficient sensitiveness to write such books would ever have made the appropriate contacts. Tolstoy lived in a great military empire in which it seemed natural for almost any young man of family to spend a few years in the army, whereas the British Empire was and still is demilitarized to a degree which continental observers find almost incredible. Civilized men do not readily move away from the centers of civilization, and in most languages there is a great dearth of what one might call colonial literature. It took a very improbable combination of circumstances to produce Kipling's gaudy tableau, in which Private Ortheris and Mrs.

* Published in a volume of essays, *The Wound and the Bow.* (Houghton Mifflin, 1941.)

Hauksbee pose against a background of palm trees to the sound of temple bells, and one necessary circumstance was that Kipling himself was only half civilized.

Kipling is the only English writer of our time who has added phrases to the language. The phrases and neologisms which we take over and use without remembering their origin do not always come from writers we admire. It is strange, for instance, to hear the Nazi broadcasters referring to the Russian soldiers as "robots," thus unconsciously borrowing a word from a Czech democrat whom they would have killed if they could have laid hands on him. Here are half a dozen phrases coined by Kipling which one sees quoted in leaderettes in the gutter press or overhears in saloon bars from people who have barely heard his name. It will be seen that they all have a certain characteristic in common:

> East is East, and West is West.
> The white man's burden.
> What do they know of England who only England know?
> The female of the species is more deadly than the male.
> Somewhere East of Suez.
> Paying the Dane-geld.

There are various others, including some that have outlived their context by many years. The phrase "killing Kruger with your mouth," for instance, was current till very recently. It is also possible that it was Kipling who first let loose the use of the word "Huns" for Germans; at any rate he began using it as soon as the guns opened fire in 1914. But what the phrases I have listed above have in common is that they are all of them phrases which one utters semi-derisively (as it might be "For I'm to be Queen o' the May, mother, I'm to be Queen o' the May"), but which one is bound to make use of sooner or later. Nothing could exceed the contempt of the *New Statesman,* for instance, for Kipling, but how many times during the Munich period did the *New Statesman* find itself quoting that phrase about paying the Dane-geld? * The fact is that Kip-

* 1945. On the first page of his recent book, *Adam and Eve,* Mr. Middleton Murry quoted the well-known lines:

> There are nine and fifty ways
> Of constructing tribal lays,
> And every single one of them is right.

He attributes these lines to Thackeray. This is probably what is known as a "Freudian error." A civilized person would prefer not to quote Kipling—*i.e.* would prefer not to feel that it was Kipling who had expressed his thought for him.

ling, apart from his snack-bar wisdom and his gift for packing much cheap picturesqueness into a few words ("Palm and Pine"—"East of Suez"—"The Road to Mandalay"), is generally talking about things that are of urgent interest. It does not matter, from this point of view, that thinking and decent people generally find themselves on the other side of the fence from him. "White man's burden" instantly conjures up a real problem, even if one feels that it ought to be altered to "black man's burden." One may disagree to the middle of one's bones with the political attitude implied in "The Islanders," but one cannot say that it is a frivolous attitude. Kipling deals in thoughts which are both vulgar and permanent. This raises the question of his special status as a poet, or verse-writer.

Mr. Eliot describes Kipling's metrical work as "verse" and not "poetry," but adds that it is "*great* verse," and further qualifies this by saying that a writer can only be described as a "great verse-writer" if there is some of his work "of which we cannot say whether it is verse or poetry." Apparently Kipling was a versifier who occasionally wrote poems, in which case it was a pity that Mr. Eliot did not specify these poems by name. The trouble is that whenever an aesthetic judgment on Kipling's work seems to be called for, Mr. Eliot is too much on the defensive to be able to speak plainly. What he does not say, and what I think one ought to start by saying in any discussion of Kipling, is that most of Kipling's verse is so horribly vulgar that it gives one the same sensation as one gets from watching a third-rate music-hall performer recite "The Pigtail of Wu Fang Fu" with the purple limelight on his face, *and yet* there is much of it that is capable of giving pleasure to people who know what poetry means. At his worst, and also his most vital, in poems like "Gunga Din" or "Danny Deever," Kipling is almost a shameful pleasure, like the taste for cheap sweets that some people secretly carry into middle life. But even with his best passages one has the same sense of being seduced by something spurious, and yet unquestionably seduced. Unless one is merely a snob and a liar it is impossible to say that no one who cares for poetry could get any pleasure out of such lines as:

> For the wind is in the palm trees, and the temple bells they say,
> "Come you back, you British soldier, come you back to Mandalay!"

and yet those lines are not poetry in the same sense as "Felix Randal" or "When icicles hang by the wall" are poetry. One can, perhaps, place Kipling more satisfactorily than by juggling with the words "verse" and "poetry," if one describes him simply as a good bad poet. He is as a poet what Harriet Beecher Stowe was as a novelist. And the mere existence of work of this kind, which is perceived by generation after generation to be vulgar and yet goes on being read, tells one something about the age we live in.

There is a great deal of good bad poetry in English, all of it, I should say, subsequent to 1790. Examples of good bad poems—I am deliberately choosing diverse ones—are "The Bridge of Sighs," "When All the World is Young, Lad," "The Charge of the Light Brigade," Bret Harte's "Dickens in Camp," "The Burial of Sir John Moore," "Jenny Kissed Me," "Keith of Ravelston," "Casabianca." All of these reek of sentimentality, and yet—not these particular poems, perhaps, but poems of this kind, are capable of giving true pleasure to people who can see clearly what is wrong with them. One could fill a fair-sized anthology with good bad poems, if it were not for the significant fact that good bad poetry is usually too well known to be worth reprinting. It is no use pretending that in an age like our own, "good" poetry can have any genuine popularity. It is, and must be, the cult of a very few people, the least tolerated of the arts. Perhaps that statement needs a certain amount of qualification. True poetry can sometimes be acceptable to the mass of the people when it disguises itself as something else. One can see an example of this in the folk poetry that England still possesses, certain nursery rhymes and mnemonic rhymes, for instance, and the songs that soldiers make up, including the words that go to some of the bugle-calls. But in general ours is a civilization in which the very word "poetry" evokes a hostile snigger or, at best, the sort of frozen disgust that most people feel when they hear the word "God." If you are good at playing the concertina you could probably go into the nearest public bar and get yourself an appreciative audience within five minutes. But what would be the attitude of that same audience if you suggested reading them Shakespeare's sonnets, for instance? Good bad poetry, however, can get across to the most unpromising audiences if the right atmosphere has been worked up beforehand. Some months back Churchill produced a great effect by quoting Clough's "Endeavour" in one of his broadcast speeches. I listened to this speech among people who could certainly not be accused of caring for poetry, and I am convinced that the lapse into verse impressed them and did not embarrass them. But not even Churchill could have got away with it if he had quoted anything much better than this.

In so far as a writer of verse can be popular, Kipling has been and probably still is popular. In his own lifetime some of his poems traveled far beyond the bounds of the reading public, beyond the world of school prize-days, Boy Scout singsongs, limp-leather edi-

tions, pokerwork and calendars, and out into the yet vaster world of
the music halls. Nevertheless, Mr. Eliot thinks it worth while to edit
him, thus confessing to a taste which others share but are not always
honest enough to mention. The fact that such a thing as good bad
poetry can exist is a sign of the emotional overlap between the intellectual and the ordinary man. The intellectual *is* different from
the ordinary man, but only in certain sections of his personality,
and even then not all the time. But what is the peculiarity of a good
bad poem? A good bad poem is a graceful monument to the obvious.
It records in memorable form—for verse is a mnemonic device,
among other things—some emotion which very nearly every human
being can share. The merit of a poem like "When All the World is
Young, Lad" is that, however sentimental it may be, its sentiment
is "true" sentiment in the sense that you are bound to find yourself
thinking the thought it expresses sooner or later; and then, if you
happen to know the poem, it will come back into your mind and
seem better than it did before. Such poems are a kind of rhyming
proverb, and it is a fact that definitely popular poetry is usually
gnomic or sententious. One example from Kipling will do:

> White hands cling to the bridle rein,
> Slipping the spur from the booted heel;
> Tenderest voices cry "Turn again!"
> Red lips tarnish the scabbarded steel:
> Down to Gehenna or up to the Throne,
> He travels the fastest who travels alone.

There is a vulgar thought vigorously expressed. It may not be true,
but at any rate it is a thought that everyone thinks. Sooner or later
you will have occasion to feel that he travels the fastest who travels
alone, and there the thought is, ready made and, as it were, waiting
for you. So the chances are that, having once heard this line, you
will remember it.

One reason for Kipling's power as a good bad poet I have already
suggested—his sense of responsibility, which made it possible for
him to have a world view, even though it happened to be a false
one. Although he had no direct connection with any political party,
Kipling was a conservative, a thing that does not exist nowadays.
Those who now call themselves conservatives are either liberals,
Fascists, or the accomplices of Fascists. He identified himself with
the ruling power and not with the opposition. In a gifted writer
this seems to us strange and even disgusting, but it did have the advantage of giving Kipling a certain grip on reality. The ruling power
is always faced with the question, "In such and such circumstances,

what would you *do?"* whereas the opposition is not obliged to take responsibility or make any real decisions. Where it is a permanent and pensioned opposition, as in England, the quality of its thought deteriorates accordingly. Moreover, anyone who starts out with a pessimistic, reactionary view of life tends to be justified by events, for Utopia never arrives and "the gods of the copybook headings," as Kipling himself put it, always return. Kipling sold out to the British governing class, not financially but emotionally. This warped his political judgment, for the British ruling class were not what he imagined, and it led him into abysses of folly and snobbery, but he gained a corresponding advantage from having at least tried to imagine what action and responsibility are like. It is a great thing in his favor that he is not witty, not "daring," has no wish to *épater les bourgeois.* He dealt largely in platitudes, and since we live in a world of platitudes, much of what he said sticks. Even his worst follies seem less shallow and less irritating than the "enlightened" utterances of the same period, such as Wilde's epigrams or the collection of cracker-mottoes at the end of *Man and Superman.*

1942

Δ

Politics vs. Literature:
an Examination of
"Gulliver's Travels"

▽

In *Gulliver's Travels* humanity is attacked, or criticized, from at least three different angles, and the implied character of Gulliver himself necessarily changes somewhat in the process. In Part I he is the typical eighteenth-century voyager, bold, practical and unromantic, his homely outlook skilfully impressed on the reader by the biographical details at the beginning, by his age (he is a man of forty, with two children, when his adventures start), and by the inventory of the things in his pockets, especially his spectacles, which make several appearances. In Part II he has in general the same character, but at moments when the story demands it he has a tendency to develop into an imbecile who is capable of boasting of "our noble Country, the Mistress of Arts and Arms, the Scourge of France," etc., etc., and at the same time of betraying every available scandalous fact about the country which he professes to love. In Part III he is much as he was in Part I, though, as he is consorting chiefly with courtiers and men of learning, one has the impression that he has risen in the social scale. In Part IV he conceives a horror of the human race which is not apparent, or only intermittently apparent, in the earlier books, and changes into a sort of unreligious anchorite whose one desire is to live in some desolate spot where he can devote himself to meditating on the goodness of the Houyhnhnms. However, these inconsistencies are forced upon Swift by the fact that Gulliver is there chiefly to provide a contrast. It is necessary, for instance, that he should appear sensible in Part I and at least intermittently silly in Part II, because in both books the essential maneuver is the same, i.e. to make the human being look ridiculous by imagining him as a creature six inches high. Whenever Gulliver is not acting as a stooge there is a sort of continuity in his character, which comes out especially in his resourcefulness and his observation of physical detail. He is much the same kind of person, with the same prose style, when he bears off the warships of Blefuscu, when he rips open the belly of the monstrous rat, and when he sails away upon the ocean in his frail coracle made from the skins of Yahoos. Moreover, it is difficult not to feel that in his shrewder moments Gulliver is simply Swift himself, and there is at least one incident in which Swift seems to be venting his private grievance against contemporary society. It will be remembered that when the Emperor of Lilliput's palace catches fire, Gulliver puts it out by urinating on it. Instead of being congratulated on his presence of mind, he finds that he has committed a capital offense by making water in the precincts of the palace, and

I was privately assured, that the Empress, conceiving the greatest Abhorrence of what I had done, removed to the most distant Side of the Court, firmly resolved that those buildings should never be repaired for her Use; and, in the Presence of her chief Confidents, could not forbear vowing Revenge.

According to Professor G. M. Trevelyan (*England under Queen Anne*), part of the reason for Swift's failure to get preferment was that the Queen was scandalized by the *Tale of a Tub*—a pamphlet in which Swift probably felt that he had done a great service to the English Crown, since it scarifies the Dissenters and still more the Catholics while leaving the Established Church alone. In any case no one would deny that *Gulliver's Travels* is a rancorous as well as a pessimistic book, and that especially in Parts I and III it often descends into political partisanship of a narrow kind. Pettiness and magnanimity, republicanism and authoritarianism, love of reason and lack of curiosity, are all mixed up in it. The hatred of the human body with which Swift is especially associated is only dominated in Part IV, but somehow this new preoccupation does not come as a surprise. One feels that all these adventures, and all these changes of mood, could have happened to the same person, and the inter-connection between Swift's political loyalties and his ultimate despair is one of the most interesting features of the book.

Politically, Swift was one of those people who are driven into a sort of perverse Toryism by the follies of the progressive party of the moment. Part I of *Gulliver's Travels*, ostensibly a satire on human greatness, can be seen, if one looks a little deeper, to be simply an attack on England, on the dominant Whig Party, and on the war with France, which—however bad the motives of the Allies may have been—did save Europe from being tyrannized over by a single reactionary power. Swift was not a Jacobite nor strictly speaking a Tory, and his declared aim in the war was merely a moderate peace treaty and not the outright defeat of England. Nevertheless there is a tinge of quislingism in his attitude, which comes out in the ending of Part I and slightly interferes with the allegory. When Gulliver flees from Lilliput (England) to Blefuscu (France) the assumption that a human being six inches high is inherently contemptible seems to be dropped. Whereas the people of Lilliput have behaved toward Gulliver with the utmost treachery and meanness, those of Blefuscu behave generously and straightforwardly, and indeed this section of the book ends on a different note from the all-round disillusionment of the earlier chapters. Evidently Swift's animus is, in the first place, against *England*. It is "your Natives" (i.e. Gulliver's fellow-countrymen) whom the King of Brobdingnag considers to be "the most pernicious Race of little odious vermin that Nature ever suffered to crawl upon the surface of the Earth," and the long passage at the end, denouncing colonization and foreign conquest, is plainly aimed at England, although the contrary is elaborately stated. The Dutch, England's allies and target of one of Swift's most famous pamphlets, are also more or less wantonly attacked in Part III. There is even what sounds like a personal note in the passage in which Gulliver records his satisfaction that the various countries he has discovered cannot be made colonies of the British Crown:

The *Houyhnhnms,* indeed, appear not to be so well prepared for War, a Science to which they are perfect Strangers, and especially against missive Weapons. However, supposing myself to be a Minister of State, I could never give my advice for invading them. . . . Imagine twenty thousand of them breaking into the midst of an *European* army, confounding the Ranks, overturning the Carriages, battering the Warriors' Faces into Mummy, by terrible Yerks from their hinder hoofs. . . .

Considering that Swift does not waste words, that phrase, "battering the warriors' faces into mummy," probably indicates a secret wish to see the invincible armies of the Duke of Marlborough treated in a like manner. There are similar touches elsewhere. Even the country mentioned in Part III, where "the Bulk of the People consist, in a Manner, wholly of Discoverers, Witnesses, Informers, Accusers, Prosecutors, Evidences, Swearers, together with their several subservient and subaltern Instruments, all under the Colours, the Conduct, and Pay of Ministers of State," is called Langdon, which is within one letter of being an anagram of England. (As the early editions of the book contain misprints, it may perhaps have been intended as a complete anagram.) Swift's *physical* repulsion from humanity is certainly real enough, but one has the feeling that his debunking of human grandeur, his diatribes against lords, politicians, court favorites, etc., has mainly a local application and springs from the fact that he belonged to the unsuccessful party. He denounces injustice and oppression, but he gives no evidence of liking democracy. In spite of his enormously greater powers, his implied position is very similar to that of the innumerable silly-clever Conservatives of our own day—people like Sir Alan Herbert, Professor G. M. Young, Lord Elton, the Tory Reform Committee, or the long line of Catholic apologists from W. H. Mallock onward: people who specialize in cracking neat jokes at the expense of whatever is "modern" and "progressive," and whose opinions are often all the more extreme because they know that they cannot influence the actual drift of events. After all, such a pamphlet as *An Argument to prove that the Abolishing of Christianity,* etc., is very like "Timothy Shy" having a bit of clean fun with the Brains Trust, or Father Ronald Knox exposing the errors of Bertrand Russell. And the ease with which Swift has been forgiven—and forgiven, sometimes, by devout believers—for the blasphemies of *A Tale of a Tub* demonstrates clearly enough the feebleness of religious sentiments as compared with political ones.

However, the reactionary cast of Swift's mind does not show itself chiefly in his political affiliations. The important thing is his attitude toward science, and, more broadly, toward intellectual curiosity. The famous Academy of Lagado, described in Part III of *Gulliver's Travels,* is no doubt a justified satire on most of the so-called scientists of Swift's own day. Significantly, the people at work in it are described as "Projectors," that is, people not engaged in disinterested research but merely on the lookout for gadgets which will save labor and bring in money. But there is no sign —indeed, all through the book there are many signs to the contrary—that "pure" science would have struck Swift as a worthwhile activity. The more serious kind of scientist has already had a kick in the pants in Part II, when the "Scholars" patronized by the King of Brobdingnag try to account for Gulliver's small stature:

> After much Debate, they concluded unanimously that I was only *Relplum Scalcath,* which is interpreted literally, *Lusus Naturae;* a Determination exactly agreeable to the modern philosophy of *Europe,* whose Professors, disdaining the old Evasion of *Occult Causes,* whereby the followers of *Aristotle* endeavoured in vain to disguise their Ignorance, have invented this wonderful Solution of All Difficulties, to the unspeakable Advancement of human Knowledge.

If this stood by itself one might assume that Swift is merely the enemy of *sham* science. In a number of places, however, he goes out of his way to proclaim the uselessness of all learning or speculation not directed toward some practical end:

> The learning of [the Brobdingnagians] is very defective, consisting only in Morality, History, Poetry, and Mathematics, wherein they must be allowed to excel. But, the last of these is wholly applied to what may be useful in Life, to the improvement of Agriculture, and all mechanical Arts so that among us it would be little esteemed. And as to Ideas, Entities, Abstractions, and Transcendentals, I could never drive the least Conception into their Heads.

The Houyhnhnms, Swift's ideal beings, are backward even in a mechanical sense. They are unacquainted with metals, have never heard of boats, do not, properly speaking, practice agriculture (we are told that the oats which they live upon "grow naturally"), and appear not to have invented wheels.* They have no alphabet, and evidently have not much curiosity about the physical world. They do not believe that any inhabited country exists beside their own, and though they understand the motions of the sun and moon, and the nature of eclipses, "this is the utmost progress of their *Astronomy.*" By contrast, the philosophers of the flying island of Laputa are so continuously absorbed in mathematical speculations

---

* Houyhnhnms too old to walk are described as being carried in "sledges" or in "a kind of vehicle, drawn like a sledge." Presumably these had no wheels.

that before speaking to them one has to attract their attention by flapping them on the ear with a bladder. They have catalogued ten thousand fixed stars, have settled the periods of ninety-three comets, and have discovered in advance of the astronomers of Europe, that Mars has two moons—all of which information Swift evidently regards as ridiculous, useless, and uninteresting. As one might expect, he believes that the scientist's place, if he has a place, is in the laboratory, and that scientific knowledge has no bearing on political matters:

> What I . . . thought altogether unaccountable, was the strong Disposition I observed in them towards News and Politics, perpetually enquiring into Public Affairs, giving their judgments in Matters of State, and passionately disputing every inch of a Party Opinion. I have, indeed, observed the same Disposition among most of the Mathematicians I have known in *Europe,* though I could never discover the least Analogy between the two Sciences; unless those people suppose, that, because the smallest Circle hath as many Degrees as the largest, therefore the Regulation and Management of the World require no more Abilities, than the Handling and Turning of a Globe.

Is there not something familiar in that phrase "I could never discover the least analogy between the two sciences"? It has precisely the note of the popular Catholic apologists who profess to be astonished when a scientist utters an opinion on such questions as the existence of God or the immortality of the soul. The scientist, we are told, is an expert only in one restricted field: why should his opinions be of value in any other? The implication is that theology is just as much an exact science as, for instance, chemistry, and that the priest is also an expert whose conclusions on certain subjects must be accepted. Swift in effect makes the same claim for the politician, but he goes one better in that he will not allow the scientist—either the "pure" scientist or the *ad hoc* investigator—to be a useful person in his own line. Even if he had not written Part III of *Gulliver's Travels,* one could infer from the rest of the book that, like Tolstoy and like Blake, he hates the very idea of studying the processes of Nature. The "Reason" which he so admires in the Houyhnhnms does not primarily mean the power of drawing logical inferences from observed facts. Although he never defines it, it appears in most contexts to mean either common sense—i.e. acceptance of the obvious and contempt for quibbles and abstractions—or absence of passion and superstition. In general he assumes that we know all that we need to know already, and merely use our knowledge incorrectly. Medicine, for instance, is a useless science, because if we lived in a more natural

way, there would be no diseases. Swift, however, is not a simple-
lifer or an admirer of the Noble Savage. He is in favor of civilization and the arts of civilization. Not only does he see the value
of good manners, good conversation, and even learning of a literary and historical kind, he also sees that agriculture, navigation,
and architecture need to be studied and could with advantages be
improved. But his implied aim is a static, incurious civilization—
the world of his own day, a little cleaner, a little saner, with no
radical change and no poking into the unknowable. More than
one would expect in anyone so free from accepted fallacies, he re-
veres the past, especially classical antiquity, and believes that modern man has degenerated sharply during the past hundred years.*
In the island of sorcerers, where the spirits of the dead can be
called up at will:

> I desired that the Senate of *Rome* might appear before me in one large
> chamber, and a modern Representative in Counterview, in another. The
> first seemed to be an Assembly of Heroes and Demy-Gods, the other a
> Knot of Pedlars, Pick-pockets, Highwaymen and Bullies.

Although Swift uses this section of Part III to attack the truthfulness of recorded history, his critical spirit deserts him as soon
as he is dealing with Greeks and Romans. He remarks, of course,
upon the corruption of imperial Rome, but he has an almost un-
reasoning admiration for some of the leading figures of the ancient
world:

> I was struck with profound Veneration at the sight of *Brutus*, and could
> easily discover the most consummate Virtue, the greatest Intrepidity and
> Firmness of Mind, the truest Love of his Country, and general Benevo-
> lence for Mankind, in every Lineament of his Countenance. . . . I had
> the honour to have much Conversation with *Brutus*, and was told, that
> his Ancestors *Junius, Socrates, Epaminondas, Cato* the younger, *Sir Thomas
> More*, and himself, were perpetually together: a *Sextumvirate*, to which all
> the Ages of the World cannot add a seventh.

It will be noticed that of these six people, only one is a Christian. This is an important point. If one adds together Swift's pessimism, his reverence for the past, his incuriosity and his horror
of the human body, one arrives at an attitude common among
religious reactionaries—that is, people who defend an unjust order

---

* The physical decadence which Swift claims to have observed may have been
a reality at that date. He attributes it to syphilis, which was a new disease in
Europe and may have been more virulent than it is now. Distilled liquors, also,
were a novelty in the seventeenth century and must have led at first to a great
increase in drunkenness.

of society by claiming that this world cannot be substantially improved and only the "next world" matters. However, Swift shows no sign of having any religious beliefs, at least in any ordinary sense of the words. He does not appear to believe seriously in life after death, and his idea of goodness is bound up with republicanism, love of liberty, courage, "benevolence" (meaning in effect public spirit), "reason" and other pagan qualities. This reminds one that there is another strain in Swift, not quite congruous with his disbelief in progress and his general hatred of humanity.

To begin with, he has moments when he is "constructive" and even "advanced." To be occasionally inconsistent is almost a mark of vitality in Utopia books, and Swift sometimes inserts a word of praise into a passage that ought to be purely satirical. Thus, his ideas about the education of the young are fathered on to the Lilliputians, who have much the same views on this subject as the Houyhnhnms. The Lilliputians also have various social and legal institutions (for instance, there are old age pensions, and people are rewarded for keeping the law as well as punished for breaking it) which Swift would have liked to see prevailing in his own country. In the middle of this passage Swift remembers his satirical intention and adds, "In relating these and the following Laws, I would only be understood to mean the original Institutions, and not the most scandalous Corruptions into which these people are fallen by the degenerate Nature of Man": but as Lilliput is supposed to represent England, and the laws he is speaking of have never had their parallel in England, it is clear that the impulse to make constructive suggestions has been too much for him. But Swift's greatest contribution to political thought in the narrower sense of the words, is his attack especially in Part III, on what would now be called totalitarianism. He has an extraordinarily clear pre-vision of the spy-haunted "police state," with its endless heresy-hunts and treason trials, all really designed to neutralize popular discontent by changing it into war hysteria. And one must remember that Swift is here inferring the whole from a quite small part, for the feeble governments of his own day did not give him illustrations ready-made. For example, there is the professor at the School of Political Projectors who "shewed me a large Paper of Instructions for discovering Plots and Conspiracies," and who claimed that one can find people's secret thoughts by examining their excrement:

Because Men are never so serious, thoughtful, and intent, as when they are at Stool, which he found by frequent Experiment: for in such Conjunctures, when he used meerly as a trial to consider what was the best Way of murdering the King, his Ordure would have a tincture of Green; but quite different when he thought only of raising an Insurrection, or burning the Metropolis.

The professor and his theory are said to have been suggested to Swift by the—from our point of view—not particularly astonishing or disgusting fact that in a recent state trial some letters found in somebody's privy had been put in evidence. Later in the same chapter we seem to be positively in the middle of the Russian purges:

> In the Kingdom of Tribnia, by the Natives called Langdon . . . the Bulk of the People consist, in a Manner, wholly of Discoverers, Witnesses, Informers, Accusers, Prosecutors, Evidences, Swearers. . . . It is first agreed, and settled among them, what suspected Persons shall be accused of a Plot: Then, effectual Care is taken to secure all their Letters and Papers, and put the Owners in Chains. These papers are delivered to a Sett of Artists, very dexterous in finding out the mysterious Meanings of Words, Syllables, and Letters. . . . Where this method fails, they have two others more effectual, which the Learned among them call *Acrostics* and *Anagrams*. *First*, they can decypher all initial Letters into political Meanings: Thus: N shall signify a Plot, B a Regiment of Horse, L a Fleet at Sea: Or, *Secondly,* by transposing the Letters of the Alphabet in any suspected Paper, they can lay open the deepest Designs of a discontented Party. So, for Example if I should say in a Letter to a Friend, *Our Brother Tom has just got the Piles,* a skilful Decypherer would discover that the same Letters, which compose that Sentence, may be analysed in the following Words: *Resist—a Plot is brought Home—The Tour.* * And this is the anagrammatic method.

Other professors at the same school invent simplified languages, write books by machinery, educate their pupils by inscribing the lesson on a wafer and causing them to swallow it, or propose to abolish individuality altogether by cutting off part of the brain of one man and grafting it on to the head of another. There is something queerly familiar in the atmosphere of these chapters, because, mixed up with much fooling, there is a perception that one of the aims of totalitarianism is not merely to make sure that people will think the right thoughts, but actually to make them *less conscious*. Then, again, Swift's account of the Leader who is usually to be found ruling over a tribe of Yahoos, and of the "favorite" who acts first as a dirty-worker and later as a scapegoat, fits remarkably well into the pattern of our own times. But are we to infer from all this that Swift was first and foremost an enemy

* Tower.

of tyranny and a champion of the free intelligence? No: his own
views, so far as one can discern them, are not markedly liberal.
No doubt he hates lords, kings, bishops, generals, ladies of fashion,
orders, titles, and flummery generally, but he does not seem to
think better of the common people than of their rulers, or to be
in favor of increased social equality, or to be enthusiastic about
representative institutions. The Houyhnhnms are organized upon
a sort of caste system which is racial in character, the horses which
do the menial work being of different colors from their masters
and not interbreeding with them. The educational system which
Swift admires in the Lilliputians takes hereditary class distinctions
for granted, and the children of the poorest classes do not go to
school, because "their Business being only to till and cultivate the
Earth . . . therefore their Education is of little Consequence to
the Public." Nor does he seem to have been strongly in favor of
freedom of speech and the press, in spite of the toleration which
his own writings enjoyed. The King of Brobdingnag is astonished
at the multiplicity of religious and political sects in England, and
considers that those who hold "opinions prejudicial to the public"
(in the context this seems to mean simply heretical opinions),
though they need not be obliged to change them, ought to be
obliged to conceal them: for "as it was Tyranny in any Government to require the first, so it was weakness not to enforce the
second." There is a subtler indication of Swift's own attitude in
the manner in which Gulliver leaves the land of the Houyhnhnms.
Intermittently, at least, Swift was a kind of anarchist, and Part
IV of *Gulliver's Travels* is a picture of an anarchistic society, not
governed by law in the ordinary sense, but by the dictates of "Reason," which are voluntarily accepted by everyone. The General Assembly of the Houyhnhnms "exhorts" Gulliver's master to get rid
of him, and his neighbors put pressure on him to make him com-
ply. Two reasons are given. One is that the presence of this unusual Yahoo may unsettle the rest of the tribe, and the other is
that a friendly relationship between a Houyhnhnm and a Yahoo
is "not agreeable to Reason or Nature, or a Thing ever heard of
before among them." Gulliver's master is somewhat unwilling to
obey, but the "exhortation" (a Houyhnhnm, we are told, is never
compelled to do anything, he is merely "exhorted" or "advised")
cannot be disregarded. This illustrates very well the totalitarian
tendency which is explicit in the anarchist or pacifist vision of society. In a society in which there is no law, and in theory no compulsion, the only arbiter of behavior is public opinion. But public opinion, because of the tremendous urge to conformity in gre-

garious animals, is less tolerant than any system of law. When human beings are governed by "thou shalt not," the individual can practice a certain amount of eccentricity: when they are supposedly governed by "love" or "reason," he is under continuous pressure to make him behave and think in exactly the same way as everyone else. The Houyhnhnms, we are told, were unanimous on almost all subjects. The only question they ever *discussed* was how to deal with the Yahoos. Otherwise there was no room for disagreement among them, because the truth is always either self-evident, or else it is undiscoverable and unimportant. They had apparently no word for "opinion" in their language, and in their conversations there was no "difference of sentiments." They had reached, in fact, the highest stage of totalitarian organization, the stage when conformity has become so general that there is no need for a police force. Swift approves of this kind of thing because among his many gifts neither curiosity nor good-nature was included. Disagreement would always seem to him sheer perversity. "Reason," among the Houyhnhnms, he says, "is not a Point Problematical, as with us, where men can argue with Plausibility on both Sides of a Question; but strikes you with immediate Conviction; as it must needs do, where it is not mingled, obscured, or discoloured by Passion and Interest." In other words, we know everything already, so why should dissident opinions be tolerated? The totalitarian society of the Houyhnhnms, where there can be no freedom and no development, follows naturally from this.

We are right to think of Swift as a rebel and iconoclast, but except in certain secondary matters, such as his insistence that women should receive the same education as men, he cannot be labeled "Left." He is a Tory anarchist, despising authority while disbelieving in liberty, and preserving the aristocratic outlook while seeing clearly that the existing aristocracy is degenerate and contemptible. When Swift utters one of his characteristic diatribes against the rich and powerful, one must probably, as I said earlier, write off something for the fact that he himself belonged to the less successful party, and was personally disappointed. The "outs," for obvious reasons, are always more radical than the "ins." * But the most essential thing in Swift is his inability to

---

* At the end of the book, as typical specimens of human folly and viciousness, Swift names "a Lawyer, a Pick-pocket, a Colonel, a Fool, a Lord, a Gamester, a Politician, a Whore-master, a Physician, an Evidence, a Suborner, an Attorney, a Traitor, or the like." One sees here the irresponsible violence of the powerless. The list lumps together those who break the conventional code, and those who keep it. For instance, if you automatically condemn a colonel, as such,

believe that life—ordinary life on the solid earth, and not some rationalized, deodorized version of it—could be made worth living. Of course, no honest person claims that happiness is *now* a normal condition among adult human beings; but perhaps it *could* be made normal, and it is upon this question that all serious political controversy really turns. Swift has much in common—more, I believe, than has been noticed—with Tolstoy, another disbeliever in the possibility of happiness. In both men you have the same anarchistic outlook covering an authoritarian cast of mind; in both a similar hostility to science, the same impatience with opponents, the same inability to see the importance of any question not interesting to themselves; and in both cases a sort of horror of the actual process of life, though in Tolstoy's case it was arrived at later and in a different way. The sexual unhappiness of the two men was not of the same kind, but there was this in common, that in both of them a sincere loathing was mixed up with a morbid fascination. Tolstoy was a reformed rake who ended by preaching complete celibacy, while continuing to practice the opposite into extreme old age. Swift was presumably impotent, and had an exaggerated horror of human dung: he also thought about it incessantly, as is evident throughout his works. Such people are not likely to enjoy even the small amount of happiness that falls to most human beings and, from obvious motives, are not likely to admit that earthly life is capable of much improvement. Their incuriosity, and hence their intolerance, spring from the same root.

Swift's disgust, rancor, and pessimism would make sense against the background of a "next world" to which this one is the prelude. As he does not appear to believe seriously in any such thing, it becomes necessary to construct a paradise supposedly existing on the surface of the earth, but something quite different from anything we know, with all that he disapproves of—lies, folly, change, enthusiasm, pleasure, love, and dirt—eliminated from it. As his ideal being he chooses the horse, an animal whose excrement is not offensive. The Houyhnhnms are dreary beasts—this is so generally admitted that the point is not worth laboring. Swift's genius can make them credible, but there can have been very few readers in whom they have excited any feeling beyond dislike. And this is not from wounded vanity at seeing animals preferred to men; for,

on what grounds do you condemn a traitor? Or again, if you want to suppress pickpockets, you must have laws, which means that you must have lawyers. But the whole closing passage, in which the hatred is so authentic, and the reason given for it so inadequate, is somehow unconvincing. One has the feeling that personal animosity is at work.

of the two, the Houyhnhnms are much liker to human beings than are the Yahoos, and Gulliver's horror of the Yahoos, together with his recognition that they are the same kind of creature as himself, contains a logical absurdity. This horror comes upon him at his very first sight of them. "I never beheld," he says, "in all my Travels, so disagreeable an Animal, nor one against which I naturally conceived so strong an Antipathy." But in comparison with what are the Yahoos disgusting? Not with the Houyhnhnms, because at this time Gulliver had not seen a Houyhnhnm. It can only be in comparison with himself, i.e. with a human being. Later, however, we are to be told that the Yahoos *are* human beings, and human society becomes insupportable to Gulliver because all men are Yahoos. In that case why did he not conceive his disgust of humanity earlier? In effect we are told that the Yahoos are fantastically different from men, and yet are the same. Swift has over-reached himself in his fury, and is shouting at his fellow-creatures: "You are filthier than you are!" However, it is impossible to feel much sympathy with the Yahoos, and it is not because they oppress the Yahoos that the Houyhnhnms are unattractive. They are unattractive because the "Reason" by which they are governed is really a desire for death. They are exempt from love, friendship, curiosity, fear, sorrow, and—except in their feelings toward the Yahoos, who occupy rather the same place in their community as the Jews in Nazi Germany—anger and hatred. "They have no Fondness for their Colts or Foles, but the Care they take, in educating them, proceeds entirely from the Dictates of *Reason*." They lay store by "Friendship" and "Benevolence," but "these are not confined to particular Objects, but universal to the whole Race." They also value conversation, but in their conversations there are no differences of opinion, and "nothing passed but what was useful, expressed in the fewest and most significant Words." They practice strict birth control, each couple producing two offspring and thereafter abstaining from sexual intercourse. Their marriages are arranged for them by their elders, on eugenic principles, and their language contains no word for "love," in the sexual sense. When somebody dies they carry on exactly as before, without feeling any grief. It will be seen that their aim is to be as like a corpse as is possible while retaining physical life. One or two of their characteristics, it is true, do not seem to be strictly "reasonable" in their own usage of the word. Thus, they place a great value not only on physical hardihood but on athleticism, and they are devoted to poetry. But these exceptions may be less arbitrary than they seem. Swift probably emphasizes the physical strength of the Houyhnhnms in order to make clear that they could never be conquered by the hated human race, while a taste for poetry may figure among their qualities because poetry appeared to Swift as the antithesis of science, from his point of view the most useless of all pursuits. In Part III he names "Imagination, Fancy, and Invention" as desirable faculties in which the Laputan mathematicians (in spite of their love of music) were wholly lacking. One must remember that although Swift was an admirable writer of comic verse, the kind of poetry he thought valuable would probably be didactic poetry. The poetry of the Houyhnhnms, he says—

> must be allowed to excel (that of) all other Mortals; wherein the Justness of their Similes, and the Minuteness, as well as exactness, of their Descriptions, are, indeed, inimitable. Their Verses abound very much in both of these; and usually contain either some exalted Notions of Friendship and Benevolence, or the Praises of those who were Victors in Races, and other bodily Exercises.

Alas, not even the genius of Swift was equal to producing a specimen by which we could judge the poetry of the Houyhnhnms. But it sounds as though it were chilly stuff (in heroic couplets, presumably), and not seriously in conflict with the principles of "Reason."

Happiness is notoriously difficult to describe, and pictures of a just and well-ordered society are seldom either attractive or convincing. Most creators of "favorable" Utopias, however, are concerned to show what life could be like if it were lived more fully. Swift advocates a simple refusal of life, justifying this by the claim that "Reason" consists in thwarting your instincts. The Houyhnhnms, creatures without a history, continue for generation after generation to live prudently, maintaining their population at exactly the same level, avoiding all passion, suffering from no diseases, meeting death indifferently, training up their young in the same principles—and all for what? In order that the same process may continue indefinitely. The notions that life here and now is worth living, or that it could be made worth living, or that it must be sacrificed for some future good, are all absent. The dreary world of the Houyhnhnms was about as good a Utopia as Swift could construct, granting that he neither believed in a "next world" nor could get any pleasure out of certain normal activities. But it is not really set up as something desirable in itself, but as the justification for another attack on humanity. The aim, as usual, is to humiliate Man by reminding him that he is weak and ridiculous, and above all that he stinks; and the ultimate motive, probably, is a kind of envy, the envy of the ghost for the living, of the man

who knows he cannot be happy for the others who—so he fears—
may be a little happier than himself. The political expression of
such an outlook must be either reactionary or nihilistic, because
the person who holds it will want to prevent society from developing in some direction in which his pessimism may be cheated.
One can do this either by blowing everything to pieces, or by avert-
ing social change. Swift ultimately blew everything to pieces in the
only way that was feasible before the atomic bomb—that is, he
went mad—but, as I have tried to show, his political aims were on
the whole reactionary ones.

From what I have written it may have seemed that I am *against*
Swift, and that my object is to refute him and even to belittle him.
In a political and moral sense I am against him, so far as I understand him. Yet curiously enough he is one of the writers I admire
with least reserve, and *Gulliver's Travels,* in particular, is a book
which it seems impossible for me to grow tired of. I read it first
when I was eight—one day short of eight, to be exact, for I stole
and furtively read the copy which was to be given me next day
on my eighth birthday—and I have certainly not read it less than
half a dozen times since. Its fascination seems inexhaustible. If I
had to make a list of six books which were to be preserved when
all others were destroyed, I would certainly put *Gulliver's Travels*
among them. This raises the question: what is the relationship between agreement with a writer's opinions, and enjoyment of his
work?

If one is capable of intellectual detachment, one can *perceive*
merit in a writer whom one deeply disagrees with, but *enjoyment*
is a different matter. Supposing that there is such a thing as good
or bad art, then the goodness or badness must reside in the work
of art itself—not independently of the observer, indeed, but independently of the mood of the observer. In one sense, therefore, it
cannot be true that a poem is good on Monday and bad on Tues-
day. But if one judges the poem by the appreciation it arouses,
then it can certainly be true, because appreciation or enjoyment is
a subjective condition which cannot be commanded. For a great
deal of his waking life, even the most cultivated person has no
aesthetic feelings whatever, and the power to have aesthetic feelings is very easily destroyed. When you are frightened, or hungry,
or are suffering from toothache or seasickness, *King Lear* is no better from your point of view than *Peter Pan.* You may know in an
intellectual sense that it is better, but that is simply a fact which
you remember: you will not *feel* the merit of *King Lear* until you
are normal again. And aesthetic judgment can be upset just as

disastrously—more disastrously, because the cause is no less readily recognized—by political or moral disagreement. If a book angers, wounds, or alarms you, then you will not enjoy it, whatever its merits may be. If it seems to you a really pernicious book, likely to influence other people in some undesirable way, then you will probably construct an aesthetic theory to show that it *has* no merits. Current literary criticism consists quite largely of this kind of dodging to and fro between two sets of standards. And yet the opposite process can also happen: enjoyment can overwhelm disapproval, even though one clearly recognizes that one is enjoying something inimical. Swift, whose world view is so peculiarly unacceptable, but who is nevertheless an extremely popular writer, is a good instance of this. Why is it that we don't mind being called Yahoos, although firmly convinced that we are *not* Yahoos?

It is not enough to make the usual answer that of course Swift was wrong, in fact he was insane, but he was "a good writer." It is true that the literary quality of a book is to some small extent separable from its subject matter. Some people have a native gift for using words, as some people have a naturally "good eye" at games. It is largely a question of timing and of instinctively knowing how much emphasis to use. As an example near at hand, look back at the passage I quoted earlier, starting "In the Kingdom of Tribnia, by the Natives called Langdon." It derives much of its force from the final sentence: "And this is the anagrammatic Method." Strictly speaking this sentence is unnecessary, for we have already seen the anagram decyphered, but the mock-solemn repetition, in which one seems to hear Swift's own voice uttering the words, drives home the idiocy of the activities described, like the final tap to a nail. But not all the power and simplicity of Swift's prose, nor the imaginative effort that has been able to make not one but a whole series of impossible worlds more credible than the majority of history books—none of this would enable us to enjoy Swift if his world view were truly wounding or shocking. Millions of people, in many countries, must have enjoyed *Gulliver's Travels* while more or less seeing its anti-human implications: and even the child who accepts Parts I and II as a simple story gets a sense of absurdity from thinking of human beings six inches high. The explanation must be that Swift's world view is felt to be *not* altogether false—or it would probably be more accurate to say, not false all the time. Swift is a diseased writer. He remains permanently in a depressed mood which in most people is only intermittent, rather as though someone suffering from jaundice or the after-effects of influenza should have the energy to write books.

But we all know that mood, and something in us responds to the expression of it. Take, for instance, one of his most characteristic works, *The Lady's Dressing Room:* one might add the kindred poem, *Upon a Beautiful Young Nymph Going to Bed.* Which is truer, the viewpoint expressed in these poems, or the viewpoint implied in Blake's phrase, "The naked female human form divine"? No doubt Blake is nearer the truth, and yet who can fail to feel a sort of pleasure in seeing that fraud, feminine delicacy, exploded for once? Swift falsifies his picture of the world by refusing to see anything in human life except dirt, folly, and wickedness, but the part which he abstracts from the whole does exist, and it is something which we all know about while shrinking from mentioning it. Part of our minds—in any normal person it is the dominant part—believes that man is a noble animal and life is worth living: but there is also a sort of inner self which at least intermittently stands aghast at the horror of existence. In the queerest way, pleasure and disgust are linked together. The human body is beautiful: it is also repulsive and ridiculous, a fact which can be verified at any swimming pool. The sexual organs are objects of desire and also of loathing, so much so that in many languages, if not in all languages, their names are used as words of abuse. Meat is delicious, but a butcher's shop makes one feel sick: and indeed all our food springs ultimately from dung and dead bodies, the two things which of all others seem to us the most horrible. A child, when it is past the infantile stage but still looking at the world with fresh eyes, is moved by horror almost as often as by wonder—horror of snot and spittle, of the dogs' excrement on the pavement, the dying toad full of maggots, the sweaty smell of grown-ups, the hideousness of old men, with their bald heads and bulbous noses. In his endless harping on disease, dirt, and deformity, Swift is not actually inventing anything, he is merely leaving something out. Human behavior, too, especially in politics, is as he describes it, although it contains other more important factors which he refuses to admit. So far as we can see, both horror and pain are necessary to the continuance of life on this planet, and it is therefore open to pessimists like Swift to say: "If horror and pain must always be with us, how can life be significantly improved?" His attitude is in effect the Christian attitude, minus the bribe of a "next world"—which, however, probably has less hold upon the minds of believers than the conviction that this world is a vale of tears and the grave is a place of rest. It is, I am certain, a wrong attitude, and one which could have harmful effects upon behavior; but something in us responds to it, as it responds to the gloomy words of the burial service and the sweetish smell of corpses in a country church.

It is often argued, at least by people who admit the importance of subject matter, that a book cannot be "good" if it expresses a palpably false view of life. We are told that in our own age, for instance, any book that has genuine literary merit will also be more or less "progressive" in tendency. This ignores the fact that throughout history a similar struggle between progress and reaction has been raging, and that the best books of any one age have always been written from several different viewpoints, some of them palpably more false than others. In so far as a writer is a propagandist, the most one can ask of him is that he shall genuinely believe in what he is saying, and that it shall not be something blazingly silly. Today, for example, one can imagine a good book being written by a Catholic, a Communist, a Fascist, a pacifist, an anarchist, perhaps by an old-style Liberal or an ordinary Conservative: one cannot imagine a good book being written by a spiritualist, a Buchmanite, or a member of the Ku Klux Klan. The views that a writer holds must be compatible with sanity, in the medical sense, and with the power of continuous thought: beyond that what we ask of him is talent, which is probably another name for conviction. Swift did not possess ordinary wisdom, but he did possess a terrible intensity of vision, capable of picking out a single hidden truth and then magnifying it and distorting it. The durability of *Gulliver's Travels* goes to show that, if the force of belief is behind it, a world view which only just passes the test of sanity is sufficient to produce a great work of art.

1946

△

Lear, Tolstoy and the Fool

▽

Tolstoy's pamphlets are the least-known part of his work, and his attack on Shakespeare * is not even an easy document to get hold of, at any rate in an English translation. Perhaps, therefore, it will

* *Shakespeare and the Drama.* Written about 1903 as an introduction to another pamphlet, *Shakespeare and the Working Classes,* by Ernest Crosby.

be useful if I give a summary of the pamphlet before trying to discuss it.

Tolstoy begins by saying that throughout life Shakespeare has aroused in him "an irresistible repulsion and tedium." Conscious that the opinion of the civilized world is against him, he has made one attempt after another on Shakespeare's works, reading and re-reading them in Russian, English, and German; but "I invariably underwent the same feelings; repulsion, weariness and bewilderment." Now, at the age of seventy-five, he has once again reread the entire works of Shakespeare, including the historical plays, and

I have felt with an even greater force, the same feelings—this time, however, not of bewilderment, but of firm, indubitable conviction that the unquestionable glory of a great genius which Shakespeare enjoys, and which compels writers of our time to imitate him and readers and spectators to discover in him non-existent merits—thereby distorting their aesthetic and ethical understanding—is a great evil, as is every untruth.

Shakespeare, Tolstoy adds, is not merely no genius, but is not even "an average author," and in order to demonstrate this fact he will examine *King Lear,* which, as he is able to show by quotations from Hazlitt, Brandes, and others, has been extravagantly praised and can be taken as an example of Shakespeare's best work.

Tolstoy then makes a sort of exposition of the plot of *King Lear,* finding it at every step to be stupid, verbose, unnatural, unintelligible, bombastic, vulgar, tedious, and full of incredible events, "wild ravings," "mirthless jokes," anachronisms, irrelevancies, obscenities, worn-out stage conventions, and other faults both moral and aesthetic. *Lear* is, in any case, a plagiarism of an earlier and much better play, *King Leir,* by an unknown author, which Shakespeare stole and then ruined. It is worth quoting a specimen paragraph to illustrate the manner in which Tolstoy goes to work. Act III, Scene 2 (in which Lear, Kent and the Fool are together in the storm) is summarized thus:

Lear walks about the heath and says words which are meant to express his despair: he desires that the winds should blow so hard that they (the winds) should crack their cheeks and that the rain should flood everything, that lightning should singe his white head, and the thunder flatten the world and destroy all germs "that make ungrateful man"! The fool keeps uttering still more senseless words. Enter Kent: Lear says that for some reason during this storm all criminals shall be found out and convicted. Kent, still unrecognized by Lear, endeavors to persuade him to take refuge in a hovel. At this point the fool utters a prophecy in no wise related to the situation and they all depart.

Tolstoy's final verdict on *Lear* is that no unhypnotized observer, if such an observer existed, could read it to the end with any feeling except "aversion and weariness." And exactly the same is true of "all the other extolled dramas of Shakespeare, not to mention the senseless dramatized tales, *Pericles, Twelfth Night, The Tempest, Cymbeline, Troilus and Cressida.*"

Having dealt with *Lear* Tolstoy draws up a more general indictment against Shakespeare. He finds that Shakespeare has a certain technical skill which is partly traceable to his having been an actor, but otherwise no merits whatever. He has no power of delineating character or of making words and actions spring naturally out of situations, his language is uniformly exaggerated and ridiculous, he constantly thrusts his own random thoughts into the mouth of any character who happens to be handy, he displays a "complete absence of aesthetic feeling," and his words "have nothing whatever in common with art and poetry."

"Shakespeare might have been whatever you like," Tolstoy concludes, "but he was not an artist." Moreover, his opinions are not original or interesting, and his tendency is "of the lowest and most immoral." Curiously enough, Tolstoy does not base this last judgment on Shakespeare's own utterances, but on the statements of two critics, Gervinus and Brandes. According to Gervinus (or at any rate Tolstoy's reading of Gervinus) "Shakespeare taught . . . that one *may be too good,*" while according to Brandes: "Shakespeare's fundamental principle . . . is that *the end justifies the means.*" Tolstoy adds on his own account that Shakespeare was a jingo patriot of the worst type, but apart from this he considers that Gervinus and Brandes have given a true and adequate description of Shakespeare's view of life.

Tolstoy then recapitulates in a few paragraphs the theory of art which he had expressed at greater length elsewhere. Put still more shortly, it amounts to a demand for dignity of subject matter, sincerity, and good craftsmanship. A great work of art must deal with some subject which is "important to the life of mankind," it must express something which the author genuinely feels, and it must use such technical methods as will produce the desired effect. As Shakespeare is debased in outlook, slipshod in execution, and incapable of being sincere even for a moment, he obviously stands condemned.

But here there arises a difficult question. If Shakespeare is all that Tolstoy has shown him to be, how did he ever come to be so generally admired? Evidently the answer can only lie in a sort of mass hypnosis, or "epidemic suggestion." The whole civilized world has somehow been deluded into thinking Shakespeare a good writer, and even the plainest demonstration to the contrary makes no impression, because one is not dealing with a reasoned opinion but with something akin to religious faith. Throughout history, says Tolstoy, there has been an endless series of these "epidemic suggestions"—for example, the Crusades, the search for the Philosopher's Stone, the craze for tulip-growing which once swept over Holland, and so on and so forth. As a contemporary instance he cites, rather significantly, the Dreyfus case over which the whole world grew violently excited for no sufficient reason. There are also sudden short-lived crazes for new political and philosophical theories, or for this or that writer, artist, or scientist—for example, Darwin who (in 1903) is "beginning to be forgotten." And in some cases a quite worthless popular idol may remain in favor for centuries, for "it also happens that such crazes, having arisen in consequence of special reasons accidentally favoring their establishment, correspond in such a degree to the views of life spread in society, and especially in literary circles, that they are maintained for a long time." Shakespeare's plays have continued to be admired over a long period because "they corresponded to the irreligious and immoral frame of mind of the upper classes of his time and ours."

As to the manner in which Shakespeare's fame *started*, Tolstoy explains it as having been "got up" by German professors toward the end of the eighteenth century. His reputation "originated in Germany, and thence was transferred to England." The Germans chose to elevate Shakespeare because, at a time when there was no German drama worth speaking about and French classical literature was beginning to seem frigid and artificial, they were captivated by Shakespeare's "clever development of scenes" and also found in him a good expression of their own attitude toward life. Goethe pronounced Shakespeare a great poet, whereupon all the other critics flocked after him like a troop of parrots, and the general infatuation has lasted ever since. The result has been a further debasement of the drama—Tolstoy is careful to include his own plays when condemning the contemporary stage—and a further corruption of the prevailing moral outlook. It follows that "the false glorification of Shakespeare" is an important evil which Tolstoy feels it his duty to combat.

This, then, is the substance of Tolstoy's pamphlet. One's first feeling is that in describing Shakespeare as a bad writer he is saying something demonstrably untrue. But this is not the case. In reality there is no kind of evidence or argument by which one can show that Shakespeare, or any other writer, is "good." Nor is there any way of definitely proving that—for instance—Warwick Deeping is "bad." Ultimately there is no test of literary merit except survival, which is itself an index to majority opinion. Artistic theories such as Tolstoy's are quite worthless, because they not only start out with arbitrary assumptions, but depend on vague terms ("sincere," "important," and so forth) which can be interpreted in any way one chooses. Properly speaking one cannot *answer* Tolstoy's attack. The interesting question is: why did he make it? But it should be noticed in passing that he uses many weak or dishonest arguments. Some of these are worth pointing out, not because they invalidate his main charge but because they are, so to speak, evidence of malice.

To begin with, his examination of *King Lear* is not "impartial," as he twice claims. On the contrary, it is a prolonged exercise in misrepresentation. It is obvious that when you are summarizing *King Lear* for the benefit of someone who has not read it, you are not really being impartial if you introduce an important speech (Lear's speech when Cordelia is dead in his arms) in this manner: "Again begin Lear's awful ravings, at which one feels ashamed, as at unsuccessful jokes." And in a long series of instances Tolstoy slightly alters or colors the passages he is criticizing, always in such a way as to make the plot appear a little more complicated and improbable, or the language a little more exaggerated. For example, we are told that Lear "has no necessity or motive for his abdication," although his reason for abdicating (that he is old and wishes to retire from the cares of state) has been clearly indicated in the first scene. It will be seen that even in the passage which I quoted earlier, Tolstoy has wilfully misunderstood one phrase and slightly changed the meaning of another, making nonsense of a remark which is reasonable enough in its context. None of these misreadings is very gross in itself, but their cumulative effect is to exaggerate the psychological incoherence of the play. Again, Tolstoy is not able to explain why Shakespeare's plays were still in print, and still on the stage, two hundred years after his death (*before* the "epidemic suggestion" started, that is); and his whole account of Shakespeare's rise to fame is guesswork punctuated by outright misstatements. And again, various of his accusations contradict one another: for example, Shakespeare is a mere entertainer and "not in earnest," but on the other hand he is constantly putting his own thoughts into the mouths of his characters. On the whole it is difficult to feel that Tolstoy's criticisms are uttered in good faith. In any case it is impossible that he should fully have

believed in his main thesis—believed, that is to say, that for a century or more the entire civilized world had been taken in by a
huge and palpable lie which he alone was able to see through.
Certainly his dislike of Shakespeare is real enough, but the reasons
for it may be different, or partly different, from what he avows;
and therein lies the interest of his pamphlet.

At this point one is obliged to start guessing. However, there
is one possible clue, or at least there is a question which may point
the way to a clue. It is: why did Tolstoy, with thirty or more plays
to choose from, pick out *King Lear* as his especial target? True
Lear is so well known and has been so much praised that it could
justly be taken as representative of Shakespeare's best work; still,
for the purpose of a hostile analysis Tolstoy would probably choose
the play he disliked most. Is it not possible that he bore an especial enmity toward this particular play because he was aware, consciously or unconsciously, of the resemblance between Lear's story
and his own? But it is better to approach this clue from the opposite direction—that is, by examining *Lear* itself, and the qualities in it that Tolstoy fails to mention.

One of the first things an English reader would notice in Tolstoy's pamphlet is that it hardly deals with Shakespeare as a poet.
Shakespeare is treated as a dramatist, and in so far as his popularity is not spurious, it is held to be due to tricks of stagecraft
which give good opportunities to clever actors. Now, so far as
the English-speaking countries go, this is not true. Several of the
plays which are most valued by lovers of Shakespeare (for instance,
Timon of Athens) are seldom or never acted, while some of the
most actable, such as *A Midsummer Night's Dream,* are the least
admired. Those who care most for Shakespeare value him in the
first place for his use of language, the "verbal music" which even
Bernard Shaw, another hostile critic, admits to be "irresistible."
Tolstoy ignores this, and does not seem to realize that a poem may
have a special value for those who speak the language in which it
was written. However, even if one puts oneself in Tolstoy's place
and tries to think of Shakespeare as a foreign poet it is still clear
that there is something that Tolstoy has left out. Poetry, it seems,
is *not* solely a matter of sound and association, and valueless outside its own language group: otherwise how is it that some poems,
including poems written in dead languages, succeed in crossing
frontiers? Clearly a lyric like "Tomorrow is Saint Valentine's Day"
could not be satisfactorily translated, but in Shakespeare's major
work there is something describable as poetry that can be separated
from the words. Tolstoy is right in saying that *Lear* is not a very

good play, as a play. It is too drawn-out and has too many characters and sub-plots. One wicked daughter would have been quite
enough, and Edgar is a superfluous character: indeed it would
probably be a better play if Gloucester and both his sons were
eliminated. Nevertheless, something, a kind of pattern, or perhaps
only an atmosphere, survives the complications and the *longueurs*.
Lear can be imagined as a puppet show, a mime, a ballet, a series
of pictures. Part of its poetry, perhaps the most essential part, is
inherent in the story and is dependent neither on any particular
set of words, nor on flesh-and-blood presentation.

Shut your eyes and think of *King Lear,* if possible without calling to mind any of the dialogue. What do you see? Here at any
rate is what I see: a majestic old man in a long black robe, with
flowing white hair and beard, a figure out of Blake's drawings (but
also, curiously enough, rather like Tolstoy), wandering through a
storm and cursing the heavens, in company with a Fool and a
lunatic. Presently the scene shifts and the old man, still cursing,
still understanding nothing, is holding a dead girl in his arms
while the Fool dangles on a gallows somewhere in the background.
This is the bare skeleton of the play, and even here Tolstoy wants
to cut out most of what is essential. He objects to the storm, as
being unnecessary, to the Fool, who in his eyes is simply a tedious
nuisance and an excuse for making bad jokes, and to the death
of Cordelia, which, as he sees it, robs the play of its moral. According to Tolstoy, the earlier play, *King Leir,* which Shakespeare
adapted

terminates more naturally and more in accordance with the moral demands of the spectator than does Shakespeare's: namely, by the King of
the Gauls conquering the husbands of the elder sisters, and by Cordelia,
instead of being killed, restoring Leir to his former position.

In other words the tragedy ought to have been a comedy, or
perhaps a melodrama. It is doubtful whether the sense of tragedy
is compatible with belief in God: at any rate, it is not compatible
with disbelief in human dignity and with the kind of "moral demand" which feels cheated when virtue fails to triumph. A tragic
situation exists precisely when virtue does *not* triumph but when
it is still felt that man is nobler than the forces which destroy
him. It is perhaps more significant that Tolstoy sees no justification for the presence of the Fool. The Fool is integral to the play.
He acts not only as a sort of chorus, making the central situation
clearer by commenting on it more intelligently than the other characters, but as a foil to Lear's frenzies. His jokes, riddles, and scraps

of rhyme, and his endless digs at Lear's high-minded folly, ranging from mere derision to a sort of melancholy poetry ("All thy other titles thou hast given away; that thou wast born with"), are like a trickle of sanity running through the play, a reminder that somewhere or other in spite of the injustices, cruelties, intrigues, deceptions, and misunderstandings that are being enacted here, life is going on much as usual. In Tolstoy's impatience with the Fool one gets a glimpse of his deeper quarrel with Shakespeare. He objects, with some justification, to the raggedness of Shakespeare's plays, the irrelevancies, the incredible plots, the exaggerated language: but what at bottom he probably most dislikes is a sort of exuberance, a tendency to take—not so much a pleasure as simply an interest in the actual process of life. It is a mistake to write Tolstoy off as a moralist attacking an artist. He never said that art, as such, is wicked or meaningless, nor did he even say that technical virtuosity is unimportant. But his main aim, in his later years, was to narrow the range of human consciousness. One's interests, one's points of attachment to the physical world and the day-to-day struggle, must be as few and not as many as possible. Literature must consist of parables, stripped of detail and almost independent of language. The parables—this is where Tolstoy differs from the average vulgar puritan—must themselves be works of art, but pleasure and curiosity must be excluded from them. Science, also, must be divorced from curiosity. The business of science, he says, is not to discover what happens but to teach men how they ought to live. So also with history and politics. Many problems (for example, the Dreyfus case) are simply not worth solving, and he is willing to leave them as loose ends. Indeed his whole theory of "crazes" or "epidemic suggestions," in which he lumps together such things as the Crusades and the Dutch passion of tulip-growing, shows a willingness to regard many human activities as mere antlike rushings to and fro, inexplicable and uninteresting. Clearly he could have no patience with a chaotic, detailed, discursive writer like Shakespeare. His reaction is that of an irritable old man who is being pestered by a noisy child. "Why do you keep jumping up and down like that? Why can't you sit still like I do?" In a way the old man is in the right, but the trouble is that the child has a feeling in its limbs which the old man has lost. And if the old man knows of the existence of this feeling, the effect is merely to increase his irritation: he would make children senile, if he could. Tolstoy does not know, perhaps, just *what* he misses in Shakespeare, but he is aware that he misses something, and he is determined that others shall be deprived of it as

well. By nature he was imperious as well as egotistical. Well after
he was grown up he would still occasionally strike his servant in
moments of anger, and somewhat later, according to his English
biographer, Derrick Leon, he felt "a frequent desire upon the slen-
derest provocation to slap the faces of those with whom he dis-
agreed." One does not necessarily get rid of that kind of temper-
ment by undergoing religious conversion, and indeed it is obvious
that the illusion of having been reborn may allow one's native
vices to flourish more freely than ever, though perhaps in subtler
forms. Tolstoy was capable of abjuring physical violence and of
seeing what this implies, but he was not capable of tolerance or
humility, and even if one knew nothing of his other writings, one
could deduce his tendency toward spiritual bullying from this single pamphlet.

However, Tolstoy is not simply trying to rob others of a pleasure
he does not share. He is doing that, but his quarrel with Shakespeare goes further. It is the quarrel between the religious and
the humanist attitudes toward life. Here one comes back to the
central theme of *King Lear,* which Tolstoy does not mention, although he sets forth the plot in some detail.

Lear is one of the minority of Shakespeare's plays that are unmistakably *about* something. As Tolstoy justly complains, much
rubbish has been written about Shakespeare as a philosopher, as
a psychologist, as a "great moral teacher," and what-not. Shakespeare was not a systematic thinker, his most serious thoughts are
uttered irrelevantly or indirectly, and we do not know to what
extent he wrote with a "purpose" or even how much of the work
attributed him was actually written by him. In the sonnets he
never even refers to the plays as part of his achievement, though
he does make what seems to be a half-ashamed allusion to his career as an actor. It is perfectly possible that he looked on at least
half of his plays as mere potboilers and hardly bothered about
purpose or probability so long as he could patch up something,
usually from stolen material, which would more or less hang together on the stage. However, that is not the whole story. To begin with, as Tolstoy himself points out, Shakespeare has a habit
of thrusting uncalled-for general reflections into the mouths of his
characters. This is a serious fault in a dramatist, but it does not
fit in with Tolstoy's picture of Shakespeare as a vulgar hack who
has no opinions of his own and merely wishes to produce the
greatest effect with the least trouble. And more than this, about
a dozen of his plays, written for the most part later than 1600,
do unquestionably have a meaning and even a moral. They re-

volve round a central subject which in some cases can be reduced
to a single word. For example, *Macbeth* is about ambition, *Othello*
is about jealousy, and *Timon of Athens* is about money. The subject of *Lear* is renunciation, and it is only by being wilfully blind
that one can fail to understand what Shakespeare is saying.

Lear renounces his throne but expects everyone to continue treat-
ing him as a king. He does not see that if he surrenders power,
other people will take advantage of his weakness: also that those
who flatter him the most grossly, i.e. Regan and Goneril, are exactly the ones who will turn against him. The moment he finds
that he can no longer make people obey him as he did before,
he falls into a rage which Tolstoy describes as "strange and unnatural," but which in fact is perfectly in character. In his madness and despair, he passes through two moods which again are
natural enough in his circumstances, though in one of them it is
probable that he is being used partly as a mouthpiece for Shakespeare's own opinions. One is the mood of disgust in which Lear
repents, as it were, for having been a king, and grasps for the first
time the rottenness of formal justice and vulgar morality. The
other is a mood of impotent fury in which he wreaks imaginary
revenges upon those who have wronged him. "To have a thousand
with red burning spits come hissing in upon 'em!", and:

> It were a delicate stratagem to shoe
> A troop of horse with felt: I'll put't in proof;
> And when I have stol'n upon these sons-in-law,
> Then kill, kill, kill, kill, kill!

Only at the end does he realize, as a sane man, that power, revenge, and victory are not worth while:

> No, no, no, no! Come, let's away to prison . . .
> . . . . and we'll wear out
> In a wall'd prison, packs and sects of great ones
> That ebb and flow by the moon.

But by the time he makes this discovery it is too late, for his death
and Cordelia's are already decided on. That is the story, and, allowing for some clumsiness in the telling, it is a very good story.

But is it not also curiously similar to the history of Tolstoy himself? There is a general resemblance which one can hardly avoid
seeing, because the most impressive event in Tolstoy's life, as in
Lear's, was a huge and gratuitous act of renunciation. In his old
age he renounced his estate, his title, and his copyrights, and made
an attempt—a sincere attempt, though it was not successful—to escape from his privileged position and live the life of a peasant.

But the deeper resemblance lies in the fact that Tolstoy, like Lear, acted on mistaken motives and failed to get the results he had hoped for. According to Tolstoy, the aim of every human being is happiness, and happiness can only be attained by doing the will of God. But doing the will of God means casting off all earthly pleasures and ambitions, and living only for others. Ultimately, therefore, Tolstoy renounced the world under the expectation that this would make him happier. But if there is one thing certain about his later years, it is that he was *not* happy. On the contrary, he was driven almost to the edge of madness by the behavior of the people about him, who persecuted him precisely *because* of his renunciation. Like Lear, Tolstoy was not humble and not a good judge of character. He was inclined at moments to revert to the attitudes of an aristocrat, in spite of his peasant's blouse, and he even had two children whom he had believed in and who ultimately turned against him—though, of course, in a less sensational manner than Regan and Goneril. His exaggerated revulsion from sexuality was also distinctly similar to Lear's. Tolstoy's remark that marriage is "slavery, satiety, repulsion" and means putting up with the proximity of "ugliness, dirtiness, smell, sores," is matched by Lear's well-known outburst:

> But to the girdle do the gods inherit,
> Beneath is all the fiends';
> There's hell, there's darkness, there's the sulphurous pit,
> Burning, scalding, stench, consumption . . . etc., etc.

And though Tolstoy could not foresee it when he wrote his essay on Shakespeare, even the ending of his life—the sudden unplanned flight across country, accompanied only by a faithful daughter, the death in a cottage in a strange village—seems to have in it a sort of phantom reminiscence of *Lear*.

Of course, one cannot assume that Tolstoy was aware of this resemblance, or would have admitted it if it had been pointed out to him. But his attitude toward the play must have been influenced by its theme. Renouncing power, giving away your lands, was a subject on which he had reason to feel deeply. Probably, therefore, he would be more angered and disturbed by the moral that Shakespeare draws than he would be in the case of some other play—*Macbeth*, for example—which did not touch so closely on his own life. But what exactly *is* the moral of *Lear?* Evidently there are two morals, one explicit, the other implied in the story.

Shakespeare starts by assuming that to make yourself powerless is to invite an attack. This does not mean that *everyone* will turn against you (Kent and the Fool stand by Lear from first to last), but in all probability *someone* will. If you throw away your weapons, some less scrupulous person will pick them up. If you turn the other cheek, you will get a harder blow on it than you got on the first one. This does not always happen, but it is to be expected, and you ought not to complain if it does happen. The second blow is, so to speak, part of the act of turning the other cheek. First of all, therefore, there is the vulgar, common-sense moral drawn by the Fool: "Don't relinquish power, don't give away your lands." But there is also another moral. Shakespeare never utters it in so many words, and it does not very much matter whether he was fully aware of it. It is contained in the story, which, after all, he made up, or altered to suit his purposes. It is: "Give away your lands if you want to, but don't expect to gain happiness by doing so. Probably you won't gain happiness. If you live for others, you must live *for others,* and not as a roundabout way of getting an advantage for yourself."

Obviously neither of these conclusions could have been pleasing to Tolstoy. The first of them expresses the ordinary, belly-to-earth selfishness from which he was genuinely trying to escape. The other conflicts with his desire to eat his cake and have it—that is, to destroy his own egoism and by so doing to gain eternal life. Of course, *Lear* is not a sermon in favor of altruism. It merely points out the results of practicing self-denial for selfish reasons. Shakespeare had a considerable streak of worldliness in him, and if he had been forced to take sides in his own play, his sympathies would probably have lain with the Fool. But at least he could see the whole issue and treat it at the level of tragedy. Vice is punished, but virtue is not rewarded. The morality of Shakespeare's later tragedies is not religious in the ordinary sense, and certainly is not Christian. Only two of them, *Hamlet* and *Othello,* are supposedly occurring inside the Christian era, and even in those, apart from the antics of the ghost in *Hamlet,* there is no indication of a "next world" where everything is to be put right. All of these tragedies start out with the humanist assumption that life, although full of sorrow, is worth living, and that Man is a noble animal—a belief which Tolstoy in his old age did not share.

Tolstoy was not a saint, but he tried very hard to make himself into a saint, and the standards he applied to literature were otherworldly ones. It is important to realize that the difference between a saint and an ordinary human being is a difference of kind and not of degree. That is, the one is not to be regarded as an imperfect form of the other. The saint, at any rate Tolstoy's kind of saint, is not trying to work an improvement in earthly life: he is trying to bring it to an end and put something different in its place. One obvious expression of this is the claim that celibacy is "higher" than marriage. If only, Tolstoy says in effect, we would stop breeding, fighting, struggling, and enjoying, if we could get rid not only of our sins but of everything else that binds us to the surface of the earth—including love—then the whole painful process would be over and the Kingdom of Heaven would arrive. But a normal human being does not want the Kingdom of Heaven: he wants life on earth to continue. This is not solely because he is "weak," "sinful," and anxious for a "good time." Most people get a fair amount of fun out of their lives, but on balance life is suffering, and only the very young or the very foolish imagine otherwise. Ultimately it is the Christian attitude which is self-interested and hedonistic, since the aim is always to get away from the painful struggle of earthly life and find eternal peace in some kind of Heaven or Nirvana. The humanist attitude is that the struggle must continue and that death is the price of life. "Men must endure their going hence, even as their coming hither: Ripeness is all"—which is an un-Christian sentiment. Often there is a seeming truce between the humanist and the religious believer, but in fact their attitudes cannot be reconciled: one must choose between this world and the next. And the enormous majority of human beings, if they understood the issue, would choose this world. They do make that choice when they continue working, breeding, and dying instead of crippling their faculties in the hope of obtaining a new lease of existence elsewhere.

We do not know a great deal about Shakespeare's religious beliefs, and from the evidence of his writings it would be difficult to prove that he had any. But at any rate he was not a saint or a would-be saint: he was a human being, and in some ways not a very good one. It is clear, for instance, that he liked to stand well with the rich and powerful, and was capable of flattering them in the most servile way. He is also noticeably cautious, not to say cowardly, in his manner of uttering unpopular opinions. Almost never does he put a subversive or skeptical remark into the mouth of a character likely to be identified with himself. Throughout his plays the acute social critics, the people who are not taken in by accepted fallacies, are buffoons, villains, lunatics, or persons who are shamming insanity or are in a state of violent hysteria. *Lear* is a play in which this tendency is particularly well marked. It contains a great deal of veiled social criticism—a point Tolstoy misses—but it is all uttered either by the Fool, by Edgar when he is pretending to be mad, or by Lear during his bouts of madness. In his sane moments Lear hardly ever makes an intelligent remark. And yet the very fact that Shakespeare had to use these subterfuges shows how widely his thoughts ranged. He could not restrain himself from commenting on almost everything, although he put on a series of masks in order to do so. If one has once read Shakespeare with attention, it is not easy to go a day without quoting him, because there are not many subjects of major importance that he does not discuss or at least mention somewhere or other, in his unsystematic but illuminating way. Even the irrelevancies that litter every one of his plays—the puns and riddles, the lists of names, the scraps of *reportage* like the conversation of the carriers in *Henry IV*, the bawdy jokes, the rescued fragments of forgotten ballads— are merely the products of excessive vitality. Shakespeare was not a philosopher or a scientist, but he did have curiosity; he loved the surface of the earth and the process of life—which, it should be repeated, is *not* the same thing as wanting to have a good time and stay alive as long as possible. Of course, it is not because of the quality of his thought that Shakespeare has survived, and he might not even be remembered as a dramatist if he had not also been a poet. His main hold on us is through language. How deeply Shakespeare himself was fascinated by the music of words can probably be inferred from the speeches of Pistol. What Pistol says is largely meaningless, but if one considers his lines singly they are magnificent rhetorical verse. Evidently, pieces of resounding nonsense ("Let floods o'erswell, and fiends for food howl on," etc.) were constantly appearing in Shakespeare's mind of their own accord, and a half-lunatic character had to be invented to use them up.

Tolstoy's native tongue was not English, and one cannot blame him for being unmoved by Shakespeare's verse, nor even, perhaps, for refusing to believe that Shakespeare's skill with words was something out of the ordinary. But he would also have rejected the whole notion of valuing poetry for its texture—valuing it, that is to say, as a kind of music. If it could somehow have been proved to him that his whole explanation of Shakespeare's rise to fame is mistaken, that inside the English-speaking world, at any rate, Shakespeare's popularity is genuine, that his mere skill in placing one syllable beside another has given acute pleasure to generation after generation of English-speaking people—all this would not have been counted as a merit to Shakespeare, but rather the contrary. It would simply have been one more proof of the irreligious, earthbound nature of Shakespeare and his admirers. Tolstoy would have said that poetry is to be judged by its meaning, and that seductive sounds merely cause false meanings to go unnoticed. At every level it is the same issue—this world against the next: and certainly the music of words is something that belongs to this world.

A sort of doubt has always hung around the character of Tolstoy, as round the character of Gandhi. He was not a vulgar hypocrite, as some people declared him to be, and he would probably have imposed even greater sacrifices on himself than he did, if he had not been interfered with at every step by the people surrounding him, especially his wife. But on the other hand it is dangerous to take such men as Tolstoy at their disciples' valuation. There is always the possibility—the probability, indeed—that they have done no more than exchange one form of egoism for another. Tolstoy renounced wealth, fame, and privilege; he abjured violence in all its forms and was ready to suffer for doing so; but it is not easy to believe that he abjured the principle of coercion, or at least the *desire* to coerce others. There are families in which the father will say to his child, "You'll get a thick ear if you do that again," while the mother, her eyes brimming over with tears, will take the child in her arms and murmur lovingly, "Now, darling, *is* it kind to Mummy to do that?" And who would maintain that the second method is less tyrannous than the first? The distinction that really matters is not between violence and non-violence, but between having and not having the appetite for power. There are people who are convinced of the wickedness both of armies and of police forces, but who are nevertheless much more tolerant and inquisitorial in outlook than the normal person who believes that it is necessary to use violence in certain circumstances. They will not say to somebody else, "Do this, that, and the other or you will go to prison," but they will, if they can, get inside his brain and dictate his thoughts for him in the minutest particulars. Creeds like pacifism and anarchism, which seem on the surface to imply a complete renunciation of power, rather encourage this habit of mind. For if you have embraced a creed which appears to be free from the ordinary dirtiness of politics—a creed from which you yourself cannot expect to draw any material advantage—surely that proves that you are in the right? And the more you are in the right, the more natural that everyone else should be bullied into thinking likewise.

If we are to believe what he says in his pamphlet, Tolstoy has never been able to see any merit in Shakespeare, and was always astonished to find that his fellow-writers, Turgenev, Fet, and others thought differently. We may be sure that in his unregenerate days Tolstoy's conclusion would have been: "You like Shakespeare—I don't. Let's leave it at that." Later, when his perception that it takes all sorts to make a world had deserted him, he came to think of Shakespeare's writings as something dangerous to himself. The more pleasure people took in Shakespeare, the less they would listen to Tolstoy. Therefore nobody must be *allowed* to enjoy Shakespeare, just as nobody must be allowed to drink alcohol or smoke tobacco. True, Tolstoy would not prevent them by force. He is not demanding that the police shall impound every copy of Shakespeare's works. But he will do dirt on Shakespeare, if he can. He will try to get inside the mind of every lover of Shakespeare and kill his enjoyment by every trick he can think of, including—as I have shown in my summary of his pamphlet—arguments which are self-contradictory or even doubtfully honest.

But finally the most striking thing is how little difference it all makes. As I said earlier, one cannot *answer* Tolstoy's pamphlet, at least on its main counts. There is no argument by which one can defend a poem. It defends itself by surviving, or it is indefensible. And if this test is valid, I think the verdict in Shakespeare's case must be "not guilty." Like every other writer, Shakespeare will be forgotten sooner or later, but it is unlikely that a heavier indictment will ever be brought against him. Tolstoy was perhaps the most admired literary man of his age, and he was certainly not its least able pamphleteer. He turned all his powers of denunciation against Shakespeare, like all the guns of a battleship roaring simultaneously. And with what result? Forty years later, Shakespeare is still there completely unaffected, and of the attempt to demolish him nothing remains except the yellowing pages of a pamphlet which hardly anyone has read, and which would be forgotten altogether if Tolstoy had not also been the author of *War and Peace* and *Anna Karenina*.

1946

Δ

In Defense of P. G. Wodehouse

▽

When the Germans made their rapid advance through Belgium in the early summer of 1940, they captured, among other things, Mr. P. G. Wodehouse, who had been living throughout the early part of the war in his villa at Le Touquet, and seems not to have realized until the last moment that he was in any danger. As he was led away into captivity, he is said to have remarked, "Perhaps after this I shall write a serious book." He was placed for the time being under house arrest, and from his subsequent statements it appears that he was treated in a fairly friendly way, German officers in the neighborhood frequently "dropping in for a bath or a party."

Over a year later, on June 25, 1941, the news came that Wodehouse had been released from internment and was living at the Adlon Hotel in Berlin. On the following day the public was astonished to learn that he had agreed to do some broadcasts of a "non-political" nature over the German radio. The full texts of these broadcasts are not easy to obtain at this date, but Wodehouse seems to have done five of them between June 26 and July 2, when the Germans took him off the air again. The first broadcast, on June 26, was not made on the Nazi radio but took the form of an interview with Harry Flannery, the representative of the Columbia Broadcasting System, which still had its correspondents in Berlin. Wodehouse also published in the *Saturday Evening Post* an article which he had written while still in the internment camp.

The article and the broadcasts dealt mainly with Wodehouse's experiences in internment, but they did include a very few comments on the war. The following are fair samples:

I never was interested in politics. I'm quite unable to work up any kind of belligerent feeling. Just as I'm about to feel belligerent about some country I meet a decent sort of chap. We go out together and lose any fighting thoughts or feelings.

A short time ago they had a look at me on parade and got the right idea; at least they sent us to the local lunatic asylum. And I have been there forty-two weeks. There is a good deal to be said for internment. It keeps you out of the saloon and helps you to keep up with your reading. The chief trouble is that it means you are away from home for a long time. When I join my wife I had better take along a letter of introduction to be on the safe side.

In the days before the war I had always been modestly proud of being an Englishman, but now that I have been some months resident in this bin or repository of Englishmen I am not so sure. . . . The only concession I want from Germany is that she gives me a loaf of bread, tells the gentlemen with muskets at the main gate to look the other way, and leaves the rest to me. In return I am prepared to hand over India, an autographed set of my books, and to reveal the secret process of cooking sliced potatoes on a radiator. This offer holds good till Wednesday week.

The first extract quoted above caused great offense. Wodehouse was also censured for using (in the interview with Flannery) the phrase "whether Britain wins the war or not," and he did not make things better by describing in another broadcast the filthy habits of some Belgian prisoners among whom he was interned. The Germans recorded this broadcast and repeated it a number of times. They seem to have supervised his talks very lightly, and they allowed him not only to be funny about the discomforts of internment but to remark that "the internees at Trost camp all fervently believe that Britain will eventually win." The general up-shot of the talks, however, was that he had not been ill treated and bore no malice.

These broadcasts caused an immediate uproar in England. There were questions in Parliament, angry editorial comments in the press, and a stream of letters from fellow-authors, nearly all of them dis-approving, though one or two suggested that it would be better to suspend judgment, and several pleaded that Wodehouse probably did not realize what he was doing. On July 15, the Home Service of the B.B.C. carried an extremely violent Postscript by "Cas-sandra" of the *Daily Mirror,* accusing Wodehouse of "selling his country." This postscript made free use of such expressions as "quisling" and "worshiping the Führer." The main charge was that Wodehouse had agreed to do German propaganda as a way of buying himself out of the internment camp.

"Cassandra's" Postscript caused a certain amount of protest, but on the whole it seems to have intensified popular feeling against Wodehouse. One result of it was that numerous lending libraries withdrew Wodehouse's books from circulation. Here is a typical news item:

> Within twenty-four hours of listening to the broadcast of Cassandra, the *Daily Mirror* columnist, Portadown (North Ireland) Urban District Council banned P. G. Wodehouse's books from their public library. Mr. Edward McCann said that Cassandra's broadcast had clinched the matter. Wodehouse was funny no longer. (*Daily Mirror.*)

In addition the B.B.C. banned Wodehouse's lyrics from the air and was still doing so a couple of years later. As late as December 1944 there were demands in Parliament that Wodehouse should be put on trial as a traitor.

There is an old saying that if you throw enough mud some of it will stick, and the mud has stuck to Wodehouse in a rather peculiar way. An impression has been left behind that Wodehouse's talks (not that anyone remembers what he said in them) showed him up not merely as a traitor but as an ideological sympathizer with Fascism. Even at the time several letters to the press claimed that "Fascist tendencies" could be detected in his books, and the charge has been repeated since. I shall try to analyze the mental atmosphere of those books in a moment, but it is important to realize that the events of 1941 do not convict Wodehouse of anything worse than stupidity. The really interesting question is how and why he could be so stupid. When Flannery met Wodehouse (released, but still under guard) at the Adlon Hotel in June, 1941, he saw at once that he was dealing with a political innocent, and when preparing him for their broadcast interview he had to warn him against making some exceedingly unfortunate remarks, one of which was by implication slightly anti-Russian. As it was, the phrase "whether England wins or not" did get through. Soon after the interview Wodehouse told him that he was also going to broadcast on the Nazi radio, apparently not realizing that this action had any special significance. Flannery comments: *

By this time the Wodehouse plot was evident. It was one of the best Nazi publicity stunts of the war, the first with a human angle. . . . Plack [Goebbels's assistant] had gone to the camp near Gleiwitz to see Wodehouse, found that the author was completely without political sense, and had an idea. He suggested to Wodehouse that in return for being released from the prison camp he write a series of broadcasts about his experiences; there would be no censorship and he would put them on the air himself. In making that proposal Plack showed that he knew his man. He knew that Wodehouse made fun of the English in all his stories and that he seldom wrote in any other way, that he was still living in the period about which he wrote and had no conception of Nazism and all it meant. Wodehouse was his own Bertie Wooster.

The striking of an actual bargain between Wodehouse and Plack seems to be merely Flannery's own interpretation. The arrangement may have been of a much less definite kind, and to judge from the broadcasts themselves, Wodehouse's main idea in making them was to keep in touch with his public and—the comedian's ruling passion —to get a laugh. Obviously they are not the utterances of a quisling of the type of Ezra Pound or John Amery, nor, probably, of a person capable of understanding the nature of quislingism. Flannery seems to have warned Wodehouse that it would be unwise to broadcast, but not very forcibly. He adds that Wodehouse (though in one broadcast he refers to himself as an Englishman) seemed to regard himself as an American citizen. He had contemplated naturalization, but had never filled in the necessary papers. He even used, to Flannery, the phrase, "We're not at war with Germany."

* *Assignment to Berlin,* by Harry W. Flannery. (Alfred A. Knopf, 1942.)

I have before me a bibliography of P. G. Wodehouse's works. It names round about fifty books, but is certainly incomplete. It is as well to be honest, and I ought to start by admitting that there are many books by Wodehouse—perhaps a quarter or a third of the total—which I have not read. It is not, indeed, easy to read the whole output of a popular writer who is normally published in cheap editions. But I have followed his work fairly closely since 1911, when I was eight years old, and am well acquainted with its peculiar mental atmosphere—an atmosphere which has not, of course, remained completely unchanged, but shows little alteration since about 1925. In the passage from Flannery's book which I quoted above there are two remarks which would immediately strike any attentive reader of Wodehouse. One is to the effect that Wodehouse "was still living in the period about which he wrote," and the other that the Nazi propaganda ministry made use of him because he "made fun of the English." The second statement is based on a misconception to which I will return presently. But Flannery's other comment is quite true and contains in it part of the clue to Wodehouse's behavior.

A thing that people often forget about P. G. Wodehouse's novels is how long ago the better-known of them were written. We think of him as in some sense typifying the silliness of the nineteen-twenties and nineteen-thirties, but in fact the scenes and characters by which he is best remembered had all made their appearance before 1925. Psmith first appeared in 1909, having been foreshadowed by other characters in earlier school stories. Blandings Castle, with Baxter and the Earl of Emsworth both in residence, was introduced in 1915. The Jeeves-Wooster cycle began in 1919, both Jeeves and Wooster having made brief appearances earlier. Ukridge appeared in 1924. When one looks through the list of Wodehouse's books from 1902 onward, one can observe three fairly well-marked periods. The first is the school-story period. It includes such books as *The Gold Bat*, *The Pothunters*, etc., and has its high spot in *Mike* (1909). *Psmith in the City*, published in the following year, belongs to this category, though it is not directly concerned with school life. The next is the American period. Wodehouse seems to have lived in the United States from about 1913 to 1920, and for a while showed signs of becoming Americanized in idiom and outlook. Some of the stories in *The Man with Two Left Feet* (1917) appear to have been influenced by O. Henry, and other books written about this time contain Americanisms (*e.g.* "highball" for "whisky and soda") which an Englishman would not normally use *in propria persona*. Nevertheless, almost all the books of this period—*Psmith, Journalist; The*

Little Nugget; The Indiscretions of Archie; Piccadilly Jim and
various others—depend for their effect on the *contrast* between English and American manners. English characters appear in an American setting, or *vice versa:* there is a certain number of purely English
stories, but hardly any purely American ones. The third period
might fitly be called the country-house period. By the early nineteen-
twenties Wodehouse must have been making a very large income,
and the social status of his characters moved upward accordingly,
though the Ukridge stories form a partial exception. The typical
setting is now a country mansion, a luxurious bachelor flat, or an
expensive golf club. The schoolboy athleticism of the earlier books
fades out, cricket and football giving way to golf, and the element
of farce and burlesque becomes more marked. No doubt many of
the later books, such as *Summer Lightning,* are light comedy rather
than pure farce, but the occasional attempts at moral earnestness
which can be found in *Psmith, Journalist;* *The Little Nugget; The
Coming of Bill; The Man with Two Left Feet* and some of the
school stories, no longer appear. Mike Jackson has turned into
Bertie Wooster. That, however, is not a very startling metamor-
phosis, and one of the most noticeable things about Wodehouse is
his *lack* of development. Books like *The Gold Bat* and *Tales of
St. Austin's,* written in the opening years of this century, already
have the familiar atmosphere. How much of a formula the writing
of his later books had become one can see from the fact that he
continued to write stories of English life although throughout the
sixteen years before his internment he was living at Hollywood and
Le Touquet.

Mike, which is now a difficult book to obtain in an unabridged
form, must be one of the best "light" school stories in English. But
though its incidents are largely farcical, it is by no means a satire on
the public-school system, and *The Gold Bat, The Pothunters,* etc., are
even less so. Wodehouse was educated at Dulwich, and then worked
in a bank and graduated into novel-writing by way of very cheap
journalism. It is clear that for many years he remained "fixated" on
his old school and loathed the unromantic job and the lower-middle-
class surroundings in which he found himself. In the early stories
the "glamour" of public-school life (house matches, fagging, teas
round the study fire, etc.) is laid on fairly thick, and the "play the
game" code of morals is accepted with not many reservations.
Wrykyn, Wodehouse's imaginary public school, is a school of a
more fashionable type than Dulwich, and one gets the impression
that between *The Gold Bat* (1904) and *Mike* (1909) Wrykyn itself
has become more expensive and moved farther from London. Psy-

chologically the most revealing book of Wodehouse's early period is *Psmith in the City*. Mike Jackson's father has suddenly lost his money, and Mike, like Wodehouse himself, is thrust at the age of about eighteen into an ill-paid subordinate job in a bank. Psmith is similarly employed, though not from financial necessity. Both this book and *Psmith, Journalist* (1915) are unusual in that they display a certain amount of political consciousness. Psmith at this stage chooses to call himself a Socialist—in his mind, and no doubt in Wodehouse's, this means no more than ignoring class distinctions— and on one occasion the two boys attend an open-air meeting on Clapham Common and go home to tea with an elderly Socialist orator, whose shabby-genteel home is described with some accuracy. But the most striking feature of the book is Mike's inability to wean himself from the atmosphere of school. He enters upon his job without any pretense of enthusiasm, and his main desire is not, as one might expect, to find a more interesting and useful job, but simply to be playing cricket. When he has to find himself lodgings he chooses to settle at Dulwich, because there he will be near a school and will be able to hear the agreeable sound of the ball striking against the bat. The climax of the book comes when Mike gets the chance to play in a county match and simply walks out of his job in order to do so. The point is that Wodehouse here sympathizes with Mike: indeed he identifies himself with him, for it is clear enough that Mike bears the same relation to Wodehouse as Julien Sorel to Stendhal. But he created many other heroes essentially similar. Through the books of this and the next period there passes a whole series of young men to whom playing games and "keeping fit" are a sufficient life work. Wodehouse is almost incapable of imagining a desirable job. The great thing is to have money of your own, or, failing that, to find a sinecure. The hero of *Something Fresh* (1915) escapes from low-class journalism by becoming physical-training instructor to a dyspeptic millionaire: this is regarded as a step up, morally as well as financially.

In the books of the third period there is no narcissism and no serious interludes, but the implied moral and social background has changed much less than might appear at first sight. If one compares Bertie Wooster with Mike, or even with the rugger-playing prefects of the earliest school stories, one sees that the only real difference between them is that Bertie is richer and lazier. His ideals would be almost the same as theirs, but he fails to live up to them. Archie Moffam, in *The Indiscretions of Archie* (1921), is a type intermediate between Bertie and the earlier heroes: he is an ass, but he is also honest, kind-hearted, athletic, and courageous. From first to last Wodehouse takes the public-school code of behavior for granted, with the difference that in his later, more sophisticated period he prefers to show his characters violating it or living up to it against their will:

> "Bertie! You wouldn't let down a pal?"
> "Yes, I would."
> "But we were at school together, Bertie."
> "I don't care."
> "The old school, Bertie, the old school!"
> "Oh, well—dash it!"

Bertie, a sluggish Don Quixote, has no wish to tilt at windmills, but he would hardly think of refusing to do so when honor calls. Most of the people whom Wodehouse intends as sympathetic characters are parasites, and some of them are plain imbeciles, but very few of them could be described as immoral. Even Ukridge is a visionary rather than a plain crook. The most immoral, or rather unmoral, of Wodehouse's characters is Jeeves, who acts as a foil to Bertie Wooster's comparative highmindedness and perhaps symbolizes the widespread English belief that intelligence and unscrupulousness are much the same thing. How closely Wodehouse sticks to conventional morality can be seen from the fact that nowhere in his books is there anything in the nature of a sex joke. This is an enormous sacrifice for a farcical writer to make. Not only are there no dirty jokes, but there are hardly any compromising situations: the horns-on-the-forehead motif is almost completely avoided. Most of the full-length books, of course, contain a "love interest," but it is always at the light-comedy level: the love affair, with its complications and its idyllic scenes, goes on and on, but, as the saying goes, "nothing happens." It is significant that Wodehouse, by nature a writer of farces, was able to collaborate more than once with Ian Hay, a serio-comic writer and an exponent (vide *Pip*, etc.) of the "clean-living Englishman" tradition at its silliest.

In *Something Fresh* Wodehouse had discovered the comic possibilities of the English aristocracy, and a succession of ridiculous but, save in a very few instances, not actually contemptible barons, earls, and what-not followed accordingly. This had the rather curious effect of causing Wodehouse to be regarded, outside England, as a penetrating satirist of English society. Hence Flannery's statement that Wodehouse "made fun of the English," which is the impression he would probably make on a German or even an American reader. Some time after the broadcasts from Berlin I was discussing them with a young Indian Nationalist who defended Wodehouse warmly.

He took it for granted that Wodehouse *had* gone over to the enemy, which from his own point of view was the right thing to do. But what interested me was to find that he regarded Wodehouse as an anti-British writer who had done useful work by showing up the British aristocracy in their true colors. This is a mistake that it would be very difficult for an English person to make, and is a good instance of the way in which books, especially humorous books, lose their finer nuances when they reach a foreign audience. For it is clear enough that Wodehouse is *not* anti-British, and not anti-upper class either. On the contrary, a harmless old-fashioned snobbishness is perceptible all through his work. Just as an intelligent Catholic is able to see that the blasphemies of Baudelaire or James Joyce are not seriously damaging to the Catholic faith, so an English reader can see that in creating such characters as Hildebrand Spencer Poyns de Burgh John Hanneyside Coombe-Crombie, 12th Earl of Dreever, Wodehouse is not really attacking the social hierarchy. Indeed, no one who genuinely despised titles would write of them so much. Wodehouse's attitude toward the English social system is the same as his attitude toward the public-school moral code—a mild facetiousness covering an unthinking acceptance. The Earl of Emsworth is funny because an earl ought to have more dignity, and Bertie Wooster's helpless dependence on Jeeves is funny partly because the servant ought not to be superior to the master. An American reader can mistake these two, and others like them, for hostile caricatures, because he is inclined to be Anglophobe already and they correspond to his preconceived ideas about a decadent aristocracy. Bertie Wooster, with his spats and his cane, is the traditional stage Englishman. But, as any English reader would see, Wodehouse intends him as a sympathetic figure, and Wodehouse's real sin has been to present the English upper classes as much nicer people than they are. All through his books certain problems are constantly avoided. Almost without exception his moneyed young men are unassuming, good mixers, not avaricious: their tone is set for them by Psmith, who retains his own upper-class exterior but bridges the social gap by addressing everyone as "Comrade."

But there is another important point about Bertie Wooster: his out-of-dateness. Conceived in 1917 or thereabouts, Bertie really belongs to an epoch earlier than that. He is the "knut" of the pre-1914 period, celebrated in such songs as "Gilbert the Filbert" or "Reckless Reggie of the Regent's Palace." The kind of life that Wodehouse writes about by preference, the life of the "clubman" or "man about town," the elegant young man who lounges all the morning in Piccadilly with a cane under his arm and a carnation in his buttonhole, barely survived into the nineteen-twenties. It is significant that Wodehouse could publish in 1936 a book entitled *Young Men in Spats*. For who was wearing spats at that date? They had gone out of fashion quite ten years earlier. But the traditional "knut," the "Piccadilly Johnny," *ought* to wear spats, just as the pantomime Chinese ought to wear a pigtail. A humorous writer is not obliged to keep up to date, and having struck one or two good veins, Wodehouse continued to exploit them with a regularity that was no doubt all the easier because he did not set foot in England during the sixteen years that preceded his internment. His picture of English society had been formed before 1914, and it was a naïve, traditional and, at bottom, admiring picture. Nor did he ever become genuinely Americanized. As I have pointed out, spontaneous Americanisms do occur in the books of the middle period, but Wodehouse remained English enough to find American slang an amusing and slightly shocking novelty. He loves to thrust a slang phrase or a crude fact in among Wardour Street English ("With a hollow groan Ukridge borrowed five shillings from me and went out into the night"), and expressions like "a piece of cheese" or "bust him on the noggin" lend themselves to this purpose. But the trick had been developed before he made any American contacts, and his use of garbled quotations is a common device of English writers running back to Fielding. As Mr. John Hayward has pointed out,* Wodehouse owes a good deal to his knowledge of English literature and especially of Shakespeare. His books are aimed, not, obviously, at a highbrow audience, but at an audience educated along traditional lines. When, for instance, he describes somebody as heaving "the kind of sigh that Prometheus might have heaved when the vulture dropped in for its lunch," he is assuming that his readers will know something of Greek mythology. In his early days the writers he admired were probably Barry Pain, Jerome K. Jerome, W. W. Jacobs, Kipling, and F. Anstey, and he has remained closer to them than to the quick-moving American comic writers such as Ring Lardner or Damon Runyon. In his radio interview with Flannery, Wodehouse wondered whether "the kind of people and the kind of England I write about will live after the war," not realizing that they were ghosts already. "He was still living in the period about which he wrote," says Flannery, meaning, probably, the nineteen-twenties. But the period was really the Edwardian age, and Bertie Wooster, if he ever existed, was killed round about 1915.

* *P. G. Wodehouse,* by John Hayward. (*The Saturday Book,* 1942.) I believe this is the only full-length critical essay on Wodehouse.

If my analysis of Wodehouse's mentality is accepted, the idea that in 1941 he consciously aided the Nazi propaganda machine becomes untenable and even ridiculous. He *may* have been induced to broadcast by the promise of an earlier release (he was due for release a few months later, on reaching his sixtieth birthday), but he cannot have realized that what he did would be damaging to British interests. As I have tried to show, his moral outlook has remained that of a public-school boy, and according to the public-school code, treachery in time of war is the most unforgivable of all the sins. But how could he fail to grasp that what he did would be a big propaganda score for the Germans and would bring down a torrent of disapproval on his own head? To answer this one must take two things into consideration. First, Wodehouse's complete lack—so far as one can judge from his printed works—of political awareness. It is nonsense to talk of "Fascist tendencies" in his books. There are no post-1918 tendencies at all. Throughout his work there is a certain uneasy awareness of the problem of class distinctions, and scattered through it at various dates there are ignorant though not unfriendly references to socialism. In *The Heart of a Goof* (1926) there is a rather silly story about a Russian novelist, which seems to have been inspired by the factional struggle then raging in the U.S.S.R. But the references in it to the Soviet system are entirely frivolous and, considering the date, not markedly hostile. That is about the extent of Wodehouse's political consciousness, so far as it is discoverable from his writings. Nowhere, so far as I know, does he so much as use the word "Fascism" or "Nazism." In left-wing circles, indeed in "enlightened" circles of any kind, to broadcast on the Nazi radio, to have any truck with the Nazis whatever, would have seemed just as shocking an action before the war as during it. But that is a habit of mind that had been developed during nearly a decade of ideological struggle against Fascism. The bulk of the British people, one ought to remember, remained anaesthetic to that struggle until late into 1940. Abyssinia, Spain, China, Austria, Czechoslovakia—the long series of crimes and aggressions had simply slid past their consciousness or were dimly noted as quarrels occurring among foreigners and "not our business." One can gauge the general ignorance from the fact that the ordinary Englishman thought of "Fascism" as an exclusively Italian thing and was bewildered when the same word was applied to Germany. And there is nothing in Wodehouse's writings to suggest that he was better informed, or more interested in politics, than the general run of his readers.

The other thing one must remember is that Wodehouse happened to be taken prisoner at just the moment when the war reached its desperate phase. We forget these things now, but until that time feelings about the war had been noticeably tepid. There was hardly any fighting, the Chamberlain Government was unpopular, eminent publicists were hinting that we should make a compromise peace as quickly as possible, trade union and Labor Party branches all over the country were passing anti-war resolutions. Afterward, of course, things changed. The Army was with difficulty extricated from Dunkirk, France collapsed, Britain was alone, the bombs rained on London, Goebbels announced that Britain was to be "reduced to degradation and poverty." By the middle of 1941 the British people knew what they were up against and feelings against the enemy were far fiercer than before. But Wodehouse had spent the intervening year in internment, and his captors seem to have treated him reasonably well. He had missed the turning-point of the war, and in 1941 he was still reacting in terms of 1939. He was not alone in this. On several occasions about this time the Germans brought captured British soldiers to the microphone, and some of them made remarks at least as tactless as Wodehouse's. They attracted no attention, however. And even an outright quisling like John Amery was afterward to arouse much less indignation than Wodehouse had done.

But why? Why should a few rather silly but harmless remarks by an elderly novelist have provoked such an outcry? One has to look for the probable answer amid the dirty requirements of propaganda warfare.

There is one point about the Wodehouse broadcasts that is almost certainly significant—the date. Wodehouse was released two or three days before the invasion of the U.S.S.R., and at a time when the higher ranks of the Nazi party must have known that the invasion was imminent. It was vitally necessary to keep America out of the war as long as possible, and in fact, about this time, the German attitude towards the U.S.A. did become more conciliatory than it had been before. The Germans could hardly hope to defeat Russia, Britain and the U.S.A. in combination, but if they could polish off Russia quickly—and presumably they expected to do so—the Americans might never intervene. The release of Wodehouse was only a minor move, but it was not a bad sop to throw to the American isolationists. He was well known in the United States, and he was—or so the Germans calculated—popular with the Anglophobe public as a caricaturist who made fun of the silly-ass Englishman with his spats and his monocle. At the microphone he could be trusted to damage British prestige in one way or another, while his release would demonstrate that the Germans were good fellows and knew how to treat their enemies chivalrously. That presumably was the calculation, though the fact that Wodehouse was only broadcasting for about a week suggests that he did not come up to expectations.

But on the British side similar though opposite calculations were at work. For the two years following Dunkirk, British morale depended largely upon the feeling that this was not only a war for democracy but a war which the common people had to win by their own efforts. The upper classes were discredited by their appeasement policy and by the disasters of 1940, and a social leveling process appeared to be taking place. Patriotism and left-wing sentiments were associated in the popular mind, and numerous able journalists were at work to tie the association tighter. Priestley's 1940 broadcasts, and "Cassandra's" articles in the *Daily Mirror*, were good examples of the demagogic propaganda flourishing at that time. In this atmosphere, Wodehouse made an ideal whipping boy. For it was generally felt that the rich were treacherous, and Wodehouse—as "Cassandra" vigorously pointed out in his broadcast—was a rich man. But he was the kind of rich man who could be attacked with impunity and without risking any damage to the structure of society. To denounce Wodehouse was not like denouncing, say, Beaverbrook. A mere novelist, however large his earnings may happen to be, is not *of* the possessing class. Even if his income touches £50,000 a year he has only the outward semblance of a millionaire. He is a lucky outsider who has fluked into a fortune—usually a very temporary fortune—like the winner of the Calcutta Derby Sweep. Consequently, Wodehouse's indiscretion gave a good propaganda opening. It was a chance to "expose" a wealthy parasite without drawing attention to any of the parasites who really mattered.

In the desperate circumstances of the time, it was excusable to be angry at what Wodehouse did, but to go on denouncing him three or four years later—and more, to let an impression remain that he acted with conscious treachery—is not excusable. Few things in this war have been more morally disgusting than the present hunt after traitors and quislings. At best it is largely the punishment of the guilty by the guilty. In France, all kinds of petty rats—police officials, penny-a-lining journalists, women who have slept with German soldiers—are hunted down while almost without exception the big rats escape. In England the fiercest tirades against quislings are uttered by Conservatives who were practicing appeasement in 1938 and Communists who were advocating it in 1940. I have striven to

show how the wretched Wodehouse—just because success and ex-
patriation had allowed him to remain mentally in the Edwardian
age—became the *corpus vile* in a propaganda experiment, and I
suggest that it is now time to regard the incident as closed. If Ezra
Pound is caught and shot by the American authorities, it will have
the effect of establishing his reputation as a poet for hundreds of
years; and even in the case of Wodehouse, if we drive him to retire
to the United States and renounce his British citizenship, we shall
end by being horribly ashamed of ourselves. Meanwhile, if we really
want to punish the people who weakened national morale at critical
moments, there are other culprits who are nearer home and better
worth chasing.

1945

△

Reflections on Gandhi

▽

Saints should always be judged guilty until they are proved innocent, but the tests that have to be applied to them are not, of
course, the same in all cases. In Gandhi's case the questions one feels
inclined to ask are: to what extent was Gandhi moved by vanity—
by the consciousness of himself as a humble, naked old man, sitting
on a praying mat and shaking empires by sheer spiritual power—
and to what extent did he compromise his own principles by entering politics, which of their nature are inseparable from coercion
and fraud? To give a definite answer one would have to study
Gandhi's acts and writings in immense detail, for his whole life was
a sort of pilgrimage in which every act was significant. But this partial autobiography,* which ends in the nineteen-twenties, is strong
evidence in his favor, all the more because it covers what he would
have called the unregenerate part of his life and reminds one that
inside the saint, or near-saint, there was a very shrewd, able person
who could, if he had chosen, have been a brilliant success as a
lawyer, an administrator, or perhaps even a businessman.

At about the time when the autobiography first appeared I remember reading its opening chapters in the ill-printed pages of

* *The Story of my Experiments with Truth.* By M. K. Gandhi. Translated
from the Gujarati by Mahadex Desai. Public Affairs Press.

some Indian newspaper. They made a good impression on me, which Gandhi himself at that time, did not. The things that one associated with him—home-spun cloth, "soul forces," and vegetarianism—were unappealing, and his medievalist program was obviously not viable in a backward, starving, overpopulated country. It was also apparent that the British were making use of him, or thought they were making use of him. Strictly speaking, as a Nationalist, he was an enemy, but since in every crisis he would exert himself to prevent violence —which, from the British point of view, meant preventing any effective action whatever—he could be regarded as "our man." In private this was sometimes cynically admitted. The attitude of the Indian millionaires was similar. Gandhi called upon them to repent, and naturally they preferred him to the Socialists and Communists who, given the chance, would actually have taken their money away. How reliable such calculations are in the long run is doubtful; as Gandhi himself says, "in the end deceivers deceive only themselves"; but at any rate the gentleness with which he was nearly always handled was due partly to the feeling that he was useful. The British Conservatives only became really angry with him when, as in 1942, he was in effect turning his non-violence against a different conqueror.

But I could see even then that the British officials who spoke of him with a mixture of amusement and disapproval also genuinely liked and admired him, after a fashion. Nobody ever suggested that he was corrupt, or ambitious in any vulgar way, or that anything he did was actuated by fear or malice. In judging a man like Gandhi one seems instinctively to apply high standards, so that some of his virtues have passed almost unnoticed. For instance, it is clear even from the autobiography that his natural physical courage was quite outstanding: the manner of his death was a later illustration of this, for a public man who attached any value to his own skin would have been more adequately guarded. Again, he seems to have been quite free from that maniacal suspiciousness which, as E. M. Forster rightly says in *A Passage to India,* is the besetting Indian vice, as hypocrisy is the British vice. Although no doubt he was shrewd enough in detecting dishonesty, he seems wherever possible to have believed that other people were acting in good faith and had a better nature through which they could be approached. And though he came of a poor middle-class family, started life rather unfavorably, and was probably of unimpressive physical appearance, he was not afflicted by envy or by the feeling of inferiority. Color feeling when he first met it in its worst form in South Africa, seems rather to have astonished him. Even when he was fighting what was in effect a color war, he did not think of people in terms of race or status. The governor of a province, a cotton millionaire, a half-starved Dravidian coolie, a British private soldier were all equally human beings, to be approached in much the same way. It is notice-able that even in the worst possible circumstances, as in South Africa when he was making himself unpopular as the champion of the Indian community, he did not lack European friends.

Written in short lengths for newspaper serialization, the auto-biography is not a literary masterpiece, but it is the more impres-sive because of the commonplaceness of much of its material. It is well to be reminded that Gandhi started out with the normal ambi-tions of a young Indian student and only adopted his extremist opinions by degrees and, in some cases, rather unwillingly. There was a time, it is interesting to learn, when he wore a top hat, took dancing lessons, studied French and Latin, went up the Eiffel Tower, and even tried to learn the violin—all this was the idea of assimilating European civilization as thoroughly as possible. He was not one of those saints who are marked out by their phenomenal piety from childhood onward, nor one of the other kind who forsake the world after sensational debaucheries. He makes full confession of the misdeeds of his youth, but in fact there is not much to con-fess. As a frontispiece to the book there is a photograph of Gandhi's possessions at the time of his death. The whole outfit could be purchased for about £5, and Gandhi's sins, at least his fleshly sins, would make the same sort of appearance if placed all in one heap. A few cigarettes, a few mouthfuls of meat, a few annas pilfered in childhood from the maidservant, two visits to a brothel (on each occasion he got away without "doing anything"), one narrowly escaped lapse with his landlady in Plymouth, one outburst of temper —that is about the whole collection. Almost from childhood onward he had a deep earnestness, an attitude ethical rather than religious, but, until he was about thirty, no very definite sense of direction. His first entry into anything describable as public life was made by way of vegetarianism. Underneath his less ordinary qualities one feels all the time the solid middle-class businessmen who were his ancestors. One feels that even after he had abandoned personal ambition he must have been a resourceful, energetic lawyer and a hardheaded political organizer, careful in keeping down expenses, an adroit handler of committees and an indefatigable chaser of sub-scriptions. His character was an extraordinarily mixed one, but there was almost nothing in it that you can put your finger on and call bad, and I believe that even Gandhi's worst enemies would admit that he was an interesting and unusual man who enriched the world simply by being alive. Whether he was also a lovable man, and whether his teachings can have much value for those who do not accept the religious beliefs on which they are founded, 1 have never felt fully certain.

Of late years it has been the fashion to talk about Gandhi as though he were not only sympathetic to the Western left-wing movement, but were integrally part of it. Anarchists and pacifists, in particular, have claimed him for their own, noticing only that he was opposed to centralism and State violence and ignoring the other-worldly, anti-humanist tendency of his doctrines. But one should, I think, realize that Gandhi's teachings cannot be squared with the belief that Man is the measure of all things and that our job is to make life worth living on this earth, which is the only earth we have. They make sense only on the assumption that God exists and that the world of solid objects is an illusion to be escaped from. It is worth considering the disciplines which Gandhi imposed on himself and which—though he might not insist on every one of his followers observing every detail—he considered indispensable if one wanted to serve either God or humanity. First of all, no meat-eating, and if possible no animal food in any form. (Gandhi himself, for the sake of his health, had to compromise on milk, but seems to have felt this to be a backsliding.) No alcohol or tobacco, and no spices or condiments even of a vegetable kind, since food should be taken not for its own sake but solely in order to preserve one's strength. Secondly, if possible, no sexual intercourse. If sexual intercourse must happen, then it should be for the sole purpose of begetting children and presumably at long intervals. Gandhi himself, in his middle thirties, took the vow of *brahmacharya*, which means not only complete chastity but the elimination of sexual desire. This condition, it seems, is difficult to attain without a special diet and frequent fasting. One of the dangers of milk-drinking is that it is apt to arouse sexual desire. And finally—this is the cardinal point— for the seeker after goodness there must be no close friendships and no exclusive loves whatever.

Close friendships, Gandhi says, are dangerous, because "friends react on one another" and through loyalty to a friend one can be led into wrong-doing. This is unquestionably true. Moreover, if one is to love God, or to love humanity as a whole, one cannot give one's preference to any individual person. This again is true, and it marks the point at which the humanistic and the religious attitude cease to be reconcilable. To an ordinary human being, love means nothing if it does not mean loving some people more than others. The autobiography leaves it uncertain whether Gandhi behaved in an inconsiderate way to his wife and children, but at any rate it makes clear that on three occasions he was willing to let his wife or a child die rather than administer the animal food prescribed by the doctor. It is true that the threatened death never actually occurred, and also that Gandhi—with, one gathers, a good deal of moral pressure in the opposite direction—always gave the patient the choice of staying alive at the price of committing a sin: still, if the decision had been solely his own, he would have forbidden the animal food, whatever the risks might be. There must, he says, be some limit to what we will do in order to remain alive, and the limit is well on this side of chicken broth. This attitude is perhaps a noble one, but, in the sense which—I think—most people would give to the word, it is inhuman. The essence of being human is that one does not seek perfection, that one *is* sometimes willing to commit sins for the sake of loyalty, that one does not push asceticism to the point where it makes friendly intercourse impossible, and that one is prepared in the end to be defeated and broken up by life, which is the inevitable price of fastening one's love upon other human individuals. No doubt alcohol, tobacco, and so forth, are things that a saint must avoid, but sainthood is also a thing that human beings must avoid. There is an obvious retort to this, but one should be wary about making it. In this yogi-ridden age, it is too readily assumed that "non-attachment" is not only better than a full acceptance of earthly life, but that the ordinary man only rejects it because it is too difficult: in other words, that the average human being is a failed saint. It is doubtful whether this is true. Many people genuinely do not wish to be saints, and it is probable that some who achieve or aspire to sainthood have never felt much temptation to be human beings. If one could follow it to its psychological roots, one would, I believe, find that the main motive for "non-attachment" is a desire to escape from the pain of living, and above all from love, which, sexual or non-sexual, is hard work. But it is not necessary here to argue whether the other-worldly or the humanistic ideal is "higher." The point is that they are incompatible. One must choose between God and Man, and all "radicals" and "progressives," from the mildest liberal to the most extreme anarchist, have in effect chosen Man.

However, Gandhi's pacifism can be separated to some extent from his other teachings. Its motive was religious, but he claimed also for it that it was a definite technique, a method, capable of producing desired political results. Gandhi's attitude was not that of most Western pacifists. *Satyagraha,* first evolved in South Africa, was a sort of non-violent warfare, a way of defeating the enemy without hurting him and without feeling or arousing hatred. It entailed such things as civil disobedience, strikes, lying down in front of railway trains, enduring police charges without running away and without hitting back, and the like. Gandhi objected to "passive resistance" as a translation of *Satyagraha:* in Gujarati, it seems, the word means "firmness in the truth." In his early days Gandhi served as a stretcher-bearer on the British side in the Boer War, and he was prepared to do the same again in the war of 1914-18. Even after he had completely abjured violence he was honest enough to see that in war it is usually necessary to take sides. He did not—indeed, since his whole political life centered round a struggle for national independence, he could not—take the sterile and dishonest line of pretending that in every war both sides are exactly the same and it makes no difference who wins. Nor did he, like most Western pacifists, specialize in avoiding awkward questions. In relation to the late war, one question that every pacifist had a clear obligation to answer was: "What about the Jews? Are you prepared to see them exterminated? If not, how do you propose to save them without resorting to war?" I must say that I have never heard, from any Western pacifist, an honest answer to this question, though I have heard plenty of evasions, usually of the "you're another" type. But it so happens that Gandhi was asked a somewhat similar question in 1938 and that his answer is on record in Mr. Louis Fischer's *Gandhi and Stalin*. According to Mr. Fischer, Gandhi's view was that the German Jews ought to commit collective suicide, which "would have aroused the world and the people of Germany to Hitler's violence." After the war he justified himself: the Jews had been killed anyway, and might as well have died significantly. One has the impression that this attitude staggered even so warm an admirer as Mr. Fischer, but Gandhi was merely being honest. If you are not prepared to take life, you must often be prepared for lives to be lost in some other way. When, in 1942, he urged non-violent resistance against a Japanese invasion, he was ready to admit that it might cost several million deaths.

At the same time there is reason to think that Gandhi, who after all was born in 1869, did not understand the nature of totalitarianism and saw everything in terms of his own struggle against the British government. The important point here is not so much that the British treated him forbearingly as that he was always able to command publicity. As can be seen from the phrase quoted above, he believed in "arousing the world," which is only possible if the world gets a chance to hear what you are doing. It is difficult to see how Gandhi's methods could be applied in a country where opponents of the régime disappear in the middle of the night and are never heard of again. Without a free press and the right of assembly, it is impossible not merely to appeal to outside opinion, but to bring a mass movement into being, or even to make your intentions known to your adversary. Is there a Gandhi in Russia at this moment? And if there is, what is he accomplishing? The Russian masses could only practice civil disobedience if the same idea happened to occur to all of them simultaneously, and even then, to judge by the history of the Ukraine famine, it would make no difference. But let it be granted that non-violent resistance can be effective against one's own government, or against an occupying power: even so, how does one put it into practice internationally? Gandhi's various conflicting statements on the late war seem to show that he felt the difficulty of this. Applied to foreign politics, pacifism either stops being pacifist or becomes appeasement. Moreover the assumption, which served Gandhi so well in dealing with individuals, that all human beings are more or less approachable and will respond to a generous gesture, needs to be seriously questioned. It is not necessarily true, for example, when you are dealing with lunatics. Then the question becomes: Who is sane? Was Hitler sane? And is it not possible for one whole culture to be insane by the standards of another? And, so far as one can gauge the feelings of whole nations, is there any apparent connection between a generous deed and a friendly response? Is gratitude a factor in international politics?

These and kindred questions need discussion, and need it urgently, in the few years left to us before somebody presses the button and the rockets begin to fly. It seems doubtful whether civilization can stand another major war, and it is at least thinkable that the way out lies through non-violence. It is Gandhi's virtue that he would have been ready to give honest consideration to the kind of question that I have raised above; and, indeed, he probably did discuss most of these questions somewhere or other in his innumerable newspaper articles. One feels of him that there was much that he did not understand, but not that there was anything that he was frightened of saying or thinking. I have never been able to feel much liking for Gandhi, but I do not feel sure that as a political thinker he was wrong in the main, nor do I believe that his life was a failure. It is curious that when he was assassinated, many of his warmest admirers exclaimed sorrowfully that he had lived just long enough to see his life work in ruins, because India was engaged in a civil war which had always been foreseen as one of the by-products of the transfer of power. But it was not in trying to smooth down Hindu-Moslem rivalry that Gandhi had spent his life. His main political objective, the peaceful ending of British rule, had after all been attained. As usual the relevant facts cut across one another. On the other hand, the British did get out of India without fighting, an event which very few observers indeed would have predicted until about a year before it happened. On the other hand, this was done by a Labor government, and it is certain that a Conservative government, especially a government headed by Churchill, would have acted differently. But if, by 1945, there had grown up in Britain a large body of opinion sympathetic to Indian independence, how far was this due to Gandhi's personal influence? And if, as may happen, India and Britain finally settle down into a decent and friendly relationship, will this be partly because Gandhi, by keeping up his struggle obstinately and without hatred, disinfected the political air? That one even thinks of asking such questions indicates his stature. One may feel, as I do, a sort of aesthetic distaste for Gandhi, one may reject the claims of sainthood made on his behalf (he never made any such claim himself, by the way), one may also reject sainthood as an ideal and therefore feel that Gandhi's basic aims were anti-human and reactionary: but regarded simply as a politician, and compared with the other leading political figures of our time, how clean a smell he has managed to leave behind!

1949

△

Second Thoughts on James Burnham

▽

James Burnham's book, *The Managerial Revolution,* made a considerable stir both in the United States and in England at the time when it was published, and its main thesis has been so much discussed that a detailed exposition of it is hardly necessary. As shortly as I can summarize it, the thesis is this:

Capitalism is disappearing, but socialism is not replacing it. What is now arising is a new kind of planned, centralized society which will be neither capitalist nor, in any accepted sense of the word, democratic. The rulers of this new society will be the people who effectively control the means of production: that is, business executives, technicians, bureaucrats, and soldiers, lumped together by Burnham under the name of "managers." These people will eliminate the old capitalistic class, crush the working class, and so organize society that all power and economic privilege remain in their own hands. Private property rights will be abolished, but common ownership will not be established. The new "managerial" societies will not consist of a patchwork of small, independent states, but of great super-states grouped round the main industrial centers in Europe, Asia, and America. These super-states will fight among themselves for possession of the remaining uncaptured portions of the earth, but will probably be unable to conquer one another completely. Internally, each society will be hierarchical, with an aristocracy of talent at the top and a mass of semi-slaves at the bottom.

In his next published book, *The Machiavellians,* Burnham elaborates and also modifies his original statement. The greater part of the book is an exposition of the theories of Machiavelli and of his modern disciples, Mosca, Michels, and Pareto: with doubtful justification, Burnham adds to these the syndicalist writer, Georges Sorel. What Burnham is mainly concerned to show is that a democratic society has never existed and, so far as we can see, never will exist. Society is of its nature oligarchical, and the power of the oligarchy always rests upon force and fraud. Burnham does not deny that "good" motives may operate in private life, but he maintains that politics consists of the struggle for power, and nothing else. All historical changes finally boil down to the replacement of one ruling class by another. All talk about democracy, liberty, equality, fraternity, all revolutionary movements, all visions of Utopia, or "the classless society," or "the Kingdom of Heaven on Earth," are humbug (not necessarily conscious humbug) covering the ambitions of some new class which is elbowing its way into power. The English Puritans, the Jacobins, the Bolsheviks, were in each case simply power-seekers using the hopes of the masses in order to win a privileged position for themselves. Power can sometimes be won or maintained without violence, but never without fraud, because it is necessary to make use of the masses, and the masses would not co-operate if they knew that they were simply serving the purposes of a minority. In each great revolutionary struggle the masses are led on by vague dreams of human brotherhood, and then, when the new ruling class is well established in power, they are thrust back into servitude. This is practically the whole of political history, as Burnham sees it.

Where the second book departs from the earlier one is in asserting that the whole process could be somewhat moralized if the facts were faced more honestly. *The Machiavellians* is sub-titled "Defenders of Freedom." Machiavelli and his followers taught that in politics decency simply does not exist and, by doing so, Burnham claims, made it possible to conduct political affairs more intelligently and less oppressively. A ruling class which recognized that its real aim was to stay in power would also recognize that it would be more likely to succeed if it served the common good, and might avoid stiffening into a hereditary aristocracy. Burnham lays much stress on Pareto's theory of the "circulation of the élites." If it is to stay in power a ruling class must constantly admit suitable recruits from below, so that the ablest men may always be at the top and a new class of power-hungry malcontents cannot come into being. This is likeliest to happen, Burnham considers, in a society which retains democratic habits—that is, where opposition is permitted and certain bodies such as the press and the trade unions can keep their autonomy. Here Burnham undoubtedly contradicts his earlier opinion. In *The Managerial Revolution,* which was written in 1940, it is taken as a matter of course that "managerial" Germany is in all ways more efficient than a capitalist democracy such as France or Britain. In the second book, written in 1942, Burnham admits that the Germans might have avoided some of their more serious strategic errors if they had permitted freedom of speech. However, the main thesis is not abandoned. Capitalism is doomed, and socialism is a dream. If we grasp what is at issue we may guide the course of the managerial revolution to some extent, but that revolution is *happening*, whether we like it or not. In both books, but especially the earlier one, there is a note of unmistakable relish over the cruelty and wickedness of the processes that are being discussed. Although he reiterates that he is merely setting forth the facts and not stating his own preferences, it is clear that Burnham is fascinated by the spectacle of power, and that his sympathies were with Germany so long as Germany appeared to be winning the war. A more recent essay, "Lenin's Heir," published in the *Partisan Review* about the beginning of 1945, suggests that this sympathy has since been transferred to the U.S.S.R. "Lenin's Heir" provoked violent controversy in the American left-wing press; I must return to it later.

It will be seen that Burnham's theory is not, strictly speaking, a new one. Many earlier writers have foreseen the emergence of a new kind of society, neither capitalist nor socialist, and probably based upon slavery: though most of them have differed from Burnham in not assuming this development to be *inevitable*. A good example is Hilaire Belloc's book, *The Servile State*, published in 1911. *The Servile State* is written in a tiresome style, and the remedy it suggests (a return to small-scale peasant ownership) is for many reasons impossible: still, it does foretell with remarkable insight the kind of things that have been happening from about 1930 onwards. Chesterton, in a less methodical way, predicted the disappearance of democracy and private property, and the rise of a slave society which might be called either capitalist or Communist. Jack London, in *The Iron Heel* (1909), foretold some of the essential features of Fascism, and such books as Wells's *The Sleeper Awakes* (1900), Zamyatin's *We* (1923), and Aldous Huxley's *Brave New World* (1930), all described imaginary worlds in which the special problems of capitalism had been solved without bringing liberty, equality, or true happiness any nearer. More recently, writers like Peter Drucker and F. A. Voigt have argued that Fascism and Communism are substantially the same thing. And indeed, it has always been obvious that a planned and centralized society is liable to develop into an oligarchy or a dictatorship. Orthodox conservatives were unable to see this, because it comforted them to assume that socialism "wouldn't work," and that the disappearance of capitalism would mean chaos and anarchy. Orthodox socialists could not see it, because they wished to think that they themselves would soon be in power, and therefore assumed that when capitalism disappears, socialism takes its place. As a result they were unable to foresee the rise of Fascism, or to make correct predictions about it after it had appeared. Later, the need to justify the Russian dictatorship and to explain away the obvious resemblances between Communism and Nazism clouded the issue still more. But the notion that industrialism must end in monopoly and that monopoly must imply tyranny is not a startling one.

Where Burnham differs from most other thinkers is in trying to plot the course of the "managerial revolution" accurately on a world scale, and in assuming that the drift toward totalitarianism is irresistible and must not be fought against, though it may be guided. According to Burnham, writing in 1940, "managerialism" has reached its fullest development in the U.S.S.R. but is almost equally well developed in Germany, and has made its appearance in the United States. He describes the New Deal as "primitive managerialism." But the trend is the same everywhere, or almost everywhere. Always *laissez-faire* capitalism gives way to planning and state interference, the mere *owner* loses power as against the technician and the bureaucrat, but socialism—that is to say, what used to be called socialism—shows no sign of emerging:

> Some apologists try to excuse Marxism by saying that it has "never had a chance." This is far from the truth. Marxism and the Marxist parties have had dozens of chances. In *Russia* a Marxist party took power. Within a short time it abandoned Socialism; if not in words, at any rate in the effect of its actions. In most European nations there were during the last months of the first world war and the years immediately thereafter, social crises which left a wide-open door for the Marxist parties: without exception they proved unable to take and hold power. In a large number of countries—*Germany, Denmark, Norway, Sweden, Austria, England, Australia, New Zealand, Spain, France*—the reformist Marxist parties have administered the governments, and have uniformly failed to introduce Socialism or make any genuine step towards Socialism. . . . These parties have, in practice, at every historical test—and there have been many—either failed Socialism or abandoned it. This is the fact which neither the bitterest foe nor the most ardent friend of Socialism can erase. This fact does not, as some think, prove anything about the moral quality of the Socialist ideal. But it does constitute unblinkable evidence that, whatever its moral quality, Socialism is not going to come.

Burnham does not, of course, deny that the new "managerial" régimes, like the régimes of Russia and Nazi Germany, may be *called* Socialist. He means merely that they will not *be* socialist in any sense of the word which would have been accepted by Marx, or Lenin, or Keir Hardie, or William Morris, or indeed, by any representative socialist prior to about 1930. Socialism, until recently, was supposed to connote political democracy, social equality, and internationalism. There is not the smallest sign that any of these things is in a way to being established anywhere, and the one great country in which something described as a proletarian revolution once happened, i.e. the U.S.S.R., has moved steadily away from the old concept of a free and equal society aiming at universal human brotherhood. In an almost unbroken progress since the early days of the Revolution, liberty has been chipped away and representative institutions smothered, while inequalities have increased and nationalism and militarism have grown stronger. But at the same time, Burnham insists, there has been no tendency to return to capitalism. What is happening is simply the growth of "managerialism," which, according to Burnham, is in progress everywhere, though the manner in which it comes about may vary from country to country.

Now, as an interpretation of what *is happening*, Burnham's theory is extremely plausible, to put it at the lowest. The events of, at any rate, the last fifteen years in the U.S.S.R. can be far more easily explained by this theory than by any other. Evidently the U.S.S.R. is not socialist, and can only be called socialist if one gives the word a meaning different from what it would have in any other context. On the other hand, prophecies that the Russian régime would revert to capitalism have always been falsified, and now seem further than ever from being fulfilled. In claiming that the process had gone almost equally far in Nazi Germany Burnham probably exaggerates, but it seems certain that the drift was away from old-style capitalism and toward a planned economy with an adoptive oligarchy in control. In Russia the capitalists were destroyed first and the workers were crushed later. In Germany the workers were crushed first, but the elimination of the capitalists had at any rate begun, and calculations based on the assumption that Nazism was "simply capitalism" were always contradicted by events. Where Burnham seems to go most astray is in believing "managerialism" to be on the up-grade in the United States, the one great country where free capitalism is still vigorous. But if one considers the world movement as a whole, his conclusions are difficult to resist; and even in the United States the all-prevailing faith in *laissez faire* may not survive the next great economic crisis. It has been urged against Burnham that he assigns far too much importance to the "managers," in the narrow sense of the word—that is, factory bosses, planners, and technicians—and seems to assume that even in Soviet Russia it is these people, and not the Communist Party chiefs, who are the real holders of power. However, this is a secondary error, and it is partially corrected in *The Machiavellians*. The real question is not whether the people who wipe their boots on us during the next fifty years are to be called managers, bureaucrats, or politicians: the question is whether capitalism, now obviously doomed, is to give way to oligarchy or to true democracy.

But curiously enough, when one examines the predictions which Burnham has based on his general theory, one finds that in so far as they are verifiable, they have been falsified. Numbers of people have pointed this out already. However, it is worth following up Burnham's predictions in detail, because they form a sort of pattern which is related to contemporary events, and which reveals, I believe, a very important weakness in present-day political thought.

To begin with, writing in 1940, Burnham takes a German victory more or less for granted. Britain is described as "dissolving," and as displaying "all the characteristics which have distinguished decadent cultures in past historical transitions," while the conquest and integration of Europe which Germany achieved in 1940 is described as "irreversible." "England," writes Burnham, "no matter with what non-European allies, cannot conceivably hope to conquer the European continent." Even if Germany should somehow manage to lose the war, she could not be dismembered or reduced to the status of the Weimar Republic, but is bound to remain as the nucleus of a unified Europe. The future map of the world with its three great super-states is, in any case, already settled in its main outlines: and "the nuclei of these great super-states are, whatever may be their future names, the previously existing nations, Japan, Germany, and the United States."

Burnham also commits himself to the opinion that Germany will not attack the U.S.S.R. until after Britain has been defeated. In a condensation of his book published in the *Partisan Review* of May-June, 1941, and presumably written later than the book itself, he says:

> As in the case of *Russia*, so with *Germany*, the third part of the managerial problem—the contest for dominance with other sections of managerial society—remains for the future. First had to come the death blow that assured the toppling of the capitalist world order, which meant above all the destruction of the foundations of the *British Empire* (the keystone of the capitalist world order) both directly and through the smashing of the European political structure, which was a necessary prop of the Empire. This is the basic explanation of the Nazi-Soviet Pact, which is not intelligible on other grounds. The future conflict between *Germany* and *Russia* will be a managerial conflict proper; prior to the great world managerial battles, the end of the capitalist order must be assured. The belief that Nazism is "decadent capitalism" . . . makes it impossible to explain reasonably the Nazi-Soviet Pact. From this belief followed the always expected war between *Germany* and *Russia*, not the actual war to the death between *Germany* and the *British Empire*. The war between *Germany* and *Russia* is one of the managerial wars of the future, not of the anti-capitalist wars of yesterday and today.

However, the attack on Russia will come later, and Russia is certain, or almost certain, to be defeated. "There is every reason to believe . . . that Russia will split apart, with the western half gravitating towards the European base and the eastern towards the Asiatic." This quotation comes from *The Managerial Revolution*. In the above-quoted article, written probably about six months later, it is put more forcibly: "The Russian weaknesses indicate that Russia will not be able to endure, that it will crack apart, and fall toward east and west." And in a supplementary note which

was added to the English (Pelican) edition, and which appears to
have been written at the end of 1941, Burnham speaks as though
the "cracking apart" process were already happening. The war, he
says, "is part of the means whereby the western half of Russia is
being integrated into the European super-state."

Sorting these various statements out, we have the following prophecies:

1. Germany is bound to win the war.
2. Germany and Japan are bound to survive as great states, and
to remain the nuclei of power in their respective areas.
3. Germany will not attack the U.S.S.R. until after the defeat of
Britain.
4. The U.S.S.R. is bound to be defeated.

However, Burnham has made other predictions besides these. In
a short article in the *Partisan Review,* in the summer of 1944, he
gives his opinion that the U.S.S.R. will gang up with Japan in
order to prevent the total defeat of the latter, while the American
Communists will be set to work to sabotage the eastern end of the
war. And finally, in an article in the same magazine in the winter
of 1944-45, he claims that Russia, destined so short a while ago to
"crack apart," is within sight of conquering the whole of Eurasia.
This article was the cause of violent controversies among the American intelligentsia. I must give some account of it here, because its
manner of approach and its emotional tone are of a peculiar kind,
and by studying them one can get nearer to the real roots of Burnham's theory.

The article is entitled "Lenin's Heir," and it sets out to show
that Stalin is the true and legitimate guardian of the Russian Revolution, which he has not in any sense "betrayed" but has merely
carried forward on lines that were implicit in it from the start. In
itself, this is an easier opinion to swallow than the usual Trotskyist
claim that Stalin is a mere crook who has perverted the Revolution to his own ends, and that things would somehow have been
different if Lenin had lived or Trotsky had remained in power.
Actually there is no strong reason for thinking that the main lines
of development would have been very different. Well before 1923
the seeds of a totalitarian society were quite plainly there. Lenin,
indeed, is one of those politicians who win an undeserved reputation by dying prematurely.* Had he lived, it is probable that he

* It is difficult to think of any politician who has lived to be eighty and still
been regarded as a success. What we call a "great" statesman normally means
one who dies before his policy has had time to take effect. If Cromwell had

would either have been thrown out, like Trotsky, or would have kept himself in power by methods as barbarous, or nearly as barbarous, as those of Stalin. The *title* of Burnham's essay, therefore, sets forth a reasonable thesis, and one would expect him to support it by an appeal to the facts.

However, the essay barely touches upon its ostensible subject matter. It is obvious that anyone genuinely concerned to show that there has been continuity of policy as between Lenin and Stalin, would start by outlining Lenin's policy and then explain in what way Stalin's has resembled it. Burnham does not do this. Except for one or two cursory sentences he says nothing about Lenin's policy, and Lenin's name only occurs five times in an essay of twelve pages: in the first seven pages, apart from the title, it does not occur at all. The real aim of the essay is to present Stalin as a towering superhuman figure, indeed a species of demigod, and Bolshevism as an irresistible force which is flowing over the earth and cannot be halted until it reaches the outermost borders of Eurasia. In so far as he makes any attempt to prove his case, Burnham does so by repeating over and over again that Stalin is "a great man"—which is probably true, but is almost completely irrelevant. Moreover, though he does advance some solid arguments for believing in Stalin's genius, it is clear that in his mind the idea of "greatness" is inextricably mixed up with the idea of cruelty and dishonesty. There are curious passages in which it seems to be suggested that Stalin is to be admired *because* of the limitless suffering that he has caused:

Stalin proves himself a "great man," in the grand style. The accounts of the banquets, staged in Moscow for the visiting dignitaries, set the symbolic tone. With their enormous menus of sturgeon, and roasts, and fowl, and sweets; their streams of liquor; the scores of toasts with which they end; the silent, unmoving secret police behind each guest; all against the winter background of the starving multitudes of besieged *Leningrad;* the dying millions at the front; the jammed concentration camps; the city crowds kept by their minute rations just at the edge of life; there is little trace of dull mediocrity or the hand of *Babbitt*. We recognize, rather, the tradition of the most spectacular of the Tsars, of the Great Kings of the Medes and Persians, of the Khanate of the Golden Horde, of the banquet we assign to the gods of the Heroic Ages in tribute to the insight that insolence, and indifference, and brutality on such a scale remove be-

---

lived a few years longer he would probably have fallen from power, in which case we should now regard him as a failure. If Pétain had died in 1930, France would have venerated him as a hero and patriot. Napoleon remarked once that if only a cannon ball had happened to hit him when he was riding into Moscow, he would have gone down to history as the greatest man who ever lived.

ings from the human level. . . . *Stalin's* political techniques show a free-dom from conventional restrictions that is incompatible with mediocrity: the mediocre man is custom-bound. Often it is the scale of his operations that sets them apart. It is usual, for example, for men active in practical life to engineer an occasional frame-up. But to carry out a frame-up against tens of thousands of persons, important percentages of whole strata of so-ciety, including most of one's own comrades, is so far out of the ordinary that the long-run mass conclusion is either that the frame-up must be true —at least "have some truth in it"—or that power so immense must be sub-mitted to—is an "historical necessity," as intellectuals put it. . . . There is nothing unexpected in letting a few individuals starve for reasons of state; but to starve, by deliberate decision, several millions is a type of action attributed ordinarily only to gods.

In these and other similar passages there may be a tinge of irony, but it is difficult not to feel that there is also a sort of fascinated admiration. Toward the end of the essay Burnham compares Stalin with those semi-mythical heroes, like Moses or Asoka, who embody in themselves a whole epoch, and can justly be credited with feats that they did not actually perform. In writing of Soviet foreign policy and its supposed objectives, he touches an even more mys-tical note:

Starting from the magnetic core of the Eurasian heartland, the Soviet power, like the reality of the One of Neo-Platonism overflowing in the descending series of the emanative progression, flows outward, west into Europe, south into the Near East, east into China, already lapping the shores of the Atlantic, the Yellow and China Seas, the Mediterranean, and the Persian Gulf. As the undifferentiated One, in its progression, descends through the stages of Mind, Soul, and Matter, and then through its fatal Return back to itself; so does the Soviet power, emanating from the in-tegrally totalitarian center, proceed outwards by Absorption (the Baltics, Bessarabia, Bukovina, East Poland), Domination (Finland, the Balkans, Mongolia, North China and, tomorrow, Germany), Orienting Influence (Italy, France, Turkey, Iran, Central and South China . . .), until it is dissipated in MHON, the outer material sphere, beyond the Eurasian boundaries, of momentary Appeasement and Infiltration (England, the United States).

I do not think it is fanciful to suggest that the unnecessary cap-ital letters with which this passage is loaded are intended to have a hypnotic effect on the reader. Burnham is trying to build up a picture of terrifying, irresistible power, and to turn a normal po-litical maneuver like infiltration into Infiltration adds to the gen-eral portentousness. The essay should be read in full. Although it is not the kind of tribute that the average Russophile would con-sider acceptable, and although Burnham himself would probably claim that he is being strictly objective, he is in effect performing an act of homage, and even of self-abasement. Meanwhile, this essay gives us another prophecy to add to the list: i.e. that the U.S.S.R. will conquer the whole of Eurasia, and probably a great deal more. And one must remember that Burnham's basic theory contains in itself a prediction which still has to be tested—that is, that whatever else happens, the "managerial" form of society is bound to prevail.

Burnham's earlier prophecy, of a German victory in the war and the integration of Europe round the German nucleus, was falsified, not only in its main outlines, but in some important details. Burnham insists all the way through that "managerialism" is not only more efficient than capitalist democracy or Marxian socialism, but also more acceptable to the masses. The slogans of democracy and national self-determination, he says, no longer have any mass appeal: "managerialism," on the other hand, can rouse enthusiasm, produce intelligible war aims, establish fifth columns everywhere, and inspire its soldiers with a fanatical morale. The "fanaticism" of the Germans, as against the "apathy" or "indifference" of the British, French, etc., is much emphasized, and Nazism is represented as a revolutionary force sweeping across Europe and spreading its philosophy "by contagion." The Nazi fifth columns "cannot be wiped out," and the democratic nations are quite incapable of projecting any settlement which the German or other European masses would prefer to the New Order. In any case, the democracies can only defeat Germany if they go "still further along the managerial road than Germany has yet gone."

The germ of truth in all this is that the smaller European states, demoralized by the chaos and stagnation of the pre-war years, collapsed rather more quickly than they need have done, and might conceivably have accepted the New Order if the Germans had kept some of their promises. But the actual experience of German rule aroused almost at once such a fury of hatred and vindictiveness as the world has seldom seen. After about the beginning of 1941 there was hardly any need of a positive war aim, since getting rid of the Germans was a sufficient objective. The question of morale, and its relation to national solidarity, is a nebulous one, and the evidence can be so manipulated as to prove almost anything. But if one goes by the proportion of prisoners to other casualties, and the amount of quislingism, the totalitarian states come out of the comparison worse than the democracies. Hundreds of thousands of Russians appear to have gone over to the Germans during the course of the war, while comparable numbers of Germans and Italians

had gone over to the Allies before the war started: the corresponding number of American or British renegades would have amounted
to a few scores. As an example of the inability of "capitalist ideol-
ogies" to enlist support, Burnham cites, "the complete failure of
voluntary military recruiting in England [as well as the entire
British Empire] and in the United States." One would gather from
this that the armies of the totalitarian states were manned by volunteers. Actually, no totalitarian state has ever so much as considered voluntary recruitment for any purpose, nor, throughout history, has a large army ever been raised by voluntary means.* It is
not worth listing the many similar arguments that Burnham puts
forward. The point is that he assumes that the Germans must win
the propaganda war as well as the military one, and that, at any
rate in Europe, this estimate was not borne out by events.

It will be seen that Burnham's predictions have not merely, when
they were verifiable, turned out to be wrong, but that they have
sometimes contradicted one another in a sensational way. It is this
last fact that is significant. Political predictions are usually wrong,
because they are usually based on wish-thinking, but they can have
symptomatic value, especially when they change abruptly. Often the
revealing factor is the date at which they are made. Dating Burnham's various writings as accurately as can be done from internal
evidence, and then noting what events they coincided with, we
find the following relationships:

In *The Managerial Revolution* Burnham prophesies a German
victory, postponement of the Russo-German war until after Britain
is defeated, and, subsequently, the defeat of Russia. The book, or
much of it, was written in the second half of 1940—i.e. at a time
when the Germans had overrun Western Europe and were bombing Britain, and the Russians were collaborating with them fairly
closely, and in what appeared, at any rate, to be a spirit of appeasement.

In the supplementary note added to the English edition of the
book, Burnham appears to assume that the U.S.S.R. is already
beaten and the splitting-up process is about to begin. This was
published in the spring of 1942 and presumably written at the end
of 1941; i.e. when the Germans were in the suburbs of Moscow.

---

* Great Britain raised a million volunteers in the earlier part of the 1914-18
war. This must be a world's record, but the pressures applied were such that
it is doubtful whether the recruitment ought to be described as voluntary. Even
the most "ideological" wars have been fought largely by pressed men. In the
English civil war, the Napoleonic wars, the American civil war, the Spanish
civil war, etc., both sides resorted to conscription or the press gang.

The prediction that Russia would gang up with Japan against the U.S.A. was written early in 1944, soon after the conclusion of a new Russo-Japanese treaty.

The prophecy of Russian world conquest was written in the winter of 1944, when the Russians were advancing rapidly in Eastern Europe while the Western Allies were still held up in Italy and northern France.

It will be seen that at each point Burnham is predicting *a continuation of the thing that is happening*. Now the tendency to do this is not simply a bad habit, like inaccuracy or exaggeration, which one can correct by taking thought. It is a major mental disease, and its roots lie partly in cowardice and partly in the worship of power, which is not fully separable from cowardice.

Suppose in 1940 you had taken a Gallup poll, in England, on the question, "Will Germany win the war?" You would have found, curiously enough, that the group answering "Yes" contained a far higher percentage of intelligent people—people with I.Q.s of over 120, shall we say—than the group answering "No." The same would have held good in the middle of 1942. In this case the figures would not have been so striking but if you had made the question, "Will the Germans capture Alexandria?" or "Will the Japanese be able to hold on to the territories they have captured?" then once again there would have been a very marked tendency for intelligence to concentrate in the "Yes" group. In every case the less gifted person would have been likelier to give a right answer.

If one went simply by these instances, one might assume that high intelligence and bad military judgment always go together. However, it is not so simple as that. The English intelligentsia, on the whole, were more defeatist than the mass of the people—and some of them went on being defeatist at a time when the war was quite plainly won—partly because they were better able to visualize the dreary years of warfare that lay ahead. Their morale was worse because their imaginations were stronger. The quickest way of ending a war is to lose it, and if one finds the prospect of a long war intolerable, it is natural to disbelieve in the possibility of victory. But there was more to it than that. There was also the disaffection of large numbers of intellectuals which made it difficult for them not to side with any country hostile to Britain. And the deepest of all, there was admiration—though only in a very few cases conscious admiration—for the power, energy, and cruelty of the Nazi régime. It would be a useful though tedious labor to go through the left-wing press and enumerate all the hostile references to Nazism during the years 1935-45. One would find, I have little doubt, that they reached their high-water mark in 1937-8 and 1944-5, and dropped off noticeably in the years 1939-42—that is, during the period when Germany seemed to be winning. One would find, also, the same people advocating a compromise peace in 1940 and approving the dismemberment of Germany in 1945. And if one studied the reactions of the English intelligentsia towards the U.S.S.R., there, too, one would find genuinely progressive impulses mixed up with admiration for power and cruelty. It would be grossly unfair to suggest that power-worship is the only motive for Russophile feeling, but it is one motive, and among intellectuals it is probably the strongest one.

Power-worship blurs political judgment because it leads, almost unavoidably, to the belief that present trends will continue. Whoever is winning at the moment will always seem to be invincible. If the Japanese have conquered South Asia, then they will keep South Asia for ever; if the Germans have captured Tobruk, they will infallibly capture Cairo; if the Russians are in Berlin, it will not be long before they are in London: and so on. This habit of mind leads also to the belief that things will happen more quickly, completely, and catastrophically than they ever do in practice. The rise and fall of empires, the disappearance of cultures and religions, are expected to happen with earthquake suddenness, and processes which have barely started are talked about as though they were already at an end. Burnham's writings are full of apocalyptic visions. Nations, governments, classes, and social systems are constantly described as expanding, contracting, decaying, dissolving, toppling, crashing, crumbling, crystallizing and, in general, behaving in an unstable and melodramatic way. The slowness of historical change, the fact that any epoch always contains a great deal of the last epoch, is never sufficiently allowed for. Such a manner of thinking is bound to lead to mistaken prophecies, because, even when it gauges the direction of events rightly, it will miscalculate their tempo. Within the space of five years Burnham foretold the domination of Russia by Germany and of Germany by Russia. In each case he was obeying the same instinct: the instinct to bow down before the conqueror of the moment, to accept the existing trend as irreversible. With this in mind one can criticize his theory in a broader way.

The mistakes I have pointed out do not disprove Burnham's theory, but they do cast light on his probable reasons for holding it. In this connection one cannot leave out of account the fact that Burnham is an American. Every political theory has a certain regional tinge about it, and every nation, every culture, has its own characteristic prejudices and patches of ignorance. There are certain problems that must almost inevitably be seen in a different perspective according to the geographical situation from which one is looking at them. Now, the attitude that Burnham adopts, of classifying Communism and Fascism as much the same thing, and at the same time accepting both of them—or, at any rate, not assuming that either must be violently struggled against—is essentially an American attitude, and would be almost impossible for an Englishman or any other western European. English writers who consider Communism and Fascism to be *the same thing*, invariably hold that both are monstrous evils which must be fought to the death: on the other hand, any Englishman who believes Communism and Fascism to be opposites will feel that he ought to side with one or the other.* The reason for this difference of outlook is simple enough and, as usual, is bound up with wish-thinking. If totalitarianism triumphs and the dreams of the geopoliticians come true, Britain will disappear as a world power and the whole of western Europe will be swallowed by some single great state. This is not a prospect that it is easy for an Englishman to contemplate with detachment. Either he does not want Britain to disappear—in which case he will tend to construct theories proving the thing that he wants—or like a minority of intellectuals, he will decide that his country is finished and transfer his allegiance to some foreign power. An American does not have to make the same choice. Whatever happens, the United States will survive as a great power, and from the American point of view it does not make much difference whether Europe is dominated by Russia or by Germany. Most Americans who think of the matter at all would prefer to see the world divided between two or three monster states which had reached their natural boundaries and could bargain with one another on economic issues without being troubled by ideological differences. Such a world picture fits in with the American tendency to admire size for its own sake and to feel that success constitutes justification, and it fits in with the all-prevailing anti-British sentiment. In practice, Britain and the United States have twice been forced into alliance against Germany, and will probably, before long, be forced into alliance against Russia: but, subjectively, a majority of Americans would prefer either Russia or

* The only exception I am able to think of is Bernard Shaw, who, for some years at any rate, declared Communism and Fascism to be much the same thing, and was in favor of both of them. But Shaw, after all, is not an Englishman, and probably does not feel his fate to be bound up with that of Britain.

Germany to Britain and, as between Russia and Germany, would prefer whichever seemed stronger at the moment.* It is, therefore, not surprising that Burnham's world-view should often be noticeably close to that of the American imperialists on the one side, or to that of the isolationists on the other. It is a "tough" or "realistic" world view which fits in with the American form of wish-thinking. The almost open admiration for Nazi methods which Burnham shows in the earlier of his two books, and which would seem shocking to almost any English reader, depends ultimately on the fact that the Atlantic is wider than the Channel.

As I have said earlier, Burnham has probably been more right than wrong about the present and the immediate past. For quite fifty years past the general drift has almost certainly been toward oligarchy. The ever-increasing concentration of industrial and financial power; the diminishing importance of the individual capitalist or shareholder, and the growth of the new "managerial" class of scientists, technicians, and bureaucrats; the weakness of the proletariat against the centralized state; the increasing helplessness of small countries against big ones; the decay of representative institutions and the appearance of one-party régimes based on police terrorism, faked plebiscites, etc.: all these things seem to point in the same direction. Burnham sees the trend and assumes that it is irresistible, rather as a rabbit fascinated by a boa constrictor might assume that a boa constrictor is the strongest thing in the world. When one looks a little deeper, one sees that all his ideas rest upon two axioms which are taken for granted in the earlier book and made partly explicit in the second one. They are:

(a) Politics is essentially the same in all ages.
(b) Political behavior is different from other kinds of behavior.

To take the second point first. In *The Machiavellians,* Burnham insists that politics is simply the struggle for power. Every great social movement, every war, every revolution, every political program, however edifying and Utopian, really has behind it the ambitions of some sectional group which is out to grab power for itself. Power can never be restrained by any ethical or religious code, but only by other power. The nearest possible approach to

* As late as the autumn of 1945, a Gallup poll taken among the American troops in Germany showed that 51 per cent "thought Hitler did much good before 1939." This was after five years of anti-Hitler propaganda. The verdict, as quoted, is not very strongly favorable to Germany, but it is hard to believe that a verdict equally favorable to Britain would be given by anywhere near 51 per cent of the American Army.

altruistic behavior is the perception by a ruling group that it will probably stay in power longer if it behaves decently. But curiously enough, these generalizations only apply to political behavior, not to any other kind of behavior. In everyday life, as Burnham sees and admits, one cannot explain every human action by applying the principle of *cui bono?* Obviously human beings have impulses which are not selfish. Man, therefore, is an animal that can act morally when he acts as an individual, but becomes unmoral when he acts collectively. But even this generalization only holds good for the higher groups. The masses, it seems, have vague aspirations toward liberty and human brotherhood, which are easily played upon by power-hungry individuals and minorities. So that history consists of a series of swindles, in which the masses are first lured into revolt by the promise of Utopia, and then, when they have done their job, enslaved over again by new masters.

Political activity, therefore, is a special kind of behavior, characterized by its complete unscrupulousness and occurring only among small groups of the population, especially among dissatisfied groups whose talents do not get free play under the existing form of society. The great mass of the people—and this is where (b) ties up with (a)—will always be unpolitical. In effect, therefore, humanity is divided into two classes: the self-seeking, hypocritical minority, and the brainless mob whose destiny is always to be led or driven, as one gets a pig back to the sty by kicking it on the bottom or by rattling a stick inside a swill-bucket, according to the needs of the moment. And this beautiful pattern is to continue for ever. Individuals may pass from one category to another, whole classes may destroy other classes and rise to the dominant position, but the division of humanity into rulers and ruled is unalterable. In their capabilities, as in their desires and needs, men are not equal. There is an "iron law of oligarchy," which would operate even if democracy were not impossible for mechanical reasons.

It is curious that in all his talk about the struggle for power, Burnham never stops to ask *why* people want power. He seems to assume that power-hunger, although only dominant in comparatively few people, is a natural instinct that does not have to be explained, like the desire for food. He also assumes that the division of society into classes serves the same purpose in all ages. This is practically to ignore the history of hundreds of years. When Burnham's master, Machiavelli, was writing, class divisions were not only unavoidable, but desirable. So long as methods of production were primitive, the great mass of the people were necessarily tied down to dreary, exhausting manual labor: and a few people had to be set free from such labor, otherwise civilization could not maintain itself, let alone make any progress. But since the arrival of the machine the whole pattern has altered. The justification for class distinctions, if there is a justification, is no longer the same, because there is no mechanical reason why the average human being should continue to be a drudge. True, drudgery persists; class distinctions are probably re-establishing themselves in a new form, and individual liberty is on the down-grade: but as these developments are now technically avoidable, they must have some psychological cause which Burnham makes no attempt to discover. The question that he ought to ask, and never does ask, is: why does the lust for naked power become a major human motive exactly *now*, when the dominion of man over man is ceasing to be necessary? As for the claim that "human nature," or "inexorable laws" of this and that, make socialism impossible, it is simply a projection of the past into the future. In effect, Burnham argues that because a society of free and equal human beings has never existed, it never can exist. By the same argument one could have demonstrated the impossibility of aeroplanes in 1900, or of motor cars in 1850.

The notion that the machine has altered human relationships, and that in consequence Machiavelli is out of date, is a very obvious one. If Burnham fails to deal with it, it can, I think, only be because his own power-instinct leads him to brush aside any suggestion that the Machiavellian world of force, fraud, and tyranny may somehow come to an end. It is important to bear in mind what I said above: that Burnham's theory is only a variant —an American variant, and interesting because of its comprehensiveness—of the power-worship now so prevalent among intellectuals. A more normal variant, at any rate in England, is Communism. If one examines the people who, having some idea of what the Russian régime is like, are strongly Russophile, one finds that, on the whole, they belong to the "managerial" class of which Burnham writes. That is, they are not managers in the narrow sense, but scientists, technicians, teachers, journalists, broadcasters, bureaucrats, professional politicians: in general, middling people who feel themselves cramped by a system that is still partly aristocratic, and are hungry for more power and more prestige. These people look toward the U.S.S.R. and see in it, or think they see, a system which eliminates the upper class, keeps the working class in its place, and hands unlimited power to people very similar to themselves. It was only *after* the Soviet régime became unmistakably totalitarian that English intellectuals, in large numbers, began to show an interest in it. Burnham, although the English Russophile intelligentsia would repudiate him, is really voicing their secret wish: the wish to destroy the old, equalitarian version of socialism and usher in a hierarchical society where the intellectual can at last get his hands on the whip. Burnham at least has the honesty to say that socialism isn't coming; the others merely say that socialism *is* coming, and then give the word "socialism" a new meaning which makes nonsense of the old one. But his theory, for all its appearance of objectivity, is the rationalization of a wish. There is no strong reason for thinking that it tells us anything about the future, except perhaps the immediate future. It merely tells us what kind of world the "managerial" class themselves, or at least the more conscious and ambitious members of the class, would like to live in. Fortunately the "managers" are not so invincible as Burnham believes. It is curious how persistently, in *The Managerial Revolution,* he ignores the advantages, military as well as social, enjoyed by a democratic country. At every point the evidence is squeezed in order to show the strength, vitality, and durability of Hitler's crazy régime. Germany is expanding rapidly, and "rapid territorial expansion has always been a sign not of decadence . . . but of renewal." Germany makes war successfully, and "the ability to make war well is never a sign of decadence but of its opposite." Germany also "inspires in millions of persons a fanatical loyalty. This, too, never accompanies decadence." Even the cruelty and dishonesty of the Nazi régime are cited in its favor, since "the young, new, rising social order is, as against the old, more likely to resort on a large scale to lies, terror, persecution." Yet, within only five years this young, rising social order had smashed itself to pieces and become, in Burnham's usage of the word, decadent. And this had happened quite largely because of the "managerial" (i.e. undemocratic) structure which Burnham admires. The immediate cause of the German defeat was the unheard-of folly of attacking the U.S.S.R. while Britain was still undefeated and America was manifestly getting ready to fight. Mistakes of this magnitude can only be made, or at any rate they are most likely to be made, in countries where public opinion has no power. So long as the common man can get a hearing, such elementary rules as not fighting all your enemies simultaneously are less likely to be violated.

But, in any case, one should have been able to see from the start that such a movement as Nazism could not produce any good or stable result. Actually, so long as they were winning, Burnham seems to have seen nothing wrong with the methods of the Nazis. Such methods, he says, only appear wicked because they are new:

There is no historical law that polite manners and "justice" shall conquer. In history there is always the question of *whose* manners and *whose* justice. A rising social class and a new order of society have got to break through the old moral codes just as they must break through the old economic and political institutions. Naturally, from the point of view of the old, they are monsters. If they win, they take care in due time of manners and morals.

This implies that literally anything can become right or wrong if the dominant class of the moment so wills it. It ignores the fact that certain rules of conduct have to be observed if human society is to hold together at all. Burnham, therefore, was unable to see that the crimes and follies of the Nazi régime *must* lead by one route or another to disaster. So also with his new-found admiration for Stalinism. It is too early to say in just what way the Russian régime will destroy itself. If I had to make a prophecy, I should say that a continuation of the Russian policies of the last fifteen years—and internal and external policy, of course, are merely two facets of the same thing—can only lead to a war conducted with atomic bombs, which will make Hitler's invasion look like a tea party. But at any rate, the Russian régime will either democratize itself, or it will perish. The huge, invincible, everlasting slave empire of which Burnham appears to dream will not be established or, if established, will not endure, because slavery is no longer a stable basis for human society.

One cannot always make positive prophecies, but there are times when one ought to be able to make negative ones. No one could have been expected to foresee the exact results of the Treaty of Versailles, but millions of thinking people could and did foresee that those results would be bad. Plenty of people, though not so many in this case, can foresee that the results of the settlement now being forced on Europe will also be bad. And to refrain from admiring Hitler or Stalin—that, too, should not require an enormous intellectual effort. But it is partly a moral effort. That a man of Burnham's gifts should have been able for a while to think of Nazism as something rather admirable, something that could and probably would build up a workable and durable social order, shows what damage is done to the sense of reality by the cultivation of what is now called "realism."

1946

△

Politics and the English Language

▽

Most people who bother with the matter at all would admit that the English language is in a bad way, but it is generally assumed that we cannot by conscious action do anything about it. Our civilization is decadent and our language—so the argument runs—must inevitably share in the general collapse. It follows that any struggle against the abuse of language is a sentimental archaism, like preferring candles to electric light or hansom cabs to aeroplanes. Underneath this lies the half-conscious belief that language is a natural growth and not an instrument which we shape for our own purposes.

Now, it is clear that the decline of a language must ultimately have political and economic causes: it is not due simply to the bad influence of this or that individual writer. But an effect can become a cause, reinforcing the original cause and producing the same effect in an intensified form, and so on indefinitely. A man may take to drink because he feels himself to be a failure, and then fail all the more completely because he drinks. It is rather the same thing that is happening to the English language. It becomes ugly and inaccurate because our thoughts are foolish, but the slovenliness of our language makes it easier for us to have foolish thoughts. The point is that the process is reversible. Modern English, especially written English, is full of bad habits which spread by imitation and which can be avoided if one is willing to take the necessary trouble. If one gets rid of these habits one can think more clearly, and to think clearly is a necessary first step toward political regeneration: so that the fight against bad English is not frivolous and is not the exclusive concern of professional writers. I will come back to this presently, and I hope that by that time the meaning of what I have said here will have become clearer. Meanwhile, here are five specimens of the English language as it is now habitually written.

These five passages have not been picked out because they are especially bad—I could have quoted far worse if I had chosen—but because they illustrate various of the mental vices from which we now suffer. They are a little below the average, but are fairly representative samples. I number them so that I can refer back to them when necessary:

(1) I am not, indeed, sure whether it is not true to say that the Milton who once seemed not unlike a seventeenth-century Shelley had not become, out of an experience ever more bitter in each year, more alien [sic] to the founder of that Jesuit sect which nothing could induce him to tolerate.

Professor Harold Laski
(Essay in *Freedom of Expression*)

(2) Above all, we cannot play ducks and drakes with a native battery of idioms which prescribes such egregious collocations of vocables as the Basic *put up with* for *tolerate* or *put at a loss* for *bewilder*.

Professor Lancelot Hogben (*Interglossa*)

(3) On the one side we have the free personality: by definition it is not neurotic, for it has neither conflict nor dream. Its desires, such as they are, are transparent, for they are just what institutional approval keeps in the forefront of consciousness; another institutional pattern would alter their number and intensity; there is little in them that is natural, irreducible, or culturally dangerous. But *on the other side,* the social bond itself is nothing but the mutual reflection of these self-secure integrities. Recall the definition of love. Is not this the very picture of a small academic? Where is there a place in this hall of mirrors for either personality or fraternity?

Essay on psychology in *Politics* (New York)

(4) All the "best people" from the gentlemen's clubs, and all the frantic fascist captains, united in common hatred of Socialism and bestial horror of the rising tide of the mass revolutionary movement, have turned to acts of provocation, to foul incendiarism, to medieval legends of poisoned wells, to legalize their own destruction of proletarian organizations, and rouse the agitated petty-bourgeoisie to chauvinistic fervor on behalf of the fight against the revolutionary way out of the crisis.

Communist pamphlet

(5) If a new spirit *is* to be infused into this old country, there is one thorny and contentious reform which must be tackled, and that is the humanization and galvanization of the B.B.C. Timidity here will bespeak canker and atrophy of the soul. The heart of Britain may be sound and of strong beat, for instance, but the British lion's roar at present is like that of Bottom in Shakespeare's *Midsummer Night's Dream*—as gentle as any sucking dove. A virile new Britain cannot continue indefinitely to be traduced in the eyes or rather ears, of the world by the effete languors of Langham Place, brazenly masquerading as "standard English." When the Voice of Britain is heard at nine o'clock, better far and infinitely less ludicrous to hear aitches honestly dropped than the present priggish, inflated, inhibited, school-ma'amish arch braying of blameless bashful mewing maidens!

Letter in *Tribune*

Each of these passages has faults of its own, but, quite apart from avoidable ugliness, two qualities are common to all of them. The first is staleness of imagery; the other is lack of precision. The writer either has a meaning and cannot express it, or he inadvertently says something else, or he is almost indifferent as to whether his words mean anything or not. This mixture of vagueness and sheer incompetence is the most marked characteristic of modern English prose, and especially of any kind of political writing. As soon as certain topics are raised, the concrete melts into the abstract and no one seems able to think of turns of speech that are not hackneyed: prose consists less and less of *words* chosen for the sake of their meaning, and more and more of *phrases* tacked together like the sections of a prefabricated henhouse. I list below, with notes and examples, various of the tricks by means of which the work of prose-construction is habitually dodged:

Dying metaphors. A newly invented metaphor assists thought by evoking a visual image, while on the other hand a metaphor which is technically "dead" (e.g. *iron resolution*) has in effect reverted to being an ordinary word and can generally be used without loss of vividness. But in between these two classes there is a huge dump of worn-out metaphors which have lost all evocative power and are merely used because they save people the trouble of inventing phrases for themselves. Examples are: *Ring the changes on, take up the cudgels for, toe the line, ride roughshod over, stand shoulder to shoulder with, play into the hands of, no axe to grind, grist to the mill, fishing in troubled waters, on the order of the day, Achilles' heel, swan song, hotbed.* Many of these are used without knowledge of their meaning (what is a "rift," for instance?), and incompatible metaphors are frequently mixed, a sure sign that the writer is not interested in what he is saying. Some metaphors now current have been twisted out of their original meaning without those who use them even being aware of the fact. For example, *toe the line* is sometimes written *tow the line.* Another example is *the hammer and the anvil,* now always used with the implication that the anvil gets the worst of it. In real life it is always the anvil that breaks the hammer, never the other way about: a writer who stopped to think what he was saying would be aware of this, and would avoid perverting the original phrase.

Operators or *verbal false limbs.* These save the trouble of picking out appropriate verbs and nouns, and at the same time pad each sentence with extra syllables which give it an appearance of symmetry. Characteristic phrases are *render inoperative, militate against, make contact with, be subjected to, give rise to, give grounds for, have the effect of, play a leading part (role) in, make itself felt, take effect, exhibit a tendency to, serve the purpose of, etc., etc.* The keynote is the elimination of simple verbs. Instead of being a single word, such as *break, stop, spoil, mend, kill,* a verb becomes a *phrase,* made up of a noun or adjective tacked on to some general-purpose verb such as *prove, serve, form, play, render.* In addition, the passive voice is wherever possible used in preference to the active, and noun constructions are used instead of gerunds (*by examination of* instead of *by examining*). The range of verbs is further cut down by means of the *-ize* and *de-* formations, and the banal statements are given an appearance of profundity by means of the *not un-* formation. Simple conjunctions and prepositions are replaced by such phrases as *with respect to, having regard to, the fact that, by dint of, in view of, in the interests of, on the hypothesis that;* and the ends of sentences are saved by anticlimax by such resounding commonplaces as *greatly to be desired, cannot be left out of account, a development to be expected in the near future, deserving of serious consideration, brought to a satisfactory conclusion,* and so on and so forth.

Pretentious diction. Words like *phenomenon, element, individual* (as noun), *objective, categorical, effective, virtual, basic, primary, promote, constitute, exhibit, exploit, utilize, eliminate, liquidate,* are used to dress up simple statement and give an air of scientific impartiality to biased judgments. Adjectives like *epoch-making, epic, historic, unforgettable, triumphant, age-old, inevitable, inexorable, veritable,* are used to dignify the sordid processes of international politics, while writing that aims at glorifying war usually takes on an archaic color, its characteristic words being: *realm, throne, chariot, mailed fist, trident, sword, shield, buckler, banner, jackboot, clarion.* Foreign words and expressions such as *cul de sac, ancien régime, deus ex machina, mutatis mutandis, status quo, gleichschaltung, weltanschauung,* are used to give an air of culture and elegance. Except for the useful abbreviations *i.e., e.g.,* and *etc.,* there is no real need for any of the hundreds of foreign phrases now current in English. Bad writers, and especially scientific, political, and sociological writers, are nearly always haunted by the notion that Latin or Greek words are grander than Saxon ones, and unnecessary words like *expedite, ameliorate, predict, extraneous, de-*

acinated, *clandestine, subaqueous,* and hundreds of others con-
tantly gain ground from their Anglo-Saxon opposite numbers.*
The jargon peculiar to Marxist writing (*hyena, hangman, cannibal,
petty bourgeois, these gentry, lackey, flunkey, mad dog, White
Guard,* etc.) consists largely of words and phrases translated from
Russian, German, or French; but the normal way of coining a new
word is to use a Latin or Greek root with the appropriate affix and,
where necessary, the size formation. It is often easier to make up
words of this kind (*deregionalize, impermissible, extramarital, non-
fragmentary* and so forth) than to think up the English words that
will cover one's meaning. The result, in general, is an increase in
slovenliness and vagueness.

Meaningless words. In certain kinds of writing, particularly in art
criticism and literary criticism, it is normal to come across long
passages which are almost completely lacking in meaning.† Words
like *romantic, plastic, values, human, dead, sentimental, natural,
vitality,* as used in art criticism, are strictly meaningless, in the sense
that they not only do not point to any discoverable object, but are
hardly ever expected to do so by the reader. When one critic writes,
"The outstanding feature of Mr. X's work is its living quality,"
while another writes, "The immediately striking thing about Mr.
X's work is its peculiar deadness," the reader accepts this as a simple
difference of opinion. If words like *black* and *white* were involved,
instead of the jargon words *dead* and *living,* he would see at once
that language was being used in an improper way. Many political
words are similarly abused. The word *Fascism* has now no meaning
except in so far as it signifies "something not desirable." The words
democracy, socialism, freedom, patriotic, realistic, justice, have each
of them several different meanings which cannot be reconciled with
one another. In the case of a word like *democracy,* not only is there

* An interesting illustration of this is the way in which the English flower
names which were in use till very recently are being ousted by Greek ones,
snapdragon becoming *antirrhinum, forget-me-not* becoming *myosotis,* etc. It is
hard to see any practical reason for this change of fashion: it is probably due
to an instinctive turning away from the more homely word and a vague feeling
that the Greek word is scientific.

† Example: "Comfort's catholicity of perception and image, strangely Whit-
manesque in range, almost the exact opposite in aesthetic compulsion, continues
to evoke that trembling atmospheric accumulative hinting at a cruel, an inexorably serene timelessness. . . . Wrey Gardiner scores by aiming at simple
bull's-eyes with precision. Only they are not so simple, and through this contented sadness runs more than the surface bittersweet of resignation." (*Poetry
Quarterly.*)

no agreed definition, but the attempt to make one is resisted from all sides. It is almost universally felt that when we call a countr democratic we are praising it: consequently the defenders of ever kind of régime claim that it is a democracy, and fear that they migh have to stop using the word if it were tied down to any one meaning Words of this kind are often used in a consciously dishonest way That is, the person who uses them has his own private definition but allows his hearer to think he means something quite differen Statements like *Marshal Pétain was a true patriot, The Soviet pres is the freest in the world, The Catholic Church is opposed to pe secution,* are almost always made with intent to deceive. Othe words used in variable meanings, in most cases more or less dis honestly, are: *class, totalitarian, science, progressive, reactionar bourgeois, equality.*

Now that I have made this catalogue of swindles and perversion let me give another example of the kind of writing that they lea to. This time it must of its nature be an imaginary one. I am goin to translate a passage of good English into modern English of th worst sort. Here is a well-known verse from *Ecclesiastes:*

I returned and saw under the sun, that the race is not to the swift, no the battle to the strong, neither yet bread to the wise, nor yet riches t men of understanding, nor yet favour to men of skill; but time and chanc happeneth to them all.

Here it is in modern English:

Objective considerations of contemporary phenomena compels the con clusion that success or failure in competitive activities exhibits no tend ency to be commensurate with innate capacity, but that a considerabl element of the unpredictable must invariably be taken into account.

This is a parody, but not a very gross one. Exhibit (3), above for instance, contains several patches of the same kind of English It will be seen that I have not made a full translation. The begin ning and ending of the sentence follow the original meaning fairl closely, but in the middle the concrete illustrations—race, battle bread—dissolve into the vague phrase "success or failure in competi tive activities." This had to be so, because no modern writer of th kind I am discussing—no one capable of using phrases like "objec tive consideration of contemporary phenomena"—would ever tabu late his thoughts in that precise and detailed way. The whole tend ency of modern prose is away from concreteness. Now analyze thes two sentences a little more closely. The first contains forty-nine words but only sixty syllables, and all its words are those of every lay life. The second contains thirty-eight words of ninety syllables: eighteen of its words are from Latin roots, and one from Greek. The first sentence contains six vivid images, and only one phrase ("time and chance") that could be called vague. The second contains not a single fresh, arresting phrase, and in spite of its ninety syllables it gives only a shortened version of the meaning contained in the first. Yet without a doubt it is the second kind of sentence that is gaining ground in modern English. I do not want to exaggerate. This kind of writing is not yet universal, and outcrops of simplicity will occur here and there in the worst-written page. Still, if you or I were told to write a few lines on the uncertainty of human fortunes, we should probably come much nearer to my imaginary sentence than to the one from *Ecclesiastes*.

As I have tried to show, modern writing at its worst does not consist in picking out words for the sake of their meaning and inventing images in order to make the meaning clearer. It consists in gumming together long strips of words which have already been set in order by someone else, and making the results presentable by sheer humbug. The attraction of this way of writing is that it is easy. It is easier—even quicker, once you have the habit—to say *In my opinion it is not an unjustifiable assumption that* than to say *I think*. If you use ready-made phrases, you not only don't have to hunt about for words; you also don't have to bother with the rhythms of your sentences, since these phrases are generally so arranged as to be more or less euphonious. When you are composing in a hurry—when you are dictating to a stenographer, for instance, or making a public speech—it is natural to fall into a pretentious, Latinized style. Tags like *a consideration which we should do well to bear in mind* or *a conclusion to which all of us would readily assent* will save many a sentence from coming down with a bump. By using stale metaphors, similes, and idioms, you save much mental effort, at the cost of leaving your meaning vague, not only for your reader but for yourself. This is the significance of mixed metaphors. The sole aim of a metaphor is to call up a visual image. When these images clash—as in *The Fascist octopus has sung its swan song, the jackboot is thrown into the melting pot*—it can be taken as certain that the writer is not seeing a mental image of the objects he is naming; in other words he is not really thinking. Look again at the examples I gave at the beginning of this essay. Professor Laski (1) uses five negatives in fifty-three words. One of these is superfluous, making nonsense of the whole passage, and in addition there is the slip—*alien* for akin—making further nonsense, and several avoidable pieces of clumsiness which increase the general vagueness. Professor

Hogben (2) plays ducks and drakes with a battery which is able to write prescriptions, and, while disapproving of the everyday phrase *put up with*, is unwilling to look *egregious* up in the dictionary and see what it means; (3), if one takes an uncharitable attitude towards it, is simply meaningless: probably one could work out its intended meaning by reading the whole of the article in which it occurs. In (4), the writer knows more or less what he wants to say, but an accumulation of stale phrases chokes him like tea leaves blocking a sink. In (5), words and meaning have almost parted company. People who write in this manner usually have a general emotional meaning—they dislike one thing and want to express solidarity with another—but they are not interested in the detail of what they are saying. A scrupulous writer, in every sentence that he writes, will ask himself at least four questions, thus: What am I trying to say? What words will express it? What image or idiom will make it clearer? Is this image fresh enough to have an effect? And he will probably ask himself two more: Could I put it more shortly? Have I said anything that is avoidably ugly? But you are not obliged to go to all this trouble. You can shirk it by simply throwing your mind open and letting the ready-made phrases come crowding in. They will construct your sentences for you—even think your thoughts for you, to a certain extent—and at need they will perform the important service of partially concealing your meaning even from yourself. It is at this point that the special connection between politics and the debasement of language becomes clear.

In our time it is broadly true that political writing is bad writing. Where it is not true, it will generally be found that the writer is some kind of rebel, expressing his private opinions and not a "party line." Orthodoxy, of whatever color, seems to demand a lifeless, imitative style. The political dialects to be found in pamphlets, leading articles, manifestoes, White Papers and the speeches of undersecretaries do, of course, vary from party to party, but they are all alike in that one almost never finds in them a fresh, vivid, homemade turn of speech. When one watches some tired hack on the platform mechanically repeating the familiar phrases—*bestial atrocities, iron heel, bloodstained tyranny, free peoples of the world, stand shoulder to shoulder*—one often has a curious feeling that one is not watching a live human being but some kind of dummy: a feeling which suddenly becomes stronger at moments when the light catches the speaker's spectacles and turns them into blank discs which seem to have no eyes behind them. And this is not altogether fanciful. A speaker who uses that kind of phraseology has gone some distance toward turning himself into a machine. The appropriate noises are coming out of his larynx, but his brain is not involved as it would be if he were choosing his words for himself. If the speech he is making is one that he is accustomed to make over and over again, he may be almost unconscious of what he is saying, as one is when one utters the responses in church. And this reduced state of consciousness, if not indispensable, is at any rate favorable to political conformity.

In our time, political speech and writing are largely the defense of the indefensible. Things like the continuance of British rule in India, the Russian purges and deportations, the dropping of the atom bombs on Japan, can indeed be defended, but only by arguments which are too brutal for most people to face, and which do not square with the professed aims of political parties. Thus political language has to consist largely of euphemism, question-begging and sheer cloudy vagueness. Defenseless villages are bombarded from the air, the inhabitants driven out into the countryside, the cattle machine-gunned, the huts set on fire with incendiary bullets: this is called *pacification*. Millions of peasants are robbed of their farms and sent trudging along the roads with no more than they can carry: this is called *transfer of population* or *rectification of frontiers*. People are imprisoned for years without trial, or shot in the back of the neck or sent to die of scurvy in Arctic lumber camps: this is called *elimination of unreliable elements*. Such phraseology is needed if one wants to name things without calling up mental pictures of them. Consider for instance some comfortable English professor defending Russian totalitarianism. He cannot say outright, "I believe in killing off your opponents when you can get good results by doing so." Probably, therefore, he will say something like this:

"While freely conceding that the Soviet régime exhibits certain features which the humanitarian may be inclined to deplore, we must, I think, agree that a certain curtailment of the right to political opposition is an unavoidable concomitant of transitional periods, and that the rigors which the Russian people have been called upon to undergo have been amply justified in the sphere of concrete achievement."

The inflated style is itself a kind of euphemism. A mass of Latin words falls upon the facts like soft snow, blurring the outlines and covering up all the details. The great enemy of clear language is insincerity. When there is a gap between one's real and one's declared aims, one turns as it were instinctively to long words and exhausted idioms, like a cuttlefish squirting out ink. In our age there is no such thing as "keeping out of politics." All issues are political issues, and politics itself is a mass of lies, evasions, folly, hatred, and schizophrenia. When the general atmosphere is bad, language must suffer. I should expect to find—this is a guess which I have not sufficient knowledge to verify—that the German, Russian and Italian languages have all deteriorated in the last ten or fifteen years, as a result of dictatorship.

But if thought corrupts language, language can also corrupt thought. A bad usage can spread by tradition and imitation, even among people who should and do know better. The debased language that I have been discussing is in some ways very convenient. Phrases like *a not unjustifiable assumption, leaves much to be desired, would serve no good purpose, a consideration which we should do well to bear in mind,* are a continuous temptation, a packet of aspirins always at one's elbow. Look back through this essay, and for certain you will find that I have again and again committed the very faults I am protesting against. By this morning's post I have received a pamphlet dealing with conditions in Germany. The author tells me that he "felt impelled" to write it. I open it at random, and here is almost the first sentence that I see: "[The Allies] have an opportunity not only of achieving a radical transformation of Germany's social and political structure in such a way as to avoid a nationalistic reaction in Germany itself, but at the same time of laying the foundations of a co-operative and unified Europe." You see, he "feels impelled" to write—feels, presumably, that he has something new to say—and yet his words, like cavalry horses answering the bugle, group themselves automatically into the familiar dreary pattern. This invasion of one's mind by ready-made phrases (*lay the foundations, achieve a radical transformation*) can only be prevented if one is constantly on guard against them, and every such phrase anaesthetizes a portion of one's brain.

I said earlier that the decadence of our language is probably curable. Those who deny this would argue, if they produced an argument at all, that language merely reflects existing social conditions, and that we cannot influence its development by any direct tinkering with words and constructions. So far as the general tone or spirit of a language goes, this may be true, but it is not true in detail. Silly words and expressions have often disappeared, not through any evolutionary process but owing to the conscious action of a minority. Two recent examples were *explore every avenue* and *leave no stone unturned,* which were killed by the jeers of a few journalists. There is a long list of flyblown metaphors which could similarly be got rid of if enough people would interest themselves in the job; and it should also be possible to laugh the *not un-* formation out of existence,* to reduce the amount of Latin and Greek in the average sentence, to drive out foreign phrases and strayed scientific words, and, in general, to make pretentiousness unfashionable. But all these are minor points. The defense of the English language implies more than this, and perhaps it is best to start by saying what it does *not* imply.

To begin with it has nothing to do with archaism, with the salvaging of obsolete words and turns of speech, or with the setting up of a "standard English" which must never be departed from. On the contrary, it is especially concerned with the scrapping of every word or idiom which has outworn its usefulness. It has nothing to do with correct grammar and syntax, which are of no importance so long as one makes one's meaning clear, or with the avoidance of Americanisms, or with having what is called a "good prose style." On the other hand it is not concerned with fake simplicity and the attempt to make written English colloquial. Nor does it even imply in every case preferring the Saxon word to the Latin one, though it does imply using the fewest and shortest words that will cover one's meaning. What is above all needed is to let the meaning choose the word, and not the other way about. In prose, the worst thing one can do with words is to surrender to them. When you think of a concrete object, you think wordlessly, and then, if you want to describe the thing you have been visualizing you probably hunt about till you find the exact words that seem to fit it. When you think of something abstract you are more inclined to use words from the start, and unless you make a conscious effort to prevent it, the existing dialect will come rushing in and do the job for you, at the expense of blurring or even changing your meaning. Probably it is better to put off using words as long as possible and get one's meaning as clear as one can through pictures or sensations. Afterward one can choose—not simply *accept*—the phrases that will best cover the meaning, and then switch round and decide what impression one's words are likely to make on another person. This last effort of the mind cuts out all stale or mixed images, all prefabricated phrases, needless repetitions, and humbug and vagueness generally. But one can often be in doubt about the effect of a word or a phrase, and one needs rules that one can rely on when instinct fails. I think the following rules will cover most cases:

(i) Never use a metaphor, simile, or other figure of speech which you are used to seeing in print.

* One can cure oneself of the *not un-* formation by memorizing this sentence: *A not unblack dog was chasing a not unsmall rabbit across a not ungreen field.*

(ii) Never use a long word where a short one will do.

(iii) If it is possible to cut a word out, always cut it out.

(iv) Never use the passive where you can use the active.

(v) Never use a foreign phrase, a scientific word, or a jargon word if you can think of an everyday English equivalent.

(vi) Break any of these rules sooner than say anything outright barbarous.

These rules sound elementary, and so they are, but they demand a deep change of attitude in anyone who has grown used to writing in the style now fashionable. One could keep all of them and still write bad English, but one could not write the kind of stuff that I quoted in those five specimens at the beginning of this article.

I have not here been considering the literary use of language, but merely language as an instrument for expressing and not for concealing or preventing thought. Stuart Chase and others have come near to claiming that all abstract words are meaningless, and have used this as a pretext for advocating a kind of political quietism. Since you don't know what Fascism is, how can you struggle against Fascism? One need not swallow such absurdities as this, but one ought to recognize that the present political chaos is connected with the decay of language, and that one can probably bring about some improvement by starting at the verbal end. If you simplify your English, you are freed from the worst follies of orthodoxy. You cannot speak any of the necessary dialects, and when you make a stupid remark its stupidity will be obvious, even to yourself. Political language—and with variations this is true of all political parties, from Conservatives to Anarchists—is designed to make lies sound truthful and murder respectable, and to give an appearance of solidity to pure wind. One cannot change this all in a moment, but one can at least change one's own habits, and from time to time one can even, if one jeers loudly enough, send some worn-out and useless phrase—some *jackboot, Achilles' heel, hotbed, melting pot, acid test, veritable inferno,* or other lump of verbal refuse—into the dustbin where it belongs.

1946

△

The Prevention of Literature

▽

About a year ago I attended a meeting of the P.E.N. Club, the occasion being the tercentenary of Milton's *Areopagitica*—a pamphlet, it may be remembered, in defense of freedom of the press. Milton's famous phrase about the sin of "killing" a book was printed on the leaflets advertising the meeting which had been circulated beforehand.

There were four speakers on the platform. One of them delivered a speech which did deal with the freedom of the press, but only in relation to India; another said, hesitantly, and in very general terms, that liberty was a good thing; a third delivered an attack on the laws relating to obscenity in literature. The fourth devoted most of his speech to a defense of the Russian purges. Of the speeches from the body of the hall, some reverted to the question of obscenity and the laws that deal with it, others were simply eulogies of Soviet Russia. Moral liberty—the liberty to discuss sex questions frankly in print—seemed to be generally approved, but political liberty was not mentioned. Out of this concourse of several hundred people, perhaps half of whom were directly connected with the writing trade, there was not a single one who could point out that freedom of the press, if it means anything at all, means the freedom to criticize and oppose. Significantly, no speaker quoted from the pamphlet which was ostensibly being commemorated. Nor was there any mention of the various books that have been "killed" in England and the United States during the war. In its net effect the meeting was a demonstration in favor of censorship.*

There was nothing particularly surprising in this. In our age, the idea of intellectual liberty is under attack from two directions. On

* It is fair to say that the P.E.N. Club celebrations, which lasted a week or more, did not always stick at quite the same level. I happened to strike a bad day. But an examination of the speeches (printed under the title *Freedom of Expression*) shows that almost nobody in our own day is able to speak out as roundly in favor of intellectual liberty as Milton could do 300 years ago—and this in spite of the fact Milton was writing in a period of civil war.

the one side are its theoretical enemies, the apologists of totalitarianism, and on the other its immediate, practical enemies, monopoly
and bureaucracy. Any writer or journalist who wants to retain his
integrity finds himself thwarted by the general drift of society rather
than by active persecution. The sort of things that are working
against him are the concentration of the press in the hands of a few
rich men, the grip of monopoly on radio and the films, the unwill-
ingness of the public to spend money on books, making it necessary for nearly every writer to earn part of his living by hackwork,
the encroachment of official bodies like the M.O.I. and the British
Council, which help the writer to keep alive but also waste his time
and dictate his opinions, and the continuous war atmosphere of the
past ten years, whose distorting effects no one has been able to
escape. Everything in our age conspires to turn the writer, and every
other kind of artist as well, into a minor official, working on themes
handed down from above and never telling what seems to him the
whole of the truth. But in struggling against this fate he gets no
help from his own side: that is, there is no large body of opinion
which will assure him that he is in the right. In the past, at any rate
throughout the Protestant centuries, the idea of rebellion and the
idea of intellectual integrity were mixed up. A heretic—political,
moral, religious, or aesthetic—was one who refused to outrage his
own conscience. His outlook was summed up in the words of the
Revivalist hymn:

> Dare to be a Daniel,
> Dare to stand alone;
> Dare to have a purpose firm,
> Dare to make it known.

To bring this hymn up to date one would have to add a "Don't" at
the beginning of each line. For it is the peculiarity of our age that
the rebels against the existing order, at any rate the most numerous
and characteristic of them, are also rebelling against the idea of
individual integrity. "Daring to stand alone" is ideologically criminal as well as practically dangerous. The independence of the writer
and the artist is eaten away by vague economic forces, and at the
same time it is undermined by those who should be its defenders.
It is with the second process that I am concerned here.

Freedom of thought and of the press are usually attacked by arguments which are not worth bothering about. Anyone who has experience of lecturing and debating knows them off backwards. Here
I am not trying to deal with the familiar claim that freedom is an
illusion, or with the claim that there is more freedom in totalitarian

countries than in democratic ones, but with the much more tenable and dangerous proposition that freedom is *undesirable* and that intellectual honesty is a form of anti-social selfishness. Although other aspects of the question are usually in the foreground, the controversy over freedom of speech and of the press is at bottom a controversy over the desirability, or otherwise, of telling lies. What is really at issue is the right to report contemporary events truthfully, or as truthfully as is consistent with the ignorance, bias and self-deception from which every observer necessarily suffers. In saying this I may seem to be saying that straightforward "reportage" is the only branch of literature that matters: but I will try to show later that at every literary level, and probably in every one of the arts, the same issue arises in more or less subtilized forms. Meanwhile, it is necessary to strip away the irrelevancies in which this controversy is usually wrapped up.

The enemies of intellectual liberty always try to present their case as a plea for discipline versus individualism. The issue truth-versus-untruth is as far as possible kept in the background. Although the point of emphasis may vary, the writer who refuses to sell his opinions is always branded as a mere *egoist*. He is accused, that is, either of wanting to shut himself up in an ivory tower, or of making an exhibitionist display of his own personality, or of resisting the inevitable current of history in an attempt to cling to unjustified privileges. The Catholic and the Communist are alike in assuming that an opponent cannot be both honest and intelligent. Each of them tacitly claims that "the truth" has already been revealed, and that the heretic, if he is not simply a fool, is secretly aware of "the truth" and merely resists it out of selfish motives. In Communist literature the attack on intellectual liberty is usually masked by oratory about "petty-bourgeois individualism," "the illusions of nineteenth-century liberalism," etc., and backed up by words of abuse such as "romantic" and "sentimental," which, since they do not have any agreed meaning, are difficult to answer. In this way the controversy is maneuvered away from its real issue. One can accept, and most enlightened people would accept, the Communist thesis that pure freedom will only exist in a classless society, and that one is most nearly free when one is working to bring such a society about. But slipped in with this is the quite unfounded claim that the Communist Party is itself aiming at the establishment of the classless society, and that in the U.S.S.R. this aim is actually on the way to being realized. If the first claim is allowed to entail the second, there is almost no assault on common sense and common decency that cannot be justified. But meanwhile, the real point has been dodged.

Freedom of the intellect means the freedom to report what one has seen, heard, and felt, and not to be obliged to fabricate imaginary facts and feelings. The familiar tirades against "escapism," and "individualism," "romanticism," and so forth, are merely a forensic device, the aim of which is to make the perversion of history seem respectable.

Fifteen years ago, when one defended the freedom of the intellect, one had to defend it against Conservatives, against Catholics, and to some extent—for they were not of great importance in England—against Fascists. Today one has to defend it against Communists and "fellow-travelers." One ought not to exaggerate the direct influence of the small English Communist Party, but there can be no question about the poisonous effect of the Russian *mythos* on English intellectual life. Because of it known facts are suppressed and distorted to such an extent as to make it doubtful whether a true history of our times can ever be written. Let me give just one instance out of the hundreds that could be cited. When Germany collapsed, it was found that very large numbers of Soviet Russians —mostly, no doubt, from non-political motives—had changed sides and were fighting for the Germans. Also, a small but not negligible proportion of the Russian prisoners and displaced persons refused to go back to the U.S.S.R., and some of them, at least, were repatriated against their will. These facts, known to many journalists on the spot, went almost unmentioned in the British press, while at the same time Russophile publicists in England continued to justify the purges and deportations of 1936-38 by claiming that the U.S.S.R. "had no quislings." The fog of lies and misinformation that surrounds such subjects as the Ukraine famine, the Spanish civil war, Russian policy in Poland, and so forth, is not due entirely to conscious dishonesty, but any writer or journalist who is fully sympathetic to the U.S.S.R.—sympathetic, that is, in the way the Russians themselves would want him to be—does have to acquiesce in deliberate falsification on important issues. I have before me what must be a very rare pamphlet, written by Maxim Litvinoff in 1918 and outlining the recent events in the Russian Revolution. It makes no mention of Stalin, but gives high praise to Trotsky, and also to Zinoviev, Kamenev, and others. What could be the attitude of even the most intellectually scrupulous Communist towards such a pamphlet? At best, the obscurantist attitude of saying that it is an undesirable document and better suppressed. And if for some reason it were decided to issue a garbled version of the pamphlet, denigrating Trotsky and inserting references to Stalin, no Communist who remained faithful to his party could protest. Forgeries almost as gross as this have been committed in recent years. But the significant thing is not that they happen, but that, even when they are known about, they provoke no reaction from the left-wing intelligentsia as a whole. The argument that to tell the truth would be "inopportune" or would "play into the hands of" somebody or other is felt to be unanswerable, and few people are bothered by the prospect of the lies which they condone getting out of the newspapers and into the history books.

The organized lying practiced by totalitarian states is not, as is sometimes claimed, a temporary expedient of the same nature as military deception. It is something integral to totalitarianism, something that would still continue even if concentration camps and secret police forces had ceased to be necessary. Among intelligent Communists there is an underground legend to the effect that although the Russian government is obliged *now* to deal in lying propaganda, frame-up trials, and so forth, it is secretly recording the true facts and will publish them at some future time. We can, I believe, be quite certain that this is not the case, because the mentality implied by such an action is that of a liberal historian who believes that the past cannot be altered and that a correct knowledge of history is valuable as a matter of course. From the totalitarian point of view history is something to be created rather than learned. A totalitarian state is in effect a theocracy, and its ruling caste, in order to keep its position, has to be thought of as infallible. But since, in practice, no one is infallible, it is frequently necessary to rearrange past events in order to show that this or that mistake was not made, or that this or that imaginary triumph actually happened. Then, again, every major change in policy demands a corresponding change of doctrine and a revaluation of prominent historical figures. This kind of thing happens everywhere, but is clearly likelier to lead to outright falsification in societies where only *one* opinion is permissible at any given moment. Totalitarianism demands, in fact, the continuous alteration of the past, and in the long run probably demands a disbelief in the very existence of objective truth. The friends of totalitarianism in this country usually tend to argue that since absolute truth is not attainable, a big lie is no worse than a little lie. It is pointed out that *all* historical records are biased and inaccurate, or, on the other hand, that modern physics has proved that what seems to us the real world is an illusion, so that to believe in the evidence of one's senses is simply vulgar philistinism. A totalitarian society which succeeded in perpetuating itself would probably set up a schizophrenic system of thought, in which the laws of common sense held good in everyday life and in certain exact sciences, but could be disregarded by the politician, the historian, and the sociologist. Already there are countless people who would think it scandalous to falsify a scientific textbook, but would see nothing wrong in falsifying an historical fact. It is at the point where literature and politics cross that totalitarianism exerts its greatest pressure on the intellectual. The exact sciences are not, at this date, menaced to anything like the same extent. This partly accounts for the fact that in all countries it is easier for the scientists than for the writers to line up behind their respective governments.

To keep the matter in perspective, let me repeat what I said at the beginning of this essay: that in England the *immediate* enemies of truthfulness, and hence of freedom of thought, are the press lords, the film magnates, and the bureaucrats, but that on a long view the weakening of the desire for liberty among the intellectuals themselves is the most serious symptom of all. It may seem that all this time I have been talking about the effects of censorship, not on literature as a whole, but merely on one department of political journalism. Granted that Soviet Russia constitutes a sort of forbidden area in the British press, granted that issues like Poland, the Spanish civil war, the Russo-German pact, and so forth, are debarred from serious discussion, and that if you possess information that conflicts with the prevailing orthodoxy you are expected either to distort it or keep quiet about it—granted all this, why should literature in the wider sense be affected? Is every writer a politician, and is every book necessarily a work of straightforward "reportage"? Even under the tightest dictatorship, cannot the individual writer remain free inside his own mind and distill or disguise his unorthodox ideas in such a way that the authorities will be too stupid to recognize them? And in any case, if the writer himself is in agreement with the prevailing orthodoxy, why should it have a cramping effect on him? Is not literature, or any of the arts, likeliest to flourish in societies in which there are no major conflicts of opinion and no sharp distinction between the artist and his audience? Does one have to assume that every writer is a rebel, or even that a writer as such is an exceptional person?

Whenever one attempts to defend intellectual liberty against the claims of totalitarianism, one meets with these arguments in one form or another. They are based on a complete misunderstanding of what literature is, and how—one should perhaps rather say *why* —it comes into being. They assume that a writer is either a mere entertainer or else a venal hack who can switch from one line of propaganda to another as easily as an organ grinder changing tunes.

But after all, how is it that books ever come to be written? Above a quite low level, literature is an attempt to influence the viewpoint of one's contemporaries by recording experience. And so far as freedom of expression is concerned, there is not much difference between a mere journalist and the most "unpolitical" imaginative writer. The journalist is unfree, and is conscious of unfreedom, when he is forced to write lies or suppress what seems to him important news: the imaginative writer is unfree when he has to falsify his subjective feelings, which from his point of view are facts. He may distort and caricature reality in order to make his meaning clearer, but he cannot misrepresent the scenery of his own mind: he cannot say with any conviction that he likes what he dislikes, or believes what he disbelieves. If he is forced to do so, the only result is that his creative faculties dry up. Nor can he solve the problem by keeping away from controversial topics. There is no such thing as genuinely non-political literature, and least of all in an age like our own, when fears, hatreds, and loyalties of a directly political kind are near to the surface of everyone's consciousness. Even a single taboo can have an all-round crippling effect upon the mind, because there is always the danger that any thought which is freely followed up may lead to the forbidden thought. It follows that the atmosphere of totalitarianism is deadly to any kind of prose writer, though a poet, at any rate a lyric poet, might possibly find it breathable. And in any totalitarian society that survives for more than a couple of generations, it is probable that prose literature, of the kind that has existed during the past four hundred years, must actually *come to an end*.

Literature has sometimes flourished under despotic régimes, but, as has often been pointed out, the despotisms of the past were not totalitarian. Their repressive apparatus was always inefficient, their ruling classes were usually either corrupt or apathetic or half-liberal in outlook, and the prevailing religious doctrines usually worked against perfectionism and the notion of human infallibility. Even so it is broadly true that prose literature has reached its highest levels in periods of democracy and free speculation. What is new in totalitarianism is that its doctrines are not only unchallengeable but also unstable. They have to be accepted on pain of damnation, but on the other hand they are always liable to be altered at a moment's notice. Consider, for example, the various attitudes, completely incompatible with one another, which an English Communist or "fellow-traveler" has had to adopt toward the war between Britain and Germany. For years before September, 1939, he was expected to be in a continuous stew about "the horrors of

Nazism" and to twist everything he wrote into a denunciation of Hitler: after September, 1939, for twenty months, he had to believe that Germany was more sinned against than sinning, and the word "Nazi," at least as far as print went, had to drop right out of his vocabulary. Immediately after hearing the 8 o'clock news bulletin on the morning of June 22, 1941, he had to start believing once again that Nazism was the most hideous evil the world had ever seen. Now, it is easy for a politician to make such changes: for a writer the case is somewhat different. If he is to switch his allegiance at exactly the right moment, he must either tell lies about his subjective feelings, or else suppress them altogether. In either case he has destroyed his dynamo. Not only will ideas refuse to come to him, but the very words he uses will seem to stiffen under his touch. Political writing in our time consists almost entirely of prefabricated phrases bolted together like the pieces of a child's Meccano set. It is the unavoidable result of self-censorship. To write in plain, vigorous language one has to think fearlessly, and if one thinks fearlessly one cannot be politically orthodox. It might be otherwise in an "age of faith," when the prevailing orthodoxy has been long established and is not taken too seriously. In that case it would be possible, or might be possible, for large areas of one's mind to remain unaffected by what one officially believed. Even so, it is worth noticing that prose literature almost disappeared during the only age of faith that Europe has ever enjoyed. Throughout the whole of the Middle Ages there was almost no imaginative prose literature and very little in the way of historical writing: and the intellectual leaders of society expressed their most serious thoughts in a dead language which barely altered during a thousand years.

Totalitarianism, however, does not so much promise an age of faith as an age of schizophrenia. A society becomes totalitarian when its structure becomes flagrantly artificial: that is, when its ruling class has lost its function but succeeds in clinging to power by force or fraud. Such a society, no matter how long it persists, can never afford to become either tolerant or intellectually stable. It can never permit either the truthful recording of facts, or the emotional sincerity, that literary creation demands. But to be corrupted by totalitarianism one does not have to live in a totalitarian country. The mere prevalence of certain ideas can spread a kind of poison that makes one subject after another impossible for literary purposes. Wherever there is an enforced orthodoxy—or even two orthodoxies, as often happens—good writing stops. This was well illustrated by the Spanish civil war. To many English intellectuals the war was a deeply moving experience, but not an experience about which they could write sincerely. There were only two things that you were allowed to say, and both of them were palpable lies: as a result, the war produced acres of print but almost nothing worth reading.

It is not certain whether the effects of totalitarianism upon verse need be so deadly as its effects on prose. There is a whole series of converging reasons why it is somewhat easier for a poet than for a prose writer to feel at home in an authoritarian society. To begin with, bureaucrats and other "practical" men usually despise the poet too deeply to be much interested in what he is saying. Secondly, what the poet is saying—that is, what his poem "means" if translated into prose—is relatively unimportant even to himself. The thought contained in a poem is always simple, and is no more the primary purpose of the poem than the anecdote is the primary purpose of the picture. A poem is an arrangement of sounds and associations, as a painting is an arrangement of brushmarks. For short snatches, indeed, as in the refrain of a song, poetry can even dispense with meaning altogether. It is therefore fairly easy for a poet to keep away from dangerous subjects and avoid uttering heresies: and even when he does utter them, they may escape notice. But above all, good verse, unlike good prose, is not necessarily an individual product. Certain kinds of poems, such as ballads, or, on the other hand, very artificial verse forms, can be composed co-operatively by groups of people. Whether the ancient English and Scottish ballads were originally produced by individuals, or by the people at large, is disputed; but at any rate they are non-individual in the sense that they constantly change in passing from mouth to mouth. Even in print no two versions of a ballad are ever quite the same. Many primitive peoples compose verse communally. Someone begins to improvise, probably accompanying himself on a musical instrument, somebody else chips in with a line or a rhyme when the first singer breaks down, and so the process continues until there exists a whole song or ballad which has no identifiable author.

In prose, this kind of intimate collaboration is quite impossible. Serious prose, in any case, has to be composed in solitude, whereas the excitement of being part of a group is actually an aid to certain kinds of versification. Verse—and perhaps good verse of its kind, though it would not be the highest kind—might survive under even the most inquisitorial régime. Even in a society where liberty and individuality had been extinguished, there would still be need either for patriotic songs and heroic ballads celebrating victories, or for elaborate exercises in flattery: and these are the kinds of poem that can be written to order, or composed communally, without necessarily lacking artistic value. Prose is a different matter, since the prose writer cannot narrow the range of his thoughts without killing his inventiveness. But the history of totalitarian societies, or of groups of people who have adopted the totalitarian outlook, suggests that loss of liberty is inimical to *all* forms of literature. German literature almost disappeared during the Hitler régime, and the case was not much better in Italy. Russian literature, so far as one can judge by translations, has deteriorated markedly since the early days of the Revolution, though some of the verse appears to be better than the prose. Few if any Russian novels that it is possible to take seriously have been translated for about fifteen years. In western Europe and America large sections of the literary intelligentsia have either passed through the Communist Party or have been warmly sympathetic to it, but this whole leftward movement has produced extraordinarily few books worth reading. Orthodox Catholicism, again, seems to have a crushing effect upon certain literary forms, especially the novel. During a period of three hundred years, how many people have been at once good novelists and good Catholics? The fact is that certain themes cannot be celebrated in words, and tyranny is one of them. No one ever wrote a good book in praise of the Inquisition. Poetry *might* survive in a totalitarian age, and certain arts or half-arts, such as architecture, might even find tyranny beneficial, but the prose writer would have no choice between silence and death. Prose literature as we know it is the product of rationalism, of the Protestant centuries, of the autonomous individual. And the destruction of intellectual liberty cripples the journalist, the sociological writer, the historian, the novelist, the critic, and the poet, in that order. In the future it is possible that a new kind of literature, not involving individual feeling or truthful observation, may arise, but no such thing is at present imaginable. It seems much likelier that if the liberal culture that we have lived in since the Renaissance actually comes to an end, the literary art will perish with it.

Of course, print will continue to be used, and it is interesting to speculate what kinds of reading matter would survive in a rigidly totalitarian society. Newspapers will presumably continue until television technique reaches a higher level, but apart from newspapers it is doubtful even now whether the great mass of people in the industrialized countries feel the need for any kind of literature. They are unwilling, at any rate, to spend anywhere near as much on reading matter as they spend on several other recreations. Probably novels and stories will be completely superseded by film and radio productions. Or perhaps some kind of low-grade sensational fiction will survive, produced by a sort of conveyor-belt process that reduces human initiative to the minimum.

It would probably not be beyond human ingenuity to write books by machinery. But a sort of mechanizing process can already be seen at work in the film and radio, in publicity and propaganda, and in the lower reaches of journalism. The Disney films, for instance, are produced by what is essentially a factory process, the work being done partly mechanically and partly by teams of artists who have to subordinate their individual style. Radio features are commonly written by tired hacks to whom the subject and the manner of treatment are dictated beforehand: even so, what they write is merely a kind of raw material to be chopped into shape by producers and censors. So also with the innumerable books and pamphlets commissioned by government departments. Even more machine-like is the production of short stories, serials, and poems for the very cheap magazines. Papers such as the *Writer* abound with advertisements of literary schools, all of them offering you ready-made plots at a few shillings a time. Some, together with the plot, supply the opening and closing sentences of each chapter. Others furnish you with a sort of algebraical formula by the use of which you can construct your plots for yourself. Others offer packs of cards marked with characters and situations, which have only to be shuffled and dealt in order to produce ingenious stories automatically. It is probably in some such way that the literature of a totalitarian society would be produced, if literature were still felt to be necessary. Imagination—even consciousness, so far as possible—would be eliminated from the process of writing. Books would be planned in their broad lines by bureaucrats, and would pass through so many hands that when finished they would be no more an individual product than a Ford car at the end of the assembly line. It goes without saying that anything so produced would be rubbish; but anything that was *not* rubbish would endanger the structure of the state. As for the surviving literature of the past, it would have to be suppressed or at least elaborately rewritten.

Meanwhile totalitarianism has not fully triumphed anywhere. Our own society is still, broadly speaking, liberal. To exercise your right of free speech you have to fight against economic pressure and against strong sections of public opinion, but not, as yet, against a secret police force. You can say or print almost anything so long as you are willing to do it in a hole-and-corner way. But what is sinister, as I said at the beginning of this essay, is that the conscious enemies of liberty are those to whom liberty ought to mean most. The big public do not care about the matter one way or the other. They are not in favor of persecuting the heretic, and they will not exert themselves to defend him. They are at once too sane and too stupid to acquire the totalitarian outlook. The direct, conscious attack on intellectual decency comes from the intellectuals themselves.

It is possible that the Russophile intelligentsia, if they had not succumbed to that particular myth, would have succumbed to another of much the same kind. But at any rate the Russian myth is there, and the corruption it causes stinks. When one sees highly educated men looking on indifferently at oppression and persecution, one wonders which to despise more, their cynicism or their shortsightedness. Many scientists, for example, are the uncritical admirers of the U.S.S.R. They appear to think that the destruction of liberty is of no importance so long as their own line of work is for the moment unaffected. The U.S.S.R. is a large, rapidly developing country which has acute need of scientific workers and, consequently, treats them generously. Provided that they steer clear of dangerous subjects such as psychology, scientists are privileged persons. Writers, on the other hand, are viciously persecuted. It is true that literary prostitutes like Ilya Ehrenburg or Alexei Tolstoy are paid huge sums of money, but the only thing which is of any value to the writer as such—his freedom of expression—is taken away from him. Some, at least, of the English scientists who speak so enthusiastically of the opportunities enjoyed by scientists in Russia are capable of understanding this. But their reflection appears to be: "Writers are persecuted in Russia. So what? I am not a writer." They do not see that any attack on intellectual liberty, and on the concept of objective truth, threatens in the long run every department of thought.

For the moment the totalitarian state tolerates the scientist because it needs him. Even in Nazi Germany, scientists, other than Jews, were relatively well treated and the German scientific community, as a whole, offered no resistance to Hitler. At this stage of history, even the most autocratic ruler is forced to take account of physical reality, partly because of the lingering-on of liberal habits of thought, partly because of the need to prepare for war. So long as physical reality cannot be altogether ignored, so long as two and two have to make four when you are, for example, drawing the blueprint of an aeroplane, the scientist has his function, and can even be allowed a measure of liberty. His awakening will come later, when the totalitarian state is firmly established. Meanwhile, if he wants to safeguard the integrity of science, it is his job to develop some kind of solidarity with his literary colleagues and not regard it as a matter of indifference when writers are silenced or driven to suicide, and newspapers systematically falsified.

But however it may be with the physical sciences, or with music, painting, and architecture, it is—as I have tried to show—certain that literature is doomed if liberty of thought perishes. Not only is it doomed in any country which retains a totalitarian structure; but any writer who adopts the totalitarian outlook, who finds excuses for persecution and the falsification of reality, thereby destroys himself as a writer. There is no way out of this. No tirades against "individualism" and "the ivory tower," no pious platitudes to the effect that "true individuality is only attained through identification with the community," can get over the fact that a bought mind is a spoiled mind. Unless spontaneity enters at some point or another, literary creation is impossible, and language itself becomes ossified. At some time in the future, if the human mind becomes something totally different from what it now is, we may learn to separate literary creation from intellectual honesty. At present we know only that the imagination, like certain wild animals, will not breed in captivity. Any writer or journalist who denies that fact—and nearly all the current praise of the Soviet Union contains or implies such a denial—is, in effect, demanding his own destruction.

1946

△

"I Write as I Please"

▽

DECLINE OF THE ENGLISH MURDER

It is Sunday afternoon, preferably before the war. The wife is already asleep in the armchair, and the children have been sent out for a nice long walk. You put your feet up on the sofa, settle your spectacles on your nose, and open the *News of the World*. Roast beef and Yorkshire, or roast pork and apple sauce, followed up by suet pudding and driven home, as it were, by a cup of mahogany-

brown tea, have put you in just the right mood. Your pipe is
drawing sweetly, the sofa cushions are soft underneath you, the
fire is well alight, the air is warm and stagnant. In these blissful
circumstances, what is it that you want to read about?

Naturally, about a murder. But what kind of murder? If one
examines the murders which have given the greatest amount of
pleasure to the British public, the murders whose story is known
in its general outline to almost everyone and which have been
made into novels and rehashed over and over again by the Sunday papers, one finds a fairly strong family resemblance running
through the greater number of them. Our great period in murder,
our Elizabethan period, so to speak, seems to have been between
roughly 1850 and 1925, and the murderers whose reputation has
stood the test of time are the following: Dr. Palmer of Rugely,
Jack the Ripper, Neill Cream, Mrs. Maybrick, Dr. Crippen, Sed-
don, Joseph Smith, Armstrong and Bywaters and Thompson. In addition, in 1919 or thereabouts, there was another very celebrated
case which fits into the general pattern but which I had better not
mention by name, because the accused man was acquitted.

Of the above-mentioned nine cases, at least four have had successful novels based on them, one has been made into a popular
melodrama, and the amount of literature surrounding them, in the
form of newspaper write-ups, criminological treatises, and reminis-
cences by lawyers and police officers, would make a considerable
library. It is difficult to believe that any recent English crime will
be remembered so long and so intimately, and not only because
the violence of external events has made murder seem unimportant, but because the prevalent type of crime seems to be changing. The principal *cause célèbre* of the war years was the so-called
Cleft Chin Murder, which has now been written up in a popular
booklet * the verbatim account of the trial was published some
time last year by Messrs. Jarrolds with an introduction by Mr.
Bechhofer Roberts. Before returning to this pitiful and sordid case,
which is only interesting from a sociological and perhaps a legal
point of view, let me try to define what it is that the readers of
Sunday papers mean when they say fretfully that "you never seem
to get a good murder nowadays."

In considering the nine murders I named above, one can start
by excluding the Jack the Ripper case, which is in a class by itself. Of the other eight, six were poisoning cases, and eight of the
ten criminals belonged to the middle class. In one way or another,

* *The Cleft Chin Murder,* by R. Alwyn Raymond, Claude Morris.

sex was a powerful motive in all but two cases, and in at least four cases respectability—the desire to gain a secure position in life, or not to forfeit one's social position by some scandal such as a divorce—was one of the main reasons for committing murder. In more than half the cases, the object was to get hold of a certain known sum of money such as a legacy or an insurance policy, but the amount involved was nearly always small. In most of the cases the crime only came to light slowly, as the result of careful investigations which started off with the suspicions of neighbors or relatives; and in nearly every case there was some dramatic coincidence, in which the finger of Providence could be clearly seen, or one of those episodes that no novelist would dare to make up, such as Crippen's flight across the Atlantic with his mistress dressed as a boy, or Joseph Smith playing "Nearer, my God, to Thee" on the harmonium while one of his wives was drowning in the next room. The background of all these crimes, except Neill Cream's, was essentially domestic; of twelve victims, seven were either wife or husband of the murderer.

With all this in mind one can construct what would be, from a *News of the World* reader's point of view, the "perfect" murder. The murderer should be a little man of the professional class—a dentist or a solicitor, say—living an intensely respectable life somewhere in the suburbs, and preferably in a semi-detached house, which will allow the neighbors to hear suspicious sounds through the wall. He should be either chairman of the local Conservative Party branch, or a leading Nonconformist and strong temperance advocate. He should go astray through cherishing a guilty passion for his secretary or the wife of a rival professional man, and should only bring himself to the point of murder after long and terrible wrestles with his conscience. Having decided on murder, he should plan it all with the utmost cunning, and only slip up over some tiny unforeseeable detail. The means chosen should, of course, be poison. In the last analysis he should commit murder because this seems to him less disgraceful, and less damaging to his career, than being detected in adultery. With this kind of background, a crime can have dramatic and even tragic qualities which make it memorable and excite pity for both victim and murderer. Most of the crimes mentioned above have a touch of this atmosphere, and in three cases, including the one I referred to but did not name, the story approximates to the one I have outlined.

Now compare the Cleft Chin Murder. There is no depth of feeling in it. It was almost chance that the two people concerned committed that particular murder, and it was only by good luck that they did not commit several others. The background was not domesticity, but the anonymous life of the dance halls and the false values of the American film. The two culprits were an eighteen-year-old ex-waitress named Elizabeth Jones, and an American army deserter, posing as an officer, named Karl Hulten. They were only together for six days, and it seems doubtful whether until they were arrested, they even learned one another's true names. They met casually in a teashop, and that night went out for a ride in a stolen army truck. Jones described herself as a strip-tease artist, which was not strictly true (she had given one unsuccessful performance in this line), and declared that she wanted to do something dangerous, "like being a gun-moll." Hulten described himself as a big-time Chicago gangster, which was also untrue. They met a girl bicycling along the road, and to show how tough he was Hulten ran over her with his truck, after which the pair robbed her of the few shillings that were on her. On another occasion they knocked out a girl to whom they had offered a lift, took her coat and handbag, and threw her into a river. Finally, in the most wanton way, they murdered a taxi-driver who happened to have £8 in his pocket. Soon afterwards they parted. Hulten was caught because he had foolishly kept the dead man's car, and Jones made spontaneous confessions to the police. In court each prisoner incriminated the other. In between crimes, both of them seem to have behaved with the utmost callousness: they spent the dead taxi-driver's £8 at the dog races.

Judging from her letters, the girl's case has a certain amount of psychological interest, but this murder probably captured the headlines because it provided distraction amid the doodle-bugs and the anxieties of the Battle of France. Jones and Hulten committed their murder to the tune of V-1, and were convicted to the tune of V-2. There was also considerable excitement because—as has become usual in England—the man was sentenced to death and the girl to imprisonment. According to Mr. Raymond, the reprieving of Jones caused widespread indignation and streams of telegrams to the Home Secretary; in her native town, "She should hang" was chalked on the walls beside pictures of a figure dangling from a gallows. Considering that only ten women have been hanged in Britain this century, and that the practice has gone out largely because of popular feeling against it, it is difficult not to feel that this clamor to hang an eighteen-year-old girl was due partly to the brutalizing effects of war. Indeed, the whole meaningless story, with its atmosphere of dance halls, movie palaces, cheap perfume, false names and stolen cars, belongs essentially to a war period.

Perhaps it is significant that the most talked-of English murder of recent years should have been committed by an American and an English girl who had become partly Americanized. But it is difficult to believe that this case will be so long remembered as the old domestic poisoning dramas, product of a stable society where the all-prevailing hypocrisy did at least ensure that crimes as serious as murder should have strong emotions behind them.

1946

SOME THOUGHTS ON THE COMMON TOAD

Before the swallow, before the daffodil, and not much later than the snowdrop, the common toad salutes the coming of spring after his own fashion, which is to emerge from a hole in the ground, where he has lain buried since the previous autumn, and crawl as rapidly as possible towards the nearest suitable patch of water. Something—some kind of shudder in the earth, or perhaps merely a rise of a few degrees in the temperature—has told him that it is time to wake up: though a few toads appear to sleep the clock round and miss out a year from time to time—at any rate, I have more than once dug them up, alive and apparently well, in the middle of the summer.

At this period, after his long fast, the toad has a very spiritual look, like a strict Anglo-Catholic toward the end of Lent. His movements are languid but purposeful, his body is shrunken, and by contrast his eyes look abnormally large. This allows one to notice, what one might not at another time, that a toad has about the most beautiful eye of any living creature. It is like gold, or more exactly it is like the golden-colored semi-precious stone which one sometimes sees in signet rings, and which I think is called a chrysoberyl.

For a few days after getting into the water the toad concentrates on building up his strength by eating small insects. Presently he has swollen to his normal size again, and then he goes through a phase of intense sexiness. All he knows, at least if he is a male toad, is that he wants to get his arms round something, and if you offer him a stick, or even your finger, he will cling to it with surprising strength and take a long time to discover that it is not a female toad. Frequently one comes upon shapeless masses of ten or twenty toads rolling over and over in the water, one clinging to another without distinction of sex. By degrees, however, they sort themselves out into couples, with the male duly sitting on the female's back. You can now distinguish males from females, because the male is smaller, darker and sits on top, with his arms tightly clasped round the female's neck. After a day or two the spawn is laid in long strings which wind themselves in and out of the reeds and soon become invisible. A few more weeks, and the water is alive with masses of tiny tadpoles which rapidly grow larger, sprout hind legs, then forelegs, then shed their tails: and finally, about the middle of the summer, the new generation of toads, smaller than one's thumbnail but perfect in every particular, crawl out of the water to begin the game anew.

I mention the spawning of the toads because it is one of the phenomena of spring which most deeply appeal to me, and because the toad, unlike the skylark and the primrose, has never had much of a boost from the poets. But I am aware that many people do not like reptiles or amphibians, and I am not suggesting that in order to enjoy the spring you have to take an interest in toads. There are also the crocus, the missel thrush, the cuckoo, the blackthorn, etc. The point is that the pleasures of spring are available to everybody, and cost nothing. Even in the most sordid street the coming of spring will register itself by some sign or other, if it is only a brighter blue between the chimney pots or the vivid green of an elder sprouting on a blitzed site. Indeed it is remarkable how Nature goes on existing unofficially, as it were, in the very heart of London. I have seen a kestrel flying over the Deptford gasworks, and I have heard a first-rate performance by a black bird in the Euston Road. There must be some hundreds of thousands, if not millions, of birds living inside the four-mile radius, and it is rather a pleasing thought that none of them pays a halfpenny of rent.

As for spring, not even the narrow and gloomy streets round the Bank of England are quite able to exclude it. It comes seeping in everywhere, like one of those new poison gases which pass through all filters. The spring is commonly referred to as "a miracle," and during the past five or six years this worn-out figure of speech has taken on a new lease of life. After the sort of winters we have had to endure recently, the spring does seem miraculous, because it has become gradually harder and harder to believe that it is actually going to happen. Every February since 1940 I have found myself thinking that this time winter is going to be permanent. But Persephone, like the toads, always rises from the dead at about the same moment. Suddenly, toward the end of March, the miracle happens and the decaying slum in which I live is transfigured. Down in the square the sooty privets have turned bright green, the leaves are thickening on the chestnut trees, the daffodils are

out, the wallflowers are budding, the policeman's tunic looks positively a pleasant shade of blue, the fish-monger greets his customers
with a smile, and even the sparrows are quite a different color,
having felt the balminess of the air and nerved themselves to take
a bath, their first since last September.

Is it wicked to take a pleasure in spring, and other seasonal
changes? To put it more precisely, is it politically reprehensible,
while we are all groaning, under the shackles of the capitalist system, to point out that life is frequently more worth living because
of a blackbird's song, a yellow elm tree in October, or some other
natural phenomenon which does not cost money and does not have
what the editors of the left-wing newspapers call a class angle?
There is no doubt that many people think so. I know by experience that a favorable reference to "Nature" in one of my articles
is liable to bring me abusive letters, and though the keyword in
these letters is usually "sentimental," two ideas seem to be mixed
up in them. One is that any pleasure in the actual process of life
encourages a sort of political quietism. People, so the thought runs,
ought to be discontented, and it is our job to multiply our wants
and not simply to increase our enjoyment of the things we have
already. The other idea is that this is the age of machines and
that to dislike the machine, or even to want to limit its domination, is backward-looking, reactionary, and slightly ridiculous. This
is often backed up by the statement that a love of Nature is a
foible of urbanized people who have no notion what Nature is
really like. Those who really have to deal with the soil, so it is
argued, do not love the soil, and do not take the faintest interest
in birds or flowers, except from a strictly utilitarian point of view.
To love the country one must live in the town, merely taking an
occasional week-end ramble at the warmer times of year.

This last idea is demonstrably false. Medieval literature, for instance, including the popular ballads, is full of an almost Georgian
enthusiasm for Nature, and the art of agricultural peoples such as
the Chinese and Japanese centers always round trees, birds, flowers,
rivers, mountains. The other idea seems to me to be wrong in a
subtler way. Certainly we ought to be discontented, we ought not
simply to find out ways of making the best of a bad job, and yet
if we kill all pleasure in the actual process of life, what sort of
future are we preparing for ourselves? If a man cannot enjoy the
return of spring, why should he be happy in a labor-saving Utopia?
What will he do with the leisure that the machine will give him?
I have always suspected that if our economic and political prob-

lems are ever really solved, life will become simpler instead of more complex, and that the sort of pleasure one gets from finding the first primrose will loom larger than the sort of pleasure one gets from eating an ice to the tune of a Wurlitzer. I think that by retaining one's childhood love of such things as trees, fishes, butterflies, and—to return to my first instance—toads, one makes a peaceful and decent future a little more probable, and that by preaching the doctrine that nothing is to be admired except steel and concrete, one merely makes it a little surer that human beings will have no outlet for their surplus energy except in hatred and leaderworship.

At any rate, spring is here, even in London, N.1, and they can't stop you enjoying it. This is a satisfying reflection. How many a time have I stood watching the toads mating, or a pair of hares having a boxing match in the young corn, and thought of all the important persons who would stop me enjoying this if they could. But luckily they can't. So long as you are not actually ill, hungry, frightened, or immured in a prison or a holiday camp, spring is still spring. The atom bombs are piling up in the factories, the police are prowling through the cities, the lies are streaming from the loudspeakers, but the earth is still going round the sun, and neither the dictators nor the bureaucrats, deeply as they disapprove of the process, are able to prevent it.

1946

A GOOD WORD FOR THE VICAR OF BRAY

Some years ago a friend took me to the little Berkshire church of which the celebrated Vicar of Bray was once the incumbent. (Actually it is a few miles from Bray, but perhaps at that time the two livings were one.) In the churchyard there stands a magnificent yew tree which, according to a notice at its foot, was planted by no less a person than the Vicar of Bray himself. And it struck me at the time as curious that such a man should have left such a relic behind him.

The Vicar of Bray, though he was well equipped to be a leaderwriter on the *Times,* could hardly be described as an admirable character. Yet, after this lapse of time, all that is left of him is a comic song * and a beautiful tree, which has rested the eyes of generation after generation and must surely have outweighed any bad effects which he produced by his political quislingism.

* An anonymous song dating from the eighteenth century. The subject is a parson who boasts that he has accommodated himself to the religious views of the reigns of Charles, James, William, Anne, and George and that, whatever king may reign, he will remain Vicar of Bray.

Thibaw, the last King of Burma, was also far from being a good man. He was a drunkard, he had five hundred wives—he seems to have kept them chiefly for show, however—and when he came to the throne his first act was to decapitate seventy or eighty of his brothers. Yet he did posterity a good turn by planting the dusty streets of Mandalay with tamarind trees which cast a pleasant shade until the Japanese incendiary bombs burned them down in 1942.

The poet, James Shirley, seems to have generalized too freely when he said that "Only the actions of the just Smell sweet and blossom in their dust." Sometimes the actions of the unjust make quite a good showing after the appropriate lapse of time. When I saw the Vicar of Bray's yew tree it reminded me of something, and afterward I got hold of a book of selections from the writings of John Aubrey and reread a pastoral poem which must have been written some time in the first half of the seventeenth century, and which was inspired by a certain Mrs. Overall.

Mrs. Overall was the wife of a Dean and was extensively unfaithful to him. According to Aubrey she "could scarcely denie any one," and she had "the loveliest Eies that were ever seen, but wondrous wanton." The poem (the "shepherd swaine" seems to have been somebody called Sir John Selby) starts off:

> Downe lay the Shepherd Swaine
> So sober and demure
> Wishing for his wench againe
> So bonny and so pure
> With his head on hillock lowe
> And his arms akimboe
> And all was for the losse of his
> Hye nonny nonny noe. . . .
> Sweet she was, as kind a love
> As ever fetter'd Swaine;
> Never such a daynty one
> Shall man enjoy again.
> Sett a thousand on a rowe
> I forbid that any showe
> Ever the like of her
> Hye nonny nonny noe.

As the poem proceeds through another six verses, the refrain "hye nonny nonny noe" takes on an unmistakably obscene meaning, but it ends with the exquisite stanza:

> But gone she is the prettiest lasse
> That ever trod on plaine.
> What ever hath betide of her
> Blame not the Shepherd Swaine.

> For why? She was her owne Foe,
> And gave herself the overthrowe
> By being so franke of her
> Hye nonny nonny noe.

Mrs. Overall was no more an exemplary character than the Vicar of Bray, though a more attractive one. Yet in the end all that remains of her is a poem which still gives pleasure to many people, though for some reason it never gets into the anthologies. The suffering which she presumably caused, and the misery and futility in which her own life must have ended, have been transformed into a sort of lingering fragrance like the smell of tobacco plants on a summer evening.

But to come back to trees. The planting of a tree, especially one of the long-living hardwood trees, is a gift which you can make to posterity at almost no cost and with almost no trouble, and if the tree takes root it will far outlive the visible effect of any of your other actions, good or evil. A year or two ago I wrote a few paragraphs in *Tribune* about some sixpenny rambler roses from Woolworth's which I had planted before the war. This brought me an indignant letter from a reader who said that roses are bourgeois, but I still think that my sixpence was better spent than if it had gone on cigarettes or even on one of the excellent Fabian Research Pamphlets.

Recently, I spent a day at the cottage where I used to live, and noted with a pleased surprise—to be exact, it was a feeling of having done good unconsciously—the progress of the things I had planted nearly ten years ago. I think it is worth recording what some of them cost, just to show what you can do with a few shillings if you invest them in something that grows.

First of all there were the two ramblers from Woolworth's, and three polyantha roses, all at sixpence each. Then there were two bush roses which were part of a job lot from a nursery garden. This job lot consisted of six fruit trees, three rose bushes and two gooseberry bushes, all for ten shillings. One of the fruit trees and one of the rose bushes died but the rest are all flourishing. The sum total is five fruit trees, seven roses and two gooseberry bushes, all for twelve and sixpence. These plants have not entailed much work, and have had nothing spent on them beyond the original amount. They never even received any manure, except what I occasionally collected in a bucket when one of the farm horses happened to have halted outside the gate.

Between them, in nine years, those seven rose bushes will have given what would add up to a hundred or a hundred and fifty months of bloom. The fruit trees, which were mere saplings when I put them in, are now just about getting in their stride. Last week one of them, a plum, was a mass of blossom, and the apples looked as if they were going to do fairly well. What had originally been the weakling of the family, a Cox's Orange Pippin—it would hardly have been included in the job lot if it had been a good plant—had grown into a sturdy tree with plenty of fruit spurs on it. I maintain that it was a public-spirited action to plant that Cox, for these trees do not fruit quickly and I did not expect to stay there long. I never had an apple off it myself, but it looks as if someone else will have quite a lot. By their fruits ye shall know them, and the Cox's Orange Pippin is a good fruit to be known by. Yet I did not plant it with the conscious intention of doing anybody a good turn. I just saw the job lot going cheap and stuck the things into the ground without much preparation.

A thing which I regret, and which I will try to remedy some time, is that I have never in my life planted a walnut. Nobody does plant them nowadays—when you see a walnut it is almost invariably an old tree. If you plant a walnut you are planting it for your grand-children, and who cares a damn for his grandchildren? Nor does anybody plant a quince, a mulberry, or a medlar. But these are garden trees which you can only be expected to plant if you have a patch of ground of your own. On the other hand, in any hedge or in any piece of waste ground you happen to be walking through, you can do something to remedy the appalling massacre of trees, espe-cially oaks, ashes, elms, and beeches, which has happened during the war years.

Even an apple tree is liable to live for about a hundred years, so that the Cox I planted in 1936 may still be bearing fruit well into the twenty-first century. An oak or a beech may live for hundreds of years and be a pleasure to thousands or tens of thousands of people before it is finally sawn up into timber. I am not suggesting that one can discharge all one's obligations towards society by means of a private re-afforestation scheme. Still, it might not be a bad idea, every time you commit an anti-social act, to make a note of it in your diary, and then, at the appropriate season, push an acorn into the ground.

And, if even one in twenty of them came to maturity, you might do quite a lot of harm in your lifetime, and still, like the Vicar of Bray, end up as a public benefactor after all.

1946

△

Why I Write

▽

From a very early age, perhaps the age of five or six, I knew that when I grew up I should be a writer. Between the ages of about seventeen and twenty-four I tried to abandon this idea, but I did so with the consciousness that I was outraging my true nature and that sooner or later I should have to settle down and write books.

I was the middle child of three, but there was a gap of five years on either side, and I barely saw my father before I was eight. For this and other reasons I was somewhat lonely, and I soon developed disagreeable mannerisms which made me unpopular throughout my schooldays. I had the lonely child's habit of making up stories and holding conversations with imaginary persons, and I think from the very start my literary ambitions were mixed up with the feeling of being isolated and undervalued. I knew that I had a facility with words and a power of facing unpleasant facts, and I felt that this created a sort of private world in which I could get my own back for my failure in everyday life. Nevertheless the volume of serious —*i.e.* seriously intended—writing which I produced all through my childhood and boyhood would not amount to half a dozen pages. I wrote my first poem at the age of four or five, my mother taking it down to dictation. I cannot remember anything about it except that it was about a tiger and the tiger had "chair-like teeth"—a good enough phrase, but I fancy the poem was a plagiarism of Blake's "Tiger, Tiger." At eleven, when the war of 1914-18 broke out, I wrote a patriotic poem which was printed in the local newspaper, as was another, two years later, on the death of Kitchener. From time to time, when I was a bit older, I wrote bad and usually unfinished "nature poems" in the Georgian style. I also, about twice, attempted a short story which was a ghastly failure. That was the total of the would-be serious work that I actually set down on paper during all those years.

However, throughout this time I did in a sense engage in literary activities. To begin with there was the made-to-order stuff which I produced quickly, easily and without much pleasure to myself. Apart from school work, I wrote *vers d'occasion*, semi-comic poems which could turn out at what now seems to me astonishing speed—at fourteen I wrote a whole rhyming play, in imitation of Aristophanes, in about a week—and helped to edit school magazines, both printed and in manuscript. These magazines were the most pitiful burlesque stuff that you could imagine, and I took far less trouble with them than I now would with the cheapest journalism. But side by side with all this, for fifteen years or more, I was carrying out a literary exercise of a quite different kind: this was the making up of a continuous "story" about myself, a sort of diary existing only in the mind. I believe this is a common habit of children and adolescents. As a very small child I used to imagine that I was, say, Robin Hood, and picture myself as the hero of thrilling adventures, but quite soon my "story" ceased to be narcissistic in a crude way and became more and more a mere description of what I was doing and the things I saw. For minutes at a time this kind of thing would be running through my head: "He pushed the door open and entered the room. A yellow beam of sunlight, filtering through the muslin curtains, slanted on to the table, where a match-box, half open, lay beside the inkpot. With his right hand in his pocket he moved across to the window. Down in the street a tortoiseshell cat was chasing a dead leaf," etc., etc. This habit continued till I was about twenty-five, right through my non-literary years. Although I had to search, and did search, for the right words, I seemed to be making this descriptive effort almost against my will, under a kind of compulsion from outside. The "story" must, I suppose, have reflected the styles of the various writers I admired at different ages, but so far as I remember it always had the same meticulous descriptive quality.

When I was about sixteen I suddenly discovered the joy of mere words, *i.e.* the sounds and associations of words. The lines from *Paradise Lost*—

> So hee with difficulty and labour hard
> Moved on: with difficulty and labour hee,

which do not now seem to me so very wonderful, sent shivers down my backbone; and the spelling "hee" for "he" was an added pleasure. As for the need to describe things, I knew all about it already. So it is clear what kind of books I wanted to write, in so far as I could be said to want to write books at that time. I wanted to write enormous naturalistic novels with unhappy endings, full of detailed descriptions and arresting similes, and also full of purple passages in which words were used partly for the sake of their sound. And in fact my first completed novel, *Burmese Days*, which I wrote when I was thirty but projected much earlier, is rather that kind of boo'

I give all this background information because I do not think on can assess a writer's motives without knowing something of his ear development. His subject matter will be determined by the age l lives in—at least this is true in tumultuous, revolutionary ages lil our own—but before he ever begins to write he will have acquire an emotional attitude from which he will never completely escap It is his job, no doubt, to discipline his temperament and avoi getting stuck at some immature stage, or in some perverse mood but if he escapes from his early influences altogether, he will hav killed his impulse to write. Putting aside the need to earn a livin; I think there are four great motives for writing, at any rate fc writing prose. They exist in different degrees in every writer, an in any one writer the proportions will vary from time to time, a cording to the atmosphere in which he is living. They are:

(1) Sheer egoism. Desire to seem clever, to be talked about, to b remembered after death, to get your own back on grown-ups wh snubbed you in childhood, etc., etc. It is humbug to pretend tha this is not a motive, and a strong one. Writers share this characte istic with scientists, artists, politicians, lawyers, soldiers, successf businessmen—in short, with the whole top crust of humanity. Th great mass of human beings are not acutely selfish. After the age about thirty they abandon individual ambition—in many cases, ir deed, they almost abandon the sense of being individuals at all— and live chiefly for others, or are simply smothered under drudger But there is also the minority of gifted, wilful people who are de termined to live their own lives to the end, and writers belong i this class. Serious writers, I should say, are on the whole more vai and self-centered than journalists, though less interested in money.

(2) Aesthetic enthusiasm. Perception of beauty in the externa world, or, on the other hand, in words and their right arrangemen Pleasure in the impact of one sound on another, in the firmness c good prose or the rhythm of a good story. Desire to share an e> perience which one feels is valuable and ought not to be missec The aesthetic motive is very feeble in a lot of writers, but even pamphleteer or a writer of textbooks will have pet words and phrase which appeal to him for non-utilitarian reasons; or he may fee strongly about typography, width of margins, etc. Above the level c a railway guide, no book is quite free from aesthetic consideration

(3) Historical impulse. Desire to see things as they are, to find ou true facts and store them up for the use of posterity.

(4) Political purpose—using the word "political" in the wides possible sense. Desire to push the world in a certain direction, t

alter other people's idea of the kind of society that they should strive after. Once again, no book is genuinely free from political bias. The opinion that art should have nothing to do with politics is itself a political attitude.

It can be seen how these various impulses must war against one another, and how they must fluctuate from person to person and from time to time. By nature—taking your "nature" to be the state you have attained when you are first adult—I am a person in whom the first three motives would outweigh the fourth. In a peaceful age I might have written ornate or merely descriptive books, and might have remained almost unaware of my political loyalties. As it is I have been forced into becoming a sort of pamphleteer. First I spent five years in an unsuitable profession (the Indian Imperial Police, in Burma), and then I underwent poverty and the sense of failure. This increased my natural hatred of authority and made me for the first time fully aware of the existence of the working classes, and the job in Burma had given me some understanding of the nature of imperialism: but these experiences were not enough to give me an accurate political orientation. Then came Hitler, the Spanish civil war, etc. By the end of 1935 I had still failed to reach a firm decision. I remember a little poem that I wrote at that date, expressing my dilemma:

> A happy vicar I might have been
> Two hundred years ago,
> To preach upon eternal doom
> And watch my walnuts grow;
>
> But born, alas, in an evil time,
> I missed that pleasant haven,
> For the hair has grown on my upper lip
> And the clergy are all clean-shaven.
>
> And later still the times were good,
> We were so easy to please,
> We rocked our troubled thoughts to sleep
> On the bosoms of the trees.
>
> All ignorant we dared to own
> The joys we now dissemble;
> The greenfinch on the apple bough
> Could make my enemies tremble.
>
> But girls' bellies and apricots,
> Roach in a shaded stream,
> Horses, ducks in flight at dawn,
> All these are a dream.

It is forbidden to dream again;
We maim our joys or hide them;
Horses are made of chromium steel
And little fat men shall ride them.

I am the worm who never turned,
The eunuch without a harem;
Between the priest and the commissar
I walk like Eugene Aram;

And the commissar is telling my fortune
While the radio plays,
But the priest has promised an Austin Seven,
For Duggie always pays.

I dreamed I dwelt in marble halls,
And woke to find it true;
I wasn't born for an age like this;
Was Smith? Was Jones? Were you?

The Spanish war and other events in 1936-7 turned the scale and thereafter I knew where I stood. Every line of serious work that I have written since 1936 has been written, directly or indirectly, *against* totalitarianism and *for* democratic socialism, as I understand it. It seems to me nonsense, in a period like our own, to think that one can avoid writing of such subjects. Everyone writes of them in one guise or another. It is simply a question of which side one takes and what approach one follows. And the more one is conscious of one's political bias, the more chance one has of acting politically without sacrificing one's aesthetic and intellectual integrity.

What I have most wanted to do throughout the past ten years is to make political writing into an art. My starting point is always a feeling of partisanship, a sense of injustice. When I sit down to write a book, I do not say to myself, "I am going to produce a work of art." I write it because there is some lie that I want to expose, some fact to which I want to draw attention, and my initial concern is to get a hearing. But I could not do the work of writing a book, or even a long magazine article, if it were not also an aesthetic experience. Anyone who cares to examine my work will see that even when it is downright propaganda it contains much that a full-time politician would consider irrelevant. I am not able, and I do not want, completely to abandon the world view that I acquired in childhood. So long as I remain alive and well I shall continue to feel strongly about prose style, to love the surface of the earth, and to take a pleasure in solid objects and scraps of useless information. It is no use trying to suppress that side of myself. The job is to reconcile my ingrained likes and dislikes with the essentially public, non-individual activities that this age forces on all of us.

It is not easy. It raises problems of construction and of language, and it raises in a new way the problem of truthfulness. Let me give just one example of the cruder kind of difficulty that arises. My book about the Spanish civil war, *Homage to Catalonia*, is, of course, a frankly political book, but in the main it is written with a certain detachment and regard for form. I did try very hard in it to tell the whole truth without violating my literary instincts. But among other things it contains a long chapter, full of newspaper quotations and the like, defending the Trotskyists who were accused of plotting with Franco. Clearly such a chapter, which after a year or two would lose its interest for any ordinary reader, must ruin the book. A critic whom I respect read me a lecture about it. "Why did you put in all that stuff?" he said. "You've turned what might have been a good book into journalism." What he said was true, but I could not have done otherwise. I happened to know, what very few people in England had been allowed to know, that innocent men were being falsely accused. If I had not been angry about that I should never have written the book.

In one form or another this problem comes up again. The problem of language is subtler and would take too long to discuss. I will only say that of late years I have tried to write less picturesquely and more exactly. In any case I find that by the time you have perfected any style of writing, you have always outgrown it. *Animal Farm* was the first book in which I tried, with full consciousness of what I was doing, to fuse political purpose and artistic purpose into one whole. I have not written a novel for seven years, but I hope to write another fairly soon. It is bound to be a failure, every book is a failure, but I do know with some clarity what kind of book I want to write. Looking back through the last page or two, I see that I have made it appear as though my motives in writing were wholly public-spirited. I don't want to leave that as the final impression. All writers are vain, selfish, and lazy, and at the very bottom of their motives there lies a mystery. Writing a book is a horrible, exhausting struggle, like a long bout of some painful illness. One would never undertake such a thing if one were not driven on by some demon whom one can neither resist nor understand. For all one knows that demon is simply the same instinct that makes a baby squall for attention. And yet it is also true that one can write nothing readable unless one constantly struggles to efface one's own personality. Good prose is like a windowpane. I cannot say with certainty which of my motives are the strongest, but I know which of them deserve to be followed. And looking back through my work, I see that it is invariably where I lacked a *political* purpose that I wrote lifeless books and was betrayed into purple passages, sentences without meaning, decorative adjectives and humbug generally.

1947

△

From "Nineteen Eighty-Four"

▽

PART I

I

It was a bright cold day in April, and the clocks were striking thirteen. Winston Smith, his chin nuzzled into his breast in an effort to escape the vile wind, slipped quickly through the glass doors of Victory Mansions, though not quickly enough to prevent a swirl of gritty dust from entering along with him.

The hallway smelt of boiled cabbage and old rag mats. At one end of it a colored poster, too large for indoor display, had been tacked to the wall. It depicted simply an enormous face, more than a meter wide: the face of a man of about forty-five, with a heavy black mustache and ruggedly handsome features. Winston made for the stairs. It was no use trying the lift. Even at the best of times it was seldom working, and at present the electric current was cut off during daylight hours. It was part of the economy drive in preparation for Hate Week. The flat was seven flights up, and Winston, who was thirty-nine and had a varicose ulcer above his right ankle, went slowly, resting several times on the way. On each landing, opposite the lift shaft, the poster with the enormous face gazed from the wall. It was one of those pictures which are so contrived that the eyes follow you about when you move. BIG BROTHER IS WATCHING YOU, the caption beneath it ran.

Inside the flat a fruity voice was reading out a list of figures which had something to do with the production of pig iron. The voice came from an oblong metal plaque like a dulled mirror which formed part of the surface of the right-hand wall. Winston turned a switch and the voice sank somewhat, though the words were still distinguishable. The instrument (the telescreen, it was called) could be dimmed, but there was no way of shutting it off completely. He moved over to the window: a smallish, frail figure, the meagerness of his body merely emphasized by the blue overalls which were the uniform of the Party. His hair was very fair, his face naturally sanguine, his skin roughened by coarse soap and blunt razor blades and the cold of the winter that had just ended.

Outside, even through the shut windowpane, the world looked cold. Down in the street little eddies of wind were whirling dust and torn paper into spirals, and though the sun was shining and the sky a harsh blue, there seemed to be no color in anything except the posters that were plastered everywhere. The black-mustachio'd face gazed down from every commanding corner. There was one on the house front immediately opposite. BIG BROTHER IS WATCHING YOU, the caption said, while the dark eyes looked deep into Winston's own. Down at street level another poster, torn at one corner, flapped fitfully in the wind, alternately covering and uncovering the single word INGSOC. In the far distance a helicopter skimmed down between the roofs, hovered for an instant like a bluebottle, and darted away again with a curving flight. It was the Police Patrol, snooping into people's windows. The patrols did not matter, however. Only the Thought Police mattered.

Behind Winston's back the voice from the telescreen was still babbling away about pig iron and the overfulfillment of the Ninth Three-Year Plan. The telescreen received and transmitted simultaneously. Any sound that Winston made, above the level of a very low whisper, would be picked up by it; moreover, so long as he remained within the field of vision which the mental plaque commanded, he could be seen as well as heard. There was of course no way of knowing whether you were being watched at any given moment. How often, or on what system, the Thought Police plugged in on any individual wire was guesswork. It was even conceivable that they watched everybody all the time. But at any rate they could plug in your wire whenever they wanted to. You had to live—did live, from habit that became instinct—in the assumption that every sound you made was overheard, and, except in darkness, every movement scrutinized.

Winston kept his back turned to the telescreen. It was safer; though, as he well knew, even a back can be revealing. A kilometer away the Ministry of Truth, his place of work, towered vast and white above the grimy landscape. This, he thought with a sort of vague distaste—this was London, chief city of Airstrip One, itself the third most populous of the provinces of Oceania. He tried to squeeze out some childhood memory that should tell him whether

London had always been quite like this. Were there always these vistas of rotting nineteenth-century houses, their sides shored up with balks of timber, their windows patched with cardboard and their roofs with corrugated iron, their crazy garden walls sagging in all directions? And the bombed sites where the plaster dust swirled in the air and the willow herb straggled over the heaps of rubble; and the places where the bombs had cleared a larger patch and there had sprung up sordid colonies of wooden dwellings like chicken houses? But it was no use, he could not remember: nothing remained of his childhood except a series of bright-lit tableaux, occurring against no background and mostly unintelligible.

The Ministry of Truth—Minitrue, in Newspeak *—was startlingly different from any other object in sight. It was an enormous pyramidal structure of glittering white concrete, soaring up, terrace after terrace, three hundred meters into the air. From where Winston stood it was just possible to read, picked out on its white face in elegant lettering, the three slogans of the Party:

WAR IS PEACE

FREEDOM IS SLAVERY

IGNORANCE IS STRENGTH.

The Ministry of Truth contained, it was said, three thousand rooms above ground level, and corresponding ramifications below. Scattered about London there were just three other buildings of similar appearance and size. So completely did they dwarf the surrounding architecture that from the roof of Victory Mansions you could see all four of them simultaneously. They were the homes of the four Ministries between which the entire apparatus of government was divided: the Ministry of Truth, which concerned itself with news, entertainment, education, and the fine arts; the Ministry of Peace, which concerned itself with war; the Ministry of Love, which maintained law and order; and the Ministry of Plenty, which was responsible for economic affairs. Their names, in Newspeak: Minitrue, Minipax, Miniluv, and Miniplenty.

The Ministry of Love was the really frightening one. There were no windows in it at all. Winston had never been inside the Ministry of Love, nor within half a kilometer of it. It was a place impossible to enter except on official business, and then only by penetrating through a maze of barbed-wire entanglements, steel doors, and hidden machine-gun nests. Even the streets leading up to its outer

---

* Newspeak was the official language of Oceania. For an account of its structure and etymology, see Appendix.

barriers were roamed by gorilla-faced guards in black uniforms, armed with jointed truncheons.

Winston turned round abruptly. He had set his features into the expression of quiet optimism which it was advisable to wear when facing the telescreen. He crossed the room into the tiny kitchen. By leaving the Ministry at this time of day he had sacrificed his lunch in the canteen, and he was aware that there was no food in the kitchen except a hunk of dark-colored bread which had got to be saved for tomorrow's breakfast. He took down from the shelf a bottle of colorless liquid with a plain white label marked VICTORY GIN. It gave off a sickly, oily smell, as of Chinese rice-spirit. Winston poured out nearly a teacupful, nerved himself for a shock, and gulped it down like a dose of medicine.

Instantly his face turned scarlet and the water ran out of his eyes. The stuff was like nitric acid, and moreover, in swallowing it one had the sensation of being hit on the back of the head with a rubber club. The next moment, however, the burning in his belly died down and the world began to look more cheerful. He took a cigarette from a crumpled packet marked VICTORY CIGARETTES and incautiously held it upright, whereupon the tobacco fell out onto the floor. With the next he was more successful. He went back to the living room and sat down at a small table that stood to the left of the telescreen. From the table drawer he took out a penholder, a bottle of ink, and a thick, quarto-sized blank book with a red back and a marbled cover.

For some reason the telescreen in the living room was in an unusual position. Instead of being placed, as was normal, in the end wall, where it could command the whole room, it was in the longer wall, opposite the window. To one side of it there was a shallow alcove in which Winston was now sitting, and which, when the flats were built, had probably been intended to hold bookshelves. By sitting in the alcove, and keeping well back, Winston was able to remain outside the range of the telescreen, so far as sight went. He could be heard, of course, but so long as he stayed in his present position he could not be seen. It was partly the unusual geography of the room that had suggested to him the thing that he was now about to do.

But it had also been suggested by the book that he had just taken out of the drawer. It was a peculiarly beautiful book. Its smooth creamy paper, a little yellowed by age, was of a kind that had not been manufactured for at least forty years past. He could guess, however, that the book was much older than that. He had seen it lying in the window of a frowsy little junk shop in a slummy quarter of the town (just what quarter he did not now remember) and had been stricken immediately by an overwhelming desire to possess it. Party members were supposed not to go into ordinary shops ("dealing on the free market," it was called), but the rule was not strictly kept, because there were various things such as shoelaces and razor blades which it was impossible to get hold of in any other way. He had given a quick glance up and down the street and then had slipped inside and bought the book for two dollars fifty. At the time he was not conscious of wanting it for any particular purpose. He had carried it guiltily home in his brief case. Even with nothing written in it, it was a compromising possession.

The thing that he was about to do was to open a diary. This was not illegal (nothing was illegal, since there were no longer any laws), but if detected it was reasonably certain that it would be punished by death, or at least by twenty-five years in a forced-labor camp. Winston fitted a nib into the penholder and sucked it to get the grease off. The pen was an archaic instrument, seldom used even for signatures, and he had procured one, furtively and with some difficulty, simply because of a feeling that the beautiful creamy paper deserved to be written on with a real nib instead of being scratched with an ink pencil. Actually he was not used to writing by hand. Apart from very short notes, it was usual to dictate everything into the speakwrite, which was of course impossible for his present purpose. He dipped the pen into the ink and then faltered for just a second. A tremor had gone through his bowels. To mark the paper was the decisive act. In small clumsy letters he wrote:

April 4th, 1984.

He sat back. A sense of complete helplessness had descended upon him. To begin with, he did not know with any certainty that this *was* 1984. It must be round about that date, since he was fairly sure that his age was thirty-nine, and he believed that he had been born in 1944 or 1945; but it was never possible nowadays to pin down any date within a year or two.

For whom, it suddenly occurred to him to wonder, was he writing this diary? For the future, for the unborn. His mind hovered for a moment round the doubtful date on the page, and then fetched up with a bump against the Newspeak word *doublethink*. For the first time the magnitude of what he had undertaken came home to him. How could you communicate with the future? It was of its nature impossible. Either the future would resemble the present, in which case it would not listen to him, or it would be different from it, and his predicament would be meaningless.

For some time he sat gazing stupidly at the paper. The telescreen had changed over to strident military music. It was curious that he seemed not merely to have lost the power of expressing himself, but even to have forgotten what it was that he had originally intended to say. For weeks past he had been making ready for this moment, and it had never crossed his mind that anything would be needed except courage. The actual writing would be easy. All he had to do was to transfer to paper the interminable restless monologue that had been running inside his head, literally for years. At this moment, however, even the monologue had dried up. Moreover, his varicose ulcer had begun itching unbearably. He dared not scratch it, because if he did so it always became inflamed. The seconds were ticking by. He was conscious of nothing except the blankness of the page in front of him, the itching of the skin above his ankle, the blaring of the music, and a slight booziness caused by the gin.

Suddenly he began writing in sheer panic, only imperfectly aware of what he was setting down. His small but childish handwriting straggled up and down the page, shedding first its capital letters and finally even its full stops:

April 4th, 1984. Last night to the flicks. All war films. One very good one of a ship full of refugees being bombed somewhere in the Mediterranean. Audience much amused by shots of a great huge fat man trying to swim away with a helicopter after him. first you saw him wallowing along in the water like a porpoise, then you saw him through the helicopters gunsights, then he was full of holes and the sea round him turned pink and he sank as suddenly as though the holes had let in the water. audience shouting with laughter when he sank. then you saw a lifeboat full of children with a helicopter hovering over it. there was a middleaged woman might have been a jewess sitting up in the bow with a little boy about three years old in her arms. little boy screaming with fright and hiding his head between her breasts as if he was trying to burrow right into her and the woman putting her arms round him and comforting him although she was blue with fright herself. all the time covering him up as much as possible as if she thought her arms could keep the bullets off him. then the helicopter planted a 20 kilo bomb in among them terrific flash and the boat went all to matchwood. then there was a wonderful shot of a childs arm going up up up right up into the air a helicopter with a camera in its nose must have followed it up and there was a lot of applause from the party seats but a woman down in the prole part of the house suddenly started kicking up a fuss and shouting they didnt oughter of showed it not in front of

*kids they didnt it aint right not in front of kids it aint until the
police turned her turned her out i dont suppose anything happened
to her nobody cares what the proles say typical prole reaction they
never—*

Winston stopped writing, partly because he was suffering from
cramp. He did not know what had made him pour out this stream
of rubbish. But the curious thing was that while he was doing so a
totally different memory had clarified itself in his mind, to the
point where he almost felt equal to writing it down. It was, he now
realized, because of this other incident that he had suddenly decided to come home and begin the diary today.

It had happened that morning at the Ministry, if anything so
nebulous could be said to happen.

It was nearly eleven hundred, and in the Records Department,
where Winston worked, they were dragging the chairs out of the
cubicles and grouping them in the center of the hall, opposite the
big telescreen, in preparation for the Two Minutes Hate. Winston
was just taking his place in one of the middle rows when two people
whom he knew by sight, but had never spoken to, came unexpectedly
into the room. One of them was a girl whom he often passed in
the corridors. He did not know her name, but he knew that she
worked in the Fiction Department. Presumably—since he had sometimes seen her with oily hands and carrying a spanner—she had some
mechanical job on one of the novel-writing machines. She was a
bold-looking girl of about twenty-seven, with thick dark hair, a
freckled face, and swift, athletic movements. A narrow scarlet sash,
emblem of the Junior Anti-Sex League, was wound several times
round the waist of her overalls, just tightly enough to bring out
the shapeliness of her hips. Winston had disliked her from the very
first moment of seeing her. He knew the reason. It was because of
the atmosphere of hockey fields and cold baths and community
hikes and general clean-mindedness which she managed to carry
about with her. He disliked nearly all women, and especially the
young and pretty ones. It was always the women, and above all the
young ones, who were the most bigoted adherents of the Party, the
swallowers of slogans, the amateur spies and nosers-out of unorthodoxy. But this particular girl gave him the impression of being
more dangerous than most. Once when they passed in the corridor
she had given him a quick sidelong glance which seemed to pierce
right into him and for a moment had filled him with black terror.
The idea had even crossed his mind that she might be an agent
of the Thought Police. That, it was true, was very unlikely. Still,

he continued to feel a peculiar uneasiness, which had fear mixed up in it as well as hostility, whenever she was anywhere near him.

The other person was a man named O'Brien, a member of the Inner Party and holder of some post so important and remote that Winston had only a dim idea of its nature. A momentary hush passed over the group of people round the chairs as they saw the black overalls of an Inner Party member approaching. O'Brien was a large, burly man with a thick neck and a coarse, humorous, brutal face. In spite of his formidable appearance he had a certain charm of manner. He had a trick of resettling his spectacles on his nose which was curiously disarming—in some indefinable way, curiously civilized. It was a gesture which, if anyone had still thought in such terms, might have recalled an eighteenth-century nobleman offering his snuffbox. Winston had seen O'Brien perhaps a dozen times in almost as many years. He felt deeply drawn to him, and not solely because he was intrigued by the contrast between O'Brien's urbane manner and his prizefighter's physique. Much more it was because of a secretly held belief—or perhaps not even a belief, merely a hope —that O'Brien's political orthodoxy was not perfect. Something in his face suggested it irresistibly. And again, perhaps it was not even unorthodoxy that was written in his face, but simply intelligence. But at any rate he had the appearance of being a person that you could talk to, if somehow you could cheat the telescreen and get him alone. Winston had never made the smallest effort to verify this guess; indeed, there was no way of doing so. At this moment O'Brien glanced at his wristwatch, saw that it was nearly eleven hundred, and evidently decided to stay in the Records Department until the Two Minutes Hate was over. He took a chair in the same row as Winston, a couple of places away. A small, sandy-haired woman who worked in the next cubicle to Winston was between them. The girl with dark hair was sitting immediately behind.

The next moment a hideous, grinding screech, as of some monstrous machine running without oil, burst from the big telescreen at the end of the room. It was a noise that set one's teeth on edge and bristled the hair at the back of one's neck. The Hate had started.

As usual, the face of Emmanuel Goldstein, the Enemy of the People, had flashed onto the screen. There were hisses here and there among the audience. The little sandy-haired woman gave a squeak of mingled fear and disgust. Goldstein was the renegade and backslider who once, long ago (how long ago, nobody quite remembered), had been one of the leading figures of the Party, almost on a level with Big Brother himself, and then had engaged in counter-revolutionary activities, had been condemned to death, and had mysteriously escaped and disappeared. The program of the Two Minutes Hate varied from day to day, but there was none in which Goldstein was not the principal figure. He was the primal traitor, the earliest defiler of the Party's purity. All subsequent crimes against the Party, all treacheries, acts of sabotage, heresies, deviations, sprang directly out of his teaching. Somewhere or other he was still alive and hatching his conspiracies: perhaps somewhere beyond the sea, under the protection of his foreign paymasters; perhaps even—so it was occasionally rumored—in some hiding place in Oceania itself.

Winston's diaphragm was constricted. He could never see the face of Goldstein without a painful mixture of emotions. It was a lean Jewish face, with a great fuzzy aureole of white hair and a small goatee beard—a clever face, and yet somehow inherently despicable, with a kind of senile silliness in the long thin nose near the end of which a pair of spectacles was perched. It resembled the face of a sheep, and the voice, too, had a sheeplike quality. Goldstein was delivering his usual venomous attack upon the doctrines of the Party—an attack so exaggerated and perverse that a child should have been able to see through it, and yet just plausible enough to fill one with an alarmed feeling that other people, less level-headed than oneself, might be taken in by it. He was abusing Big Brother, he was denouncing the dictatorship of the Party, he was demanding the immediate conclusion of peace with Eurasia, he was advocating freedom of speech, freedom of the press, freedom of assembly, freedom of thought, he was crying hysterically that the revolution had been betrayed—and all this in rapid polysyllabic speech which was a sort of parody of the habitual style of the orators of the Party, and even contained Newspeak words: more Newspeak words, indeed, than any Party member would normally use in real life. And all the while, lest one should be in any doubt as to the reality which Goldstein's specious claptrap covered, behind his head on the telescreen there marched the endless columns of the Eurasian army— row after row of solid-looking men with expressionless Asiatic faces, who swam up to the surface of the screen and vanished, to be replaced by others exactly similar. The dull, rhythmic tramp of the soldiers' boots formed the background to Goldstein's bleating voice.

Before the Hate had proceeded for thirty seconds, uncontrollable exclamations of rage were breaking out from half the people in the room. The self-satisfied sheeplike face on the screen, and the terrifying power of the Eurasian army behind it, were too much to be borne; besides, the sight or even the thought of Goldstein produced fear and anger automatically. He was an object of hatred more constant than either Eurasia or Eastasia, since when Oceania was at war with one of these powers it was generally at peace with the other. But what was strange was that although Goldstein was hated and despised by everybody, although every day, and a thousand times a day, on platforms, on the telescreen, in newspapers, in books, his theories were refuted, smashed, ridiculed, held up to the general gaze for the pitiful rubbish that they were—in spite of all this, his influence never seemed to grow less. Always there were fresh dupes waiting to be seduced by him. A day never passed when spies and saboteurs acting under his directions were not unmasked by the Thought Police. He was the commander of a vast shadowy army, an underground network of conspirators dedicated to the overthrow of the State. The Brotherhood, its name was supposed to be. There were also whispered stories of a terrible book, a compendium of all the heresies, of which Goldstein was the author and which circulated clandestinely here and there. It was a book without a title. People referred to it, if at all, simply as *the book*. But one knew of such things only through vague rumors. Neither the Brotherhood nor *the book* was a subject that any ordinary Party member would mention if there was a way of avoiding it.

In its second minute the Hate rose to a frenzy. People were leaping up and down in their places and shouting at the tops of their voices in an effort to drown the maddening bleating voice that came from the screen. The little sandy-haired woman had turned bright pink, and her mouth was opening and shutting like that of a landed fish. Even O'Brien's heavy face was flushed. He was sitting very straight in his chair, his powerful chest swelling and quivering as though he were standing up to the assault of a wave. The dark-haired girl behind Winston had begun crying out "Swine! Swine! Swine!" and suddenly she picked up a heavy Newspeak dictionary and flung it at the screen. It struck Goldstein's nose and bounced off; the voice continued inexorably. In a lucid moment Winston found that he was shouting with the others and kicking his heel violently against the rung of his chair. The horrible thing about the Two Minutes Hate was not that one was obliged to act a part, but that it was impossible to avoid joining in. Within thirty seconds any pretense was always unnecessary. A hideous ecstasy of fear and vindictiveness, a desire to kill, to torture, to smash faces in with a sledge hammer, seemed to flow through the whole group of people like an electric current, turning one even against one's will into a grimacing, screaming lunatic. And yet the rage that one felt was an abstract, undirected emotion which could be switched from one

object to another like the flame of a blowlamp. Thus, at one moment Winston's hatred was not turned against Goldstein at all, but,
on the contrary, against Big Brother, the Party, and the Thought
Police; and at such moments his heart went out to the lonely, de-
rided heretic on the screen, sole guardian of truth and sanity in a
world of lies. And yet the very next instant he was at one with the
people about him, and all that was said of Goldstein seemed to him
to be true. At those moments his secret loathing of Big Brother
changed into adoration, and Big Brother seemed to tower up, an
invincible, fearless protector, standing like a rock against the hordes
of Asia, and Goldstein, in spite of his isolation, his helplessness, and
the doubt that hung about his very existence, seemed like some
sinister enchanter, capable by the mere power of his voice of wrecking the structure of civilization.

It was even possible, at moments, to switch one's hatred this way
or that by a voluntary act. Suddenly, by the sort of violent effort
with which one wrenches one's head away from the pillow in a
nightmare, Winston succeeded in transferring his hatred from the
face on the screen to the dark-haired girl behind him. Vivid, beautiful hallucinations flashed through his mind. He would flog her to
death with a rubber truncheon. He would tie her naked to a stake
and shoot her full of arrows like Saint Sebastian. He would ravish
her and cut her throat at the moment of climax. Better than before,
moreover, he realized *why* it was that he hated her. He hated her
because she was young and pretty and sexless, because he wanted to
go to bed with her and would never do so, because round her sweet
supple waist, which seemed to ask you to encircle it with your arm,
there was only the odious scarlet sash, aggressive symbol of chastity.

The Hate rose to its climax. The voice of Goldstein had become
an actual sheep's bleat, and for an instant the face changed into
that of a sheep. Then the sheep-face melted into the figure of a
Eurasian soldier who seemed to be advancing, huge and terrible,
his submachine gun roaring, and seeming to spring out of the surface of the screen, so that some of the people in the front row
actually flinched backwards in their seats. But in the same moment,
drawing a deep sigh of relief from everybody, the hostile figure
melted into the face of Big Brother, black-haired, black mustachio'd,
full of power and mysterious calm, and so vast that it almost filled
up the screen. Nobody heard what Big Brother was saying. It was
merely a few words of encouragement, the sort of words that are
uttered in the din of battle, not distinguishable individually but
restoring confidence by the fact of being spoken. Then the face of

Big Brother faded away again, and instead the three slogans of the Party stood out in bold capitals:

WAR IS PEACE

FREEDOM IS SLAVERY

IGNORANCE IS STRENGTH.

But the face of Big Brother seemed to persist for several seconds on the screen, as though the impact that it had made on everyone's eyeballs were too vivid to wear off immediately. The little sandy-haired woman had flung herself forward over the back of the chair in front of her. With a tremulous murmur that sounded like "My Savior!" she extended her arms toward the screen. Then she buried her face in her hands. It was apparent that she was uttering a prayer.

At this moment the entire group of people broke into a deep, slow, rhythmical chant of "B-B! . . . B-B! . . . B-B!" over and over again, very slowly, with a long pause between the first "B" and the second—a heavy, murmurous sound, somehow curiously savage, in the background of which one seemed to hear the stamp of naked feet and the throbbing of tom-toms. For perhaps as much as thirty seconds they kept it up. It was a refrain that was often heard in moments of overwhelming emotion. Partly it was a sort of hymn to the wisdom and majesty of Big Brother, but still more it was an act of self-hypnosis, a deliberate drowning of consciousness by means of rhythmic noise. Winston's entrails seemed to grow cold. In the Two Minutes Hate he could not help sharing in the general delirium, but this subhuman chanting of "B-B! . . . B-B!" always filled him with horror. Of course he chanted with the rest: it was impossible to do otherwise. To dissemble your feelings, to control your face, to do what everyone else was doing, was an instinctive reaction. But there was a space of a couple of seconds during which the expression in his eyes might conceivably have betrayed him. And it was exactly at this moment that the significant thing happened—if, indeed, it did happen.

Momentarily he caught O'Brien's eye. O'Brien had stood up. He had taken off his spectacles and was in the act of resettling them on his nose with his characteristic gesture. But there was a fraction of a second when their eyes met, and for as long as it took to happen Winston knew—yes, he *knew!*—that O'Brien was thinking the same thing as himself. An unmistakable message had passed. It was as though their two minds had opened and the thoughts were flowing from one into the other through their eyes. "I am with you," O'Brien seemed to be saying to him. "I know precisely what you are feeling. I know all about your contempt, your hatred, your disgust. But don't worry, I am on your side!" And then the flash of intelligence was gone, and O'Brien's face was as inscrutable as everybody else's.

That was all, and he was already uncertain whether it had happened. Such incidents never had any sequel. All that they did was to keep alive in him the belief, or hope, that others besides himself were the enemies of the Party. Perhaps the rumors of vast underground conspiracies were true after all—perhaps the Brotherhood really existed! It was impossible, in spite of the endless arrests and confessions and executions, to be sure that the Brotherhood was not simply a myth. Some days he believed in it, some days not. There was no evidence, only fleeting glimpses that might mean anything or nothing: snatches of overheard conversation, faint scribbles on lavatory walls—once, even, when two strangers met, a small movement of the hands which had looked as though it might be a signal of recognition. It was all guesswork: very likely he had imagined everything. He had gone back to his cubicle without looking at O'Brien again. The idea of following up their momentary contact hardly crossed his mind. It would have been inconceivably dangerous even if he had known how to set about doing it. For a second, two seconds, they had exchanged an equivocal glance, and that was the end of the story. But even that was a memorable event, in the locked loneliness in which one had to live.

Winston roused himself and sat up straighter. He let out a belch. The gin was rising from his stomach.

His eyes refocused on the page. He discovered that while he sat helplessly musing he had also been writing, as though by automatic action. And it was no longer the same cramped awkward handwriting as before. His pen had slid voluptuously over the smooth paper, printing in large neat capitals—

DOWN WITH BIG BROTHER
DOWN WITH BIG BROTHER
DOWN WITH BIG BROTHER
DOWN WITH BIG BROTHER
DOWN WITH BIG BROTHER

over and over again, filling half a page.

He could not help feeling a twinge of panic. It was absurd, since the writing of those particular words was not more dangerous than the initial act of opening the diary; but for a moment he was tempted to tear out the spoiled pages and abandon the enterprise altogether.

He did not do so, however, because he knew that it was useless. Whether he wrote DOWN WITH BIG BROTHER, or whether he refrained from writing it, made no difference. Whether he went on with the diary, or whether he did not go on with it, made no difference. The Thought Police would get him just the same. He had committed—would still have committed, even if he had never set pen to paper—the essential crime that contained all others in itself. Thoughtcrime, they called it. Thoughtcrime was not a thing that could be concealed forever. You might dodge successfully for a while, even for years, but sooner or later they were bound to get you.

It was always at night—the arrests invariably happened at night. The sudden jerk out of sleep, the rough hand shaking your shoulder, the lights glaring in your eyes, the ring of hard faces round the bed. In the vast majority of cases there was no trial, no report of the arrest. People simply disappeared, always during the night. Your name was removed from the registers, every record of everything you had ever done was wiped out, your one-time existence was denied and then forgotten. You were abolished, annihilated: *vaporized* was the usual word.

For a moment he was seized by a kind of hysteria. He began writing in a hurried untidy scrawl:

theyll shoot me i dont care theyll shoot me in the back of the neck i dont care down with big brother they always shoot you in the back of the neck i dont care down with big brother—

He sat back in his chair, slightly ashamed of himself, and laid down the pen. The next moment he started violently. There was a knocking at the door. . . .

Appendix

THE PRINCIPLES OF NEWSPEAK

Newspeak was the official language of Oceania and had been devised to meet the ideological needs of Ingsoc, or English Socialism. In the year 1984 there was not as yet anyone who used Newspeak as his sole means of communication, either in speech or writing. The leading articles in the *Times* were written in it, but this was a tour de force which could only be carried out by a specialist. It was expected that Newspeak would have finally superseded Oldspeak (or Standard English, as we should call it) by about the year 2050. Meanwhile it gained ground steadily, all Party members tending to use Newspeak words and grammatical constructions more and more in their everyday speech. The version in use in 1984, and embodied in the Ninth and Tenth Editions of the Newspeak dictionary, was a provisional one, and contained many superfluous words and archaic formations which were due to be suppressed later. It is with the final, perfected version, as embodied in the Eleventh Edition of the dictionary, that we are concerned here.

The purpose of Newspeak was not only to provide a medium of expression for the world view and mental habits proper to the devotees of Ingsoc, but to make all other modes of thought impossible. It was intended that when Newspeak had been adopted once and for all and Oldspeak forgotten, a heretical thought—that is, a thought diverging from the principles of Ingsoc—should be literally unthinkable, at least so far as thought is dependent on words. Its vocabulary was so constructed as to give exact and often very subtle expression to every meaning that a Party member could properly wish to express, while excluding all other meanings and also the possibility of arriving at them by indirect methods. This was done partly by the invention of new words, but chiefly by eliminating undesirable words and by stripping such words as remained of unorthodox meanings, and so far as possible of all secondary meanings whatever. To give a single example. The word *free* still existed in Newspeak, but it could only be used in such statements as "This dog is free from lice" or "This field is free from weeds." It could not be used in its old sense of "politically free" or "intellectually free," since political and intellectual freedom no longer existed even as concepts, and were therefore of necessity nameless. Quite apart from the suppression of definitely heretical words, reduction of vocabulary was regarded as an end in itself, and no word that could be dispensed with was allowed to survive. Newspeak was designed not to extend but to *diminish* the range of thought, and this purpose was indirectly assisted by cutting the choice of words down to a minimum.

Newspeak was founded on the English language as we now know it, though many Newspeak sentences, even when not containing newly created words, would be barely intelligible to an English-speaker of our own day. Newspeak words were divided into three distinct classes, known as the A vocabulary, the B vocabulary (also called compound words), and the C vocabulary. It will be simpler to discuss each class separately, but the grammatical peculiarities of the language can be dealt with in the section devoted to the A vocabulary, since the same rules held good for all three categories.

The A vocabulary. The A vocabulary consisted of the words needed for the business of everyday life—for such things as eating, drinking, working, putting on one's clothes, going up and down stairs, riding in vehicles, gardening, cooking, and the like. It was composed almost entirely of words that we already possess—words like *hit, run, dog, tree, sugar, house, field*—but in comparison with the present-day English vocabulary, their number was extremely small, while their meanings were far more rigidly defined. All ambiguities and shades of meaning had been purged out of them. So far as it could be achieved, a Newspeak word of this class was simply a staccato sound expressing *one* clearly understood concept. It would have been quite impossible to use the A vocabulary for literary purposes or for political or philosophical discussion. It was intended only to express simple, purposive thoughts, usually involving concrete objects or physical actions.

The grammar of Newspeak had two outstanding peculiarities. The first of these was an almost complete interchangeability between different parts of speech. Any word in the language (in principle this applied even to very abstract words such as *if* or *when*) could be used either as verb, noun, adjective, or adverb. Between the verb and the noun form, when they were of the same root, there was never any variation, this rule of itself involving the destruction of many archaic forms. The word *thought,* for example, did not exist in Newspeak. Its place was taken by *think,* which did duty for both noun and verb. No etymological principle was followed here; in some cases it was the original noun that was chosen for retention, in other cases the verb. Even where a noun and verb of kindred meaning were not etymologically connected, one or other of them was frequently suppressed. There was, for example, no such word as *cut,* its meaning being sufficiently covered by the noun-verb *knife.* Adjectives were formed by adding the suffix *-ful* to the noun-verb, and adverbs by adding *-wise.* Thus, for example, *speedful* meant "rapid" and *speedwise* meant "quickly." Certain of our present-day adjectives, such as *good, strong, big, black, soft,* were retained, but their total number was very small. There was little need for them, since almost any adjectival meaning could be arrived at by adding *-ful* to a noun-verb. None of the now-existing adverbs was retained, except for a very few already ending in *-wise;* the *-wise* termination was invariable. The word *well,* for example, was replaced by *goodwise.*

In addition, any word—this again applied in principle to every word in the language—could be negatived by adding the affix *un-,* or could be strengthened by the affix *plus-,* or, for still greater emphasis, *doubleplus-.* Thus, for example, *uncold* meant "warm," while *pluscold* and *doublepluscold* meant, respectively, "very cold" and "superlatively cold." It was also possible, as in present-day English, to modify the meaning of almost any word by prepositional affixes such as *ante-, post-, up-, down-,* etc. By such methods it was found possible to bring about an enormous diminution of vocabulary. Given, for instance, the word *good,* there was no need for such a word as *bad,* since the required meaning was equally well—indeed, better—expressed by *ungood.* All that was necessary, in any case where two words formed a natural pair of opposites, was to decide which of them to suppress. *Dark,* for example, could be replaced by *unlight,* or *light* by *undark,* according to preference.

The second distinguishing mark of Newspeak grammar was its regularity. Subject to a few exceptions which are mentioned below, all inflections followed the same rules. Thus, in all verbs the preterite and the past participle were the same and ended in *-ed.* The preterite of *steal* was *stealed,* the preterite of *think* was *thinked,* and so on throughout the language, all such forms as *swam, gave, brought, spoke, taken,* etc., being abolished. All plurals were made by adding *-s* or *-es* as the case might be. The plurals of *man, ox, life* were *mans, oxes, lifes.* Comparison of adjectives was invariably made by adding *-er, -est* (*good, gooder, goodest*), irregular forms and the *more, most* formation being suppressed.

The only classes of words that were still allowed to inflect irregularly were the pronouns, the relatives, the demonstrative adjectives, and the auxiliary verbs. All of these followed their ancient usage, except that *whom* had been scrapped as unnecessary, and the *shall, should* tenses had been dropped, all their uses being covered by *will* and *would.* There were also certain irregularities in word-formation arising out of the need for rapid and easy speech. A word which was difficult to utter, or was liable to be incorrectly heard, was held to be ipso facto a bad word; occasionally therefore, for the sake of euphony, extra letters were inserted into a word or an archaic formation was retained. But this need made itself felt chiefly in connection with the B vocabulary. *Why* so great an importance was attached to ease of pronunciation will be made clear later in this essay.

The B vocabulary. The B vocabulary consisted of words which had been deliberately constructed for political purposes: words, that is to say, which not only had in every case a political implication, but were intended to impose a desirable mental attitude upon the person using them. Without a full understanding of the principles of Ingsoc it was difficult to use these words correctly. In some cases they could be translated into Oldspeak, or even into words taken from the A vocabulary, but this usually demanded a long para-phrase and always involved the loss of certain overtones. The B words were a sort of verbal shorthand, often packing whole ranges of ideas into a few syllables, and at the same time more accurate and forcible than ordinary language.

The B words were in all cases compound words.* They consisted of two or more words, or portions of words, welded together in an easily pronounceable form. The resulting amalgam was always a noun-verb, and inflected according to the ordinary rules. To take a single example: the word *goodthink,* meaning, very roughly, "orthodoxy," or, if one chose to regard it as a verb, "to think in an orthodox manner." This inflected as follows: noun-verb, *good-think;* past tense and past participle, *goodthinked;* present partici-ple, *goodthinking;* adjective, *goodthinkful;* adverb, *goodthinkwise;* verbal noun, *goodthinker.*

The B words were not constructed on any etymological plan. The words of which they were made up could be any parts of speech, and could be placed in any order and mutilated in any way which made them easy to pronounce while indicating their derivation. In the word *crimethink* (thoughtcrime), for instance, the *think* came second, whereas in *thinkpol* (Thought Police) it came first, and in the latter word *police* had lost its second sylla-ble. Because of the greater difficulty in securing euphony, irreg-ular formations were commoner in the B vocabulary than in the A vocabulary. For example, the adjectival forms of *Minitrue, Mini-pax,* and *Miniluv* were, respectively, *Minitruthful, Minipeaceful,* and *Minilovely,* simply because *-trueful, -paxful,* and *-loveful* were slightly awkward to pronounce. In principle, however, all B words could inflect, and all inflected in exactly the same way.

Some of the B words had highly subtilized meanings, barely in-telligible to anyone who had not mastered the language as a whole. Consider, for example, such a typical sentence from a *Times* lead-ing article as *Oldthinkers unbellyfeel Ingsoc.* The shortest render-ing that one could make of this in Oldspeak would be: "Those whose ideas were formed before the Revolution cannot have a full emotional understanding of the principles of English Socialism." But this is not an adequate translation. To begin with, in order to grasp the full meaning of the Newspeak sentence quoted above, one would have to have a clear idea of what is meant by *Ingsoc.* And, in addition, only a person thoroughly grounded in Ingsoc

---

* Compound words, such as *speakwrite,* were of course to be found in the A vocabulary, but these were merely convenient abbreviations and had no special ideological color.

could appreciate the full force of the word *bellyfeel,* which implied a blind, enthusiastic acceptance difficult to imagine today; or of the word *oldthink,* which was inextricably mixed up with the idea of wickedness and decadence. But the special function of certain Newspeak words, of which *oldthink* was one, was not so much to express meanings as to destroy them. These words, necessarily few in number, had had their meanings extended until they contained within themselves whole batteries of words which, as they were sufficiently covered by a single comprehensive term, could now be scrapped and forgotten. The greatest difficulty facing the compilers of the Newspeak dictionary was not to invent new words, but, having invented them, to make sure what they meant: to make sure, that is to say, what ranges of words they canceled by their existence.

As we have already seen in the case of the word *free,* words which had once borne a heretical meaning were sometimes retained for the sake of convenience, but only with the undesirable meanings purged out of them. Countless other words such as *honor, justice, morality, internationalism, democracy, science,* and *religion* had simply ceased to exist. A few blanket words covered them, and, in covering them, abolished them. All words grouping themselves round the concepts of liberty and equality, for instance, were contained in the single word *crimethink,* while all words grouping themselves round the concepts of objectivity and rationalism were contained in the single word *oldthink.* Greater precision would have been dangerous. What was required in a Party member was an outlook similar to that of the ancient Hebrew who knew, without knowing much else, that all nations other than his own worshiped "false gods." He did not need to know that these gods were called Baal, Osiris, Moloch, Ashtaroth, and the like; probably the less he knew about them the better for his orthodoxy. He knew Jehovah and the commandments of Jehovah; he knew, therefore, that all gods with other names or other attributes were false gods. In somewhat the same way, the Party member knew what constituted right conduct, and in exceedingly vague, generalized terms he knew what kinds of departure from it were possible. His sexual life, for example, was entirely regulated by the two Newspeak words *sexcrime* (sexual immorality) and *goodsex* (chastity). *Sexcrime* covered all sexual misdeeds whatever. It covered fornication, adultery, homosexuality, and other perversions, and, in addition, normal intercourse practiced for its own sake. There was no need to enumerate them separately, since they were all equally culpable, and, in principle, all punishable by death. In the C vocabulary, which consisted of scientific and technical words, it might be necessary to give specialized names to certain sexual aberrations, but the ordinary citizen had no need of them. He knew what was meant by *goodsex*—that is to say, normal intercourse between man and wife, for the sole purpose of begetting children, and without physical pleasure on the part of the woman; all else was *sexcrime*. In Newspeak it was seldom possible to follow a heretical thought further than the perception that it *was* heretical; beyond that point the necessary words were nonexistent.

No word in the B vocabulary was ideologically neutral. A great many were euphemisms. Such words, for instance, as *joycamp* (forced-labor camp) or *Minipax* (Ministry of Peace, i.e., Ministry of War) meant almost the exact opposite of what they appeared to mean. Some words, on the other hand, displayed a frank and contemptuous understanding of the real nature of Oceanic society. An example was *prolefeed,* meaning the rubbishy entertainment and spurious news which the Party handed out to the masses. Other words, again, were ambivalent, having the connotation "good" when applied to the Party and "bad" when applied to its enemies. But in addition there were great numbers of words which at first sight appeared to be mere abbreviations and which derived their ideological color not from their meaning but from their structure.

So far as it could be contrived, everything that had or might have political significance of any kind was fitted into the B vocabulary. The name of every organization, or body of people, or doctrine, or country, or institution, or public building, was invariably cut down into the familiar shape; that is, a single easily pronounced word with the smallest number of syllables that would preserve the original derivation. In the Ministry of Truth, for example, the Records Department, in which Winston Smith worked, was called *Recdep,* the Fiction Department was called *Ficdep,* the Teleprograms Department was called *Teledep,* and so on. This was not done solely with the object of saving time. Even in the early decades of the twentieth century, telescoped words and phrases had been one of the characteristic features of political language; and it had been noticed that the tendency to use abbreviations of this kind was most marked in totalitarian countries and totalitarian organizations. Examples were such words as *Nazi, Gestapo, Comintern, Inprecorr, Agitprop.* In the beginning the practice had been adopted as it were instinctively, but in Newspeak it was used with a conscious purpose. It was perceived that in thus abbreviating a name one narrowed and subtly altered its meaning, by cutting out most of the associations that would otherwise cling to it. The words

Communist International, for instance, call up a composite picture of universal human brotherhood, red flags, barricades, Karl Marx, and the Paris Commune. The word Comintern, on the other hand, suggests merely a tightly knit organization and a well-defined body of doctrine. It refers to something almost as easily recognized, and as limited in purpose, as a chair or a table. *Comintern* is a word that can be uttered almost without taking thought, whereas *Communist International* is a phrase over which one is obliged to linger at least momentarily. In the same way, the associations called up by a word like *Minitrue* are fewer and more controllable than those called up by *Ministry of Truth.* This accounted not only for the habit of abbreviating whenever possible, but also for the almost exaggerated care that was taken to make every word easily pronounceable.

In Newspeak, euphony outweighed every consideration other than exactitude of meaning. Regularity of grammar was always sacrificed to it when it seemed necessary. And rightly so, since what was required, above all for political purposes, were short clipped words of unmistakable meaning which could be uttered rapidly and which roused the minimum of echoes in the speaker's mind. The words of the B vocabulary even gained in force from the fact that nearly all of them were very much alike. Almost invariably these words —*goodthink, Minipax, prolefeed, sexcrime, joycamp, Ingsoc, bellyfeel, thinkpol,* and countless others—were words of two or three syllables, with the stress distributed equally between the first syllable and the last. The use of them encouraged a gabbling style of speech, at once staccato and monotonous. And this was exactly what was aimed at. The intention was to make speech, and especially speech on any subject not ideologically neutral, as nearly as possible independent of consciousness. For the purposes of everyday life it was no doubt necessary, or sometimes necessary, to reflect before speaking, but a Party member called upon to make a political or ethical judgment should be able to spray forth the correct opinions as automatically as a machine gun spraying forth bullets. His training fitted him to do this, the language gave him an almost foolproof instrument, and the texture of the words, with their harsh sound and a certain wilful ugliness which was in accord with the spirit of Ingsoc, assisted the process still further.

So did the fact of having very few words to choose from. Relative to our own, the Newspeak vocabulary was tiny, and new ways of reducing it were constantly being devised. Newspeak, indeed, differed from almost all other languages in that its vocabulary grew smaller instead of larger every year. Each reduction was a gain, since the smaller the area of choice, the smaller the temptation to take thought. Ultimately it was hoped to make articulate speech issue from the larynx without involving the higher brain centers at all. This aim was frankly admitted in the Newspeak word *duckspeak,* meaning "to quack like a duck." Like various other words in the B vocabulary, *duckspeak* was ambivalent in meaning. Provided that the opinions which were quacked out were orthodox ones, it implied nothing but praise, and when the *Times* referred to one of the orators of the Party as a *doubleplusgood duckspeaker* it was paying a warm and valued compliment.

The C vocabulary. The C vocabulary was supplementary to the others and consisted entirely of scientific and technical terms. These resembled the scientific terms in use today, and were constructed from the same roots, but the usual care was taken to define them rigidly and strip them of undesirable meanings. They followed the same grammatical rules as the words in the other two vocabularies. Very few of the C words had any currency either in everyday speech or in political speech. Any scientific worker or technician could find all the words he needed in the list devoted to his own speciality, but he seldom had more than a smattering of the words occurring in the other lists. Only a very few words were common to all lists, and there was no vocabulary expressing the function of Science as a habit of mind, or a method of thought, irrespective of its particular branches. There was, indeed, no word for "Science," any meaning that it could possibly bear being already sufficiently covered by the word *Ingsoc.*

From the foregoing account it will be seen that in Newspeak the expression of unorthodox opinions, above a very low level, was well-nigh impossible. It was of course possible to utter heresies of a very crude kind, a species of blasphemy. It would have been possible, for example, to say *Big Brother is ungood.* But this statement, which to an orthodox ear merely conveyed a self-evident absurdity, could not have been sustained by reasoned argument, because the necessary words were not available. Ideas inimical to Ingsoc could only be entertained in a vague wordless form, and could only be named in very broad terms which lumped together and condemned whole groups of heresies without defining them in doing so. One could, in fact, only use Newspeak for unorthodox purposes by illegitimately translating some of the words back into Oldspeak. For example, *All mans are equal* was a possible Newspeak sentence, but only in the same sense in which *All men are redhaired* is a possible Oldspeak sentence. It did not contain a grammatical error, but it expressed a palpable untruth, i.e., that all men are of equal size, weight, or strength. The concept of political equality no longer existed, and this secondary meaning had accordingly been purged out of the word *equal*. In 1984, when Oldspeak was still the normal means of communication, the danger theoretically existed that in using Newspeak words one might remember their original meanings. In practice it was not difficult for any person well grounded in *doublethink* to avoid doing this, but within a couple of generations even the possibility of such a lapse would have vanished. A person growing up with Newspeak as his sole language would no more know that *equal* had once had the secondary meaning of "politically equal," or that *free* had once meant "intellectually free," than, for instance, a person who had never heard of chess would be aware of the secondary meanings attaching to *queen* and *rook*. There would be many crimes and errors which it would be beyond his power to commit, simply because they were nameless and therefore unimaginable. And it was to be foreseen that with the passage of time the distinguishing characteristics of Newspeak would become more and more pronounced—its words growing fewer and fewer, their meanings more and more rigid, and the chance of putting them to improper uses always diminishing.

When Oldspeak had been once and for all superseded, the last link with the past would have been severed. History had already been rewritten, but fragments of the literature of the past survived here and there, imperfectly censored, and so long as one retained one's knowledge of Oldspeak it was possible to read them. In the future such fragments, even if they chanced to survive, would be unintelligible and untranslatable. It was impossible to translate any passage of Oldspeak into Newspeak unless it either referred to some technical process or some very simple everyday action, or was already orthodox (*goodthinkful* would be the Newspeak expression) in tendency. In practice this meant that no book written before approximately 1960 could be translated as a whole. Prerevolutionary literature could only be subjected to ideological translation—that is, alteration in sense as well as language. Take for example the well-known passage from the Declaration of Independence:

> *We hold these truths to be self-evident, that all men are created equal, that they are endowed by their Creator with certain inalienable rights, that among these are life, liberty and the pursuit of happiness. That to secure these rights, Governments are instituted among men, deriving their powers from the consent of the gov-*

erned. That whenever any form of Government becomes destruc-
tive of those ends, it is the right of the People to alter or abolish
it, and to institute new Government. . . .

It would have been quite impossible to render this into Newspeak while keeping to the sense of the original. The nearest one
could come to doing so would be to swallow the whole passage up
in the single word *crimethink*. A full translation could only be an
ideological translation, whereby Jefferson's words would be changed
into a panegyric on absolute government.

A good deal of the literature of the past was, indeed, already
being transformed in this way. Considerations of prestige made it
desirable to preserve the memory of certain historical figures, while
at the same time bringing their achievements into line with the
philosophy of Ingsoc. Various writers, such as Shakespeare, Milton,
Swift, Byron, Dickens, and some others were therefore in process
of translation; when the task had been completed, their original
writings, with all else that survived of the literature of the past,
would be destroyed. These translations were a slow and difficult
business, and it was not expected that they would be finished before the first or second decade of the twenty-first century. There
were also large quantities of merely utilitarian literature—indispensable technical manuals and the like—that had to be treated in the
same way. It was chiefly in order to allow time for the preliminary
work of translation that the final adoption of Newspeak had been
fixed for so late a date as 2050.

1949

△

"Such, Such Were the Joys . . ."

▽

I

Soon after I arrived at Crossgates (not immediately, but after a
week or two, just when I seemed to be settling into the routine
of school life) I began wetting my bed. I was now aged eight, so
that this was a reversion to a habit which I must have grown out
of at least four years earlier.

Nowadays, I believe, bed-wetting in such circumstances is taken for granted. It is a normal reaction in children who have been removed from their homes to a strange place. In those days, however, it was looked on as a disgusting crime which the child committed on purpose and for which the proper cure was a beating. For my part I did not need to be told it was a crime. Night after night I prayed, with a fervor never previously attained in my prayers, "Please God, do not let me wet my bed! Oh, please God, do not let me wet my bed!" but it made remarkably little difference. Some nights the thing happened, others not. There was no volition about it, no consciousness. You did not properly speaking *do* the deed: you merely woke up in the morning and found that the sheets were wringing wet.

After the second or third offense I was warned that I should be beaten next time, but I received the warning in a curiously roundabout way. One afternoon, as we were filing out from tea, Mrs. Simpson, the headmaster's wife, was sitting at the head of one of the tables, chatting with a lady of whom I know nothing, except that she was on an afternoon's visit to the school. She was an intimidating, masculine-looking person wearing a riding habit, or something that I took to be a riding habit. I was just leaving the room when Mrs. Simpson called me back, as though to introduce me to the visitor.

Mrs. Simpson was nicknamed Bingo, and I shall call her by that name for I seldom think of her by any other. (Officially, however, she was addressed as Mum, probably a corruption of the "Ma'am" used by public-school boys to their housemasters' wives.) She was a stocky square-built woman with hard red cheeks, a flat top to her head, prominent brows and deepset, suspicious eyes. Although a great deal of the time she was full of false heartiness, jollying one along with mannish slang ("*Buck* up, old chap!" and so forth), and even using one's Christian name, her eyes never lost their anxious, accusing look. It was very difficult to look her in the face without feeling guilty, even at moments when one was not guilty of anything in particular.

"Here is a little boy," said Bingo, indicating me to the strange lady, "who wets his bed every night. Do you know what I am going to do if you wet your bed again?" she added, turning to me. "I am going to get the Sixth Form to beat you."

The strange lady put on an air of being inexpressibly shocked, and exclaimed "I-should-think-so!" And here occurred one of those wild, almost lunatic misunderstandings which are part of the daily experience of childhood. The Sixth Form was a group of older boys who were selected as having "character" and were empowered to beat smaller boys. I had not yet learned of their existence, and I misheard the phrase "the Sixth Form" as "Mrs. Form." I took it as referring to the strange lady—I thought, that is, that her name was Mrs. Form. It was an improbable name, but a child has no judgment in such matters. I imagined, therefore, that it was *she* who was to be deputed to beat me. It did not strike me as strange that this job should be turned over to a casual visitor in no way connected with the school. I merely assumed that "Mrs. Form" was a stern disciplinarian who enjoyed beating people (somehow her appearance seemed to bear this out) and I had an immediate terrifying vision of her arriving for the occasion in full riding kit and armed with a hunting whip. To this day I can feel myself almost swooning with shame as I stood, a very small, round-faced boy in short corduroy knickers, before the two women. I could not speak. I felt that I should die if "Mrs. Form" were to beat me. But my dominant feeling was not fear or even resentment: it was simply shame because one more person, and that a woman, had been told of my disgusting offense.

A little later, I forget how, I learned that it was not after all "Mrs. Form" who would do the beating. I cannot remember whether it was that very night that I wetted my bed again, but at any rate I did wet it again quite soon. Oh, the despair, the feeling of cruel injustice, after all my prayers and resolutions, at once again waking between the clammy sheets! There was no chance of hiding what I had done. The grim statuesque matron, Daphne by name, arrived in the dormitory specially to inspect my bed. She pulled back the clothes, then drew herself up, and the dreaded words seemed to come rolling out of her like a peal of thunder:

"REPORT YOURSELF to the headmaster after breakfast!"

I do not know how many times I heard that phrase during my early years at Crossgates. It was only very rarely that it did not mean a beating. The words always had a portentous sound in my ears, like muffled drums or the words of the death sentence.

When I arrived to report myself, Bingo was doing something or other at the long shiny table in the ante-room to the study. Her uneasy eyes searched me as I went past. In the study Mr. Simpson, nicknamed Sim, was waiting. Sim was a round-shouldered curiously oafish-looking man, not large but shambling in gait, with a chubby face which was like that of an overgrown baby, and which was capable of good humor. He knew, of course, why I had been sent to him, and had already taken a bone-handled riding crop out of the cupboard, but it was part of the punishment of reporting yourself that you had to proclaim your offense with your own lips. When I had said my say, he read me a short but pompous lecture, then seized me by the scruff of the neck, twisted me over and began beating me with the riding crop. He had a habit of continuing his lecture while he flogged you, and I remember the words "you dir-ty lit-tle boy" keeping time with the blows. The beating did not hurt (perhaps as it was the first time, he was not hitting me very hard), and I walked out feeling very much better. The fact that the beating had not hurt was a sort of victory and partially wiped out the shame of the bed-wetting. I was even incautious enough to wear a grin on my face. Some small boys were hanging about in the passage outside the door of the ante-room.

"D'you get the cane?"

"It didn't hurt," I said proudly.

Bingo had heard everything. Instantly her voice came screaming after me:

"Come here! Come here this instant! What was that you said?"

"I said it didn't hurt," I faltered out.

"How dare you say a thing like that? Do you think that is a proper thing to say? Go in and REPORT YOURSELF AGAIN!"

This time Sim laid on in real earnest. He continued for a length of time that frightened and astonished me—about five minutes, it seemed—ending up by breaking the riding crop. The bone handle went flying across the room.

"Look what you've made me do!" he said furiously, holding up the broken crop.

I had fallen into a chair, weakly sniveling. I remember that this was the only time throughout my boyhood when a beating actually reduced me to tears, and curiously enough I was not even now crying because of the pain. The second beating had not hurt very much either. Fright and shame seemed to have anesthetized me. I was crying partly because I felt that this was expected of me, partly from genuine repentance, but partly also because of a deeper grief which is peculiar to childhood and not easy to convey: a sense of desolate loneliness and helplessness, of being locked up not only in a hostile world but in a world of good and evil where the rules were such that it was actually not possible for me to keep them.

I knew that bed-wetting was (a) wicked and (b) outside my control. The second fact I was personally aware of, and the first I did not question. It was possible, therefore, to commit a sin without knowing that you committed it, without wanting to commit it, and without being able to avoid it. Sin was not necessarily something that you did: it might be something that happened to you. I do not want to claim that this idea flashed into my mind as a complete novelty at this very moment, under the blows of Sim's cane: I must have had glimpses of it even before I left home, for my early childhood had not been altogether happy. But at any rate this was the great, abiding lesson of my boyhood: that I was in a world where it was *not possible* for me to be good. And the double beating was a turning-point, for it brought home to me for the first time the harshness of the environment into which I had been flung. Life was more terrible, and I was more wicked, than I had imagined. At any rate, as I sat on the edge of a chair in Sim's study, with not even the self-possession to stand up while he stormed at me, I had a conviction of sin and folly and weakness, such as I do not remember to have felt before.

In general, one's memories of any period must necessarily weaken as one moves away from it. One is constantly learning new facts, and old ones have to drop out to make way for them. At twenty I could have written the history of my schooldays with an accuracy which would be quite impossible now. But it can also happen that one's memories grow sharper after a long lapse of time, because one is looking at the past with fresh eyes and can isolate and, as it were, notice facts which previously existed undifferentiated among a mass of others. Here are two things which in a sense I remembered, but which did not strike me as strange or interesting until quite recently. One is that the second beating seemed to me a just and reasonable punishment. To get one beating, and then to get another and far fiercer one on top of it, for being so unwise as to show that the first had not hurt—that was quite natural. The gods are jealous, and when you have good fortune you should conceal it. The other is that I accepted the broken riding crop as my own crime. I can still recall my feeling as I saw the handle lying on the carpet—the feeling of having done an ill-bred clumsy thing, and ruined an expensive object. *I* had broken it: so Sim told me, and so I believed. This acceptance of guilt lay unnoticed in my memory for twenty or thirty years.

So much for the episode of the bed-wetting. But there is one more thing to be remarked. This is that I did not wet my bed again—at least, I did wet it once again, and received another beating, after which the trouble stopped. So perhaps this barbarous remedy does work, though at a heavy price, I have no doubt.

Crossgates was an expensive and snobbish school which was in process of becoming more snobbish, and, I imagine, more expensive. The public school with which it had special connections was Harrow, but during my time an increasing proportion of the boys went on to Eton. Most of them were the children of rich parents, but on the whole they were the unaristocratic rich, the sort of people who live in huge shrubberied houses in Bournemouth or Richmond, and who have cars and butlers but not country estates. There were a few exotics among them—some South American boys, sons of Argentine beef barons, one or two Russians, and even a Siamese prince, or someone who was described as a prince.

Sim had two great ambitions. One was to attract titled boys to the school, and the other was to train up pupils to win scholarships at public schools, above all Eton. He did, towards the end of my time, succeed in getting hold of two boys with real English titles. One of them, I remember, was a wretched little creature, almost an albino, peering upward out of weak eyes, with a long nose at the end of which a dewdrop always seemed to be trembling. Sim always gave these boys their titles when mentioning them to a third person, and for their first few days he actually addressed them to their faces as "Lord So-and-so." Needless to say he found ways of drawing attention to them when any visitor was being shown round the school. Once, I remember, the little fair-haired boy had a choking fit at dinner, and a stream of snot ran out of his nose onto his plate in a way horrible to see. Any lesser person would have been called a dirty little beast and ordered out of the room instantly: but Sim and Bingo laughed it off in a "boys will be boys" spirit.

All the very rich boys were more or less undisguisedly favored. The school still had a faint suggestion of the Victorian "private academy" with its "parlor boarders," and when I later read about that kind of school in Thackeray I immediately saw the resemblance. The rich boys had milk and biscuits in the middle of the morning, they were given riding lessons once or twice a week, Bingo mothered them and called them by their Christian names, and above all they were never caned. Apart from the South Americans, whose parents were safely distant, I doubt whether Sim ever caned any boy whose father's income was much above £2,000 a year. But he was sometimes willing to sacrifice financial profit to scholastic prestige. Occasionally, by special arrangement, he would take at greatly reduced fees some boy who seemed likely to win scholarships and thus bring credit on the school. It was on these terms that I was at Crossgates myself: otherwise my parents could not have afforded to send me to so expensive a school.

I did not at first understand that I was being taken at reduced fees; it was only when I was about eleven that Bingo and Sim began throwing the fact in my teeth. For my first two or three years I went through the ordinary educational mill: then, soon after I had started Greek (one started Latin at eight, Greek at ten), I moved into the scholarship class, which was taught, so far as classics went, largely by Sim himself. Over a period of two or three years the scholarship boys were crammed with learning as cynically as a goose is crammed for Christmas. And with what learning! This business of making a gifted boy's career depend on a competitive examination, taken when he is only twelve or thirteen, is an evil thing at best, but there do appear to be preparatory schools which send scholars to Eton, Winchester, etc., without teaching them to see everything in terms of marks. At Crossgates the whole process was frankly a preparation for a sort of confidence trick. Your job was to learn exactly those things that would give an examiner the impression that you knew more than you did know, and as far as possible to avoid burdening your brain with anything else. Subjects which lacked examination value, such as geography, were almost completely neglected, mathematics was also neglected if you were a "classical," science was not taught in any form—indeed it was so despised that even an interest in natural history was discouraged—and the books you were encouraged to read in your spare time were chosen with one eye on the "English Paper." Latin and Greek, the main scholarship subjects, were what counted, but even these were deliberately taught in a flashy, unsound way. We never, for example, read right through even a single book of a Greek or Latin author: we merely read short passages which were picked out because they were the kind of thing likely to be set as an "unseen translation." During the last year or so before we went up for our scholarships, most of our time was spent in simply working our way through the scholarship papers of previous years. Sim had sheaves of these in his possession, from every one of the major public schools. But the greatest outrage of all was the teaching of history.

There was in those days a piece of nonsense called the Harrow History Prize, an annual competition for which many preparatory schools entered. At Crossgates we mugged up every paper that had been set since the competition started. They were the kind of stupid question that is answered by rapping out a name or a quotation. Who plundered the Begams? Who was beheaded in an open boat? Who caught the Whigs bathing and ran away with their clothes? Almost all our historical teaching was on this level. History was a series of unrelated, unintelligible but—in some way that was never explained to us—important facts with resounding phrases tied to them. Disraeli brought peace with honor. Clive was astonished at his moderation. Pitt called in the New World to redress the balance of the Old. And the dates, and the mnemonic devices! (Did you know, for example, that the initial letters of "A black Negress was my aunt: there's her house behind the barn" are also the initial letters of the battles in the Wars of the Roses?) Bingo, who "took" the higher forms in history, revelled in this kind of thing. I recall positive orgies of dates, with the keener boys leaping up and down in their places in their eagerness to shout out the right answers, and at the same time not feeling the faintest interest in the meaning of the mysterious events they were naming.

"1587?"

"Massacre of St. Bartholomew!"

"1707?"

"Death of Aurangzeeb!"

"1713?"

"Treaty of Utrecht!"

"1773?"

"The Boston Tea Party!"

"1520?"

"Oh, Mum, please, Mum—"

"Please, Mum, please, Mum! Let me tell him, Mum!"

"Well; 1520?"

"Field of the Cloth of Gold!"

And so on.

But history and such secondary subjects were not bad fun. It was in "classics" that the real strain came. Looking back, I realize that I then worked harder than I have ever done since, and yet at the time it never seemed possible to make quite the effort that was demanded of one. We would sit round the long shiny table, made of some very pale-colored, hard wood, with Sim goading, threatening, exhorting, sometimes joking, very occasionally praising, but always prodding, prodding away at one's mind to keep it up to the right pitch of concentration, as one might keep a sleepy person awake by sticking pins into him.

"Go on, you little slacker! Go on, you idle, worthless little boy! The whole trouble with you is that you're bone and horn idle. You eat too much, that's why. You wolf down enormous meals, and then when you come here you're half asleep. Go on, now, put your back into it. You're not *thinking*. Your brain doesn't sweat."

He would tap away at one's skull with his silver pencil, which, in my memory, seems to have been about the size of a banana, and which certainly was heavy enough to raise a bump: or he would pull the short hairs round one's ears, or, occasionally, reach out under the table and kick one's shin. On some days nothing seemed to go right, and then it would be: "All right, then, I know what you want. You've been asking for it the whole morning. Come along, you useless little slacker. Come into the study." And then whack, whack, whack, whack, and back one would come, red-wealed and smarting—in later years Sim had abandoned his riding crop in favor of a thin rattan cane which hurt very much more— to settle down to work again. This did not happen very often, but I do remember more than once being led out of the room in the middle of a Latin sentence, receiving a beating and then go-ing straight ahead with the same sentence, just like that. It is a mistake to think such methods do not work. They work very well for their special purpose. Indeed, I doubt whether classical educa-tion ever has been or can be successfully carried on without cor-poral punishment. The boys themselves believed in its efficacy. There was a boy named Beacham, with no brains to speak of, but evidently in acute need of a scholarship. Sim was flogging him towards the goal as one might do with a foundered horse. He went up for a scholarship at Uppingham, came back with a conscious-ness of having done badly, and a day or two later received a se-vere beating for idleness. "I wish I'd had that caning before I went up for the exam," he said sadly—a remark which I felt to be contemptible, but which I perfectly well understood.

The boys of the scholarship class were not all treated alike. If a boy were the son of rich parents to whom the saving of fees was not all-important, Sim would goad him along in a comparatively fatherly way, with jokes and digs in the ribs and perhaps an oc-casional tap with the pencil, but no hair-pulling and no caning. It was the poor but "clever" boys who suffered. Our brains were a gold mine in which he had sunk money, and the dividends must be squeezed out of us. Long before I had grasped the nature of my financial relationship with Sim, I had been made to under-stand that I was not on the same footing as most of the other boys. In effect there were three castes in the school. There was the mi-nority with an aristocratic or millionaire background, there were the children of the ordinary suburban rich, who made up the bulk of the school, and there were a few underlings like myself, the sons of clergymen, Indian civil servants, struggling widows and the like. These poorer ones were discouraged from going in for "extras" such as shooting and carpentry, and were humiliated over clothes and petty possessions. I never, for instance, succeeded in getting a cricket bat of my own, because "your parents wouldn't be able to afford it." This phrase pursued me throughout my schooldays. At Crossgates we were not allowed to keep the money we brought back with us, but had to "give it in" on the first day of term, and then from time to time were allowed to spend it under supervision. I and similarly placed boys were always choked off from buying expensive toys like model aeroplanes, even if the necessary money stood to our credit. Bingo, in particular, seemed to aim consciously at inculcating a humble outlook in the poorer boys. "Do you think that's the sort of thing a boy like you should buy?" I remember her saying to somebody—and she said this in front of the whole school; "You know you're not going to grow up with money, don't you? Your people aren't rich. You must learn to be sensible. Don't get above yourself!" There was also the weekly pocket-money, which we took out in sweets, dispensed by Bingo from a large table. The millionaires had sixpence a week, but the normal sum was threepence. I and one or two others were only allowed twopence. My parents had not given instructions to this effect, and the saving of a penny a week could not conceivably have made any difference to them: it was a mark of status. Worse yet was the detail of the birthday cakes. It was usual for each boy, on his birthday, to have a large iced cake with candles, which was shared out at tea between the whole school. It was provided as a matter of routine and went on his parents' bill. I never had such a cake, though my parents would have paid for it readily enough. Year after year, never daring to ask, I would miserably hope that this year a cake would appear. Once or twice I even rashly pretended to my companions that this time I *was* going to have a cake. Then came teatime, and no cake, which did not make me more popular.

Very early it was impressed upon me that I had no chance of a decent future unless I won a scholarship at a public school. Either I won my scholarship, or I must leave school at fourteen and become, in Sim's favorite phrase, "a little office boy at forty pounds a year." In my circumstances it was natural that I should believe this. Indeed, it was universally taken for granted at Crossgates that unless you went to a "good" public school (and only about fifteen schools came under this heading) you were ruined for life. It is not easy to convey to a grown-up person the sense of strain, of nerving oneself for some terrible, all-deciding combat, as the date of the examination crept nearer—eleven years old, twelve years old, then thirteen, the fatal year itself! Over a period of about two years, I do not think there was ever a day when "the exam," as I called it, was quite out of my waking thoughts. In my prayers it figured invariably: and whenever I got the bigger portion of a wishbone, or picked up a horseshoe, or bowed seven times to the new moon, or succeeded in passing through a wishing-gate without touching the sides, then the wish I earned by doing so went on "the exam" as a matter of course. And yet curiously enough I was also tormented by an almost irresistible impulse *not* to work. There were days when my heart sickened at the labors ahead of me, and I stood stupid as an animal before the most elementary difficulties. In the holidays, also, I could not work. Some of the scholarship boys received extra tuition from a certain Mr. Batchelor, a like-able, very hairy man who wore shaggy suits and lived in a typical bachelor's "den"—booklined walls, overwhelming stench of tobacco —somewhere in the town. During the holidays Mr. Batchelor used to send us extracts from Latin authors to translate, and we were supposed to send back a wad of work once a week. Somehow I could not do it. The empty paper and the black Latin dictionary lying on the table, the consciousness of a plain duty shirked, poi-soned my leisure, but somehow I could not start, and by the end of the holidays I would only have sent Mr. Batchelor fifty or a hundred lines. Undoubtedly part of the reason was that Sim and his cane were far away. But in term time, also, I would go through periods of idleness and stupidity when I would sink deeper and deeper into disgrace and even achieve a sort of feeble defiance, fully conscious of my guilt and yet unable or unwilling—I could not be sure which—to do any better. Then Bingo or Sim would send for me, and this time it would not even be a caning.

Bingo would search me with her baleful eyes. (What color were those eyes, I wonder? I remember them as green, but actually no human being has green eyes. Perhaps they were hazel.) She would start off in her peculiar, wheedling, bullying style, which never failed to get right through one's guard and score a hit on one's better nature.

"I don't think it's awfully decent of you to behave like this, is it? Do you think it's quite playing the game by your mother and father to go on idling your time away, week after week, month after month? Do you *want* to throw all your chances away? You know your people aren't rich, don't you? You know they can't af-ford the same things as other boys' parents. How are they to send you to a public school if you don't win a scholarship? I know how proud your mother is of you. Do you *want* to let her down?"

"I don't think he wants to go to a public school any longer," Sim would say, addressing himself to Bingo with a pretense that I was not there. "I think he's given up that idea. He wants to be a little office boy at forty pounds a year."

The horrible sensation of tears—a swelling in the breasts, a tickling behind the nose—would already have assailed me. Bingo would bring out her ace of trumps:

"And do you think it's quite fair to *us*, the way you're behaving? After all we've done for you? You *do* know what we've done for you, don't you?" Her eyes would pierce deep into me, and though she never said it straight out, I did know. "We've had you here all these years—we even had you here for a week in the holidays so that Mr. Batchelor could coach you. We don't *want* to have to send you away, you know, but we can't keep a boy here just to eat up our food, term after term. *I* don't think it's very straight, the way you're behaving. Do you?"

I never had any answer except a miserable "No, Mum," or "Yes, Mum" as the case might be. Evidently it was *not* straight, the way I was behaving. And at some point or other the unwanted tear would always force its way out of the corner of my eye, roll down my nose, and splash.

Bingo never said in plain words that I was a non-paying pupil, no doubt because vague phrases like "all we've done for you" had a deeper emotional appeal. Sim, who did not aspire to be loved by his pupils, put it more brutally, though, as was usual with him, in pompous language. "You are living on my bounty" was his favorite phrase in this context. At least once I listened to these words between blows of the cane. I must say that these scenes were not frequent, and except on one occasion they did not take place in the presence of other boys. In public I was reminded that I was poor and that my parents "wouldn't be able to afford" this or that, but I was not actually reminded of my dependent position. It was a final unanswerable argument, to be brought forth like an instrument of torture when my work became exceptionally bad.

To grasp the effect of this kind of thing on a child of ten or twelve, one has to remember that the child has little sense of proportion or probability. A child may be a mass of egoism and rebelliousness, but it has not accumulated experience to give it confidence in its own judgments. On the whole it will accept what it is told, and it will believe in the most fantastic way in the knowledge and power of the adults surrounding it. Here is an example.

I have said that at Crossgates we were not allowed to keep our own money. However, it was possible to hold back a shilling or two, and sometimes I used furtively to buy sweets which I kept hidden in the loose ivy on the playing-field wall. One day when I had been sent on an errand I went into a sweetshop a mile or more from the school and bought some chocolates. As I came out of the shop I saw on the opposite pavement a small sharp-faced man who seemed to be staring very hard at my school cap. Instantly a horrible fear went through me. There could be no doubt as to who the man was. He was a spy placed there by Sim! I turned away unconcernedly, and then, as though my legs were doing it of their own accord, broke into a clumsy run. But when I got round the next corner I forced myself to walk again, for to run was a sign of guilt, and obviously there would be other spies posted here and there about the town. All that day and the next I waited for the summons to the study, and was surprised when it did not come. It did not seem to me strange that the headmaster of a private school should dispose of an army of informers, and I did not even imagine that he would have to pay them. I assumed that any adult, inside the school or outside, would collaborate voluntarily in preventing us from breaking the rules. Sim was all-powerful, and it was natural that his agents should be everywhere. When this episode happened I do not think I can have been less than twelve years old.

I hated Bingo and Sim, with a sort of shamefaced, remorseful hatred, but it did not occur to me to doubt their judgment. When they told me that I must either win a public school scholarship or become an office boy at fourteen, I believed that those were the unavoidable alternatives before me. And above all, I believed Bingo and Sim when they told me they were my benefactors. I see now, of course, that from Sim's point of view I was a good speculation. He sank money in me, and he looked to get it back in the form of prestige. If I had "gone off," as promising boys sometimes do, I imagine that he would have got rid of me swiftly. As it was I won him two scholarships when the time came, and no doubt he made full use of them in his prospectuses. But it is difficult for a child to realize that a school is primarily a commercial venture. A child believes that the school exists to educate and that the schoolmaster disciplines him either for his own good, or from a love of bullying. Sim and Bingo had chosen to befriend me, and their friendship included canings, reproaches, and humiliations, which were good for me and saved me from an office stool. That was their version, and I believed in it. It was therefore clear that

I owed them a vast debt of gratitude. But I was *not* grateful, as I very well knew. On the contrary, I hated both of them. I could not control my subjective feelings, and I could not conceal them from myself. But it is wicked, is it not, to hate your benefactors? So I was taught, and so I believed. A child accepts the codes of behavior that are presented to it, even when it breaks them. From the age of eight, or even earlier, the consciousness of sin was never far away from me. If I contrived to seem callous and defiant, it was only a thin cover over a mass of shame and dismay. All through my boyhood I had a profound conviction that I was no good, that I was wasting my time, wrecking my talents, behaving with monstrous folly and wickedness and ingratitude—and all this, it seemed, was inescapable, because I lived among laws which were absolute, like the law of gravity, but which it was not possible for me to keep.

III

No one can look back on his schooldays and say with truth that they were altogether unhappy.

I have good memories of Crossgates, among a horde of bad ones. Sometimes on summer afternoons there were wonderful expeditions across the Downs, or to Beachy Head, where one bathed dangerously among the chalk boulders and came home covered with cuts. And there were still more wonderful midsummer evenings when, as a special treat, we were not driven off to bed as usual but allowed to wander about the grounds in the long twilight, ending up with a plunge into the swimming bath at about nine o'clock. There was the joy of waking early on summer mornings and getting in an hour's undisturbed reading (Ian Hay, Thackeray, Kipling, and H. G. Wells were the favorite authors of my boyhood) in the sunlit, sleeping dormitory. There was also cricket, which I was no good at but with which I conducted a sort of hopeless love affair up to the age of about eighteen. And there was the pleasure of keeping caterpillars—the silky green and purple puss-moth, the ghostly green poplar-hawk, the privet hawk, large as one's third finger, specimens of which could be illicitly purchased for sixpence at a shop in the town—and, when one could escape long enough from the master who was "taking the walk," there was the excitement of dredging the dew-ponds on the Downs for enormous newts with orange-colored bellies. This business of being out for a walk, coming across something of fascinating interest and then being dragged away from it by a yell from the master, like a dog jerked onward by the leash, is an important feature of school life, and helps to build up the conviction, so strong in many children, that the things you most want to do are always unattainable.

Very occasionally, perhaps once during each summer, it was possible to escape altogether from the barrack-like atmosphere of school, when Brown, the second master, was permitted to take one or two boys for an afternoon of butterfly hunting on a common a few miles away. Brown was a man with white hair and a red face like a strawberry, who was good at natural history, making models and plaster casts, operating magic lanterns, and things of that kind. He and Mr. Batchelor were the only adults in any way connected with the school whom I did not either dislike or fear. Once he took me into his room and showed me in confidence a plated, pearl-handled revolver—his "six-shooter," he called it—which he kept in a box under his bed. And oh, the joy of those occasional expeditions! The ride of two or three miles on a lonely little branch line, the afternoon of charging to and fro with large green nets, the beauty of the enormous dragon flies which hovered over the tops of the grasses, the sinister killing-bottle with its sickly smell, and then tea in the parlor of a pub with large slices of pale-colored cake! The essence of it was in the railway journey, which seemed to put magic distances between yourself and school.

Bingo, characteristically, disapproved of these expeditions, though not actually forbidding them. "And have you been catching *little butterflies?*" she would say with a vicious sneer when one got back, making her voice as babyish as possible. From her point of view, natural history ("bug-hunting" she would probably have called it) was a babyish pursuit which a boy should be laughed out of as early as possible. Moreover it was somehow faintly plebeian, it was traditionally associated with boys who wore spectacles and were no good at games, it did not help you to pass exams, and above all it smelt of science and therefore seemed to menace classical education. It needed a considerable moral effort to accept Brown's invitation. How I dreaded that sneer of *little butterflies!* Brown, however, who had been at the school since its early days, had built up a certain independence for himself: he seemed able to handle Sim, and ignored Bingo a good deal. If it ever happened that both of them were away, Brown acted as deputy headmaster, and on those occasions, instead of reading the appointed lesson for the day at morning chapel, he would read us stories from the Apocrypha.

Most of the good memories of my childhood, and up to the age of about twenty, are in some way connected with animals. So far as Crossgates goes, it also seems, when I look back, that all my good memories are of summer. In winter your nose ran continually, your fingers were too numb to button your shirt (this was an especial misery on Sundays, when we wore Eton collars), and there was the daily nightmare of football—the cold, the mud, the hideous greasy ball that came whizzing at one's face, the gouging knees and trampling boots of the bigger boys. Part of the trouble was that in winter, after the age of about ten, I was seldom in good health, at any rate during term time. I had defective bronchial tubes and a lesion in one lung which was not discovered till many years later. Hence I not only had a chronic cough, but running was a torment to me. In those days, however, "wheeziness," or "chestiness," as it was called, was either diagnosed as imagination or was looked on as essentially a moral disorder, caused by overeating. "You wheeze like a concertina," Sim would say disapprovingly as he stood behind my chair; "You're perpetually stuffing yourself with food, that's why." My cough was referred to as a "stomach cough," which made it sound both disgusting and reprehensible. The cure for it was hard running, which, if you kept it up long enough, ultimately "cleared your chest."

It is curious, the degree—I will not say of actual hardship, but of squalor and neglect, that was taken for granted in upper-class schools of that period. Almost as in the days of Thackeray, it seemed natural that a little boy of eight or ten should be a miserable, snotty-nosed creature, his face almost permanently dirty, his hands chapped, his nails bitten, his handkerchief a sodden horror, his bottom frequently blue with bruises. It was partly the prospect of actual physical discomfort that made the thought of going back to school lie in one's breast like a lump of lead during the last few days of the holidays. A characteristic memory of Crossgates is the astonishing hardness of one's bed on the first night of term. Since this was an expensive school, I took a social step upwards by attending it, and yet the standard of comfort was in every way far lower than in my own home, or indeed, than it would have been in a prosperous working-class home. One only had a hot bath once a week, for instance. The food was not only bad, it was also insufficient. Never before or since have I seen butter or jam scraped on bread so thinly. I do not think I can be imagining the fact that we were underfed, when I remember the lengths we would go in order to steal food. On a number of occasions I remember creeping down at two or three o'clock in the morning through what seemed like miles of pitch-dark stairways and passages—barefooted, stopping to listen after each step, paralyzed with about equal fear of Sim, ghosts and burglars—to steal stale bread from the pantry. The assistant masters had their meals with us, but they had somewhat better food, and if one got half a chance it was usual to steal left-over scraps of bacon rind or fried potato when their plates were removed.

As usual, I did not see the sound commercial reason for this under-feeding. On the whole I accepted Sim's view that a boy's appetite is a sort of morbid growth which should be kept in check as much as possible. A maxim often repeated to us at Crossgates was that it is healthy to get up from a meal feeling as hungry as when you sat down. Only a generation earlier than this it had been common for school dinners to start off with a slab of un-sweetened suet pudding, which, it was frankly said, "broke the boys' appetites." But the underfeeding was probably less flagrant at preparatory schools, where a boy was wholly dependent on the official diet, than at public schools, where he was allowed—indeed, expected—to buy extra food for himself. At some schools, he would literally not have had enough to eat unless he had bought regular supplies of eggs, sausages, sardines, etc.; and his parents had to al-low him money for this purpose. At Eton, for instance, at any rate in College, a boy was given no solid meal after midday dinner. For his afternoon tea he was given only tea and bread and butter, and at eight o'clock he was given a miserable supper of soup or fried fish, or more often bread and cheese, with water to drink. Sim went down to see his eldest son at Eton and came back in snobbish ecstasies over the luxury in which the boys lived. "They give them fried fish for supper!" he exclaimed, beaming all over his chubby face. "There's no school like it in the world." Fried fish! The habitual supper of the poorest of the working class! At very cheap boarding schools it was no doubt worse. A very early memory of mine is of seeing the boarders at a grammar school—the sons, probably, of farmers and shopkeepers—being fed on boiled lights.

Whoever writes about his childhood must beware of exaggera-tion and self-pity. I do not want to claim that I was a martyr or that Crossgates was a sort of Dotheboys Hall. But I should be fal-sifying my own memories if I did not record that they are largely memories of disgust. The overcrowded, underfed, underwashed life that we led *was* disgusting, as I recall it. If I shut my eyes and say "school," it is of course the physical surroundings that first come back to me: the flat playing field with its cricket pavilion and the little shed by the rifle range, the draughty dormitories, the dusty splintery passages, the square of asphalt in front of the gymnasium, the raw-looking pinewood chapel at the back. And at almost every point some filthy detail obtrudes itself. For example, there were the pewter bowls out of which we had our porridge. They had overhanging rims, and under the rims there were accumulations of sour porridge, which could be flaked off in long strips. The porridge itself, too, contained more lumps, hairs and unexplained black things than one would have thought possible, unless someone were putting them there on purpose. It was never safe to start on that porridge without investigating it first. And there was the slimy water of the plunge bath—it was twelve or fifteen feet long, the whole school was supposed to go into it every morning, and I doubt whether the water was changed at all frequently—and the always-damp towels with their cheesy smell: and, on occasional visits in the winter, the murky sea water of the local Baths, which came straight in from the beach and on which I once saw floating a human turd. And the sweaty smell of the changing room with its greasy basins, and, giving on this, the row of filthy, dilapidated lavatories, which had no fastenings of any kind on the doors, so that whenever you were sitting there someone was sure to come crashing in. It is not easy for me to think of my schooldays without seeming to breathe in a whiff of something cold and evil-smelling—a sort of compound of sweaty stockings, dirty towels, faecal smells blowing along corridors, forks with old food between the prongs, neck-of-mutton stew, and the banging doors of the lavatories and the echoing chamber-pots in the dormitories.

It is true that I am by nature not gregarious, and the W.C. and dirty-handkerchief side of life is necessarily more obtrusive when great numbers of human beings are crushed together in small space. It is just as bad in an army, and worse, no doubt, in a prison. Besides, boyhood is the age of disgust. After one has learned to differentiate, and before one has become hardened—between seven and eighteen, say—one seems always to be walking the tightrope over a cesspool. Yet I do not think I exaggerate the squalor of school life, when I remember how health and cleanliness were neglected, in spite of the hoo-ha about fresh air and cold water and keeping in hard training. It was common to remain constipated for days together. Indeed, one was hardly encouraged to keep one's bowels open, since the aperients tolerated were Castor Oil or another almost equally horrible drink called Liquorice Powder. One was supposed to go into the plunge bath every morning, but some boys shirked it for days on end, simply making themselves scarce when the bell sounded, or else slipping along the edge of the bath among the crowd, and then wetting their hair with a little dirty water off the floor. A little boy of eight or nine will not necessarily keep himself clean unless there is someone to see that he does it. There was a new boy named Hazel, a pretty, mother's darling of a boy, who came a little before I left. The first thing I noticed about him was the beautiful pearly whiteness of his teeth. By the end of that term his teeth were an extraordinary shade of green. During all that time, apparently, no one had taken sufficient interest in him to see that he brushed them.

But of course the differences between home and school were more than physical. That bump on the hard mattress, on the first night of term, used to give me a feeling of abrupt awakening, a feeling of: "This is reality, this is what you are up against." Your home might be far from perfect, but at least it was a place ruled by love rather than by fear, where you did not have to be perpetually on your guard against the people surrounding you. At eight years old you were suddenly taken out of this warm nest and flung into a world of force and fraud and secrecy, like a goldfish into a tank full of pike. Against no matter what degree of bullying you had no redress. You could only have defended yourself by sneaking, which, except in a few rigidly defined circumstances, was the unforgivable sin. To write home and ask your parents to take you away would have been even less thinkable, since to do so would have been to admit yourself unhappy and unpopular, which a boy will never do. Boys are Erewhonians: they think that misfortune is disgraceful and must be concealed at all costs. It might perhaps have been considered permissible to complain to your parents about bad food, or an unjustified caning, or some other ill-treatment inflicted by masters and not by boys. The fact that Sim never beat the richer boys suggests that such complaints were made occasionally. But in my own peculiar circumstances I could never have asked my parents to intervene on my behalf. Even before I understood about the reduced fees, I grasped that they were in some way under an obligation to Sim, and therefore could not protect me against him. I have mentioned already that throughout my time at Crossgates I never had a cricket bat of my own. I had been told this was because "your parents couldn't afford it." One day in the holidays, by some casual remark, it came out that they had provided ten shillings to buy me one: yet no cricket bat appeared. I did not protest to my parents, let alone raise the subject with Sim. How could I? I was dependent on him, and the ten shillings was merely a fragment of what I owed him. I realize now, of course, that it is immensely unlikely that Sim had simply stuck to the money. No doubt the matter had slipped his memory. But the point is that I assumed that he had stuck to it, and that he had a right to do so if he chose.

How difficult it is for a child to have any real independence of
attitude could be seen in our behavior towards Bingo. I think it
would be true to say that every boy in the school hated and feared
her. Yet we all fawned on her in the most abject way, and the top
layer of our feelings toward her was a sort of guilt-stricken loyalty.
Bingo, although the discipline of the school depended more on her
than on Sim, hardly pretended to dispense justice. She was frankly
capricious. An act which might get you a caning one day, might
next day be laughed off as a boyish prank, or even commended
because it "showed you had guts." There were days when everyone cowered before those deepset, accusing eyes, and there were
days when she was like a flirtatious queen surrounded by courtier-
lovers, laughing and joking, scattering largesse, or the promise of
largesse ("And if you win the Harrow History Prize I'll give you
a new case for your camera!"), and occasionally even packing three
or four favored boys into her Ford car and carrying them off to a
teashop in town, where they were allowed to buy coffee and cakes.
Bingo was inextricably mixed up in my mind with Queen Elizabeth, whose relations with Leicester and Essex and Raleigh were
intelligible to me from a very early age. A word we all constantly
used in speaking of Bingo was "favor." "I'm in good favor," we
would say, or "I'm in bad favor." Except for the handful of wealthy
or titled boys, no one was permanently in good favor, but on the
other hand even the outcasts had patches of it from time to time.
Thus, although my memories of Bingo are mostly hostile, I also
remember considerable periods when I basked under her smiles,
when she called me "old chap" and used my Christian name, and
allowed me to frequent her private library, where I first made acquaintance with *Vanity Fair*. The high-water mark of good favor
was to be invited to serve at table on Sunday nights when Bingo
and Sim had guests to dinner. In clearing away, of course, one had
a chance to finish off the scraps, but one also got a servile pleasure
from standing behind the seated guests and darting deferentially
forward when something was wanted. Whenever one had the chance
to suck up, one did suck up, and at the first smile one's hatred
turned into a sort of cringing love. I was always tremendously proud
when I succeeded in making Bingo laugh. I have even, at her command, written *vers d'occasion,* comic verses to celebrate memorable
events in the life of the school.

I am anxious to make it clear that I was not a rebel, except by
force of circumstances. I accepted the codes that I found in being.
Once, towards the end of my time, I even sneaked to Brown about
a suspected case of homosexuality. I did not know very well what

homosexuality was, but I knew that it happened and was bad, and that this was one of the contexts in which it was proper to sneak. Brown told me I was "a good fellow," which made me feel horribly ashamed. Before Bingo one seemed as helpless as a snake before a snake-charmer. She had a hardly varying vocabulary of praise and abuse, a whole series of set phrases, each of which promptly called forth the appropriate response. There was *"Buck* up, old chap!"*, which inspired one to paroxysms of energy; there was "Don't *be* such a fool!" (or, "It's path*etic,* isn't it?"), which made one feel a born idiot; and there was "It isn't very straight of you, is it?", which always brought one to the brink of tears. And yet all the while, at the middle of one's heart, there seemed to stand an incorruptible inner self who knew that whatever one did—whether one laughed or sniveled or went into frenzies of gratitude for small favors—one's only true feeling was hatred.

IV

I had learned early in my career that one can do wrong against one's will, and before long I also learned that one can do wrong without ever discovering what one has done or why it was wrong. There were sins that were too subtle to be explained, and there were others that were too terrible to be clearly mentioned. For example, there was sex, which was always smoldering just under the surface and which suddenly blew up into a tremendous row when I was about twelve.

At some preparatory schools homosexuality is not a problem, but I think that Crossgates may have acquired a "bad tone" thanks to the presence of the South American boys, who would perhaps mature a year or two earlier than an English boy. At that age I was not interested, so I do not actually know what went on, but I imagine it was group masturbation. At any rate, one day the storm suddenly burst over our heads. There were summonses, interrogations, confessions, floggings, repentances, solemn lectures of which one understood nothing except that some irredeemable sin known as "swinishness" or "beastliness" had been committed. One of the ringleaders, a boy named Horne, was flogged, according to eyewitnesses, for a quarter of an hour continuously before being expelled. His yells rang through the house. But we were all implicated, more or less, or felt ourselves to be implicated. Guilt seemed to hang in the air like a pall of smoke. A solemn, black-haired imbecile of an assistant master, who was later to be a Member of Parliament, took the older boys to a secluded room and delivered a talk on the Temple of the Body.

"Don't you realize what a wonderful thing your body is?" he said gravely. "You talk of your motor-car engines, your Rolls Royces and Daimlers and so on. Don't you understand that no engine ever made is fit to be compared with your body? And then you go and wreck it, ruin it—for life!"

He turned his cavernous black eyes on me and added sadly:

"And you, whom I'd always believed to be quite a decent person after your fashion—you, I hear, are one of the very worst."

A feeling of doom descended upon me. So I was guilty too. I too had done the dreadful thing, whatever it was, that wrecked you for life, body and soul, and ended in suicide or the lunatic asylum. Till then I had hoped that I was innocent, and the conviction of sin which now took possession of me was perhaps all the stronger because I did not know what I had done. I was not among those who were interrogated and flogged, and it was not until the row was well over that I even learned about the trivial accident that had connected my name with it. Even then I understood nothing. It was not till about two years later that I fully grasped what that lecture on the Temple of the Body had referred to.

At this time I was in an almost sexless state, which is normal, or at any rate common, in boys of that age; I was therefore in the position of simultaneously knowing and not knowing what used to be called the Facts of Life. At five or six, like many children, I had passed through a phase of sexuality. My friends were the plumber's children up the road, and we used sometimes to play games of a vaguely erotic kind. One was called "playing at doctors," and I remember getting a faint but definitely pleasant thrill from holding a toy trumpet, which was supposed to be a stethoscope, against a little girl's belly. About the same time I fell deeply in love, a far more worshiping kind of love than I have ever felt for anyone since, with a girl named Elsie at the convent school which I attended. She seemed to me grown up, so I suppose she must have been fifteen. After that, as so often happens, all sexual feelings seemed to go out of me for many years. At twelve I knew more than I had known as a young child, but I understood less, because I no longer knew the essential fact that there is something pleasant in sexual activity. Between roughly seven and fourteen, the whole subject seemed to me uninteresting and, when for some reason I was forced to think of it, disgusting. My knowledge of the so-called Facts of Life was derived from animals, and was therefore distorted, and in any case was only intermittent. I knew that animals copulated and that human beings had bodies resembling those of animals: but that human beings also copulated I only knew, as it were reluctantly, when something, a phrase in the Bible perhaps, compelled me to remember it. Not having desire, I had no curiosity, and was willing to leave many questions unanswered. Thus, I knew in principle how the baby gets into the woman, but I did not know how it gets out again, because I had never followed the subject up. I knew all the dirty words, and in my bad moments I would repeat them to myself, but I did not know what the worst of them meant, nor want to know. They were abstractly wicked, a sort of verbal charm. While I remained in this state, it was easy for me to remain ignorant of any sexual misdeeds that went on about me, and to be hardly wiser even when the row broke. At most, through the veiled and terrible warnings of Bingo, Sim and all the rest of them, I grasped that the crime of which we were all guilty was somehow connected with the sexual organs. I had noticed, without feeling much interest, that one's penis sometimes stands up of its own accord (this starts happening to a boy long before he has any conscious sexual desires), and I was inclined to believe, or half-believe, that *that* must be the crime. At any rate, it was something to do with the penis—so much I understood. Many other boys, I have no doubt, were equally in the dark.

After the talk on the Temple of the Body (days later, it seems in retrospect: the row seemed to continue for days), a dozen of us were seated at the long shiny table which Sim used for the scholarship, under Bingo's lowering eye. A long, desolate wail rang out from a room somewhere above. A very small boy named Ronald, aged no more than about ten, who was implicated in some way, was being flogged, or was recovering from a flogging. At the sound, Bingo's eyes searched our faces, and settled on me.

"You see," she said.

I will not swear that she said, "You see what you have done," but that was the sense of it. We were all bowed down with shame. It was *our* fault. Somehow or other we had led poor Ronald astray: *we* were responsible for his agony and his ruin. Then Bingo turned upon another boy named Heath. It is thirty years ago, and I cannot remember for certain whether she merely quoted a verse from the Bible, or whether she actually brought out a Bible and made Heath read it; but at any rate the text indicated was:

"Who shall offend one of these little ones that believe in me, it were better for him that a millstone were hanged about his neck, and that he were drowned in the depth of the sea."

That, too, was terrible. Ronald was one of these little ones; we had offended him; it were better that a millstone were hanged about our necks and that we were drowned in the depth of the sea.

"Have you thought about that, Heath—have you thought what it means?" Bingo said. And Heath broke down into tears.

Another boy, Beacham, whom I have mentioned already, was similarly overwhelmed with shame by the accusation that he "had black rings round his eyes."

"Have you looked in the glass lately, Beacham?" said Bingo. "Aren't you ashamed to go about with a face like that? Do you think everyone doesn't know what it means when a boy has black rings round his eyes?"

Once again the load of guilt and fear seemed to settle down upon me. Had *I* got black rings round my eyes? A couple of years later I realized that these were supposed to be a symptom by which masturbators could be detected. But already, without knowing this, I accepted the black rings as a sure sign of depravity, *some* kind of depravity. And many times, even before I grasped the supposed meaning, I have gazed anxiously into the glass, looking for the first hint of that dreaded stigma, the confession which the secret sinner writes upon his own face.

These terrors wore off, or became merely intermittent, without affecting what one might call my official beliefs. It was still true about the madhouse and the suicide's grave, but it was no longer acutely frightening. Some months later it happened that I once again saw Horne, the ringleader who had been flogged and expelled. Horne was one of the outcasts, the son of poor middle-class parents, which was no doubt part of the reason why Sim had handled him so roughly. The term after his expulsion he went on to South Coast College, the small local public school, which was hideously despised at Crossgates and looked upon as "not really" a public school at all. Only a very few boys from Crossgates went there, and Sim always spoke of them with a sort of contemptuous pity. You had no chance if you went to a school like that: at the best your destiny would be a clerkship. I thought of Horne as a person who at thirteen had already forfeited all hope of any decent future. Physically, morally and socially he was finished. Moreover I assumed that his parents had only sent him to South Coast College because after his disgrace no "good" school would have him.

During the following term, when we were out for a walk, we passed Horne in the street. He looked completely normal. He was a strongly built, rather good-looking boy with black hair. I im-

mediately noticed that he looked better than when I had last seen
him—his complexion, previously rather pale, was pinker—and that
he did not seem embarrassed at meeting us. Apparently he was
not ashamed either of having been expelled, or of being at South
Coast College. If one could gather anything from the way he looked
at us as we filed past, it was that he was glad to have escaped from
Crossgates. But the encounter made very little impression on me.
I drew no inference from the fact that Horne, ruined in body and
soul, appeared to be happy and in good health. I still believed in
the sexual mythology that had been taught me by Bingo and Sim.
The mysterious, terrible dangers were still there. Any morning the
black rings might appear round your eyes and you would know
that you too were among the lost ones. Only it no longer seemed
to matter very much. These contradictions can exist easily in the
mind of a child, because of its own vitality. It accepts—how can it
do otherwise?—the nonsense that its elders tell it, but its youthful
body, and the sweetness of the physical world, tell it another story.
It was the same with Hell, which up to the age of about fourteen
I officially believed in. Almost certainly Hell existed, and there
were occasions when a vivid sermon could scare you into fits. But
somehow it never lasted. The fire that waited for you was real
fire, it would hurt in the same way as when you burnt your finger,
and *for ever,* but most of the time you could contemplate it without bothering.

v

The various codes which were presented to you at Crossgates—religious, moral, social and intellectual—contradicted one another if
you worked out their implications. The essential conflict was between the tradition of nineteenth-century ascetism and the actually existing luxury and snobbery of the pre-1914 age. On the one
side were low-church Bible Christianity, sex puritanism, insistence
on hard work, respect for academic distinction, disapproval of self-
indulgence: on the other, contempt for "braininess" and worship
of games, contempt for foreigners and the working class, an almost
neurotic dread of poverty, and, above all, the assumption not only
that money and privilege are the things that matter, but that it
is better to inherit them than to have to work for them. Broadly,
you were bidden to be at once a Christian and a social success,
which is impossible. At the time I did not perceive that the various ideals which were set before us cancelled out. I merely saw
that they were all, or nearly all, unattainable, so far as I was concerned, since they all depended not only on what you did but on
what you *were.*

Very early, at the age of only ten or eleven, I reached the conclusion—no one told me this, but on the other hand I did not simply make it up out of my own head: somehow it was in the air I breathed—that you were no good unless you had £100,000. I had perhaps fixed on this particular sum as a result of reading Thackeray. The interest on £100,000 a year (I was in favor of a safe 4 per cent) would be £4,000, and this seemed to me the minimum income that you must possess if you were to belong to the real top crust, the people in the country houses. But it was clear that I could never find my way into that paradise, to which you did not really belong unless you were born into it. You could only *make* money, if at all, by a mysterious operation called "going into the City," and when you came out of the City, having won your £100,000, you were fat and old. But the truly enviable thing about the top-notchers was that they were rich while young. For people like me, the ambitious middle class, the examination passers, only a bleak, laborious kind of success was possible. You clambered upward on a ladder of scholarships into the Home Civil Service or the Indian Civil Service, or possibly you became a barrister. And if at any point you "slacked" or "went off" and missed one of the rungs in the ladder, you became "a little office boy at forty pounds a year." But even if you climbed to the highest niche that was open to you, you could still only be an underling, a hanger-on of the people who really counted.

Even if I had not learned this from Sim and Bingo, I would have learned it from the other boys. Looking back, it is astonishing how intimately, intelligently snobbish we all were, how knowledgeable about names and addresses, how swift to detect small differences in accents and manners and the cut of clothes. There were some boys who seemed to drop money from their pores even in the bleak misery of the middle of a winter term. At the beginning and end of the term, especially, there was naively snobbish chatter about Switzerland, and Scotland with its ghillies and grouse moors, and "my uncle's yacht," and "our place in the country," and "my pony" and "my pater's touring car." There never was, I suppose, in the history of the world a time when the sheer vulgar fatness of wealth, without any kind of aristocratic elegance to redeem it, was so obtrusive as in those years before 1914. It was the age when crazy millionaires in curly top hats and lavender waistcoats gave champagne parties in rococo houseboats on the Thames, the age of diabolo and hobble skirts, the age of the "knut" in his gray bowler and cutaway coat, the age of *The Merry Widow*, Saki's novels, *Peter Pan* and *Where the Rainbow Ends*, the age when people talked about chocs and cigs and ripping and topping and heavenly, when they went for divvy week-ends at Brighton and had scrumptious teas at the Troc. From the whole decade before 1914, there seems to breathe forth a smell of the more vulgar, un-grown-up kinds of luxury, a smell of brilliantine and crème de menthe and soft-centered chocolates—an atmosphere, as it were, of eating everlasting strawberry ices on green lawns to the tune of the Eton Boating Song. The extraordinary thing was the way in which everyone took it for granted that this oozing, bulging wealth of the English upper and upper-middle classes would last for ever, and was part of the order of things. After 1918 it was never quite the same again. Snobbishness and expensive habits came back, cer-tainly, but they were self-conscious and on the defensive. Before the war the worship of money was entirely unreflecting and un-troubled by any pang of conscience. The goodness of money was as unmistakable as the goodness of health or beauty, and a glit-tering car, a title, or a horde of servants was mixed up in people's minds with the idea of actual moral virtue.

At Crossgates, in term time, the general bareness of life enforced a certain democracy, but any mention of the holidays, and the con-sequent competitive swanking about cars and butlers and country houses, promptly called class distinctions into being. The school was pervaded by a curious cult of Scotland, which brought out the fundamental contradiction in our standard of values. Bingo claimed Scottish ancestry, and she favored the Scottish boys, en-couraging them to wear kilts in their ancestral tartan instead of the school uniform, and even christened her youngest child by a Gaelic name. Ostensibly we were supposed to admire the Scots be-cause they were "grim" and "dour" ("stern" was perhaps the key word), and irresistible on the field of battle. In the big schoolroom there was a steel engraving of the charge of the Scots Greys at Waterloo, all looking as though they enjoyed every moment of it. Our picture of Scotland was made up of burns, braes, kilts, spor-rans, claymores, bagpipes, and the like, all somehow mixed up with the invigorating effects of porridge, Protestantism, and a cold cli-mate. But underlying this was something quite different. The real reason for the cult of Scotland was that only very rich people could spend their summers there. And the pretended belief in Scottish superiority was a cover for the bad conscience of the oc-cupying English, who had pushed the Highland peasantry off their farms to make way for the deer forests, and then compensated them by turning them into servants. Bingo's face always beamed with innocent snobbishness when she spoke of Scotland. Occasionally she even attempted a trace of Scottish accent. Scotland was a private paradise which a few initiates could talk about and make outsiders feel small.

"You going to Scotland this hols?"

"Rather! We go every year."

"My pater's giving me a new gun for the twelfth. There's jolly good black game where we go. Get out, Smith! What are you listening for? You've never been in Scotland. I bet you don't know what a black-cock looks like."

Following on this, imitations of the cry of a black-cock, of the roaring of a stag, of the accent of "our ghillies," etc., etc.

And the questionings that new boys of doubtful social origin were sometimes put through—questionings quite surprising in their mean-minded particularity, when one reflects that the inquisitors were only twelve or thirteen!

"How much a year has your pater got? What part of London do you live in? Is that Knightsbridge or Kensington? How many bathrooms has your house got? How many servants do your people keep? Have you got a butler? Well, then, have you got a cook? Where do you get your clothes made? How many shows did you go to in the hols? How much money did you bring back with you?" etc., etc.

I have seen a little new boy, hardly older than eight, desperately lying his way through such a catechism:

"Have your people got a car?"

"Yes."

"What sort of car?"

"Daimler."

"How many horsepower?"

(Pause, and leap in the dark.) "Fifteen."

"What kind of lights?"

The little boy is bewildered.

"What kind of lights? Electric or acetylene?"

(A longer pause, and another leap in the dark.) "Acetylene."

"Coo! He says his pater's car's got acetylene lamps. They went out years ago. It must be as old as the hills."

"Rot! He's making it up. He hasn't got a car. He's just a navvy. Your pater's a navvy."

And so on.

By the social standards that prevailed about me, I was no good, and could not be any good. But all the different kinds of virtue seemed to be mysteriously interconnected and to belong to much the same people. It was not only money that mattered: there were also strength, beauty, charm, athleticism, and something called "guts" or "character," which in reality meant the power to impose your will on others. I did not possess any of these qualities. At games, for instance, I was hopeless. I was a fairly good swimmer and not altogether contemptible at cricket, but these had no prestige value, because boys only attach importance to a game if it requires strength and courage. What counted was football, at which I was a funk. I loathed the game, and since I could see no pleasure or usefulness in it, it was very difficult for me to show courage at it. Football, it seemed to me, is not really played for the pleasure of kicking a ball about, but is a species of fighting. The lovers of football are large, boisterous, nobbly boys who are good at knocking down and trampling on slightly smaller boys. That was the pattern of school life—a continuous triumph of the strong over the weak. Virtue consisted in winning: it consisted in being bigger, stronger, handsomer, richer, more popular, more elegant, more unscrupulous than other people—in dominating them, bullying them, making them suffer pain, making them look foolish, getting the better of them in every way. Life was hierarchical and whatever happened was right. There was the strong, who deserved to win and always did win, and there were the weak, who deserved to lose and always did lose, everlastingly.

I did not question the prevailing standards, because so far as I could see there were no others. How could the rich, the strong, the elegant, the fashionable, the powerful, be in the wrong? It was their world, and the rules they made for it must be the right ones. And yet from a very early age I was aware of the impossibility of any *subjective* conformity. Always at the center of my heart the inner self seemed to be awake, pointing out the difference between the moral obligation and the psychological *fact*. It was the same in all matters, worldly or other-worldly. Take religion, for instance. You were supposed to love God, and I did not question this. Till the age of about fourteen I believed in God, and believed that the accounts given of him were true. But I was well aware that I did not love him. On the contrary, I hated him, just as I hated Jesus and the Hebrew patriarchs. If I had sympathetic feelings toward any character in the Old Testament, it was towards such people as Cain, Jezebel, Haman, Agag, Sisera: in the New Testament my friends, if any, were Ananias, Caiaphas, Judas, and Pontius Pilate. But the whole business of religion seemed to be strewn with psychological impossibilities. The Prayer Book told you, for example, to love God and fear him: but how could you love someone whom you feared? With your private affections it was the same. What you *ought* to feel was usually clear enough, but the appropriate emotion could not be commanded. Obviously it was my duty to feel grateful toward Bingo and Sim; but I was not grateful. It was equally clear that one ought to love one's father, but I knew very well that I merely disliked my own father, whom I had barely seen before I was eight and who appeared to me simply as a gruff-voiced elderly man forever saying "Don't." It was not that one did not want to possess the right qualities or feel the correct emotions, but that one could not. The good and the possible never seemed to coincide.

There was a line of verse that I came across, not actually while I was at Crossgates, but a year or two later, and which seemed to strike a sort of leaden echo in my heart. It was: "The armies of unalterable law." I understood to perfection what it meant to be Lucifer, defeated and justly defeated, with no possibility of revenge. The schoolmasters with their canes, the millionaires with their Scottish castles, the athletes with their curly hair—these were the armies of the unalterable law. It was not easy, at that date, to realize that in fact it *was* alterable. And according to that law I was damned. I had no money, I was weak, I was ugly, I was unpopular, I had a chronic cough, I was cowardly, I smelt. This picture, I should add, was not altogether fanciful. I was an unattractive boy. Crossgates soon made me so, even if I had not been so before. But a child's belief of its own shortcomings is not much influenced by facts. I believed, for example, that I "smelt," but this was based simply on general probability. It was notorious that disagreeable people smelt, and therefore presumably I did so too. Again, until after I had left school for good I continued to believe that I was preternaturally ugly. It was what my schoolfellows had told me, and I had no other authority to refer to. The conviction that it was *not possible* for me to be a success went deep enough to influence my actions till far into adult life. Until I was about thirty I always planned my life on the assumption not only that any major undertaking was bound to fail, but that I could only expect to live a few years longer.

But this sense of guilt and inevitable failure was balanced by something else: that is, the instinct to survive. Even a creature that is weak, ugly, cowardly, smelly, and in no way justifiable still wants to stay alive and be happy after its own fashion. I could not invert the existing scale of values, or turn myself into a success, but I could accept my failure and make the best of it. I could resign myself to being what I was, and then endeavor to survive on those terms.

To survive, or at least to preserve any kind of independence, was essentially criminal, since it meant breaking rules which you yourself recognized. There was a boy named Johnny Hall who for some months oppressed me horribly. He was a big, powerful, coarsely handsome boy with a very red face and curly black hair, who was for ever twisting somebody's arm, wringing somebody's ear, flogging somebody with a riding crop (he was a member of the Sixth Form), or performing prodigies of activity on the football field. Bingo loved him (hence the fact that he was habitually called by his Christian name), and Sim commended him as a boy who "had character" and could "keep order." He was followed about by a group of toadies who nicknamed him Strong Man.

One day, when we were taking off our overcoats in the changing-room, Hall picked on me for some reason. I "answered him back," whereupon he gripped my wrist, twisted it round, and bent my fore-arm back upon itself in a hideously painful way. I remember his handsome, jeering red face bearing down upon mine. He was, I think, older than I, besides being enormously stronger. As he let go of me a terrible, wicked resolve formed itself in my heart. I would get back on him by hitting him when he did not expect it. It was a strategic moment, for the master who had been "taking" the walk would be coming back almost immediately, and then there could be no fight. I let perhaps a minute go by, walked up to Hall with the most harmless air I could assume, and then, getting the weight of my body behind it, smashed my fist into his face. He was flung backward by the blow and some blood ran out of his mouth. His always sanguine face turned almost black with rage. Then he turned away to rinse his mouth at the washing-basins.

"_All right!_" he said to me between his teeth as the master led us away.

For days after this he followed me about, challenging me to fight. Although terrified out of my wits, I steadily refused to fight. I said that the blow in the face had served him right, and there was an end of it. Curiously enough he did not simply fall upon me then and there, which public opinion would probably have supported him in doing. So gradually the matter tailed off, and there was no fight.

Now, I had behaved wrongly, by my own code no less than his. To hit him unawares was wrong. But to refuse to fight afterward, knowing that if we fought he would beat me—that was far worse: it was cowardly. If I had refused because I disapproved of fighting, or because I genuinely felt the matter to be closed, it would have been all right; but I had refused merely because I was afraid. Even my revenge was made empty by that fact. I had struck the blow in a moment of mindless violence, deliberately not looking far ahead and merely determined to get my own back for once and damn the consequences. I had had time to realize that what I did was wrong, but it was the kind of crime from which you could get some satisfaction. Now all was nullified. There had been a sort of courage in the first act, but my subsequent cowardice had wiped it out.

The fact I hardly noticed was that although Hall formally challenged me to fight, he did not actually attack me. Indeed, after receiving that one blow he never oppressed me again. It was perhaps twenty years before I saw the significance of this. At the time I could not see beyond the moral dilemma that is presented to the weak in a world governed by the strong: Break the rules, or perish. I did not see that in that case the weak have the right to make a different set of rules for themselves; because, even if such an idea had occurred to me, there was no one in my environment who could have confirmed me in it. I lived in a world of boys, gregarious animals, questioning nothing, accepting the law of the stronger and avenging their own humiliations by passing them down to someone smaller. My situation was that of countless other boys, and if potentially I was more of a rebel than most, it was only because, by boyish standards, I was a poorer specimen. But I never did rebel intellectually, only emotionally. I had nothing to help me except my dumb selfishness, my inability—not, indeed, to despise myself, but to *dislike* myself—my instinct to survive.

It was about a year after I hit Johnny Hall in the face that I left Crossgates for ever. It was the end of a winter term. With a sense of coming out from darkness into sunlight I put on my Old Boy's tie as we dressed for the journey. I well remember the feeling of that brand-new silk tie round my neck, a feeling of emancipation, as though the tie had been at once a badge of manhood and an amulet against Bingo's voice and Sim's cane. I was escaping from bondage. It was not that I expected, or even intended, to be any more successful at a public school than I had been at Crossgates. But still, I was escaping. I knew that at a public school there would be more privacy, more neglect, more chance to be idle and self-indulgent and degenerate. For years past I had been resolved—unconsciously at first, but consciously later on—that when once my scholarship was won I would "slack off" and cram no longer. This resolve, by the way, was so fully carried out that between the ages of thirteen and twenty-two or -three I hardly ever did a stroke of avoidable work.

Bingo shook hands to say good-bye. She even gave me my Christian name for the occasion. But there was a sort of patronage, almost a sneer, in her face and in her voice. The tone in which she said good-bye was nearly the tone in which she had been used to say *little butterflies.* I had won two scholarships, but I was a failure, because success was measured not by what you did but by what you *were.* I was "not a good type of boy and could bring no credit on the school. I did not possess character or courage or health or strength or money, or even good manners, the power to look like a gentleman."

"Good-bye," Bingo's parting smile seemed to say; "it's not worth quarreling now. You haven't made much of a success of your time at Crossgates, have you? And I don't suppose you'll get on awfully well at a public school either. We made a mistake, really, in wasting our time and money on you. This kind of education hasn't much to offer to a boy with your background and outlook. Oh, don't think we don't understand you! We know all about those ideas you have at the back of your head, we know you disbelieve in everything we've taught you, and we know you aren't in the least grateful for all we've done for you. But there's no use in bringing it all up now. We aren't responsible for you any longer, and we shan't be seeing you again. Let's just admit that you're one of our failures and part without ill-feeling. And so, good-bye."

That at least was what I read into her face. And yet how happy I was, that winter morning, as the train bore me away with the gleaming new silk tie around my neck! The world was opening before me, just a little, like a gray sky which exhibits a narrow crack of blue. A public school would be better fun than Crossgates but at bottom equally alien. In a world where the prime necessities were money, titled relatives, athleticism, tailor-made clothes, neatly brushed hair, a charming smile, I was no good. All I had gained was a breathing space. A little quietude, a little self-indulgence, a little respite from cramming—and then, ruin. What kind of ruin I did not know: perhaps the colonies or an office stool, perhaps prison or an early death. But first a year or two in which one could "slack off" and get the benefit of one's sins, like Doctor Faustus. It is the advantage of being thirteen that you cannot only live in the moment, but do so with full consciousness, foreseeing the future and yet not caring about it. Next term I was going to Wellington. I had also won a scholarship at Eton, but was uncertain whether there would be a vacancy, and I was going to Wellington first. At Eton you had a room to yourself—a room which might even have a fire in it. At Wellington you had your own cubicle, and could make cocoa in the evenings. The privacy of it, the grown-upness! And there would be libraries to hang about in, and summer afternoons when you could shirk games and mooch about the countryside alone, with no master driving you along. Meanwhile there were the holidays. There was the .22 rifle that I had bought the previous holidays (the Crackshot, it was called, costing twenty-two and sixpence), and Christmas was coming next week. There were also the pleasures of overeating. I thought of some particularly voluptuous cream buns which could be bought for twopence each at a shop in our town. (This was 1916, and food-rationing had not yet started.) Even the detail that my journey-money had been slightly miscalculated, leaving about a shilling over—enough for an unforeseen cup of coffee and a cake or two somewhere on the way—was enough to fill me with bliss. There was time for a bit of happiness before the future closed in upon me. But I did know that the future was dark. Failure, failure, failure—failure behind me, failure ahead of me—that was by far the deepest conviction that I carried away.

VI

All this was thirty years ago and more. The question is: Does a child at school go through the same kind of experiences nowadays?

The only honest answer, I believe, is that we do not with certainty know. Of course it is obvious that the present-day *attitude* towards education is enormously more humane and sensible than that of the past. The snobbishness that was an integral part of my own education would be almost unthinkable today, because the society that nourished it is dead. I recall a conversation that must have taken place about a year before I left Crossgates. A Russian boy, large and fair-haired, a year older than myself, was questioning me.

"How much a year has your father got?"

I told him what I thought it was, adding a few hundreds to make it sound better. The Russian boy, neat in his habits, produced a pencil and a small notebook and made a calculation.

"My father has over two hundred times as much money as yours," he announced with a sort of amused contempt.

That was in 1915. What happened to that money a couple of years later, I wonder? And still more I wonder, do conversations of that kind happen at preparatory schools now?

Clearly there has been a vast change of outlook, a general growth of "enlightenment," even among ordinary, unthinking middle-class people. Religious belief, for instance, has largely vanished, dragging ther kinds of nonsense after it. I imagine that very few people nowadays would tell a child that if it masturbates it will end in the lunatic asylum. Beating, too, has become discredited, and has even been abandoned at many schools. Nor is the underfeeding of children looked on as a normal, almost meritorious act. No one now would openly set out to give his pupils as little food as they could do with, or tell them that it is healthy to get up from a meal as hungry as you sat down. The whole status of children has improved, partly because they have grown relatively less numerous. And the diffusion of even a little psychological knowledge has made it harder for parents and schoolteachers to indulge their aberrations in the name of discipline. Here is a case, not known to me personally, but known to someone I can vouch for, and happening within my own lifetime. A small girl, daughter of a clergyman, continued wetting her bed at an age when she should have grown out of it. In order to punish her for this dreadful deed, her father took her to a large garden party and there introduced her to the whole company as a little girl who wetted her bed: and to underline her wickedness he had previously painted her face black. I do not suggest that Bingo and Sim would actually have done a thing like this, but I doubt whether it would have much surprised them. After all, things do change. And yet—!

The question is not whether boys are still buckled into Eton collars on Sunday, or told that babies are dug up under gooseberry bushes. That kind of thing is at an end, admittedly. The real question is whether it is still normal for a school child to live for years amid irrational terrors and lunatic misunderstandings. And here one is up against the very great difficulty of knowing what a child really feels and thinks. A child which appears reasonably happy may actually be suffering horrors which it cannot or will not reveal. It lives in a sort of alien under-water world which we can only penetrate by memory or divination. Our chief clue is the fact that we were once children ourselves, and many people appear to forget the atmosphere of their own childhood almost entirely. Think for instance of the unnecessary torments that people will inflict by sending a child back to school with clothes of the wrong pattern, and refusing to see that this matters! Over things of this kind a child will sometimes utter a protest, but a great deal of the time its attitude is one of simple concealment. Not to expose your true feelings to an adult seems to be instinctive from the age of seven or eight onward. Even the affection that one feels for a child, the desire to protect and cherish it, is a cause of misunderstanding. One can love a child, perhaps, more deeply than one can love another adult, but is rash to assume that the child feels any love in return. Looking back on my own childhood, after the infant years were over, I do not believe that I ever felt love for any mature person, except my mother, and even her I did not trust, in the sense that shyness made me conceal most of my real feelings from her. Love, the spontaneous, unqualified emotion of love, was something I could only feel for people who were young. Toward people who were old—and remember that "old" to a child means over thirty, or even over twenty-five—I could feel reverence, respect, admiration, or compunction, but I seemed cut off from them by a veil of fear and shyness mixed up with physical distaste. People are too ready to forget the child's *physical* shrinking from the adult. The enormous size of grownups, their ungainly, rigid bodies, their coarse wrinkled skins, their great relaxed eyelids, their yellow teeth, and the whiffs of musty clothes and beer and sweat and tobacco that disengage from them at every movement! Part of the reason for the ugliness of adults, in a child's eyes, is that the child is usually looking upward, and few faces are at their best when seen from below. Besides, being fresh and unmarked itself, the child has impossibly high standards in the matter of skin and teeth and complexion. But the greatest barrier of all is the child's misconception about age. A child can hardly envisage life beyond thirty, and in judging people's ages it will make fantastic mistakes. It will think that a person of twenty-five is forty, that a person of forty is sixty-five, and so on. Thus, when I fell in love with Elsie I took her to be grown up. I met her again, when I was thirteen and she, I think, must have been twenty-three; she now seemed to me a middle-aged woman, somewhat past her best. And the child thinks of growing old as an almost obscene calamity, which for some mysterious reason will never happen to itself. All who have passed the age of thirty are joyless grotesques, endlessly fussing about things of no importance and staying alive without, so far as the child can see, having anything to live for. Only child life is real life. The schoolmaster who imagines he is loved and trusted by his boys is in fact mimicked and laughed at behind his back. An adult who does not seem dangerous nearly always seems ridiculous.

I base these generalizations on what I can recall of my own childhood outlook. Treacherous though memory is, it seems to me the chief means we have of discovering how a child's mind works. Only by resurrecting our own memories can we realize how incredibly distorted is the child's vision of the world. Consider this, for example. How would Crossgates appear to me now, if I could go back, at my present age, and see it as it was in 1915? What should

I think of Bingo and Sim, those terrible, all-powerful monsters?
I should see them as a couple of silly, shallow, ineffectual people,
eagerly clambering up a social ladder which any thinking person
could see to be on the point of collapse. I would be no more
frightened of them than I would be frightened of a dormouse.
Moreover, in those days they seemed to me fantastically old,
whereas—though of this I am not certain—I imagine they must have
been somewhat younger than I am now. And how would Johnny
Hall appear, with his blacksmith's arms and his red, jeering face?
Merely a scruffy little boy, barely distinguishable from hundreds
of other scruffy little boys. The two sets of facts can lie side by side
in my mind, because these happen to be my own memories. But it
would be very difficult for me to see with the eyes of any other
child, except by an effort of the imagination which might lead me
completely astray. The child and the adult live in different worlds.
If that is so, we cannot be certain that school, at any rate boarding
school, is not still for many children as dreadful an experience
as it used to be. Take away God, Latin, the cane, class distinctions
and sexual taboos, and the fear, the hatred, the snobbery and the
misunderstanding might still all be there. It will have been seen
that my own main trouble was an utter lack of any sense of proportion or probability. This led me to accept outrages and believe
absurdities, and to suffer torments over things which were in fact
of no importance. It is not enough to say that I was "silly" and
"ought to have known better." Look back into your own childhood
and think of the nonsense you used to believe and the trivialities
which could make you suffer. Of course my own case had its individual variations, but essentially it was that of countless other
boys. The weakness of the child is that it starts with a blank sheet.
It neither understands nor questions the society in which it lives, and
because of its credulity other people can work upon it, infecting
it with the sense of inferiority and the dread of offending against
mysterious, terrible laws. It may be that everything that happened
to me at Crossgates could happen in the most "enlightened" school,
though perhaps in subtler forms. Of one thing, however, I do feel
fairly sure, and that is that boarding schools are worse than day
schools. A child has a better chance with the sanctuary of its home
near at hand. And I think the characteristic faults of the English
upper and middle classes may be partly due to the practice, general
until recently, of sending children away from home as young as
nine, eight or even seven.

I have never been back to Crossgates. In a way it is only within
the last decade that I have really thought over my schooldays,

vividly though their memory has haunted me. Nowadays, I believe it would make very little impression on me to see the place agair if it still exists. And if I went inside and smelt again the inky dusty smell of the big schoolroom, the rosiny smell of the chapel the stagnant smell of the swimming bath and the cold reek of th lavatories, I think I should only feel what one invariably feel in revisiting any scene of childhood: How small everything ha grown, and how terrible is the deterioration in myself!

195

Books by George Orwell

available in paperbound editions from
Harcourt Brace Jovanovich, Inc.

DOWN AND OUT IN PARIS AND LONDON (HPL 54)

BURMESE DAYS (HPL 62)

A CLERGYMAN'S DAUGHTER (HPL 37)

KEEP THE ASPIDISTRA FLYING (HPL 38)

THE ROAD TO WIGAN PIER (HB 240)

HOMAGE TO CATALONIA (HB 162)

COMING UP FOR AIR (HPL 44)

DICKENS, DALI & OTHERS (HB 188)

A COLLECTION OF ESSAYS (HPL 48)

THE ORWELL READER: FICTION, ESSAYS AND REPORTAGE (HB 42)

THE COLLECTED ESSAYS, JOURNALISM AND LETTERS
OF GEORGE ORWELL:

I. An Age Like This, 1920–1940 (HB 209)

II. My Country Right or Left, 1940–1943 (HB 210)

III. As I Please, 1943–1945 (HB 211)

IV. In Front of Your Nose, 1945–1950 (HB 212)

Four volumes, boxed set (HB 218)